GATHERED GUESTS

CONCORDIA ACADEMIC PRESS

GATHERED GUESTS

A GUIDE TO WORSHIP IN THE LUTHERAN CHURCH

TIMOTHY H. MASCHKE

CONCORDIA PUBLISHING HOUSE · SAINT LOUIS

ACADEMIC PRESS

To Robert and Ruth;
Sharon;
Jedidiah, Benjamin, and Nathanael.
You have taught me much!
2 Timothy 3:14

Library of Congress Cataloging-in-Publication Data

Maschke, Timothy, 1947–
    Gathered guests : a guide to worship in the Lutheran Church / Timothy H. Maschke.
        p. cm.
Includes bibliographical references.
    ISBN 0-570-04276-3
   1. Public worship—Lutheran Church. 2. Lutheran Church—Liturgy. I. Title.
    BX8067.A1M375 2003
    264′.041—dc21   2003005584

2   3   4   5   6   7   8   9   10   12   11   10   09   08   07   06   05

CONTENTS

ABBREVIATIONS

AC	Augsburg Confession
Ap.	Apology of the Augsburg Confession
Christian Worship	Milwaukee: Northwestern, 1993.
ELCA	Evangelical Lutheran Church of America
K-W	*The Book of Concord*. Edited by Robert Kolb and Timothy J. Wengert. Translated by Charles Arand et al. Minneapolis: Fortress, 2000. Quotations used with permission.
LC	Large Catechism
LCMS	The Lutheran Church—Missouri Synod
Lutheran Book of Worship	Inter-Lutheran Commision on Worship. Minneapolis: Augsburg; Philadelphia: Board of Publication, LCA, 1978.
The Lutheran Hymnal	Evangelical Lutheran Synodical Conference of North America. St. Louis: Concordia, 1941.
Lutheran Worship	Commission on Worship, LCMS. St. Louis: Concordia, 1982. Quotations used with permission.
Lutheran Worship: Agenda	Commission on Worship, LCMS. St. Louis: Concordia, 1984. Quotations used with permission.
Lutheran Worship: Altar Book	Commission on Worship, LCMS. St. Louis: Concordia, 1982. Quotations used with permission.

LW	Luther, Martin. *Luther's Works*. American Edition. General editors Jaroslav Pelikan and Helmut T. Lehmann. 56 vols. St. Louis: Concordia; Philadelphia: Muhlenberg and Fortress, 1955–86. Quotations used with permission.
RSV	Revised Standard Version
SA	Schmalkald Articles
SD	Solid Declaration
This Far by Faith	Minneapolis: Augsburg Fortress, 1999.
WA	Luther, Martin. *D. Martin Luthers Werke. Kritische Gesamtausgabe. Schriften.* 68 vols. Weimar: Hermann Böhlaus Nachfolger, 1883–1999.
WELS	Wisconsin Evangelical Lutheran Synod
Worship Supplement	Commission on Worship, the LCMS. St. Louis: Concordia, 1969.

LIFE, LITURGY, AND THEOLOGY

I have always been interested in worship. Since my days attending a Lutheran high school, I've collected orders of service and been fascinated with what happens in worship. My theological training has made me increasingly aware of the intimate connection between theology and worship. This association is not something new nor is it revolutionary, yet this connection needs to be stated clearly at the beginning of this book. Woven throughout *Gathered Guests* is the concept that how we pray indicates what we believe. How did I come to this recognition, and, more important, why is it a valid concern for the worshiping life of God's gathered guests?

Probably no Latin theological phrase has been touted as flippantly in recent years as *lex orandi, lex credendi* ("law of praying, law of believing"). The historical origin and the various understandings and applications of this phrase help explain why the study of worship is important for the life of the church and for an individual's spirituality. A decade ago, evangelical Christian author Robert Webber stated a concern for Americans and particularly U.S. church members that merits repeating:

> We Americans are a-historical. Most of us know very little about history and probably care even less . . . . Unfortunately, most churches in this country have the same mentality. This is especially true of conservative Protestant churches . . . . Unfortunately, when it comes to worship, there is a terrible price to pay for this attitude. When we cut ourselves off from the rich treasury of resources and from the collective spirituality of God's people throughout the ages, we diminish our vision of God. We isolate ourselves from what God would do in the world through us, his church.[1]

It is always good to look at the historical roots of our understandings, and in this instance, I want to look particularly at the origin of this salient phrase *lex orandi, lex credendi*.

In the early fifth century, a lay monk named Prosper of Aquitaine was a literary disciple and defender of Augustine. Facing a controversy over Baptism, Prosper penned the original adage: *legem credendi lex statuat supplicandi* ("the rule of believing establishes the rule of supplicating").[2] As part of his argument for salvation by grace alone, Prosper demonstrated that the reason the church prays for all people is that faith is purely the result of God's grace. Thus the liturgy underscored the belief of the church. Augustine had made similar proofs of doctrine from the liturgy.[3]

Although Prosper's phrase is clear in its context, the concept has taken on a life of its own. Three distinct ways have developed for interpreting and applying the basic truth articulated by Prosper:

1. An individual's worship life creates and affects beliefs.

2. An individual's beliefs creates and affects worship practices.

3. An individual's worship life and beliefs will have reciprocal effects on each other.

These three perspectives have historical precedents as well as contemporary manifestations.

WORSHIP LIFE CREATES AND AFFECTS BELIEFS

Arius (A.D. 256–336), an early Christian teacher who began to lead people away from the true biblical faith, understood that a Christian community's worship life had a powerful affect on its beliefs.[4] To introduce his aberrations about Christ's origin, Arius set his beliefs to music, using tunes from the marketplace to infect the people's thinking and theological consciousness. As a result of the popular jingles, Arianism was difficult to eradicate in Asia Minor.[5] A century or so later when Nestorius, bishop of Constantinople (ca. A.D. 428), forbade his people from speaking of Mary as "God-bearer," only allowing them to call her "Christ-bearer," a theological battle erupted. His devotional directions were considered denials of the doctrine of the nature (actually the two natures) of Christ. As a result of this Nestorian heresy, the Chalcedonian Definition[6] quickly reasserted the phrase "God-bearer" into the liturgical confessions of the church.[7] These accounts illustrate the interpretation of Prosper's statement that is especially common among Roman Catholics: Worship life establishes doctrine.[8] Eastern Orthodox Christians hold a similar view.[9]

A more recent and concrete illustration of this phenomenon is the 1950 doctrinal statement by Pope Pius XII that established the bodily assumption of Mary as an official teaching of the Roman Catholic Church.[10] This doctrine states that Mary is physically in heaven. It flows out of the worship life of Catholics, who have prayed to Mary for centuries. Such devotion is verified and undergirded by the papal affirmation, but it was based on the practices of the church over many centuries, not on any biblical evidence.[11] Similarly, many modern Protestant groups continue to seek

Christian unity through external worship practices rather than through agreement on biblical teachings.[12]

BELIEFS CREATE AND AFFECT WORSHIP LIFE

The second way to view the phrase *lex orandi, lex credendi* takes an opposite perspective. As a result of many heretical worship practices in the early church, ecclesiastical and doctrinal control was often rigidly exercised over the liturgy. The Reformation era brought about a recognition of the dogmatic value of liturgy.[13] John Calvin, particularly, made the Second Commandment foundational for all worship practices of those who followed his style of reform. Idolatry of any type was carefully avoided, including the idolatry of the liturgy as Calvin saw it.[14]

Recently, Robert Webber has stated pointedly and correctly that a theology of worship affects the actions of worship.[15] Certainly the early American revival preachers used an approach to evangelistic worship with a particular theological goal. Preparatory songs "warmed people up to worship," then the preachers gave extended and persuasive sermons that ended with an exhortation to "accept Christ." A physical act of coming forward and being "smitten in the Spirit" concluded the services. Recent evangelical worship styles continue this mechanical and manipulative approach to worship in the guise of American informality and liturgical minimalism, yet such practices clearly show that theology affects worship practices.

David Luecke, though Lutheran, has adopted the paradigm of Reformed Protestantism in his book *Evangelical Style and Lutheran Substance*. After citing various styles of evangelistic worship, Luecke offers some strong theological reservations about certain styles. He concludes that Lutherans can only use one style, arguing that only "experiential 'contact' Pietism . . . has a rightful place in Lutheran theology and history."[16] Thus he seems to fall into the category of Protestant worship leaders who think that theology is the only determinant of worship style.

WORSHIP LIFE AND BELIEFS AFFECT EACH OTHER

The third way to interpret Prosper's phrase is a middle position that acknowledges the validity of the two previous views yet shows that each is deficient in its neglect of the opposite. Lutherans have navigated this middle course between the proverbial and mythical Scylla and Charybdis. For centuries Lutherans have reflected the mutuality of both doctrine and devotional life. Theology and worship are significantly interrelated.

In 1522, Martin Luther wrote his *Prayer Book* in which he illustrated the close connection between devotional life and doctrinal formulations.[17] This booklet was revised and remained in print for the next 70 years as a way to maintain doctrinal integrity through worship practices. Similarly, Luther recognized that changing certain parts of the liturgy was necessary for doctrinal purity, especially when he discovered that the biblical emphasis in the Lord's Supper was on God's gift to humanity rather than on the sacrificial responses of humans toward God.[18]

A mutual relationship always exists between liturgy and doctrine because liturgy communicates doctrine and affects the lives of those who worship. Vilmos Vajta demonstrates Luther's understanding of worship and summarizes it well.

> Rites and ceremonies indeed form a training school of faith. To this extent, the pedagogical view is true to Luther. While ceremonies cannot create the faith, they can point to it. They are the scaffolding needed for building the church, but must not be confused with the church itself. They can serve to bring the immature (the young and simple folk) in the orbit of the Word and Sacrament where faith is born. As long as man is "external," such outward orders will be needed for the sake of love, for love and order belong together.[19]

What occurs in worship affects doctrine, and the doctrine of the church should be evident in its worship, according to Luther.

The Danish Lutheran theologian Regin Prenter has carried on Luther's approach of relating theology and liturgy. In a masterful article titled "Liturgy and Theology," Prenter exhibits this uniquely Lutheran approach: "The liturgy of the Church is theological. It speaks to God and man about God and man. . . . The theology of the Church is liturgical, a part of the liturgy in the wider sense. . . . It serves God and neighbor."[20] The separation of the two has detrimental effects, warns Prenter:

> If liturgy is separated from theology, i.e., if it is no longer in its essence "theology" or true witness to the revelation of God, it then becomes an end in itself, a "good work," performed with the intention of pleasing God. . . . If, on the other hand, theology is separated from liturgy, i.e., if it is no longer seen as a part of the liturgy of the Church, part of the living sacrifice of our bodies in the service of God and our fellow men, it, too, becomes an end in itself, a human wisdom competing with and sometimes even rejecting the revelation of God. . . . These two dangers arising out of the neglect of the essential unity of liturgy and theology are, I think, imminent in our present situation in the Lutheran Church.[21]

Thus there is an intimate relation between what is done on a Sunday in a Lutheran church and what it means to be Lutheran.

Lutheran theologian Peter Brunner also underscores the mutuality of doctrine and worship. In introductory comments to his classic book *Worship in the Name of Jesus*, he states: "The church's doctrine on worship will determine which liturgical order it employs, which it leaves to freedom of choice, and which it rejects."[22] On the other hand, Brunner also states that "if the dogmatic statements do not simultaneously express what takes place in the concrete worship service in which we take part, this worship will find itself in a bad way. It would then cease to be the worship instituted by God and Christ."[23] To be a Lutheran means to retain the mutual tension between worship life and doctrine. It means I will evaluate what I do in worship in light of what the Bible teaches. It also means that I will evaluate my worship practices to be sure they reflect what I wish to teach.

In recent years doctrinal concerns within the LCMS were a significant consideration in the discussions to adopt a hymnal in 1978. The issue of theology and worship came together as one hymnal project was rejected and another proposed. This concern developed because of denominational history. The LCMS in convention has agreed to the following condition for membership: "4. Exclusive use of doctrinally pure agenda, hymnbooks, and catechisms in church and school."[24] Such a statement demonstrates the recognition of the mutual relationship between doctrine and worship, as well as the importance of education.

This book is written from the perspective that God's gathered guests come together because God calls us by His Gospel. We are gathered in His name to receive His Word and Meal. We respond in praise and prayers and works of service. This gathering time provides us with the power for living and believing. The worship service ends, but our service continues throughout the week as we live out our faith in Christ in our daily lives.

GATHERED GUESTS

As readers will quickly recognize, *Gathered Guests* is a textbook. It is intended for informed laity and college-age students who want to know more about worship practices in the Lutheran Church. I have designed this book as a practical guide to worship—written by a Lutheran theologian, pastor, and teacher—to provide biblical and theological answers to the perennial question "What is worship?" and, particularly, to the question "What is Lutheran worship?"

How Lutherans worship has been determined by a long and distinguished tradition. The chapters of this book address topics under a variety of categories. After looking at various dimensions of worship from a Lutheran perspective, part 1 will introduce the church year and a hierarchy of traditions to use when evaluating one's personal worship life. In part 2 the origins and development of Christian liturgy as practiced by Lutherans are explained in light of the larger Christian tradition. Part 3 provides a glimpse into the integral place that music, art, and architecture have in the worship life of every congregation. Part 4 offers suggestions for various approaches to seasonal services—Advent, Epiphany, Lent, and Holy Week—and occasional services, such as Baptism, confirmation, weddings, funerals, and Morning and Evening Prayer. Guidelines for public prayer and public reading of Scripture are augmented in part 5 with discussions of various roles of leadership and service in the church's worship life. Finally, part 6 provides practical suggestions for organizing a worship committee and planning for both small-group worship and variety in worship.

Some of the chapters are more practical; others are theoretical or historical. My goal in each chapter is to handle the subject matter in the way I believe best informs the interested reader about Lutheran worship. In almost all chapters, readers will benefit from exploring the parenthetical Scripture passages because they are the foundation and focus of Lutheran worship life. While all the topics are related to the overall theme of worship, this book does not need to be read from cover to cover. Rather, it can serve as a reference work and resource for further study by God's gathered guests.

ACKNOWLEDGMENTS

I want to express my appreciation and thanks to the many people who have contributed to this work, especially to those teachers I have had over the years and to those whom I have taught. *Gathered Guests* began more than a decade ago when I was asked to teach a course on worship for lay leaders. Dr. John Boubel encouraged me to expand the work he had developed for the course, which I gladly did. Since that time, I have taught the course on Lutheran worship at least annually at Concordia University Wisconsin. Therefore, I thank my many students for their insights and responses to various dimensions of the book as emphases developed over the years. Some of my classroom rhetoric has remained in the final edition. I want to thank especially the students who took REL 221 Lutheran Worship during the 2000 fall semester for their honest critical responses to a rough draft of this book. I should also mention my appreciation of Nathan Grepke, a graduate of Concordia University Wisconsin, who spent many hours preparing some of the illustrations found in this book.

My friend and former colleague Dr. Joel Heck of Concordia University at Austin first suggested the idea of publishing a book on worship. His experience in publishing and his honest reaction to several chapters provided encouragement and is most appreciated. In addition, Dr. Steve Mueller, Concordia University, Irvine, California, made helpful suggestions on several chapters for which I am thankful.

Other theologians, pastors, colleagues, and friends have influenced this work in ways I am often unaware. I have also benefited from the editorial support and encouragement of the staff at Concordia Publishing House, particularly Dawn Weinstock and her patience in the process. Any errors or mistakes in this book, however, are my own, and I take full responsibility for all that remain, if factual or theological, and I ask the reader's charity.

Besides thanking my teachers and those I've taught, several other people have provided special insights and perspectives that have proved helpful in my understanding of the Lutheran way of worshiping. My parents, the Rev. Robert and Ruth Maschke, were my first teachers as they modeled worship and music and life. I cannot express sufficient gratitude to my family for their support and training. My wife, Sharon, has quietly spurred me on in this project, encouraging me to express in print issues we discussed across the kitchen table. My sons, Jedidiah, Benjamin, and Nathanael, have been my teachers, as well as my students, as they grew up before my eyes (and behind my back) over the past decades. Therefore, this book is dedicated to my family.

Finally, I thank God for gathering me as one of His guests through the miraculous waters of Baptism and for continuing to sustain me through the body and blood of my Lord Jesus Christ. Jesus' death gives me life, and His Spirit continues to nurture my faith as that relationship with Christ grows and changes and matures. God has blessed me richly, and this book is one small way to express my gratitude for His grace.

S.D.G.
Timothy Maschke
Pentecost 2001

Notes

1. Webber, *Signs of Wonder*, 9–10.

2. For centuries the phrase had been attributed to Pope Celestine I (A.D. 422–432) in *capitula Coelestini* (Patrologia latina 51:205–12); see also Muller, *Dictionary of Latin and Greek Theological Terms*, 175. More correctly, Federer, *Liturgie und Glaube*, 13–16, attributes the authorship to Prosper and cites M. Cappuyns, "L'origine des Capitula pseudo-célestiniens contre se semi-pélagianisme," *Revue bénédictine* 41 (1929): 156–70. See also Wainwright, *Doxology*, 225–26; and Church, "The Law of Begging," 448–49, who cites P. de Letter, ed., *St. Prosper of Aquitaine: Defense of St. Augustine* (Ancient Christian Writers 32; Westminster: Newman, 1963), 183: "Let the rule of prayer lay down the rule of faith."

3. Wainwright, *Doxology,* 227, cites more than two dozen such references in Augustine's writings.

4. Grillmeier, *Christ in Christian Tradition*, 1:219–48.

5. González, *History of Christian Thought*, 272–90.

6. A church council, meeting in Chalcedonia in A.D. 451, reaffirmed the Nicene Creed as being sufficiently clear. However, against the views of Nestorius and his opponent, Eutyches, the council further clarified the position that in the one person Jesus Christ two natures exist "without confusing them, without changing them, without dividing them, and without separating them" (Grillmeier, *Christ in Christian Tradition*, 1:542–57).

7. Grillmeier, *Christ in Christian Tradition*, 1:451–72, 520–57.

8. Wainwright, *Doxology*, 251. Kavanagh, *On Liturgical Theology*, deals with this most clearly.

9. Ware, *Orthodox Church*, 271, quotes Georges Florovsky: "Christianity is a liturgical religion. The Church is first of all a worshiping community. Worship comes first, doctrine and discipline second."

10. Pius XII apostolic constitution "Munificentissimus Deus," 1 November 1950, mentioned in *The Documents of Vatican II* (ed. Walter M. Abbott; New York: Herder & Herder, 1966), 90.

11. Wainwright, *Doxology*, 238.

12. Pfatteicher, "Still to Be Tried," 22, states that concept succinctly: "The point of having one book is to have one church."

13. Fagerberg, *What Is Liturgical Theology?*, 3–45, 112–13.

14. John Calvin, *Institutes of the Christian Religion*, 1.11.9–11; 2.8.11; 4.10.19; 4.10.24; 4.10.30.

15. Webber, *Signs of Wonder*, 32–33, 146.

16. Luecke, *Evangelical Style and Lutheran Substance*, 92.

17. LW 43:3–45.

18. LW 53:11, 61.

19. Vajta, *Luther on Worship*, 175.

20. Prenter, "Liturgy and Theology." Originally published in Mandus A. Egge, ed., *Liturgy, Theology, and Music in the Lutheran Church* (Minneapolis: International Choral Union, 1959), 151.

21. Prenter, "Liturgy and Theology," 141.

22. Brunner, *Worship in the Name of Jesus*, 24.

23. Brunner, *Worship in the Name of Jesus*, 27. Vajta, *Luther on Worship*, ix, cites an article by Brunner in which Brunner states: "Liturgy is dogma prayed and confessed." See Peter Brunner, "Die Ordnung des Gottesdienstes an Sonn- und Feiertagen," in *Der Gottesdienst an Sonn- und Feiertagen: Untersuchungen zur Kirchen agende*, I, 1 (Gütersloh: n.p., 1949), 10.

24. *Handbook of The Lutheran Church—Missouri Synod*, Constitution, Article VI.4.

PART 1

DIMENSIONS OF WORSHIP

CHAPTER 1

WHAT IS WORSHIP?

I t's time for church!" From infancy I have attended church regularly. As a child, going to church was a time to learn more about Jesus, to sing hymns, sometimes to sit beside the organ while my mother played, or sometimes to sit in a pew with a friend while my father preached. I saw babies and adults baptized. I watched my parents during Communion, particularly as they returned from the altar. Church also evokes sounds for me, particularly hymns played on an old pump organ and on a pipe organ. I remember the pianist in a mission church and a harp concert one memorable Sunday. Going to church always meant a sermon, a main feature of the service. It was why we went to church: to hear about God's love for us in Jesus. Now I hear people talking about "worship" in the same way we used to speak of "going to church."

What do Lutherans mean by *worship?* Most often it refers to Sunday church services, and worship is indeed what happens on Sundays. Yet the concept of worship goes beyond an hour's activity on Sunday (or any other day of the week, for that matter). Lutherans understand worship as something more than what occurs on Sunday. It is a matter of God's gracious gift of faith, and the resulting activities that flow from that gift. Such faith-based activity is most evident in Sunday services as we gather as God's guests to receive from Him and to express our thanks and praise to Him. For that reason the focus of this book will concentrate on Sunday worship, though a variety of worship ideas and practices will be presented.

This chapter will look at the concept of worship in a manner that should provide more to think about the next time you attend church. In addition, you will have an opportunity to read in both the Old and New Testaments what God thought about worship. Finally, this chapter will look briefly at how contemporary Lutherans understand worship, the elements necessary to make a worship service Lutheran, and why worship remains an important activity for all Christians.

THE FOUR DIMENSIONS OF LUTHERAN WORSHIP

The concept of worship for Lutherans is multidimensional. There is no one way to express the fullness of the concept of worship in a single word or equivalent concept, though many have tried. This is true when we study the biblical ideas and our historical heritage, as well as when we reflect on present Lutheran worship practices.

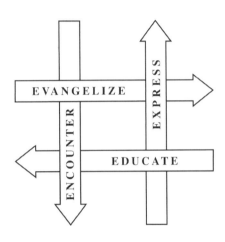

The concept of worship has two clear directions and four distinct dimensions.[1] Worship is God's service to us as His gathered guests and our faith-full response to Him in Christ. Worship is also an opportunity to grow and develop as a community and for the community to be empowered to go out into the world. Therefore, Lutheran worship can be described as being upward, downward, outward, and inward—or to put it in the words of this chapter, Lutheran worship is encounter, expression, education, and evangelism.

ENCOUNTER

The first dimension of Lutheran worship is *encounter*.[2] Walter Buszin, a formative worship leader and Lutheran seminary instructor of a previous generation, writes:

> In her services of corporate worship the Christian Church presents the eternal verities of God's holy and infallible Word, exhorts to high regard for Christian doctrine and to the application of Biblical teaching, receives the benefits of the blessed Sacraments, and enjoys the fellowship which has its roots in the very Gospel of Christ Jesus.[3]

Lutherans understand worship as a profound encounter with God and His manifold gifts to His people. God comes to His gathered guests with numerous blessings from on high.

In many ways Lutherans are unique in their approach to worship. James White, an authority on Protestant worship, distinguishes between two classical approaches to worship—one that places an emphasis on human feelings and one that emphasizes the people's work.[4] He says of the first category of worshipers that people seek to "get something" from a service, usually an emotional reaction. Feelings judge the worship experience. Such an evaluative measure and approach to worship is relatively recent, growing out of Pietism (seventeenth century), Methodism (eighteenth century), Revivalism (nineteenth century), and Fundamentalism (twentieth century) with their emphasis on humanity and human experience (decision). The second approach, one evident in the larger catholic tradition, views worship as work to be done in God's service. People plan to give their time, talents, and treasures as part of the community's natural response, in obedience to God, and from grateful hearts (as offering). Neither of these approaches are clearly or distinctly Lutheran, however. A third perspective views worship as an opportunity to receive the blessings, comfort, and gifts from God and then to respond in gratitude. Lutheran worshipers are gathered guests whose worship involves feelings and work but, most important, the opportunity to receive tremendous benefits from a great and gracious God.[5] Worship as encounter calls to mind the Lutheran emphasis on the means of grace, the Word and Sacraments. Lutheran worship is boldly and unashamedly sacramental worship, but it is important to understand that such an encounter is somewhat peculiar, even among many Protestants.[6]

Encounter is actually the first half of what Lutheran liturgical theologian Peter Brunner considers the two dimensions of worship, which can be described as revelation and response. Following earlier Lutherans, Brunner uses the German word *Gottesdienst* to describe worship. This word has a unique double sense because it is made up of two words—*divine* or God's (*Gottes*) and *service* (*dienst*). The term "Divine Service" thus can refer to both God's service to us as well as our service to God.[7] Luther insightfully commented on this dimension of worship when he wrote: "We [keep holy days] so that people will have time and opportunity on such days of rest, which otherwise would not be available, to attend worship services, that is, so that they may assemble to hear and discuss God's Word and then to offer praise, song, and prayer to God."[8]

Worship is also an encounter with the blessings God has given His gathered guests as expressed in particular symbols, people, actions, locations, relationships, and, ultimately, faith. Visualize what you see in a worship setting—a cross or crucifix, an altar, a pulpit, candles, a Bible, special cloth hangings (paraments), and, perhaps, works of art in the form of banners or stained-glass windows. We encounter many symbols in a worship setting. We also encounter people—the pastor, other worshipers, guests and visitors, ushers and greeters, musicians and choir members, young children and older adults, those with much and those who have little. Some of these people have special roles in the service that encourage a variety of additional encounters. The actions we encounter in worship become evident once the service begins—standing, singing, sitting, and speaking are common. Some worshipers cross themselves, kneel for prayers, raise their hands in praise, and respond verbally to the preacher. Worship activities are normally conducted in a building that is specifically designed for the gathering of God's people. Some congregations, however, meet in public buildings or in private houses or even in funeral homes. Whatever the specific location, each is designed or rearranged to enable people to encounter God's blessings. Finally, the relationships we encounter in worship are numerous—friends, family members, strangers, leaders, followers, contributors, and participants. We may be in all of these relationships and more when we participate in various worship services and encounter those who gather in God's name to pray, praise, and give thanks.

Most important, we encounter our triune God—our faith relationship with Him is what worship is all about. Vilmos Vajta's description of Luther's understanding of worship applies equally to us: "Revelation and worship constitute one and the same reality: fellowship between God and man on the earthly level."[9] Worship is an encounter with the grace-revealing God who is known most clearly in His Son, Jesus, who sends us His faith-strengthening Spirit. This encounter is central to all worship and is the vital element of whatever else occurs in church.

EXPRESSION

Worship is also an *expression* of our faith or a response to what God has done for us in Christ. Psalm 96 (particularly vv. 7–9) captures the essence of this dimension of worship in a most engaging manner. The psalmist wrote:

> Ascribe to the LORD, O families of nations,
>   ascribe to the LORD glory and strength.
> Ascribe to the LORD the glory due His name;
>   bring an offering and come into His courts.
> Worship the LORD in the splendor of His holiness;
>   tremble before Him, all the earth.

Psalms are written in a Hebrew poetic style characterized by parallelism—a second line repeats or parallels a thought from the first line. The parallelism in these particular verses from Psalm 96 draws the thoughts together and develops an idea that focuses on the key theme. The psalmist directs us to an understanding of true worship. The first line of the first verse is not a clear or complete thought because it does not tell the "families of nations" what should be ascribed. The second line of the verse completes the thought: God deserves our ascription of praise because of His awesome glory and omnipotent strength. The next verse becomes more focused. We are not to ascribe just any glory to God; instead, we are to ascribe the unique glory reflected in His name. Included in that ascription of praise are physical activities that express the worshipers' self-recognition as creatures of the great Creator. Finally, the idea of worship is expressed, but not any worship; rather, it is worship that reflects God's holiness, His uniqueness, His utter "otherness." Notice that as the psalmist expands and expounds on ascribing to God His worthiness, he culminates with an expression of awe and reverence before the gracious Almighty One. This is the essence of worship as response.

The English word for *worship* comes from the Anglo-Saxon word *weorthscipe*. *Weorthscipe* referred to the worthiness of someone or something—quite literally *weorth* (worth) plus *scipe* (ship), indicating worth-ship or worthiness. As is true of all Christians, we express our worship by ascribing to God the fact that He is truly worthy of our praise. Once we have encountered God's blessings and grace as His gathered guests, we want to express our gratitude to Him in worship.

Two Old Testament words are often translated as *worship.* One has to do with bowing down, falling down with faces to the ground, or prostrating oneself (2 Chronicles 7:3). The other has to do with adoration and service (Exodus 23:24–25). Both are responses to God and His benevolence. In the New Testament the word translated as *worship* is used to describe one's whole life (Romans 12:1) and is centered in the Christian's response to the living Word and God's Word. Worship is our grateful and thankful response to God for coming to us in His Word and Sacraments. Therefore, the second dimension of Lutheran worship is one of joyous and grateful response.

There are inward expressions as well as outward expressions in corporate worship. We experience worship through our senses and respond through these same senses, especially as we communicate with others. Sounds of praise are heard and felt. Our eyes see visual expressions of the faith—lights and furnishings—that set the mood for worship and direct our attention to God's presence and promises. Some Lutheran congregations use incense to visualize the prayers of the people and to connect the sense of smell to the worship experience.

Evelyn Underhill, an influential author on contemporary spiritual life and worship, described worship in almost mystical terms when she said that it is predominantly what people do before God. She spoke of "the response of the creature to the Eternal" and an acknowledgment of God as transcendent.[10] She meant that once we encounter God, there is a natural tendency to respond to Him. Even pagans respond in various ways to their understandings of God. Yet Lutheran Christians understand God as revealed most clearly in Jesus Christ, so our response is different from that of non-Christians. Our response is always *coram Deo* (before God), as Luther said, because we always stand before a God who is gracious to us in Jesus.

The word *celebration* has become popular in recent years to describe large worship gatherings or events. While a wonderful word when connected to our Christian response, James White expresses some caution about using *celebration* as a synonym for Christian worship.

> [Celebration] is frequently used in secular contexts and seems to have developed a vagueness that makes it rather meaningless unless used with a specific object so that one knows what is being celebrated. Since the 1920s the word has been linked to such indefinite notions as celebration of life, joy, a new day, or other equally vacuous objects. It seems better to use it to describe Christian worship only when the object is clear so as to have a definite content and form. If one speaks of celebration of the eucharist or celebration of Christmas, the content may be clear. Christian worship is subject to pastoral, theological, and historical norms; many kinds of celebration easily elude all of these.[11]

As an expression of faith, worship can be a celebration of God's gifts to His gathered guests. We celebrate the life, death, and resurrection of our Savior. We celebrate "the communion of saints and forgiveness of sins." We celebrate the joy of a renewed life in Christ and the hope of eternity. We celebrate the opportunity to be edified by God's Spirit.

EDUCATION

Worship is also *education* or *edification*. Luther recognized this dimension of worship early in the Reformation. He exhorted the Livonians to "consider the edification of the lay folk" as he helped them reform their worship practices.[12] A year later, in his German Mass, Luther explained the purpose of carefully conducted liturgical worship practices: "They are essential especially for the immature and the young who must be *trained and educated* in the Scripture and God's Word daily so that they may become familiar with the Bible, grounded, well versed, and skilled in it, ready to defend their faith and in due time to teach others and to increase the kingdom of Christ."[13] Luther saw the abuse of worship practices in his day, yet he also recognized the profound ability of good liturgical worship to maintain the faith in the face of false "prophets" who proclaimed rigid adherence to a mechanical form of worship or who advocated total freedom from any constraints in the area of liturgy.[14]

As education, worship teaches the faith and nurtures the faithful because it is Word-oriented. Ralph Smith writes, "Worship is a safe learning environment because the Word of God has primary place in this gathering."[15] The fellowship of believers, gathered in the name of Jesus, fosters the work of the Spirit. Lutheran worship is Word-centered worship. Sermons based on the readings of the day and the use of liturgical texts are rooted in the divine biblical revelation. The Sacrament of the Altar is administered according to Christ's intent and institution. In such a context God becomes the teacher of His gathered guests.

Often neglected in the worship life of a congregation and the church as a whole, children learn easily to pray, to confess their sins and their faith, and to respond to God with song and financial gifts in a worship setting. In fact, I never intentionally taught my three sons the Lord's Prayer or the Apostles' Creed; instead, they learned these expressions of the Christian faith through regular attendance and participation in Sunday worship services. They were taught to participate in the service, and they knew the words of the liturgy long before they could actually read the texts in the hymnal or service folder. Children learn much by participating in the regular routine of the liturgy.

In a study of children in worship, Shirley Morgenthaler notes that children require predictability, which liturgical worship provides.

> For liturgy to be predictable for children, it must have an element of sameness and structure. While this sameness can be dynamic, it needs to contain sameness to be accessible to the child (and to the visitor or new Christian). . . . The absence of many of the historic elements of the liturgy in many of the churches surveyed indicates . . . that children's needs may not fully be served by the diminution of ritual and predictability in those worship services.[16]

Luther was also interested in training the young. His liturgical renovations were not radical because he knew that children learned by rote repetition. He wanted children particularly to learn the faith through encounters with God's Word Sunday after Sunday. Then they and their parents could express their faith in Jesus' redemption through weekly activities and be instruments for extending God's kingdom by gathering other guests. This emphasis on liturgical ritual as a link to children and to new Christians leads to the final dimension of worship—worship as it relates to evangelism.

EVANGELISM

Worship is always *evangelism* or *witnessing*. This is the fourth dimension of Christian worship in a Lutheran context. Whatever we do in worship expresses our faith so others may see. In this regard, there is a dramatic dynamic at work in worship. As noted in the preface, our worship affects our witness and our witness affects our worship. Early in the fifth century Prosper of Aquitaine coined the phrase *lex orandi est lex credendi et agendi*. To rephrase, he believed that "the pattern of prayer is the pattern of faith and action." When Prosper lived, the Christian church already recognized that an individual's faith is affected by what occurs in the worship service. Worship practices form the faith of the community. The clearest recent evidence of this approach is the 1950 establishment of the Roman Catholic doctrine that Mary is bodily in heaven. Part of the rationale for that dogmatic statement was that the people had been praying to Mary for centuries, so she must be there.[17] Therefore, the Catholic church officially acknowledged that Mary is in heaven to hear prayers directed to her. As people worship, so they believe. The opposite statement is also true: As people believe, so they worship. Many churches that grew out of the Protestant Reformation have assumed this view. Whether charismatic demonstrations of the Spirit's presence or quiet and methodical responses to a preacher, worshipers demonstrate their faith through their worship practices.[18]

Lutherans see a two-way relationship between evangelism and worship. Worship affects witness and witness affects worship. Paul Bosch underscores the closeness of faith and Lutheran worship when he says, "True worship . . . has to do with life in faith . . . . What happens in the cult [that is, the worship practices], then, is preparation, proclamation and enactment of what ought to happen every day."[19] What we do on Sunday affects our daily lives, and our daily relationship with God affects our expressions of worship on Sundays.

Commenting on the activity of early Christians, Frank C. Senn notes that even "the very *style* of Christian worship made a witness to the revealed truth."[20] He goes on to say how extremely important the continuing expression of Word and Sacrament is to the witnessing of the Christian church. But Senn also underscores the significance of hospitality, which is one major expression of the Christian faith according to Patrick Kiefert, who states:

> Public worship is the single most important factor in active church participation for the first-time visitor as well as the vast majority of members of any congregation . . . . Many who recognize the importance of public worship in a vibrant congregation and of effective evangelism decide to make radical changes in their public worship. This approach, although it meets with some success, is not entirely sound. When this approach succeeds, it does so primarily because it rediscovers ancient wisdom about public worship . . . . The beginnings of Christian liturgy around the Lord's table emphasized hospitality to the stranger . . . . The effective use of ritual . . . can be an extremely effective way of bridging the private and public dimensions of our lives. It can also structure into our worship hospitality to the stranger . . . . Instead of thinking of the congregation primarily

as a family, we can balance this image with that of the church as a company of strangers . . . . The gospel's vision affirms impersonal, public interaction, since the gospel is primarily a public event. It is a public announcement of God's word. It opens the private to the public and builds a bridge between them . . . . In short, ritual, which according to the intimate society, is the enemy of healthy human interaction, is instead a key ingredient to good public worship.[21]

In no uncertain terms Kiefert stresses the necessity of liturgical worship and its accompanying ritual, which bridges the gap between believers and nonbelievers, members and nonmembers so all can receive the life-changing Word of God.

The word *ritual* is often used negatively. Admittedly, some rituals can become meaningless actions, particularly if worship leaders fail to educate worshipers. However, ritual often carries much meaning.[22] A sports event has much ritual. A young child's nightly bedtime routine takes on necessary ritual dimensions, such as kissing a stuffed animal or saying evening prayers. None of these are negative rituals. Kiefert shows us the benefits of such ritual. He describes experiencing a close bond with members of the men's choir at a congregation he attended while doing graduate work in Germany. The bond was created, he recalls, through the simple ritual of a cordial greeting with a hearty handshake that occurred before each rehearsal. Such a use of ritual encourages evangelism and outreach in a positive way.

David Gleason reiterates the importance of doing the liturgy well. He shows how good liturgical worship will speak to the unchurched in our contemporary society:

> The unchurched we strive to reach for Christ are children of an age that is often characterized by highly sophisticated aural *and* visual communication. Seeing is as important to learning and understanding as hearing. They are enticed by the graphic and the colorful, by action and movement. The very nature of the historic liturgy of the church as ritualized encounter with God is, likewise, characterized by verbal *and* visual communication. It is the liturgy of the Word and Sacraments, of the spoken and enacted Word, of the Word preached and made visible in earthy elements. It is filled with the color of churchly vesture and with the movement of ritual action. Inquirers to faith find the visual and enacted communication of the Word something to which they can readily relate. It draws them in and encourages them to join with believers in actively doing worship. The realization that the sounds and sights for the liturgy belong to a tradition passed on through generations of witness to apostolic faith, grounds their doing of the liturgy in faithfulness to that witness. They discover a sense of belonging, of belonging to a community of believers which transcends the moment by being intimately tied to the entire heritage of the church catholic, of belonging to the reality of God alive and at work among his people.[23]

Good liturgical worship done well will attract the unchurched and will provide an opportunity for the unchurched to hear God's gracious will for them and to experience the gathered guests of God. Stephen Hower, pastor of a large Lutheran congregation, avows that "worship is the number-one way in which God's people are fed. [But] the congregation is not the mission. It is established by God to accomplish the mission [which is] to save the lost and strengthen the saved to live bold and courageous lives of Christian witness before a non-believing world."[24] Similarly, a Lutheran professor wrote several years ago, "We do not worship in order to gain converts but rather we evangelize in order to gain worshipers."[25]

BIBLICAL BASIS FOR WORSHIP

The four dimensions of worship have a significant biblical basis, which can be seen in the variety of worship-related concepts found in both the Old and New Testaments. This biblical basis is the foundation on which all worship activities are conducted among God's gathered guests. The biblical foundation for worship may be self-evident to many Christians, but Lutherans seek to retain and explain the scriptural foundation for all that is said and done. Various biblical terms describe worship and worship activities, so we will look at these to familiarize ourselves with God's directives and gifts.

Two words used in the Old Testament for worship were mentioned previously. In addition to these words, which mean "bowing down in adoration" and "humble service," the Old Testament also speaks of various activities related to worshiping and praising God for what He has done (1 Chronicles 16:1–4).

1. Sacrifices or burnt offerings were made by the people (the Hebrew words *zebach* and *olah* in, for example, Leviticus 7 and 2 Chronicles 2:4; 31:3).
2. Major festivals were celebrated by the people, including Passover (Exodus 12; Numbers 2 and 28; Deuteronomy 16; Ezra 6:19) and the Day of Atonement (Exodus 30; Numbers 29; Leviticus 23). During these occasions, the people or priests presented sacrifices (Leviticus 4–9), offered incense (Exodus 30 and 40), and pronounced blessings (Numbers 6:23–26).
3. Public prayers and praises were offered that expressed the people's love and gratitude to God (Deuteronomy 11:13).

In the New Testament several significant words relate to worship, but the Greek word *latreia* is the most frequently used.[26] The English word *idolatry* has the same root. Paul used *latreia* in Romans 9:4 when he spoke of the ritual activities commanded by God in the Old Testament. Later, in Romans 12:1, Paul uses the word to speak of the Christian's entire existence before God as one's spiritual worship. It is in this second sense that we encounter another dimension of worship: Life itself is worshipful for the redeemed Christian. For example, Luke quoted Paul in Acts 24:14 when he said that the whole Christian life is "worship." In Philippians 3:3, Paul joined the Philippian congregation in worship. Later, he said to young Timothy (2 Timothy 1:3) that his devotional life is worshipful. Similarly, in Romans 1:9, Paul used *latreia* when he called his missionary work a "service to God." All these verses use the same word to denote worship as response to God.

Several other New Testament words relate in specific ways to worship. For example, *proskynein* refers to adoration of God. It literally means "to kiss the ground." Although not translated as *worship*, *proskynein* is used to denote a specific dimension of paying homage to God (Matthew 4:10; Luke 4:8; John 4:23; Revelation 5:14). Worship involves more than our minds and lips; our whole body may be involved. *Prosphora* refers to the offerings the early Christians made to God. This active word refers to someone bringing something to God. The writer to the Hebrews (10:10) spoke of God offering Christ for us. Early Christians, such as the first-century Christian pastor and teacher Clement of Rome, used *prosphora* to refer to Christ's gifts to God for us.[27]

Luther translated the Greek word *sebesthai* as "to be worshipful" (*Gottesdienst erzeigen*). Although connected with idols (*sebasma* was an "object of worship" in the ancient world), Luther understood *sebesthai* as a service rightfully due to the only true God, as evident in its use in Acts 17:23 and 2 Thessalonians 2:4. *Sebein* is also used in Matthew 15:9; Mark 7:7; Acts 18:13; and Acts 19:27, where it communicates a clear sense of the kind of worship that should be given to God alone. *Sebein* is also used to describe the activity of the first-century God-fearers, those Gentiles who converted to Judaism (Acts 13:50; 16:14; 17:4; 18:7). A final word for worship, *thusia*, is used for both Christian and pagan offerings. Paul spoke of a "living sacrifice" in Romans 12:1 (see also Hebrews 13:15), as well as pagan worship (1 Corinthians 10:20).

Peter Brunner notes that when Christians speak of worship, it is often in the context of a Christian assembly.[28] The gathering of God's people around Word and Sacraments, prayer and praise constitutes the living worship of the New Testament people. Thus Lutherans often speak of "going to church" rather than "going to worship." Our whole lives are worship, while our assemblies around Word and Sacraments are particular places where we receive and respond, witness and educate.

The primary emphasis in Lutheran worship is the corporate activity directed in grateful response to a gracious God; worship is a manifestation of the assembly of believers, the body of Christ. Undoubtedly, this is why early Christians called the first part of their worship service *synaxis,* or "assembled gathering."[29] Luther Reed acknowledged the importance of corporate worship: "No matter what other activities the church may engage in, public worship is essential to its life and mission. Common assembly and worship foster spiritual development and perpetuate the common faith."[30] This assembly has become an assembly because of God's activity. In the miracle of Baptism in the name of the Father, Son, and Holy Spirit, women and men, girls and boys, babies and the aged are marked as family members of the household of faith. In worship, the triune God is invoked and confessed, listened to and prayed to as God's people gather in His presence. The Christian assembly is unique because it is trinitarian and creedal. In its worship, the Christian community confesses this uniqueness to the world.

WHY WORSHIP?

After looking at four dimensions of worship and at biblical concepts associated with worshipful activities, we turn our attention to four reasons for worship, which can be arranged in two pairs of relationships.

First, God acts. (See right.) As we see His creation and, most important, as we understand His grace in Christ Jesus, our Lord and Savior, we recognize the dynamic involvement of our creating, redeeming, and sanctifying God. Worship begins with God entering our world in love.

Second, as a result of God's actions, we want and need to respond to Him. (See right.) There is a natural human desire to express feelings of awe and wonderment in particular ways. According to many modern sociologists, ritual is an important part of the human experience. Worship, therefore, is a proper response to God's activities for us, to us, and in us.

Third, God commands that we worship Him. This may be more obvious than we think. God has given many commands, some of which we do not always understand. As we mature in the faith, we find that God's commands are good. He has commanded that we worship Him, that we take time to be with Him, that we come together with other believers to respond to His work in our lives. This quality time with God is His gracious will and loving wish for us.

Fourth and finally, in obedience to God we worship. Because of our sinful condition, we do not always "feel" like worshiping. However, despite our feelings, God wants our physical, emotional, and spiritual selves to come into His presence. Our worship is not merely for ourselves, but for Him who loved us enough to send His Son and Spirit.

Thus we return to the multidimensional dynamic of Lutheran worship: Our worship is from God to us and from us back to God. Two decades ago, Norman Nagel expressed this dynamic in his introduction to the hymnal *Lutheran Worship*: "Our Lord speaks and we listen . . . . The rhythm of our worship is from him to us, and then from us back to him. He gives his gifts, and together we receive and extol them. We build one another up as we speak to one another in psalms, hymns, and spiritual songs."[31]

Who is the audience?

A provocative question that focuses on what worship actually involves is: "When we worship, who is the audience?" This is a critical question in light of the many contemporary activities that are called worship. Someone correctly answered this question with "God is and we are!" How will this paradoxical concept affect your worship expectations and your worship activities?

Some Questions to Consider

1. Describe the four dimensions of worship as you have experienced them in the past year.

2. What are the two senses of "Divine Service"? Why is this double sense important for understanding worship from a Lutheran perspective?

3. How is worship an encounter? With whom? With what?

4. What does the liturgy express about the worshipers? About the object or subject of their worship?

5. How and what does worship teach? How is this edifying?

6. To what does worship witness? How does your congregation's worship life express the faith of your community as gathered guests?

7. Which biblical concepts of worship help you appreciate the fullness of the biblical revelation on worship?

8. How do the four reasons for worship parallel our human existence as saints and sinners?

Notes

1. I thank Robert Christian and Walter Schoedel for depicting this multidimensional idea, which I had in mind for many years but was unable to visualize until I saw it in their booklet *Worship Is*, 19.

2. Van Loon, *Encountering God*, emphasizes the significance of encounter as the dynamic dimension of Lutheran worship. Similarly, Pfatteicher, *Liturgical Spirituality*, concludes with the emphasis that liturgical worship is an encounter with God that changes worshipers, causing them to grow and develop a deeper relationship with and faithfulness to the God of glory and grace.

3. Buszin, "Genius of Lutheran Corporate Worship," 260.

4. James White, *Protestant Worship and Church Architecture*, 3–15.

5. Former LCMS president A. L. Barry stated, "The purpose of [Lutheran] worship, therefore, is to be gathered by God around His gifts" ("Lutheran Worship: 2000 and Beyond").

6. More than a decade ago, the liberal mainline Protestant magazine *Christian Century* carried an article that said Christian "worship on . . . every Sunday . . . will include both Word and Supper, not one or the other" (Paul Westermeyer, "The Practical Life of the Church Musician," *Christian Century* [13–20 September 1989]: 813). In response, John Chamberlain of Goucher College, Townson, Maryland, wrote a letter to the editor that stated in part: "I have no complaint if those in the sacramentalist tradition find their spiritual experience in the correspondence of symbols in profane space to reality in sacred space. If Christ becomes present for them in the natural bread and wine, I rejoice; it is good that believers be joined to their Lord. But I resent being told that my faith is fundamentally flawed unless that is the way Christ becomes present to me. I am offended by the claim that the Eucharist is the central act of Christian worship. I am a Christian and I worship, and if I receive communion more than three or four times a year I find it monotonous and cheapened. Christ comes to me in the sacred story explored afresh in Scripture and sermon in the community of believers; my spirit is left out of balance by a service in which Scripture and sermon are preparatory to a Eucharist . . . . The Reformers quite deliberately sought to replace the medieval metaphors of space with biblical metaphors of time—to return to the Jewish concept of a God who is revealed primarily in history rather than primarily in nature. I do not condemn sacramentalism; I do say that it is not characteristic of the Protestant heritage or central to Protestant spirituality" ("Eucharist Nonessential," 941–42). How different this is for Lutheranism, which is unapologetically sacramental.

7. Brunner, *Worship in the Name of Jesus*, emphasizes these dimensions of "sacrament" and "sacrifice," particularly in part 2.

8. LC, "Ten Commandments," 84 (K-W, 397).

9. Vajta, *Luther on Worship*, 15.

10. Underhill, *Worship*, 3, 10, and especially chapter 1, "The Nature of Worship."

11. James White, *Protestant Worship and Church Architecture,* 36.

12. "Christian Exhortation to the Livonians," LW 53:47.

13. "German Mass and Order of Service (1526)," LW 53:62 (*my emphasis*).

14. See background information from Brecht, *Martin Luther: Shaping and Defining the Reformation*, 119–35, 157–72.

15. Smith, "Worship as Transformation," 346.

16. Becker, Morgenthaler, and Bertels, "Children in Worship," *Lutheran Education* 133:5, 254.

17. See *Gathered Guests* preface for more details.

18. Wright, *Community of Joy*, 55, recognizes that "worship styles, on the other hand, communicate the substance of faith."

19. Bosch, *Worship Workbench*, 7.

20. Senn, *Witness of the Worshiping Community*, 11 (*Senn's emphasis*).

21. Kiefert, *Worship and Evangelism*, 8, 11, 26, 28, 30.

22. In worship, a helpful distinction is made between ritualism and ceremony. The written form of a service is called "the rite" because it precisely lays out the words to be spoken or sung. Sometimes these rites are rigidly followed, which results in ritualism, an emphasis on the actions. Actually, the rite has been prepared to help worship leaders conduct the "ceremony," which is the actions done in the service by the leaders and the congregation, such as standing or kneeling. In the current context, the concept of ritual is closer to the concept of ceremony because it communicates a greater spiritual content and concern.

23. Gleason, "Liturgy: An Evangelism Advantage," 147 (*Gleason's emphasis*).

24. Parker, "Worship Wars," [*Lutheran Witness*] news release of the LCMS.

25. Truemper, "Evangelism: Liturgy *versus* Church Growth," 32.

26. *Latreia* is used in Hebrews 9:1, 6 to refer to the priestly functions in the temple, as well as in Hebrews 8:5; 9:9; 10:2; 13:10.

27. Clement of Rome, "To the Corinthians," 36.1, in *Apostolic Fathers,* 2:111, 290.

28. Brunner, *Worship in the Name of Jesus,* 17–19.

29. Grisbrooke, "Synaxis," 501. See *Gathered Guests* chapters 7 and 15 for more information on the Service of the Word.

30. Reed, *Lutheran Liturgy* (rev. ed.), 3.

31. [Nagel], introduction to *Lutheran Worship,* 6.

CHAPTER 2

THE LUTHERAN
LITURGICAL TRADITION

Lutherans have always had a unique relationship with tradition.[1] On the one hand, Lutherans have never felt bound by any one tradition. On the other hand, tradition has played a significant role in the understanding and practice of worship. Such a paradoxical relationship needs to be explained, particularly as it relates to the contemporary Lutheran worship scene. Undoubtedly, the Lutheran appreciation for tradition is strong because Lutheran worship is biblically based and Gospel centered. Yet several other reasons support our cherished traditions. Overall, we can say that as God's gathered guests, Lutherans have enjoyed a full and rich tradition of worship for more than half a millennium.

TRADITION: WHO NEEDS IT?

Traditions surround us. Every family has its own traditions. This usually becomes obvious when a young child visits a friend's house or a young person vacations with another family or a young adult goes away to school. We call many of these personal traditions "habits." People outside of one's immediate family may do things differently; they have their own traditions. Some couples discover unique family traditions only after they marry. Sometimes they even find them to be a source of conflict until they can be resolved with new traditions. Some personal or family traditions are good; others are indifferent; some may be detrimental to our physical or even our spiritual lives.

The church also has traditions: some good, some indifferent, and some detrimental. St. Paul, for example, used the Greek word for tradition, *paradosis*, in 1 Corinthians 11:23 to describe the institution of the Lord's Supper, a tradition the

35

church had received from the Lord Himself. St. Paul told the Thessalonians to maintain those traditions they had received from him (2 Thessalonians 2:15; 3:6). He also warned the Colossians (2:8) to beware of human traditions that can draw people away from Christ.

Such biblical tradition was almost lost for a generation or two in the early church prior to the formation of the canon of Scripture around A.D. 150. As Oscar Cullmann so insightfully concludes in an article on tradition:

> By subordinating all subsequent tradition to the canon, the Church once and for all saved its apostolic basis. It enabled its members to hear, thanks to this canon, continually afresh and throughout all the centuries to come the authentic word of the apostles, a privilege which no oral tradition, passing through Polycarp or Papius, could have assured them.[2]

Lutherans have taken great pains to reject one form of tradition, the Tradition of the Catholic Church. Spelled with a capital T, this Tradition refers to established rules and doctrines that have no clear scriptural foundation yet are held as divinely ordered.[3] Martin Luther fought against Catholic Tradition,[4] but he recognized the importance of biblical tradition and cherished the Gospel tradition he had received.[5] However, Luther saw a discontinuity between the Gospel or scriptural tradition and the suppressive and oppressive Tradition of the Catholic Church of his day. In 1522, Luther spoke of two opposing church traditions—the apostolic tradition of the Gospel message of salvation through Christ alone and the papal traditions that claimed divine institution but emphasized human merit. Luther maintained this distinction throughout his life.[6]

The other kind of catholic tradition (note the lowercase letters) provides a conscientiously biblical link for confessional Lutherans. This tradition is the Gospel tradition, the biblical tradition, the creedal tradition, the confessional tradition that keeps its focus on Jesus Christ as Lord and Savior of all. That is why the *Book of Concord* asserts: "Furthermore, we gladly keep the ancient traditions set up in the church because they are useful and promote tranquility, and we interpret them in the best possible way, by excluding the opinion that they justify."[7]

FOUR REASONS TO FOLLOW TRADITION

Four reasons can be given to explain why most Christians, and particularly Lutheran Christians, retain many elements of this cherished Gospel tradition. We will look at these reasons and illustrate their meaningfulness for God's gathered guests.

TRADITION MEDIATES THE WORD TO US

Most of us have come to know Jesus Christ through tradition (the Greek word for tradition, *paradosis,* literally means "to pass down" something), whether it was the tradition of the church or (for most of us) the message passed down by our Christian parents. Someone "handed down" to us the message of God's love and forgiveness. As Luther scholar Kenneth Hagen writes: "Tradition is the transitive process by means of which the Christian past is renewed in the living present and made available to the open future. . . . As Christians we live and have our being in the tradition of the Gospel testified in Scripture, transmitted in and by the Church through the power of the Holy Spirit."[8] We certainly would not want to eliminate such a significant tradition from the Christian community.

TRADITION SHOWS OUR RESPECT FOR THE PAST

When we become mature, we no longer "fight" our parents. This is also true with the tradition of the church. Tradition is not "the dead faith of those who are living"; instead, it is the "living faith of those who have died." We respect those who have gone before us. Not that we follow them blindly, but in their historical context, we hold traditions in love and esteem. G. K. Chesterton shed some light on this aspect of tradition in his classic book *Orthodoxy*:

> Tradition may be defined as an extension of the franchise. Tradition means giving votes to the most obscure of all classes, our ancestors. It is the democracy of the dead. Tradition refuses to submit to the small and arrogant oligarchy of those who merely happen to be walking about. All democrats object to men being disqualified by the accident of birth; tradition objects to their being disqualified by the accident of death . . . . Tradition asks us not to neglect a good man's opinion, even if he is our father.[9]

Chesterton recognized the great contribution made by those who had gone before him and the chronic contemporary need for not becoming haughty about the particulars of the present.

TRADITION REPRESENTS THE "GREATER CHURCH"

The greater church is visible and invisible, militant and triumphant, past and present. Tradition gives us a sense of personal and corporate identity. Thus in one sense, the Lutheran respect for tradition shows a respect for ourselves as part of a greater community of saints. We confess in the Apostles' Creed: "I believe in the holy Christian Church, the communion of saints." We cherish this communion through our good use of tradition. We are part of something larger than our local congregation or even our denomination. We are part of the body of Christ. Our songs join us with the "angels and archangels and with all the company of heaven," as the pastor reminds us in the Preface of the Holy Communion service.

Illustrative of this practice is the fact that at the time of the Reformation, the Lutheran reformers retained a collect for Maundy Thursday that had been composed in 1264 by Thomas Aquinas for the Feast of Corpus Christi. Lutherans vehemently opposed the feast because it emphasized the adoration of the communion wafer, yet Aquinas's collect was retained because it most beautifully expressed the Lutheran understanding of Christ's real presence in the Sacrament. As Luther Reed states: "The address to our Lord himself is unusual and appropriate, and the content of the prayer is thoroughly evangelical and satisfying, though the emphasis has been changed from contemplation to reception."[10]

TRADITION PROVIDES PERSPECTIVE IN OUR CHANGING WORLD

Much of society is experiencing rapid change, so much so that we speak of "future shock." Actually, it is not "future" at all but a present recognition of the megachanges that have occurred within our lifetimes. In such times as this we need a sense of continuity and solidarity. Tradition provides us with a powerful acknowledgment that change is neither new nor is it always bad or good. Scripture tells us that only God does not change (Hebrews 7:21; 13:8). With our eyes opened to past traditions, we can expect the changes of the present and be hope-filled as we anticipate the future.

SIX LEVELS OF TRADITION

Paul Bosch describes six levels of tradition in worship settings. These six levels can be considered a hierarchy of traditions, the first being the most important and the last being the least valuable. Although the descriptions of these levels of tradition are neither complete nor always distinct, they provide a concrete means to evaluate worship practices. As you read these descriptions, you may wish to add your own ideas or illustrations of each level.

BIBLICAL TRADITIONS

The content of worship should enable us to respond to God's saving activity. We know this divine work only through the mediation of sacred Scripture. The Old and New Testaments provide evidence for worship practices, albeit not as complete or as thorough as many of us would wish. "The biblical tradition is the history of God, the history of the Word made flesh in the Man of God's own choosing; THE

TRADITION biblically grounded is the life of the Triune God; the Tradition is the faith of Christ handed down in the life of the Church (*ab Abel* [from Abel])."[11]

From the Old Testament we learn of the importance of the liturgical assembly.[12] God called and gathered His people together around Word and sacrifice. "The assembly was a dialogical event. God's initiative and revelation in the Scriptures constituted one aspect of the assembly; the people's response in a profession of faith, sacrifice or . . . prayer of blessing or thanksgiving completed the action."[13] The Old Testament accounts of worship emphasize ritual and liturgy. Several chapters of the Pentateuch are devoted to the vestments worn by the priests and Levites (Exodus 28–29; 39; Leviticus 8–9). The Book of Psalms provides a wealth of resources from the worship life of the Hebrew people over several centuries, and it has been used for Jewish and Christian worship for millennia. Although incense had various purposes, the Bible tells us that God loves the smell of incense (Exodus 30) and that it symbolizes our prayers (Psalm 141:2; Revelation 8:4). The sacrificial system described in many places of the Old Testament points to the long-awaited Anointed One (the Messiah) who would come to be the final sacrifice, Jesus the Christ.[14]

In the New Testament we see lay participation in worship (1 Timothy 2:1–10). We also see an interesting emphasis on orderliness (1 Corinthians 14:40). The Eucharist ("breaking of bread," "the Lord's Supper") is celebrated frequently (Acts 2:42; 1 Corinthians 11:26). The New Testament also emphasizes the Good News that Christ has come and that He continues to be present when believers gather together in His name (Matthew 18:20). Psalms, hymns, and spiritual songs continue to be sung, along with prayers and readings from Scripture (Colossians 3:16–17).

In both Testaments we see the communal nature of worship. Israel gathered together around the tabernacle, even to the point of encamping on all sides of the structure (Numbers 2), literally demonstrating the centrality of corporate worship. The New Israel (Galatians 6:16), the church, continues the practice by celebrating *koinonia* (fellowship) with one another and with the Savior (1 Corinthians 10:14–17).

Biblical worship is Christocentric. God's saving activity in Christ is the central focus of all that is said and done. Paul reminded the Colossians that their previous worship had been a shadow of the one to come (Colossians 2:16–17). Christ is the Great Liturgist (Hebrews 8:2, 6). More important, Christ is always the "main event" (Revelation 14; 21) in the great liturgy of God's gathered guests.

Finally, biblical worship is temporal (that is, this worldly). Pagan worshipers emphasized the mystical and the spiritual aspects of life and nature.[15] Such worship, however, could not affect the lives of those followers: It was altogether otherworldly. The Bible reminds us that ethics and life are important so mysticism and spiritualism do not dominate biblical worship. Biblical worship affects the daily lives of those who worship the God who is, who was, and who is to come (Revelation 1:8), but it also is super-temporal (pointing beyond this life).

CATHOLIC TRADITIONS

The word *catholic* means several things—whole, integral, ecumenical, universal. The word in Greek literally means "throughout the whole [world]." In the creeds Luther substituted the word *Christian,* which is the connotation here. There is a larger Christian tradition than merely the Lutheran practice of it. This tradition goes back to Scripture, but it continued after the Scriptures were written. Many examples in the early church illustrate this tradition.

Basic for catholic tradition is trinitarian, creedal worship. When psalms are used in corporate Christian worship, for example, a trinitarian doxology is added to underscore the Christian understanding of God. We recite and profess the creeds regularly in our Lutheran worship life so we will recall the hard-fought theological debates of the early church.[16]

Catholic worship is also sacramental. The biblical tradition points to a regular practice of Holy Communion, but the early church provides greater details of its celebration.[17] The separation of the *Agape* ("love") feast from the Sunday morning Eucharist was a significant event, though when this occurred is now hidden in the shadows of history. Baptism and Holy Absolution are also important elements in the worship life of Christians throughout the world because they convey the forgiveness of sins through the Word of God inherent in them. Through these means of grace, the Spirit comes to us with the blessings of salvation.

Early Christians recognized the need for ritual and structure, following Paul's exhortation for orderliness (1 Corinthians 14:40). Therefore, the catholic tradition is clearly liturgical, a word that refers to the work of the people. Early Christians worshiped together and participated in the liturgy, yet this worship was not the same thing as family devotions. It was much more formal and communal.[18]

Over the centuries this catholic tradition grew, developed, and (regrettably) became distorted and overly concerned with human activities rather than God's actions as He comes to His gathered guests. Over time, a clergy-laity dichotomy developed. This was one of several aspects of the tradition that the Reformation sought to change.

CONFESSIONAL OR LUTHERAN TRADITIONS

This level of tradition looks at what can be called "non-Protestant" Lutheranism. Lutherans have maintained a distinction in many biblical doctrines that places them between Protestant and Catholic poles. For example, John Calvin and Huldrych Zwingli, while recognizing the significance of the Lord's Supper, believed that the finite cannot contain the infinite; therefore, bread and wine cannot bring us the body and blood of Christ. Their Reformed worship became merely a memorial service. Roman Catholics said that the elements of bread and wine change into the body and blood of Christ. Lutherans believe Christ is really present in, with, and under the elements.

A significant aspect of the confessional or Lutheran tradition is the understanding that catholic is not bad. Luther was Roman Catholic and did not desire to leave the church. Although excommunicated, he continued to seek to reform the church to an earlier, more pure, state, not establish a new "religion." Frank C. Senn reports this dimension of Lutheran tradition as follows: "What stands out in the Lutheran church orders, especially when compared with the orders and practices of other Reformation churches, is what Jaroslav Pelikan called 'a critical reverence' for the received catholic tradition. The concern of Luther and other reformers was to make worship consonant with Holy Scripture."[19] Lutherans continue to respect with a critical eye the traditional elements received from the larger church. In many ways this level of tradition includes many aspects of the higher levels of tradition, particularly the biblical.

Lutheran confessional worship emphasizes the means of grace. The Word of God, the Lord's Supper, Baptism, and Holy Absolution are not human inventions. Rather, they are God's gifts to His people.[20] Thus, Lutherans have emphasized Word and Sacraments as important aspects of Sunday worship.[21]

Preaching is an important aspect of Protestant worship, yet Lutherans have a particular emphasis in their preaching—the message from a Lutheran pulpit will always contain Law and Gospel (a biblical tradition). A Lutheran sermon clearly communicates both doctrines of Scripture; without both there is actually neither.[22] Coupled with this emphasis on preaching is the Lutheran self-understanding that believers are both saints and sinners. A confessional service or a preparatory service is normal in Lutheran liturgy because it recognizes this sinful condition and seeks God's forgiving aid for our worship life as His gathered guests.

Probably as noteworthy as liturgical worship and preaching in the language of the people is Luther's contribution of congregational hymns. Luther recognized the great opportunity that song provides to bring a message to the hearts and minds of

Lutheran Chorales

people.[23] Praising God with doctrinally sound hymns, especially with Lutheran chorales, has been a benchmark of Lutheran worship.

NATIONAL, SYNODICAL, OR DENOMINATIONAL TRADITIONS

The fourth level of tradition has various expressions, all centered on a limited geographic context. For our purposes we can speak of a synodical tradition that is peculiarly that of the LCMS. One could readily recognize distinctions at this level of tradition if one traveled to Scandinavia, Europe, or Africa and participated in a Lutheran worship service. The distinction may also be evident if one attended a worship service in an ELCA or WELS congregation. The LCMS has a noble tradition in the area of worship. Much of the traditions recognized throughout Lutheranism as middle-of-the-road positions have grown from this synodical tradition, which originated within a confessionally conservative German immigrant population.

Among the elements or examples of this tradition are the hymnals of the LCMS. *The Lutheran Hymnal* has stood the test of time, serving the LCMS for more than half a century. *Worship Supplement* contributed much during the days of liturgical renewal in the 1960s. *Lutheran Worship* is recognized for its substantively conservative yet innovative contribution to worship life in LCMS congregations. Similarly, *Hymnal Supplement 98* is making significant contributions to an expanded tradition that will culminate in a new hymnal by 2010. Plans for a new hymnal continue to reflect this synodical level of tradition.

Theological issues also affect worship practices at this level of tradition. For example, consider the LCMS statement on church fellowship practices. Because the LCMS recognizes the importance of public witness, certain worship practices, such as participation in ecumenical services, are to be avoided. The level of involvement granted to women in worship is also affected by theological considerations.[24]

The LCMS also has synodical idiosyncrasies, such as the Festival of St. Laurence.[25] Congregation members might wonder about the inclusion of such an obscure early Christian saint. However, a member of the committee that developed *Lutheran Worship* attended St. Lorenz, Frankenmuth, Michigan,[26] which was named for St. Laurence, the patron of the poor. This saint was recognized by some of the founders of the LCMS, so he is once again remembered in *Lutheran Worship*.

Perhaps one of the most obvious, yet least recognized, elements in synodical tradition is congregational autonomy, which has become a hallmark of the LCMS. This autonomy affects the worship life of every congregation and is evident immediately when visiting a neighboring congregation. No two LCMS congregations do everything the same.

PAROCHIAL, LOCAL, CONGREGATIONAL, OR PASTORAL TRADITIONS

The congregational nature of the LCMS provides a logical bridge to the fifth level of tradition. Each congregation has its own parish history. This history affects certain practices, such as service times, length of services, and even what occurs in the service. Because of greater community awareness, each congregation has an opportunity to plan services that will serve the particular community of God's gathered guests in which it is located.

Sometimes the congregational dimension contradicts higher levels of tradition. For example, some congregations do not offer Holy Communion every week, though that is a common practice. A variety of worship resources are used by some congregations, yet as a Synod, the member congregations of the LCMS have agreed to "walk together" and use "doctrinally pure agenda [and] hymnbooks" for worship.[27]

Specific pastoral sensitivities, coupled with local concerns, are reflected in local worship services. The number of handicapped or elderly members may affect Communion distribution practices. The employment or occupation of the membership may affect worship times and days on which services are offered. On the basis of pastoral concern for the gathered guests, pastors may also consider the length of their sermons or services. Certainly children's sermons are a worship element that varies from pastor to pastor and from congregation to congregation. Whether the congregation stands, sits, or kneels is often determined more by pastoral than by congregational or even synodical traditions.

PERSONAL TRADITIONS

The lowest level in the hierarchy of worship traditions is the personal level, yet it is probably the most set and the least likely to change. For example, your choice of service times is usually personal, but it also is habitual. You can recognize other personal traditions when a pastor either picks or fails to pick a favorite hymn. I recall one kind woman, a German-Russian immigrant, who attended a congregation my father served as pastor. She sat in the last pew every Sunday. One summer my father wanted the congregation to sit closer to the chancel, so he used a red rope to cordon off the last five rows of pews. The next Sunday as my brother and I served as ushers, we witnessed this woman enter church in her black dress and babushka, survey the scene, and without touching the rope, literally limbo under the barrier to sit defiantly in her pew! Needless to say, the rope was removed and my dad abandoned his attempt to move people closer to the chancel. Undoubtedly, you can determine more personal traditions from your own experience.

WHY A WORSHIP HIERARCHY?

This worship hierarchy is important because we can seek to move toward higher levels of tradition rather than remain at a lower level. As we recognize and use higher levels of tradition, we discover that we can include more of them in our worship experiences with beneficial results. For many worshipers, personal or congregational traditions are hardest to change. We "like" them, though there are logical and theological reasons why a biblical or catholic tradition may strengthen our relationship with Jesus Christ. In our postmodern society in which relationships seem to dominate, the higher worship traditions are often ignored or rejected rather than cherished and celebrated. As Lutheran Christians we have opportunities to expand and enhance our worship life by recognizing the hierarchy of traditions.

THE LUTHERAN WORSHIP TRADITION

When we speak of Lutheran worship, we need to recall that the Reformation neither destroyed nor offered innovations of worship practices; rather, it sought to restore the church to an earlier, more biblical, approach to worship. Luther is often criticized for being too conservative in the changes he made in the worship arena. His conservative approach, however, meant he kept everything that was not contrary or destructive to the Gospel. He recognized the great benefit of the "catholic" worship tradition in which he had been trained. The Lutheran confessional documents, especially the Augsburg Confession and the Apology of the Augsburg Confession, reiterate the fact that Lutherans kept the "catholic" worship tradition. Specifically, these confessional documents mention weekly Communion services and the use of other traditional worship aids, such as vestments and candles. To be Lutheran means to use these traditions wisely in the local congregation to feed and strengthen the people of God with His Word and Sacraments.

Luther's emphasis on the biblical doctrine of the priesthood of all believers stands as another mark of Lutheran worship. Luther recognized that clergy had no extra powers to bring prayers before the throne of God. Each Christian could pray, praise, and give thanks. Therefore, the whole congregation could participate in the worship life of God's gathered guests.

In many ways the Lutheran tradition of worship is still a "middle of the road" position within Christendom. James White places Lutherans as a "right wing" preservationist position within Protestant traditions on worship.[28] However, in the much larger perspective of Christian worship, Lutherans have been centrist, which is illustrated by the following diagram.

Pentecostal Baptist Reformed **Lutheran** Episcopal Roman Catholic Orthodox

As Lutherans reclaim their voice in the larger arena of Christianity, this centrist aspect of Lutheran worship will become increasingly important. Lutherans have many worship traditions to offer even as we continue to learn about other traditions.

PROTESTANT WORSHIP TRADITIONS

James White places various Protestant traditions of worship in the following general categories: Lutheran, Reformed, Free Church (sixteenth-century continental), Anglican, Free Church (seventeenth-century England), Quaker, Methodist, Free Church (nineteenth-century American), and Pentecostal.[29]

Lutheran worship, says White, is marked by a strong scriptural emphasis. A guiding motif for Luther was to restore the ancient practices of Christian worship to their rightful place in the life of the Christian congregation. In addition, White notes, Luther's own love of music and concern for preaching is characteristic of Lutheran worship. Thus congregational singing, reading Scripture in the language of the people, and preaching so the Gospel is clearly heard are encouraged. Traditional practices that were neither condemned nor commanded in Scripture were allowed in Lutheran congregations in contrast to the tendency of other reformers who rejected all extrabiblical practices. Finally, Christian art and liturgical ceremonies were retained in Lutheran churches unless they clearly detracted from the Gospel.

Reformed worship grew out of the Zwingli, Calvin, Bucer, and Knox reformations in Switzerland and Scotland, explains White. These reformers used Scripture as the sole guide to all forms of worship, yet in a legalistic and normative manner. Preaching was essential, though strongly didactic and emphasizing the moral improvement of the disciplined community. Originally, music was not allowed, except for the singing of psalms. Ceremonies in worship and the use of liturgical art was minimal, if used at all, and then only as a means to emphasize or dramatize the spoken Word.

The more radical reformation among the Anabaptists and Spiritualists in Switzerland led to a Free Church movement in which purity was the predominant emphasis. The name "Free Church" was applied because these churches were not recognized by the government and so were free of government intervention.

Preaching in these churches remained important, but they practiced only "believer's baptism." The Lord's Supper was celebrated infrequently and only as a memorial meal. A love for hymnody about martyrdom was one characteristic of this earliest form of Free Church worship. In North America, the variety of Baptist churches is evidence of the strongly independent nature of this form of the Free Church movement.

During the founding decades of the Anglican Church, worship was considered a means to achieve national unity. The *Book of Common Prayer* shaped the piety of the people by emphasizing the daily office for both laity and clergy. Human tradition was coupled with Scripture and human reason to serve as an authoritative tripod for determining worship practices. Later, particularly in the nineteenth century, expository preaching and majestic hymnody developed among some Anglicans into highly sophisticated worship practices, as did a certain form of sacramental piety.

The Puritans of England established a second kind of free church worship when they rejected all human tradition in their Anglican experience. Preaching again became prominent but with a stronger moral dimension. Each congregation was free to order its own worship life with a minimum of ceremony, and only psalms were used as hymnody.

George Fox developed the Quaker tradition, which rejected all outward forms of Anglican worship. The "inner light" of the Spirit was a primary feature of Quaker teachings. Sermons, prayers, hymns, and even Scripture were secondary to the personal experience of enlightenment. Communion could be celebrated without bread and wine because it was considered only "spiritual food." The key feature of a Quaker service was the peculiar silence as the "lights" (members) gathered to form the mystical body of Christ.

A worship tradition passed down from John Wesley also grew out of the Anglican and Free Church movements, but it took a more pragmatic and methodical approach (thus the name *Methodist*). James White calls Wesley's approach "pragmatic traditionalism" because Wesley used whatever worked from the *Book of Common Prayer* but added "love feasts," "night watches," and some ancient practices of hymnody. In addition, Wesley developed new hymns to correspond with his fervent preaching style and extemporaneous praying. Although a strong emphasis on frequent Communion marked Wesley's ministry, this did not develop in the North American Wesleyan tradition nor is it a significant element in contemporary Methodist worship.

A third form of Free Church movement, according to White, grew out of the frontier activities of the circuit rider missionaries. The freedom to follow God's

Word and to "do what works" dominated this form of worship tradition. Evangelistic preaching was the key method for making converts, and whatever worked to produce the desired result was deemed acceptable and even "of God." This approach is evident in Revivalism and many present-day "evangelical" denominations that emphasize personal decision and conversion experiences. Congregations in this tradition are independent of one another, and their worship forms and practices are as varied as the people who meet together. The significance of denominationalism in North America can find many roots in this third form of Free Church activity.

Pentecostalism is the most recent Protestant worship tradition. Beginning in the early twentieth century, it has its roots in Methodism and some Free Church movements of the previous century. No formal worship orders are used, though its informality follows a familiar pattern of preaching and is dominated by hymnody. Speaking in tongues usually marks the worship experiences in Pentecostal congregations, as does spontaneous congregational participation. While the sacraments are possible elements in worship, the emphasis on the Spirit's action predominates.

As Lutherans gather for worship, they are part of a larger Christian worship tradition, yet they emphasize a specific aspect of that tradition. They are part of the larger Christian community that believes in Christ as Lord and Savior, yet they desire to emphasize the free gift of salvation by faith alone. The Lutheran liturgical tradition keeps its focus on God's actions as He comes to His gathered guests through Word and Sacraments and on our response to God with prayers and praise.

SOME QUESTIONS TO CONSIDER

1. Why is the issue of tradition somewhat problematic for Lutherans? What tradition is rejected by Lutherans?

2. Explain the four reasons for following Christian traditions.

3. Distinguish between a biblical and a catholic tradition. Are there any similarities? Give illustrations from the history of the Christian church.

4. Distinguish between a confessional and national tradition. Are there any similarities? Give illustrations from your own experience.

5. Why are parochial and personal traditions the most difficult to change? Is it ever necessary to change them? Why or why not?

6. How is the Lutheran tradition of worship a middle position in Christianity? Give some illustrations.

7. What makes the Lutheran worship tradition Gospel-centered?

NOTES

1. The general structure and ideas for this chapter grew out of Bosch, *Worship Workbench*, 10–12.

2. Cullmann, "Tradition," 96–97. Cullmann also notes that the claim for episcopal succession in the case of Polycarp and Papius was a less effective safeguard against distortions when considering the Apostolic Fathers than the later writings of Irenaeus, for example, who had a canon on which to rely.

3. See Chemnitz, "Second Topic: Concerning Traditions," in *Examination of the Council of Trent*, 1:217–307. Chemnitz discusses various kinds of tradition, showing that most traditions are good and beneficial. Only a tradition that is counter to the Gospel is to be rejected.

4. See SA XV, 1, where Luther wrote, "That the papists say human [traditions] help attain the forgiveness of sins or merit salvation is unchristian and damnable" (K-W, 326).

5. Gritsch, "Martin Luther's View of Tradition," 61–75. Gritsch notes that Luther used the word *tradition* and its derivations almost 400 times in his writings.

6. "On the Councils and the Church," LW 41:3–178 (= WA 50:509–653).

7. Ap. XV, 38 (K-W, 229).

8. Hagen, introduction to *Quadrilog*, 3.

9. Chesterton, "Ethics of Elfdom," 48.

10. Reed, *Lutheran Liturgy* (rev. ed.), 503.

11. Hagen, introduction to *Quadrilog*, 3.

12. Maertens, *Assembly for Christ*, 1–36.

13. Vincie, "Liturgical Assembly," 129.

14. See Hummel's introduction to the Old Testament, *The Word Becoming Flesh*.

15. See, for example, Schneidau, *Sacred Discontent*.

16. See Kelly, *Early Christian Creeds*, for the background to these liturgical and confessional statements of faith.

17. Dix, *Shape of the Liturgy*, 36–156.

18. Richardson, "The Didache," in *Early Christian Fathers*, 161–79.

19. Senn, *Christian Liturgy*, 354.

20. AC XXIV, 1–10; Ap. XXIV, 1–8 (K-W, 68, 258).

21. See *Gathered Guests* chapter 5 for a thorough explanation of this dual nature of Lutheran worship.

22. See particularly thesis 4 in Walther, *Proper Distinction between Law and Gospel*, 60–69.

23. "Preface to Georg Rhau's *Symphoniae Iucundae* (1538)," LW 53:321–24.

24. See Commission on Theology and Church Relations, the LCMS, *Nature and Implications of the Concept of Fellowship* and *Women in the Church*.

25. See *Lutheran Worship*, p. 117, for the Propers for this festival, which is observed on August 10.

26. St. Lorenz was named after the "home" church in Germany of a particular group of immigrants.

27. See *Handbook of The Lutheran Church—Missouri Synod*, Constitution, Article VI.4: "Exclusive use of doctrinally pure agenda, hymnbooks, and catechisms in church and school."

28. James White, *Introduction to Christian Worship*, 43.

29. James White, "Classification of Protestant Traditions of Worship," 264–72.

CHAPTER 3

THE CHURCH YEAR

GOD'S TIME IN OUR TIME

As Lutheran Christians gather for worship, they do so with a strong sense of time and history because Lutherans have followed a worship calendar handed down through the centuries. In this chapter you will learn the background of the historic liturgical calendar and why Lutherans have set aside certain dates for particular consideration and celebration.

TIME CONSCIOUSNESS

Humans have always been time-conscious. Whether it is glancing at a clock in the classroom or at work, or letting the pastor know how long the sermon was, we are conscious of time passing. Light and darkness regulate our days. Daily life is ordered by the activities of work and rest. Seasons change in a regular way from times of growth to times of death, which we often perceive as an "end" of time.

God established this time consciousness. Genesis 1 shows the centrality of time, which God created when He instituted "evening and . . . morning—the first day" (Genesis 1:5). God set the time-markers in the heavens on the fourth day "to separate the day from the night, and [to] let them serve as signs to mark seasons and days and years" (Genesis 1:14). God rested on the seventh day as a model for us (Exodus 20:8–11).

The Hebrew people followed God's directives and celebrated time in significant ways. The English word *holiday* comes from the idea of a day being set apart (the Hebrew concept of "holy") from regular activities. The day of rest was established by God as a day to recall His creativity and His grace (Genesis 2:2–3; Exodus 20:11). As the people of Israel experienced God's care, He asked them to set apart particular days of remembrance—Passover (Leviticus 23:4–8), Firstfruits (Leviticus 23:9–14), Weeks (Leviticus 23:15–22), Trumpets (Leviticus 23:23–25), Tabernacles (Leviticus

23:33–43), and the Day of Atonement (Leviticus 16). Each of these days was to be special, a day distinctly different from the normal days of the year, as evidenced by its particular activities, which focused on God's gifts, promises, and blessings.

A CHRISTIAN CALENDAR

Christians retain this sense of time. Our seven-day week continues to recall God's incomparable creation of the world. Some Jewish festivals were adapted to the Christian community's time consciousness. The early Christians also recalled the historic time-related events that were important to their faith, especially events in the life of Jesus. They realized that God entered our world "when the time had fully come" (Galatians 4:4). Mark tells us that Jesus' first sermon was about time: "The time has come . . . the kingdom of God is near" (Mark 1:15). In his Gospel, Luke also reminds us of the timeliness of Christ's arrival: "In the time of Herod king of Judea" (Luke 1:5); "[the census] took place while Quirinius was governor of Syria" (Luke 2:2). The evangelist John also reports specific historical settings for our Lord's ministry (John 10:22–23). A Sunday close to Passover is now celebrated as the festival of the Resurrection of Our Lord (Luke 24:1). The Jewish harvest festival of Pentecost is remembered now as the birthday of the Christian church (Acts 2:1).

Christians also have added their own unique celebrations and adapted others to trinitarian understandings. For example, Easter did not become an extension of the Jewish Passover celebration; instead, it is an event by which Christians identify themselves as distinctly new creations. Easter is the Son's Day of Days. The Nativity of Our Lord, celebrated on December 25, is the second great Christian feast and is most clearly the Father's Day. On this day, God gives His most precious gift of life to the world in the person of His Son, Jesus. Finally, Pentecost has been separated from the Easter season and is celebrated with a specific focus on the Spirit's presence, power, and purpose. Thus Pentecost is the Spirit's Day. Celebrations of the Epiphany and Transfiguration of Our Lord also recall Jesus' ministry in power and glory. Trinity Sunday reminds us of the great controversies and struggles in the first three centuries of Christianity as the church sought to clarify and articulate the biblical revelation of God's unity in three distinct persons. As time passed, notable church leaders were remembered on their death day, underscoring the fact that death is actually an entrance or birth into the new life with Christ in heaven.

This sacred calendar of holidays is retained in Christian churches throughout the world for several reasons. First, a regular calendar is helpful to "keep the memories alive." Just as God commanded the Jewish people to recall how He had delivered them in the past, so Christians continue to keep these important memories alive in their communities as Jesus had encouraged His disciples to do (Luke 22:19). Second, following their Jewish predecessors, Christians consider the regularity of the holidays as "teaching moments" for followers of Christ. In Judaism, the Passover meal begins with a question that highlights the teaching moment as the youngest child asks, "Why is this night different from all other nights?" The answer spurs the recollection and retelling of God's redemption of the children of Israel from Egypt. Similarly, Christians see in the events of Christ's life timely moments to tell and retell the Good News. Finally, Christians recognize that this life is not an end in itself. Christ's victory over death means that daily life focuses beyond the mundane to eternity. A calendar of Christian events unites believers with the past and the future in the present. Thus the Christian community has adopted and adapted the Jewish calendar for its worship and faith life.

Following the same reasoning, Lutherans have retained the liturgical calendar, albeit adapted to a fuller Christ-centered theological and historical tradition. Lutherans join other Christians in following the Christian calendar so we may remember, nurture, and celebrate our shared Christian faith. Lutherans have made several changes to this calendar that are appropriate to our historic and theological needs, yet we have kept alive the enduring traditions that are most beneficial and edifying. As Edward Horn explains:

> The church has always impoverished itself when it has abandoned the church year, or attempted to reconstruct it. In the sixteenth century the conservative reformers were aware of this fact and retained the church year, eliminating only those festivals which were felt to be unwarranted on the basis of the teachings of Christ. The more radical reformers discarded the historic year . . . . The result has been that Protestant America, excepting the liturgical churches, has had an impoverished background.[1]

In this chapter, we will look at the church year as it has been used among Christians for centuries and particularly as Lutherans have used it for almost half a millennium.

The History and Development of the Church Year

Sunday

Basic to the Christian calendar is the first day of the week, Sunday. Yet as we sometimes forget, this day was not the day of worship among the children of Israel. The Hebrews were obedient to God's command to remember *shabbat*, the day of rest (Exodus 23:1–12), which was a weekly celebration of God's rest after the six-day creation (Genesis 2:2–3). In addition to the Sabbath, God set aside various holidays so the children of Israel could recall His continuing care for them and particularly His promises to them.

The early Christians continued the Jewish practice of Sabbath and other celebrations, but they did not observe them out of a sense of blind obedience. Instead, Christians took time for God in response to the continuing presence of the resurrected Christ and the gift of His Spirit. For Christians, a particularly significant change in the Jewish worship tradition was the adaptation of the weekly time to gather in Jesus' name. Instead of continuing the Sabbath rest (on Saturday), the Christian community's focus shifted the day to the Son's Day, "the first day of every week" (1 Corinthians 16:2), which is Sunday. A recollection of the first day of creation when God separated light from darkness was poignantly connected to the first day of re-creation (resurrection), which gave that day new meaning. Sunday was no longer merely a new *shabbat*, but it recalled the day Christ arose from the dead (Matthew 28:1–6; Mark 16:2–6; Luke 24:1–3; John 20:1–8). This day was known as "the Lord's Day" (Revelation 1:10), a concept retained in several Romance languages.[2]

Early in the second century, Bishop Ignatius of Antioch (ca. A.D. 35–107) identified his fellow Christians as those who "ceased to keep the Sabbath and lived by the Lord's Day."[3] About the same time, a manual for early Christian instruction, *The Didache*, reminded Christians: "On the day of the Lord come together, break bread and hold eucharist."[4] Thus it was that Sunday became the central feature of the Christian calendar.

THE CHURCH CALENDAR

The present arrangement of the church year will be followed in this chapter for ease in understanding the history surrounding the various holidays and celebrations. The actual historical development of the calendar (see diagram on p. 53) began with the celebration of Easter and its season, then Christmas and its season was highlighted, and finally distinctions were made among the festivals, the days of preparation, and the days of celebration. More details will be provided on a variety of services that can be used for special occasions related to these times, as well as information on the use of liturgical colors and the specific colors associated with the times in the church year.

Advent

The present calendar of the church begins with Advent (from the Latin *adventus*, which means "coming"). During this season, Christians throughout the world prepare for

The Church Calendar

Christmas. In western Christianity, this four-week preparation for Christmas[5] begins with the fourth Sunday before December 25 or the Sunday closest to the Feast of St. Andrew, which is observed on November 30.

Advent seems to have been established by A.D. 550, though practices varied across Europe for centuries thereafter. Apparently originating in fifth-century Gaul, Advent was first celebrated over a six-week period.[6] The four-week season was officially established by Pope Gregory the Great (pope from A.D. 590–604) and was considered a joyful festival season (during which the vestments and paraments were white). Only a century or so later, however, the theological emphasis shifted toward an anticipation of Christ's second coming, and the theme of preparation began to dominate the church's thinking. A short time later, the penitential nature of the season became central to the worship activities of Advent.[7]

The season of Advent shares some of the same qualities typically associated with Lent: Some congregations postpone weddings until after Christmas and the Gloria in Excelsis is omitted until Christmas Eve. The preparatory and penitential aspects of Advent focus on Christ's second coming as judge of the world on the Last Day. Despite the penitential tone, Advent is a time for holy joy and preparation that emphasizes four advents or comings: the prophetic coming that pointed to Christ's birth, the incarnate coming of Christ in Bethlehem, the sacramental coming of Christ in Word and Sacraments, and the eschatological coming of Christ at the end of the world. These themes may be developed throughout Advent in numerous ways and with a variety of services, for example the Service of Evening Prayer with its Service of Light.[8]

Christmas and Its Season

For early Christians, the Savior's birth was second in importance only to His resurrection on Easter Sunday. Therefore, from earliest times Christians took time to reflect on God's great and gracious gift of Himself. The date of Christmas, however, fluctuated among March 25, January 6, and December 25.[9] December 25 apparently was selected as the date because it coincided with a pagan winter solstice festival known as the birth of the invincible sun (*natalis solis invicti*). Christians quickly adapted this festival to the birth of the truly invincible Son of God, whom "the darkness has not overcome" (John 1:5 RSV).

However, Thomas Talley suggests another ancient reason to calculate December 25 as the date of Christ's birth, one that dates from the early fourth century. Citing the ancient belief that calculating the date of conception is more significant, Talley emphasizes that an older tradition places the date of the annunciation on March 25, and December 25 is nine months after this date. The choice of March 25 as the date of the annunciation was calculated from the biblical narrative of Mary's visit to Elizabeth, which occurred after John the Baptist's conception.[10] In addition, by following a somewhat mystical ancient logic in which famous persons were said to have lived in complete years, a person's death date was often considered to be his day of conception. Because the early church calculated that the first Good Friday occurred on March 25, this way of thinking meant Christ was conceived on the same date.[11]

Despite what occurs in our commercial markets, the season of Christmas continues after December 25, a period known traditionally as the "Twelve Days of Christmas." This nearly two-week season includes a number of minor festivals: The festival of St. Stephen, the first martyr, occurs on December 26. St. John, apostle and evangelist, is remembered on December 27. The death of the babies in Bethlehem is observed on December 28, which is the Feast of the Holy Innocents. The circumcision and naming of Jesus on the eighth day after His birth (Luke 2:21) is celebrated on January 1. The Christmas season culminates on January 6 with the most ancient nativity festival, the Epiphany of Our Lord.

Epiphany and Its Season

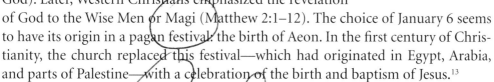

Epiphany is one of the oldest seasons in the Christian church year, second only to the Easter season.[12] This Season of Lights emphasizes Jesus' manifestation (the Greek word is *epiphany*) as God and man. The earliest Christians called the festival of the Epiphany the *Theophany* (revelation of God). Later, Western Christians emphasized the revelation of God to the Wise Men or Magi (Matthew 2:1–12). The choice of January 6 seems to have its origin in a pagan festival, the birth of Aeon. In the first century of Christianity, the church replaced this festival—which had originated in Egypt, Arabia, and parts of Palestine—with a celebration of the birth and baptism of Jesus.[13]

Epiphany may include as many as nine Sundays, depending on the date of Easter. The season begins with the Baptism of Our Lord. Included in Epiphany is Jesus' first miracle, the changing of water into wine at the wedding at Cana, which John reports in his Gospel: "He thus revealed [*ephanerosen*] His glory, and His disciples put their faith in Him" (John 2:11). The season ends with the Festival of the Transfiguration,[14] which is a significant and uniquely Lutheran contribution to the Christian calendar and is now celebrated by several Protestant denominations. This festival commemorates the moment on the Mount of Transfiguration when three of Jesus' disciples glimpsed their Lord in divine splendor, seeing Him as the center of the Law (Moses) and the Prophets (Elijah). Thus Jesus was manifested fully to His chosen disciples before He went to Jerusalem for the Passover. Johannes Bugenhagen, Luther's pastor and colleague, introduced Transfiguration Sunday to the Lutheran community in the sixteenth century.[15]

Epiphany offers several excellent opportunities for evangelism emphases. The focus on light and on Jesus' miracles presents numerous possibilities for relating

Christ's presence and purpose to contemporary society. A Service of Light to which members are encouraged to bring guests and visitors could underscore and manifest this Epiphany theme of evangelism.

In earlier Christian calendars, preparation Sundays for Lent were included at the end of the Epiphany season. These pre-Lenten Sundays were sometimes referred to as the "-gesima" Sundays because of the Greek endings of the titles for these Sundays—Septuagesima (70th), Sexagesima (60th), and Quinquagesima (50th). Finally church officials realized that not only did these Sundays make the Lent season "too long," but they were redundant—a preparation time *for* Lent during the "-gesima" Sundays prior to the preparation time *of* Lent.[16]

Lent

Easter celebrates the chief event in the life of Christ and was the major celebration among early Christians. However, Easter required a period of preparation. The 40-day preparation prescribed for baptismal candidates became known as Lent (from the Latin word for "spring"). During this period, the candidates were examined (the "scrutinies," as the questioning was often called) in preparation for Baptism at the Easter (or Paschal) Vigil. In A.D. 325, the Council of Nicaea recorded the first reference to the specific number of days for Lent: 40. Later, these 40 days were associated with Jesus' 40 days in the desert prior to His temptation (Matthew 4) and to the 40 years the children of Israel spent in the wilderness (Numbers 14:34). A few years after the council, in A.D. 329, the father of orthodox Christianity, Bishop Athanasius (ca. A.D. 296–373), asked his congregation in his paschal letter to keep a fast of 40 days.[17] This seems to be one of the earliest statements about a Lenten season. In the fifth century, Pope Leo the Great explained to his congregation in a Lenten sermon that "Lent was appointed to prepare souls for a fruitful commemoration of the mystery of Easter; as a time of inner purification and sanctification, of penance for sins past, of breaking off of sinful habits, of the exercise of virtues, especially almsgiving, reconciliation and the laying aside of enmity and hatred."[18]

Ash Wednesday begins the observance of Lent. The placing of ashes on the foreheads of God's gathered guests was practiced in France in the sixth century and was universally adopted as a sign of penitence and as a reminder of human mortality by the tenth century.[19] During Lent, alleluias are discontinued and the Gloria in Excelsis is not

sung. Already in the fourth century these liturgical omissions had become common practice.[20] Some early Lutheran congregations also forbade the playing of an organ and officiating at wedding services during the season.[21]

Interestingly, the Sundays during this season are not "of Lent" but "in Lent." Thus the Sundays retain an Easter tone and may be less solemn than the midweek services that Lutheran congregations typically offer. In earlier centuries of Christianity, Lenten fasts were extended from six to more than eight weeks, but Saturdays, Sundays, and the days of Holy Week were not considered part of Lent.[22] The observances of Lent are concrete reminders of the greater solemnity of this season, yet Lutherans emphasize the Gospel of Christ as central even to this penitential season.

Holy Week

Culminating the preparatory time of Lent is Holy Week, which begins with Passion Sunday and ends with Good Friday. The practice of celebrating throughout this particular week seems to have grown from a three-day event, the *Triduum* (Latin for "three days")—Maundy Thursday, Good Friday, and Easter Eve. Observed in Jerusalem, the Triduum pre-dates the 40-day Lenten season.[23] As increasing numbers of pilgrims attended services in the ancient city on these days, additional special services were added throughout the week. In notes she made about her trip to Jerusalem,[24] the fourth-century Spanish nun Egeria recalled the worship activities of this "Great Week" that had developed by A.D. 385. Apparently under the leadership of Bishop Cyril of Jerusalem (bishop from approximately A.D. 351 to 386), the historic sites in and around Jerusalem that were connected to Jesus' life, death, and resurrection became locations for special services to mark the events of Holy Week. These services provided opportunities for further catechetical instruction.[25] After the pilgrims visited the sites and participated in the services, they carried the moving experiences to their home territories and congregations. Thus the practice of stations of the cross and Lenten services spread throughout Europe.

Palm Sunday (from *Palmarum*, a Latin word that means "of the palms") was a Roman Catholic designation adapted after the Reformation in some Lutheran churches and only used in North American churches in the past century. The palm procession, which recalls Jesus' triumphant entry into Jerusalem, dates to pilgrim practices in Jerusalem in the fourth century. The use of palms, however, dates to Jesus' own lifetime, when they were used as symbols of hope, life, and victory.[26] Because the complete account of the Lord's passion from Matthew, Mark, or Luke is often read, this Sunday is also called Passion Sunday. (The passion according to John is normally reserved for use on Good Friday.)

In Lutheran circles, weekday services during Holy Week center particularly on Jesus' dialogues in chapters 12–18 of the Gospel of John. Johannes Bugenhagen prepared a passion history for use at Matins and Vespers during Holy Week that became popular among Lutherans for centuries.[27] At least one sixteenth-century Lutheran congregation in Brandenburg, Germany, followed Jesus' practice of footwashing.[28] Depending on pastoral and local circumstances, Lutheran congregations may wish to continue the practice after the Maundy Thursday sermon. Maundy Thursday was originally a preparation day for the paschal event. The name comes from the Latin phrase in John 13:34. In this section of Scripture, Jesus gives His disciples a new commandment: *mandatum novum. Maundy* is an Anglicized distortion of the Latin word for "command."

Besides recalling the footwashing and new command by Jesus, on Maundy Thursday Lutherans recognize the Jewish Seder setting of Jesus' institution of the Sacrament of the Altar. The third cup in the Jewish Passover observation is called "the cup of salvation." The significance of Christ's institution of the Lord's Supper and the benefits of the Sacrament, as well as the biblical understanding of Christ's presence in, with, and under the bread and wine, are clearly articulated in Lutheran congregations on this memorable day.

At the conclusion of the Maundy Thursday service, after the congregation has received the Sacrament of the Altar and the final prayers are said, the altar is stripped—all the linens, paraments, ornaments, vessels, and candles are removed. The congregation is encouraged to sing or read Psalm 22 as these items are taken from the chancel. The Benediction may not be spoken on Maundy Thursday to indicate that as part of the *Triduum* the service continues the next day.

Good Friday is the most solemn of all days in the Christian church (similar to Yom Kippur in the Jewish faith), yet a note of joy remains as the title of the day indicates: "Good" Friday. In some denominations, the Lord's Supper is not offered on Good Friday because it was celebrated the previous evening. This adds to the emphasis on mourning and fasting. Some Lutheran congregations, however, keep a less somber observance of this holy day by offering Holy Communion, ringing bells, and using the organ for congregational singing.

Easter Sunday and Its Season

For the early church, Easter was the chief festival. In the first century, Christians recalled Jesus' death as the Passover Lamb during the Jewish celebration of Passover, or Pascha, but His resurrection was the real cause for celebration. For several generations a debate raged concerning the date of Christ's resurrection. Known as the Quartodeciman (14th-day) Controversy, the debate was whether the Jewish dating of Passover on the 14th day of the lunar month of Nisan should be used as the date of Easter. Because this date could fall on any day of the week according to this method, Easter  could be celebrated on a Wednesday. In the fourth century, a decision was finally made: "Never on any day other than the Lord's Day should the mystery of the Lord's resurrection from the dead be celebrated, . . . on that day alone we should observe the end of the Paschal fast."[29] For Western Christians, Easter was finally set as the first Sunday after the first full moon after the vernal (spring) equinox.[30] Thus Easter serves as a fulcrum for the liturgical calendar for almost half the year.

Easter is a victory celebration, a time for all Christians to proclaim boldly their faith in a risen and victorious Savior. As Christians meet one another on Easter morning, the traditional greeting "He's risen!" is answered with "He's risen, indeed!" and festive chills often run down the spines of the gathered guests as they celebrate their Lord's victory.

For the early Christians, Easter was not merely a day, it was (and is) a whole season that also includes the celebration of Jesus' ascension. As one student wrote, "This is not only the focal point of our faith (the intellectual side), but this is really when the church parties (the emotional side)." The 50 days between Easter and Pentecost, known as the "Great Fifty Days,"[31] was the first liturgical season observed in the first three centuries of the church. This 50-day celebration is a week-of-weeks, renewed in *Lutheran Worship* by emphasizing the Sundays "of Easter." The season's length is fitting because we are dedicating one seventh of the year to the Lord's resurrection.

In many congregations, this festival season marks the beginning of vacation season and the conclusion of many church programs. How do we refrain from making the weeks after Easter "vacation time"? Can there be a sincere and meaningful celebration of Easter for 50 days? What elements of Easter Sunday can be extended throughout these weeks? Most pastors know that each Sunday of Easter has a special emphasis, yet many Lutheran worshipers are unaware of the images and events of the Easter season. Several Sundays recount Jesus' miraculous and mysterious post-Easter appearances. Perhaps this sense of mystery could be reintroduced. In ancient times, the Second Sunday of Easter was known as White Sunday because the recently baptized wore their white robes all week as a sign of their baptismal renewal. After the Reformation some Lutheran congregations held confirmation on this Sunday, continuing a German custom that dates to the ninth century.[32] Also noteworthy is the Fourth Sunday of Easter, which recalls the many references in John's Gospel to Jesus as Good Shepherd. This image of Jesus has profound significance because the concept of being lost and found still resonates, even in an urban environment. Such activities and emphases offer additional possibilities for respecting and reemphasizing the Easter season.

Ascension Day is celebrated 40 days after Easter, which means it falls on a Thursday. Until the fourth century, many Christians celebrated Jesus' ascension in conjunction with His gift of the Holy Spirit at Pentecost.[33] *The Apostolic Constitutions*, written at the end of the fourth century, directs Christians to "celebrate the feast of ascension of the Lord" 40 days after Easter, citing Acts 1:3 in support of the practice.[34]

The final Sunday of Easter anticipates the sending of the Holy Spirit. A congregation may choose to emphasize the anticipation that the early Christians experienced as they awaited this event. In some ways, this can be compared to a little Advent as Christians remember the hopeful and expectant anticipation of the first Christians as they awaited the Spirit's powerful presence. Throughout the Easter season, readings from the Book of Acts emphasize the rapid spread of the joyous Good News of Jesus' victory over sin and death and the consequent growth of the Christian community throughout the world.

Pentecost and Its Season

The Jewish spring harvest festival, known as Pentecost (Greek for "50th," named for the 50th day after Passover), was adapted by early Christians to commemorate the first great harvest of believers for Christ. Pentecost was the "birthday" of the Christian church as the Holy Spirit came upon the disciples and they gave their compelling witness to many people about their resurrected

Lord (Acts 2:1–41). For the first Christians, the celebration of Pentecost was second only to Easter in its importance, which is confirmed by its early date of origin. Beginning at least in the second century, Christians who had not been baptized at the Easter Vigil were baptized on Pentecost (Acts 2:41).

The emphasis on the Holy Spirit and the disciples' communication to all nationalities makes Pentecost an ideal festival for mission emphasis. The use of a variety of Bible translations for the assigned readings is one way to emphasize the Spirit's vital activity in the life of the Christian community. Pentecost also offers a prime opportunity for a congregation's members to celebrate the diversity of cultures present in the community. For example, the children could prepare banners with words of praise in languages spoken in the community. These banners could be part of a festive Pentecost procession. The activity of the Holy Spirit, as emphasized in the Lutheran Confessions, may also be underscored on this Sunday.

In a sermon preached in A.D. 386, John Chrysostom effectively summed up the liturgical year: "For if Christ had not been born into flesh he would not have been baptized, which is the Theophany [Epiphany], he would not have been crucified [some texts add: and risen], which is the Pascha, he would not have sent down the Spirit, which is the Pentecost."[35] If a paschal candle is used during the Easter season, usually it is moved near the baptismal font on Pentecost to mark the continuing presence and work of the Holy Spirit through the means of grace. This action can become a significant event in the life of God's gathered guests and a visual aid for children and new members.

After the fourth-century church delineated the relationship of the Father, Son, and Holy Spirit, the doctrine of the Trinity was recognized as orthodox. The three ecumenical creeds—the Apostles', the Nicene, and the Athanasian—were introduced into the liturgical life of congregations throughout Europe. The Sunday following Pentecost, the octave of Pentecost, became known as Trinity Sunday in the tenth century. Two popes with the name of Alexander (II in the eleventh century and III in the twelfth century) tried to suppress this special day, arguing that every Sunday celebrated the Trinity. But Pope John XXII (d. 1334) established 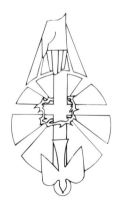 the Festival of the Holy Trinity for the whole Christian church.[36] Following that title, the season inappropriately became known as Trinity season. Because all other seasons of the church year are named after festivals, *Lutheran Worship* and most liturgical churches have restored the title of this season to its more traditional "Season of Pentecost." The Sundays are identified as Sundays *after* Pentecost. During this season, God's activity in the church is emphasized.

Because the Pentecost season is "ordinary," as the Roman Catholic Church identifies it,[37] congregations may choose to observe some of the lesser festivals of the season. When significant saint days or commemorations fall on Sundays, worship leaders could highlight these to inject variety in worship and offer teaching moments about the breadth of the church's life and work. These noteworthy days enable God's gathered guests to reflect on how we worship with "angels and all the company of heaven."

Saint Days and Lesser Festivals

The long tradition of liturgical worship provides an additional resource for the liturgical calendar—saint days and other appropriate holy days. In addition to the three festivals of Easter, Pentecost, and Epiphany, Christians of the first four centuries recalled the anniversaries of local martyrs. Edward Horn explains the significance of employing Christian models of the past:

> Almost every congregation in the first four centuries had its own roll of those who had suffered and died for the faith. It was only natural that the dates of their sacrifice should be commemorated in their churches . . . . Their names were read at the services and commemorative services on their "days" were sometimes held in the cemeteries or catacombs beside their graves.[38]

These dates of the martyred Christians were often called their "birthdays" into eternity. One of the first to be placed on a list was Polycarp, bishop of Smyrna, who died in A.D. 156 and whose martyrdom was recounted in several congregations.[39]

A better term for recognizing the contributions of these faithful early Christian believers is "commemoration" of the saints. A calendar of commemorations is valuable to Lutherans for several reasons, as Philip Pfatteicher indicates.

> The calendar of commemorations is a kind of genealogical exploration of who one's spiritual ancestors have been. It is a way of encouraging people to examine the personal stories of certain women and men to learn of the richness and the potential of human life lived by the grace of God in Jesus Christ. A study of the calendar is at once a course in theology, church history (and sometimes political history as well), spirituality, and prayer. Such a calendar can convey something of the breadth of Christian history and provide a rich assorted variety of the young and old, learned and ignorant, people of action and contemplatives, whose common denominator is simply that the grace of God worked mightily within them.[40]

Such commemorations, then, literally draw together our memories so we can express our thanks to God for His gracious Spirit, as well as receive encouragement in our own activities. Luther said that it is important for Christians to recall the saints because they are excellent models for our faith and life, concrete examples of following Christ. In 1527, Luther wrote some *Festpostils*, or meditations, for the commemorations of St. Mary Magdalene, St. Lawrence, the Assumption and Nativity of the Virgin Mary, St. Catherine, the Decollation [Beheading] of St. John the Baptist, the Invention and the Exaltation of the Holy Cross, St. Barbara, St. Nicholas, and St. Anne, though he objected to some of these festivals at other times.[41]

Luther's colleague Philipp Melanchthon explained the Lutheran viewpoint of saints in the Apology of the Augsburg Confession:

> Even though the great things that the saints have done serve as examples to people in their public or private life, as a means of strengthening faith and as an incentive to imitate them in public affairs, no one has searched for such examples in the true stories of the saints. It is indeed helpful to hear how the saints administered public affairs, how they underwent calamities and dangers, how holy individuals came to the aid of kings in times of great danger, how they taught the gospel and did battle with heretics.[42]

Therefore, Lutherans have continued to celebrate the faith of some who have joined the Church Triumphant. Central for Lutherans is November 1, All Saints' Day, especially because it follows Reformation Day.

Luther reduced the number of saint days and holidays on the Lutheran liturgical calendar by eliminating those that were most distant from Christ's life and work,[43] yet the variety of minor festivals on the present Lutheran liturgical calendar is astounding.[44] This variety is flexible and offers numerous opportunities for local distinctions.

When Lutheran congregations celebrate saint days, they often do so on a Sunday. This is sometimes referred to as celebrating "within the octave" of the feast—the Sunday within the liturgical week of the festival day. This practice and title comes from the original concept of the seven-day week. Early Christians emphasized the new creation theme by referring to the week as an "octave" of eight days—from Sunday to Sunday. A celebration within that eight-day week would occur in the "octave" of the festival. Thus Reformation is often celebrated either the Sunday before October 31 or the Sunday after but always within the octave of Reformation Day.

Lutherans do not celebrate as many saint days or Marian festivals as Roman Catholics and some within the High Anglican tradition. However, Luther and Lutherans have retained several Marian days because the emphasis was placed on

Jesus' life. These festivals include the Annunciation, the Purification of Mary (Presentation of Our Lord), and the Visitation. In recent years some Lutheran groups have considered popular political leaders to be worthy of celebration.[45] Caution should be used, however, because individuals should be remembered for their exemplary faith in Jesus Christ, not merely their productive and active social lives.

Lutheran congregations could introduce the observation of saint days by beginning with the saint after whom the church is named, such as St. Paul (January 25), St. Luke (October 18), St. John (December 27), or even Holy Cross (September 14). Such commemorations may offer opportunity for the congregation to think about their mission activities, as well as to connect with a higher liturgical tradition. Another saint day that many congregations commemorate is Michaelmas, or the Day of St. Michael and All Angels (September 29). Most Lutherans retained this day because it provides pastors with the opportunity to highlight the biblical teachings about angels and their ministry. Luther preached on Michaelmas more than a half-dozen times.[46]

Most Lutheran congregations observe the celebration of the Lutheran Reformation on October 31. An increasing number are beginning to celebrate the signing of the Augsburg Confession on June 25. Such an observance enables better understanding of our Lutheran history and encourages a renewed commitment to and sharing of the Good News of God's love in Christ for the whole world.

In addition to biblical saint days and celebrating key dates in the organization of the Lutheran Church, Lutherans recall the ways God has used individuals to bless the church. These days commemorate the lives of church leaders, such as Martin Luther (February 28), Wilhelm Löhe (January 2), and C. F. W. Walther (May 7), as well as the lives of martyrs (Perpetua, March 7; Polycarp, February 23; and Hus, July 6), missionaries (Patrick, March 17), renewers of the church (Agricola, April 10), renewers of society (Lydia, January 27; Lawrence, August 10), pastors and bishops (Chrysostom, September 13; Bugenhagen, April 20), theologians and teachers (Athanasius, May 2; Melanchthon, June 25), and artists and scientists (Cranach, April 6; Bach, July 28; and Copernicus, May 24).

Sunday of the Fulfillment

The Last Sunday after Pentecost, also called the Sunday of the Fulfillment and Christ the King Sunday, is a recent festival of Roman Catholic origin. It emphasizes the culminating vision and propitious expectation of the Lord's return in triumph, which mirrors Luther's suggestion that the last three Sundays of the church year be observed by reading Matthew 25:15–28 (the

abomination of desolation), Matthew 25:31–46 (the last judgment), and Matthew 5:1–12 (the Beatitudes, which were used in remembrance of those who had died in the faith). The latter remembrance was designed to replace the Roman Catholic observance of All Saints' and All Souls' Days on November 1 and 2. By the end of the sixteenth century, Matthew 24:1–13 (the parable of the foolish and wise virgins) became the customary reading for this last Sunday of the church year.[47]

The church year ends with an eschatological emphasis; thus it is again ready to begin the church year with its similar Advent themes.[48] This liturgical calendar was essentially complete by the end of the sixth century, though additions and emphases continue to be transmuted.[49] Christians continue to follow the festival half of the year, as well as the church's half of the year, so they may grow in faith and in gratitude as God's gathered guests.

This review of the origin of the church year and the special days of remembrance reminds us how important it is to see the bigger picture. We worship with a host of witnesses in the faith, both those gathered with us in a congregation and those gathered to be with the Lord in heaven. We are part of Christ's great holy Christian church, the communion of saints, God's gathered guests, as we participate in the great liturgical tradition of the Divine Service.

SOME QUESTIONS TO CONSIDER

1. Why is a liturgical calendar a comfortable means to organize the cycle of worship and Gospel proclamation?

2. Why have Lutherans retained the Christian calendar and the church year?

3. Describe the chief characteristics of Advent and the Christmas season.

4. What unique contribution have Lutherans made to the liturgical calendar in the Epiphany season? Explain the benefit of this contribution.

5. How does Lent serve the Easter season? What aspects of Lent differentiate it from the Easter season?

6. What one major thing differentiates the Pentecost season from the other seasons? How can this season be made "more interesting"?

7. Why does the Lutheran liturgical calendar have commemoration days? How can the Gospel be clearly proclaimed in such a context?

NOTES

1. Edward Horn, *Christian Year*, 26.

2. For example, the Latin term for Sunday, *dominica dies* ("Lord's Day"), became *Domingo* in Spanish, *Dimanche* in French, and *Domenica* in Italian.

3. Ignatius, "Letter to the Magnesians," 9.1, in *Early Christian Fathers*, 96.

4. Lake, "The Didache," 14.1, in *Apostolic Fathers*, 1:331.

5. Actually, Advent may vary between three and four full weeks, but it always includes four Sundays. The last week in Advent may be short, depending on when Christmas occurs during that week.

6. Buxton, "Advent," 1.

7. Cobb, "History of the Christian Year," 416.

8. See *Hymnal Supplement 98*, pp. 17–22.

9. Hickman et al., *Handbook of the Christian Year*, 23, suggest that "the dates of January 6 and December 25 may have originated in winter solstice celebrations according to the ancient Egyptian and Julian (Roman) calendars, respectively . . . . On the other hand, these dates may have been calculated using traditions regarding the date of Jesus' death and identifying the day of his death with that of his conception."

10. Talley, *Origins of the Liturgical Year*, 91–95. See also Roll, "Christmas Then and Now," 505–21, especially 509–12, 515.

11. Edward Horn, *Christian Year*, 67.

12. Edward Horn, *Christian Year*, 82, says Epiphany dates to the second century, when it served both as a commemoration of Jesus' baptism and of His birth.

13. Edward Horn, *Christian Year*, 17.

14. Reed, *Lutheran Liturgy* (rev. ed.), 485–86, indicates that the observance of the Festival of Transfiguration seems to date from a proclamation by Pope Calixtus III in 1456. Less than a century later, Johannes Bugenhagen and Veit Dietrich, Luther's colleagues, preached on this theme for the Sixth Sunday after Epiphany.

15. Pfatteicher, *Commentary*, 221.

16. Lutherans have generally followed the revisions introduced in the 1969 Roman Missal. Horn, *Christian Year*, 95–99, provides background to the three and a half weeks of pre-Lent. For interested persons, Pfatteicher has prepared a table of the liturgical calendar before and after 1969 in *Commentary*, 23–24.

17. Dix, *Shape of the Liturgy*, 355, notes that Athanasius's plea for such a celebration increased in intensity until A.D. 339. In that year, he begged his congregation in Alexandria, Egypt, to follow the 40-day fast so they would not be mocked by the rest of the Christian world for their neglect.

18. Edward Horn, *Christian Year*, 103, without further reference to the original source.

19. Pfatteicher, *Commentary*, 224.

20. Cabrol, *Year's Liturgy*, 1:102, reported that, in his Monastic Rule, Basil already required his monks to cease singing the Alleluia during Lent.

21. Senn, *Christian Liturgy*, 343.

22. Dix, *Shape of the Liturgy*, 355.

23. Pfatteicher, *Commentary*, 232.

24. Wilkinson, *Egeria's Travels*, 132–33.

25. Dix, *Shape of the Liturgy*, 348–53.

26. See 1 Maccabees 13:51; Revelation 7:9.

27. Edward Horn, *Christian Year*, 114.

28. Edward Horn, *Christian Year*, 120.

29. Eusebius, *History of the Church*, 230.

30. Dates for Easter until 2020 are as follows: March 27, 2005; April 16, 2006; April 8, 2007; March 23, 2008; April 12, 2009; April 4, 2010; April 24, 2011; April 8, 2012; March 31, 2013; April 20, 2014; April 5, 2015; March 27, 2016; April 16, 2017; April 1, 2018; April 21, 2019; and April 12, 2020.

31. Some early Christian writers, such as Eusebius, spoke of this 50-day festival as "Pentecost" (50th), though that was not a common designation.

32. Pfatteicher, *Commentary*, 291.

33. Tertullian, "On Baptism," in *Ante-Nicene Fathers*, 3:678; and Eusebius, *Life of Constantine the Great*, in *The Nicene and Post-Nicene Fathers*, ser. 2, 1:557.

34. "Constitutions of the Holy Apostles," V, III, xix, in *The Ante-Nicene Fathers*, ed. Alexander Roberts and James Donaldson (1886; repr., Peabody, Mass.: Hendrickson, 1995), 7:448.

35. John Chrysostom, *Opera Omnia*, ed. Bernard de Montfaucon (Paris: Gaume, 1834), 1:608, quoted in Hickman et al., *Handbook of the Church Year*, 24.

36. Reed, *Lutheran Liturgy* (rev. ed.), 519.

37. In the Roman Catholic Church, these Sundays are called the "Sundays in Ordinary Time."

38. Edward Horn, *Christian Year*, 17–18.

39. "Martyrdom of Polycarp," in *Early Christian Fathers*, 141–58.

40. Pfatteicher, *Festivals and Commemorations*, 16.

41. Edward Horn, *Christian Year*, 180.

42. Ap. XXI, 36 (K-W, 243).

43. In 1568, Pope Pius V did something similar by reducing to 150 the number of saints on the church calendar. However, by the time of Vatican II that number had more than doubled and another reduction was made, though with more local flexibility. Senn, *Christian Liturgy*, 660, adds that after Vatican II the Roman calendar had "only thirty-three feast days (including feasts of the Lord), with sixty-three obligatory and ninety-five optional commemorations."

44. See *Lutheran Worship*, p. 9.

45. This is especially evident in Pfatteicher and Messerli, *Manual on the Liturgy*; see also Pfatteicher, *Festivals and Commemorations*.

46. Luther preached on the Michaelmas Gospel (Matthew 18:1–10) or Epistle (Revelation 12:7–12) in 1520 (WA 9:477f.), 1530 (WA 32:552–55), three times in 1531 (WA 34/1:222–42, 243–69, 270–87), 1532 (WA 36:333–38), 1539 (WA 47:853–58), and 1544 (WA 49:570–87).

47. Senn, *Christian Liturgy*, 344.

48. Edward Horn, *Christian Year*, 24, writes that "the lessons from the last Sunday after Trinity in both Lutheran and Anglican use are reminiscent of the centuries when Advent was a longer season."

49. Klauser, *Short History of the Western Liturgy*, 9.

PART 2

THE LUTHERAN LITURGY

CHAPTER 4

THE ORIGINS AND DEVELOPMENT OF CHRISTIAN LITURGY BEFORE THE REFORMATION

W hen Lutherans worship, they participate as gathered guests in a great histor-ical and liturgical lineage. The worship services conducted in congregations throughout Lutheranism actually have a history that precedes Lutheranism. Lutheran worship has roots in the larger arena of Christian worship. As we saw in chapter 2, we can consider several higher traditions. Elements of Lutheran Sunday services recall Old Testament and New Testament practices. They also echo early Christian worship forms and draw us into the great "host of witnesses" mentioned in Hebrews 12. Frank C. Senn describes how present Lutheran worship practices come from many parts of the past:

> Christian liturgy retains traces of the various cultures through which it has passed and to which it has been adapted. We chant a Hebrew "Amen," sing Greek canticles, pray the rhythms of Latin rhetoric, assemble in Gothic build-ings, listen to German chorale preludes, and extend an American handshake at the greeting of peace.[1]

To understand the origins of Lutheran worship, we need to look at early Christian worship practices, then see what unique contributions Lutheranism has made to the present worship life of congregations.

A general form of worship has developed throughout the history of Chris-tianity, and it serves as a constant and central focus for God's gathered guests. This form is a corporate gathering of God's faithful people around the Word of God and the Sacrament of the Altar. The setting for these two activities has varied throughout history, yet it shows a similarity across a wide geographic and chronological space. Such remarkable similarity with creative variety makes the study of the history of worship an interesting endeavor.

"In spite of the constant flux and variation," notes John Harper, a historian of Christian liturgy, "it is possible to perceive . . . phases in the history of worship in the Western Church."[2] He delineates the first few centuries as (1) the formative period, followed by (2) an adaptive period as Christianity spread and adapted to the outer limits of the Roman Empire and as monasticism developed. Beginning during the eighth and ninth centuries, there was a movement toward a (3) medieval Roman-Frankish Rite under Charlemagne (ca. A.D. 742–814). Included in this period was the distribution of the late-medieval Roman rite of the twelfth-century Curia accomplished by the mendicant friars, especially the Franciscans in the thirteenth century. With the Council of Trent's response to the Protestant Reformation in the sixteenth century, a (4) codified period was established in Catholicism and Protestantism experienced a restorative period with unique individual or denominational emphases. We will look at Lutheran developments of the liturgy with special focus on developments in North America as many Lutherans migrated across the Atlantic in the eighteenth and nineteenth centuries. Beginning in the last half of the twentieth century, there is a period of (5) revision of the major western liturgical traditions.

THE FORMATIVE PERIOD

During the time of the New Testament, Christians worshiped in various ways, though little is actually recorded in Scripture. Two types of worship seem to have existed nearly simultaneously. Luther Reed suggests two terms to describe the worship practices of this formative period—a Jerusalem type and a Gentile type.[3]

THE JERUSALEM TYPE

Worship practices of the Jerusalem type were strongly influenced by the synagogue experiences of Jesus and His disciples, as well as the continuing practice of Christians who had converted from Judaism.[4] This type of worship was marked by regular attendance at the temple, along with a more intimate family-style worship that included a festive meal. For example, Acts 2:42, 46 states: "They devoted themselves to the apostles' teaching and to the fellowship, to the breaking of bread and to prayer. . . . Every day they continued to meet together in the temple courts. They broke bread in their homes and ate together with glad and sincere hearts."[5] These two liturgical emphases in the Jerusalem style of worship show a basic content comparable to the Word and Sacrament structure of modern Christian worship.

The Service of the Word in early Christianity had three dominant themes: praise, prayer, and proclamation.[6] The emphasis on the reading and exposition of the Scriptures in a setting of praise and prayer is "a direct inheritance from the Jewish Synagogue."[7] The Catholic liturgical scholar Fernand Cabrol says that "the christian *synaxis* [the Service of the Word] bears an astonishing resemblance to the Synagogue service and is made up of the same elements."[8] Hebraic expressions found in the Old Testament, such as "hallelujah," "amen," and "hosanna," as well as greetings of peace, were part of the common responses to the Word and illustrate this Jewish connection.

The weekly Jewish Sabbath meal gave early Christians the opportunity to recall the Lord's meals with His disciples. More important, it encouraged Christians to celebrate Christ's gifts given at His Last Supper.[9] Luther Reed explains the rationale for carrying some content of Jewish worship into the fledgling Christian community:

> Christians were discriminating in their use of Jewish elements. They retained the Old Testament teaching concerning the one true God and whatever was not antagonistic to the Christian faith. In addition to Hebrew formulas, such as Amen, Alleluia, Hosanna, Peace be with you, and doxologies, they took over the observance of the week and of the great festivals, Easter and Pentecost, though with different meanings. Minor details, such as ablutions, the use of oil and incense, the imposition of hands, standing in prayer, were also retained.[10]

In his historical analysis of early Christian worship, John Harper claims that "Jerusalem remained an influential center until the seventh century."[11]

THE GENTILE TYPE

The second pattern of worship in New Testament times is referred to as the Gentile type, which Luther Reed suggests developed perhaps 20 years after Christ's ascension.[12] These alternate worship experiences were not daily but weekly "Lord's Day" assemblies for educational discussions. The gatherings included a special meal, identified as the Eucharist (Greek for "thanksgiving"), and, perhaps additionally, *Agape* meals—a kind of church potluck—which are especially noted in Corinth.[13] These Gentile services were held in the houses of local patrons and involved a defined social group in Roman times with the father always serving as the head of all religious activities.[14] Charismatic activities are occasionally reported within this style of worship, but perhaps because of the pagan connotations, St. Paul recommended a more orderly service (1 Corinthians 14).[15] The emphasis in this Gentile type of worship was consistently on the body of Christ, as the church thought of itself as it gathered around Word and eucharistic and *Agape* meals.[16]

In both the Jerusalem and the Gentile type of early Christian worship, the Psalter was freely and fully used.[17] "New songs" (Ephesians 5:19; Colossians 3:16; Revelation 5:9) were also introduced as Christians sought to praise and proclaim the wonders of God's love in Christ in new and clear ways. Creedal statements are also evident in several New Testament passages and served as part of the worship life of first-century Christian communities.[18] These creedal statements gradually became more distinctly trinitarian as Christianity grew and drew away from its Jewish roots.

Numerous examples and references to liturgical structure are provided in the writings of the early church fathers, beginning in the first half of the second century. The larger groups involved in corporate worship required a more orderly form. St. Paul had wisely advised, "Everything should be done in a fitting and orderly way. . . . For God is not a God of disorder but of peace" (1 Corinthians 14:40, 33a). Early Christians heeded Paul's advice and found suitable structure for their practices as the church grew, enabling greater participation by all worshipers.

In the second century, Sunday worship with the Lord's Supper, or Eucharist, was standard. *The Didache (The Teaching of the Apostles)*, an early manual of instruction, describes an *Agape* meal (potluck) that included a Communion service. This shows a new synthesis of Jewish-Christian worship. A prayer from *The Didache* exemplifies the unifying character of public eucharistic worship and includes the following sentence: "As this piece [of bread] was scattered [as grain] upon the hills and then was brought together and made one, so let your Church be brought together from the ends of the earth into your Kingdom. For yours is the glory and the power through Jesus Christ forever."[19]

The double focus on Word and Sacrament in the worship service becomes increasingly evident throughout the second century. Reading from the Word of God was followed by a homily, then the celebration of the Sacrament of the Altar. In addition, prayers were said and hymns were sung throughout the service. The Service of the Word, following the synagogue practice of *lectio continua*—continual reading from a biblical book—included readings from the Old Testament and the "memoirs of the apostles" (a reference to either the Gospels or the Epistles). The whole congregation of believers participated in the service as they sang songs and affirmed the prayers of the community. Undoubtedly they used the short Hebrew exclamation "amen," or they sang the Hebrew "hallelujah" (Praise Yahweh) or the Greek plea "Kyrie eleison" (Lord, have mercy). Most likely they also prayed the Our

Father.[20] These early Christian communities also practiced close(d) Communion, particularly as persecutions became more common.[21]

In the third century more information about the worship service is available from primary sources. The early Christian teacher Hippolytus (A.D. 160–235) wrote *Apostolic Tradition*, which gives an early form of the Communion service.[22] Selections from Holy Scripture were read aloud as the people gathered in homes and assembly halls.[23] Following a kiss of peace, the bread and wine were offered, then came several preparatory sentences. A Communion prayer, known as the Great Thanksgiving (or Eucharist), included a consecration of the elements with the Words of Institution and a summary of the Christian faith. This prayer consisted of several sentences of thanksgiving to God, a narrative of the institution (*verba*), and the first appearance of a remembrance (*anamnesis*) and an invocation of the Holy Spirit (*epiclesis*) connected to the Supper, which Eastern Christians adopted into their liturgy.[24] The people then brought their offerings to the altar, and Communion prayers were followed by the distribution of the bread and the wine. A blessing and dismissal concluded the service. The structure and words of this Communion liturgy offer striking similarities to present-day Communion services in many liturgical worship books.

Another third-century writer, the lay theologian Tertullian (A.D. 150–240), describes *Agape* meals as evening socials distinct from the eucharistic services held in the early morning. The Sunday morning services Tertullian describes included readings from the Law, Prophets, Gospels, and Letters of the Apostles. The Prayer of the Faithful, a significant part of the worship service, was said while standing with arms outstretched rather than kneeling, an indication of a truly humble demeanor in that age, as well as being in conformity to St. Paul's directives in 1 Timothy 2:8.[25]

Worship was becoming more formal as Christians gathered around Word and Sacraments. Various individuals, lay and clergy, including women, were involved in these services.[26] Gradually, respect for Christ's continuing presence in the gathered community was shown as worshipers stood for the reading of the Gospel and for reception of the Communion elements.[27] These early practices blossomed into elaborate services of praise, prayer, and proclamation in the next centuries.

THE ADAPTIVE PERIOD

When the Roman Emperor Constantine announced the Edict of Milan in A.D. 313, he not only declared Christianity to be an acceptable religious expression in his empire, he also radically altered the conduct of worship by Christians.[28] Fernand Cabrol categorizes the resulting change in the worship practices of the common people of that time: "incense, flowers, vessels of gold and silver, lamps, crowns, lights, linen, silk, music, processions, festival days passed from the altars of the vanquished to the altar of the Victor."[29] Thus during this period the worship styles of the pagans were adopted and adapted by the Christians. (This same adaptive practice surfaces again in Luther's approach to the liturgy when he distinguished between "essentials" and "nonessentials" during the Reformation.)

A noteworthy adaptation during this period is the selection of the date for Christmas: December 25. Although now obscured by time, some scholars believe this date was chosen so a Christian celebration would correspond to the pagan festival of the birth of the invincible sun (*natalis solis invicti*), which was celebrated around the winter solstice. Other scholars have clearly and convincingly demonstrated that the early Christians used a sophisticated method to calculate Christmas, and it also fell on December 25.[30] In either case, by the middle of the fourth century the date was set.[31] In addition to this one date, a rather impressive calendar of remembrances developed over the next several centuries. This church calendar became fairly standardized by the end of this adaptive period.[32]

Because of the popularity and acceptance of Christianity, much more information is available on Christian worship during the adaptive period than is available from the formative period. Several documents on church worship orders from the fourth century have been preserved. For example, Egeria (or Etheria), a nun from Spain, recounted her pilgrimage to Egypt and Jerusalem around A.D. 380. She reports in detail the worship practices of the Christian community in Jerusalem, particularly those services around the festivals of Christmas and Easter. During this same time, the great theologians Basil (A.D. 330–79), Jerome (A.D. 331–420), Ambrose (A.D. 340–97), Chrysostom (A.D. 345/347–407), and Augustine (A.D. 354–430) wrote or spoke about worship. We also have two anonymous documents, the *Apostolic Church Order* and the *Apostolic Constitutions,* from this adaptive period that describe the worship life and practices of vigorous Christian communities.

With all this information, what emerges is a sense of careful structure to worship and a form of the liturgy that was always in two basic parts. For example, the *Apostolic Constitutions* describes a two-part worship service: the Liturgy of the Word and the Liturgy of the Upper Room.[33] After several introductory prayers, readings from the Law, Prophets, Epistles, Acts, and Gospels are interspersed with psalms sung by cantors. The sermon followed the readings and hymns, then the catechumens (those who were not yet baptized and, therefore, not yet full members) were dismissed. The second part of the service began with prayers by the deacon, then by the bishop. An offertory occurred and was followed by the Communion liturgy.

With increased adaptation in the worship life of God's gathered guests, diversity grew during these centuries. "In addition to the Roman Rite," reports John Harper, "important traditions emerged in the Ambrosian (Milan), Celtic (Ireland and northern Britain), Gallican (France), and Mozarabic (Spain) liturgies of the first millennium."[34] As each group adapted the basic form to its particular cultural demands, each of these national or provincial forms of the liturgy offered its own emphasis within the basic liturgical structure of Word and Sacrament.

One of the most significant adaptations of the liturgy occurred in Italy at the turn of the fourth century. The traditional language of the liturgy (Greek) changed to the vernacular of the people (Latin). An example is provided by Ambrose (Bishop of Milan A.D. 374–97), who routinely used Latin as the language of the liturgy, as well as in his preaching.[35] Until that time, the liturgy was spoken and sung in Greek, the cosmopolitan language of the then-known world. However, Ambrose understood the need for clear communication and used the local Latin dialect for liturgy and preaching. Only a vestige of this great Greek heritage remains in our contemporary liturgies: the Kyrie. The word *Kyrie* means "Lord" in Greek and is often used as the title of the ancient refrain "Lord, have mercy" (Kyrie, eleison).

The mention of Ambrose draws attention to another adaptation, or emphasis, that arose in this adaptive period. Sermons became increasingly popular features of the Christian worship service. Exposition of biblical texts had always been part of worship, even in Jewish circles. But during the fourth and fifth centuries, the most significant theologians—John Chrysostom, Basil, Ambrose, Augustine, and Jerome—were also gifted preachers, known for their expository style. Augustine, a rhetorician, said his conversion to Christianity was the result of visiting Ambrose's church in Milan to study his oratorical style. Augustine noted that after a while the style did not draw him to Ambrose's church; instead, the Gospel content of the messages he heard from the pulpit of this great preacher brought him back.[36]

Adaptations were also made in response to heresies that threatened the orthodoxy of fourth-century Christianity. This is particularly evident in the forms of prayers used in worship. Increasingly these prayers, or collects, concluded with trinitarian doxologies in response to the Arian controversies in the fourth and subsequent centuries. The singing of the Te Deum Laudamus and the Quicunque Vult (the Athanasian Creed) were direct results of confessional struggles around this time period.[37] The use of the Lord's Prayer became a part of the liturgical order during Communion at this time because Ambrose and Augustine both mention it in their writings as customary.[38]

Although processions during worship had been common since Old Testament times, Gospel processions were introduced in the fifth century with great fanfare. On the practical side, these processions enabled worship assistants to carry biblical texts to the various readers who were seated in the chancel area. But the processions also provided a miniparade on special feast days as the community assembled for the celebration, something the people not only enjoyed but also expected because it was the custom in the secular arena.

By the sixth century, under Pope Gregory the Great (A.D. 590–604), a new adaptation becomes evident in the role of the clergy. Because of the new theological emphasis on the "sacrifice" of the Mass, the ordained clergy were given more authority and visibility in worship. According to the seemingly logical rationale of Gregory's advisors, only priests could offer sacrifices; therefore, they must be given special privileges, prestige, and recognition. At this same time the Litany (the Deacon's Prayer) was reduced to only the words of the Kyrie, thereby limiting the need for lay assistants in the liturgical service. Under Pope Gregory and his successors, the use of liturgical chant (unaccompanied musical responses) developed into what became known as "Gregorian chant." Finally, during this century the Agnus Dei was introduced into the liturgy by Pope Sergius I (A.D. 681–701) after he visited among Syrian Christians, who used it during the breaking of the eucharistic bread.[39]

Adaptations also occurred regarding the selection of readings. The Syrian and Armenian churches reflected an older synagogue practice of using three readings in their services—one from the Law, one from a Prophet, and one from the New Testament. By contrast, in the West only one Old Testament reading was used and two readings came from the New Testament: an Epistle lesson and a reading from a Gospel. Inexplicably, by the seventh century only the New Testament readings were used.[40] In the sixth and seventh centuries, elaborate additions to the simpler form of the service become evident. "Stational" readings, which refers to the practice of various assisting ministers reading at different locations or stations in the chancel, were introduced. A subdeacon would read the Epistle, and a deacon would read the Gospel. At such a service the deacon would kiss the bishop's feet as a sign of devotion and service, then ask for a blessing before reading the Scriptures. Before the Gospel reading, the Gospel book would be brought to the deacon untouched by human hands (it was held through the chasuble). This procession included two torchbearers and two subdeacons (one subdeacon served as a thurifer, the assisting minister who carries the incense). The deacon would kiss the Gospel book before reading. Formal greetings between the presiding minister and the people, along with Gospel acclamations, were also added. The sign of the cross, standing to listen, and "the putting aside of canes, sticks, and swords, and the removal of headgear" were other adaptations introduced during this period.[41]

Although there was much variety during this adaptive period, two orders of service were becoming standard. By the end of the seventh century, the Gallican Mass, which originated in the area of present-day France, was widely used in Europe outside of Rome. In this form of the liturgy, the role of lay assistants was more extensive. The deacon, for example, would introduce the petitions during the prayers and administer the cup at Communion. In addition, this order of service "was more sensuous, symbolical, and dramatic than the Roman Rite of the same period, and much lengthier," as William Maxwell explains. "It abounded in propers, and was by far the most flexible rite known. Its ceremonial was elaborate and splendid, and its use of incense copious."[42]

In addition to this elaborate order of service, which provided much variety for individual communities, a simpler Roman order was being formulated. The following description provides some interesting insights about the structure of this early Christian service. John Harper explains:

> The document known as *Ordo Romanus I* (late seventh century) is a description of a Papal Mass celebrated at a church in Rome: it may be considered a prototype of the form of Mass that came to be codified in the Middle Ages. . . . Its contents encompass a compilation of items adopted, expanded, or truncated over at least 400 years. A crude summary shows something of this process: Entrance psalm (from Papal Mass procession in basilicas, c. 430), *Kyrie* as Litany (c. 495, later truncated), *Gloria in excelsis* (at Lauds, c. 340; at Mass, c. 500), Collect (c. 440), Readings (originally three or four, but only two by about the fifth century), Psalm between readings (by fourth century), Alleluia (spreads from Eastertide use, sixth century); Homily (from earliest times, but disappeared by seventh century), Dismissal of Catechumens (formalized in fourth century, disappeared in sixth century); Prayers of the Faithful (solemn prayers of second century, displaced by opening Litany in c. 495); Peace (before Offertory in second century, transferred to before Communion by fifth century), Offertory (wide range of offerings before fourth century); Thanksgiving (eucharistic prayer, earliest texts from second century); inclusion of *Sanctus* in eucharistic prayer (c. 400); Lord's Prayer (fourth century); Communion (with psalms from fourth century); Prayer after Communion (fourth century).[43]

A comparison with the form of Lutheran worship practiced in the twentieth and twenty-first centuries shows remarkable similarities.

THE MEDIEVAL PERIOD

Although this next period covers a length of time equal to the two previous sections combined, there is less to say about the development of worship forms. If anything, little changed. One author has described this period as a time of liturgical deterioration.[44]

Two major shapes of the liturgy vied for prominence at the beginning of this medieval period. Mentioned in passing was the Gallican form of the Mass. Common in Gaul (later to become France and, therefore, sometimes referred to as "Frankish"), this form allowed diversity, variation, and elaboration. The Gallican orders provided a wide repertoire of readings and prayers to be selected for the various feasts and local celebrations, as well as regular Sunday worship. The Gallican service books also incorporated material borrowed from the East, as well as Spain and the British Isles (Celtic).[45]

The Gallican Rite at the beginning of the eighth century would have appeared as follows:

Entrance songs or psalms

Call for silence with greeting and response

Triple Sanctus and Kyrie (sung; a fifth-century importation from the East)

Benedictus or Gloria in Excelsis (said or sung; a sixth-century importation from the East)

Collect before the Reading

Reading from a Prophecy or an Old Testament reading

Canticle from Daniel (Benedicite Omnia Operum or other canticle)

Reading from Acts or an Epistle

Prayer of Blessing and Sanctus (sung)

Gospel (procession with lights and incense, along with sung responses)

Chant (Kyrie or triple Sanctus after the Gospel)

Sermon

Deacon's Prayer (in litany form)

Dismissal of Catechumens

Offertory (offering gifts and Communion elements collected and prepared while a psalm is sung) and Litany of the Faithful (names of those who have died are recalled)

Collect after the Naming

Kiss of Peace and Collect of Peace

Salutation and Communion Preface

Prayer of Consecration (much variety allowed but always included the Proper Preface, Sanctus, Collect, Words of Institution, Collect of Invocation)

Breaking of Bread (into nine pieces to form a cross, followed by a collect spoken quietly, during which an antiphon is sung)

Lord's Prayer (with added prayers expanding on "deliver us from evil" in connection to the communion)

Bishop's Blessing of the People

Communion of the People (while Psalm 34 is sung)

Prayer of Thanksgiving

Dismissal (by the deacon)[46]

In comparison to the Roman Rite described earlier, this service is similar in general structure but allows more congregational participation.

During the last two centuries of the first millennium, pressure was placed on the Frankish lands to use the Roman liturgy, though with some northern European adaptations.[47] Thus the simpler (but more rigid) Roman Rite gained supremacy over the more elaborate (yet more ancient) Gallican Rite.[48] This Roman Rite was actually a modification of a service developed for the Curia, the papal administrators in Rome who did not wish to take time for elaborate services but wanted only to fulfill their responsibilities as clerics of the church, serving in the pope's chapel.[49]

One significant addition to the Roman Rite during this time was the inclusion of the Nicene Creed.[50] The Roman service also had collects, graduals, an offertory, and a silent Eucharistic Prayer with a strong emphasis on the "sacrificial mystery" (anticipating the later Roman Catholic teaching of transubstantiation). The practices of the reservation and adoration of the host grew out of this emphasis. "The celebration of the medieval Mass centered on the priest," notes John Harper. "Corporate elements of the early Church's celebration were omitted or abbreviated . . . . The eucharist assembly ceased to exist."[51]

The consequences of this last aspect of medieval worship were significant. Private devotions replaced a sense of corporate worship among the various worshipers. Thus a significant distinction between the priests, the laity, and even the monks became harmfully evident in the church's liturgical life, as well as in the social lives of these classes. The laypeople were no longer worshipers; instead, they became passive observers of those who were doing the work of the liturgy.

The priests, already deeply involved in leading worship, were given special prayers to use as private devotions during the liturgy. They had time to do so because professional choirs made up of other clergy took over much of the liturgy. For example, prayers at the Offertory, during the Sanctus, and before and after Communion were added to the sacramentaries (books that provided priests with the directions and texts for conducting the liturgy). Most of these prayers were spoken inaudibly, often while choirs were singing expansive responsories.[52]

Increasingly, the laity was being left out of the worship activities. Well-trained choirs and professional soloists (cantors) sang the traditional congregational responses. In addition to the laity's lack of involvement, the use of Latin as the language of the liturgy meant the services grew more distant from the regular life of the worshipers who spoke a variety of local dialects or languages. Therefore, something had to be offered in place of liturgical participation. That something was private devotion through the recitation of the rosary.[53]

The monasteries added to the separation of the liturgy from the general population. As monasteries grew in power and importance, they also elaborated on the liturgy, their main reason for existing and their chief work for God. For example, private masses were not only allowed but were encouraged because they provided funds to maintain the increasing number of monasteries and convents. Even when some monastic orders, such as the monks at Cluny, carried out drastic and necessary reforms, these same orders gradually left a legacy in which their elaborate liturgical forms dominated and added suffocating accretions to the originally simple Roman service.[54]

Yet the monastic movement was not altogether detrimental to the worship life of the people. The mendicant orders—the Dominicans and the Franciscans—were especially influential in encouraging the spread of liturgical piety and practice.[55] "The liturgy was a basis for their pastoral mission outside the walls of the friary, rather than an end in itself."[56] As they traveled throughout the countryside, the friars encouraged the simple Roman order of service. Because of their missionary zeal and willing adaptation, local variety persisted throughout much of this medieval period. Texts of the introits, graduals, lessons, prayers, blessings, ceremonies, and liturgical colors varied among distinctive regions and ethnic districts.

Despite this variety, the overall "structure and order [of worship] were relatively stable from the mid-eleventh century."[57] But this structure and order became more grand and more elaborate than that evident at the beginning of the medieval period. This elaboration was the result of the new aesthetic emphasis in art and architecture known as Gothic.[58] Gothic art, music, and architecture—introduced around the eleventh century—affected the liturgy because it emphasized the glory and exaltation of human achievements. Stability and grandeur were combined.

Over the eight centuries of this medieval period, the Roman Mass became the recognized standard for Christian worship, though in three forms—the Pontifical Mass, the High Mass, and the Low Mass. The Pontifical Mass was celebrated by a bishop and was almost completely sung by the assisting clergy as the choir. The High Mass was celebrated by a priest, who was assisted by a deacon, subdeacon, servers, and a highly trained choir. The choir sang the required musical responses. The Low Mass was a considerably abridged service, and a priest performed all parts of the liturgy.[59] The Low Mass became the standard for most laypeople in Europe at that time. "This period tells us that when solid theological, ecclesiological, and liturgical foundations are absent in our liturgical activities, autumn has come and winter is not far away."[60] From its earliest Christian origins, worship practices budded, blossomed, then faded. The great jewel of God's Word became only a small part of the great event of the sacrifice of the Mass. Finally, the mysteries of the Sacrament became the key event, and the Word of God was nearly lost. This was the worship life and liturgical context into which Luther was born at the end of the fifteenth century.

SOME QUESTIONS TO CONSIDER

1. Identify the five general periods into which the history of worship can be placed.

2. Compare and contrast the Jerusalem type and the Gentile type of New Testament Christian worship.

3. What is the historic double focus for all liturgical worship, a focus established in the first three centuries of Christian worship?

4. How did Constantine's Edict of Milan affect Christian worship practices?

5. What was the original language of worship among early Christians? What vestige of that language do we have in our present Lutheran liturgical services?

6. Compare the *Ordo Romanus* with the Divine Service in *Lutheran Worship*. Identify the common features.

7. What were the consequences of the elaborate worship practices of the medieval Mass?

NOTES

1. Senn, "Spirit of the Liturgy," 25.

2. Harper, *Forms and Orders*, 11. Although this chapter does not follow Harper's structure, information on the medieval liturgy is drawn from his study.

3. Reed, *Lutheran Liturgy* (rev. ed.), 25.

4. Recent scholarship has done much to help Christians understand their roots in Judaism. The influence of synagogue worship has been documented in Oesterly, *Jewish Background of Christian Liturgy*, as well as in Dugmore, *Influence of the Synagogue*. However, some recent studies have seriously questioned the reality of a standard in the synagogue worship life of first-century Judaism.

5. See also Luke 24:50–53; Acts 5:42.

6. Martin, *Worship in the Early Church*, 23–27. I altered Martin's third term to "proclamation" for alliterative purposes only.

7. William Maxwell, *History of Christian Worship*, 2.

8. Cabrol, *Prayer of the Early Christians*, xxi.

9. Senn, *Christian Liturgy*, 55–58, which draws on Di Sante, *Jewish Prayer*.

10. Reed, *Lutheran Liturgy* (rev. ed.), 36.

11. Harper, *Forms and Orders*, 16.

12. Reed, *Lutheran Liturgy* (rev. ed.), 25.

13. See Acts 20:7; 1 Corinthians 10:16; 11:20; 16:2.

14. Volz, *Pastoral Life and Practice*, 62.

15. Quasten, *Music and Worship*, 59–62, notes several early Christian sources that sought to avoid the "enthusiasm" of paganism for a more worthy praise of Christ.

16. Reed, *Lutheran Liturgy* (rev. ed.), 25.

17. Quasten, *Music and Worship*, 121, indicates that such usage of the psalms in the Gentile-type service was designed to offset the common devotional songs used in pagan homes.

18. Evidence of New Testament hymns and creedal formulations have been identified by many scholars. See, for example, Romans 13:11–12; 1 Corinthians 2:9; Ephesians 5:14; Philippians 2:5–11; Colossians 1:15–20; 1 Timothy 3:16; 2 Timothy 2:11–13; Revelation 5:9–10, 12.

19. Richardson, "The Didache," 9.4, in *Early Christian Fathers*, 175.

20. William Maxwell, *History of Christian Worship*, 13, draws this from Justin Martyr, "First Apology," 65–67, in *Early Christian Fathers*, 285–86.

21. Elert, *Eucharist and Church Fellowship*, 75–83. See also Richardson, "The Didache," 9.5, in *Early Christian Fathers*, 175.

22. Hippolytus, *Treatise on the Apostolic Tradition*, iv.1–13 (pp. 6–9).

23. Van Dijk, "Bible in Liturgical Use," 222.

24. Reed, *Lutheran Liturgy* (rev. ed.), 33–34. See *Worship Supplement*, p. 46, for an English translation of this prayer.

25. See Tertullian, *De Oratione* (*On Prayer*), for details as cited in Reed, *Lutheran Liturgy* (rev. ed.), 34–35. Tertullian also gives an early commentary on the Lord's Prayer.

26. See Quasten, *Music and Worship*, 75–86; and Volz, *Pastoral Life and Practice*, 180–211.

27. William Maxwell, *History of Christian Worship*, 16.

28. The rescript issued at Nicomedia by Licinius on 13 June 313 simply stated: "When we, Constantine Augustus and Licinius Augustus, met so happily in Milan, and considered together all that concerned the interest and security of the State, we decided . . . to grant to Christians and to everybody the free power to follow the religion of their choice, in order that all that is divine in the heavens may be favorable and propitious towards us and towards all who are placed under our authority" (Lactantius, *De mortibus persecutorum*, xlviii). See also Eusebius, *Ecclesiastical History*, X.v.

29. Cabrol, *Prayer of the Early Christians*, xiii, cites what he calls "the pompous phraseology of Chateaubriand" from his *Etudes historiques*, t.II, 101.

30. Roll, "Christmas Then and Now," 505–21, shows that early Christians calculated Christ's death as March 25 on the Julian solar calendar. Because of the saving significance of Christ's incarnation, they believed His conception also would have occurred on March 25, making His birthday December 25.

31. Roll, "Christmas Then and Now," 509, notes that the earliest attestation to December 25 is the calendrical almanac of Furius Dionysius Philocalus, which is known as the *Chronograph*.

32. Dix, *Shape of the Liturgy*, 333–34, 347–60.

33. William Maxwell, *History of Christian Worship*, 27f., provides a general scheme of the worship service that is drawn from Book 8 of the *Apostolic Constitutions*.

34. Harper, *Forms and Orders*, 17. Interested students will find informative details on this variety in William Maxwell, *History of Christian Worship*; Senn, *Christian Liturgy*; and in chapter 4 of *Twenty Centuries of Christian Worship* (vol. 2 of *Complete Library of Christian Worship*, ed. Robert E. Webber).

35. Reed, *Lutheran Liturgy* (rev. ed.), 44, attributes this to a scholarly conjecture by the Benedictine monk Odo Casel, which Reed says has been generally accepted by most scholars. Jungmann, *Early Liturgy*, 205–6, however, suggests that this transition occurred earlier, perhaps already in the middle of the third century. The official change came under Pope Damasus I (d. 384), according to Chupungco, "History of the Liturgy until the Fourth Century," 105.

36. Augustine, *Confessions of Saint Augustine*, V.14, (pp. 130–32).

37. Piepkorn, *Roman Catholic, Old Catholic, Eastern Orthodox*, 148–51.

38. Dix, *Shape of the Liturgy*, 131.

39. Van Dijk, "Bible in Liturgical Use," 243.

40. Van Dijk, "Bible in Liturgical Use," 224.

41. Van Dijk, "Bible in Liturgical Use," 229–30.

42. William Maxwell, *History of Christian Worship*, 48. Maxwell describes a reconstruction of a typical Gallican service in some detail (pp. 49–51).

43. Harper, *Forms and Orders*, 111.

44. Senn, *Christian Liturgy*, 211. Senn titles this chapter "Medieval Liturgical Deterioration."

45. Leonard, "Gallican Liturgy," 63–64.

46. Adapted from William Maxwell, *History of Christian Worship*, 49–50; Senn, *Christian Liturgy*, 138, 186–87, and Leonard, "Gallican Liturgy," 63–64.

47. Harper, *Forms and Orders*, 17.

48. Reed, *Lutheran Liturgy* (rev. ed.), 52f.

49. Harper, *Forms and Orders*, 18.

50. William Maxwell, *History of Christian Worship*, 65.

51. Harper, *Forms and Orders*, 113.

52. William Maxwell, *History of Christian Worship*, 69–71.

53. Walsh, "Rosary," 471–72.

54. Chupungco, "History of the Roman Liturgy until the Fifteenth Century," 147.

55. Chupungco, "History of the Roman Liturgy until the Fifteenth Century," 149.

56. Harper, *Forms and Orders*, 30.

57. Harper, *Forms and Orders*, 114.

58. *Goth* was the Germanic equivalent of the Latin *gens*, which means "people." See Senn, *Christian Liturgy*, 174.

59. William Maxwell, *History of Christian Worship*, 63f.

60. Chupungco, "History of the Roman Liturgy until the Fifteenth Century," 151.

CHAPTER 5

THE ORIGINS OF LUTHERAN LITURGY

REFORMATION AND POST-REFORMATION
LITURGICAL CONTRIBUTIONS

Christians have always recognized the centrality of corporate worship. Lutherans have rejoiced in their deep roots in this fertile soil of Christian worship. The legacy inherited by Martin Luther and his followers came from the early Christian synagogue and home-church experience and was passed down through many hands over hundreds of years. This tradition grew, changed, was corrupted, and was reformed many times throughout many generations. From simple services of Scripture readings and the Lord's Supper to ones so elaborately overlaid with distracting accretions that something had to be done, the church has struggled with how to worship God in spirit and truth, in purity and orthodoxy. God's gathered guests want and need to receive the promised blessings of their Host and to respond to His gracious gifts.

The shape of the liturgy that Luther experienced in his early years was that of the medieval Mass. This shape reflected the early Christian structure of Word and Sacrament, but by Luther's time the involvement of the people was minimal. The service itself had become "a dramatic spectacle, culminating not in communion, but in the miracle of transubstantiation, and marked by adoration, not unmixed with superstition, at the elevation."[1] The clergy now dominated the worship life and, in most cases, were the only ones involved in actual worship activities. Scripture readings, if any, were in Latin and, therefore, were not understood by the common people, who stood as silent and ignored worshipers. Sermons were nonexistent or, if given on holidays, were merely comments on the legendary lives of saints. The time for reform had come.

Luther's experience of the need for reform is evident in his comments in 1523 to a congregation in Leisnig or Wittenberg:

> The service now in common use everywhere goes back to genuine Christian beginnings, as does the office of preaching. But as the latter has been perverted by the spiritual tyrants, so the former has been corrupted by the hypocrites. As we do not on that account abolish the office of preaching, but aim to restore it again to its right and proper place, so it is not our intention to do away with the service, but to restore it again to its rightful use.[2]

Thus Luther set about to suggest some changes so the Gospel could be heard by God's gathered guests.

The Lutheran Reformation

For Luther, the presence of Christ, whose life and death justified the world, was central in theology and practice. Therefore, Word and Sacrament, the two places where God is present with His love and forgiveness, are central to the life of the Christian community. Luther's emphasis on preaching and teaching demonstrated the centrality of the Word. In his Ninety-five Theses (1517), Luther repeated the phrase, "Christians are to be taught . . . ."[3] Several years later he wrote that every time Christians gather for worship, the Holy Scriptures should be read and the glorious Gospel proclaimed.[4]

In 1520, Luther preached a sermon in which he stated that the Lord's Supper ought "to be celebrated daily throughout Christendom."[5] In the Supper, communicants recognize and receive the very presence of the Lord; it is God's gracious gift to His beloved people. In his 1520 treatise "On the Babylonian Captivity of the Church," Luther condemned the Roman Church's manipulative use of the sacramental system, which required people to come continually to church to receive God's grace. In opposition to that situation, he urged a vernacular service and repudiated transubstantiation, withholding the cup from the laity, and the Mass as a good work and a sacrifice. Luther said that all believers can give to God is a "sacrifice of praise" because the greatest sacrifice was Christ Himself, given once and for all.[6]

Luther chose to reform the Mass rather than to substitute a new "reformation" service. In December 1523, Luther introduced his "reformed common service" with his *Formula missae et communionis* ("Form of Mass and Communion"). In doing so, he distinguished between essentials and nonessentials. The latter elements were acceptable practices that clearly showed Christian liberty. Hearing the Word, however, was essential. Therefore, Scripture passages and the sermon were to be read and preached in the vernacular (though for daily chapel services on the campus of Wittenberg University, Luther still encouraged reading Scripture in Hebrew and Greek for the sake of the students). Communion in both kinds was reintroduced to attest to the completeness of the sign. Congregational participation, especially in the singing of hymns, was introduced to emphasize the priesthood of all believers. Thus the parish became the primary location for pastoral care, and the liturgy was directed to the people of the parish.[7]

The following service outline shows Luther's careful delineation of essentials and nonessentials:[8]

> Introit
> Kyrie (nine times)
> Gloria in Excelsis
> Collect of the Day
> Epistle
> Gradual of two verses and Alleluia (or a Sequence Hymn, but only for
>   the Nativity and Pentecost)
> Gospel (lights and incense optional)
> Nicene Creed (sung)
> Sermon (the Creed could be sung after the Sermon as the elements were
>   prepared during the Offertory)
> Offertory
> Preface
> Verba (sung, read aloud, or read silently)
> Sanctus and Elevation (during "Blessed Is He")
> Our Father
> Pax
> Communion
> Agnus Dei
> Communion
> Final Collect
> Salutation
> Benedicamus
> Benediction

In this service Luther showed his "radically conservative" nature of reforming, retaining "the use of the Latin language along with the optional use of lights, incense, and vestments."[9] However, he eliminated the most theologically abhorrent part of the service: the Canon of the Mass. During this main prayer of the Mass, saints were invoked and the idea that the priest was offering a sacrifice for the people's sins was communicated to the worshipers. As Frank C. Senn notes:

> By retaining the outward ceremonial act of the elevation at the place where it usually would have occurred, Luther was able to effect a radical change in the rite of the mass: the virtual elimination of the canon and the relocation of the *Verba institutionis* [words of institution] . . . . This stroke of pastoral genius has to be unequalled in the history of liturgy: to have effected a radical revision of the heart of the Mass without the worshipers necessarily noticing any outward change.[10]

The changes in worship were done in the content, not in the form, of the liturgy.

Luther was not alone in seeing the need for reform. Several others attempted to reform the Mass, but they failed to produce a truly German Mass. One such effort was a Germanized liturgy prepared in 1522 by Carmelite prior Kaspar Kantz.[11] In 1525, Luther introduced another service, his *Deutsche Messe und Gottes-dienstes* ("German Mass and Divine Service"), that included more congregational singing. The following outline gives the basic shape of this service.[12]

> Hymn or German Introit
>
> Kyrie (three times; it is unclear why Luther eliminated the Gloria in Excelsis)
>
> Collect (sung facing the altar)
>
> Epistle (sung facing the people)
>
> German hymn
>
> Gospel
>
> Apostles' Creed (Luther versified the Nicene Creed;[13] the offerings were gathered at this time and the altar prepared for Communion)
>
> Sermon (normally on the Gospel)
>
> Lord's Prayer (paraphrased)[14]
>
> Exhortation to Communicants[15]
>
> Consecration (sung) and Distribution of Bread
>
> German Sanctus[16]
>
> Consecration and Distribution of Wine
>
> German Agnus Dei or another hymn
>
> Post-Communion Collect
>
> Aaronic Benediction

Luther used this service for an entire year in Wittenberg before publishing it in 1526.

A comparison of the two outlines of Luther's services reveals a peculiar practice: a double distribution of the Communion elements. Luther believed such a practice affirmed the real presence of Christ, who was the actual host of the Meal. By participating in the service, the worshipers experienced that first Lord's Supper and became contemporaries with Christ and Christ with them.[17] In addition, Christ was truly with the worshipers at their own altars.[18] That is also why Luther suggested that "the priest should always face the people as Christ doubtlessly did in the Last Supper."[19]

In addition to these two Services of Holy Communion, Luther produced two baptismal rites (1523 and 1526), an Order of Marriage (1529), an Order of Confession, a German and Latin Litany (1529), and an Ordination Rite.[20] These services, along with several dozen hymns, reflect Luther's burning desire that the people hear the Gospel in all their worship activities.

While most Lutheran churches accepted the principles of Luther's liturgical reform, they did not follow Luther's services mechanically or legalistically. Most congregations rejected Luther's omission of the Gloria in Excelsis, as well as his split Verba, the double distribution of the elements, the elevation of the host, and his paraphrased portions of the liturgy. Instead of his Exhortation to Communicants, the ancient Preface was restored in most Lutheran congregations.

The Lutheran confessors clearly assert that no break with Rome was considered, and they certainly did not innovate or propose drastic changes in the arena of worship practices. In fact, the Augsburg Confession states: "Our churches are falsely accused of abolishing the Mass. In fact, the Mass is retained among us and is celebrated with the greatest reverence. Almost all the customary ceremonies are also retained, except that German hymns, added for the instruction of the people, are interspersed here and there among the Latin ones."[21] Philipp Melanchthon reiterated this in the Apology of the Augsburg Confession.

> We do not abolish the Mass but religiously retain and defend it. Among us the Mass is celebrated every Lord's day and on other festivals, when the sacrament is made available to those who wish to partake of it, after they have been examined and absolved. We also keep traditional liturgical forms, such as the order of readings, prayers, vestments, and other similar things.[22]

Thus the Lutheran Reformation did not produce a radical change in the worship life of the people, but it did change its focus. Word and Sacrament clearly became the focal point for worshipers because through them came the Good News of God's forgiving love in Christ. Participation by the worshipers through song and prayer added to this emphasis. Worship was no longer a burdensome drudgery, an obligation; instead, it was a joyous privilege and an opportunity to receive generous blessings from God and respond to His gracious presence.

As a result of the intimate connection Luther recognized between evangelical doctrine and liturgical practice, Lutherans have always been concerned that worship practices reflect biblical doctrine. This importance is seen in the years following the official reading of the Augsburg Confession (1530). The most influential of Luther's followers in the area of worship was his colleague and pastor at Wittenberg, Johannes Bugenhagen (1485–1558). Bugenhagen, along with Melanchthon (1497–1560) and Justus Jonas (1493–1555), prepared "church orders" for nearly a dozen congregations or regions in Germany during the time of the Reformation. "No fewer than 135 church orders appeared between 1523 (*Formula Missae*) and 1555 (Peace of Augsburg)," many of them influenced by Bugenhagen.[23] These church orders regulated church life, laying out the details of administrative structure, as well as guiding the liturgical materials to be used in Lutheran worship.

In one of his first church orders, the Brunswick Orders of 1528, which was prepared for northern Germany and Denmark, Bugenhagen proposed the following order of service: Introit (Psalm 34 or another psalm); Kyrie and Gloria (pastor intones and choir continues); Collect and Epistle; a Gradual (sung by choirboys); Gospel reading; Creed (pastor begins, "I believe in one God," and congregation continues with Luther's chorale, "We all believe in one true God"); Sermon; announcements and encouragement to pray for the state; German hymn or psalm (communicants enter chancel, and after preparing the elements, the pastor exhorts communicants); Preface (using traditional propers in Latin); Sanctus (by choir in Latin); Lord's Prayer (sung in German by pastor with congregation responding with "Amen"); Words of Institution; distribution (after Agnus Dei, other German hymns are sung); Luther's Post-communion collect; the Aaronic Benediction.[24] In comparing this service to those of Luther, one sees a conflation of his *Formula Missae* and his German Mass. This basic order would become a standard practice for Lutheran services throughout the rest of the century and a mark of Luther's legacy.

OTHER WORSHIP REFORMS

The Reformation affected not only Lutherans, but also all of western Christendom. Although we do not have the space to discuss the variety of worship reforms that occurred during this period of change, the following reforming movements should be mentioned because they affected the worship life of the times.

The Swiss reformer Huldrych Zwingli (1484–1531), trained as a humanist, created a service that was extremely didactic. His carefully prepared prayers were doctrinal expositions of belief rather than devotional petitions and doxological words of praise. The presence of Christ in the Lord's Supper was stated, but the celebration of this Meal was never the norm. In fact Communion was offered only infrequently because it was not considered a means of grace. In 1523, Zwingli presented his revision of the Mass in *An Attack on the Canon of the Mass*. The emphasis, even in the Communion liturgy and particularly in the prayers, was on the Word.[25] Two years later Zwingli abolished the use of eucharistic vestments, as well as music. Such a radical approach resulted in an empty corporate worship life because a balance of Word and Sacrament had been neglected. *Balance*

John Calvin (1509–1564), on the other hand, introduced a less radical approach to his French followers in Strasbourg and Geneva. Adapting much from Martin Bucer (1491–1551), Calvin added a clear emphasis on frequent Communion, though the Genevan magistrates rejected such a practice.[26] He published *Form of Prayers and Manner of Administering the Sacraments according to Ancient Church Usage* in early 1540, which included the following order of service:

Scripture Sentence (Psalm 124:8)

Confession of Sins and Prayer for Pardon (the reading of the Law may have been introduced here)

Absolution

Metrical Psalm (sung, or Hymn of Praise)

Collect for Illumination

Reading (may be from a Gospel)

Sermon

Collection of Alms

Intercessions

Lord's Prayer (in a lengthy paraphrase)

Preparation of Elements

Apostles' Creed (sung)

Words of Institution

Exhortation

Consecration Prayer

Breaking of Bread and Distribution (psalms may be sung or Scripture read)

Nunc Dimittis (introduced in Strasbourg by Calvin but not mentioned in later services)

Post-Communion Collect

Aaronic Benediction[27]

Calvin attempted to take the two parts of the liturgy and unite the service into one, simple, flowing experience.

In 1531, Thomas Cranmer (1489–1556), who later became Archbishop of Canterbury, visited Germany for a year and a half. During that time, he studied Lutheran forms of worship and Luther's liturgical principles. In 1547, Cranmer produced the *Book of Common Prayer*, which contained the "Order for Communion," which was almost identical to Lutheran practices in Germany.[28] Luther's influence is evident in the fact that Communion was distributed in both kinds, a major revision of the Canon of the Mass eliminated the sacrificial language, and the eucharistic prayers only spoke of "a sacrifice of praise and thanksgiving."[29]

Finally, the Roman Catholic liturgy, which had become increasingly standardized, was formalized at the Council of Trent (1545–1563). As a result of the Council of Trent (and the availability of efficient printing presses), all liturgical books used in Catholic congregations were revised, standardized, and published exclusively by the Curia. This Latin (or Tridentine, named after the Council of Trent) Mass remained normative throughout the Catholic world for the next four centuries.[30]

Lutheran Orthodoxy and Pietism after the Reformation

The generation following Luther was blessed with many orthodox thinkers and clear writers. Among them was the "second Martin," Martin Chemnitz (1522–1586), who helped establish Luther's biblical positions in a time of internecine battles among the reformer's Protestant and Lutheran successors. Johann Gerhard (1582–1637), leader among the succeeding generation of Lutheran theologians, continued the clear articulation of Lutheran doctrine and encouraged continued practice of the faith. These orthodox teachers provided a solid edifice built on Luther's evangelical foundation.[31]

The vitality of the Lutheran Reformation was undercut, however, within a century of Luther's initial reform activities. Most destructive was the Thirty Years' War (1618–1648), which broke out initially when the Catholic king Maximilian of Bavaria tried forcibly to restore Catholicism throughout Europe. Thankfully, the Swedish Lutheran King Gustavus Adolphus (1594–1632) provided military relief for the German Lutherans, who continued to suffer from incidental battles until a final settlement was reached. During these 30 years, church buildings and their contents suffered irreparable damage and the people's worship life was disrupted and nearly eliminated. By some accounts, as much as half the population died or emigrated from German lands during this period. After these devastating and demoralizing years, congregational life took on a mechanical expression of the previously

vital Reformation faith. Unfortunately, to restore some sense of ecclesiastical continuity, Lutheran leaders tried to impose rules for attending church and the Lord's
Supper. Worship was explained as fulfilling the Law of God.[32] Such legalistic rigidity
only created a greater spiritual vacuum.[33]

This vacuum was filled by a movement known as Pietism. In 1675, Philipp
Spener (1635–1705) published a proposal for revitalizing Lutheranism from its cold
institutionalism. His booklet *Pious Desires* offered suggestions for increased Bible
study groups, lay leadership in congregations, living the Christian faith, expressing
Christian love for the world, and revitalizing seminary instruction to include spiritual formation and practical experience.[34] While Spener's ideas were good, the practical results had several far-reaching negative consequences. Under Spener's
disciple, the capable organizer A. H. Francke (1663–1727), Pietism revitalized many
segments of Lutheranism, but a separatist attitude also developed, primarily
because of Spener's idea of "little churches" or cell groups. These groups often
rejected not only pastoral leadership and supervision, but also the need for Scripture as the Spirit's promised vehicle. Bible study replaced the Lord's Supper, and the
traditional liturgical forms of worship were rejected and replaced by free-flowing
subjective extemporaneous styles of worship that were no longer identifiable as
Lutheran.

Despite Pietism's influence, an enclave of Lutheran orthodox worship
remained in Leipzig well into the eighteenth century. This was the city of Johann
Sebastian Bach (1685–1750), the greatest Lutheran composer.[35] "In Bach's Leipzig
there were daily public prayers, a weekly Eucharist with a great many communicants, and a rich observance of the church year."[36] The orders of service were similar
to that of the Reformation church orders. Ministers used traditional vestments,
including the chasuble for Holy Communion. The spiritual depth of the gathered
guests in Leipzig underscores the benefits of solid worship practices in times of
uncertainty.

In addition to Pietism, with its rejection of rigidity for its own methodological
structure of Christian spirituality, Rationalism also undercut the orthodox Lutheran
liturgical life. Growing out of the 18th-century Enlightenment, Rationalism
attempted to move away from the church's traditions, as well as to avoid pure piety.
Rationalism replaced piety and tradition with human reason, yet reason quickly
gave way to a more rigid antisupernaturalism and a stronger deistic sentimentality
than had ever been experienced in Christendom. Luther Reed summarizes the consequences of Rationalism on Lutheran worship by noting that the services "ranged
in character from empty sentimentality to moralizing soliloquy and verbosity."[37]

LUTHERANS IN NORTH AMERICA

During the eighteenth century, Lutherans began coming to North America in increasing numbers. Many influences had undercut the Lutheran liturgical heritage of the Reformation—especially Pietism, Rationalism, and anti-Romanism. These same influences were at work on the Lutheran immigrants in the Americas, which meant they lacked a certainty of what it meant to be Lutheran in this "new world."[38]

One of the greatest North American Lutheran leaders was Henry Melchior Muhlenberg (1711–1787). He had been sent by the Pietist school of Halle to help establish Lutheran congregations in colonial America, particularly in Pennsylvania.[39] Muhlenberg's English Liturgy, which he developed for his own congregations as well as the congregations of the Pennsylvania Ministerium, was a composite of the German services he remembered and a printed order from St. Mary's German Lutheran Church in London.[40] The basic form became known as the Common Service.

As the number of Lutherans increased in the American colonies, the orders of service brought from various European congregations and districts were modified. Many of these changes were the result of attempts by Samuel Schmucker (1799–1873) to "Americanize" Lutheranism. He sought to eliminate those practices most clearly identified as "Lutheran" that Schmucker and others claimed were roadblocks to evangelism. These practices included the pastor's declaration of absolution and the regular celebration of the Lord's Supper. Influenced by the desire among some new Lutherans to be truly ecumenical, Schmucker also initiated changes in the worship practices of North American Lutherans to break "down the partition wall between the Lutherans and the Reformed which is only based upon prejudice."[41] These efforts resulted in a dilution of Lutheran identity and a lack of clarity in the Gospel proclamation through Word and Sacrament. Fortunately, in the middle of the nineteenth century, the Ministerium of Pennsylvania took bold steps and carefully developed an English translation of the German liturgy, restoring to Lutherans in North America a more fully developed classic liturgy of the Reformation.

During the second quarter of the nineteenth century, many immigrants from Saxony, who had left Germany because of Rationalism and a government-imposed church union with Reformed congregations, arrived in the central United States. They brought with them two major service forms—a Saxon *Agenda* and an *Agenda* prepared by Wilhelm Löhe (1808–1872). Both agendas reflected a more orthodox and confessional understanding of Lutheran worship. In his introduction to his *Agenda*, Löhe explained to F. C. Wyneken (1810–1876) that, after studying approximately 200 church orders, he was presenting a consensus that reflected the best orthodox Lutheran usage. In addition to the chief service of Holy Communion, Löhe's *Agenda* included the daily offices of Matins, Lauds, Prime, Vespers, and Compline, along with Luther's Litany, General Prayers, and the rites of Baptism, confirmation, marriage, Communion of the sick, and installation of a pastor.[42]

C. F. W. Walther, first president of the LCMS, after supervising a new song-book for his immigrant congregations, turned his attention to the preparation of orders of service. In 1856, a *Church Agenda* (*Kirchen-Agende*) was issued. It provided services for many occasions, particularly for the main Sunday service, *Der Hauptgottesdienst* (literally, the "Chief Divine Service"). This was a more formal German service than Muhlenberg had developed or than that included in the Saxon *Agenda*. It followed closely the Common Service, which would be adopted in the mid-1880s by several other Lutheran synods in North America. Through several avenues, this service came down to the Evangelical Lutheran Synodical Conference of North America in *The Lutheran Hymnal*, as well as to those Lutherans who developed the *Service Book and Hymnal* and most recently *Christian Worship*, the hymnal for WELS congregations.

THE PERIOD OF REVISION

The history of North American hymnbooks is beyond the purview of this book, but needless to say, it is varied and interesting.[43] About the middle of the twentieth century, a new interest in liturgy arose throughout Christendom. Liturgical movements flourished among Catholics, Lutherans, and Episcopalians, as well as among several nonliturgical denominations. Many of these movements quickly recognized the close ties between worship and doctrine. Believing that worship could move groups together, the ecumenically minded leaders in some denominations were especially cognizant of the impact that worship forms could have on the church.

Two branches of Lutheran hymnals grew in somewhat parallel fashion in the latter half of the twentieth century. In 1941, the LCMS published *The Lutheran Hymnal*, prepared by all six member denominations of the Inter-Synodical Committee of Hymnology and Liturgics of the Evangelical Lutheran Synodical Conference of North America. This joint project of six synods (Missouri, Ohio, Wisconsin, Illinois, Minnesota, and the Norwegian) employed the Common Service of the previous century, which exhibited the best English-language liturgy of the time.[44] Two years later, several Lutheran groups proposed a Joint Commission on the Liturgy. Because the LCMS had just completed its hymnal, President John Behnken declined the invitation; however, "bodies, representing about two-thirds of Lutherans in North America, did respond positively."[45] As a result of these efforts, the *Service*

Book and Hymnal of the Lutheran Church in America was produced in 1958. As expected, joint worship practices led to corporate mergers among several Lutheran groups. Of the eight Lutheran bodies that had worked on this hymnal project, four formed the ALC and the other four became the LCA.[46] In 1959, the LCMS initiated discussions with these same Lutheran churches to develop a joint hymnal for all North American Lutherans. Again, because the *Service Book and Hymnal* had just been published, there was no great desire on the part of the other Lutheran groups for such a project. Instead, the LCMS developed its *Worship Supplement*, which was published in 1969.

Meanwhile, Pope John XXIII (1881–1963) called the Roman Catholic Church together for the Second Vatican Council, which opened on October 11, 1962, and concluded on December 8, 1965. One major emphasis of this council was the introduction of worship variations through the "Constitution on the Sacred Liturgy." Lay participation in worship (including the possibility of receiving Communion in both kinds), liturgy in the language of the people, and a greater emphasis on Scripture readings (along with sermons) were a few of the momentous changes. Protestants took note of and were invited to consider these changes in light of their own traditions, particularly the use of a common liturgical calendar.[47]

In early 1966, as a result of synodical convention resolutions in the summer of 1965, Oliver Harms (1901–1980), president of the LCMS, invited the ALC and the LCA to form a joint worship commission. This group became the Inter-Lutheran Commission on Worship (ILCW). Beginning in 1969, the ILCW produced several study documents, which were to be reviewed by local Lutheran congregations and national synods.[48] Regrettably, because theological controversy erupted nationally within the LCMS during the early 1970s, most LCMS congregations paid little attention to these liturgical studies. However, throughout this period of upheaval in the LCMS, plans continued simultaneously among other North American Lutherans for a joint hymnal.

In 1977, the LCMS rejected the proposed *Lutheran Book of Worship* on theological grounds, though church politics were also involved as an underlying cause of the rejection.[49] The ALC and the LCA, along with the new AELC (a group that broke away from the LCMS shortly before this hymnal was rejected), adopted *Lutheran Book of Worship*. Ten years later, in 1988, these three Lutheran bodies formed the ELCA.

LUTHERAN WORSHIP

The LCMS hymnal and service book *Lutheran Worship*, published in 1982, is a modified version of *Lutheran Book of Worship*. Some of the changes are beneficial, and some were politically or personally expedient for those involved. Regardless of the reason, the result was "something old, something new, something borrowed, something blue."

"SOMETHING OLD"

Within *Lutheran Worship* are many elements from earlier hymnals and traditions. The traditional introits and collects have been saved for posterity; the familiar Common Service, or "Order of Holy Communion," appears as Divine Service I; and the daily offices of Matins and Vespers were included. In addition, the Bidding Prayer and Luther's Litany, as well as many familiar hymns from *The Lutheran Hymnal*, were retained.

"SOMETHING NEW"

While keeping much that was good from the previous hymnal, several settings of the Divine Service were added to *Lutheran Worship*. In addition, a full Rite of Baptism was placed in the liturgical section of the book. New texts for 23 hymns were supplied, along with newer settings of Matins and Vespers, titled "Morning Prayer" and "Evening Prayer." A distinct service without Communion was eliminated, as were most Elizabethan pronouns. Rubrics (directions) printed in red helped make the format of the liturgy clearer. One major change to the services was the addition of assisting ministers, indicated in the liturgy by $\boxed{\textbf{A}}$, as well as the reference to a presiding minister, indicated by $\boxed{\textbf{P}}$. These additions were meant "to expand . . . the corporate quality of worship."[50]

"SOMETHING BORROWED"

The musical settings of Divine Service II in *Lutheran Worship* were taken from *Lutheran Book of Worship*. The biblical translation for the Psalter and other scriptural references were from the New International Version. More than 130 hymns included in *Lutheran Worship* are common hymns listed by the Consultation on Ecumenical Hymnody and appear in 26 other denominational hymnals.[51]

"SOMETHING BLUE"

The cover of *Lutheran Worship* reverted to the blue color of an older edition of *The Lutheran Hymnal*, though in a more attractive and contemporary shade!

THE FUTURE FOR WORSHIP IN THE LUTHERAN CHURCH

With the increasing use of computers and photocopiers, with the availability of a variety of worship resources on CD-ROM, with the increasing use of copyright licenses, will hymnals become a thing of the past? In a publication by the LCMS Commission on Worship, the question was raised whether there is a future for the liturgy and for hymnals.[52] The answer was a resounding yes! By the end of the first decade of the third millennium, a new hymnal will be available for congregations of the LCMS, but it will not be the "same old thing." And there will always be a need for new worship resources as "each generation receives from those who went before and . . . adds what best may serve its own day . . . ."[53]

The evidence over the past decade shows an increase in publication of hymnal materials and supplements. The LCMS prepared a Hispanic hymnal in the late 1980s. In 1993, WELS presented its carefully prepared update of the Common Service in *Christian Worship*. In 1997, the ELCA prepared *With One Voice*, a supplement to *Lutheran Book of Worship*. In 1998, the LCMS introduced *Hymnal Supplement 98* for study and use in anticipation of its new hymnal. In 1999, Augsburg Fortress published *This Far by Faith*, a culturally sensitive hymnal for African American congregations. Many other denominations also have produced hymnals and liturgical resources in recent years.

Several issues will be raised as new resources are received or rejected by God's gathered guests. How does the church express its careful critique of the dominant culture of its society? How can the devotional lives of Christians be enhanced through corporate worship? What impact do various special-interest movements have on the church's worship life? Can the church seek unity in the Spirit through a celebrated diversity of worship practices?

Lutherans will always seek new ways to express the eternal truths of God's love and grace in Christ. Lutheran Christians understand that our corporate worship expresses our corporate faith. What we say and do in church expresses our doctrinal understandings, and worship affects our daily lives. We always need resources that unite the great catholic tradition of worship with contemporary expressions of faith in God the Father, who sent His only Son to redeem the world and whose unifying and edifying Spirit continues to work through Word and Sacraments.

SOME QUESTIONS TO CONSIDER

1. What was Luther's approach to reforming worship life? Can that principle still be used when looking at the contemporary worship life of congregations?

2. List five distinct features in Luther's orders of service compared to those normally conducted at the time.

3. How did Bugenhagen retain Luther's tradition of worship? How did he change it?

4. What changes did other Protestant reformers make to the liturgy? Why were their changes different?

5. How were Pietism and Rationalism harmful to the worship life of some post-Reformation Lutherans?

6. What worship needs did Lutherans in North America face? How were these needs met?

7. Describe the period of revision in Lutheran worship in the last part of the twentieth century as compared to the earlier periods identified by John Harper in the previous chapter.

8. How is *Lutheran Worship* something old, something new, something borrowed, and something blue?

9. Why are new hymnals still necessary? Why is it a great time to study worship?

NOTES

1. William Maxwell, *History of Christian Worship*, 72.
2. "Concerning the Order of Public Worship," LW 53:11.
3. "Ninety-Five Theses," LW 31:29–30, theses 42–51.
4. "Concerning the Order of Public Worship," LW 53:11.
5. Luther's "Sermon on Good Works," cited in William Maxwell, *History of Christian Worship*, 74.
6. "On the Babylonian Captivity of the Church," LW 36:3–126.
7. Harper, *Forms and Orders*, 31.
8. LW 53:19–40; WA 12:205–20.
9. Senn, "Luther's Revision of the Eucharistic Canon," 101.
10. Senn, *Christian Liturgy*, 278–79.
11. William Maxwell, *History of Christian Worship*, 76.
12. See *Lutheran Worship*, pp. 197–98, for an adaptation of this service that uses hymns, including several by Luther. Luther's German service is found in LW 53: 61–90; WA 19:72–113.
13. *Lutheran Worship*, 213.
14. *Lutheran Worship*, 431.
15. *The Lutheran Hymnal*, 47.
16. *Lutheran Worship*, 214.
17. The altarpiece by Lucas Cranach the Elder in St. Mary's, Luther's home church in Wittenberg, shows Luther at the Passover table with Christ and the disciples.
18. See Maschke, "Contemporaneity," 165–82. For a detail of the Wittenberg altarpiece, see Maschke, "Contemporaneity," 168.
19. LW 53:69.
20. Spinks, *Luther's Liturgical Criteria*, 3. See LW 53 for several of these orders of service.

21. AC XXIV, 1–2 (K-W, 69).

22. Ap. XXIV, 1 (K-W, 258).

23. Senn, *Christian Liturgy*, 330, 332.

24. Senn, *Christian Liturgy*, 332–33.

25. William Maxwell, *History of Christian Worship*, 82.

26. Bouwsma, *John Calvin*, 24, 217.

27. William Maxwell, *History of Christian Worship*, 112–19. Maxwell calls the paraphrase of the Lord's Prayer "long and tiresome" (115).

28. From Cranmer's *Book of Common Prayer*, U.S. Lutherans would get their "English" translation of the Common Service 300 years later, which explains the use of King James English in several versions of the Divine Service, including those in *The Lutheran Hymnal*. See Precht, "Worship Resources in Missouri Synod's History," 103.

29. William Maxwell, *History of Christian Worship*, 146.

30. The Second Vatican Council set new guidelines for worship in its "Constitution on the Sacred Liturgy" (4 December 1964).

31. Preus, *Theology of Post-Reformation Lutheranism*, 15–19.

32. Kalb, *Theology of Worship*, 10–64, details this aspect in two chapters.

33. The spiritual vacuum was not complete. The orthodox theologian Johann Gerhard produced a corpus of doctrinally pure yet spiritually nurturing devotional materials. Paul Gerhardt (1606–1676) similarly produced a great number of orthodox, confessional, yet spiritually vital hymns during these years. Most notable and influential was *True Christianity* by Johann Arndt (1555–1621). This book articulated a Lutheran spirituality comparable with that of Luther.

34. Spener, *Pia Desideria*.

35. See Pelikan, *Bach among the Theologians*, for an enjoyable exposition of Bach's life and influence.

36. James White, "Lutheran Worship," 75.

37. Reed, *Lutheran Liturgy* (rev. ed.), 148. See Senn, *Christian Liturgy*, 542–44, for examples drawn from Jeremiah F. Ohl, "The Liturgical Deterioration of the Seventeenth and Eighteenth Centuries," in *Memoirs of the Lutheran Liturgical Association* IV (1901–1902): 75–78.

38. Precht, "Worship Resources," 77–89.

39. See Tappert and Doberstein, *Journals of Henry Melchior Muhlenberg*, for the life and work of this Lutheran leader.

40. Reed, *Lutheran Liturgy* (rev. ed.), 166. Reed also gives an outline and description of the order of service (pp. 167–68).

41. Cited by Reed, *Lutheran Liturgy* (rev. ed.), 171.

42. Precht, "Worship Resources," 85.

43. See Schalk, *God's Song in a New Land*.

44. Precht, "Worship Resources," 104.

45. Senn, *Christian Liturgy*, 626.

46. Senn, *Christian Liturgy*, 626.

47. Abbott, "Constitution on the Sacred Liturgy," 133ff.

48. Precht, "Worship Resources," 108–10.

49. Sauer, "Special Hymnal Review Committee," 117, notes that a new bylaw was passed that called for approval of all worship books by the Synod in convention. See also Sauer, "Special Hymnal Review Committee," 120–26.

50. Commission on Worship, the LCMS, *Guide to Introducing* Lutheran Worship, 23–24, shows the concept of worship leadership expressed by this change. Fred L. Precht, "Commission on Worship," in *Lutheran Worship: History and Practice* (ed. Fred L. Precht; St. Louis: Concordia, 1993), 136, states the viewpoint of the Commission: "*Lutheran Worship* envisions laypeople serving as assisting ministers, as such representing the congregation as they lead in prayer, assist in the reading of the Word of God and in the distribution of the chalice at the Communion. Serving as cantor might also be considered as an assisting minister role. Such service is a visible picture of the priesthood of believers sharing a common response to God's truth."

51. Precht, "Commission on Worship," 138.

52. Paul Grime, Richard Stuckwisch, and Jon D. Vieker, eds., *Through the Church the Song Goes On* (St. Louis: Commission on Worship, the LCMS, 1999) provides two essays under the sectional theme "The Future of Hymnals."

53. [Nagel,] introduction to *Lutheran Worship*, 6.

CHAPTER 6

WHAT IS A LUTHERAN LITURGY?

When Lutherans gather in church as worshiping guests, a unique event transpires. The introduction to *Lutheran Worship* describes it this way:

> Our Lord speaks and we listen. His Word bestows what it says. Faith that is born from what is heard acknowledges the gifts received with eager thankfulness and praise. Music is drawn into this thankfulness and praise, enlarging and elevating the adoration of our gracious giver God. Saying back to him what he has said to us, we repeat what is most true and sure. . . . The rhythm of our worship is from him to us, and then from us back to him.[1]

God comes to us as we come into His presence. This is the essence of the German word *Gottesdienst*. This "Divine Service" or "God's service" is a two-way event characterized by the dual nature of Lutheran worship: the gracious giving and the responsive receiving, sometimes referred to as the sacramental and the sacrificial elements of worship. This concept of *Gottesdienst* summarizes the whole flow of Lutheran corporate worship and outlines the liturgy of the Divine Service.

In this chapter we will look at the basic structure of the traditional Mass form, as well as some peculiar emphases that help to identify Lutheran worship from that of other denominations.

THE LITURGY OF WORSHIP

WHY LITURGY?

Lutheran worship is structured in a particular way because we understand from the Bible that God is a God of order and not chaos (Genesis 1:1–2). In the New Testament, Paul encouraged the Corinthian congregation to do everything "in a fitting and orderly way" (1 Corinthians 14:40). While rigid uniformity is not demanded, Lutherans have found that a regular pattern of worship with a clear structure encourages an orderly service, particularly as more people travel yet seek a sense of home in a new church setting. As part of the greater catholic tradition, Lutherans have retained the longstanding Christian tradition of liturgical worship.[2]

The title of this section speaks of "the liturgy of worship" and not merely "the liturgy." As a gathering of worshiping guests, Lutherans desire some structure to aid corporate worship. The leaders of the service usually determine and maintain the structure, a practice followed in most "nonliturgical" churches as well. (Although identified as nonliturgical, most of these churches meticulously follow a regularized routine of ritual at every service.) This structure may be held in common by the members of the congregation in the form of an agreed upon hymnal. This approach is the common practice within the Lutheran church because of its strong emphasis on the priesthood of all believers.

Form and function have been the topic of some recent discussion of worship. Is the Lutheran worship form merely a structure to carry out our desire to respond to God, or is this function aided by form? While the answers are debated, Lutherans have maintained that form and function work hand in hand: Our form of worship communicates our doctrinal content and functions as a means to express our formal teachings. Form follows function and function follows form, and the liturgy provides both.

WHAT IS "LITURGY"?

Using its Greek roots, *liturgy* is usually defined as "the work of the people."[3] We can see the origin of our English word *liturgy* (Greek *leitourgia*) in the two Greek words from which we get *laity* (Greek *laos*) and *energy* (Greek *ergon*). Originally *leitourgia* referred to the political obligations performed by the citizens for the sake of the community, such as participation in public service projects or payment of taxes. Yet when Christians adapted the word, they understood it in a positive sense of willing service to God because of what He had done first for them. When the energy of God's Spirit-endowed people is tapped, worship is conducted in a proper, Spirit-guided way. People respond to God's revelation and worship Him "in spirit and truth" (John 4:24). In Hebrews 1:14, the angels are called liturgical spirits or "ministering spirits." Similarly, the writer to the Hebrews speaks of Christ, exalted at the Father's right hand, as the liturgist of the true heavenly sanctuary (8:2, 6). Thus liturgy is the act of God's people responding to the act of our Divine Liturgist. As a result of God's activity, Paul considered his apostolic service to be a liturgy too (Romans 15:16; Philippians 2:17).

When we speak of *the* liturgy, we mean the corporate structure of the worship experience and practice, which is centered in hearing God's Word and the proper administration of the Sacraments. This liturgy is more than what we do; it is how we do it. The liturgy is a vehicle for receiving God's beneficent aid, as well as for our expression of gratitude for His grace. In a sense, the liturgy can be compared to breathing: God's Spirit comes to us (we inhale) and we express our spiritual response back to God (we exhale).

Several years ago the Commission on Worship of the LCMS prepared a concise statement that defined liturgy. This helpful statement is worthy of repetition in full: "[Liturgy] is the design or pattern through which the congregation gathers to hear and receive anew the Gospel promise in Word and Sacrament, and then to respond collectively to the abundant gifts and gracious presence of the Triune God."[5] Notice that this definition underscores the fact that the liturgy is a beneficial pattern to help God's people do what God would have us do. This definition also maintains the responsive nature of Lutheran worship as a corporate or collective activity before our triune God.

WHAT IS BASIC IN LUTHERAN WORSHIP?

As innovations come from different areas of society and with varying qualities (and theologies), it is important to understand what is basic in Lutheran worship. What elements are essential elements in a traditional Lutheran service of Word and Sacrament? The Commission on Worship of the LCMS has produced a statement and guide to answer this question.[6]

The style of liturgy is not ours alone; it is the "public work of the whole people of God."[7] At times congregations and worship leaders think they can "do their own thing" when it comes to worship. In some ways this is true, but in others it is a form of idolatry. Christian worship and liturgy trace their roots through a history of Christian expressions. Frank C. Senn writes:

> Christian liturgy retains traces of the various cultures through which it has passed and to which it has been adapted. We chant a Hebrew "Amen," sing Greek canticles, pray the rhythms of Latin rhetoric, assemble in Gothic buildings, listen to German chorale preludes, and extend an American handshake at the greeting of peace . . . . Since liturgy is a public statement of the church's identity, it requires the distinctive contribution of each group of people within the church. At the same time the spirit of self-sacrifice requires each group to realize that they are not the totality of the church.[8]

Thus much can be contributed by and much needs to be appreciated in the Lutheran liturgical tradition.

Many congregations wonder what variety in liturgy is possible. Some of this will be discussed later, but it is helpful to look at the wealth of resources for variety within the Lutheran liturgical tradition. First, the "OR" sections within the various orders of service provide options. For example, there are alternate choices for the Hymn of Praise, Offertory, and Post-Communion Canticle. Second, the various settings of the Divine Service provide variety. Third, variety can be constructed with additions or deletions within the liturgical structure. Philip Pfatteicher and Carlos Messerli's *Manual on the Liturgy* provides guidelines on the use of specific parts of the liturgy and when they may be eliminated throughout the church year.[9] Fourth, variety may be introduced by substituting or alternating portions of the liturgy with hymns or spiritual songs, an option especially helpful for people who desire to use contemporary Christian music. However, when using contemporary Christian music, the theological content of the song should correspond to the content of the liturgical section being replaced. For example, many contemporary praise songs may be substituted for the Hymn of Praise, but one is hard-pressed to find as many possibilities to replace the liturgical texts of the Sanctus or the Kyrie. Pastoral care and caution should be exercised.

Why be concerned? Consider again Prosper of Aquitaine's argument that faith is affected by worship life and that the church's worship practices establish its theology. In recent years, Prosper's idea—formulated in the Latin phrase *lex orandi, lex credendi*—has been popularized by Anglican theologian Geoffrey Wainwright.[10] Wainwright suggests that Catholics follow Prosper's formula and that Protestants view the relationship in reverse—doctrine affects worship. Lutherans, however, see the relationship in both directions—what we do in worship affects doctrine *and* doctrine affects and should be evident in worship. Perhaps another way to view this issue is to analyze your response to these statements:

1. How we worship indicates what we believe.

2. As we believe, so we worship.

If a congregation sees God as cold, transcendent, and out of touch with His people, its worship may reflect this view by being cold and mechanical. On the other hand, if a congregation's worship life is dynamic, vibrant, and centered in Word and Sacraments, those people will grow spiritually by the empowering Gospel. Lutheran worship recognizes the biblical and historical nature of the incarnation; thus it holds to a traditional and liturgical form. Yet there is variety and vibrancy in Lutheran worship as songs, hymns, and spiritual songs unite the congregation in praising God for all His gifts, especially the gift of His Son.

The Structure of the Service

Traditionally, there are two major parts of a Christian order of service. The early Jerusalem type of worship emphasized Scripture and sacrifice. A decade or two after the Christian church began, the Gentile type of worship, which emphasized message and Meal, grew in significance. In both cases, Word and Sacrament received equal emphasis as the central resources for the Christian community. Through the means of grace, believers received God's gracious forgiveness and the strength for continuing one's Christian vocation. Lutheran worship has retained these two parts of a Christian worship service.

These two emphases have had various names over the centuries. (See below.) Today, the most common names are the Service of the Word and the Service of the Sacrament. These two titles clearly describe the emphasis of each part of the service and help worshipers focus on each segment appropriately. In earlier times, especially in areas influenced by the Roman Catholic Church, the parts of the service were often designated "Ante-Communion" and "Communion." These names emphasized Communion as the main event, while the Service of the Word was merely preparatory. Such a designation, though sometimes used by Lutheran writers, misrepresents a Lutheran understanding of both parts of the Divine Service.

First Part	**Second Part**
Service of the Word	Service of the Sacrament
Ante-Communion	Communion
Mass of the Catechumens	Mass of the Faithful

An even earlier designation for the two parts of the Divine Service was the "Mass of the Catechumens" and the "Mass of the Faithful." These names actually described the worshipers' relationship to the body of Christ. Because catechumens were still learning what God had done for them, their worship focused on education. However, the faithful, after being reminded of God's continuing blessing, received Christ's body and blood for the forgiveness of sins. Thus the Mass of the Catechumens emphasized the instructional nature of the Service of the Word and was for all people, including those not yet fully qualified as members by Baptism. The catechumens were then dismissed from the Mass of the Faithful because they could not experience "the mysteries" (the Latin word is *sacramentum*) until after appropriate instruction. Some congregations may still witness an exodus after the Offertory and prior to the Lord's Supper because a generation or two ago some pastors followed this ancient practice and dismissed those who did not intend to or could not yet commune. A more private Communion service after the Service of the Word was conducted for those who remained. (Divine Service I and II in *Lutheran Worship* still allow this practice; however, it is strongly discouraged.) This custom arose from the early church's concern for practicing close(d) Communion.

WORD AND SACRAMENT

Lutheran worship has always had a double focus. *Der Hauptgottesdienst* (the "Chief Divine Service") is both God's service to us and our service back to God in grateful response. This duality does not hide the mystery that God is active in both. His gift to us in Jesus evokes in us a proper response of thanks, praise, worship, and service. This duality in worship is sometimes distinguished by the words "sacramental" and "sacrificial." The sacramental elements are those actions in which God comes to the people; the sacrificial elements are those actions in which the people respond to God. The emphasis on the Word and the Sacrament of the Altar reflects the Lutheran concern for the Gospel's proclamation and the empowerment for living and serving as congregation members go out into the world as witnesses.

The pattern of Word followed by Sacrament is not only part of the catholic and confessional history of Lutheranism, the pattern also has theological and practical dimensions. As Luther discussed the reforms of the liturgy and the emphasis on the Word, he said: "It seems particularly fitting to preach before mass. For properly speaking, the mass consists in using the Gospel and communing at the table of the Lord."[11] Thus Lutherans have generally retained the practice of offering Communion only after the Service of the Word.[12] Where this is not practiced in a Lutheran congregation, legitimate questions can be raised regarding the appropriateness or the purpose of opposing a tradition that goes back almost two millennia in Christian worship practices.

WHAT IS A LUTHERAN LITURGY?

As noted earlier, the LCMS Commission on Worship prepared a statement in the early 1990s that defined "liturgy." Here is the more complete context of that definition:

> As applied to Christian worship, the "service of God," [liturgy] is the design or pattern through which the congregation gathers to hear and receive anew the Gospel promise in Word and Sacrament, and then to respond collectively to the abundant gifts and gracious presence of the Triune God. Liturgy recognizes above all that the primary "action" of Christian worship is not ours, but God's . . . . The Christian liturgy attempts to relate everything in the worship service to the central event and proclamation of the church: what a merciful God has done

through the life, death, and resurrection of Jesus Christ to forgive our sins, incorporate us into His family, and make us heirs of the kingdom of heaven.[13]

The ancient Greeks used the word *liturgy* to describe a particular form of corporate activity and responsibility. The New Testament uses the word and its derivatives to designate a proper response of "service," "ministry," and "worship" (Luke 1:23; Philippians 2:17; Hebrews 9:21). Thus liturgy designates the work performed by people for others, specifically, God's royal priesthood responding to His empowering blessings as they prepare to serve in the world.

With this basic and common understanding of liturgy, we move to what makes a Lutheran liturgy distinct. Although many activities in a Lutheran service reflect the long tradition of Christian worship, some significant characteristics distinguish a Lutheran worshiping community from other Christian groups. While most Christian denominations hold the following ideas in common, the strong emphasis and engaging selection is peculiar to the Lutheran Church. Lutherans recognize a close relationship between their faith as articulated in doctrinal statements and their faith as expressed in worship and life. Therefore, the following descriptive adjectives help identify God's gathered guests who come to worship with a committed Lutheran outlook.

TRINITARIAN

Lutherans follow a creedal tradition in worship as we recall the great and gracious gifts from the Father, Son, and Holy Spirit. The Father has called us together and encourages us to gather. We gather "in the name of the Son" to celebrate His life-giving death and resurrection; it is His Word that we preach and believe and His body and blood that we receive. Finally, the Holy Spirit "calls, gathers, [and] enlightens"[14] us as God's gathered guests around Word and Sacraments.

CHRISTOLOGICAL

Lutheran Christians understand that Christ comes to us in worship. He speaks to us and we hear His Word—the Word of Scripture, the Word of the Gospel, the Word made flesh. While much recent literature on worship deals with people's responses to God and His sovereign will or the Holy Spirit and His manifestations, Lutheran worship is centered in Jesus, who is the object of our worship. We come to worship because "we would like to see [and hear!] Jesus" (John 12:21). We come into His presence and, through Word and Sacraments, are strengthened for faith and life. God's forgiving love in Christ is central to Lutheran sermons, as well as key to understanding the Lutheran use of the sacraments.

EVANGELICAL

The word *evangelical* has been adopted by many Protestant denominations in North America, yet it is originally a Lutheran designation. The word refers to our Gospel emphasis. Lutheran worship is not only Christ-centered, it also proclaims the Gospel. God has declared sinners acceptable and forgiven because of Jesus' perfect life and death and confirming resurrection and ascension (Romans 4:25). Lutherans desire to share this life-giving Good News of God's love and forgiveness for a dying sinful world. The Sunday sermon has a central place in the worship of Lutherans, particularly because the sermon speaks a word of forgiveness, life, and hope through Christ. Luther said that any assembly in which God's Word is not preached is not worship.[15]

CATHOLIC OR ECUMENICAL

Lutheran worship grows out of its roots in Roman Catholic worship. While many Protestant churches reject anything associated with Catholicism, Lutherans hold that much good has been received from that tradition. Yet the body of Christ is more than a denomination. The Greek word *katholikos* has a sense of something that extends throughout the whole. Lutheran worship is open to the whole world and seeks to be a tool for extending Christ's kingdom. With that understanding, Lutheran worship has a missionary dimension in the evangelistic and educational emphases of faith life and worship practices. Lutheran worship is designed to bring the living voice of God to a people who are dying because they do not know Him.

HISTORICAL

Lutherans respect the past. As a denomination with strong European roots, Lutherans look to their past for ideas in the present. They also recognize mistakes made in the past and determine to avoid similar mistakes in the present or future. Lutherans worship with an eye on time and eternity. Lutherans in worship are aware of a bigger picture that involves more people and places and times than the present situation. Lutheran worship leaders seek to avoid a parochial approach to worship. Worship is "with angels and archangels and with all the company of heaven," as the pastor says in the Common Preface of the Holy Communion liturgy.[16]

LITURGICAL

Lutherans follow an established pattern of worship so all worshipers can participate in the service in some way.[17] Lutherans follow a meaningful structure and a set order for services. First-century Christians were liturgical in their worship practices (remember that Paul encouraged the Corinthians to do things in an orderly way).

The word *liturgy* refers to the work of the laity or work for the common good. Liturgy is the beneficial structure in which God comes to His gathered guests through Word and Sacraments and the people give an orderly response before God.[18]

TRADITIONAL OR CREEDAL

Lutherans clearly follow a tradition that traces its roots through the ancient creeds to the Bible. In the early church, the writer Irenaeus emphasized the necessity of following the already established tradition of the church as displayed in the Apostles' Creed.[19] Lutherans continue to follow this creedal tradition in worship as we recall the great and gracious gifts from the Father, Son, and Holy Spirit.

CONTEMPORARY

We worship in the present, though our eyes are also on the past and the future. Everything we do is "contemporary," that is, "with the times." Although debates rage about this word, Lutheran worship certainly is for the present. It should never be a mere relic of the past or a symbol of some bygone era, nor should it be some cute innovative fad that speaks for a moment in time before being dismissed as passé. What Lutheran worshipers say and do on Sunday has relevance for the rest of the week. Worship affects the daily living of the Gospel. It is a "now" event for God's gathered guests.

We have demonstrated how Lutheran worship is biblical and traditional, and we have underscored the confessional nature of Lutheran worship—both as a confession of faith and of life. The structure of Lutheran worship follows the traditional Mass form, yet the emphasis is distinct. In addition, several characteristics of Lutheran worship mark it as unique: It is trinitarian, Christological, evangelical, catholic, historical, liturgical, traditional, and contemporary. With this background, we are now ready to look at the two-part worship service in detail.

SOME QUESTIONS TO CONSIDER

1. Briefly describe the dual nature of Lutheran worship as expressed in the introduction to *Lutheran Worship*.
2. Differentiate the three designations for the two parts of the Divine Service.
3. List three parts of a service that are sacramental and three that are sacrificial. To what do these two categories refer?
4. What is the relationship between form and function of the liturgy?
5. How is Christ our liturgist? How are we liturgists?

6. How do Lutherans understand *liturgy*? Explain it in less than 50 words.

7. Describe the essential parts of a Lutheran worship service.

8. Choose three characteristics of Lutheran worship and explain why they distinguish worship as Lutheran.

Notes

1. [Nagel,] introduction to *Lutheran Worship*, 6.

2. See *Gathered Guests* chapter 2 for a more detailed explanation of the rationale for this practice.

3. The Greek word *leitourgia* and its derivations are used more than a dozen times in the New Testament. The word is used as a verb (Acts 13:2; Romans 15:27; Hebrews 10:11), as well as a noun (Luke 1:23; 2 Corinthians 9:12; Philippians 2:17, 30; Hebrews 8:6; 9:21) and an adverb (Hebrews 1:14). In addition, persons are identified as "liturgists" (*leitourgoi*) of God (Romans 13:6; 15:16; Philippians 2:28; Hebrews 1:7; 8:2). Each of these uses of *leitourgia* expresses something about one's service in response to God's actions.

4. Strathmann, "leitourgeo, leitourgia, leitorgos, leitourgikos," *Theological Dictionary of the New Testament*, 4:215–31.

5. Commission on Worship, the LCMS, "What Is Liturgy?" 5.

6. The document concludes: "This statement is recommended to the parishes and people of The Lutheran Church—Missouri Synod as a guide and a discussion piece. It may be photocopied as needed" (Commission on Worship, the LCMS, "What Is Liturgy?").

7. Commission on Worship, the LCMS, "What Is Liturgy?" 5.

8. Senn, "Spirit of the Liturgy," 25.

9. Pfatteicher and Messerli, *Manual on the Liturgy*, 211.

10. See Wainwright, *Doxology*, 218–83.

11. "Order of Mass and Communion for the Church at Wittenberg," LW 53:25.

12. Some Lutheran congregations have begun to place the Service of the Sacrament before the Service of the Word, which demonstrates a misunderstanding of the unified yet distinct contribution each means of grace makes to the worshiping community.

13. Commission on Worship, the LCMS, "What Is Liturgy," 5.

14. SC, "The Creed," 6 (K-W, 355).

15. "German Mass," LW 53:68–69.

16. *Lutheran Worship*, p. 146.

17. Ludwig, *Sacred Paths*, 431, makes this association: "Liturgical denominations include the Roman Catholic, Eastern Orthodox, Anglican, and Lutheran churches; nonliturgical groups would be Baptists, Quakers, and the variety of free evangelical churches. Somewhere in between are such groups as the Methodists and the Calvinist (Presbyterian, Reformed) churches, who do not emphasize the traditional liturgies and sacraments but do follow commonly accepted forms of worship."

18. Three biblical references use the verb form *leitourge*: Acts 13:2; Romans 15:27; Hebrews 10:11. Six passages use the noun *leitourgia*: Luke 1:23; 2 Corinthians 9:12; Philippians 2:17, 30; Hebrews 8:6; 9:21. One uses the adjectival form *leitourgikos*: Hebrews 1:14. There are five references to the servant *leitourgos*: Romans 13:6; 15:16; Philippians 2:28; Hebrews 1:7; 8:2.

19. Irenaeus, "Selections from the work *Against Heresies*," I.10.1–2, in *Early Christian Fathers*, 360. Later in the same book, Irenaeus shows how the tradition is biblical too.

CHAPTER 7

THE SERVICE OF THE WORD

The Lutheran liturgy is a gift received from our Lutheran heritage. We cherish it as a vehicle for us both to acquire God's gifts to us and to express our grateful responses to Him. In this chapter we will look at the Divine Service in detail. The structure of the liturgy can be viewed as an outline or a format to follow so all the things that will build up the body of Christ in the congregation are included. Knowing that Lutheran theology is formative, the liturgical structure affirms the truths that we believe about God's grace, the importance of the Gospel, how we express our gratitude to God, the proper use of the Sacrament of the Altar, and the life of prayer. As God's gathered guests, we cherish our time together.

Lutheran Worship has served the LCMS as its hymnal for several decades. Although some congregations still use *The Lutheran Hymnal* and others adopted *Lutheran Book of Worship*, the next two chapters of this book will explain the Divine Service as found in *Lutheran Worship*. The detailed explanations of the service that follow can be applied to other liturgical worship orders with only minor changes because the basic structure is the same for all liturgical services in the Lutheran tradition.[1]

Three forms of the Divine Service are included in *Lutheran Worship*. The explanations in this chapter and in chapter 8 follow Divine Service II, though occasional references to Divine Service I and Divine Service III are also made.

RUBRIC, RITE, AND CEREMONY

When we study the liturgy, especially liturgical texts, several words need to be explained. Three—*rubric, rite,* and *ceremony*—relate to participation in the service. Although some portions of the liturgy are read or sung by the officiant or worship leader, much of the liturgy is sung or spoken by the congregation. The directions for leading worship—determining who sings or says what at a specific point in the service—are called *rubrics*. The word *rubric* comes from the Latin

115

word *ruber*, which means "red." Traditionally rubrics were—and in *Lutheran Worship* and more recent hymnals still are—printed in red ink. Printed in the *rite*, the written form of the service, rubrics give the prescribed liturgical wording to be spoken or sung. The rite is prepared to aid the leader in conducting the *ceremony*, which is the actions done in the service by the leaders and the congregation. These actions might include whether the congregation stands or kneels or what kind of procession is conducted at a particular point in the service.

Rubrics can be divided into two types. Some rubrics say something "may" *option* occur, which means the direction is optional and appropriate substitutions or deletions are indicated. Other rubrics indicate that something "is" done, or the item is merely indicated (for example, the sermon) and is not an option. The "is" rubric (older versions of the rite said "shall") indicates a substitution is irregular and a deletion should not be made under normal circumstances because the element is basic to the structure of the service. By way of illustration, rubric 7 in Divine Service II reads: *not option*

The COLLECT OF THE DAY is chanted or said; the salutation may precede it.[2]

These directions indicate that the Collect of the Day is part of the regular structure of the service and should be said, but the method is optional, as indicated by the use of *or*. The Salutation, however, may be omitted. Because this particular instruction combines both types of rubrics, it demonstrates the flexibility within the liturgical structure.

THE PREPARATION　*Confession*

To prepare for the reception of the Lord's Supper, many congregations in the Lutheran tradition, particularly within the last century, have introduced a confessional service prior to the actual Service of the Word.[3] In Divine Service I, the preparatory nature of confession and absolution is clearly indicated in the rite.[4] In earlier eras, this portion of the service normally occurred in another location, often in the church's undercroft or side chapel. This earlier practice was actually a Service of Confession and Exhortation to Communion that was offered to those who had already announced their desire to commune or who had decided to receive the Sacrament that morning.

Today, the pastor may communicate the preparatory nature of this portion of the service by the location from which he conducts it. For example, the pastor can lead this confessional service from the entrance of the church. If done in this manner, the congregation faces the back of the church until the processional hymn draws the people's attention to the chancel. More commonly, this preparatory service is conducted from outside the Communion rail or from the bottom step of the chancel.[5] In any case, the location of the worship leader clearly indicates that this is a separate part of the worship activity.

The following numbered sections match the rubrics of Divine Service II as found in *Lutheran Worship*. Where the liturgy offers options, the text addresses each option as a separate entry, as noted by the addition of a letter to the rubric number.

1.A. HYMN

The use of "may" in this rubric indicates that an opening hymn before the Invocation is not necessary. The inclusion of this hymn often depends on local congregational preference and practice. When the opening hymn appears later in the service, as suggested by the rite, meditation prior to confession can be done with reverence and solemnity. If a procession will be included during the ceremony, it occurs during the Entrance Hymn,[6] which signals the beginning of the Service of the Word. If a hymn is used at this initial point in the service, one addressed to the Holy Spirit or a trinitarian hymn is most appropriate. Hymns included in the section "Beginning of Service"[7] draw the attention of worshipers to the activities that will occur during the service and to God's gracious promise of His presence.

1.B. INVOCATION

When does a worship service begin? The service does not begin with the lighting of candles, the ringing of bells, the start of the prelude, or the conclusion of the preservice music. In one sense, the service begins at the Invocation. The gathered guests have assembled and now hear and recall the name of Him who promises to be with us always (Matthew 28:20).

In such a context, the Invocation confesses that God has put His holy name on His people in Holy Baptism and so has promised to remain with them, especially where two or three are gathered in Jesus' name, according to the Father's will (Matthew 18:19–20; 28:19–20). Christians use God's name properly by speaking the words of the Lord, receiving His gifts, and praising Him in worship and prayer. When we speak, God listens. Call out His name, and God hears (Psalm 91:15). The Holy Spirit works through the Word to leave no room for doubt that we, indeed, are God's redeemed people in His house, receiving His gifts to His glory.

At the Invocation the members of the congregation may make the sign of the cross on themselves, a sign first placed on each gathered guest at the time of his or her Baptism. The Invocation reminds us that only through faith can we come into God's house and approach God's heavenly throne. We invoke God only because we have been made one of God's gathered guests through the waters of Baptism. The sign of the cross is also a physical action that draws the whole self into the act of worship. Some people may consider this is a "Catholic" practice, and in the past this connotation caused many Lutherans to abandon its use. Yet Luther suggested the sign of the cross as a daily practice, directing in his Small Catechism that the head of the household should teach the family the Morning and Evening Prayers in this way:

> In the morning, when you get up, make the sign of the holy cross and say:
>
> In the name of ✠ the Father and of the Son and of the Holy Ghost. Amen.[8]

The sign of the cross is made by placing the thumb and first two fingers of the right hand together as a reminder of the Trinity. Touch your head at the naming of the Father, then bring your hand to the middle of your chest (over your heart) at the name of the Son. At the name of the Holy Spirit touch your right shoulder, then your left shoulder. This last step is different from the way Roman Catholics cross themselves and follows the more ancient practice of the Eastern Orthodox churches. (See diagram.)

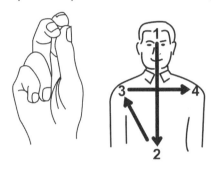

As the Invocation is said, recall your Baptism and the fact that through Baptism you are a "holy priest" and a child of God (Matthew 28:18–20; 1 Peter 2:9). Some Lutheran congregations have moved their baptismal fonts to the entrance of the church, which has encouraged worshipers to recall their Baptism. Worshipers may make the sign of the cross as they enter the sanctuary.

The pastor should use the words of the Invocation as printed in the rite. Our Lord puts His promises where His words are, as with the words, "This is My body." Departing from the words in Matthew 28:19—" in the name of the Father, and of the Son, and of the Holy Spirit"—introduces room for doubt. Accordingly, variations such as "God the Father, God the Son . . ." are strongly discouraged for the same reason that we do not readily modify the Words of Institution. Similarly, the use of "We begin in . . ." is inaccurate because the whole service is conducted in God's presence. The congregation's "Amen" (Hebrew for "I concur" or "I agree") confesses that the worshipers have no doubt of God's presence and intent, namely, to call His people together in Word and Sacrament—"the holy things for the holy ones"—and save them from the fallen world.

1.C. INVITATION TO CONFESSION

Lutheran liturgical practice throughout the past century provides a general confessional service at the beginning of the Divine Service. The practice of examining one's life was called *confession* in Luther's day, and it was done on a regular basis.[9] Because of misunderstandings and some misuse, a general confession was introduced in Lutheran churches in later centuries.[10]

The pastor may speak this invitation to confession from the back of the church, from beside the baptismal font, or from the congregation's side of the communion rail. The worship leader says, "If we say we have no sin, we deceive ourselves and the truth is not in us." To this the congregation responds, "But if we confess our sins, God, who is faithful and just, will forgive our sins and cleanse us from all unrighteousness."[11] This invitational verse is from 1 John 1:8–9 and directs the gathered guests to the scriptural roots of confession and, more important, to the assurance of full and free absolution through Christ. God's gracious promise to forgive all our sins gives His gathered guests confidence to make an honest and complete confession.

2.A. SILENCE BEFORE CONFESSION

After the invitation to confession, the rubric suggests a time for silent reflection, a nearly lost art in Christian corporate worship. Especially among North Americans, silence is rare. Music typically surrounds us at work and in most public settings. Traffic noise and subtle electronic sounds are almost everywhere. Some churches have even adopted the practice of playing the organ during prayers. As a result, many people do not know how to be silent before the Lord (Psalm 46:10).

Luther spoke of meditation (*meditatio*) as a second element in the making of a theologian. To introduce a congregation to the practice of meditation, worship leaders may instruct the congregation about the practice and purpose of being quiet and thinking about God's Word. It is advisable to begin with short periods of silence, 10 to 15 seconds, which can "feel" rather long without an explanation. The worship leader may specifically guide worshipers to ponder the words of the invitation to confess, to think through the Ten Commandments, or to confess privately those sins they know and feel in their hearts. As the congregation becomes accustomed to the use of silence, the time may be extended to a half minute or a minute before oral confession.

2.B. CONFESSION

Most Lutherans are familiar with the practice of corporate confession. However, in Luther's day private and individual confession outside of the worship setting was typical. There was also a practice called *Offene Schuld* (literally, "open guilt"). Although Luther did not use such a preparatory service in his liturgical orders, his exhortation to communicants exhibits a confessional nature.[12]

The general confession is just that, a confession of sins in general without reference to specific sins. This confession clearly places the need for Christ at the center of the worshipers' thoughts and words. Not only is the doctrine of original sin acknowledged, but the many sins committed or omitted are also recognized. Only through Christ is there forgiveness and the possibility of living Christlike lives in God's presence.

In recent years worship leaders have tried to develop alternative forms of confession to greater and lesser success. Innovation should be undertaken with care. Some confessions can be distracting and even harmful. For example, in a semihumorous article on confession, Browne Barr reflects on a "contemporary" confession of sins that required worshipers to confess the "sin" of using "fitted sheets."[13] His point was that the idea of confessing specific sins became a distraction rather than a help to godly worship and heartfelt confession. *Lutheran Worship* provides several alternative wordings of the general confession if variety is desired.[14]

The confession provides worshipers with a time and a text to lead them into the dark depths of their souls and to recognize their need for Jesus, the light of the world. While debates continue about exact wording, the theological content should reflect the biblical truths of the corruption of our human nature and our failure to fulfill God's double command to love Him and our neighbor, as well as our recognition of our doomed and damned condition apart from Christ. Only then will we hear the pastoral absolution as a word of Good News.

3.A. ABSOLUTION

The Office of the Keys is given to the Christian church. A Christian congregation by the command of Christ calls pastors to carry out the Office of the Keys publicly in His name and on behalf of the congregation. In this portion of the service, the Lutheran theology of the pastoral office is underscored as the pastor says, "As a called and ordained servant of the Word I therefore forgive you all your sins . . ."[15] In Divine Service I, the pastor adds the phrase, "in the stead [place] and by the command of my Lord Jesus Christ . . ."[16] Through these statements, the pastor clearly speaks the word of forgiveness on God's behalf. Luther reminds us in the Small Catechism that we receive forgiveness from the pastor as from God Himself.[17] According to some Lutheran confessional documents, Holy Absolution is a third sacrament.[18] The biblical warrants from Matthew 16:19; John 20:21–23; and 2 Corinthians 2:10 strongly support the Lutheran practice of Absolution.

3.B. DECLARATION OF GRACE

An alternative to Absolution is the second statement in this rubric, which expresses the graciousness of God in a more descriptive but less powerful form. As stated in Divine Service I, this second response to the confession of sins is identified as the Declaration of Grace. Rather than forgiving the sins of the confessing congregation, the pastor or worship leader assures worshipers of God's forgiving grace. When a nonordained person leads this part of the service, the Declaration of Grace is used.

Curiously, the tradition behind the usage of these two forms of Absolution is unclear. Many congregations follow the practice from *The Lutheran Hymnal*, where the Declaration of Grace is used when Holy Communion is not offered. Yet the logical time to use the Absolution is when there is no Sacrament of the Altar because there would still be one sacramental event in the service. The pastoral leadership of the congregation makes the final decision on which form to use.

To the Declaration of Grace, *Lutheran Worship* adds, "May the Lord, who has begun this good work in us, bring it to completion in the day of our Lord Jesus Christ."[19] This statement comes from Philippians 1:6. This Declaration of Grace or the Absolution concludes the preparatory service, and the Service of the Word begins immediately.

THE SERVICE OF THE WORD

Three options are available to the worship leader at this point. The Service of the Word may begin with a pastoral or choral introduction or the congregation may join in jubilant song.

4.A. INTROIT OF THE DAY

The Introit of the Day marks the actual beginning of the Service of the Word. The Introit, from the Latin word for "he enters in," was originally a practical rubric to begin the service. When the priest entered the church, the people stopped their activities in the nave of the church and assembled around the chancel. During this time, the choir sang a selection from a psalm, known as the *Introit*.

The Introit was originally an entire psalm sung antiphonally (one "choir" responding to the other) by a double choir or between the pastor and the people.[20] In the *Formula Missae*, Luther preferred the use of a whole psalm instead of shortened verses.[21] However, the Introit later was shortened to one verse, as in *The Lutheran Hymnal*. *Lutheran Worship* offers a longer Introit with selected Scripture verses and a section of a psalm that introduces the theme for the day or sets the tone for the season.

The Introit is the first of the Propers, those portions of the service that change (or are "proper") each Sunday or season of the church year. The Propers contrast with the ordinary (from the Latin *ordo*, which means "regular order") portions of the liturgy, which do not change. The Propers—Introit, Collect, the readings, Gradual, and Verse—along with the colors of the church year, underscore particular worship themes from the liturgical calendar. The Propers for each Sunday and for most special days in the church year are included in *Lutheran Worship*.[22]

After the Absolution and during the Introit, the pastor enters the chancel and goes to his chair or to the *ambo*,[23] from which he may conduct the rest of the Service of the Word. The altar is not the center of attention for the Service of the Word; instead, the reading table, ambo, or Table of the Word, from which the Scriptures are read and the sermon is preached, is central.

4.B. Entrance Hymn

A preferable alternative to the Introit is the Entrance Hymn. The purpose of this hymn is to unify the congregation for vibrant worship. Selected stanzas of an Entrance Hymn may be sung by the choir or divided among the worshipers as a way to add a festive quality to the hymn. Especially appropriate for festival Sundays, the Entrance Hymn affords the possibility of fanfares and celebrative processional music. Processions recall how the crowds followed or welcomed Jesus on His travels, especially on Palm Sunday. A procession provides a visible means to highlight a central theme or festival occasion in the life of God's gathered guests, satisfying a congregation's desire to do "more" in the regular order of service. If a procession is used, select an Entrance Hymn with a clear meter so those processing can walk at a comfortable pace.

When planning a procession, the order of the participants communicates the significance of the event. The procession begins with the processional cross, which symbolizes that the Christian church follows the Lord. The crucifer walks deliberately, neither too slowly nor too quickly. If candles, called torches when they are carried, are used, the torchbearers normally follow the crucifer.[24] The cross and torches are carried in a vertical position, preferably with one hand grasping the staff of the cross or torch at face level and the other at waist level. The candles and cross should be elevated above the eye level of the standing congregation.[25]

The occasion will determine the order of additional participants in the procession. A Palm Sunday procession may include children carrying palm branches or balloons. A congregation's anniversary service may emphasize leaders of the congregation or longtime members. A Mission Sunday procession could highlight the nations in which the congregation supports missionaries or in which the congregation might serve as individuals carry flags from these nations. The special speaker might follow these individuals. Choirs, members of various organizations, or other distinguished guests may also process between the crucifer and the final member of the procession. Regardless of the makeup of the processional group, the last person to enter the sanctuary is normally the presiding minister.[26] The congregation should stand when the cross enters the sanctuary, facing it as it is carried from the rear of the church to the chancel, where it is placed in its stand.

4.C. PSALM

A third option to begin the Service of the Word is the use of the appointed Psalm of the Day. This option may be followed occasionally to provide variety or to use a festival psalm setting with choir and instruments. However, the Psalm may be better used later in the service at the time of the Scripture readings. Occasionally, the appointed psalm is a slightly longer version of the Introit and is closer in theme to the readings of the day.

5.A. KYRIE

From the joyous song of entrance, the tone of the service shifts with the Kyrie. This ancient prayer represents the last remnant of the earliest Christian orders of service, which were in Greek, the language used for Christian worship for the first 300 years of the church. The phrase *Kyrie eleison* means "Lord, have mercy." It recalls the petitions for help and healing spoken to Jesus during His lifetime (Matthew 15:22; Mark 10:46–52; Luke 17:13). Although many pagan cultures around the Mediterranean used this praise-shout, Christians felt confident that it was an appropriate element for their worship of Him who is Lord and Savior.[27]

The Kyrie was traditionally spoken by laypeople and was known as the Deacon's Prayer. Some early forms of the Kyrie included a place for special petitions prior to the acclamation, a form that still may be observed today according to congregational tradition. In Luther's day, the earlier expanded form of the Kyrie had been reduced to a simple threefold plea, with the second plea made to Christ: "Lord, have mercy; Christ, have mercy; Lord, have mercy."[28] *Lutheran Worship* has now restored the Kyrie to the assisting minister. The congregation is invited by the assisting minister to pray for specific gifts of peace, and the whole congregation prays, "Lord, have mercy."

The present form of the Kyrie serves as a congregational acclamation of praise as Jesus is present with His people. The prayers focus on the desire for true peace, which Christ alone gives. Each petition asks for a dimension of peace, beginning with salvation and concluding with peace among those assembled as God's gathered guests.

5.B. OMISSION OF THE KYRIE

The "may" rubric suggests that the Kyrie need not be included in every service. The Kyrie may be omitted during the Sundays after Epiphany, after Pentecost, and on festivals.[29] In addition, a hymnic setting may be substituted for the Kyrie on occasion. One possible substitute is the medieval hymn "Kyrie, God Father."[30]

6.A. HYMN OF PRAISE: GLORIA IN EXCELSIS

An outburst of joy and praise immediately follows the Kyrie as the mood of the service quickly changes. The Gloria in Excelsis, a traditional hymn of the church, recalls the angelic choir's praise at the coming of the Christ Child (Luke 2:14). The hymn itself is Christological, praising the Father for His gift and extolling Christ's self-sacrifice as He returns to the Father, concluding with a trinitarian doxology.[31] The hymn is known as the Greater Gloria, in contrast to the Gloria Patri, which concludes psalms and canticles (scriptural songs). Because of its close connection to Christmas, the Gloria in Excelsis is typically used as the Hymn of Praise from Christmas through the Sunday of the Transfiguration and for the Sundays after Pentecost.

Other versifications of the Gloria in Excelsis may be used, such as Luther's hymn "All Glory Be to God Alone"[32] and Nikolaus Decius's hymn "All Glory Be to God on High."[33]

6.B. HYMN OF PRAISE: THIS IS THE FEAST

"This Is the Feast," which has become popular in Lutheran congregations since its inclusion in *Lutheran Worship*,[34] is taken from ideas, phrases, and images in Revelation (5:9–13; 15:2–4; 19:4–9). The images of the Passover deliverance and Christ's Easter victory in this hymn of praise anticipate the great messianic banquet. The image of Christ as the Lamb who was slain and who now reigns in triumphant glory unites this hymn with the Gloria in Excelsis. Because of the Easter imagery, "This Is the Feast" is recommended for the Great Fifty Days of Easter and on all festivals.

6.C. OMISSION OF THE HYMN OF PRAISE

Normally, no hymn of praise is sung during Advent and Lent. This practice accentuates the solemn and penitential nature of these seasons. However, during Advent the canticle "Oh, Come, Oh, Come, Emmanuel"[35] may be sung, and "The Royal Banners Forward Go"[36] may be used during Lent.

7.A. SALUTATION

The Service of the Word continues with a traditional greeting among Christians. This responsive dialogue unites the people and the pastor in corporate worship. The Hebrew greeting "Shalom alechum! Alechum shalom!" (Peace be with you) is still heard in Israeli streets. Christians replaced the Hebrew wish for peace, *shalom*, with the peacegiver Himself.[37] "The Lord be [or *is*] with you" may be said prior to the Collect of the Day.

The Salutation has been interpreted in several ways,[38] but its underlying emphasis is the existence of a special relationship between the pastor and the congregation. The response "And also with you," or "And with your spirit," confirms this caring relationship. This is not a prayer but an exchange of mutual love and respect. The Salutation is a much stronger greeting than the "Good morning!" often expressed from the chancel prior to a Sunday liturgy. The Salutation signifies a spiritual tie between pastor and people that the Lord alone brings.

7.B. COLLECT OF THE DAY

From a gracious greeting, the Service of the Word moves to prayer as the gathered guests approach God's throne. The word *collect* has an uncertain origin. Some suggest that it indicates the people had "collected" themselves and were acknowledging the assembly through prayer. More probable is the interpretation that these ancient prayers "collect" the thoughts of the day for the people in the form of a five-part petition: invocation, reason, petition, result, and trinitarian termination.

The Collect of the Day helps the gathered guests focus on a central theme drawn from the readings of the day. There is a specific collect for each Sunday and festival of the church year.[39] In many ways these collects remind us that our prayers are not ours alone, but they are the prayers of the whole church—past, present, and future. After the pastor chants or speaks the prayer, the congregation joins in speaking or singing the Hebrew affirmation "Amen." In this way the gathered guests endorse the prayer the pastor has led and acknowledge their participation in the liturgy as royal priests.

8.A. OLD TESTAMENT READING

The actual Service of the Word begins with this reading. The reclamation of reading from the Old Testament reminds us of Luther's strong commitment to this Testament and his exhortation to "find Christ" in its books. There are two sets of readings provided in *Lutheran Worship*: a one-year series from the Western Catholic tradition[40] and a three-year series adapted from the Consultation on Common Texts, an ecumenically oriented set of lessons that covers more of Scripture.[41] In the three-year series, the Old Testament Reading is tied thematically to the Gospel of the Day.

The Old Testament Reading may be done from the lectern, ambo, or altar. If read from the altar, the Old Testament Reading and the Epistle are read from the liturgical "south," that is, on the front-left side or Epistle side of the altar as the minister faces the congregation. Traditionally, this first reading was read by the subdeacon. In modern practice, a resource for worship produced by the LCMS indicates that "the first two readings may be read by lay persons."[42]

8.B. ALTERNATE READING FROM THE BOOK OF ACTS

During the Easter season, the three-year series takes its first reading from the Book of Acts because it is the "new" history of the church. Readers should be careful when introducing this reading during the Easter season. The rubric indicates an introduction such as: "The Reading from the Book of Acts for _____ is from the _____ chapter." An alternative introduction for this first reading, which could be used in every season, is, "The first reading for _____ is from _____."

8.C. "THIS IS THE WORD OF THE LORD"

After the Old Testament or first reading, the rubric suggests that the lector indicate the end with the phrase, "This is the Word of the Lord." Divine Service I adds a congregational response: "Thanks be to God!"[43] Congregations are encouraged to adopt the practice of responding with this acclamation after the completion of each Scripture reading.

9.A. GRADUAL OF THE SEASON

After the first reading, a response may be given by the congregation or a choir. The word for this response, *gradual*, comes from the Latin word *gradus,* which means "step." Music may have been needed during earlier ages of Christian worship as the subdeacon brought the Bible or lectionary into the chancel for the next readings or as the New Testament was brought toward the altar. Whatever its origin, the Gradual provides a response to the Old Testament Reading.

The Gradual is the third Proper, and it normally is the same for an entire season of the church year rather than crafted for one day. This short selection from Scripture, normally sung by the choir, continues the liturgical theme of the day. As an alternative, choral anthems may be sung at this time with a text that reflects the theme of the service.

9.B. PSALM OF THE DAY

Instead of the Gradual, the appointed Psalm is most appropriately used at this time. The use of a psalm recalls the ancient congregational practice of singing all the psalms each week (which is still done in some monasteries) or at least singing through the psalter once each year. Choral settings of the psalms are available, but congregational chanting can be uplifting. *Lutheran Worship* contains sixty-one psalms[44] that have been "pointed" (or marked) for ease of chanting and are taken from the New International Version.[45]

10. EPISTLE READING

After the Gradual, the congregation is ready to hear a word from the New Testament. The second lesson recalls the early Christian tradition of reading from the "memoirs of the apostles."[46] The Epistle Reading may be read from the liturgical "south," as was the Old Testament Reading. In some congregations, this reading is read from the side of the chancel from which the sermon is preached. It may be read either by the deacon or by a lay reader.

The Epistle selection frequently follows the biblical tradition of *lectio continua* ("continuous reading"), with modifications because of the omission of some weekday readings. For a series of Sundays, especially during the Pentecost season, the Epistle Reading will come from the same book. For example, in Series A of the three-year series, the Book of Romans is read for 16 weeks, skipping only a few sections. In the three-year series, no attempt was made to coordinate the Epistle Reading with the Gospel of the Day. If the themes coincide, it is serendipitous.

During the festival half of the church year, the Epistle Reading in the one-year series reflects one of the main themes of the day, as does the Gospel. The central themes of most festival services receive a strong emphasis from the first lesson, the Psalm, the second lesson, and finally, from the theme-setting Gospel.

10.B. "THIS IS THE WORD OF THE LORD"

After the Epistle or second reading, the rubric suggests that the lector again indicate the end with the phrase, "This is the Word of the Lord."

11.A. ALLELUIA VERSE

In preparation for the reading of the Gospel, another short piece of music is sung by the choir or congregation. Combined with the *alleluias*, the congregation sings a portion of John 6:68, recalling Peter's response to Jesus, who had asked the disciples if they were going to leave Him. In this Verse, the gathered guests join the Old Testament believers who sang the *Hallel* (praise) Psalms (Psalm 104–50) as a joyous cry of the faithful community. The Great Hallelujah Psalms (Psalm 113–18) were probably used during the Passover season and, therefore, by Jesus and His disciples on Maundy Thursday. The same *Hallelujah*, which simply means "Praise the Lord," continues throughout eternity (Revelation 19:6). *Alleluia* (the Greek form of the Hebrew word) is the church's "perpetual voice . . . just as the memorial of [Christ's] passion and victory is perpetual," Luther reminded us.[47] Luther also suggested the singing of a hymn between the Epistle and the Gospel readings.

A choir or soloist may sing the Alleluia Verse. Actually, the singing of the Alleluia Verse is part of the important liturgical responsibility of the choir. The choir may occasionally sing a longer anthem or hymn stanza, which helps the congregation anticipate the Gospel. This also was the place in the liturgy where Johann Sebastian Bach's cantatas were sung.[48]

At the singing of the appropriate Verse, the congregation stands in anticipation of the Gospel Reading. The practice of standing for the Gospel dates to at least the fourth century and is similar in purpose to standing for the Invocation: As gathered guests we acknowledge our Host and His words to us. Standing also reminds the gathered guests that the Word, Jesus Christ, is truly present.[49]

11.B. LENTEN VERSE

During the Lenten season, a verse from Joel 2:13 replaces the Alleluia Verse. It recalls the Old Testament hope and our fulfilled joy even in the solemn Lenten season. During the Lenten and Advent seasons, *alleluias* are omitted to stress the penitential nature of the season.[50]

11.C. GOSPEL PROCESSION

On festival days, during the singing of the Verse, the minister may process into the congregation, carrying the Bible, which visualizes the words of St. John: "The

Word became flesh and made His dwelling among us" (John 1:14). In the fifth century, Augustine already admonished his congregation, "Let us listen to the Gospel just as if the Lord himself were present."[51] Luther, following Augustine, spoke of the importance of recognizing the presence of Christ in the Gospel: "For the preaching of the Gospel is nothing else than Christ coming to us, or we being brought to him."[52] As the congregation faces the reader, the worshipers model the gathering of all people from around the world to hear the Lord's message and worship Him.

The Gospel procession is composed of the presiding minister, the bookbearer, and two torchbearers.[53] As appropriate music is played or as the Verse is sung, the bookbearer, accompanied by the torchbearers, moves to the altar to retrieve the Bible that had been deposited there prior to the service or after the Entrance Hymn. Led by the bookbearer, the group moves about one-third of the way down the center aisle. (See diagram.) The bookbearer stands between the torchbearers,[54] turns to face the presiding

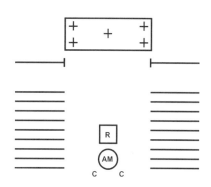

minister, and opens the Bible to the appropriate place.[55] A modest fanfare may be used for the procession and as the group returns to the chancel. Occasionally Lutheran churches use richly decorated Gospel texts for these processions, which illustrate the great respect worshipers hold for the Bible as the Word of God.

If there is no Gospel procession and if the Gospel is not read from the pulpit or the lectern, the Gospel may be read from the liturgical "north" side of the altar, that is, on the front-right side or Gospel side of the altar as the minister faces the congregation. The pastor may move to this position during the Verse.

12.A. GOSPEL ANNOUNCEMENT

The Gospel is announced simply and clearly. Elaborate explanations and introductions are inappropriate because the Word is sufficient. If a brief introduction is used, it should draw listeners into the context of the reading. The sung response to the announcement of the Gospel—"Glory to you, O Lord"[56]—reflects the Old Testament expectation and understanding of the Lord's glorious presence in the midst of His people.

Lutherans are beginning to participate in the tradition of making the sign of the cross with the thumb on the forehead, mouth, and breast as the Gospel Reading is announced. This may be especially appropriate for the minister, who also may pray silently, "May the Lord be on my mind [cross the forehead], on my lips [cross the mouth], and in my heart [cross the chest]. Amen."

12.b. Gospel Reading

The Gospel Reading is the central reading for any day in the church year and should never be omitted. "Normally the Gospel is read by the preacher from the place of preaching, especially if the Sermon is to be based on the Gospel."[57] If pew Bibles are used, page numbers may appear in the bulletin. Printed readings in the bulletin or provided as inserts may draw attention away from the proclaimed Word. Whenever the Gospel is read, care should be taken to pronounce the words clearly. Luther even delineated melodic lines so the Gospel could be chanted, thus communicating clearly the truth and power of God's Word.[58]

13. Gospel Response

After the conclusion of the Gospel Reading is announced, the congregation again bursts into a joyous response: "Praise to you, O Christ."[59] In contrast to the Old Testament imagery of the Lord's glory, the congregation responds to the Gospel Reading by praising Christ, who fulfills God's promises and is the incarnate Messiah. This rubric emphasizes that God's gathered guests have heard the Good News that God came to them in Jesus Christ.

14. Hymn of the Day

Following the Gospel Reading and its response, the congregation joins in a corporate hymn of praise. This chief hymn of the day (*Hauptlied* in German) is a distinctive liturgical contribution made by the Lutheran Church. These specially selected hymns provide commentary on the readings and were prescribed in the sixteenth century for Lutheran congregations. Although sometimes referred to as the Sermon Hymn, the Hymn of the Day actually augments the readings to focus the congregation's thoughts on the theme of the day. It could be considered another Proper. *Lutheran Worship* lists these hymns according to the readings.[60] As many as four hymns may be listed, depending on how closely the hymn texts match the pericopes of the day. An unfamiliar hymn may be introduced to the congregation prior to the service. Explanations that show the connection between the hymn text and the readings may help to underscore the theme of worship as edification.

15. Sermon

Since postexilic times Jews met to hear readings from the Holy Scriptures and commentaries on the texts in the vernacular (Nehemiah 8:8). Jesus continued that practice (Luke 4:16–30), as did the early Christians (Acts 20:7). Lutherans are also people of the Word. In contrast to Reformed churches, where "the Word" refers only to Scripture, Lutherans also understand "the Word" as the proclamation of the Gospel. Luther said that no gathering of worshipers should omit a sermon or homily (a simple, less formal conversation on Scripture).[61] The Sermon, therefore, is never an option. Here, God's people hear from God Himself in the voice of the preacher.

The proclamation of God's love in Christ for the whole world is the highpoint of the Service of the Word. During the Sermon, the living voice of the Gospel is delivered for the continuing life of the gathered guests, which prepares worshipers for scattering into the world for the remainder of the week. Yet the Sermon may not always be in the form of a lecture. Dramatic dialogues or chancel dramas may introduce or emphasize a central theme of the readings and serve as a commentary for the proclamation of the Gospel.

The Sermon may be on any of the readings, though traditionally the Sermon is an exposition of the Gospel Reading. Law and Gospel are two messages that should be clearly heard in Lutheran sermons, whether the message is based on a passage from the Old or the New Testament. The Law is not merely information about what God wants. It convicts hearers of sin in their hearts. Likewise, the Gospel is not merely a mention of Jesus or of God's general love for the world. It proclaims God's gift of forgiveness, life, and salvation through faith in Jesus.

The location of the Sermon in the worship service may vary. Luther suggested in his *Formula Missae* that it be placed after the Creed or immediately before the Service of Holy Communion. In his German Mass, Luther suggested that the Sermon follow the Creed. *Lutheran Worship* follows a tradition dating to Reformation times, when several Lutheran communities placed the Sermon before the Creed.[62]

The Sermon may conclude with the Votum: "The peace of God, which transcends all understanding, will guard your hearts and minds in Christ Jesus" (Philippians 4:7). Because the Sermon is followed by the Creed in Divine Service II, it is better to omit the Votum, which is a mini-Benediction that concludes the Service of the Word in Divine Service I.

Children's sermons have become increasingly popular. While this practice can be beneficial, be careful that the message clearly proclaims Law and Gospel. Objects may be used to communicate clearly the central truth in the Scriptures of the day.

16. Creed

After the Sermon the congregation stands to confess its trinitarian faith. The Creed is a summary of and a reply to the Word, affirming the people's response to the Sermon. *Credo* is Latin for "I believe." Three ecumenical or catholic creeds are used in Lutheran congregations: the Apostles' Creed, the Nicene Creed, and the Athanasian Creed. By using these creeds regularly in worship, Lutherans show that they are not a sect but a confidently biblical and confessing movement in the greater Christian community throughout the world.

The rubric in *Lutheran Worship* indicates that any of the creeds may be used and in a variety of formats—including hymnic settings. During some festivals, worship leaders may chant a creed, using one note as the chant tone. Several choral settings of the creeds also are available. (If the text of the creed in a choral setting is not in English, translations may be provided in the worship folder.) The sign of the cross is appropriate at the end of any of the creeds, reminding worshipers of the resurrection hope built on the cross of Christ.

16.A. Nicene Creed

The Nicene Creed is traditionally used during Holy Communion services and on major church festivals, though some Lutheran orders of service suggest the use of the Apostles' Creed for Communion and the Nicene Creed for festivals. With increasingly frequent administration of the Lord's Supper, the Nicene Creed has become the most familiar creed to many Lutheran worshipers.

The Nicene Creed grew out of a need to clarify the doctrines of the Trinity and the deity of Christ, which were addressed at the Council of Nicaea in A.D. 325. Later modifications at the Council of Constantinople in A.D. 381 removed some of the specific condemnations mentioned in the original Nicene Creed, which means we actually confess the Niceno-Constantinopolitan Creed (obviously a mouthful too cumbersome for regular use). In the original Greek text of the creed, the wording was in the first-person plural, "We believe . . ." This wording underscores the corporate nature of this ecumenical creed as worshipers join Christians of all times and all places in confessing the common Christian faith. Luther also used this grammatical choice in his paraphrase of the creed, "We All Believe in One True God, Maker."[63]

Several phrases in the Nicene Creed underscore the Christological emphasis of Jesus' eternal deity: "God of God, Light of Light, very God of very God, begotten, not made." In addition, this creed avers the complete equality of the Son with the

Father in the phrase "of one substance with the Father by whom all things were made."[64]

Some Lutherans use the adjective *Christian* to define *church* in the Nicene Creed instead of the more traditional adjective *catholic*. Luther adopted the German practice of defining the church as "one, holy, Christian, and apostolic" in his catechisms, instead of the ancient and universally established phraseology "one, holy, catholic, and apostolic." Luther recognized that the word *catholic* had a denominational connotation and that the word *Christian* (which in German is *christliche*) communicated more accurately the true sense of the creed. Luther, therefore, substituted *Christian* for *catholic* because the German word *allgemeine* was not as clear as *christliche*. Swedish, Norwegian, Danish, French, and Spanish Lutherans have retained the more traditional word *catholic*. However, the German Lutheran practice has continued in North America and remains in *Lutheran Worship*.

A chanted version of the Nicene Creed is available in a plainsong setting in *Lutheran Worship*.[65] The minister may intone the first few words, and the congregation joins him for the rest of the creed.

16.B. APOSTLES' CREED

The Apostles' Creed is the baptismal creed of the gathered guests and summarizes the Christian faith in the most simple, scriptural, and apostolic terms. If a Baptism was conducted prior to the Preparatory Service, the creed may be omitted. Some congregations place the Baptism at this point in the service. In such circumstances, the congregation joins in the baptismal creed.

The Apostles' Creed is used on nonfestival Sundays and, according to some worship books, during the "green seasons" of the church year—the Sundays after Epiphany and Pentecost. The alternate readings of this and the Nicene Creed underscore the ecumenical nature of these creeds as nonsectarian statements to which all true Christians adhere. A hymnic setting of the Apostles' Creed is available.[66]

16.C. QUICUNQUE VULT (ATHANASIAN CREED)

The Athanasian Creed[67] is confessed only occasionally by congregations, most often on Trinity Sunday. Some scholars have suggested that this statement of faith was never a spoken creed but a poetic affirmation of faith; others have argued that it is hymnic and should be sung. The first two words of this statement, "Whoever wishes" (*Quicunque vult*), are retained as the Latin title.

Named after Athanasius (A.D. 296–373), the great defender of trinitarian theology, this creed originated in Gaul (France) a century or so after his death. Therefore, the creed is misnamed for two reasons: It is neither by Athanasius nor was it officially adopted as a creed of the Christian church. However, this creed affirms traditional Christian beliefs, and Athanasius's defense of Christ's divinity and the equality of the persons of the Trinity deserves the attention of God's gathered guests.

17. A QUESTIONABLE "OPTION"

The Chief Divine Service ("*Hauptgottesdienst*") is a service of Word *and* Sacrament. The early church and the Lutheran reformers celebrated Holy Communion every Sunday, holy day, and any other time the congregation desired.[68] A later Reformed tradition separated the Service of Communion from the Service of the Word,[69] so weekly Communion was not the norm for Lutheran congregations for several generations. To end the worship service without the Sacrament terminates the movement from God's gracious words to God's gracious action in the Lord's Supper.

If a service centered around the Word alone is desired, *Lutheran Worship* provides alternatives in Matins (and Morning Prayer) and Vespers (and Evening Prayer), along with three services of "Prayer and Preaching" in *Worship Supplement.*[70]

18. PRAYERS

After confessing their faith, the gathered guests now approach their Host in confident faith and trust. As a royal priesthood, they bring their requests and petitions to God's heavenly throne (Matthew 18:19). Their concern is for all people as they offer prayers, supplications, and thanksgivings (1 Timothy 2:1–4). Prayer, therefore, is one of the central activities of God's gathered guests (Acts 2:42).

The worship leader may wish to gather petitions immediately after the Creed if there is no system to gather requests prior to the service. Petitions, thanksgiving, supplications, and intercessions are made for the whole church, as well as for local needs. Worshipers may stand for these prayers as a sign of their membership in the priesthood of all believers. Kneeling is appropriate during the Lenten season. As part of his pastoral and priestly office, the presiding minister concludes the prayers.

18.A. PRAYERS: RESPONSIVE FORM

Diaconal ministry is especially evident in the responsive form of the prayers as the congregation is not only invited to pray for special needs, but actually prays. The assisting minister, identified with [A] , is traditionally a lay deacon who gathers the prayers, petitions, and thanksgivings and presents them to the congregation for prayer. In the simplest form of responsive praying, the deacon states the desired content of the petition as a "bidding," such as "for _____ that _____." The specific situation or person follows the word *for*, and following *that* is an articulation of the desired result (for example, "For those who are ill, that they may find healing and wholeness in Christ's presence"). The "bidding" may be followed by silence so each parishioner can offer a personal prayer or the deacon may offer a brief petition. The deacon then continues, "Lord, in your mercy" or "Let us pray to the Lord." The congregation responds with either "hear our prayer" or "Lord, have mercy."[71] These two responses provide variety and are not assigned to any specific season.

If the congregation is small, the pastor may invite worshipers to announce prayer requests. As the pastor formulates the prayer, he will want to expand requests and praises to include those of "the whole people of God in Christ Jesus."[72]

18.B. PRAYERS: COLLECT FORM

The second form of prayers uses a collect form for the petitions. In this format the congregation listens as the worship leader, usually the pastor, prays for a series of concerns in the General Prayer of the Church.[73] When there is no Communion, the General Prayer is an adaptation of a prayer used in the Orthodox-Catholic Apostolic Church before the Holy Door and at Matins. The origins of this prayer have been lost to time.[74] The General Prayer may be divided into a series of several collects, using a modified termination to indicate to the congregation the end of a specific collect.[75]

19.A. OFFERING

Once the prayers have been completed, God's gathered guests respond to God's Word with grateful hearts and with their lives (Romans 12:1–2; 2 Corinthians 8:9). The offerings are symbolic of their spiritual condition. In the early church the offerings were not only monetary, but also "in kind." Gifts from the field (grain and vegetables, oil and flowers, wool and flax), as well as gifts from the forest (honey, furs, wood, fruits and berries), were offered to the Lord. Initially placed at the entrance of the church, the offerings were symbolically brought forward during the Offertory Hymn and placed on a side table. The loaves of bread and the flasks of wine for the Lord's Supper were selected from these gifts, and the rest of the offerings were used for the poor.

In our modern settings, the gathering of the congregation's gifts should be done with dignity and discretion rather than overt pomp. As the gifts are gathered, the presiding minister may prepare for Holy Communion. Normally, the Communion elements are reserved on a side table (called a credence table) until this point in the service. If this is the case, only a veiled chalice is placed on the altar prior to the Service of the Sacrament. This indicates that the Lord's Supper will be served. The corporal (a white cloth) is spread on the altar, and all the utensils (chalice and flagon/cruets, paten, and ciborium/pyx) are brought to the altar. (See diagram.) If assisting ministers are available, everyone shares the task of preparing for Communion.

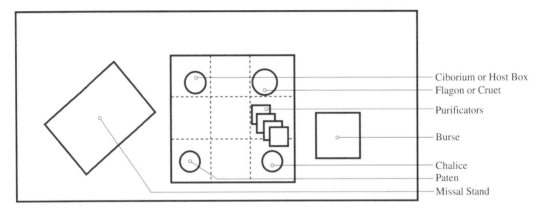

19.B. OTHER OFFERINGS

As the offering is gathered, music may be played. Organists have traditionally played voluntaries. In earlier centuries, musicians composed voluntaries as special offerings to God and to the congregation; they would not be paid for these compositions (thus the general category of "voluntary"). This is an appropriate time for members of the body of Christ to bring personal offerings of musical praise. Children, young adults, or dramatic groups may offer presentations, dance, solos, or duets.

The congregation's creativity and generosity can be expanded and celebrated at this point in the service. In addition to monetary gifts to the congregation, quilts prepared for distribution, food for relief pantries, and monetary gifts for mission projects may be offered to the Lord during this portion of the liturgy.

20.A. OFFERTORY HYMN

After the offering has been gathered, the congregation joins in a hymn of praise. Three hymns are available in *Lutheran Worship*: "Let the Vineyards Be Fruitful, Lord,"[76] "What Shall I Render to the Lord,"[77] and "Create in Me."[78] The latter was incorrectly understood as a response to the Sermon in *The Lutheran Hymnal*. Some congregations follow their own tradition and use a familiar hymn on stewardship.

20.B. OFFERTORY PROCESSION

During the Offertory Hymn, individuals (or families) can join the ushers to bring the offerings to the Lord. Along with the offering, these individuals may bring forward the bread and wine for the Eucharist. As mentioned previously, the ancient church observed the custom of offering gifts "in kind." Some congregations still invite volunteers to make or buy the bread and the wine for Communion and to bring these as personal gifts of gratitude. A loaf (1 Corinthians 10:17) of pita bread or matzo and white wine are appropriate.[79]

A famous mosaic in the Italian city of Ravenna shows the Emperor Justinian and the Empress Theodora carrying a loaf of bread and a flask of wine in an Offertory Procession with many other worshipers. In many African congregations a lively and rhythmic dance is observed as representative members of the congregation bring their offerings to the altar. Some North American Lutheran congregations follow this participatory practice, drawing beneficial ideas from other cultures to include in their liturgical practices.

The Service of the Word is now complete, and the congregation anticipates the second half of the service, the Service of the Sacrament. The foundation built on God's words of promise is now ready for an edifice of faith, fellowship, and thanksgiving.

SOME QUESTIONS TO CONSIDER

1. Explain the meaning and purpose of *rubric*. How does it function in a worship rite?

2. List three places in the liturgy where the sign of the cross may be made. Why are these appropriate places?

3. Why do Lutherans often have a Preparatory Service prior to the Service of the Word? How does the Declaration of Grace differ from Absolution? Which is a more "Lutheran" statement?

4. Describe three Propers and explain their function and purpose in the Divine Service.

5. How does the Hymn of Praise function in the Divine Service? What alternate hymns can be used in place of the liturgical hymn?

6. What four Scripture readings are appointed for a Sunday? How are they related to one another?

7. What is the high point of the Service of the Word? How do the parts of the Service of the Word build toward this high point?

NOTES

1. As evidence for this, Pfatteicher and Messerli, *Manual on the Liturgy*, has been used for years in conjunction with *Lutheran Worship*. Precht, *Lutheran Worship: History and Practice*, presupposes many of the principles and details for conducting the liturgy that are found in *Manual on the Liturgy*.

2. *Lutheran Worship*, pp. 159, 183.

3. AC XXIV, 6; AC XXV, 1; Ap. XXIV, 1; and LC, "Brief Exhortation to Confession," 29 (K-W, 69, 72–73, 258, 479).

4. See *Lutheran Worship,* p. 136.

5. Commission on Worship, the LCMS, "Notes on the Liturgy," in *Lutheran Worship: Agenda*, 27. See illustrations that indicate the location of worship leaders in Pfatteicher and Messerli, *Manual on the Liturgy*, 196–98.

6. See rubric 4, *Lutheran Worship*, pp. 159, 179.

7. See *Lutheran Worship*, 196–207.

8. *Lutheran Worship*, p. 305.

9. "Short Order of Confession," LW 53:116–18.

10. Precht, "Confession and Absolution," 370, notes: "Granted that Luther never made confession and absolution a requirement for coming to the Lord's Table, his linking the free element of confession and absolution to the obligatory examination regarding doctrine and life resulted, however, in this type of confession becoming a preparation for the reception of Holy Communion."

11. *Lutheran Worship*, pp. 158, 178.

12. In "German Mass," LW 53:80, Luther notes that "the admonition itself has since become a public confession." Cf. WA 19:96.

13. Barr, "Prayers of Confession," 844.

14. See *Lutheran Worship*, pp. 136f., 264, 308, 310.

15. *Lutheran Worship*, pp. 158, 178.

16. *Lutheran Worship*, p. 137.

17. "We receive absolution, or forgiveness, from the pastor as from God Himself, and in no wise doubt, but firmly believe, that by it our sins are forgiven before God in heaven" (*Lutheran Worship*, p. 304).

18. Ap. XII, 41; Ap. XIII, 4 (K-W, 193, 219).

19. *Lutheran Worship,* pp. 159, 179.

20. Reed, *Lutheran Liturgy* (rev. ed.), 261.

21. LW 53:22.

22. See *Lutheran Worship*, pp. 10–123.

23. The Latin word *ambo* means "both" (*ambivalent* and *ambiguous* both have roots from this word). An ambo is a piece of chancel furniture that serves as both a reading table and a pulpit. It is becoming increasingly popular in Lutheran churches.

24. Candles used for processions are usually positioned atop poles. See Pfatteicher and Messerli, *Manual on the Liturgy*, 204.

25. Be careful that wax does not drip from the candles onto the torchbearers or onto worshipers. Also avoid using a military style (elbow of one arm extending horizontally) when holding a candle or cross.

26. Consider that in wedding processions the bride, the "focal point" of the procession, enters the church last. For a procession during an ordination service, the guest pastors enter before the candidate, who enters immediately before the last person in the procession, the ordinator (normally the District president or bishop).

27. Reed, *Lutheran Liturgy* (rev. ed.), 268.

28. "German Mass," LW 53:72.

29. Pfatteicher and Messerli, *Manual on the Liturgy*, 211.

30. *Lutheran Worship*, 209. This hymn is a ninth-century chant tune adapted to a twelfth-century Latin text of the Kyrie.

31. Reed, *Lutheran Liturgy* (rev. ed.), 273, quotes Luther as saying that the Gloria in Excelsis "did not grow, nor was it made on earth, but it came down from heaven."

32. *Lutheran Worship*, 210.

33. *Lutheran Worship*, 215.

34. Several years ago, Pope John Paul II used the setting of "This Is the Feast" by Richard Hillert (Divine Service II: First Setting in *Lutheran Worship*) for a pontifical mass held in the United States.

35. *Lutheran Worship*, 1.

36. *Lutheran Worship*, 2.

37. See Ruth 2:4; Luke 1:28; Galatians 6:18; Philippians 4:23; 2 Thessalonians 3:16; 2 Timothy 4:22; Philemon 25.

38. Pfatteicher, *Commentary*, 125–27; and Reed, *Lutheran Liturgy* (rev. ed.), 277f.

39. See *Lutheran Worship*, pp. 10–123.

40. Reed, *Lutheran Liturgy* (rev. ed.), 291, says: "The mature judgment of the church has retained [the historic pericopes] because their use is a guarantee of sound and complete teaching of fundamental Christian truth. Altogether they constitute a solid block of fundamental material about which the services of a particular day or season are constructed. They are a most important part of the common liturgical inheritance of the universal church, with a continuous history of nearly fifteen hundred years."

41. See Consultation on Common Texts, *Common Lectionary*, for further explanation of the content and purpose of the selected readings.

42. Commission on Worship, the LCMS, *Narrative for Adults*, 6. To uphold the Lutheran view of the public authority of the pastoral office in the Divine Service, the pastor customarily reads the Gospel lesson. This wise tradition separates the Lutheran view of the pasoral office from the Reformed position. However, such a custom is not identified in Holy Scripture.

43. *Lutheran Worship*, p. 140. It is unclear why Divine Service I has a congregational response to the announcement of the completion of the first reading while Divine Service II omits the response. Divine Service I omits the congregational response to the announcement of the completion of the Epistle Reading.

44. See *Lutheran Worship*, pp. 313–65.

45. See *Lutheran Worship*, pp. 366–68, for instructions on how to chant the psalms.

46. Justin Martyr, "First Apology," 67, in *Early Christian Fathers*, 287.

47. "Formula of the Mass and Communion," LW 53:24.

48. Pelikan, *Bach among the Theologians*, 9–12.

49. Langer, "From Study of Scripture to a Reenactment of Sinai," 57, says that in Jewish worship "the presence of the scroll ritually marks God's presence." Bradshaw, "Use of the Bible in Liturgy," 35, reports that Christians adapted this view. Bradshaw says the Bible is "a sacramental expression of Christ's presence in the assembly" (35).

50. The Eastern Orthodox churches never omit the Alleluia Verse. Luther also questioned the omission of the Alleluia Verse, saying in his *Formula Missae* that "the Alleluia is the perpetual voice of the church" (LW 53:24).

51. Augustine, "Sermon on St. John's Gospel" 30.1, in *Nicene and Post-Nicene Fathers*, vol. 7 (First Series)

trans. James Innes, ed. Philip Schaff (Peabody, Mass.: Hendrickson, 1994), 186 (*author's paraphrase*).

52. "Brief Instruction," LW 35:121.

53. Although the note in Precht, *Lutheran Worship: History and Practice*, 413 indicates that the crucifer leads the way, the Bible replaces the crucifix as the symbol of Christ's presence. Thus the bookbearer usually leads the Gospel procession. If the bookbearer leads, the crucifer is not used.

54. If a bookbearer is not used, the reader may carry the Bible.

55. See Pfatteicher and Messerli, *Manual on the Liturgy*, 221–23.

56. *Lutheran Worship*, pp. 165, 184.

57. Pfatteicher and Messerli, *Manual on the Liturgy*, 221. Beginning about the fourth century, the deacon replaced the lector as the reader of the Gospel. In Jerusalem, the bishop read the Gospel each Sunday.

58. "German Mass," LW 53:74–78.

59. *Lutheran Worship*, pp. 165, 185.

60. See *Lutheran Worship*, p. 976ff. Unfortunately, the index is at the end of the hymnal rather than included with the Propers.

61. LW 53:11.

62. Reed, *Lutheran Liturgy* (rev. ed.), 302, indicates that Leipzig (1534), Brandenburg (1540), and Cologne (1543) followed this practice.

63. *Lutheran Worship*, 213.

64. *Lutheran Worship*, pp. 141–42.

65. *Lutheran Worship*, 4.

66. "We All Believe in One True God, Father " (*Lutheran Worship*, 212).

67. *Lutheran Worship*, pp. 134–35.

68. Ap. XXIV, 1 (K-W, 258).

69. Senn, *Christian Liturgy*, 364–65.

70. *Worship Supplement* was a study document prepared by the LCMS Commission on Worship. It has been an LCMS worship resource since the 1970s.

71. *Lutheran Worship*, pp. 168, 187.

72. *Lutheran Worship*, pp. 167, 187.

73. *Lutheran Worship*, p. 132f.

74. Reed, *Lutheran Liturgy* (rev. ed.), 661.

75. See *Lutheran Worship*, pp. 220–21, 232–33. Note that Matins and Vespers distinguish between collect terminations.

76. The text in *Lutheran Worship*, pp. 168f. or 187f., is by John Arthur and alludes to Isaiah 5:1; Hosea 10:1; Ezekiel 19:10; Psalm 23:5; Revelation 14:15; John 6:48.

77. The text in *Lutheran Worship*, pp. 169f. or 188, is from one of the Hallel Psalms—Psalms 116:12, 17, 13–14, 19. It is traditionally associated with Holy Communion because the Hallel Psalms probably were sung by Jesus and His disciples on Maundy Thursday.

78. The text in *Lutheran Worship*, pp. 175 or 194f., is a portion of Psalm 51. This text is the Offertory in *The Lutheran Hymnal* and is sung after the Votum, apparently as a response to the Sermon.

79. Recipes for unleavened bread often are available through altar guild organizations.

CHAPTER 8

THE SERVICE OF THE SACRAMENT

The second major focus of the Divine Service is the service and celebration of Holy Communion, which is one of the unique marks of the Christian community.[1] By it the members are connected to the body of Christ (1 Corinthians 10:16–17; 11:27–29). As God's gathered guests, Lutherans faithfully receive the precious body and blood of Jesus "in, with, and under" the bread and wine. Perhaps more than any other part of the Divine Service, the Service of the Sacrament is filled with the mystery of God, as well as the concrete assurance of His grace. Early Christians recognized this and used the Latin phrase for mystery, *sacramentum*, when speaking of this gift. This Sacrament was reserved for the mature in faith who had been baptized and properly instructed. The Sacrament strengthens our personal faith and gives witness to our corporate faith. The Lutheran emphasis on Word and Sacrament is most evident in this second part of the worship service. Each half of the Divine Service deserves thoughtful preparation and conscientious practice; neither part should be rushed or truncated.

In this chapter we will complete our look at the Divine Service, following the rubrics of Divine Service II. The detailed explanations of the service that follow can be applied to other liturgical worship orders with only minor changes because the basic structure is the same for all liturgical services in the Lutheran tradition.

SERVICE OF THE SACRAMENT

21.A. PREFACE

The second half of the Divine Service begins with an ancient dialogue. Martin Luther preferred a freestanding altar so the congregation could hear and observe this portion of the service and carry on a meaningful conversation with the pastor.[2] This dialogue between the pastor and congregation is the oldest and least changed portion of the Lutheran liturgy. Some of the most ancient liturgies of the Christian church include an almost identical greeting that begins with "The Lord be with you" and concludes with, "It is right to give him thanks and praise."[3] Chanting this portion of the liturgy helps worshipers ponder this unique conversation.

21.B. SALUTATION

As the pastor and people ask that the Lord be present with one another, they are reminded of the special relationship they have with one another. In this Salutation, a mutual caring and a mutual sharing becomes explicit. The Salutation invites participation and attention. It also imparts a blessing and a bond of love as it communicates a strong relationship in Christ.

21.C. *SURSUM CORDA*

The phrase "Lift up your hearts" (Latin, *sursum corda*) and the response "We lift them to the Lord" are from Lamentations 3:41 and Psalm 86:4.[4] This part of the Preface reflects our responsive anticipation of God's most powerful gift to us—Himself. Dating to second-century worship practices, this dialogue helped the congregation focus on those spiritual things from "above" (Colossians 3:1–2; John 11:41). The hearts of the gathered guests are to receive and their minds are to reflect on the greatness of God's love, which caused Him to send His Son into this world.

21.D. EUCHARIST

The Preface continues with the exhortation "Let us give thanks to the Lord."[5] The Greek word *eucharist* means "thanksgiving," which is our appropriate response to God's promises to us. Jesus also prayed a prayer of thanksgiving or blessing before breaking bread (Matthew 14:19; Luke 22:19; 24:30; 1 Corinthians 11:24). The Jewish tradition of blessing (*berakah*) the bread before it is eaten seems to be the model adopted and adapted by the early Christians. The people respond to this invitation by acknowledging that such thanksgiving is right and proper.

22.A. PROPER PREFACE

After the general introductory remarks, the liturgy continues with a specific focus. In early forms the Preface recalled the history of salvation, beginning with creation and moving through Christ's life and the institution of the Holy Supper. Later, particularly in the West, the Roman Mass at this point in the service focused on an aspect of salvation appropriate to the specific season of the church year.[6]

These seasonal prefaces provide concrete reasons for giving thanks in light of God's actions through the life of Christ.

All the Proper Prefaces conclude with the acknowledgment of our corporate praise. At this point in the liturgy, we confess that worship is not limited by time or space. As God's gathered guests we join the unending worship experience "with angels and archangels and with all the company of heaven."[7] Our weekly worship joins the perpetual worship of the angelic choirs and the invisible church of all ages. We might recall the words of Hebrews 12:1: "We are surrounded by . . . a great cloud of witnesses." Thus the Proper Preface prepares worshipers to join in the eternal song of heaven.

22.B. SANCTUS AND BENEDICTUS

As a Hymn of Praise was sung prior to the Service of the Word, so now a Hymn of Praise is sung before the Sacrament. "Holy, holy, holy" (*sanctus, sanctus, sanctus* in Latin) is the great angelic hymn described in the theophany of Isaiah 6:3. The prophet describes the seraphim gathered around the throne of God, chanting a confession of God's supreme "otherness" (this is one meaning of the word *holy*) and separateness from all that He created. The six-winged seraphim covered their faces in the presence of God's divine glory, yet Isaiah was privileged to witness this event. We also are able to participate in this inspired adoration as our worship takes on a supertemporal nature (literally, "above time") and becomes truly eternal. In a hymn setting for his German Mass, Luther depicted this scene from Isaiah, describing the awesome sights, sounds, and smells of the occasion.[8] In the churches of the Reformation era, three boys often sang this hymn as they knelt before the altar.[9]

In Divine Service II the Lord is described as "God of power and might." In Divine Service I the more ancient title is used: "God of Sabaoth." This phrase refers to God as a powerful and divine warrior who comes with His angelic armies to free His people, as described in Psalm 89:5–18 and as used in Romans 9:29 and James 5:4. This descriptive phrase also has a more general sense because it suggests God's omnipotence (Mark 4:41).

Immediately appended to the Sanctus is the Hosanna and the Benedictus. In Psalm 118:25–26, a form of *hosanna* is translated "O Lord, save us" and is coupled with the Benedictus, "Blessed is He." The people of Jerusalem sang these messianic verses as Jesus entered Jerusalem on Palm Sunday. These words of Jesus' first-century disciples and followers are also our hymns of praise as Jesus comes to us in the mystery and marvel of the Sacrament of the Altar. The sign of the cross may again be made at this time.

Luther placed his German Sanctus[10] after the Words of Institution to emphasize the Lutheran recognition of the real presence in the Sacrament of the Altar. (Most Reformed churches have removed any reference to Psalm 118 from their Communion services because they reject the real presence of Christ in the elements, that is, that we receive the body and blood of Christ in, with, and under the bread and wine.) A Lutheran tradition that has been lost in most congregations is to bow during the singing of the Sanctus and to make the sign of the cross at the Benedictus. These two actions provide a physical response to the awesome awareness of God's graciousness in Christ. They could be reintroduced in a variety of ways, including during catechetical instruction.

23. PRAYER: EUCHARISTIC

The prayer that follows the angelic hymn is a new element in Lutheran rites. Picking up the theme of the Benedictus, the pastor more specifically praises God for His gift of Jesus. Luther removed a long and misleading prayer, known as the Canon of the Mass, from his orders of service. The Canon included prayers to saints and for the dead. In addition, the medieval Eucharistic Prayer included several references to the Lord's Supper as a sacrifice of Christ to God being performed by the priest. In earlier Christian orders of service, the prayer at this point in the service included the Words of Institution (1 Corinthians 11:23–26), along with a recital of God's redemptive activity.[11] The Eucharistic Prayer in Divine Service II conforms to God's injunction to "give thanks" before the breaking of bread. We gather at the Table with Jesus Himself. Just as Jesus prayed a prayer of blessing before the Meal, before He fed the 5,000 (Matthew 14:13–21), before He fed the 4,000 (Matthew 15:29–38), and at other times in His ministry (Luke 9:10–17; 24:13–31), so the pastor prays now.

The Eucharistic Prayer traditionally had two parts, *anamnesis* and *epiclesis* (Greek for "remembering" and "invoking"), though the theological relevance of the latter is diminished since the Reformation. With words drawn from John 3:16, the pastor recalls God's mercy and grace. Because we want to "do this in remembrance" (*anamnesis*) of Christ, we recall the reason for His incarnation, then we thank God for the redemption He prepared. The invocation, as used in this prayer, differs from that of most other church orders. We do not call down the Holy Spirit on the elements, as the Greek Orthodox liturgy requires for the consecration of the elements and as many ancient Eucharistic Prayers state.[12] Instead, we ask for the Spirit's continuing aid in making us worthy recipients of the Sacrament—that is, as He strengthens our faith. Luther's remarks are significant in this matter: "a person who has faith in these words . . . is really worthy and well prepared."[13] Thus it is faith strengthened by the Spirit that makes for worthiness, not the Spirit's presence in the elements. Here is another example where Lutheran theology comes through clearly and correctly in the liturgy. The Spirit prepares our hearts to receive Jesus, our Redeemer and Lord.

23.B. PRAYER: OUR FATHER

Early in Christian worship practice, the Our Father (also known as the Lord's Prayer) was associated with the Lord's Supper. The petition for "daily bread" was often understood as the spiritual food received in Holy Communion. In a concrete yet spiritual manner, this prayer recognizes that God's full and free forgiveness is to be shared with others. We are to go into the world as God's kingdom bearers, instruments of His will.

Either the 1789 translation of the Our Father found in the American *Book of Common Prayer* or the recent translation by the International Consultation on English Texts may be used. An occasional change in usage may encourage worshipers to think about the meaning of the words. Even Luther paraphrased the Our Father because it had become so mechanical and mystical in his time.[14] Some contemporary musical settings of the Our Father, which repeat "hallowed be thy name," are good, though perhaps theologically weak in the repetition of only one petition.

From the seventh century, the Our Father was said only by the priest. This practice continued in most Reformation era churches and was included in C. F. W. Walther's service for the LCMS. It was also the practice in *The Lutheran Hymnal*. However, following some German and more recent North American examples, *Lutheran Worship* returned the Our Father to the people. The pastor may take the *orans* (Latin for "praying") position as an indication of his intercessory role and bring his hands together at the chest at the conclusion of the prayer.

24. WORDS OF INSTITUTION

Sometimes referred to as the *Verba* (Latin for "the words"[15]), the pastor uses Christ's own words (1 Corinthians 11:24–25) to consecrate, or set apart, the bread and wine for God's special use. The pastor may simply make the sign of the cross on the elements, or he may hold the bread and the cup in his hands as he makes the sign of the cross on each. Whatever ritual action is used, it should demonstrate that Jesus is present with His gathered guests. Time and space are bridged, and the past is a contemporary experience as we hear the words of our Lord.[16]

Lutherans confess and believe that Christ gives His body and blood "in, with, and under" the consecrated physical elements of bread and wine. The elements deserve respect because of their divinely mandated function. Again the Good News is proclaimed that our sins are forgiven by Christ Himself and we receive the benefits of His saving act on Calvary.

25.A. GREETING OF PEACE

Jesus' Easter greeting (John 20:19) is recalled as the pastor clearly states the proclamation of peace—"The peace of the Lord be with you always"[17]—which is based on 1 Corinthians 16:23 and 2 Corinthians 13:13. Luther suggested that this was another point in the service at which the gathered guests receive a statement of absolution. The pastor may express the peace and the congregation responds in a manner similar to the Salutation earlier in the service.

25.B. SHARING OF THE PEACE

An equally effective communication of the peace invites all worshipers to exchange the words of peace with those around them. Some feel the chaos that results as people reach across pews or walk down the aisles disrupts the solemn flow of the liturgy. Originally, the peace was exchanged at the conclusion of the Service of the Word. However, the rationale for moving the exchange of peace seems to be theological—this action demonstrates the Fifth Petition of the Lord's Prayer.[18]

In 1 Corinthians 11, Paul expresses the need for communal forgiveness and reconciliation. On numerous occasions, the apostles suggested that Christians greet one another with "a holy kiss" (Romans 16:16; 1 Corinthians 16:20; 2 Corinthians 13:12; 1 Thessalonians 5:26) or "a kiss of love" (1 Peter 5:14). The sharing of the peace is an opportunity for the worshipers to be reconciled and to express the great love they have for one another.

26. AGNUS DEI

Jesus is the Lamb of God who takes away the sin of the world. John the Baptist pointed to the Paschal "Lamb of God" (Latin, *Agnus Dei*[19]) at the beginning of Jesus' earthly ministry (John 1:29; cf. Isaiah 53:7; Ephesians 2:13–15). We are reminded in this canticle[20] that Jesus alone is the one who was our sacrifice for sin and through whom we have access to God's mercy and peace. In this scriptural song we adore the one who comes to us as the Lamb slain for sinners.

During this first Communion hymn, the presiding minister and those assisting him may commune. It is also appropriate at this time to prepare the bread and wine for distribution. In fact, the Agnus Dei originally was included in the liturgy so the bread, brought forward during the Offertory, could be broken into pieces for distribution. All activities during this hymn should be performed in a dignified and respectful manner, anticipating the reception of Christ's body and blood. The canticle is a devotional moment in the liturgy that provides the congregation time to savor the words as the worshipers recall God's gracious gift of Himself.

27. HYMNS DURING DISTRIBUTION

Congregations normally sing several hymns, which are listed in the worship folder or on the hymn board, during the distribution of the Communion elements. Some organists and congregations develop a pattern of singing several stanzas of a hymn before pausing for an interlude, for example, after every third stanza. Such an arrangement may work well in a small congregation, but it may confuse newer members and visitors. If breaks are made within a hymn, it may be best to note them in the bulletin. In general, it is easier to sing all the stanzas of a hymn, then offer a postlude to the hymn or a prelude to the next hymn.

A second option is the use of special music. Choirs and soloists can provide music appropriate for the time of the church year and for the Sacrament of the Altar. Texts should clearly communicate the mystery and the blessings of the Sacrament.

A third option for the use of this time is to allow the congregation to sit in silence.[21] Some congregations may encourage their musicians to receive the Sacrament with the rest of the congregation during this period of silence. This quiet time allows the congregation to meditate on the words "The body of Christ for you . . . the blood of Christ for you" and to reflect on the great mystery occurring among God's gathered guests.

28. COMMUNION DISTRIBUTION

Distributing the Communion elements, while a practical concern, should be done in a dignified and respectful manner. However, a wise worship leader will evaluate the circumstances of the service, the architectural layout of the chancel and nave, and the makeup of the communicants when planning for distribution. A congregation's board of elders may want to address distribution practices on a periodic basis, evaluating the method and considering alternative approaches.

Numerous methods of distribution are possible. The congregation may receive the Sacrament kneeling or standing. They may receive it in a continuous method—communicants walk to a "station" to receive each element, then return to their seats—or they may come by "tables" to the altar rail. Congregations may distribute the wine in a chalice or common cup or use individual glasses or chalices. Even the bread may take on various forms—a loaf would follow the Pauline imagery, while wafers bring to mind matzo, the bread prepared for the Jewish Passover. Some congregations that desire easier reception for older members have returned to an earlier practice in which all recipients stand to receive the Sacrament as a symbol of joy. Other congregations have introduced the practice of standing to commune during Easter and kneeling during Advent and Lent. None of these practices are divisive of the unity we celebrate and share at the Lord's Table. To deepen the sense of oneness and unity in Christ that the Sacrament provides, many congregations use a continuous method of distribution. One campus pastor called this the *upsilon* approach, named after the Greek uppercase letter Υ, which is similar to the English capital letter Y. The communicants would receive the bread from the pastor, then split to receive the wine from one of two assistants positioned to his right and left. Regardless of the method, the pace of distribution should communicate dignity and respect because the gathered guests are receiving the greatest of gifts from the Host—Himself!

Regardless of how the communicants receive the Sacrament, the presiding minister usually distributes the bread so the practice of close(d) Communion can be followed. (Under normal conditions, the pastor knows the members of the congregation.) Assistants, if available, distribute the wine, passing over anyone to whom the pastor does not give the bread. Most congregations ask visitors who wish to commune to meet with the pastor prior to the service. A pastor may seek out visitors to meet with them after the service in unusual situations.

During distribution, the bread may be placed in the communicant's right hand, which is placed on top of the left hand, before being raised to the mouth.[22] The wafer also may be placed directly in the communicant's mouth. If there are no assistants, the pastor returns to the altar after distributing the bread and takes the chalice or individual cups to distribute the wine. If assisting ministers are available, they follow behind the pastor with the wine. Congregation members may be encouraged to assist the minister as he delivers the chalice by gently holding its base to guide it to their mouth. After the cup is shared, the minister wipes the chalice's rim with a purificator and turns the chalice slightly for the next communicant. The chalice may be wiped more thoroughly at the altar. If individual cups are used, they should be received in a reverent manner and returned to the server in a similar fashion.[23] Communicants may again make the sign of the cross either before or after receiving the elements as a reminder of their own continuing baptismal relationship with God.

Rather than using red wine for Communion as if it were a symbol of Christ's blood, Luther encouraged the use of white wine to avoid the Zwinglian symbolic misunderstanding. Communion is a matter of faith and not of sight. The white wine used may vary with congregations and tastes; however, a fuller-bodied wine is preferable for its alcohol content. The issue of nonalcoholic wine has been raised in recent years. Because of present distilling practices, wine that has been dealcoholized (sometimes called "nonalcoholic" wine) is acceptable for the Sacrament of the Altar. Grape juice that has been made to look and taste like wine (referred to as nonalcoholic "wine") should be avoided.[24]

Bas-relief of St. Andrew

More recently a concern has been raised regarding individuals who have a serious allergy to wheat flour. At the present time, no acceptable solution for gluten-free Communion bread has been offered.[25] However, Luther's suggestion that it is better to receive only one kind than to be forced to receive both elements may be worthy of further study.[26]

Children may approach the altar with their parents so they may witness this sacred event. Such a practice means young children do not need to be left unattended in the pews or parents do not need to commune separately. The pastor may give a blessing or a reminder of Baptism as he lays his hands on each child's head. To indicate that they will not commune, children may cross their arms over their chests, thus forming the sign of an X-cross, which is known as the St. Andrew cross. This posture also may help keep little hands under control.

29. DISMISSAL

After communicants have received the bread and wine, the pastor dismisses them. The words of the Dismissal—"The body and blood of our Lord strengthen and preserve you steadfast in the true faith to life everlasting. Go in peace."[27]—may be spoken to each "table" or at the end of the distribution. Under the best circumstances, one common Dismissal at the end of Communion will be heard more clearly than an individual Dismissal at each table. A common Dismissal also provides a sense of unity as the whole congregation hears the good news of God's gracious gift in the Sacrament.

30. "AMEN"

The congregation responds to the Dismissal with an affirmation of the truth it has confessed. This response by communicants is a "may" rubric, but those who choose to respond are recognizing the blessings received in the Sacrament.

31.A. POST-COMMUNION CANTICLE: THANK THE LORD

The natural response after receiving a gift is to give thanks. The supernatural gift of God's forgiving grace in Christ elicits a grateful response from all communicants. "Thank the Lord" is a "new song" in *Lutheran Worship*. The text is based on the opening verses of Psalm 105. In ancient times Psalms 34 and 145 were sung as the people communed. An appropriate response to receiving the Sacrament, this canticle illustrates the evangelistic emphasis of the liturgical service. Because this song includes the *alleluia*, it is not used during the Lenten or Advent seasons.

31.B. POST-COMMUNION CANTICLE: NUNC DIMITTIS

Traditionally used in the services of Compline and Vespers, Simeon's Song (Luke 2:25–32) is a distinctively Lutheran contribution to the Communion liturgy of Western Christianity.[28] Simeon's beautiful expression of spiritual satisfaction is repeated by the congregation in appreciation for the manifestation of God's salvation. This canticle is most appropriately sung during the Advent and Lenten seasons.[29]

32. POST-COMMUNION COLLECT

Both of the collects offered in *Lutheran Worship* underscore the blessings of the Sacrament. The first is from Luther's German Mass and is found in most Lutheran liturgies. After giving thanks, the dual blessing of the Sacrament is recognized—strengthening of faith and strengthening for loving service to others. Other collects may be used, especially those prepared for Maundy Thursday. Divine Service I introduces the Post-Communion Collect as the pastor chants or speaks the words of Psalm 136:1: "Oh, give thanks to the Lord, for he is good." The congregation responds with "And his mercy endures forever."[30] As during other collects, the presiding minister or assisting minister may take the *orans* position. At the termination, his hands come together until the *amen* is said or sung.

33. BENEDICTION

Following the directives of Numbers 6:22–27, the pastor speaks the trinitarian blessing on the people. The last word of the liturgy comes from God, who hosted the service. The Benediction is more than a prayer or a wish. By His most holy name, the Benediction bestows God's blessing on the people for the rest of the week. To rephrase the Benediction as a wish removes the divine significance of our Host's parting declaration to His gathered guests. The Aaronic Benediction (Numbers 6:24–26) is a uniquely Lutheran choice, yet it underscores the continuity of praise with all God's people. The congregation may sing the *amen* if the pastor chants the Benediction. Worshipers also may make the sign of the cross on themselves as the pastor makes it over the whole congregation.

The Service of the Sacrament is a high point in the Lutheran liturgy because in it the gathered guests receive the very God whose house they have entered. Whether it is in the words or in the silence, the gathered guests receive again and again the forgiveness of their sins in Christ. All that is done in this half of the liturgy is done to God's glory and for the extension of His kingdom.

SOME QUESTIONS TO CONSIDER

1. What is historically significant about the Preface in the Service of the Sacrament? How do the several verses and responses function together?

2. How does the singing of the Sanctus serve as a supertemporal (or eternal) act of the gathered guests?

3. Explain the two parts of the Eucharistic Prayer as used in *Lutheran Worship*.

4. Why is the Verba a key element in the Lutheran understanding and practice of the Lord's Supper?

5. What alternatives are possible during the distribution of the Sacrament of the Altar? List some benefits and some drawbacks of specific practices.

6. Evaluate your congregation's distribution practices. What changes could be made? Why might your congregation's present practice be the best possible practice?

7. What contributions did Lutherans make to the post-Communion liturgy?

NOTES

1. Reed, *Lutheran Liturgy* (rev ed.), 322, notes: "Mohammedans and Jews worship God; philosophers and theorists of all kinds preach and teach . . . . But none of them, however much they may quote from Holy Scripture, include the Holy Sacrament in their ritual. Instinctively this is recognized and respected as a divine institution committed to the church and to the church alone."

2. See LW 53:69.

3. *Lutheran Worship*, pp. 170, 189. For example, around A.D. 215, Hippolytus recorded in his *Apostolic Tradition* (iv.3) a dialogue between the worship leader and the congregation that is similar to the first three responses in the Preface. See Dix and Chadwick, *Treatise on the Apostolic Tradition*, 7.

4. *Lutheran Worship*, pp. 170, 189.

5. *Lutheran Worship*, pp. 170, 189.

6. See *Lutheran Worship*, pp. 146–48, for the wording of the Proper Preface for each season of the church year. Regrettably, there is no reference to these pages in the settings of Divine Service II.

7. *Lutheran Worship*, p. 146.

8. LW 53:82–83. An English version appears as *Lutheran Worship*, 214. Luther's hymn mentions the smoke of incense ascending around God's heavenly throne and filling the scene. If incense is used as part of a service of Holy Communion, this is the time to incense the altar in remembrance of this marvelous vision of heaven. Luther's hymn may be used instead of the Sanctus, as may Gerard Moultrie's hymn "Let All Mortal Flesh Keep Silence" (*Lutheran Worship*, 241).

9. "German Mass," LW 53:60.

10. *Lutheran Worship*, 214.

11. Reed, *Lutheran Liturgy* (rev. ed.), 334–55, devotes a whole chapter to "The Recension of the Canon." Pfatteicher, *Commentary*, 163–84, also devotes significant space to a discussion of the use of several of these prayers, including the Great Thanksgiving.

12. Reed, *Lutheran Liturgy* (rev. ed.), 358–63, points out that by the middle of the third century references to an invocation of the Holy Spirit on the gifts of the congregation are found at this point in the service. See also Pfatteicher and Messerli, *Manual on the Liturgy*, 237–38.

13. SC, "Sacrament of the Altar," 9–10 (K-W, 363).

14. See *Lutheran Worship*, 431.

15. The Words of Institution, Verba, were described in various ways in the church's history. They were called the *Verba Testamenti* (Words of the Testament), underscoring the promise given in the Sacrament. *Verba Institutionis* (Words of Institution) refers to the actions of the priest as he consecrated the elements. Luther spoke of the *Verba Benedictionis* (Words of Blessing) to emphasize the Gospel promise and consequence as the powerful and living Word of God affected the believer.

16. See "Babylonian Captivity of the Church," LW 36:52.

17. *Lutheran Worship*, pp. 171, 191.

18. When I was in college, we followed the directives of our Lord in Matthew 5:23–24 by exchanging the peace prior to the Lord's Supper. On one occasion a classmate, who was always rather light-hearted, turned to face the person behind him to exchange a handshake of peace and found himself face-to-face with the wife of a faculty member with whom he had had a well-known dispute. At that moment he experienced the full meaning of reconciliation before coming to the altar of the Lord. Later, he acknowledged to the rest of us that the encounter was one of the most meaningful experiences of reconciliation that he had experienced.

19. Pronounced "og-noos" or "an-yus day-ee," not like someone's personal name.

20. A canticle is a liturgical song taken from the Bible, for example, the Magnificat or Nunc Dimittis. See *Lutheran Worship*, p. 369, for a complete listing of canticles and chants.

21. Pfatteicher and Messerli, *Manual on the Liturgy*, 246. Cf. Reed, *Lutheran Liturgy* (rev. ed.), 377.

22. Cyril of Jerusalem describes communicants as "making the left hand a throne for the right, and hollowing the palm of the right to receive the body of Christ." Cited by Reed, *Lutheran Liturgy* (rev. ed.), 376, from W. E. Scudamore, *Notitia Eucharistica*, 2d ed. (London: Rivingtons, 1876), 721.

23. Reed, *Lutheran Liturgy* (rev. ed.), 374–75. In general, the use of disposable or plastic cups may inaccurately communicate a lack of respect for the Lord's Supper, especially if a trash receptacle is pro-

vided for communicants as they leave the altar area. After the service, the sacramental elements are to be handled in a manner decided on by the congregation—a manner that connotes great respect for the Sacrament. The most common way to handle the elements is to place the bread in a pyx and the wine in a sacrarium/piscina (a special sink that leads directly to the ground, which is also used to properly dispose of baptismal water). If the Communion elements are consumed by those assisting in the distribution, be careful not to offend worshipers or abuse the elements.

24. See the opinion of the Department of Systematic Theology, Concordia Seminary, St. Louis, in "Is 'Non-Alcoholic Wine' Really Wine?" 4–6. The use of grape juice has increasingly been questioned in Lutheran circles, and this article constructively addresses concerns in a North American context.

25. Zemler-Cizewski, "Eucharist and the Consequences of Celiac Disease," 237–48.

26. "Order of Mass and Communion," LW 53:35.

27. *Lutheran Worship*, pp. 173, 192.

28. Reed, *Lutheran Liturgy* (rev. ed.), 379, notes that the Greek church uses the Nunc Dimittis at the close of the Communion liturgy.

29. According to the rubric in Divine Service I, the canticle may or may not be sung. See *Lutheran Worship*, p. 152. This is different from the rubric in Divine Service II.

30. *Lutheran Worship*, p. 153.

PART 3

WORSHIP, MUSIC, AND THE ARTS

CHAPTER 9

ART IN THE LORD'S SERVICE

GLIMPSING GOD'S GLORY

God has created His world with beauty, and the crown of His creation, human-ity, has been blessed with aesthetic sensitivities. People love beautiful things. Whether it is in the grandeur or simplicity of nature or in the multitude of daz-zlingly creative expressions made by human hands, God's people delight in those things that bring pleasure to the senses and an awareness of deeper truths. Perhaps in ways distinct from other Protestant traditions, Lutherans delight in beautiful things in the area of worship.[1]

We will look at liturgical art as a special form of expressing gratitude to God. Specific types of visual art will be discussed as they have been used in Christian communities for nearly two millennia. Finally, a few of the innumerable Christian symbols will be presented, along with an explanation of liturgical colors as they are used throughout the church year.

LITURGICAL ART

To express gratitude to God, His gathered guests offer Him the best they have. In the Old Testament, God's people prepared the tabernacle in the wilderness under God's direction. The children of Israel presented Aaron and Moses with their gold and silver and their finest cloth. With these gifts, skilled workers carried out God's designs for vessels and furnishings to be used as His people worshiped Him (Exo-dus 31). In the New Testament, Paul gives a more general encouragement to think about those things that are noble, pure, or lovely (Philippians 4:8). In several places, the Book of Revelation reveals the vivid beauty and golden glory of the awesome heavenly sanctuary (4:1–6; 5:6–8; 8:1–5; 14:1–3; 22:1–6).

Searching the Old Testament provides a wealth of information associated with the worship life of the people of Israel. From the blue and scarlet cloth of the tabernacle to the golden angels covering the ark of the covenant, the Hebrew people adored God with the finest works of art (Exodus 25–28; 35–39). The description of Solomon's temple (1 Kings 6) and the imagery of Ezekiel's vision of the perfect temple (Ezekiel 40–44) affirm that beauty and artistic expression are to be used for God's glory.[2]

The artistic furnishings in the ancient places of worship were designed to help the children of Israel recall God's activities in their personal lives and in their corporate history. Perhaps the large bronze basin in the courtyard of the worship center perhaps reminded the people of their escape from Egypt through the Red Sea (Exodus 30:17–21). The Bread of the Presence may have reminded the worshipers of the divine bread, the manna, that God had provided in the wilderness (Exodus 37:10–16). The altar of incense and the lampstands possibly brought to mind the pillars of cloud and fire that led the Israelites throughout their wilderness wanderings (Exodus 37:17–29). Certainly, the ark of the covenant localized the presence of God, and it contained the tablets of the Law received by Moses on Mount Sinai (Exodus 37:1–9). The Most Holy Place brought to mind the holy mountain that only Moses could ascend, just as the high priest was the only one who could enter the Most Holy Place, and then only once each year (Exodus 36:8–38).

The Christian church has a long and impressive tradition of expressing that which is holy in art. Tapestries and hangings brightened the dark interiors of early and medieval churches and cathedrals. For centuries, sculptures and paintings were commissioned and given prominence within the worship space of Christian communities. One need only think of Michelangelo's work in the Sistine Chapel in Rome or daVinci's *Last Supper* to recognize the contribution of art to the church. Luther wrote in his preface to the *Wittenberg Hymnal* (1524): "I am not of the opinion, as are the heterodox, that for the sake of the Gospel all arts should be rejected and eliminated; rather, I feel strongly that all the arts, and particularly music, should be placed in the service of Him who has created and given them."[3]

A distinction between liturgical art and religious art should be noted. Frank C. Senn distinguishes these two kinds of art when he suggests that liturgical art draws its subjects from the liturgy itself, that is, from the mystery of redemption. Furthermore, Senn suggests that liturgical art does not seek to shock or to attempt to be too contemporary, which may make it easily dated or meaningless. Liturgical art, Senn concludes, is evocative. In a symbolic manner, liturgical art points beyond itself to draw from the observer a response of faith in the object being viewed (for example, a crucifix) and, more important, in the grace of God in Christ that is being portrayed. Therefore, liturgical art is timeless and enduring, not conventional or banal.[4]

Liturgical art manifests a peculiar distinction from all other forms of art, whether secular or sacred. The objects of liturgical art are, for the most part, practical objects—books, vessels, buildings, sculptures, furnishings, etc.—that assist the gathered guests as they offer thanksgiving to God and receive His gifts. These objects are special because they are used for devotional purposes. As Peter Brunner states: "The ornamentation must be a sign of the veneration of the present Lord. It is a sign of the joyous surrender of the congregation to its Lord. . . . Unless we take account of the real presence of Jesus in worship, this must appear as extravagance, just as Mary's ointment did to Judas."[5]

PRINCIPLES FOR CHOOSING LITURGICAL ART[6]

After describing the distinctive nature of liturgical art, it is helpful to look at some principles that can help us more clearly identify, select, and appreciate liturgical art.

1. Good liturgical art draws the attention of worshipers to the object of their worship, not to itself. While items of artistic creativity have much to offer, worshipers' attention should not focus on the piece of art; that would be idolatry. The images, symbols, and accessories of worship must never compete with the primary focus of worship: God Himself and the gifts He provides. Avoid ostentation in any form of art.

2. Liturgical art supports a rich theological life and liturgical spirituality. Liturgical art creates an environment that is markedly and noticeably different from that in one's home. Liturgical art produces a sense of being in God's presence and causes those who observe the work of art to think about God and His gracious presence in Christ.[7] Objects of liturgical art in a Lutheran context should orient the worshipers toward Word and Sacraments as the vehicles of Christ's faith-creating Spirit and should proclaim God's love for the world in Christ.

3. The design of liturgical art exhibits a sensitivity to the liturgical space. Well-designed and carefully placed objects with appropriate colors that complement the worship environment will emphasize the oneness of the assembly. A worship setting may become easily cluttered. Unless artists are aware of the whole liturgical space, designs and patterns can become distractions to the centrality of Word and Sacrament.

4. The liturgical artist "speaks for the community rather than to it, aiming not at self-expression but at capturing the essence of that which makes the community one."[8] The liturgical artist must be so comfortable with the medium employed that the theological content of the piece is central. The artist is not

trying to communicate his or her own message but to draw worshipers together to receive and to respond to God's warnings and promises. The "artistic statement" in a piece of art should represent the whole community of faith.

5. Although contemporary expressions may be used, excellent and salutary liturgical art creates a sense of timelessness. Art that is too time-bound will become passé and no longer speak a word from God.[9] Liturgical art is more symbolic in the sense that it is pictorially didactic rather than a representational portrayal of a spiritual reality. For example, a cross or crucifix communicates the essence of God's act of reconciliation, though it does not depict the actual cross used for Christ's crucifixion.

6. A Gospel emphasis is most desirable in Lutheran liturgical art. Peter Brunner summarizes this point: "The work of art which results from the belief in the Gospel will . . . indicate symbolically the movement into which the creature is transferred by Jesus' cross and resurrection, the movement leading from the beginning, passing through the lost condition, and approaching the final transformation and liberation."[10] For example, a judgment scene may be depicted so the flowing blood of Christ covers the believing soul, or illustrations of God's gracious and sacramental gifts may be more dominant than portrayals of Christian vocations.

7. Natural materials usually produce a more convincing depiction of reality than synthetic replications. The use of wood and stone instead of plastic and concrete enables the worshiper to recall the Creator as the one behind the work. This principle is not meant to eliminate the use of manmade products but to make sure that manmade media do not stand in the way of true and orthodox worship.

CHRISTIAN ART FORMS

EARLY CHRISTIAN PAINTINGS

The first evidence of Christian art is wall paintings in early Christian meetinghouses. The first Christians met in homes after abandoning the temple and being rejected by local synagogues. These homes often were adapted for larger assemblies by removing a wall between two rooms. The remaining walls of such house churches often displayed depictions of biblical people, such as Adam and Eve, and David and Goliath; portrayals of Jesus' ministry; and confessions of faith, such as "There is one God in heaven."[11]

A century later, Christians in Rome decorated the burial vaults, or catacombs, with symbols and illustrations of the faith. As Robert Milburn explains, "The Christians on the whole preferred to make their approach to Heaven less by the avenue of beauty than by symbolic allusion to the hope that was in themselves. Nor did they often attempt to portray the mysterious character of the Divine as did the followers of Dionysus."[12] Among the images portrayed on the walls of the Roman catacombs are vine and branches, loaves and bread, a lamb, a shepherd boy with a lamb on his shoulders, banquet scenes, praying figures, and many Old Testament stories. Catacomb paintings continued even after Constantine and his successors allowed open expression of the Christian faith.

Early Christian paintings used fresco and tempera techniques, which required special preparation of the walls prior to painting. Fresco painting applied color to the final coat of plaster while it was still moist so the pigments penetrated the surface. The tempera technique involved applying paint to an almost hardened surface with the help of some fixative, such as milk or egg whites. These two painting techniques developed into high art forms during the Middle Ages and the Renaissance.

ICONS

Icons—paintings created specifically for service to the church—are a peculiar and recognizable liturgical art form.[13] *Icon* is a Greek word that means "image." According to the Orthodox churches, these stylized images of biblical figures and events are not painted but "written." The artisans are called iconographers rather than painters. According to a tradition held by Eastern Orthodox Christians, who have supported this form of liturgical art for more than fifteen centuries, Luke was the first iconographer, and they believe he crafted six hundred icons.

For more than a century, controversy surrounded the creation and use of icons as iconoclasts (literally, "icon destroyers") sought to eliminate all art from churches. In A.D. 787, an ecumenical church council approved the use of icons to assist in worship, though not as objects of worship.[14] Constantinople and Thessalonica were the centers of iconic production from about A.D. 700 to A.D. 850. During the next centuries, three additional sites developed equal claim for the highest level of technical, theological, and aesthetically masterful icon production: Mount Athos in Greece, the island of Patmos, and Mount Sinai. The icons from these five centers became the models for almost all other icons produced throughout the world to the present day.

An icon is often referred to as a "window into heaven." The original purpose of such liturgical art was to communicate the faith visually to an illiterate people. For example, the gold background on which the objects of veneration seemed to float communicated a sense of a holy reality, thus inspiring awe-filled worship.[15] The images themselves were stylized to serve as reminders of the event or person portrayed, not to function as portraits.

As icons became increasingly important in the worship life of Eastern Orthodox congregations, a special railing was built to hold these pieces of liturgical art. The railing is still a feature of modern Orthodox architecture. Known as an *iconostasis* (or icon stand), this railing is located in front of the altar and separates the altar from the view of the worshiping community. The icons on the iconostasis are displayed in a specific arrangement. (See diagram.) The icon of Christ is always flanked by icons of Mary and John the Baptist. A second row of taller and narrower icons is displayed within arches. These icons depict angels, apostles, the Twelve Great Feasts from the life of the Lord, and perhaps locally familiar saints. A large crucifix is painted above the icons, and the scene of the annunciation is usually painted on a folding door in the center.[16]

Crucifixion of Christ

Patriarchs and Prophets of the Old Testament					
Twelve Apostles					
Six most important events in life of Virgin Mary		Lord's Supper	Six most important events in Christ's life		
Archangel Gabriel upon north door	St. Nicholas	Theotokos	Holy Doors	Christ	Saint of the Church, or John Baptist	Archangel Michael upon the south door

Although not common in Lutheran churches, the icon remains a significant form of liturgical art and demonstrates the distinction between religious art and liturgical art.

MOSAICS

In ancient times, artisans used small pieces of tile, colored glass, or a variety of stones to create floor and wall decorations, often depicting scenes from everyday life or mythological stories. Following the artistic custom of the Greeks and Romans, Christian artists used this art form to beautify churches and homes. The wall and floor decorations they created were intended for worshipful contemplation. An early Christian church in the Italian city of Aquileia that dates to A.D. 315 has a richly decorated mosaic floor. Included in these mosaic images are birds and fish, cupids and maidens, fruits and flowers, trees and palm branches. This church, built by Bishop Theodore, required significant offerings from generous donors (most of whom were women). Their portraits also are included in the mosaic. The Good Shepherd is featured in this floor, along with images related to the Lord's Supper. "Here youths and maidens hold a basket of loaves or grapes or flowers, while, in a large square panel which dominates the whole composition, a dark-robed angel, clasping the wreath and palm-branch which denote victorious perseverance, stands behind the heaped-up loaves and the wine-jar."[17] This floor, while extraordinary in its quality, illustrates the finely developed liturgical art form of mosaic installation.

More outstanding than mosaic floors are the ceiling designs of many ancient churches. Churches in the great centers of Christianity—Jerusalem, Constantinople, Rome, Thessalonica, and in northern Africa—display unique examples of the mosaic artisans' skills. The biblical scenes they portray enhanced the worship life of those who assembled in these structures. The mosaic in the apse of St. Apollinare Nuovoin Classe, a lavishly decorated church in Ravenna, is one of the most renowned of the fourth century. It depicts numerous biblical themes, including the transfiguration of Christ, the Good Shepherd, the Last Judgment, and the pastoral office of St. Apollinare. "Throughout the composition historical realism is subordinated to timeless abstraction."[18]

Today, this art form continues to be used in a variety of settings. Mosaic floors and walls can be seen in churches throughout the world, employing an art form designed to draw the worshiper into the timeless presence of God.

CARVINGS

Carved stone sculpture was a highly developed art form in the Greco-Roman world, yet stone carvings are rare in early Christian art. The exceptions are beautifully sculpted sarcophagi that depict the Good Shepherd and other biblical images. Beginning in the fifth century, ivory and wood were carved into book covers for worship books. These covers are known as diptychs, many of which have survived the ravages of time. Metal, ivory, and jewels were added to the covers of Gospel books used in worship processions.[19] Talented and acclaimed craftsmen in the Christian community created these carvings. Sculpted figures of ivory, wood, and later of stone—including crucifixes, angels, and figures of Christ and the saints— were considered major works of art in Christian communities from the fourth century to the present.

Particularly during the Romanesque architectural period, carved stone columns and doorways provided a lasting legacy of this liturgical art form. The doorways of many churches built in this period were exquisitely designed to communicate the realities and hopes of the Christian life. Christ is often portrayed on His royal throne of judgment with an arrangement of the major virtues and vices positioned on each side.[20] Later Gothic sculptors developed stone carving into a highly decorative art form. Their figures invited viewers to meditate on the focus of the liturgical scene, usually Christ.

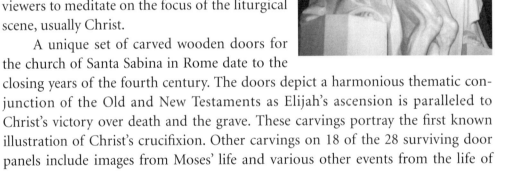

A unique set of carved wooden doors for the church of Santa Sabina in Rome date to the closing years of the fourth century. The doors depict a harmonious thematic conjunction of the Old and New Testaments as Elijah's ascension is paralleled to Christ's victory over death and the grave. These carvings portray the first known illustration of Christ's crucifixion. Other carvings on 18 of the 28 surviving door panels include images from Moses' life and various other events from the life of Christ.[21]

Perhaps the most significant example of carving is the use of lumber for churches in Scandinavia. Stave churches—built between the eleventh and thirteenth centuries—are named for the narrow strips of wood used in their construction. These ornate and uniquely designed churches combined the skilled carpentry of shipbuilding with sensitivities to the liturgical and climatic restrictions of northern Christian communities.[22]

In addition to stave churches, throughout the Renaissance and Reformation periods and into the modern era, altars, pulpits, chairs, and screens often were sculpted from wood and exhibit great liturgical consciousness and artistic craftsmanship. Most modern Christian communities exhibit some form of carving.

METALWORK

From the golden calf in Exodus 32 to the elaborate temple furnishings described in 1 Kings 5–7, metalwork has been used liturgically for millennia. Early Christian communities undoubtedly used household utensils for Communion vessels during the first centuries; however, by the fourth century, cups (chalices), plates (patens), and spoons were made specifically for liturgical use in churches. Each of these items displayed some liturgical marking, such as Christ's monogram (*Chi-Rho*) or a Christian symbol (such as the Greek letters *alpha* and *omega*, A Ω, or a cross, ✠). Elaborate patens have been found in Syria that depict Christ distributing the Sacrament to His disciples.[23] Specialized plates and cups were the products of liturgical artists who used their skills to produce vessels for the Lord's service.

Chalice   Ciborium

Copper and brass were used to construct practical items for liturgical use, such as lamps, censers, and crosses. Around the twelfth century, candleholders were introduced, replacing oil lamps. Sometimes used as torches during processions, candleholders often were extremely tall so they could be seen throughout the church.[24] Brass and iron gates and railings also appeared at the entrances to the nave and sanctuary.

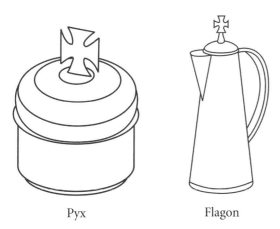

Pyx   Flagon

Most congregations today have vessels used for distribution of the Sacrament and for other purposes in a worship service. Chalices and patens, flagons, ciboriums, and pyxes used for the Lord's Supper aver the importance of Christ's presence with us, thus they should be carefully designed and well constructed. Most Communion vessels are lined with silver or gold for ease in cleaning and purifying.[25] Flower vases and stands can also be found in most sanctuaries. Processional crosses offer artists numerous creative possibilities for artistic and liturgical expression. Crosses of wood or metal are most common. The corpus (the figure of Christ's crucified body that is placed on the cross) may be either of the same material or of a contrasting material—for example, a ceramic figure of Christ may be placed on a wooden or metal cross.

Metalwork introduced into the church's worship space is typically useful and unobtrusive, exhibiting a timelessness that communicates the Christian faith and the eternal hope of God's gathered guests.

STAINED GLASS

For centuries, Egyptians, Greeks, and Romans glazed windows and cast glass objects, but staining or coloring glass was not achieved until the twelfth century. This process provided increased opportunity for liturgical art. The creation of a large window required not only the production of great amounts of glass, but also the construction of a metal framework to support the glass and lead joints. The staining and etching of the glass created a halo effect as light streamed through the colored glass, softening the image for the viewer. The earliest windows still in existence are mosaic-like in appearance and display a simplicity that has rarely been duplicated.

As glass production increased and became more sophisticated, different styles of stained glass developed. Some artists tried to recreate paintings of biblical stories or allegorical descriptions of theological truths in windows. Regrettably, innumerable stained-glass windows were lost after the Reformation as followers of the radical reformers destroyed all visual religious objects in the name of the First Commandment. The two world wars of the twentieth century also destroyed many priceless and irreplaceable windows.[26]

Many churches built in the nineteenth and early twentieth centuries incorporated pictures and designs in stained glass that lack the vitality of earlier windows, both in quality of glass and in color and design. Yet the art form continues as new techniques develop. Some artisans follow an innovative process of setting pieces of glass in a concrete mixture; others follow a more traditional style of constructing pictures from glass. The pastel-colored glass panels common in

churches built around the 1960s are being replaced with more traditional designs that communicate biblical stories and themes.

TEXTILES

Most common today, but not specifically recognized as liturgical art in earlier centuries, is the use of cloth and textiles. Textiles were not used for specific liturgical purposes until approximately the seventh century when Christians began weaving detailed illustrations of biblical scenes into linen curtains.[27] Because textiles perish easily, little is known of the earliest Christian vestments or of the earliest liturgical use of cloth. However, embroidered altar cloths of linen and silk baptismal garments prepared by Egyptian weavers have been preserved from early centuries of the church. Today, textiles are not only used for vestments and banners, but also for carpeting and padding for seating.

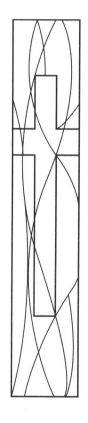

Since the 1960s, Christian churches have increasingly used banners in worship settings. These works of textile art provide opportunities to communicate clearly the Gospel message. As one banner maker reports, "The excitement engendered by the liturgical renewal in the sixties brought forth a flood of expressions, especially the return of the banner." Yet this designer adds, "The billboard sloganism that crept into fabric art has hopefully seen its day and been permitted to die a happy death."[28] Instead of serving as slogan-bearers, banners can visibly communicate what words alone cannot convey.

The placement of banners and other fabric art in the sanctuary should not distract from the liturgical focal points and actions of the gathered guests. While large-scale tapestries and bolts of cloth (15 to 30 feet in length) can be used effectively to convey the sense of a season or the significance of a celebration, care should be taken that they do not overpower the altar, pulpit, and baptismal font.

It is best to change banners regularly so they do not outlive their usefulness and impact. Banners created for specific celebrations will rarely apply in other circumstances or settings. Unless created professionally as a tapestry, most banners will begin to fade or fall apart after a few years of use, whether periodic or regular. Paper banners created for a specific event, then thrown away, are becoming increasingly popular.

GRAPHIC DESIGN

Besides large-scale artwork, smaller works of art are produced regularly for use in churches. Church bulletins with attractive covers are a major tool for communicating scriptural themes for worship. Done well, they continue to communicate this message throughout the week. The contents of these printed worship folders enable worshipers to participate fully in the service.

In the area of graphic arts, much more can be done on a local level than has been possible in the past. With the aid of digital photography and color printing, pictures by local artists or congregation members can be used as bulletin covers. Congregation members with artistic abilities and computer skills may provide images for bulletins as well as for banners for God's gathered guests.

PROJECTED IMAGES

Some congregations now use a screen to project images and words within the sanctuary. These churches believe the use of printed orders of service cause people to sing into the folder or not to sing at all. When words are projected people look up and sing their praises more confidently. Care must be exercised though because a display in a visually obscure location may result in frustration and nonparticipation. When using overhead projectors, PowerPoint presentations, or slides and videos, remember the medium is not the message; rather, it conveys a message from God's Word.

Instead of cumbersome screens or large blank walls, other congregations are using rear-projected images on a special screen to provide better viewing. The costs of renovation to accommodate rear projection may be a major concern, as well as the architectural "damage" that can result when the sanctuary is altered. James White notes that "where projections are possible, a wall can be whatever we want to project on it. 'Okay, we'll have the Sistine Chapel this week, but for next week's lessons Big Sur would work better.' We are limited only by the horizons of our imaginations."[29] Whether or not such an approach is always best, the possibilities are numerous for enhancing worship with visual displays; however, it is best to maintain an emphasis on the gifts of God and His caring presence with His gathered guests.

OTHER ART FORMS THAT ENHANCE WORSHIP

In addition to the art forms already mentioned, seasonal objects of art or visual displays may be used. Most congregations use an Advent wreath to help members anticipate the festival of Christmas. Christmas ornaments displayed on a church tree can be related to Christ's life and ministry, such as a manger, star, cross, shepherd's staff, and crown. A cross made from the trunk of the previous year's Christmas tree can carry significant meaning for those who worship during the Lenten season. Veiling the crucifix during Lent is an ancient tradition and can effectively communicate the absence of art as a form of Lenten self-sacrifice. Palm branches and lilies may be used to add an aesthetic quality to special services on Palm Sunday and Easter. Whatever objects are used in worship, they should not trivialize the message of God's most generous gift of Himself. Discolored or old objects, whether made from paper, cloth, or plastic, should be replaced by genuine items of beauty.[30]

LITURGICAL COLORS

Color communicates psychologically because certain colors are associated with common human experiences or emotions. For example, red is associated with blood and fire, white with purity, gold with royalty and festivity, green with growth, and dark colors with despair and mourning.

The church has passed down a tradition of colors that correspond to the seasons of the church year.[31] In studies conducted toward the end of the twentieth century, scientists documented the effects that various colors have on people. Liturgical colors communicate well when they are understood and used appropriately. Therefore, the following section briefly explains the colors used throughout the liturgical year.

WHITE

This color signifies celebration, purity, innocence, and gladness. White is associated with key events in our Lord's life, particularly His birth and baptism and the Easter season. It is also used for days dedicated to nonmartyred saints. The Latin word for white, *alba,* is the name for a liturgical gown worn by worship leaders, a gown that is reminiscent of the traditional baptismal dress. White is, therefore, associated with Baptism and confirmation, as well as with Trinity Sunday.

GREEN

For obvious reasons, green depicts growth and fulfillment (foliage and ripening fruit). Green is used through the octave of (or the week surrounding) Epiphany and its season, during the octave of Trinity, and throughout the Pentecost season. Just as colors in nature change, the liturgical color green can change in shade and hue as the light green of spring deepens throughout summer and may become almost drab in the early fall.

BLUE

For the last century or two, blue has become a Marian color (Mary is usually depicted wearing a blue garment). Yet after World War II, Scandinavian Lutherans used blue to depict hope and the joyous anticipation of Christ's return. In the last quarter of the twentieth century, blue has become popular in North American usage as a color for the Advent season.

PURPLE OR VIOLET

These colors are a sign of royalty and self-disciplined responsibility. In ancient times, purple was an expensive color to produce because the cloth was dyed in the "blood" of a snail (*murex*). Such a colorization process required much self-sacrifice, not only on the part of the snails but also by the purchaser of this expensive cloth (Acts 16:14). Thus the use of purple was a symbol of penitence. Purple is used during the 40 days of Lent and as an alternate color for Advent. It is also occasionally used for funerals.

RED

Because it is associated with blood and fire, the latter reminiscent of the Spirit's presence at Pentecost, red is used for Pentecost and for days dedicated to martyrs. It is also used for festivals of renewal in the Holy Spirit—such as Reformation and missions—and often for ordination rites (though some denominations use white).

SCARLET

A variant of red and purple, almost blood-red in hue, scarlet is a solemn color. Scarlet may be used during Holy Week. The "royal purple" used in earlier centuries was a deep scarlet, almost maroon.

GOLD

A regal color, gold shows ultimate sacrifice. Gold is an alternate color only for the days of Easter and Christmas. It is sometimes also used as an alternate color on Trinity Sunday. If used at other times, it should be reserved for special celebrations.

BLACK

Black is associated with ashes and thus repentance. Black may be used on Ash Wednesday, or, if the altar is not stripped on Maundy Thursday, it may be used on Good Friday. In some denominations black is suggested for the Advent season, as well as the days between Transfiguration Sunday and Ash Wednesday.

EARTH TONES, GRAYS, AND OTHER COLORS

These colors are often used in conjunction with the basic liturgical colors. In addition the opposite colors on a color wheel provide contrasting yet complementary colors for a variety of uses in the worship service and church setting.

LITURGICAL SYMBOLS[32]

From animals, birds, insects, trees, flowers, and plants to religious figures, objects, and events, liturgical artists have tried to communicate about God's gifts to His gathered guests. The following brief catalog only touches on the vast number of symbols artists have used to communicate God's truths to His people.

AΩ

Alpha and omega are the first and last letters of the Greek alphabet. Jesus uses these letters to refer to Himself and to His constant presence with the church (see Revelation 1:8; 21:6; 22:13. Cf. Isaiah 44:6).

ANGEL

Appearing as human beings, these divine messengers and helpers are depicted in various ways. The addition of wings comes from the account in Isaiah 6 of the seraphim who encircle God's throne, singing "Holy, holy, holy."

BREAD

Often accompanied by a cup or chalice, a loaf of bread may represent the presence of Christ in the Sacrament of the Altar, or it may depict the Word of God on which His gathered guests feed (Matthew 4).

CHI-RHO

Jesus' official title in Greek is *Christ*, which means "the Anointed." The first two letters of that title are the Greek capital letters *X* (*chi*) and *P* (*rho*). These two letters—sometimes incorrectly called by their English equivalents—are the monogram for Christ, the one who came as God's anointed prophet, priest, and king.

CROSS

There are numerous kinds of crosses, each with its own history and significance. Whole books have been written to describe the meaning of each style. Five traditional crosses are the Latin cross ✝; the Greek cross with its equal arms ✚; the St. Andrew's cross with its diagonal arms ✖; the *tau* cross, T, which is named after the Greek letter; and the Greek Orthodox cross ☦, which has extra crossbars that represent the placard placed on the cross above Jesus' head and the footrest.

CRUCIFIX

The placement of the body of Christ on a cross reminds us of Paul's words "we preach Christ crucified" (1 Corinthians 1:23). In most situations the crucifix depicts Christ's suffering. However, some congregations place a victorious Christ, robed and crowned, on the cross to indicate His victory over sin, death, and the devil.

DOVE

The Holy Spirit is often represented as a dove, recalling Jesus' baptism when the Spirit descended from heaven "like a dove" (Matthew 3:16).

EYE

Representing God's presence and knowledge of all things, this symbol is often displayed inside a triangle to signify the Trinity.

FIRE OR TONGUES OF FIRE

At Pentecost, the Holy Spirit descended on each disciple like a tongue of fire (Acts 2:3–4). The number of tongues of fire depicted in liturgical art is usually seven, which represent the fruit of the Spirit (Galatians 5:22–23). Sometimes the number depicted is nine, which represent the gifts of the Spirit (1 Corinthians 12:8–10).

FISH

The Greek word for fish, *IXΘΥΣ*, was used by early Christians as a confession of faith. The Greek capital letter *iota*, *I*, stands for Jesus' name in Greek (*Ιησους*). The *X* is the Greek capital letter *chi*, which stands for *Christ*. The Greek letter *theta*, *Θ* in its capital form, is the first letter in the Greek word *theou*, which means "God's." The capital letter *upsilon*, *Υ*, is the first letter of the Greek word *Υιος*, which means "Son." And the ending capital Greek letter *sigma*, *Σ*, appears to be a sideways *M* and stands for "Savior" (*Σωτηρ*).

GRAPES AND GRAIN

Symbols for the products of the land that are used to make the elements of the Lord's Supper (wine and bread), these two foods can also represent God's gift of the produce of the land.

HAND

If a hand is depicted with the fingers pointing down, it is a symbol of God's creation and blessing. If the fingers are pointing up, the hand is a symbol of the Good Shepherd's blessing.

I-H-S

In ancient times, the first two letters and the last letter of a name were often used to abbreviate the name. In Greek, *Jesus* is spelled *Ιησους*. Thus the letters *I-H-S* became an abbreviation of Jesus' name, which means "Savior" or "Rescuer" (Matthew 1:21). Other explanations for this symbol include an abbreviation of the Latin phrase *Iesus hominum Salvator*, "Jesus, Savior of humanity." Sometimes this symbol is modified as *I-H-C* because the final Greek letter looks something like the English letter *c*.

INRI

These were the first letters of the four Latin words placed above Jesus' head when He was crucified (John 1:19–21). The words stated that this man was Jesus of Nazareth, the King of the Jews—*Iesus Nazarenus Rex Iudaeorum*.

LAMB

Combining the imagery of Christ's ministry and His victory, early Christians used lambs and a shepherd to depict themselves and Jesus, the Lamb of God who takes away the sin of the world (Revelation 5:6ff.).

SERPENT

The powers of evil, particularly Satan (Genesis 3), are depicted by a serpent, as in Psalm 91. Conversely, in John 3 the serpent on a cross refers to Christ's crucifixion.

SHELL

Baptism is often depicted by a scallop shell and three drops of water, a reminder of the trinitarian Baptism.

SHIP

Recalling Noah's ark and the disciples' fishing boats, this image became a symbol of hope, salvation, and immortality. It also depicts the church itself, particularly when the mast is shaped like a cross.

STAR

Associated with Jesus' birth (Numbers 24:17; Matthew 2), stars can represent Christian witness to the world (Daniel 12:3). The six-pointed star may be combined with the cross and the *Chi-Rho* as the "saving sign."

TREE OR TREE OF LIFE

The image of a tree recalls the words of Psalm 1:3, which describes a righteous person. Early Christians used this symbol to portray the relationship of the Word of God and the believer (Revelation 22:2).

TRIANGLE

The church's teaching of the Trinity is often represented by an equilateral triangle. Each person of the Trinity is equal to the others, yet Father, Son, and Holy Spirit are one God.

THE ROLE OF THE LITURGICAL ARTIST

As an artist who creates art in the context of worship, "the efforts of all who minister in giving shape to a liturgical environment are to create a worship space that speaks of both *mystery* and *hospitality*. The space should inspire us with wonder and awe and also help us feel comfortable and at home."[33]

A liturgical artist is often a trained professional, thus an individual interested in preparing liturgical art usually seeks professional training to master a particular media. Such training also will provide a deeper understanding of the theological foundations for worship. While the theological content of works of art used in the worship setting is of primary concern, James White notes that "it is far better to use a secular artist of great talent than one who is pious but whose work is mediocre."[34] After all, a talented artist will listen to the community and produce a work that meets the needs of the worship setting. Many artists are being trained in both areas and can provide expertise to local parishes.[35]

A liturgical artist is aware of liturgical space, as well as of the piece of art itself. Frank C. Senn has suggested that sometimes less is more. If a competent liturgical artist cannot be employed to evoke a sense of mystery and holiness, perhaps a plain white wall behind the altar is best.[36] Poor placement of liturgical art or a poorly designed setting can result in a sense of clutter rather than a sense of awe and worship. A liturgical artist can help a congregation understand the close relationship of form and function.

A liturgical artist is also a person of worship. Thomas Simons and James Fitzpatrick note: "The arts or artists must never take over the flow or rhythm of the worship; however, the arts can definitely enhance the celebration and inspire the assembly at prayer."[37] A liturgical artist recognizes that Word and Sacrament are central in Lutheran worship. The importance of enhancing a formal setting with images that communicate the faith of the gathered guests is paramount.

A liturgical artist is an assisting minister of the church. Worship is always directed to God, and art should aid in such worshipful devotion. Paul Hoon reminds us that artists need to understand their role as assisting in the Lord's service. He warns that we must call into question "the conscious or unconscious affirmation [which] art commonly makes that the reality which Christianity names 'God' is most authentically experienced as Beauty rather than as the Holy."[38] There is a grander perspective required of liturgical art. The liturgical artist is not interested in beauty for its own sake but in the ways beauty assists the congregation to recognize the holy. From a Lutheran perspective, the liturgical artist will also help worshipers perceive the graciousness of God in Christ.

A liturgical artist is involved in a servant ministry. "The art work must be capable of bearing the sacred, the wonderfully holy, and of serving the needs of the liturgy itself. Taken together, the arts form a serving environment for the worship of God by the community of faith."[39] All that is done in the area of liturgical art is done to the glory of God and to praise His name.

Finally, it is good to hear from a teacher who has studied Christian worship for more than a generation. James White reminds us that just as pastors spend much time preparing a sermon, which is heard only once, so church leaders should not back away from spending adequate time in communicating visually to a broader segment of the community.[40] Even when items are disposable, such as paper banners and weekly bulletins, the focus on God's gracious message for His gathered guests will reap great benefits.

Some Questions to Consider

1. Cite five biblical examples that support the use of art in the context of worship.

2. What distinguishes liturgical art from religious art? Give one additional characteristic of liturgical art not listed in this chapter.

3. What is the difference between painting a picture and writing an icon? What did some eighth-century Christians find wrong with icons?

4. Name five media used for liturgical art that can be found in your home congregation. Why do these items fall under the category of liturgical art?

5. What liturgical color is currently in use in your church? What color was used prior to the present color? What is the significance of these colors?

6. Do you have, or do you know someone who has, jewelry with Christian symbolism? Name five items and describe the Christian symbol.

7. Describe the role of Christian artists, particularly as such artists employ their skills to construct liturgical art.

Notes

1. In Finney, *Seeing beyond the Word*, it is stated that Calvinists lay claim to a meager visual tradition, one that is fairly idiosyncratic and sporadic.

2. For more on the use of architecture to glorify God, see *Gathered Guests* chapter 11.

3. Luther, *Sämmtliche Schriften*, 10:1424; translated in Halter, *Practice of Sacred Music*, 11.

4. Senn, *Christian Liturgy*, 606.

5. Brunner, *Worship in the Name of Jesus*, 278, notes that Wilhelm Löhe recognized this analogy of Mary's pure ointment (John 12:1–5) to ornamentation in worship, which he may have learned from Rupert of Deutz.

6. These principles are adapted from Simons and Fitzpatrick, *Ministry of Liturgical Environment*, 34.

7. Brunner, *Worship in the Name of Jesus*, 280–81, says the following about pictorial art: "The picture in particular must assume the function of reminding the congregation that the pneumatic presence of the salvation-event becomes a reality in this place through Word and Sacrament. Like the house of worship as a whole, the picture in this place will prove of special help to the congregation to concentrate on God and to meet the Word of God with a collected mind. But this picture will also be helpful in opening heart and mind for petition and praise to God."

8. White and White, *Church Architecture*, 157 (*White and White's emphasis*).

9. A review of magazine advertisements from an earlier generation demonstrates how many artistic expressions are time-bound and how images can become dated.

10. Brunner, *Worship in the Name of Jesus*, 259–60.

11. Milburn, *Early Christian Art*, 10–12.

12. Milburn, *Early Christian Art*, 27.

13. Kalokyris, *Essence of Orthodox Iconography*, 13–20.

14. The victory in A.D. 787 is often called the Triumph of Orthodoxy. Yet the Iconoclastic Controversy, as this sometimes bloody conflict was called, continued for more than 50 years. In A.D. 843, the iconodules (those who venerated icons instead of worshiping them) were finally vindicated.

15. Kalokyris, *Essence of Orthodox Iconography*, 102.

16. Weitzmann, Chatzidakis, and Radojcic, *Icons*, 7–8.

17. Milburn, *Early Christian Art*, 117.

18. Milburn, *Early Christian Art*, 175.

19. Milburn, *Early Christian Art*, 242–47.

20. Clowney and Clowney, *Exploring Churches*, 48, note that churches as far removed as England, Spain, and France had similar judgment scenes, perhaps crafted by itinerant sculptors who traveled throughout Europe to ply their artistic vocations.

21. Milburn, *Early Christian Art*, 107–9.

22. Strzygowski, *Early Church Art*, 77–142, gives many illustrations and explanations of stave churches.

23. Milburn, *Early Christian Art*, 253–63.

24. Pocknee and Randall, "Candles, Lamps and Lights," 137–39.

25. Periodically replating chalices with gold or silver is recommended to eliminate unsightly oxidation spots that may result as the metal wears away. See Gent and Sturges, *Altar Guild Book*, 34.

26. Clowney and Clowney, *Exploring Churches*, 66–67.

27. Milburn, *Early Christian Art*, 285.

28. Simons and Fitzpatrick, *Ministry of Liturgical Environment*, 32, 35.

29. James White, *Introduction to Christian Worship*, 73.

30. Simons and Fitzpatrick, *Ministry of Liturgical Environment*, 17, add: "The Church and its worship should provide us with relief from the world of plastic, provided our local parish has not given in to the current style of disposability: plastic flowers, electric vigil lights, wood painted to look like marble, paper napkin purificators, and so on."

31. Pope Innocent III (1198–1216) established a uniform description of liturgical colors for the Roman Catholic Church, which has changed little during the past millennium: white for feasts, red for martyrs, black for penitential seasons, and green at other times.

32. Several resources provide adequate explanations of most liturgical symbols. The following books give further information: Appleton and Bridges, *Symbolism in Liturgical Art*; Ferguson, *Signs and Symbols*; and Newton and Neil, *2000 Years of Christian Art*.

33. Simons and Fitzpatrick, *Ministry of Liturgical Environment*, 20 (*Simons and Fitzpatrick's emphasis*).

34. James White, *Introduction to Christian Worship*, 156.

35. Christians in the Visual Arts (CIVA) is an international organization whose artists draw on the theological foundations of the Christian faith to produce religious and liturgical art. CIVA may be contacted at P.O. Box 18117, Minneapolis, MN 55418-0117. The organization's web site is www.civa.org.

36. Senn, *Christian Liturgy*, 606, alludes to a remark by Brunner in *Worship in the Name of Jesus*, 281.

37. Simons and Fitzpatrick, *Ministry of Liturgical Environment*, 20.

38. Hoon, *Integrity of Worship*, 64.

39. Simons and Fitzpatrick, *Ministry of Liturgical Environment*, 20.

40. James White, *Introduction to Christian Worship*, 75.

CHAPTER 10
Vestments in the Lord's Service
Dress for the Occasion

Guests usually dress for the occasion. For a casual affair, guests may wear slacks, T-shirts, or other comfortable clothes. If the event is more formal, guests usually appear in suits and dresses. Tuxedos and formal gowns are worn to proms and most weddings to mark these as significant events. News reports regularly comment on the elaborate attire worn by Hollywood stars as they parade into award ceremonies and movie premieres.

Uniforms also are a common sight. They identify the unique function or role of the wearer. Teams are recognized by uniform colors and mascots. Officials for sporting events often wear some variation of a black-and-white uniform. Police officers, health services personnel, and prison inmates typically wear identifying garments. Even gang members have particular clothing items or styles of dress that serve as "uniforms" for those involved in this subculture.

In the same way as other individuals who serve in an official capacity, pastors and other worship leaders wear clothes appropriate for their roles among God's gathered guests. These garments are not costumes because pastors are not playing a role in some show. Instead, pastors and other worship assistants are servants of the Host, fulfilling their official duty for Him as they bring God's gifts to His gathered guests. The vestments worn by these individuals connect God's people to the history of the Christian faith and are symbolic reminders of the truths of God's revelation.

A Brief History of Vestments

Throughout the centuries, worship leaders have worn specific garments to indicate either their office or their liturgical function. These garments also mark significant events in the worship life of God's gathered guests. The English word *vestment*

comes from the Latin word *vestimentum*, which means "clothing." Vestments are
the official clothing or "uniforms" for worship leaders and assistants. Vestments
remove the "humanity" from these individuals as they direct attention to the ministerial office or liturgical function. For example, a pastor may wear a business suit
during the week as he goes about his tasks. However, when he leads the congregation in worship before the throne of God, the pastor stands in vestments before the
people as Christ's representative. He holds an office that dates to biblical times.
Therefore, the pastor's attire demonstrates his role, responsibility, and ancient connection.

Those who lead and those who assist in Lutheran worship services wear a wide
variety of garments. From the simple black robe of the academic classroom to the
colorful regalia of the high Swedish Mass, Lutherans retain a spectrum of garments
appropriate for the worship setting.

BIBLICAL PRECEDENCE

Vestments played a significant role in Old Testament worship. In Exodus
28:2–3, God told the people of Israel, and Moses specifically, "You shall make holy
garments for Aaron your brother, for glory and for beauty. And you shall speak to
all who have ability, whom I have endowed with an able mind, that they make
Aaron's garments to consecrate him for My priesthood" (RSV). In response to God's
command, Exodus 39:1 reports: "And of the blue and purple and scarlet stuff they
made finely wrought garments, for ministering in the holy place; they made the
holy garments for Aaron; as the LORD had commanded Moses" (RSV).

The high priest, as the leader of the worshiping assembly, wore a unique garment to signify his role in the worship
life of Israel. (See illustration.) This garment was of the highest quality because it served the grandest purpose: to give
God glory and to mark the singular activity of worshiping
God. In addition to the high priest, the Levites, who were the
temple assistants, wore particular garments while serving the
Lord. Young Samuel annually received such a garment from
his mother while he served in the temple with Eli, the high
priest (1 Samuel 2).

The Gospel writers record that Jesus wore a tuniclike
garment (Matthew 5:40). Jesus was wearing this calf-length
outer shirt (Greek, *chiton*) when He was arrested in Gethsemane (John 19:23). John wrote that the souls of those who
had been martyred received a similar white robe (Revelation

6:11), which reminded them that they had been redeemed and cleansed in the blood of the Lamb (Revelation 7:14). John tells us that "fine linen stands for the righteous acts of the saints" (Revelation 19:8b).

While there is no command to follow Old or New Testament styles of dress in worship, the church followed these biblical precedents, making slight adaptations throughout the centuries.

THE PRACTICE OF THE EARLY CHURCH

From the time of the apostles, clergy wore the style of clothing common to the well-dressed people of imperial Rome. As Christianity became the dominant religion during the fourth and fifth centuries, clergy continued to wear the common garb of professionals of the late Roman Empire. During these early centuries, Old Testament liturgical vestments were strictly avoided.[1] The first evidence of a garment designed specifically for liturgical use in the Christian church is reported around A.D. 330. Emperor Constantine gave a robe of gold tissue to Macarius, bishop of Jerusalem, to wear as he presided over baptisms during the Easter Vigil.[2] Jerome (A.D. 341–420) spoke of the garments he wore for church as something different from his everyday clothing, referring to his churchly apparel as a "suit of clean clothes."[3] By the sixth century, a church council meeting in Narbonne dictated that the alb was the official vestment for Christian worship.[4]

By the seventh century, clergy wore three specific vestments—the alb, the stole, and the chasuble—as signs of their ecclesiastical office.[5] These gracefully flowing garments were distinctively nonbarbarian in style, emphasizing the Roman "civility" of the Christian clergy in contrast to the barbarians, who had introduced military trousers into contemporary society. About a century later, during the Carolingian period (A.D. 700–986), rich brocades and delicate embroidery were added to clerical vestments. Orphreys—narrow bands of floral or geometric designs—were incorporated along the hems of the garments worn by the clergy, which mimicked a style popular with public officials of the same era.[6]

As the distinction between the clergy and the laity became more pronounced, vestments became more unique as the church assigned special duties and roles to the clergy. Not only in style, but also in design and ornamentation, vestments became different. Some of the later ornateness of medieval vestments can be traced to the fact that they were gifts from royalty, who relished lavish decoration. For example, in England, Queen Matilda, wife of William the Conqueror, bequeathed "to the Abbey of the Holy Trinity my tunic worked at Winchester by Alderet's wife and the mantle embroidered with gold, which is in my chamber, to make a cope. Of my two golden girdles, I give that which is ornamented with emblems for the purpose of suspending the lamb before the great altar."[7] Thus it was that the clergy received elegant materials from which they made distinctive garments.

LUTHERAN PERSPECTIVES

Martin Luther wore the vestments of the medieval priest in most of his worship activities even after his break with Rome. However, because he preached frequently for the University of Wittenberg's daily services, he often came straight from the classroom, still wearing his academic gown, for the exposition of the Word. This double use of academic robes for worship and for teaching continues in some Protestant denominations. On the other hand, Luther's colleague Andreas Bodenstein von Karlstadt rebelled against clerical distinctions, threw out all vestments, and even wore feathers in his hat during a service of Holy Communion in Wittenberg. Following the Anabaptists and Enthusiasts of his day, Karlstadt considered vestments to be symbols of papal tyranny.

In general, however, Lutherans viewed vestments as *adiaphora*, meaning they were neither commanded nor forbidden by God's Word. Some Lutheran congregations, following Luther's pastor, Johannes Bugenhagen, retained some of the traditional vestments of the church, particularly the chasuble. Other Lutheran congregations, for example, many in Scandinavia, considered vestments to be symbols of continuity with the Roman Catholic Church. As expressions of opposition to the radical reformers, the Enthusiasts, and some of the Calvinists, Scandinavian Lutherans maintained the traditional vestments.[8] A few Lutheran congregations followed a more Reformed tradition and adopted an academic robe for all worship activities.

For the half-century following Luther's death, most Lutheran congregations continued to provide "Mass vestments" for their pastors. These vestments included an alb with stole and chasuble, as well as a dalmatic for the deacon who assisted in worship. One concern was whether Lutheran clergy should wear the cassock and surplice, which in many areas were perceived to be "papistic" garments. Despite this connection, the cassock and surplice were used throughout the sixteenth century for preaching, for public ministry to the sick and homebound, and for funerals.[9]

Early in the seventeenth century, pastors who did not wear at least a surplice for the Lord's Supper were suspected of being Calvinists. Surplices were used by the officiant and the altar boys who assisted in the service. One of the most detailed records of Lutheran vestments comes from the sacristan's records of St. Nicholas Church in Leipzig. More than 20 chasubles were used throughout the year, including one of green velvet with an embroidered image of Jesus' triumphal entry into Jerusalem, which was used for Advent; one of white damask with a crucifix; one of black velvet with a crucifix, which was used for Good Friday; one of red-brown velvet with a symbol of the Holy Trinity embroidered in pearls and gems, which was used for Pentecost; and one of red velvet embroidered with a Madonna and Child.[10] In addition, copes in various colors continued to be used by Lutheran bishops in Denmark and Norway for ordinations and other special occasions.

During the difficult years of the late seventeenth century, a group broke from many of the traditional practices of Lutheranism. These Pietists, as they became known, followed the continuing Reformed or Calvinist practices, as well as the Rationalist tendencies of the day. Pietists rejected all clerical vestments, opting for the common dress of the academic elite—a black gown. Sometimes called Geneva gowns because of their Reformed origin, these vestments became the standard dress for many early Lutheran clergy in North America.

Throughout European Lutheranism, several distinct liturgical vestments were retained. The alb, surplice, stole, and chasuble seem to have been used regularly in several regions. Arthur Piepkorn reports that "the use of white surplices and colored chasubles embroidered with golden crosses was general at this period in Saxony, Brunswick, the territory of Brandenburg-Nuremberg and elsewhere."[11] At the same time the academic or preaching gown was becoming more prominent among Protestants. By the end of the eighteenth century, most northern European Lutheran pastors had ceased using chasubles; only a few retained the surplice for preaching and liturgical functions. European Rationalism and a gradual Protestantizing of North American Lutheran churches had a negative influence on most Lutheran clergy of that era.

By the nineteenth century, the black preaching gown and the bands (two white tabs of linen that overlapped the collar) had become the regular apparel for most North American and European Protestant clergy. (See illustration.) Some Lutheran congregations kept the alb, stole, and chasuble, but they were the exceptions to the rule. Thus for more than a century the preaching gown was considered the only vestment for use during Lutheran worship. Along with anti-Roman Protestants from Europe, many North American Protestant groups adopted the common garments of contemporary society. Most Lutheran clergy of the nineteenth and early twentieth centuries followed this general social custom.

The 1950s witnessed a new interest in liturgy, which caused a shift in liturgical dress among Lutherans. Luther Reed and his associates reintroduced the cassock with surplice and stole to North American Lutheranism.[12] A decade or so later, the alb with stole was introduced and found almost universal acceptance. The use of the chasuble, though it has a long history in Lutheranism, has not been as universally accepted as the alb. Today there is no universal vestment for Christian worship. Looking through commercial church supply catalogs underscores the lack of uniformity. The alb, stole, and chasuble are available in a variety of styles. Liturgical colors, as well as national, ethnic, and even political images, are incorporated into the designs. Although many different kinds of vestments are available, not all items are edifying or appropriate for God's people to use; therefore, vestments should be chosen with discretion.

John Pless reiterates two significant reasons vestments have been retained in Lutheran congregations. First, vestments are emblems of the office of the holy (public) ministry. Vestments cover the man so the congregation sees not the person but the promises of God proclaimed and purveyed by the pastor. Second, the historic vestments visualize the connection and continuity with the Christian community. We stand as gathered guests "with prophets, apostles, martyrs, and confessors of all times and places."[13]

LITURGICAL VESTMENTS

Because each vestment signifies something in the worshiping life of God's gathered guests, the following provides the meaning or significance of liturgical vestments traditionally used by Lutherans.

FOR ALL WORSHIP PARTICIPANTS

The Alb

The basic garment for all formal worship participants—ordained or nonordained, female or male—is the alb.[14] Acolytes, choir members, organists, assisting ministers, lectors, and clergy may wear this vestment. It is the undergarment for all other liturgical vestments and is a reminder of the white baptismal robe worn by the earliest Christians.[15] The alb is derived from the *tunica linea* (woolen tunic) or *tunica alba* (white tunic), an ankle-length garment worn in Roman times. Originally, this tuniclike garment, also known as the *chiton* or *colobium* (depending on whether it had sleevelike openings), was white or off-white. (The Latin word *alb* means "white" and describes the color of the natural linen rather than the type of garment itself.) In its traditional form, this garment looked like a nightshirt, though it had a rope belt called a cincture (*cingulum*) or girdle. A hood, known as an amice (from the Latin word *amictus,* which is derived from *amicio*, "to wrap around"), was folded to form a detachable collar on the otherwise collarless alb.[16]

During the pre-Germanic period of the Christian church's history, pants were considered barbaric. Only after invading tribesmen brought Rome to its knees did military-style trousers appear among the lower classes. Before this time, particularly during the second and third centuries, the upperclass aristocracy of Rome wore the *tunica alba* or the long *colobium*, which conferred dignity on the wearer because the garment's length made it impossible to perform manual labor. Near the end of the third century, long sleeves and decorative stripes were added to this garment. From the fourth to the eleventh century, all ranks of the clergy wore the plain alb. Around the twelfth century, the alb underwent a significant change, following the design of the tunics worn by Anglo-Saxon nobles and civilians.[17] From this time on, the alb disappeared under the highly ornate outer vestments, which became exclusive marks of the medieval clergy.[18]

The alb has regained visibility and widespread use in Roman Catholic, Episcopal, and Lutheran churches during the last half of the twentieth century. The present-day alb is worn like a coat and fastens with snaps, buttons, or Velcro. A belt or cincture (rope belt) is worn at the waist. "The alb, plain or with apparels, and with only minor changes in fashion (e.g., amplitude of cut, use of lace or other decoration) has continued to be worn until the present day and, in a sense, is to be thought of as the archetypal 'white robe' of Christianity."[19]

FOR THE PRESIDING MINISTER

Cassock and Surplice

Lutherans have adopted the traditional vestment of the cassock and surplice with a clergy stole from several sources. However, the cassock is not a vestment in the technical sense. Rather, it was the street dress of the Roman citizenry, which was introduced to the Roman military around the third century by Emperor Marcus Aurelius Antoninus Bassianus. Variations of this long tunic with close-fitting sleeves were common in Persia and among Jews living in the East.[20]

The cassock, a close-fitting, ankle-length black garment with narrow sleeves and a cutout collar, was adapted from early monastic dress. Around the eleventh century, the *caracalla*, as this cloak was called, became known in Italy as a *casacca* and in France as a *casaque,* which was anglicized as *cassock*. This black undergarment functioned as the daily dress of the medieval clergy.[21] In the great monastic period of the church, friars and monks distinguished their orders by the style and color of their garments or habits—brown, black, or off-white. Some Lutheran pastors explain the origin of the cassock as a combination of the monastic alb and the Renaissance/Reformation academic gown; however, there is no evidence for this genesis. The cassock may be in a Latin (or Roman) style with buttons down the front or in an Anglican (or Jesuit) style with fasteners at the shoulder and a cincture or sash at the waist.

The surplice is a modification of the alb that dates to about the eleventh century. During the Middle Ages, clergy spent long hours in unheated cathedrals or monastic chapels in northern Europe. The priests or monks would don fur- or fleece-lined cassocks for their daily prayer services. However, it could be difficult to put on an alb quickly over such bulky cassocks. The narrow-fitting albs also caused clerics to look bulbous when wearing fur-lined cassocks. Therefore, a modified alb was designed to cover the cassock and to provide a more dignified, flowing appearance. Called the *superpellicium*, this modified alb eventually became the *surplice*, a word derived from the Latin words *super* (which means "over") and *pellis* ("pelts, fur, or skins"). Thus the practice of wearing both a cassock and surplice developed.[22]

Originally, the surplice was a white, floor-length garment without a cincture. The sleeves were fuller and looser than the alb, and the opening for the head was usually round. By the thirteenth century, various orders of clergy wore the surplice for the administration of the Sacrament and during other portions of the worship service, such as processions. The length of the surplice changed over the next three centuries, gradually growing shorter. After the Reformation, some conservative Lutheran clergy wore simple floor-length surplices while more liberal clergy wore shorter, more elaborate, and even lace-trimmed surplices (sometimes called cottas). Because the surplice replaced the alb, nearly floor-length surplices are appropriate and are worn over a cassock.[23]

The surplice as a vestment for Holy Communion dates to an Anglican event near the end of the sixteenth century known as the Elizabethan Settlement. As a compromise between those who wanted to do away with vestments and those who desired to retain the full traditional vestments of Roman Catholicism, the surplice became standard in Anglican liturgical practice.[24] This usage came into North

American Lutheranism in the middle of the twentieth century through the liturgical movement. Most recently, the cassock and surplice as noneucharistic vestments were adopted from low Anglican usage at Morning and Evening Prayer.[25] In Lutheran congregations the cassock and surplice are normally worn for non-Communion services, especially Matins and Vespers. Pastors may wear stoles with the cassock and surplice. If nonordained assistants wear the cassock and surplice, they do not wear a stole.

The clergy shirt with a Roman collar is a relatively recent adaptation of the cassock.[26] Collar styles follow either a Roman Catholic style (sometimes referred to as "tab tops" because of the white plastic insert) or an Anglican style (sometimes referred to as "round collar"). Normally these shirts are black, though church supply houses offer a variety of colors—red for cardinals, purple for bishops, brown and gray for some Catholic religious orders.[27] There is no universally recognized style or color among Lutheran clergy.

Stole

Perhaps the most recognizable of the distinctive clergy vestments is the stole, the scarflike cloth that is draped over a pastor's shoulders. This vestment originated in pre-Christian times. In the civilized world of the Greeks and Romans, renowned philosophers and notable scholars wore a large shawl-like garment known as the *pallium* over their tunics. This garment gradually became smaller, and by the fourth century, it was the size of a scarf. Roman senators wore this scarf as a symbol of their official responsibilities and as the badge of a Roman dignitary.[28]

The earliest name given to this vestment is *orarium*, which is related to the Latin word for prayer (*ora*).[29] The stole was worn by those designated to lead public prayer—priests and deacons—and may have had its origin in the prayer shawls of late Judaism. The word *stole* comes from a Greek word (*stola*) that denotes a long, flowing robe, similar to those worn by the Jewish scribes in the Gospel accounts (Mark 12:38; cf. Revelation 6:11; 7:9, 13).

Gradually, all worship leaders wore the *orarium*. However, in A.D. 343, the Council of Laodicea prohibited subdeacons from wearing the stole.[30] A century later the stole was used in France (around A.D. 425) as a badge of office among the hierarchy of clergy. However, Pope Celestine I rebuked the French clergy, saying that "bishops [should be] distinguished by life not robes, by purity of heart not by elegance."[31] By the end of the fifth century, all clergy used the stole as a liturgical vestment. The Council of Mayence (A.D. 813) prescribed the stole as the distinguishing mark of the priestly vocation and commanded that it be worn at all times, even when traveling.

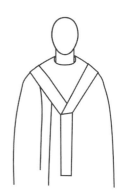

Around the ninth century, another style of the stole, distinct from the scarflike garment, was introduced. It looked like the English letter *Y* in the front and back with the top serving as the yoke. This double-Y stole became known as an "episcopal pallium" because it was worn chiefly by bishops and archbishops. During this same time, a longer stole (between 9 feet and 12 feet in length) was worn with one end draped down from the left shoulder and the other end drawn around the back, turned over at the middle of the breast, then placed over the left shoulder.[32]

During the Middle Ages, a small *pallium* stole was given personally by the popes of Rome to their representatives (particularly bishops and archbishops) as a symbol of pontifical appointment. All stoles were decorated with at least one cross and sometimes seven or more crosses. Stoles were sometimes made from purple cloth to indicate the office of bishop. By the tenth century, tassels and small bells, as well as fringes, were added as ornamentation, particularly to those stoles worn by bishops.[33]

Lutherans have retained the use of the stole.[34] Because Lutherans understand that pastors hold the office of the public ministry, the stole is a visible sign of their official responsibilities. Recent explanations for the stole include the belief that it represents the "easy yoke" of our Lord (see Matthew 11:30). The stole is usually given to a pastor at the time of his ordination. It is considered a preaching vestment and was reintroduced to Lutheran churches in the 1950s from the Anglican Oxford Movement of the early 1900s. Stoles are worn over the alb or cassock and surplice for official pastoral acts—weddings, burials, confession and absolution, the Service of the Word, and preaching. The stole need not be worn for daily prayer services.[35]

Clergy can wear a stole in two distinct ways. Pastors of parishes normally wear a stole as a yoke. When a pastor or bishop is the presiding minister, that is, the pastor who leads the worshiping community, he may wear a longer stole and cross it over his chest during the Service of the Word. When the Communion liturgy begins and the chasuble is placed over the alb, the longer stole is uncrossed and becomes visible under the chasuble.[36]

Stoles always match the paraments in the liturgical color of the day. Designs and symbols on the stoles may vary, depending on the season of the church year. Unusual colors or ostentatious symbols may draw attention to the stole rather than to the message being proclaimed through the liturgy and the sermon. Traditional stoles designed with symbols of the liturgical season, the pastoral office, or with any of the vast variety of crosses may be best.

Chasuble

In many Lutheran congregations, the main vestment for the presiding minister at services of Holy Communion is the chasuble, which comes from the Latin word *casula*, which means "little castle" or "little house" (*casa* in Latin). A poncholike outer garment of Greco-Roman origin, this flowing vestment, sometimes confused with the paenula (a capelike garment worn by Roman nobility), has a rich tradition. Worn in ancient times by common folk and senators alike, the chasuble fulfills a purpose similar to a contemporary outer coat. Philo the Jew, writing about A.D. 49, said the chasuble provided the wearer with a portable home and was suitable for travelers, soldiers, peasants, monks, and others who were obliged to be in the open air.[37] The chasuble was without sleeves and without an opening in the front, which distinguishes it from the paenula (see the description of the cope below).

Augustine of Hippo (A.D. 354–430) seems to be the first to mention the *casula* as a clerical vestment, yet he indicates that laypeople also possessed such a garment. From this reference, liturgical scholars assume that the *casula* developed into a garment particularly attractive to ascetics and monks because these individuals spent considerable time outside or in unheated buildings. During the early fifth century, the chasuble became a liturgical vestment for Communion with the stole arranged around the shoulders of the presiding minister.[38]

The chasuble remained a full-flowing vestment until around the tenth century; in the Eastern Orthodox churches, it remains so today. Sometime during the tenth century, chasubles became short and pointed in front and long and wide in back. This design probably developed because it freed the clergy from excess cloth around their hands and arms as they officiated at the altar. Although full chasubles (later called "Gothic") continued to be worn for centuries, one notable change occurred around the fourteenth century. Chest-sized "fiddle-back" chasubles, so named because the cut resembled the body of the stringed instrument, were introduced because the "art" of gracefully wearing draped clothing was being lost among the clergy and society in general.[39] "Fiddle-back" chasubles looked like large bibs and were used until after the Reformation, even in many European Lutheran congregations.[40]

The full-bodied nearly floor-length chasubles, sometimes misnamed Byzantine-style by church supply houses, are used most frequently in Christian churches in both the East and the West. Chasubles are worn in the liturgical color of the day and may be decorated with bands in a contrasting color or pattern. Some chasubles have a symbol embroidered or appliqued on the front and back. Only worn by ordained pastors, a chasuble may be worn during the whole service if it is put on after the Absolution during the Entrance Hymn. Normally, however, the pastor vests with the chasuble during the Offertory, prior to preparing for Communion.[41]

A white chasuble, often purchased by a Lutheran congregation as its first Communion vestment, offers versatility. A stole in the liturgical color of the season may be worn over the chasuble, reminiscent of the early bishop's pallium. The use of a chasuble for Christmas or Easter would highlight the festival Communion service experience of God's gathered guests.

Cope or Cape

The cope is a garment for special occasions that dates from Roman times. This liturgical vestment developed from an outer garment worn by Roman citizens on formal occasions. It was known as a paenula or pancho. (See illustration below.) The hooded cape, most often made of a full circle of wool, was a practical garment designed to keep the wearer warm in unheated buildings or warm and dry when outside in inclement weather. Paul's request for his cloak in Troas was probably a request for his paenula (2 Timothy 4:13).

Early Christian records indicate that already in the fourth century bishops wore the *paenula* for liturgical purposes, as well as on official visits.[42] Capes were often elaborately decorated. Because of its liturgical use, the whole vestment was renamed *cope*. Originally a practical element of the cope, the hood has undergone several adaptations during the past centuries. Some hoods were detachable so they could match the liturgical color of the season. From the time of the Reformation, an imitation or stylized hood has been developed that appears as a decorative panel around the back yoke of the shoulders, ending with a tassel at the center.[43]

White copes may be used for many occasions, though traditionally this vestment would be in the liturgical color of the season. The worship leader may wear the cope to add dignity, solemnity, or festivity to a

procession or service. The cope is the most majestic of the noneucharistic vestments. (See illustration.)

The cope may be worn for any festival occasion, particularly when processing outdoors in cooler climates. For a festival service at which the Lord's Supper is not offered, the cope would be an appropriate way to express the festive nature of the gathering. Even for a festival at which the Lord's Supper is celebrated, the cope may be worn by the presiding minister during the Service of the Word. The cope is also appropriate for occasional services, such as weddings, funerals, and confirmations.[44] On festive occasions when the presiding minister wears a chasuble, assisting ministers may wear copes.

Preaching Gown

The preaching gown is an "un-vestment."(See illustration on p. 183.) A plain black robe was worn by university professors and students for at least a century before and after the Reformation. In England professors and students at Oxford and Cambridge still wear the academic gown for special occasions. Students often were given gowns as they matriculated from preparatory school. The various styles of gowns distinguished the level of academic standing—the bachelor had an open sleeve, the master had a pocketed sleeve, and the doctor had a fully closed sleeve.

Both Luther and Calvin were professors, thus they often wore their academic gowns when preaching for the daily chapel services at their respective universities. For chapel services in Christian universities, this is still appropriate. Unfortunately the black gown became a symbol of Rationalism, which rapidly took root in Reformation soil in the eighteenth century. Worship no longer was considered an opportunity to join with the saints and angels through Word and Sacrament; instead, it was an educational experience that focused on moral exhortation and practical exposition for Christian living. This is evident particularly in the fact that pastors of the Reformed tradition have retained the preaching gown, though many have adopted the doctoral robe. Lutheran pastors who choose to wear the black robe do so as an academic vestige of the Enlightenment, rather than as a liturgical sign of the pastoral office.

The Bands

Some Lutheran pastors retain the use of a split collar, known as the "bands" (*Beffchen*).[45] Originating from sixteenth-century white ties, Lutheran pastors offered an allegorical explanation that the bands represent the preaching of Law and

Gospel. Some Lutheran pastors wear these bands as the only addition to the black preaching gown. (See illustration on p. 183.)

FOR ASSISTING MINISTERS[46]

The Alb

As mentioned previously, the alb may be worn by all who assist in worship services.[47] Whether worn by assisting ministers who help with Communion, by acolytes who light candles, or by members of the choir, the alb symbolizes the baptismal foundation on which all Christian worship is based. If a congregation has not had assisting ministers vest in an alb, the change should be explained. The simplicity and uniformity of the alb also provides an inexpensive vestment for all who help serve God's gathered guests in worship.

Cassock and Surplice

Although most often associated with ordained clergy, the cassock and surplice is appropriate for use by any worship assistant.[48] The stole is not worn by nonordained assistants because the stole identifies the clergy. Acolytes or altar boys (and girls) in cassocks and short surplices are frequently seen in Lutheran congregations. Avoid purchasing red cassocks for acolytes because red is worn only by Roman Catholic cardinals (just as a purple cassock is worn by Catholic bishops and a white cassock by the pope).

A cassock without sleeves is called a *rochet* and is often used by choir directors and organists so they can keep their arms free. As an alternative to a rochet, a choir director or organist may select a loose surplice with sleeves that close at the wrist.

Deacon's Stole

Although distinct from the symbol of the pastoral office, the deacon's stole represents the church's recognition of professional (certified) lay leaders in a congregation. The deacon's stole is worn over the left shoulder with both ends hanging down the right side.[49] This stole is held in place with a cincture or more securely by a small chain or cord attached at the waist. The deacon's stole should be in the liturgical color of the day and may be decorated with appropriate symbols of the season.

Dalmatic and Tunic

Like the chasuble, the dalmatic and tunic began as ordinary garments in the province of Dalmatia (considered a barbarian region of the Roman Empire at the time of the early Christians).

Comparable to suit coats today, the dalmatic was worn over an undergarment (the alb) as a tunic. This tunic, or *tunica*, was the traditional garment of the Roman working class.[50]

Around the turn of the second century and in the early third century, several eccentric Roman emperors popularized this garment by wearing it at their coronations. At first the general Roman populace thought the dalmatics were uncivilized and barbarian because they had large sleeves, but the upper classes of imperial Rome quickly adopted the garment. Soon after, the common citizens embraced the fashion. For decoration, stripes of red, russet, or purple went up the front and down the back, with two rows on each sleeve set near the hem.

Christians adopted this garment, too, because it was more utilitarian and egalitarian. Several frescoes in early Christian churches show Jesus in a dalmatic, a garment that ended above the knees and had short sleeves. Paintings in the catacombs also depict saints and the Good Shepherd with arms raised, wearing sleeved garments in the style of the dalmatic. Constantine used the dalmatic as a mark of a bishop's teaching authority within the state. From the fourth to the ninth century, bishops and even popes wore a dalmatic over an alb but under the chasuble. The dalmatic, however, was not considered a liturgical vestment because clergy and laity, male and female, wore this style of dress. Around the seventh century, the dalmatic fell out of use by the laity, but the lower-ranked clergy retained it as a distinguishing mark of their office.[51]

Usually a decorative orphrey (a panel or strip of decorative cloth) was added to the dalmatic along the hem and sleeves and often on the front. By the ninth century, the decoration became more varied and elaborate with tassels appended to the traditional stripes or orphries and beautifully embroidered designs in gold and silk thread.[52]

Deacons—apostolicly appointed assistants in the New Testament and later professional lay leaders of congregations—adopted the dalmatic in the late sixth century as their distinctive apparel, but they made the sleeves slightly longer and larger. A subdeacon may wear a less decorated dalmatic known as a tunic. Nonordained assisting ministers also may wear the dalmatic. The dalmatic is worn only during the Service of the Sacrament. The vestment should match the color of the day as worn by the presiding minister. To differentiate between a tunic and a dalmatic, worn respectively by the subdeacon and deacon, a horizontal line is often added to the dalmatic across the chest and back of the garment, or the dalmatic may have more ornamentation than the tunic.

Choir Robes

The most misunderstood and misused vestment is the choir robe. Some robes are pseudoliturgical vestments, following the design of vestments normally worn only by high officials in some denominations. Other choir robes have fake academic hoods, euphemistically called "collars," and come in liturgical colors rather than academic colors. Colored albs (an anachronism because the word *alb* means "white") are occasionally purchased for choirs. For practical reasons the traditional white or off-white alb may be the best vestment (and investment) for a congregation. Albs in a variety of sizes may be purchased for use by assisting ministers, choir members, and acolytes. Such usage would underscore the baptismal basis for Christian participation in all activities of God's gathered guests.

Paraments

Tapestries, hangings, altar coverings, and vesture are some of the more familiar forms of liturgical art. This precious heritage remains evident as exquisite and edifying designs in cloth continue to enhance the liturgy. While *vestments* are the clothing for the worship leaders, *paraments* are the "clothing" for sanctuary furnishings. As Frank C. Senn points out, Lutherans have come late to the use of paraments. Previous Lutheran practice had been to cover the altar with a simple white linen,[53] but practices have changed. The following descriptions refer to the furniture rather than to the parament because congregations have many options, depending on the size, location, and visibility of the furnishings.

Altar

As with a formal table setting, a tablecloth is used to cover the altar mensa (the top of the altar table). This practice began in the Middle Ages when stone altars were covered with a waxed linen cloth called cerecloth (literally "waxed" cloth) to prevent the damp stone from ruining any cloths placed on top. In modern times, the cerecloth has been replaced by a heavy linen cloth that may have a frontal attached to it. A fair linen is placed on top of the heavy linen. The fair linen matches the altar dimensions exactly or is a little longer than the mensa, extending down the two sides by approximately three inches. Five crosses,

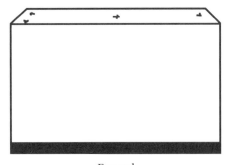

Frontal

reminiscent of Jesus' five wounds, are embroidered on the fair linen, which symbolizes the burial cloth of Jesus.

A frontal is a piece of fabric in the liturgical color of the season that covers all or part of the front of the altar. (See illustration on p. 194.) A frontal may be hung from the altar, or, in the case of a large freestanding altar, it may be a rectangular cloth that is carefully draped to the floor (called Laudian or Jacobean because of its Anglican origin). Small frontlets, or superfrontals, may be placed over the frontal to hide the rod or hooks that hold the frontal to the altar.

Symbols placed on the frontal may be associated with the season of the church year or with the Lord's Supper. Sometimes words appear on the frontal, such as *Alleluia* or the phrase "Holy, holy, holy."

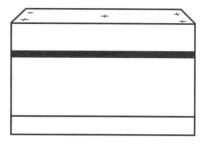

Superfrontal

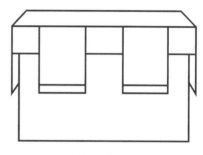

Frontlets

Lutheran congregations avoid the phrase "Do this in remembrance of Me" on the altar frontal because Reformed churches use this phrase to deny Christ's real presence in the Sacrament. On full-sized frontals, a scene or symbols from the church year are common.

PULPIT AND LECTERN

Some congregations display a hanging for the pulpit and/or lectern that matches the altar frontal. This hanging is called an antependium (from the Latin *antependulus*, which means "hanging before"). If used, the antependium may hang from the top of the bookstand, or when in the form of a large bookmarker (generally three inches wide), it hangs from one side of the bookstand. Any symbols on the antependia typically emphasize the Word of God, the life of our Lord, or other scriptural images. A variety of options from early Christian art or designs by contemporary Christian artists may be considered.

Lutherans have retained many of the traditional garments of the church catholic, as well as adapting to new situations and adopting styles of dress that communicate our understanding of God's gifts and His presence. The use of vestments underscores the distinction between daily routine and the time we set aside to assemble as God's gathered guests.

SOME QUESTIONS TO CONSIDER

1. Other than those mentioned in this chapter, list uniforms or vestments that are distinguishing marks for contemporary offices or professions.

2. How do Lutherans follow a biblical tradition by retaining special vestments for worship leaders and assistants?

3. Describe the origin of the alb as a liturgical vestment and its benefits as a form of liturgical dress.

4. Why do the cassock and surplice have uncertain places as Lutheran vestments? What are their origins? When are they worn? Who wears them?

5. How has the stole changed through the centuries? What is its continuing significance for clergy?

6. When is a chasuble worn? What are some alternative vestments for the same part of the service?

7. Why should assisting ministers wear some kind of vestment? What vestments might they wear?

8. How do paraments differ from vestments? Describe the paraments used in your church during the past week, including any symbols and colors.

NOTES

1. Boyd, "Vestments," 34.

2. Dix, *Shape of the Liturgy*, 399.

3. Cited in Cope, "Vestments," 523.

4. Norris, *Church Vestments*, 17.

5. Dix, *Shape of the Liturgy*, 403, reports that in A.D. 633 the Council of Toledo ordered the restoration of the alb, stole, and chasuble to a priest who had been defrocked.

6. Dolby, *Church Vestments*, 49.

7. Cited in Margaret Lane, "Parson's Plumage," *The [London] Daily Telegraph* (25 January 1985): 12, a review of Janet Mayo, *A History of Ecclesiastical Dress* (Batsford, 1985).

8. Piepkorn, *Survival of the Historic Vestments*, 8–10.

9. Piepkorn, *Survival of the Historic Vestments*, 12–24.

10. Piepkorn, *Survival of the Historic Vestments*, 41–42.

11. Piepkorn, *Survival of the Historic Vestments*, 64.

12. Senn, *Christian Liturgy*, 624.

13. Pless, "Leaders of Worship," 223.

14. Norris, *Church Vestments*, 8.

15. In the *Apostolic Tradition of Hippolytus* (xxi.20), the newly baptized received robes to signify their new life in Christ. See Dix and Chadwick, *Treatise on the Apostolic Tradition*, 38.

16. Cope, "Vestments," 524, indicates that the amice became "an essential mass vestment from the eighth century onwards." The amice is also called a *humerale* or shawl.

17. Norris, *Church Vestments*, 15–17, 19–20.

18. Dolby, *Church Vestments*, 34.

19. Cope, "Vestments," 524.

20. Norris, *Church Vestments*, 165.

21. Norris, *Church Vestments*, 166.

22. Dolby, *Church Vestments*, 121.

23. Norris, *Church Vestments*, 168–69.

24. Reed, *Lutheran Liturgy* (rev. ed.), 136.

25. Senn, *Christian Liturgy*, 624.

26. Dolby, *Church Vestments*, 173, notes that no such clergy garments were known until the seventeenth century.

27. Although church supply houses provide clergy shirts in a variety of colors and styles, selections are best made wisely and judiciously.

28. Norris, *Church Vestments*, 24–26.

29. Some scholars connect the word *orarium* to the long towel used for the hands and mouth (*os, oris*). Others associate it with a scarf used to keep one's head and neck warm. This towel or scarf was known as a *sudarium*. A Greek transliteration of this latter word is used for the linen cloth placed over Jesus' head at the time of His burial (John 20:7).

30. Barnett, *The Diaconate*, 202.

31. Dix, *Shape of the Liturgy*, 401.

32. Norris, *Church Vestments*, 27–31.

33. Norris, *Church Vestments*, 32–34.

34. Piepkorn, *Survival of the Historic Vestments*, 3, 119–20.

35. Pless, "Leaders of Worship," 224.

36. Pfatteicher and Messerli, *Manual on the Liturgy*, 159, provides a diagram that illustrates various ways to wear the stole, as well as how a deacon's stole is worn.

37. Norris, *Church Vestments*, 61.

38. Norris, *Church Vestments*, 60–61.

39. Norris, *Church Vestments*, 79–81.

40. For a visual history of the chasuble, see *The New Westminster Dictionary of Liturgy and Worship* (ed. J. G. Davies; Philadelphia: Westminster, 1986), 528–29, which illustrates more than five dozen distinct styles of chasubles.

41. Commission on Worship, the LCMS, "Notes on the Liturgy," in *Lutheran Worship: Altar Book* (St. Louis: Concordia, 1982), 26.

42. Norris, *Church Vestments*, 59.

43. Dolby, *Church Vestments*, 103–4.

44. Many Lutheran congregations with a cemetery on their premises provide a black cope or cape for their pastor to use while officiating at committal services.

45. Piepkorn, *Survival of the Historic Vestments*, 111.

46. Commission on Worship, the LCMS, "Notes on the Liturgy," 11, provides additional information on vestments appropriate for those assisting in the worship service.

47. Pless, "Leaders of Worship," 224.

48. Pless, "Leaders of Worship," 224.

49. Norris, *Church Vestments*, 91, notes that around the middle of the twelfth century the deacon wore his stole unfastened at the hip. The two ends were looped over the shoulder on the left side under the dalmatic. This is still the style in many Eastern Orthodox churches.

50. Norris, *Church Vestments*, 43.

51. Norris, *Church Vestments*, 45–46.

52. Norris, *Church Vestments*, 48.

53. Senn, *Christian Liturgy*, 607.

CHAPTER 11

ARCHITECTURE IN THE LORD'S SERVICE

EXPRESSING ECCLESIASTICAL AWE

Architecture provides another avenue to express God's glory and the theology of the worshiping community. Church buildings are specifically designed as places for God's guests to gather. They provide the setting for the activities of God and His people. The unique witness of a church building to the surrounding community often goes unrecognized, yet Christian architectural settings are significant for the liturgy and life of God's people.

Architects Donald Bruggink and Carl Droppers state the issue most clearly in their book *Christ and Architecture*: "Architecture for churches is a matter of gospel. A church that is interested in proclaiming the Gospel must also be interested in architecture, for year after year the architecture of the church proclaims a message that either augments the proclaimed Word or conflicts with it."[1] Architecture and theology go hand in hand, and it is important to understand what is being communicated, both intentionally and unintentionally. The theological significance of a church building is one of its most important functions. "This may be the one quality which distinguishes it from any other building," notes the LCMS Commission on Architecture.[2]

Winston Churchill once said that "we shape our buildings and then our buildings shape us."[3] The architecture and the arrangement of objects in a building determines who will meet whom, who will listen to whom, and who will see whom. A building's architecture even controls actions.[4] Space communicates—whether in its clutter or simplicity, or in its ability to make us feel restless or comfortable. Space shapes us and our attitudes. "Those whose ministry is the liturgical environment must first be sensitive to all of the ramifications of the role that space plays in our life and for the formative quality of the spaces we occupy. We then see that space and worship work together and are important in creating an atmosphere for a people at prayer."[5]

THE HOUSE OF THE CHURCH OR THE HOUSE OF THE LORD

The church is the body of Christ, God's people gathered around Word and Sacraments. The church is built on the apostles and prophets, with Christ as the cornerstone, as St. Paul explains in Ephesians 2. The church is people, and these people gather to recount God's blessings to them and to receive His promises and forgiveness anew. When we speak of churches, we also mean the specific places that house the gathered people of God.

The place where God's people worship is important. Numerous passages in the Old Testament describe the preparation, ornamentation, and arrangement of the tabernacle (Exodus 25–27; 31). The careful building requirements for the temple are explained in 1 Kings 6–7 and 1 Chronicles 28–29. Even the elaborate furnishings of these places of worship were designed to send a significant message to the worshipers.[6] In one of his visions, Ezekiel described with exquisite detail the ideal temple (Ezekiel 40–44).

In the New Testament, Jesus ignored Peter's building proposal on the Mount of Transfiguration (Matthew 17), but He did not reject it. Later Jesus spoke of tearing down and rebuilding the temple, a reference to His body (John 2:19–21). After the first Easter, early Christians continued to meet in the temple as a place to recall God's enduring blessings (Luke 24:53; Acts 2:46). The writer to the Hebrews encouraged his readers to participate in the worship life of the gathered guests, the Christian community (Hebrews 10:25). Finally, the Book of Revelation concludes with visions of heaven without a temple because, as John explained, "the Lord God Almighty and the Lamb are its temple" (Revelation 21:22).

From earliest times, Christians met in local synagogues and in the homes of the wealthy. Synagogues were Jewish community centers for biblical training and theological discussion, so Christians found them to be convenient and appropriate places in which to meet. Paul frequently began his missionary work in such gathering places (Acts 17–18). Synagogues were arranged with seats around three walls and a central reading table for the scrolls of the Old Testament. These reading tables were undoubtedly used by the first Christians to read Paul's letters along with the Law and the Prophets.

Gregory Dix, an authority on early Christian worship, suggested that Christians met in the homes of wealthy members. The homes were constructed with an atrium (courtyard) in the center, a vestibule entrance (called the *tablinum*, which included a shrine and a chair), a large dining room, and a living area.[7] An archaeological discovery in an Iranian community known as Dura-Europos uncovered one of the earliest Christian homes, which dates to the middle of the third century.

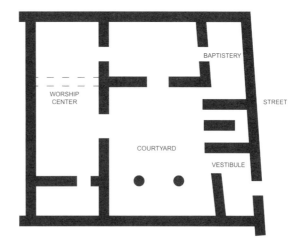

Floor plan of Christian house-church in Dura-Europos.

Clearly the home was used as a worship center by Christians.[8] The details of this discovery confirm major points in Dix's hypothesis.

When the persecution of Christians began, believers were forced to meet in secret sites. The most renowned examples of these sites are in Rome, where Christians met in the vast maze of underground catacombs. Until the end of the third century, the site where Christians gathered for worship was generally known as the *domus ecclesiae* (house of the church), rather than the house of God (*domus Dei*).[9] The focus was on the people as God's gathered guests (the true church), not on the place in which they gathered (the house).

In A.D. 313, Emperor Constantine gave the church official approval and Christianity became a public religion.[10] Thereafter, large assemblies gathered for religious occasions, and sacred things began to take precedence over the sacred message. Larger facilities for worship were required because of the influx of converts. Rather than mimicking the intimate shrines typical of pagan worship, Christians took a different approach for their building projects. The newly approved Christian communities adapted the design of the Greco-Roman meeting hall. These public buildings served communities as grand banquet halls, marketplaces, official audience halls, or even imperial forums. Christians experimented with the design of these buildings for their churches.

Gradually the style of the imperial building, known as a *basilica* (which means "king's hall" and comes from the Greek word for king, *basileus*), became the standard structure for Christian churches. Rather quickly, Emperor Constantine designated the basilica style as the appropriate style for the church's gathering place because it was associated with dignity, authority, and simplicity. The imposing structure consisted of a huge hall, up to 70 feet wide, a vaulted ceiling, and at each end a semicircular wall (called an apse). In the civic buildings, the magistrates' chairs were placed at one end of the hall and a statue of the emperor at the other. In their buildings, Christians removed the emperor's statue and seated the worship leaders, particularly the bishop, in the area reserved for the magistrates. Thus the humble house church was replaced by a corporatelike structure for much of the rest of Christian history.

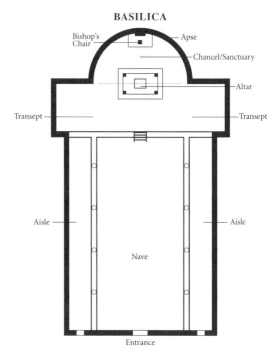

As Christians adapted the basilica style to their worship needs, the apse provided an unanticipated but necessary acoustic benefit. The apse served as an architectural megaphone for the proclamation of God's Word. In the West, the altar often was positioned in front of the apse, closer to the people, though the bishop's seat or throne (the Latin word was *cathedra*), from which he preached, remained in the apse for acoustic purposes.[11] A grand entrance area (the narthex[12]) frequently replaced the apse at the other end of the building. The interior of a Christian basilica was often brighter than the secular basilica because the designers increased the number of windows above the side aisles and added elaborate decorations—such as paintings and mosaics—on the ceilings, walls, and floors. From the fourth through the sixth centuries, many pagans were baptized into the Christian community, thus baptisms became a regular feature of congregational life and often included whole families. Adequate space was required for these frequent services, thus the baptistery was added to the basic design.

In the sixth century the Byzantine style of architecture was most prevalent. Hagia Sophia, the famous church built in Constantinople (present-day Istanbul) by Emperor Justinian, epitomizes this style of church. The building is shaped like a Greek cross (four equal-length arms) with the main altar in the center. The congregation gathers around the sides. A huge dome, symbolizing the heavens, dominates the structure as sunlight reflects through the many windows onto the silver and gold and the mosaics. Combined with innumerable candles and clouds of incense, the visual effect creates a sense of awesome mystery surrounding the presence of God.

Around the middle of the sixth century, a screened wall called an iconostasis became common in Eastern churches.[13] The iconostasis was a rail or high screen on which icons of Jesus and early Christians were placed. Eastern Orthodox churches later expanded and raised this screen between the altar and the congregation so it separated the priest from the people as a reminder of the Most Holy Place in the Old Testament tabernacle and temple.

In the West, railings were built around the chancel at about this same time as a way to distinguish between and also to separate the holy and the secular, the place for the clergy and the place for the populace. This emphasis on separation and distinction was enhanced when Pope Gregory the Great (A.D. 590–604) elevated the role of the clergy over the laity by affirming the priest's power to transubstantiate the elements of Holy Communion. That is, Gregory declared that the priest could change the physical elements of bread and wine into the true body and blood of Christ during the Sacrament of the Altar.

Increasingly, Christian churches in Europe were built so the people faced east, the direction of the rising sun and of the holy city of Jerusalem. This practice became a formal requirement in the Middle Ages. Orienting (literally, "East-ing") churches continues within the liturgical and architectural language of church buildings to this day. The result is that the entrance of a church (the narthex) is considered the "liturgical west" of the building and the altar area (the chancel) is the "liturgical east" of the building.

By the tenth century, the congregation's involvement in worship had diminished to that of mere observation. The clergy no longer conducted the liturgy "on behalf of" the people, they celebrated the Mass "instead of" the congregation. Large choirs composed of clergy or aspiring clergy played an ever greater role in worship, often supplanting the congregation. Thus a specially designated area for choirs developed within the basilica. Some of the great medieval and monastic churches had larger choir areas than the area designated for the worshiping congregation.

In some communities, church buildings took on the shape of two distinct rooms. The clergy, frequently consisting of cloistered monks, isolated themselves from the laypeople, though they shared a common altar. Thus the freestanding altar was split down the middle so the clergy could participate on one side, the laity on the other. As a result the altar appeared to be moved against a wall. In addition, the clergy moved from behind the altar, where they had always faced the people, to a liturgical setting in which they had to turn their backs on the people to face the altar. This practice continued into the middle of the twentieth century.[14]

In medieval Europe the Byzantine basilica was adapted and became known as a Romanesque structure. Romanesque buildings had a fortresslike appearance and seemed to symbolize the strength of the Roman Empire. Of uncertain origin, this style spread quickly during the eleventh and twelfth centuries. The round-arched buildings were different from the basilicas in two significant ways: their roofs and the elaborate carvings. The timber roofs of the basilica were replaced with grand tunnel vaults of massive masonry. Coupled with this increased use of stone, which required extremely thick walls and supporting columns, were ornate carvings of dramatic scenes and geometric shapes. These stone carvings were intended to make the ominous buildings aesthetically attractive and to advertise what was happening inside, as well as to remind worshipers of life's seriousness. Paul and Tessa Clowney descriptively summarize this perspective: "The solidity and imagination of Romanesque architecture reflects both the seriousness with which the church was viewed and also the magical world which medieval man saw all around him."[15]

In the eleventh century, elevated pulpits appeared in church construction throughout the West. Prior to this time, preachers sat on the cathedra, or bishop's chair, which was located in the apse. From there a clear proclamation of the Word was possible in the basilica. Around the time of the great preacher John Chrysostom (A.D. 347–407), a *bema* (or platform) extended from the front of the elevated altar so the preacher could be closer to the people.[16] Chrysostom would then walk into the midst of the congregation to preach.[17] Pulpits in larger cathedrals became increasingly elaborate (and lofty) as steps and railings were added in the twelfth century.[18]

During the twelfth century, candles and a cross were regularly placed on altars. Prior to this time, candles (usually referred to as torches) and the cross were carried only during the entrance procession; then they were placed on stands in the chancel. An ancient tradition of the church forbade placing anything on the altar except that which was specifically needed for the celebration of Holy Communion.[19] Like the pulpit, candlestands also grew in size and became more elaborate over time.

Architectural styles became more varied during the Middle Ages as building skills became more sophisticated and construction materials became more diverse. The strong, solid, and heavy Romanesque style of church architecture gave way to the more airy and aspiring Gothic style of the late Middle Ages. Communities across Europe began to vie for recognition through the height and prominence of their cathedral (the main community church where the bishop had his throne). Almost all medieval cathedrals were characterized by a cruciform shape. The main worship area for the laity was called the nave. Aisles ran parallel with the nave, often separated by large columns that supported the massive roof or vaulted ceiling. Two transepts, extensions to the north and south of the nave, formed the arms of these cross-shaped churches. The grand chancel at the head of the building was raised by several steps at the east end where the clergy or choir would gather around the main altar.

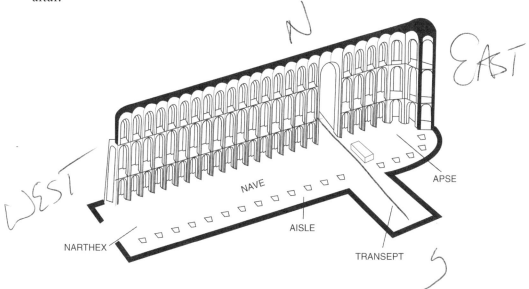

Originating in France, Gothic architecture spread throughout Europe during the twelfth through fourteenth centuries (and later, by mimicry, to North America in the nineteenth century). The word *Gothic* was first used in the seventeenth century as a pejorative term, meaning these buildings were "like the uncultured Goth," highly ostentatious but lacking in refinement. Begun in Paris under Abbot Suger, the Gothic Cathedral of St. Denis exuded a sense of order, lightness, and weightlessness, which became an attractive source of inspiration for several generations of architects.[20] This first Gothic church seemed to defy gravity when compared with the massive interiors of Romanesque churches. By using supportive pointed arches and carefully placed exterior buttresses, new possibilities for church architecture were realized in Gothic architecture. "The result is a space with the three features which were to become the hallmarks of the Gothic style: verticality, achieved through height and visual stress on vertical lines; lightness, created by large windows and slender buttressing; and unity, with all the architectural details integrated into one whole."[21] Today, such Gothic monuments are still in evidence throughout France (Amiens, Beauvais, Chartres, Paris, and Strasbourg), Germany (Cologne and Freiburg), and England (Cambridge and Winchester).

"Church architecture of the late medieval period focused on the altar as shrine,"[22] explains Keith Pecklers, a Benedictine scholar. Two distinct parts of the building were clearly differentiated, even by church law—the chancel in which the monks sang the daily office (therefore, this section was also known as the choir) and the nave for the laity. Even in Western European churches, a large partition—known as a rood-screen (*rood* refers to the crucifix affixed to the main beam over the chancel)—served as a divider that blocked the view of the altar from the laity.[23] As a result of this architectural feature, side chapels grew in popularity so the laity could observe the priests as they conducted private masses. Sometimes the choir area and organ took a central place in the nave and blocked the congregation's view of the chancel.[24]

Cathedrals were major community centers and often featured high towers. These towers extended the visibility of the cathedral and allowed the bells to be heard for great distances. Two arrangements were most common for church towers. One arrangement positioned a tower at the west end of the church, which is apparent in many older churches, even in the United States. The other arrangement featured a set of towers at the west end of the church and a larger central tower at the crossing of the transepts, often above the main altar. Spires were often positioned atop the towers, which symbolized human aspirations for heavenly things.[25]

During the Renaissance, architects displayed their skills as distinguished artists rather than merely as construction practitioners. As a result, the human dimension of the building became more significant, and the lofty ceiling of the Gothic cathedral was reduced to a more humanly proportional setting. This is perhaps most evident in the Basilica of St. Peter's in Rome, which was commissioned by Pope Julius II in the early 1500s and completed a century later. Every famous architect of that era worked on this building, which was designed to portray the human contact point for divinity.[26]

Around the fifteenth century, seating became a more common feature in many churches. Prior to this worshipers occasionally walked around during the service for their private devotional times, particularly if they could not understand the Latin liturgy. If a preacher was exceptionally good or the worshipers were unable to stand for long periods of time, congregation members would bring their own chairs to the service. After the Reformation, seats were arranged around the pulpit, which was often attached to a column in the nave. Only later were pews fixed in place. Beginning around the eighteenth century, some pews were considered private property and sold to families in the community.[27]

At the time of the Reformation, several additional changes occurred in church buildings. Although pulpits were evident in churches before the Reformation, the prominence of the pulpit became a hallmark of Protestant buildings. Similarly, Reformed churches frequently returned to a simpler style of construction that emphasized the church as a meeting place rather than as an elaborate temple. As a result of an iconoclastic attitude among some early Protestant reformers, beautiful stained-glass windows, exquisite wall paintings, and impressive sculptures were removed or destroyed. By contrast, Martin Luther and his followers were not only tolerant of art and artistic expressions of the Gospel, but they encouraged its use in worship.[28] As a result, the Lutheran Church adapted a variety of styles from its Catholic roots while reestablishing preaching as a major feature of corporate worship. With the introduction of congregational singing, organ lofts also developed in the sixteenth century, especially in Protestant countries.

One interesting ecclesiastical architectural feature developed after the Reformation in England. William Laud (1573–1645), archbishop of Canterbury, is credited with fixing the altar permanently on the east wall. At that time the altar was being profaned by a variety of uses, so Laud initiated a rule that the altar should have rails around it. This shift emphasized the altar as the central feature for Anglican worship, rather than the pulpit, which had been an increasingly common focus of attention among Anglican preachers. This Anglican influence on ecclesiastical architecture remains to this day, even in North America.

Beginning in the seventeenth century, another style of architecture was introduced to church buildings: the elaborate architecture of the Baroque period (and its more refined form, Rococo). At first the Baroque was a return to an earlier Byzantine (circular) style of design, except that the ornamentation and elaborate arch work prohibits such comparison. "Baroque architecture was theatrical, known for its flamboyant movement, color, and detail, and its twisted columns. . . . Nothing was simple in Baroque churches. Everything was designed to create effects and awaken the senses."[29] This period also included the heyday of the theater, so the church took on theatrical dimensions, particularly in its decorations. Even the gilding found in Baroque churches was portrayed as providing a more heavenly backdrop for the liturgy. One of the most famous examples of Baroque architecture is the church of the Fourteen Saints (*Vierzehnheiligen*) in the region of Bavaria, Germany. The building is almost a metaphor for the gates of heaven. The lavishly tex-

tured interior walls and the dramatic scenes painted on the ceiling draw the worshiper into the mystery and majesty of the glorious realms above.

In England, the rood-screen was often left intact (because organ pipes had frequently been built on them) and separated the church building into two rooms: the
nave for the preaching of the Word and the choir for the Lord's Supper.[30] This can
still be observed in many Anglican and Episcopal churches in Europe and North
America.

Sir Christopher Wren (1632–1723), noted British architect, experimented with
a variety of architectural styles that would provide a suitable environment for hearing the sermon. He introduced the "auditory church," which had several galleries
that emphasized hearing over seeing. One of his designs provided seating for as
many as 2,000 people.[31] This increased emphasis on preaching led to a more prominent pulpit in a more acoustically accommodating setting, even in Roman Catholic
churches.[32]

Since the nineteenth century, a variety of ecclesiastical architecture styles have
flourished in quiet competition. Gothic, Renaissance, Reformation, and Baroque
styles have grown together and been adapted to a variety of settings in Europe and
North America. The Protestant spirit of independence has given rise to a perplexing
variety of architectural combinations in an attempt to communicate various distinctions and emphases of Christian theology and life.

In North America a few additional architectural features developed. Pew boxes
emerged as a distinct feature of New England churches, along with a gallery around
three sides of the nave for greater emphasis on hearing. The altar, desk, and pulpit
were concentrated in the front of the church. In the North American frontier, many
Lutheran congregations built a significantly raised pulpit above a highly ornate
altar, which symbolized a Word and Sacrament orientation.[33]

A neoclassicism arose in the late eighteenth century and influenced nine-
teenth- and twentieth-century architecture. Stately Ionic columns supported domed
ceilings and round arches to create a central forum for worshipers. A renewed interest in classical antiquity among architects of the era enabled key elements of the
Greek temple to shape Christian houses of worship in a peculiar way. Churches
built around this time are usually wider than they are deep, and the pews are often
set in a semicircular floor plan.

In North America today ecclesiastical architecture is as diverse as the denominations that enlist ideas for new church buildings. Revivalism of earlier traditional
styles (neo-Romanesque, neoclassical, and neo-Gothic, to name a few), as well as
extremely creative designs that have no ecclesiastical precedent, have been built in

the twentieth century.[34] Many congregations follow a pattern they have seen in other churches without investigating the theological message of the architecture. This may be most apparent as auditoriums or theaters have become models for some of the newest church construction among North America's megachurches. "The word 'auditorium' is often used in reference to churches, and the personality of a preacher is too often the prime element in the service. Passive worship becomes the norm, though in fact passive worship is a contradiction in terms."[35] Any congregation contemplating a building or a renovation project should consider its mission and how it will do that mission at that location.

Modern church architecture has been marked by its use of an increasing variety of construction materials. The massive walls of the earlier cathedrals are no longer necessary, but many would say that the practical boxlike, factory-shaped buildings of the twentieth-century Bauhaus school are not attractive either. Glass, concrete, steel, and fabrications of a variety of other materials can be used in endless ways by architects. A sense of informality and a sense of community are two contemporary themes becoming architecturally evident in modern churches. These two themes, reminiscent of the early Christian communities, are giving impetus to new "houses for the church" (*domus ecclesia*), as God's people continue to gather to worship Him.

SIGNIFICANT SPACES FOR WORSHIP

When considering the architecture of a church, the most important concern is the interior space. After all, the interior of the church is where the gathered guests assemble to receive God's blessings and to respond to His gifts. Therefore, three significant spaces are often identified for special consideration—the altar area, the area for the baptismal font, and the area for the pulpit. Two of these are sacramental spaces, the third is proclamation space.

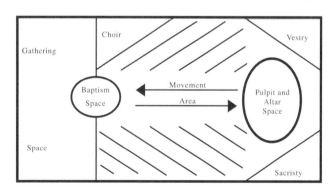

These three areas are key for communicating a theology of worship and a theology of God's gathered guests. Where the altar, the pulpit, and the font are located and how they are emphasized architecturally reveals much about the theology and beliefs of the people who are constructing the building. The location of these spaces also greatly affects the next generation's theological perspectives.

THE SACRAMENTAL SPACE OF THE ALTAR

The location and size of the altar communicates much about the theology and beliefs of those who worship in the sanctuary. In most Lutheran churches the altar occupies the most prominent place in the church, yet it is normally accessible to all the people. High altars with large railings, as in older Roman Catholic churches, communicate a sense of distance and a separation that is foreign to Lutheran theology. As noted earlier, Eastern Orthodox churches create a kind of Most Holy Place with an iconostasis, which intentionally blocks the altar from the view of the worshipers. In contrast, altars in non-Lutheran Protestant traditions are often diminutive tables that may even be removed for most corporate worship services. Lutheran churches generally have an altar of significant size and visual prominence, yet one that does not overshadow the pulpit.

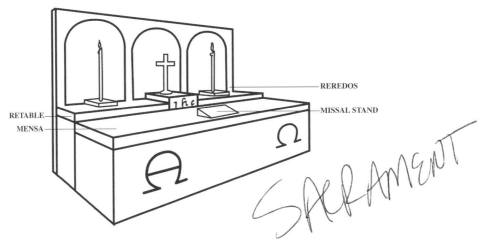

The illustration above shows the various parts of an altar that is located at the liturgical east of the chancel. Some churches have an elaborate reredos (a carved wooden panel or set of panels) or a dossal curtain (a floor- or altar-to-ceiling drapery or curtain, sometimes combined with a wooden latticework frame or support) behind the altar. Other churches have elaborate stained-glass windows or intricate mosaic images that visually designate the altar as a focal point. However, such items should not detract from the altar itself as a place where God's gifts are placed.

The altar is not a stand for papers, miscellaneous books, flowers, or other items not used for the Service of the Sacrament. These other items may be placed on the retable (a stepped platform behind the altar), if it is available, or on appropriately crafted stands, called credence tables, that are placed along a side or back wall in the chancel. The altar is for the bread and wine of Holy Communion and perhaps for a Bible and an altar book. If so desired, two candles may be placed on the altar to represent the two natures of Christ. If a crucifix is not present in the chancel behind the altar, one may be placed on the altar. The altar communicates a place of reception: God's gifts of the means of grace are distributed from this location.

In recent years altars have been moved away from the wall to provide the image of a table around which God's people gather. Particularly when using a free-standing altar, worship leaders should ensure that the least number of items are placed on the table to avoid clutter. Even the Communion elements are best brought to the altar during the Offertory with only a veiled chalice placed on the altar prior to the Service of the Sacrament. Side tables may hold the collection plates and other items for the worship service.

THE PROCLAMATION SPACE OF THE PULPIT

Preaching is the central activity for the communication of the Gospel. In many ways the pulpit emphasizes the Lutheran understanding of the pastoral office as a preaching office (*Predigtamt*) as compared to the Protestant emphasis on the person who holds the office. The proclamation of God's Word is the greatest activity in the church, and the pulpit is a visible witness to the importance of preaching God's forgiving grace in Christ.

In Christian churches the pulpit has been placed in various prominent locations. In the early church, the preaching chair was elevated behind the altar in the apse (to aid the preacher acoustically). Some preachers desired a preaching stand in front of the altar. During the Reformation, the pulpit was elevated over the people on one side of the nave away from the chancel. The pulpit's location carries significant theological implications. From the worshipers' perspective, the right side of the chancel is called the liturgical south. It represents the Epistle side of the church. A pulpit located on the right side emphasizes the didactic nature of evangelical preaching. A pulpit located on the liturgical north, which is called the Gospel side, emphasizes God's forgiving grace in Christ.

In some Lutheran congregations in Germany and North America, the pulpit was built over and behind the altar, creating a duality of focus (see illustration on next page).[36] More recent ideas about the location of the pulpit include the use of a freestanding altar with a pulpit-reading table built into the back of the altar. No design is completely satisfactory, so Lutheran congregations continue to struggle

with the question of how to communicate the centrality of both Word and Sacraments.

Sometimes the pulpit has been augmented with
a lectern or reading stand. While the lectern is a helpful piece of furniture in a large chancel, particularly
when several people read the Scripture readings,
more congregations are adopting the ambo, a reading
and preaching stand.[37] An ambo allows the reading
and the preaching of the Word to come from the
same place and elevates the theological significance of
Scripture reading and preaching.

THE SACRAMENTAL SPACE OF THE FONT

Besides the altar and the pulpit, a third significant space is the area set aside for baptisms. Early
baptisms occurred in the waters of a river (Acts 8) or,
perhaps, in the *mikvahs* (ceremonial bathing pools) of Jewish synagogues. As Christians began to meet in homes, bathing areas were renovated to meet the needs for
baptisms inside the house churches.[38]

As a result of increased numbers of baptisms in the fourth century, baptismal
fonts were featured prominently at the entrance of church buildings as a visible
sign that Baptism was the entrance to the Christian community. These baptismal
fonts often had six or eight sides, which was symbolic of the day of Christ's death
(the sixth day of the week) and the day of His resurrection (the eighth day). Early
Christian architects also designed cross-shaped fonts into which the candidates
stepped or were carried. An ancient cross-shaped font, now in the Museum of
Bardo in Tunis, was lined and surrounded by mosaics with images of the flood and
Noah's ark.[39]

As larger spaces were needed for multiple baptisms, baptisteries developed as
separate buildings that adjoined the narthex or chancel of a cathedral. Baptisteries
were often built in the shape of a pagan funerary mausoleum or tomb, thus associ-
ating Baptism with the biblical imagery of Christ's death and resurrection (Romans
6). In medieval cathedrals baptismal fonts were almost always positioned near the
entrance to the church.[40] Within the past two decades, the entrance of the church is
again becoming an increasingly common location for the baptismal font in
Lutheran churches. This location serves as a sign that Baptism is the entrance into
the family of God and a reminder to all worshipers of the continuing blessings of
Baptism. This location emphasizes the communal nature of the Sacrament of Holy

Baptism. Baptism is not a private act in the life of a lone Christian. Therefore, locating the font at the entrance of the church visually underscores that through Baptism a person is brought into the community of God's gathered guests.

Most early Christian fonts contained enough water so the baptized could stand in knee-deep water.[41] The font itself was large enough to allow for immersion of infants and to hold sufficient water for adults to have their entire bodies washed.[42] Luther explained that Baptism communicates the imagery of drowning and dying to sin and rising to new life.[43] Although the amount of water does not determine the effects of Baptism, traditional baptismal fonts are often too small and inconspicuous to adequately communicate such strong biblical and catechetical imagery.

THREE THEOLOGICAL EMPHASES

The design of a church should "accommodate the liturgy"; it should also "symbolize the doctrines."[44] Thus a congregation should carefully consider the architectural design of its worship space. As has been noted, Word and Sacraments are central to the worship experience of most Christian communities. Because of differing theological emphases, we can identify three basic interior designs in Western Christian architecture.

SACRAMENTAL EMPHASIS

Catholic theology and its resultant architecture can be called "sacramental." In Catholic churches the altar has the most prominent position and dominates the worshipers' view.[45] A lesser focus on the reading and preaching of the Word is usually evident by the size and position of the pulpit and/or lectern. Catholic architects have used a variety of means to emphasize the significance of the altar—size, elevation, or a canopy placed over the altar.[46] The centrality of the altar communicates the importance of the Lord's Supper as the primary means of grace for the congregation.

PROCLAMATIONAL EMPHASIS

Protestant theology and its architectural expression can be called "proclamational." The placement of the pulpit or preaching table centers the worshipers' attention on the speaker.[47] A small memorial table for use in an occasional Communion service is usually placed in a less prominent location.[48] Even when the altar may be at the center of the chancel, the pulpit is often larger in size and, though off to one side, clearly overshadows the altar. In Calvin's Geneva, the Church of St.

Pierre was remodeled to move the pulpit into the nave. On Sundays when Communion was served, a table was brought in; when an occasional Baptism was administered, a small basin was used.[49] The chief focus of St. Pierre was the pulpit.

Episcopal churches share a commitment to the Protestant emphasis on preaching and the Catholic emphasis on the Sacrament of the Altar. As a result many Episcopal (or Anglican) church buildings emphasize the altar; others emphasize the pulpit. Perhaps one of the best examples of a building that tries to communicate a dual emphasis on Word and Sacrament is the Church of the Redeemer in Baltimore, Maryland.[50] The altar is placed forward in the midst of the worshiping community, and the pulpit and lectern are on the rear corners of the chancel. Although there is an attempt to bring equity between the two, the altar takes precedence theologically and visually.

Dual Emphasis

In contrast to the Church of the Redeemer, consider Kramer Chapel on the campus of Concordia Theological Seminary in Fort Wayne, Indiana.[51] Designed by Eero Saarinen, the chapel features an altar set toward the back of the chancel as one focal point for the worshipers' attention. The pulpit and lectern are at the front edge of the chancel, just above the steps to the chancel. At this position they visually complement the altar in prominence. This is an attempt to communicate confessional Lutheran theology and its strong emphasis on the proclamation of the Word, as well as the administration of Holy Communion.[52]

Because of a dual emphasis on Word and Sacrament, Lutherans have struggled with how to communicate these theological emphases architecturally so altar and pulpit stand together.[53] After the Reformation, the *Kanzelaltar* (literally, pulpit-altar) was developed in Germany as a single place where verbal and sacramental actions could occur with equal emphasis.[54] During the post-Reformation era, as Lutheran churches were being built or formerly Catholic churches were being renovated, the pulpit-altar spread throughout the Lutheran heartland. Unfortunately, the rise of Pietism and Rationalism—both of which denigrated the means of grace—caused this structural distinction, which clearly embodied Lutheran theology, to be abandoned, especially as various earlier architectural styles were revived.

Some Lutheran congregations in rural North America adapted the idea of elevating the pulpit above the altar from Reformation era buildings. In such church buildings, the altar is usually larger and more impressive than in a building designed for a Reformed congregation. The *Frauenkirche* ("Virgin's Church," which was built on the site of the older Catholic Church of Our Lady) in Dresden, Germany, was designed and rebuilt by the Lutheran citizens of Dresden as a bold statement of faith. Known officially as the Evangelical Cathedral of Saints Peter and Paul, it was begun in 1726 to rival St. Peter's Basilica in Rome. Commissioned as chief architect, George Bähr designed an octagonal structure with seven balconies in which 3,500 worshipers could gather to hear the Word and participate in the Sacrament of the Altar. The church stood as a confession of the evangelical Lutheran faith until it was destroyed on April 15, 1945, in a bombing raid on Dresden.[55] Recently Our Savior Lutheran Church in Houston, Texas, built a sanctuary that is an excellent model of orthodox Lutheran theology and creative architectural integrity.[56] These churches exemplify the Lutheran emphasis on Word and Sacrament. While different congregations have unique structures, some architectural emphases communicate more clearly the centrality of this dual theological emphasis.

OTHER SPACES FOR WORSHIP

Three additional areas in the church building should be evaluated. These are the "gathering space," where the people assemble before and after the service; the "processional space," where ministers and worship participants enter the sanctuary; and the "worship space," the actual place where the people assemble to participate in the various worship activities. "Preparation space" is also necessary as a site for storage and preparation of items used in worship.

GATHERING SPACE

In our society a sense of community and a sense of intimacy vie for equal emphasis. A gathering space offers congregations several options to accomplish both. In many older church buildings little space was provided for the worshipers to gather before the service. Usually, the gathering occurred outside of the church building in a churchyard or on the parking lot. As people have become more sensitive to and secluded from the natural environment, however, less time is spent outside. Therefore, consideration is now given to where worshipers may gather.

The gathering space, or narthex, should be large enough so worshipers may greet one another before and after the service. Some congregations have renovated their structure to add such a meeting space. The space should be attractive yet not distracting from the worship space. It should offer comfortable traffic flow for those entering or exiting the sanctuary. Depending on the area of the country, space for hanging coats may be needed. When seeking a proper place to display a national flag, the gathering space is one of the best locations for a congregation to witness its allegiance. The gathering space also can serve as the location for a wedding party to greet guests and for the placement of a casket for viewing prior to a funeral. The baptismal font also may be located near this space, at the entrance to the worship space.

PROCESSIONAL SPACE

Processional space is often ignored, yet it is necessary for corporate worship. Processional space refers to those areas used for movement before, during, and after the service. How the congregation moves in and out of the church communicates much about how worshipers gather and scatter. Normally processional space is a central aisle, but that may not be the only option available to a congregation.

Processional possibilities encourage a congregation to consider the width and the length of the aisle.[57] Accessibility also deserves consideration. Congregations considering renovations should test whether a wheelchair can easily move into the worship space and whether movement in the processional space is possible if wheelchairs are present. In addition, if a congregation uses banners in processions or large groups often process, such as choirs, this may influence the width of the processional space or aisles. If candlestands are placed along the central aisle for Evening Prayer or for candlelight services, sufficient space should be available so worshipers do not bump the stands as they enter or depart the nave. As a congregation evaluates its side aisles, it may ask: Will these aisles be used for dismissal? Should side aisles provide the same access to the sanctuary as the central aisle?

Remember that processional space enables movement of wedding guests and the bridal party; it allows movement of mourners and the casket at funerals; it permits baptismal groups to enter the worship space; and it provides an avenue for confirmands and communicants to approach the altar. All these processional occasions invite worshipers to visualize themselves as a pilgrim people who follow the Lord Jesus, who is represented by the processional cross.

WORSHIP SPACE

The most significant space for a congregation is the worship space or nave. The word *nave* comes from the Latin *navis*, which means "ship." Early in the history of the Christian church the ark was commonly used as a symbol of salvation (1 Peter 3:20–21). Many churches with wood-beamed ceilings were intentionally constructed to look like inverted ship's hulls. As the early Christians taught, the one holy Christian church is the ship into which the saved are brought and in which they travel until they reach their heavenly home.

Several factors should be considered when evaluating the main worship space.

The nave is the area in which the congregation will spend most of its gathered time. Aesthetic, acoustic, visual, and physical concerns unite in regard to this site. Included in this evaluation of the worship space is the location of the musicians—the choir, organist, and other instrumentalists. Architecturally, it is important to understand that congregation members sing better when the music that leads them comes from behind. There is a psychological and emotional advantage to music that supports the congregation rather than "comes at them" from the front, particularly if music is recognized as our response to God's gifts to us.

Comfortable seating is a significant consideration when discussing worship space. Padded pews, though a rather recent innovation, do little to dampen the acoustics because there is little difference between people sitting on hard pews or padded pews. Increasingly, chairs are being used in smaller churches and for the area near the chancel in larger churches to provide greater flexibility in seating. It is best to replace metal folding chairs with permanent seating (chairs or pews) whenever possible.

The visual and aesthetic state of a church building is important too. Avoid a busyness in the décor; instead, worshipers should experience a sense of calm and comfort. The colors and design of the walls and ceilings may project a heavenly glow. Avoid visual obstructions or distractions that diminish the focus on the chancel, including bright windows behind the altar that may obscure the view of the minister at the altar or pulpit.

All these concerns regarding the worship space are important so the Word and Sacraments can take their rightful position of prominence among God's gathered guests.

PREPARATION SPACE

Perhaps one of the most neglected yet most necessary spaces for congregational worship is preparation space. Preparation is usually done in rooms—known as sacristies—located alongside the chancel. Sacristies are normally designed for the preparation and storage of Communion elements, candles, paraments, and altar cloths. Wise churchly practice suggests the sacristy might have running water, as well as a piscina or sacrarium[58] for the disposal of baptismal water and the Communion wine that remains in the chalice. However, God's Word does not include such requirements concerning the sacristy.

In addition to the working sacristy, another sacristy, sometimes called a vestry, is desirable for the pastor's preservice preparation and vesting. The vestry may serve as the pastor's office, but it should be easily accessible to the chancel. Some pastors prefer a vestry near the entrance to the church so they can greet people prior to the service, as well as be present for a procession at the beginning of the service.

THREE BASIC SHAPES FOR A CHURCH

Although there has always been variety within the basic structure of church buildings, most architectural consultants now identify three basic shapes: the processional or axial, the antiphonal, and the radial church.

PROCESSIONAL OR AXIAL

Chancel

The processional or axial building allows each congregation member to face the front of the building, the traditional location of both the altar and pulpit. If there is a center aisle, this style of church is designated as "axial," which is a beneficial shape if one wants to maintain order and to focus the worshipers' attention. Traditionally, the basilica plan is a symbol of the church militant in ordered rank and file.[59] This style communicates that the church is in the world but not "of the world" (John 17) as it directs the attention of the worshipers forward. In a sense, the arrangement protects the worshiper from the world as the community gathers before the Lord. Its beauty is such that it invites outsiders inside.

The negative aspect of the axial or processional design is that there is a sense of coldness and detachment from other individuals. Only the backs of other worshipers can be seen. A sense of shared communal worship is lost when face-to-face contact is avoided. This structure also requires an elevated altar and pulpit so the worshipers, even when sitting, can see and hear adequately.

ANTIPHONAL

Ambo

The antiphonal style of church design grew from the monastic tradition of daily devotional services in which the worshipers responded to one another by singing the psalms and reciting corporate prayers responsively. In this style of church, the ambo (pulpit/lectern or reading table) is at one end of the structure, and half the congregation faces the other half, like monastic choirs. This design facilitates a sense of intimacy among the worshipers, yet

Altar

it retains the focus on the altar (though normally this shape was used only for the Service of the Word). The altar is located opposite the ambo.

The difficulty with the antiphonal style is its lack of flexibility. Little can be done if large groups need to be accommodated. In addition, while it offers the intimacy of face-to-face contact, such proximity can be distracting. The focus may be taken from Word and Sacrament and placed on other worshipers.

RADIAL

The radial form is sometimes called the church "in the round" because it features the altar in the center of the gathered guests. Several adaptations of this basic shape are possible, but the focus is on the central altar as the congregation gathers on three or four sides. Otto Bartning, a famous German architect, proposed that the long, narrow processional or axial plans of traditional buildings are inappropriate to a Christian understanding of worship and the church. The proper view of the gathered congregation, Bartning said, is that of a cohesive community of clergy and laypeople (all priests) whose members are aware of their unity as the body of Christ, the family of God, the household of believers.[60] Thus the church in the round symbolizes "a family of believers .... The circle denotes the oneness of God and eternity under God."[61] Bartning's *Stern Kirche* in Germany exhibits his architectural goal.[62] Frank Lloyd Wright's Greek Orthodox Church of the Annunciation in Milwaukee, Wisconsin, is such a circular church, yet it retains the Eastern Orthodox chancel area with an enclosed altar area at one side.

A more pragmatic, modern, multipurpose approach to the worship setting is suggested by the church architect E. A. Sövik. He calls his design a "centrum," which is "a place for more than one purpose, and must be so seen, and so used. . . . In the first place, we must be reminded that the Christian community is a pilgrim community that has no certain resting place . . . . In the second place, we may hope that the church can supply the comfort of permanence in a world of change."[63] The multipurpose facility that Sövik proposed and built provides ample room for a variety of activities but allows a specific place for the gathered guests. A distinct disadvantage of such a multipurpose room is that the worship space is not permanent and must be set up each time a service is planned.

Whatever God's gathered guests do as they design their places of worship, they may recall the following: "A Christian congregation assembles (at least once each week) to worship the Lord in prayer and song and to be instructed in the Scriptures . . . . It is done to please God. Any part of this sacred act which is done to please the congregation or glorify man is not an act of worship."[64]

EVALUATING A CONGREGATION'S WORSHIP SPACE

Rarely does a congregation have the opportunity to build a new worship facility. Only "once every several generations"[65] can a congregation acquire the funding to renovate an existing building. Therefore, when the time comes, certain considerations should be made regarding the congregation's needs prior to any final decision. Four areas should be evaluated when assessing a congregation's worship space: visibility, audibility, flexibility, and simplicity.[66]

VISIBILITY

Lighting in a church is often the most neglected yet most important aspect of visibility and flexibility. Where lights are located, how they are controlled, and how much flexibility is possible are important issues to address. Sufficient lighting provides adequate illumination during the day, as well as during evening services. The ability to change lighting quality and intensity and to provide a variety of effects both in the chancel and in the nave should be reviewed when an architectural change to the nave is considered.

With modern structural steel and concrete, large columns in the middle of the worship space no longer need to be features in new church construction. Older buildings with columns along side aisles may result in obstructed views. Congregational leaders will want to consider how the worship activities of the congregation—particularly how the liturgy is conducted and how the pastor preaches—may become more visible to worshipers in such settings. Similarly, balconies often create difficult lines of sight, and an architect may be able to eliminate these problems when renovations are considered.

AUDIBILITY

The effective production and use of sound in a church is more significant than the lighting. Modern sound equipment provides great advantages over the large cathedrals with only an apse to aid the preacher's voice. Acoustics systems that provide quality sound yet do not dominate the sanctuary visually are highly recommended. Sound equipment should be checked before every service, including the strength of batteries used in portable microphones. In addition, trained personnel should monitor the settings of the sound system throughout the service. Musicians also may need to have their voices or instruments amplified. Care should be taken that such amplification does not overwhelm worshipers but assists the natural sounds of the voices and instruments.

Whether a church should have padded or hardwood pews is often a topic of debate. Most acoustical consultants advise that the sound varies little between a congregation with padded pews and one with fully occupied hardwood pews. More important acoustically are the surfaces of the floor, walls, and ceiling. Carpeting can deaden the sound of a worshiping congregation's praises and responses. A less-carpeted worship space requires less amplification. A worship space with a carpeted central aisle and hard surfaces under the seats or pews is probably a good compromise for most churches. Acoustical consultants can provide congregations with a variety of resources to meet every local need for sound.

FLEXIBILITY

The flexibility of many congregational worship spaces is limited. Here is where newer churches sometimes have an advantage. Congregations evaluating their worship space often realize they could use the space in the nave to a greater advantage if they had more flexible seating. Pews, though traditional because they can seat various numbers of worshipers, are not easy to rearrange. Chairs provide more flexibility and are being introduced in congregations of all sizes. Interlocking chairs can be set in traditional arrangements, yet they provide flexibility when other uses are required for the same space. Mission congregations might move from metal folding chairs to a more permanent worship plan that employs the flexibility of interlocking chairs. Larger congregations may find that they can improve the flexibility of the worship space by removing several pews from the front of the church and replacing them with chairs designed specifically for worship.

Flexibility in the chancel is also possible. Some congregations use large portable pulpits and lecterns to enlarge the chancel space for dramas or other non-liturgical uses of the facilities. However, too much flexibility can create a sense of chaos before a service and a sense of uncertainty surrounding the means of grace. Removable altar railings are one means to provide flexible alternatives in most chancels.

In recent years some Lutheran congregations have introduced projection screens in the chancel. This innovation facilitates corporate singing from a variety of sources other than a hymnal or songbook. Preachers may use these screens to provide an outline for the message as well. Lutheran congregations will want to evaluate the central importance of Word and Sacrament in worship before adding expensive projection equipment. The location and visual attractiveness of this equipment should be weighed against the possibility that it removes the focus of the congregation from the Word and Sacraments. On the other hand, such a screen can be used during the worship service to feature works of liturgical art that will edify the congregation and underscore the Gospel's proclamation.

SIMPLICITY

Simplicity of form and design is paramount in the design of a church's worship space. Cluttered altar areas and chancels may make worshipers uneasy. Music stands and equipment should be removed from a congregation's worship setting after use. Flower stands and seasonal decorations should be attractive but not distracting from the altar and pulpit. When an object has served its purpose, it should be removed from the chancel.

The architecture that surrounds and supports the liturgy of the church aids significantly in communicating the theology of God's people and their response to His gracious gifts. As God's gathered guests, Lutheran worshipers unite to focus their attention on these gifts, to be strengthened in their faith, to be encouraged as a pilgrim community, and to be challenged for continued service to God in the world.

SOME QUESTIONS TO CONSIDER

1. What effect does architecture have on our general activities and attitudes? Give three illustrations of how architecture can provide elevating or transcendent experiences.

2. How does the house church in Dura-Europos illustrate the early concept of a Christian assembly?

3. Why was the basilica chosen as a model for Christian churches in contrast to pagan shrines? How did this choice advance Christianity?

4. What place did preaching have in early, medieval, and Reformation churches? How did the buildings change with each new era?

5. Describe the sacramental and proclamational spaces in your congregation. Explain what is good about those spaces. What could be changed and why?

6. How do theological distinctions among mainline Christian denominations affect the architecture of their churches? Give an illustration of one distinction from your own experience.

7. Why is it important to consider gathering space, worship space, and processional space? How do these spaces affect God's gathered guests?

8. List the advantages and disadvantages of the three basic church shapes.

9. If you were granted $5 million to renovate your home congregation, how would you undertake the project? What would you change, and what would you keep?

NOTES

1. Bruggink and Droppers, *Christ and Architecture*, 1. See especially the first chapter, "Theological Architecture."

2. Commission on Church Architecture, the LCMS, *Architecture and the Church*, 12.

3. Simons and Fitzpatrick, *Ministry of Liturgical Environment*, 10, without reference to source.

4. In 1983, Concordia University Wisconsin moved from a small Milwaukee campus to a 100-acre campus with a large chapel. (The chapel and campus were built by the Roman Catholics in the 1960s.) This move had a significant effect on student chapel services. The change from an intimate chapel with seating for less than 200 worshipers to a chapel that could accommodate more than 700 caused students to speak of a "cold" chapel and a desire to return to the comforts of the former campus.

5. Simons and Fitzpatrick, *Ministry of Liturgical Environment*, 15.

6. See *Gathered Guests* chapter 9.

7. Dix, *Shape of the Liturgy*, 16–27.

8. See Hopkins and Baur, *Excavations at Dura-Europos*; Rostovtzeff, *Dura-Europos and Its Art*; and Kraeling, *The Christian Building*.

9. Jungmann, *Public Worship*, 56, as well as Jungmann, *Early Liturgy*, 17.

10. The rescript issued at Nicomedia by Licinius on 13 June 313 simply stated: "When we, Constantine Augustus and Licinius Augustus, met so happily in Milan, and considered together all that concerned the interest and security of the State, we decided . . . to grant to Christians and to everybody the free power to follow the religion of their choice, in order that all that is divine in the heavens may be favorable and propitious towards us and towards all who are placed under our authority" (Lactantius, *De mortibus persecutorum*, xlviii). See also Eusebius, *Ecclesiastical History*, X.v.

11. Senn, *Christian Liturgy*, 164–65, notes the distinction between the Byzantine church and the Roman basilica.

12. This Greek word refers to a reedy plant sometimes carried by nobles and public officials. When the officials gathered to enter a public building (basilica), the meeting place outside the main room became known as the narthex. Thus the gathering space of a church is often referred to as the narthex.

13. For more information and an illustration of an iconostasis, see the discussion in *Gathered Guests* chapter 9.

14. Jungmann, *Early Liturgy*, 137–38, suggests that the freestanding altar, at which the clergy faced east, caused the people to turn their backs to the altar as they faced east with the priests for prayer. Beginning in about the fifth century, churches increasingly were built with the apse at the east so the clergy and laity both faced the same direction for prayer. This provides one possible explanation for altars positioned at the far wall of the chancel.

15. Clowney and Clowney, *Exploring Churches*, 46.

16. MacDonald, *Early Christian and Byzantine Architecture*, plate 8, illustrates an early Christian chancel with an extended pulpit.

17. In the east, Emperor Justinian (A.D. 483–565) rebuilt St. Sophia in Constantinople with a large pulpit of rare marble. The pulpit was decorated with gold and had a platform large enough for his coronation and a choir space below (see Milburn, *Early Christian Art*, 123).

18. Clowney and Clowney, *Exploring Churches*, 26, have an illustration of such a pulpit.

19. Hammond, *Liturgy and Architecture*, 38.

20. Gerson, *Abbot Suger and Saint-Denis*, 3–40.

21. Clowney and Clowney, *Exploring Churches*, 61.

22. Pecklers, "History of the Roman Liturgy," 155.

23. The remnant of this divider is the reredos and dossal curtain, which appear behind altars that are not freestanding. Many congregations adopted this architectural construction unaware that it was only a "half altar."

24. The clearest illustration of such architecture is Lincoln Cathedral in England. Similarly, the Cathedral of Mexico City has a large organ and choir loft in the nave.

25. Clowney and Clowney, *Exploring Churches*, 12–13.

26. The following architects and artists were involved: Bernardo Rosselini (1409–1464) began the project before it was suspended for half a century. Bramante (d. 1514), Raphael (d. 1520), Peruzzi (d. 1536), Sangallo (d. 1546), and Michelangelo (d. 1564) worked to complete the basilica.

27. Travelers in the Eastern United States need only visit a few New England churches to see the pew boxes associated with many Puritan and Congregational churches.

28. "I am not of the opinion, as are the heterodox, that for the sake of the Gospel all arts should be rejected and eliminated; rather, I feel strongly that all the arts, and particularly music, should be placed in the service of him who has created and given them" (Luther, *Sämmtliche Schriften*, 10:1424, translated in Halter, *Practice of Sacred Music*, 11).

29. Pecklers, "History of the Roman Liturgy," 162.

30. Bruggink and Droppers, *Christ and Architecture*, 86.

31. Davies, "Architectural Setting," 34.

32. Pecklers, "History of the Roman Liturgy," 155, also notes that the first such church that emphasized preaching was the Church of Gesu in Rome, built by the Jesuits between 1568 and 1575.

33. See comments on the *Kanzelaltar* on pp. 211–12, 214.

34. One of the most unique and famous buildings is Le Corbusier's Chapel of Notre Dame du Haut in France.

35. Clowney and Clowney, *Exploring Churches*, 86.

36. Architects of the Reformed tradition also have produced some attractive pulpit-altars, as is evident in Bruggink and Droppers, *Christ and Architecture*. However, the altars are often more diminutive than those in most Lutheran congregations.

37. The word *ambo*, according to Milburn, *Early Christian Art*, 123, comes from a Greek word for "raised-up place," or reading desk. Others have attributed the word to the Latin word for "both." Thus the word refers to the fact that this large podium is used both for Scripture readings and for preaching.

38. Goranson, "7 vs. 8," 22–33, 44.

39. Milburn, *Early Christian Art*, 205.

40. The tradition of making the sign of the cross with holy water grew from the practice of worshipers recalling their Baptism as they entered the church building.

41. Milburn, *Early Christian Art*, 204.

42. An early liturgical handbook describes the baptismal scene this way: "Give public instruction . . . and then baptize in running water 'in the name of the Father and of the Son and of the Holy Spirit.' If you do not have running water, baptize in some other. If you cannot in cold, then in warm. If you

have neither, then pour water on the head three times 'in the name of the Father and of the Son and of the Holy Spirit'" (Richardson, "The Didache," vii, in *Early Christian Fathers*, 174).

43. LC, "Baptism," 65 (K-W, 464–65).

44. Commission on Architecture, the LCMS, *Architecture and the Church*, 12.

45. Liturgical Commission of the Roman Catholic diocese of Superior, Wisc., "Diocesan Building Directives," 7–9, 43–44 (cited in Hammond, *Liturgy and Architecture*, 36), states: "[The Christian altar] must possess absolute prominence over all else contained by the church . . . It must be the unchallenged focal point of the building."

46. Simons and Fitzpatrick, *Ministry of Liturgical Environment*, 24, note that "the altar is holy and sacred. [It] is central to the Eucharistic celebration. This should be reflected in its location."

47. Bruggink and Droppers, *Christ and Architecture*, 94, say that "to achieve an unmistakable visual statement concerning the indispensability of the Word, by far the most exciting architectural opportunities lie in the sounding board" (a large architectural canopy above and behind the pulpit). Bruggink and Droppers also provide many visual examples of a variety of Reformed church buildings, along with some Roman Catholic buildings, that clearly illustrate this emphasis.

48. A visit to the Crystal Cathedral in Orange, California, illustrates this emphasis, as does watching many prominent television evangelists.

49. Davies, "Architectural Setting," 34.

50. See the illustration in Commission on Architecture, the LCMS, *Architecture and the Church*, 98.

51. See the illustration in Commission on Architecture, the LCMS, *Architecture and the Church*, 96.

52. A similar placement of the altar, pulpit, and lectern is evident in the Chapel of St. Timothy and St. Titus on the campus of Concordia Seminary, St. Louis, Missouri.

53. As an example, consider Trinity Lutheran Church, Altenburg, Missouri, and Concordia Lutheran Church, Frohna, Missouri, which feature both altar and pulpit in the center, a style imported from Germany. James White (*Documents of Christian Worship*, 58, 63, 65) also illustrates an early North American Lutheran building with this architectural distinction. While this architectural feature is particularly true of Lutherans, some other sacramental Protestant groups—such as Episcopalians and some Reformed and Methodist congregations—have sought to convey architecturally the duality of Word and Sacrament. See Commission on Architecture, LCMS, *Architecture and the Church*, 90–102.

54. Mai, *Der Evangelische Kanzelaltar*, 201.

55. See Magirius, *Dresden: Die Frauenkirche*.

56. I wish to thank the Rev. Lawrence White, pastor of Our Savior, Houston, Texas, for sharing some of his plans and ideas.

57. See *Gathered Guests* chapter 7 for a discussion of the use of processions in the liturgy.

58. *Piscina* and *sacrarium* are used nearly synonymously to refer to a special sink that allows its contents to flow directly onto the ground. Most church architects have experience in constructing this receptacle for consecrated elements.

59. Commission on Architecture, the LCMS, *Architecture and the Church*, 12.

60. Sövik, *Architecture for Worship*, 29–30.

61. Commission on Architecture, the LCMS, *Architecture and the Church*, 13.

62. Sövik, *Architecture for Worship*, 30.

63. Sövik, *Architecture for Worship*, 70.

64. Commission on Architecture, the LCMS, *Architecture and the Church*, 13.

65. Mauk, *Places for Worship*, 10.

66. Simons and Fitzpatrick, *Ministry of Liturgical Environment*, 22.

CHAPTER 12
MUSIC IN THE LORD'S SERVICE

When people gather for special occasions, song often springs forth. Whether it is a birthday party or a ball game or even impromptu dinner gatherings, music and song are part of the pageantry of community celebrations. This phenomenon is also true when God's gathered guests assemble for worship. But how does music affect the theology and practice of worship in a Lutheran setting?

MUSIC IN WORSHIP

Music is intimately connected with Christian worship. When God's gathered guests assemble, singing and worship cannot be separated. Because of God's gracious gifts to His people, particularly through the forgiveness accomplished in Jesus' life, death, and resurrection, Lutheran worshipers join Christians throughout the world to offer God joyous and grateful praise. *Hallelujahs* sung in a grand corporate setting with magnificent musical accompaniment seem a fitting offering to God. Music also enhances the central feature of Lutheran worship, the Word of God. Consider Psalm 33:2–4: "Praise the LORD with the harp; make music to Him on the ten-stringed lyre. Sing to Him a new song; play skillfully, and shout for joy. For the word of the LORD is right and true; He is faithful in all He does." Martin Luther once said, "The Word of God will go to the heart more directly when it is sung."[1]

Throughout the history of Christianity, music has had a twofold purpose: the glorification of God and the edification of His people.[2] These purposes are accomplished particularly through the creation of musical settings for biblical texts. Until the middle of the eighteenth century, around the time of Johann Sebastian Bach's death, music was chiefly prepared and performed in the church for the Lord's service. From a biblical perspective, worship and music have gone together for generations.[3] From the edges of the Red Sea (Exodus 15:2–21) to the steps of the Lamb's throne (Revelation 15:1–4), God's people have gathered before Him to proclaim

His praises in psalms, hymns, and spiritual songs. Lutherans are part of this great Judeo-Christian history of song.

In the Old Testament, tabernacle and temple worship involved singers and music (1 Chronicles 25; Ezra 3:10–11). The Book of Psalms, the perpetual hymnbook of God's faithful people, provides numerous examples of music used in worship as believers expressed faith, hope, and trust in God. Because the psalms express almost every human emotion and devotional theme, these 150 songs of faith have been sung more than any other texts in Judeo-Christian worship. The prophets, particularly Isaiah, depict the angels of heaven singing praises to God eternally (Isaiah 6).

In the New Testament, music continued to unite believers in eternal worship of God. Jesus sang a hymn with His disciples after instituting the Lord's Supper (Matthew 26:30; Mark 14:26). Paul and Silas witnessed to their faith as they sang in prison (Acts 16:25). The early Christian congregations were encouraged by Paul to sing "psalms, hymns and spiritual songs" (Colossians 3:16; Ephesians 5:19). James advised early Christians, "Is anyone happy? Let him sing songs of praise" (5:13). Finally, the Revelation to John depicts choirs of angels and believers praising and proclaiming the Victor and His victory (Revelation 4:8, 11; 5:9–14; 7:9–12).

Scriptural paraphrases, usually referred to as canticles, have dominated the worship life of Christians for centuries as God's gathered guests have sung the songs of Miriam and Moses, of Hannah and Hezekiah, as well as selections from Isaiah, Proverbs, Acts, Paul's epistles, and Revelation. These great hymns of the church reflect the natural response of God's people to His gifts. Particularly significant are the songs of the New Testament that the church has incorporated into her liturgy. Mary sang a magnificent song of humble praise in response to the angel's announcement of Christ's birth through her (the Magnificat is taken from Luke 1:46–55). Zechariah sang a song of praise and prophecy in response to the announcement of the name of his son, John the Baptist, the forerunner of the Christ (the Benedictus is taken from Luke 1:68–79). The angel choir sang a joyous song extolling the birth of Christ (the Gloria in Excelsis is taken from Luke 2:14). Simeon, the aged sage, sang a hope-filled song in response to holding his Savior in the temple (the Nunc Dimittis is taken from Luke 2:29–32). The whole of heaven joins in praise of God's gift of salvation in Christ, the Lamb, in the final book of the New Testament. From Revelation come several variations in recent hymnology: "Worthy Is Christ" (taken from Revelation 5:12, 9, 13; 7:10, 12; 19:4, 6–9),[4] "Worthy Is the Lamb" (Dignus est Agnus is taken from Revelation 5, 15, 19),[5] and "This Is the Feast" (taken from Revelation 5:9–13; 19:4–9).[6] In addition to these biblical texts, the Te Deum Laudamus, though composed sometime after the New Testament, has acquired the status of a canticle because it enables the redeemed people of God to praise the Father, Son, and Holy Spirit for the gift of salvation through Christ, who will return as judge.[7]

Accounts of singing portions of the Christian liturgy enter the literary record around A.D. 200. Hippolytus (ca. A.D. 170–236) describes the singing of the Hymn of Light.[8] In contrast to pagan music, Christian music was not offered to placate God or to please the worshipers; it was an act of love and devotion in response to God's activity in Christ.[9] Early in the second century, with the rise of popular heretical songs,[10] the Christian church encouraged singing biblically based, orthodox texts. Songs such as "Shepherd of Tender Youth"[11] by Clement of Alexandria (ca. A.D. 160–ca. A.D. 215) were originally written as guides for converts.[12] These songs were sung in Greek until the early fourth century, when Latin hymns were written to oppose Arianism.[13] Ambrose's (A.D. 340–397) great morning hymn "O Splendor of the Father's Light" and evening hymn "O Trinity, O Blessed Light," along with "Savior of the Nations Come," survive in *Lutheran Worship* from among almost one hundred hymns attributed to his composition.

Singing during these first few centuries of Christian worship was normally in unison.[14] The first bishop of Antioch, Ignatius (ca. A.D. 35–107), wrote: "Every one of you should become a choir so that, singing together in harmony [and] taking your pitch from God, you may in unison with one voice sing praise through Jesus Christ to the Father."[15] Similarly, Bishop Clement of Rome (A.D. 92–103) wrote: "We, then, should assemble with one accord, [and] with one heart should cry out without ceasing to Him as with one mouth."[16] Three hundred years later, the great preacher John Chrysostom (ca. A.D. 347–407) instructed his congregation about the significance of their singing:

> The psalm which occurred just now in the office blended all voices together, and caused one single fully harmonious chant to arise; young and old, rich and poor, women and men, slaves and free, all sang one single melody . . . . All the inequalities of social life are here banished. Together we make up a single choir in perfect equality of rights and of expression whereby earth imitates heaven. Such is the noble character of the Church.[17]

As Christians gathered for worship each week, they continued the practice of singing and praising God together. However, as music changed throughout the centuries, gifted individuals and groups took on the roles and responsibilities of cantor and choir. In part, the origins of these roles can be explained by the rarity of books, which meant most music for worship had to be memorized. Particularly for elaborate services, choirs had to memorize tremendous amounts of musical and textual material.[18] Gradually, music became profoundly edifying and something that was enjoyed by the worshipers but not something in which they participated. The choirs took over the function of the worshiping community. Yet from the great theologians of the Middle Ages came such congregational hymns as "O Sacred Head, Now Wounded" (Bernard of Clairvaux, 1091–1153) and "All Creatures of Our God and King" (Francis of Assisi, 1182–1226).

Church music after the twelfth century grew rapidly. From simple unison chant to elaborate descants and multivoiced choirs, the music employed for worship became more diverse and multifaceted. Yet by the fifteenth century, music had taken on a life of its own, one almost separate from the liturgical service for which it was intended. Luther Reed's comment is noteworthy: "Counterpoint was carried on through single and double, augmented and diminished, direct, inverted, and retrograde, until it obscured the rhythm and the words and almost broke under its own weight."[19] Similarly, Gregory Dix noted that the medieval approach to worship reduced the participation of the people to merely seeing and hearing, which resulted in worshipers who were further removed from the liturgy and relegated to thinking and feeling through personal private devotions.[20]

Luther understood the importance of music in worship.[21] In his essay "Concerning Music," Luther asserted: "I am not pleased with those who, like all the fanatics, despise music. Music is a gift of God, not of men. Music drives away the devil and makes people happy; in the presence of music one forgets all hate, unchastity, pride, and other vices. After theology I accord to music the highest place and the greatest honor."[22] As a result of his position on music, Luther reintroduced congregational singing to the worship life of the church. In a letter to a colleague in 1523, Luther said, "Following the example of the Prophets and Church Fathers, I intend to supply German psalms or religious songs, so that the Word of God may live among the people also in musical form."[23] Fifteen years later, in a preface for a publication of music for several voices, Luther wrote:

> Experience testifies that, after the Word of God, only music deserves to be praised as the mistress and governess of the emotions of the heart . . . by which human beings are ruled and often torn asunder as if by their masters. A greater praise of music than this we cannot imagine. . . . It is out of consideration for this power of music that the Fathers and Prophets willed, and not in vain, that nothing be more closely bound up with the Word of God than music.[24]

No wonder one of the most respected and revered church musicians was Lutheran:

Head
Heart

Johann Sebastian Bach (1685–1750). Bach provided the church with choral settings of the highest caliber, as well as instrumental settings for important Lutheran texts.[25]

With the spread of the Reformation, tremendous changes occurred in the field of music for worship.[26] Bach and a few other Lutheran hymnwriters, such as Paul Gerhardt (1606–1676) and composer Johann Crüger (1598–1662), demonstrated the balance between head and heart that Luther had embodied throughout his lifetime. Within a century after Luther's death, a dichotomy seems to have occurred, and for the most part, music moved out of the church. The great polyphonic music of the late sixteenth century—with its multiple choirs, organs, and orchestras—nearly overwhelmed the liturgy. Clifford Howell comments critically about the Baroque era: "Music had become the mistress, rather than the handmaid, of liturgy; it submerged the whole Mass in a beautiful sea of sound, in which the liturgy was carried on unobtrusively in the depths, without any significance, coming to the surface of attention only when the music paused briefly at the Elevation."[27]

Coupled with this expansion in overtly and overly elaborate music for worship was the rise of Pietism, which centered its attention on the subjective, emotional, and immediately personal experience of the worshipers. Pietism weakened the objective Lutheran truths of salvation by grace through faith in Christ. As Luther Reed explains:

> The struggle for personal consciousness of conversion and regeneration led to an undervaluation of the objective means of grace .... Hymns based on objective facts of redemption were discarded for others expressive of immediate, personal experience. New and emotional tunes displaced the more vigorous chorales. Operatic arias and sentimental solos supplanted the impersonal polyphonic chorus music of the choir.[28]

More details and dimensions to the history of music in worship could be given, but this must suffice to indicate the importance of music for Christian worship. The diversity of forms and practices resulting from the Reformation and from the Enlightenment can be explored in greater depth through specialized study.[29]

A review of recent Lutheran hymnbooks discloses a clear emphasis on congregational song and the means of grace.[30] Liturgical services and the Propers for the church year take a prominent position at the beginning of these service books. Psalms and prayers usually follow. The bulk of these books, however, is centered on hymnody for the gathered guests. Hymns are arranged by the liturgical seasons, as well as thematically according to the central teachings of the Christian church. The congregation is corporately yet personally involved in the whole activity of worshiping the triune God through music. The essence of music in Lutheran worship has been well stated by Carl Halter:

> To love, respect, and use the gifts which God has given His Church in times past; to discard forms when they breathe a spirit contrary to Scripture; to create new forms when the need arises. Lutheranism occupies a middle position which is able to make the best of two worlds—old and new. Lutheranism at its best is neither tradition-bound nor immaturely contemptuous of the past.[31]

A Lutheran understanding of music for worship straddles the extremes yet offers a sensible position for nurturing new songs, as well as for singing the enduring scriptural songs of salvation.

Music is more expressive than speech and provides an intensification of emotions as tempo, pitch, volume, melody, harmony, and rhythm combine in a multitude of methods and styles. While this dimension of music may be abused, as Calvin and Zwingli recognized, which caused them to restrict or reject music for worship, Luther clearly distinguished music in general from church music, which had at its center the Word of God.[32] The function of music as a means to proclaim the Word is a key feature of church music. Robin Leaver explains the proclamational dimension of music this way:

> Sometimes this [proclamation] is done through the single voice of the cantor or minister, sometimes through the combined voice of choir and instruments, and sometimes through instrumental music alone. And then there is that unique proclamation of the whole people of God when they join their voices in one, in psalmody and hymnody, as they proclaim their response of faith to God and give witness of that faith to each other.[33]

This purposeful dimension of music for worship helps clarify the distinction sometimes unrecognized between secular music and church music.

Pope Paul VI in 1972 said, "Singing fashions a community, as the harmony of voices fosters the harmony of hearts. It eliminates differences of age, origin, and social class and it brings everyone into one accord in praising God, Creator of the universe and Father of us all."[34] Carl Schalk reiterates this theme: "True congregational song is song that unites the gathered assembly in common praise and prayer. . . . Above all it is a song that gathers the individual voices into one grand choir of praise as these respond to God's Word, acclaim the Gospel, and sing of their salvation in Christ."[35]

While there is no such thing as "Lutheran" music, some characteristics that grew out of the Lutheran Reformation can serve as hallmarks of the Lutheran practice of music in worship. Music in Lutheran worship is noted by the following adjectives: doxological (it focuses on praising the Trinity), scriptural (the texts are rooted in God's Word), liturgical (it fits into the ordered Communion service within the pattern of the church year), proclamational (it communicates the Gospel of Jesus Christ), participatory (the congregation actively sings), pedagogical (it teaches the truth of God's love and forgiveness in Christ), traditional (it is built on the best of the past), eclectic (it employs styles and practices from various sources that aid the Gospel), creative (it eagerly explores new expressions), and it aspires to excellence (it desires and seeks to give God the best).[36]

THE CHURCH MUSICIAN

While the pastor normally leads the corporate worship services in a congregation, the ministry of music is extremely important for the participation of God's gathered guests. The minister of music and the pastor work together and need a common understanding of the history, purpose, and practice of Lutheran worship, as well as an understanding of the wealth of liturgical resources available to the congregation.[37]

Most congregations depend on at least one main musician, usually an organist. The organist's chief function is to support the congregation's singing with strong, sensitive control. The organist should love the liturgy and recognize the great Lutheran treasure of music for worship, which is readily available for corporate and choral song and instrumental accompaniment. Through the effective use of musical introductions, tempo choices, registration settings, and harmonies, organists enhance the worship life and serve as ministers of music.[38] As the congregation becomes familiar with various parts of the liturgy, the organist may vary and embellish the accompaniment on festive occasions to stimulate further the congregation's faith-filled singing.[39] Solo organ music is often performed prior to and after the service and perhaps during the gathering of the offerings, at which time it is called a voluntary. For centuries Lutheran organists have used the prelude to acquaint the congregation with new hymn tunes, as well as to introduce the theme of the service through the use of melodies associated with liturgical and hymn texts.

The church musician is often a multitalented person who fulfills the responsibilities of a cantor.[40] The cantor is sensitive to the tastes of the people he or she serves.[41] Yet the church musician has particular responsibilities "to choose the music to be sung and played, to teach it, and to conduct its performance. No musician can accept responsibility for the music of the church if part or all of these functions are taken over by someone else."[42] A church musician or minister of music often has a positive, optimistic personality that is inspiring and motivating, fair, sincere, and modest. The capacity to grow in skills and knowledge are requisites a congregation will not only cherish but also encourage, in a conscientious cantor.

It is best when the organist and choir director of a Lutheran congregation are Lutheran because the background of the musician becomes evident in the choice of music and the way in which it is performed. As Hugo Gehrke states: "The richer the background in Lutheran doctrine, mores, and music, the more nearly will the musician approach the true ideal of a Lutheran musician and servant of God in the church."[43]

Other musicians besides the organist and choir director may contribute to the musical life of a congregation as they offer their services to the Lord at a specific congregation or for particular services under the direction of the church musician. The service of these musicians is an opportunity to praise God with the particular gifts with which He has endowed them, rather than an opportunity to perform. The spirit of humble service will be evident in all that musicians do to enhance the worship life of the congregation through the gift of music.

Congregational Singing

The congregation is not merely an audience; instead, the gathered guests participate in the glorious task of worshiping God. The chief activity in this worship is singing, which Luther reintroduced and emphasized. The singing or chanting of the traditional songs of the "ordinary" of the Divine Service is "the chief liturgical assignment of the people."[44] Joseph Gelineau, whose psalm settings are used throughout the world, writes: "The liturgy is the shared activity of a people gathered together. No other sign rings out this communal dimension so well as singing."[45]

Working together, the pastor and the church musician will seek to enhance the worship life of the congregation and extend the pastoral ministry to the gathered guests through sensitive musical selections and opportunities to experience the wealth of the church's musical tradition. In most Lutheran hymnbooks, this tradition includes a broad and eclectic base of historic, ethnic, and cultural sources.[46] A goal for every Lutheran worship leader should be that the whole congregation joins in singing God's praises. After all, the psalmist said, "Come, let us sing for joy to the LORD; let us shout aloud to the Rock of our salvation" (Psalm 95:1).

Chant

For millennia, participation in corporate worship involved chanting. Usually the clergy led the congregation's worship by chanting words to which the congregation sang a response in almost echo fashion. In the Old Testament, sung portions of

Scripture appear to have been used based on accounts of tabernacle and temple worship (1 Chronicles 16). These melodic texts without harmony followed the rhythm and accent of the spoken word but offered a musical dimension that enhanced the words for the hearers. Jewish Christians continued to follow the practice of chanting psalms and other biblical texts originally learned at the temple and synagogue.

The actual sounds of early chant are unknown because musical notation was not developed until the eighth or ninth century. From biblical and extrabiblical evidence, chant may have followed an echo pattern in which the congregation repeated what the leader sang, or it could have been a regular response that was repeated by the congregation after a section of text was sung by the leader (Psalm 136). Some scholars have suggested that chant could have been a kind of dialogue between leader and congregation or between two parts of the congregation.[47] In all cases, congregational involvement was important in chant.

Chant was how the liturgy was conducted for most early Christians. Whether in small intimate settings or in large spacious areas with great numbers of people, music unified early Christian worship, just as it had Jewish worship.[48] Thus chant served as a characteristic feature of Christian worship, particularly the chanting of psalms or at least a psalm between the readings.[49] Joseph Gelineau writes, "Chant may be considered the form of singing that is best adapted to Christian worship."[50] These chants became increasingly standardized as Christianity spread throughout the Mediterranean region.

With the development of more involved chant forms after Ambrose (A.D. 340–397) and Gregory the Great (A.D. 540–604), liturgical and musical materials became more organized and elaborate so congregational participation gradually diminished. Gregory is credited with establishing schools for readers, which developed into the tradition of the *schola cantorum* (school of singers).[51] Particularly with the standardization of various chants around the late sixth century, adaptations and elaborations of the basic plainchant and Gregorian chant continued until the thirteenth century, when other forms of music gained precedence. As polyphonic music (multiple pitches and harmonies) developed during the high Middle Ages and early Renaissance, choirs took over the major portions of liturgical song from the congregation.[52] Luther retained chant in his orders of service, though he added congregational hymns as an additional dimension to the congregation's worship practice.[53]

As a result of anti-Catholic sentiment among some Lutherans in the past century, much of the use of chant was lost. The traditional chanted dialogue between the pastor and congregation in the German services of the nineteenth and early twentieth centuries were not continued when the English service was introduced. The reclamation of a modified form of chant in Lutheran congregations at the end of the twentieth century has returned to the pastor and people some liturgical, sung conversations. The sung dialogues between pastor and people can enhance corporate worship and keep idiosyncratic styles from surfacing.

Contemporary approaches to chant are twofold. One approach repeats a long and cherished method. *Lutheran Worship* takes this approach with the Psalms.[54] The names of the ten chant "tones" follow traditional Greek nomenclature. Most Introits and Psalms for a designated Sunday have the same tone, which can also be used for the Gradual. The syllables or words of the text are sung to one note (the reciting tone), and the chant concludes with a two- or three-note phrase ending.[55] The easiest way to introduce chant to a group is to demonstrate several verses. Another approach to chant uses contemporary accompaniments, augmented by a sound system, to create a new sound. This approach is evident in the dated (though still used) *Chicago Folk Service*.[56] The refrains or choruses of many contemporary Christian songs follow this pattern and can be adapted to the liturgy of the church.

MUSIC OF THE LITURGY

• Congregational songs are usually of two kinds: hymns and music of the liturgy, though the five chief songs of the liturgy—the Kyrie, the Hymn of Praise, the Creed, the Sanctus, and the Agnus Dei—were also prepared as hymns by the Lutheran reformers.[57] The music of the liturgy offers numerous opportunities for the gathered guests to raise their voices in praise to God.

The Entrance Hymn sets the tone for the service and should be selected carefully. The alternative to the Entrance Hymn is the Introit—either a selected verse from a psalm or a whole psalm may be sung by the congregation or choir.[58] Handbells pitched to the chant tone for the psalm add a festive dimension to the Introit or Psalm of the Day when used in a procession on the great festivals of the church year. Instruments may be used to accompany and embellish an Entrance Hymn as well.

The Kyrie—also called the Diaconal Prayer or Litany—is sung responsively by the congregation and worship leader. Familiarity with this form of prayer enables the congregation to participate optimally. When the words, music, and patterns become second nature, the congregation may be better able to focus on the content of the petitions. Special petitions may be added prior to the final acclamation.

The Hymn of Praise, which follows the Kyrie, allows the congregation to express its joy at being in God's presence. Traditionally this hymn is the Gloria in

Excelsis and begins with the angels' Christmas chorus (Luke 2:14). Other canticles, more recently labeled as "liturgical songs,"[59] may be substituted as appropriate to the season of the church year—particularly the hymns from the Book of Revelation "This Is the Feast" or "Worthy Is Christ."

Perhaps more than any other part of the Service of the Word, the Psalm of the Day or the Gradual provides the opportunity for the congregation to join in songs, hymns, and spiritual songs. The Gradual normally is composed of selected Scripture verses that are used throughout a season of the church year. The congregation can learn the Gradual and sing it joyfully each Sunday after the first lesson is read. The Psalm of the Day picks up a theme from the readings and follows the ancient practice of singing from the Psalter in response to the reading of Scripture. This response may be antiphonal (one group alternates with another) or responsorial[60] (a single voice alternates with a group). The choir or cantor can determine the thematic link with the other texts and emphasize the theme with an antiphon.[61] Various musical settings of the psalms provide simple refrains for the congregation that draw out the liturgical theme. A director of music may even compose a psalm response for the congregation. The church musician should be familiar with three types of psalm settings: Gregorian, Anglican, and Gelineau.[62] In addition, the Protestant tradition handed down by John Calvin featured psalm-only singing for nearly 200 years. Church music from this Reformed tradition provides a wealth of versified psalms set to metrical tunes designed for hymn singing.[63] Erik Routley, however, notes that only sixteen psalms are ever sung in their entirety, even in Scottish worship services, which are strongly Calvinistic in origin.[64]

During Morning and Evening Prayer (Matins and Vespers), the psalms serve as texts for meditation. Therefore, they may be sung in a different style than that used during a regular Sunday worship service. A slower pace is more appropriate with time for silent meditation after each psalm. A variety of musical forms may be used during these services because a series of psalms in the same style can become monotonous rather than meditative. Antiphons by a choir or cantor may also be included before and after the chief psalm or at other times when the psalms are sung. Seasonal responsories would be appropriate for such antiphons.

The Salutation may occur as a sung dialogue between the pastor and the people. If chanted, organ accompaniment is required only if the pastor needs to hear the key change. The congregation's response may follow without intonation by the organist, though accompaniment supports a heartfelt response.

The Alleluia Verse and Gospel Procession may include liturgical chant and congregational participation. In festival seasons, the Alleluia Verse and Gospel Procession can incorporate the seasonal verse between the alleluias. That is, the congregation may sing the Alleluia Verse, then the choir or cantor may sing an extended verse. The traditional Alleluia Verse may also be sung as the Gospel Procession returns to the chancel. On Christmas, Easter, and Pentecost, hymns may be used in place of the traditional verse or the traditional Sequence Hymns may be used: "Of the Father's Love Begotten";[65] "Christians, to the Paschal Victim" or "Christ the Lord Is Risen Today; Alleluia";[66] and "Come, Holy Ghost, Our Souls Inspire."[67]

The Offertory allows numerous expressions of praise in a variety of musical offerings. Traditionally, a psalm verse was sung with an antiphon appropriate to the church year. A portion of Psalm 51—"Create in me"—or another psalm selection may also be sung. A choir may sing one of several offertory psalms, but alternative texts are also possible. Instrumental "offerings" may be made or an organ voluntary played as the congregation gives its monetary offerings.

The Communion Preface is one of the most ancient dialogues between worship leader and congregation. The simple musical accompaniment provides a dignified setting for the biblical texts, which invite the congregation to join the heavenly hosts in praising God as earthly worshipers anticipate His presence in the Sacrament.

The Sanctus and Benedictus are almost always grouped together liturgically. The Sanctus recalls Isaiah's great vision as he beheld the seraphim continually praising God before His heavenly throne (Isaiah 6:3). The Benedictus (Mark 11:9) recalls the joyous throngs of Jerusalem who welcomed Jesus. Both songs may be sung by the choir or the congregation or in combination for special occasions. These two songs are a musical and liturgical highpoint in the service as God's people anticipate receiving the Lord Himself in the Sacrament.

The Agnus Dei is the first Communion hymn, a hymn of adoration that draws out the congregation's faith and its hope. A variety of settings and arrangements are possible for the choir and congregation. Extended choral settings may be used for festival services, particularly if the worship leader treats the Agnus Dei as a distribution hymn.[68]

Music during the distribution of the Lord's Supper should underscore the central theme of the service, as well as the theological significance of the sacramental meal. Hymns designated for the congregation are best sung as a unit rather than stopped after a few stanzas only to restart after an interval. Such a practice may make it difficult for those returning from the altar to rejoin the congregation in singing. The time during Communion distribution is also an opportunity for the choir to acquaint the congregation with an unfamiliar hymn in its entirety. Special compositions offered during this portion of the service may include cantatas, though the music should not detract from the Sacrament.

The Post-Communion Canticle, which in Lutheran congregations is tradition-ally the Nunc Dimittis, allows the congregation to express its joy at being in Christ's presence. This Song of Simeon (Luke 2:29–32) underscores the eucharistic (thanks-giving) dimension of the service. A new canticle, "Thank the Lord and Sing His Praise," provides an alternative contemporary scriptural song that has become pop-ular in Lutheran congregations. Various settings of each canticle are available for congregational or choral use. Among the earliest practices of singing during Com-munion was the use of Psalms 145 and 34 during distribution and the Gloria Patri at the conclusion of the Sacrament. This may be another alternative to the tradi-tional canticles.

No closing hymn is necessary for worship because the Lord's blessing con-cludes the service. If music is needed for the pastor or choir to recess, the organist may play one stanza of a hymn used in the service prior to the recessional.

HYMNS

Hymnody has become the primary vehicle to express the priesthood of all believers in Lutheran theology. Luther understood that hymn singing actively engaged people in the liturgy. A noteworthy Lutheran contribution to the participa-tion of worshipers in the liturgy is substitution. Luther substituted German songs or hymns for the Latin texts of the liturgy.[69] Substitution continues to this day.

Because the chief function of music in worship is to communicate the truths of God's Word to His gathered guests, hymn selection is vitally important in Lutheran worship services.[70] In contrast to chant, hymns offer greater balance between music and text, and the musical harmony adds depth to the melodic lines. Pericopal preaching and liturgical planning that follows the church year enables worship leaders to select from a wide variety of hymn texts. Besides the Hymn of the Day, the Entrance Hymn holds the place of greatest importance because it reflects the theme of the service, as well as the particular Sunday's place in the litur-gical year.

The text of a hymn should be the key factor in its selection. Peter Brunner suc-cinctly states, "In a tangible, forceful, and impressive form the hymn visualizes and presents the message of salvation, or individual, important segments of it."[71] A hymn should be selected because it says something about God and His activity for humanity or because it provides worshipers with a concrete expression of their spir-itual lives. The best texts are rich in biblical and poetic imagery, and the best tunes

CONCORDANCE

feature strong melodies and rhythmic interest. Most pastors select hymns that follow a central theme of their message or of the day's worship, thus the hymn texts closely reflect the Scripture readings or themes of the liturgical season. A concordance to the hymnbook is a useful tool for researching themes or phrases in hymns.[72] Also helpful is a resource such as *Lutheran Worship: Hymnal Companion*, which provides background information on hymn texts and tunes, as well as biographical information on authors, translators, composers, and arrangers.[73]

Hymns should be selected with the congregation in mind. Entrance and closing hymns that are familiar to the congregation will set a jubilant tone for the service and leave worshipers with a joyous message as they depart. Hymns should also be appropriate to the season of the church year. New hymns, unfamiliar texts, or more challenging tunes are best introduced during the service, usually between the readings. During Communion distribution, a variety of hymns that suit the occasion and the Sacrament may be selected.

In recent years cultural considerations have increasingly become a concern when selecting hymns because hymns are one avenue to express cultural diversity. In fact, most hymnals contain hymns from a variety of sources.[74] A Lutheran statement on worship and culture describes worship as transcultural, contextual, countercultural, and cross-cultural.[75] Hymns reflect this multidimensional aspect of worship, and, with careful selection as noted above, they can be beneficial to a congregation.[76]

Hymns are sacred poetry set to music. Therefore, the tunes are also relevant for consideration. Most people judge whether they like a hymn by the tune rather than the text. Tunes also should reflect the time of the liturgical year. During the more somber and reflective periods, particularly Advent and Lent, solemn-sounding tunes are most appropriate. On the other hand, Easter requires bright and joyous tunes connected with all the celebrative texts. Similarly, an Entrance Hymn may offer a spirited setting as it leads the congregation into the theme for the day. If a closing hymn is used, it directs the people back into the world with the use of a more animated and enthusiastic tune.

The organist is crucial to a congregation's successful and enthusiastic singing of hymns. The accuracy and pace of an organ accompaniment can enhance or detract from a congregation's faithful worship. No single registration reflects the character of every hymn or even the content of all the stanzas of a hymn. Introductions to hymns also may be varied. Sometimes preludes for the Hymn of the Day will be appropriate; at other times a brief intonation of a few bars of the melody will be sufficient. Similarly, consistency of rhythm and articulation of phrases will advance the congregation's appreciation of hymn singing. Recognizing the textual nuances of a hymn can provide ample opportunities for organ variations within each hymn.

Some tunes are not easily learned by a congregation, yet the texts may be edifying. Consider selecting an alternate tune in such cases, which is possible by noting the hymn's metrical setting.[77] A text can often be sung to the tune of another hymn because they have the same meter. It is important that the change of tune is understood by the organist and the liturgist. A worship leader should go through the text with the new tune because on occasion the metrical settings may match but the rhythmic poetry does not. A music director may have a repository of tunes in addition to the congregation's hymnbook from which additional alternate tunes may be selected.

Much more can be said about the origin, development, writing, and harmonizing of hymns, an area of study called hymnology. Several resources are available to aid worship leaders and interested laypeople as they seek more information about hymns.[78]

Introducing New Hymns

There is no easy way to introduce new hymns, but it is always helpful to plan ahead. Unfamiliar hymns or new tunes can be introduced by the pastor and music director by alerting the congregation to the new hymn and the reasons for its introduction. The tune also may be used prior to the service or even as a prelude or voluntary the Sunday before it is introduced. A rehearsal prior to the service may help make a new song or portion of the liturgy singable by the majority of the congregation's members. Some ministers of music suggest that the congregation be "seeded" with choir members or children from the school or Sunday school who have already learned the new hymn or liturgical selection.[79] In this way, congregation members hear others near them who are singing strongly, which may help worshipers join in the new song more enthusiastically.

Another suggestion is to take a full month to introduce a new hymn or musical setting. The organist may play the music for several Sundays as a prelude, interlude, or postlude. A choir, especially a children's choir, may sing the hymn during the liturgy for the first week. The congregation may join in on the last stanza on the next Sunday. Finally, the congregation may sing the hymn several Sundays in a row. The hymn may be repeated a month or two later and at least once a year after that so the congregation remembers it.

The congregation's musical inclinations will play a large role in hymn selection. It is best not to have more than one new or difficult hymn in each service. Repeating difficult hymns over a period of time helps the congregation learn the hymn. However, worship planners must be careful not to overuse a hymn, whether it is new to the repertoire or an old favorite. One way to provide diversity follows a uniquely Lutheran approach: Hymn stanzas may be sung in alternation between the congregation and the choir. Occasionally the organ may "sing" a stanza as well.[80] This method may keep a new hymn or an old standard from becoming routine.

The Hymn of the Day

Beginning in sixteenth-century Lutheranism, a hymn was selected specifically to match the pericopal Scripture readings for each Sunday in the church year. This Hymn of the Day is not merely a sermon hymn or a paraphrase of the Gospel reading; instead, it corresponds to the Propers for the day.[81] Many of these hymns are Lutheran chorales.

Lutheran chorales are a unique body of texts and melodies that grew out of the Reformation and quickly spread throughout European Lutheranism. The texts spoke of sin and salvation, confession and forgiveness, subjugation and rescue, death and resurrection, this world and the world to come. The tunes were often drawn from Latin hymns and the folk-song literature of Luther's day. These ruggedly rhythmic, yet metric, melodies provided a characteristic vitality to early Lutheran worship. In 1599, Philipp Nicolai (1556–1608) presented two melodies to the church—"Wake, Awake, for Night Is Flying" (*Wachet auf*) and "O Morning Star, How Fair and Bright" (*Wie shön leuchtet*)—which have been known ever since as the king and queen of chorales.[82]

Contemporary Songs and Traditional Hymns

Creativity and artistic skills in the service of God and His people have been encouraged in every age.[83] Contemporary songs often display a wide spectrum of quality and character. These songs should be carefully critiqued before selection. Contemporary songs frequently represent contemporary sounds and ideas. They may speak to the present generation in a way no other hymn can do. On the other hand, some contemporary songs may also (and for the same reason) be absolutely "out of touch" just as quickly. An example of such an "in" and "out" are the antiwar songs of the 1960s. The oft-heard argument that Luther borrowed secular barroom songs for his hymn tunes has been definitively and decisively disproved.[84]

Because something is new does not make it good nor is something that is old necessarily bad. Traditional hymns are often preferred because they represent texts and tunes that have staying power. The words, though not necessarily profound, have touched the hearts of many people in a variety of life situations, and the tunes have remained singable for generations. Hymns have stood the test of time; contemporary songs are typically offered for the moment.

Lutheran chorales, when placed against most contemporary songs, often exhibit stronger tunes and express deeper theological truths. Richard Hillert states the issue constructively:

> Where the church has . . . lost sight of its liturgical heritage . . . nothing better
> can be expected than the kind of traditionless music for traditionless worship
> that has characterized some of the church's music making. Apathy and lack of
> identity with a clearly understood liturgical heritage and musical tradition invite
> the kind of indiscriminate influences from secular sources that are sometimes
> introduced in the name of innovation. Contemporary church music is in need
> of the element of innovation, but not of the wrong kind. Innovation has no
> value for its own sake but is significant and meaningful only when it is rooted
> directly in a real tradition—and in a profound understanding of and apprecia-
> tion for that tradition. Without tradition there is nothing to be innovative
> about.[85]

Thus contemporary songs and traditional hymns need to stand beside each other in a friendly tension between the best of the past and the best of the present for the sake of the future.

THE ROLE OF THE CHOIR

The ministry of the choir is that of serving the worshiping community by leading its response to God's gracious work. The ministry of the choir dates back nearly three thousand years to the time of David, when he appointed Levites as singers (1 Chronicles 15). Solomon also used singers at the dedication of the temple (2 Chronicles 5:12–14). Choir members should view themselves as servants and assistants, not as performers. They are gifted individuals who praise the Lord with their special and God-given talents. They are also communicators—both to the director about the feeling and perceptions of the congregation and to the congregation about the practice and purpose of music in worship. Part of the choir's role is to be a teacher. The congregation learns by hearing the choir and through the choir's assistance.[86]

The choral portions of the service frequently include the unvarying portions of Christian worship, such as the Kyrie, the Gloria in Excelsis, the Sanctus, the Agnus Dei, and the Te Deum Laudamus (in Matins). More traditionally, the choir may sing the Introit, the Gradual, the Alleluia Verse, the Tract (which replaces the Alleluia during Lent) or Sequence Hymn,[87] and the Offertory. The choir also may sing during the distribution of Holy Communion.[88] Occasionally, a musical setting of a Creed and the Our Father may enhance a specific service.[89] These choral portions of the liturgy are particularly edifying for festival services, and a wealth of musical resources from the fourteenth to the twentieth centuries are available to contemporary choirs.[90]

Choral music is distinguished from other liturgical music because it provides a higher and deeper musical development of the text. The choir lifts the worshipers to a more exalted level of praise and proclamation of divine truth. This can be done in various ways, particularly when the choir sings more elaborate settings of the liturgy or chorales in alternate stanzas with the congregation.[91]

In the history of church music, motets developed from an earlier chant tradition. This occurred during the thirteenth and fourteenth centuries when a second melody was added. Later, more voices were added until the church enjoyed the lasting legacy of such master composers as Orlando di Lasso (ca. 1532–1594) and Giovanni Palestrina (ca. 1525–1594). Motets and other styles of music have been designated "attendant" music because such pieces are not central or critical to the service, yet they can enhance the worship of God's gathered guests.[92]

The chorale motet developed during the Lutheran Reformation. Based on Luther's chorales—hymns that featured congregational participation—Lutheran composers developed expanded polyphonic versions of these familiar texts and congregational tunes. These motets or cantatas enhanced the worship life of Lutheran congregations for generations.

Some choirs perform anthems—a development within Anglican worship—that may be thematically related to the service but often are based on general texts. Anthems are less liturgically related to worship and are closer to secular music in their origin and purpose. The operatic oratorios of George Frederic Handel (1685–1759) may also fit into this genre on a monumental scale. Erik Routley commendably explains that "anthems at their best are expositions of Scripture through music."[93]

The placement of the choir in the sanctuary is important. Locating the choir in the chancel, evident in many Protestant churches, dates only from the mid-nineteenth-century revivals of Charles Finney, though there is some precedence in the monastic choirs of medieval cathedrals.[94] Not only does this location separate the choir from the congregation, it also gives the appearance of entertainment rather than worship. Hugo Gehrke notes that churches that locate the organ and choir in a rear balcony have found significant benefits: The focal point of the altar is maintained; the choir, organ, and congregation blend better; and robes and processions by the choir are not necessary every Sunday.[95]

Rehearsals are a required dimension of the ministry of music. An average rehearsal should be no longer than 90 minutes, including an opening and closing prayer. The director may prepare a plan for practice that includes a brief time to warm up. Singing should be the priority at practice, not conversation. Familiar and new music may be included in each rehearsal. Choir directors will want to choose edifying texts and music, not look for clever accompaniments or theatrical sound tracks. Variety in composition is also important. A choir director may also want to include at least one Bach chorale annually in a Lutheran congregation.

Ministers of music may arrange for a choir or soloist to serve the congregation at each service. (A soloist has the same role as a choir in the service.) Choirs may be organized around various needs, purposes, or even seasons of the church year.[96] Some congregations have found that summer choirs work well to introduce new members to the regular choir. The congregation might consider a youth, men's, or couples' group during the summer months.

INSTRUMENTS OF PRAISE

While much of the music of worship is accomplished with the human voice, instruments have always been involved in assisting God's gathered guests as they respond in praise.

THE ORGAN

From its origin in Alexandria around 250 B.C., organs have been used in a variety of public gatherings.[97] According to records, the sounds of ancient organs must have been more like calliopes than what we associate with modern pipe organs. In earlier eras the organ was seldom considered appropriate for Christian worship, perhaps because of its raucous sounds, its undeveloped methods of notation, or its association with secular settings, particularly the theater and the circus. However, for some undiscovered reason, around the tenth century the pipe organ became an accepted instrument in churches. Within three centuries, every major cathedral possessed at least one organ.[98] By the sixteenth century, organ builders had developed instruments that could perform with softer tones and were more harmonically pleasing. Some organ music even replaced chanted portions in the worship service in Roman Catholic churches. By the seventeenth and eighteenth centuries, the finest organs were built to play the great works of Johann Pachelbel (1653–1706), Dietrich Buxtehude (1637–1707), and Johann Sebastian Bach (1685–1750). Today the organ has a repertoire more deeply connected with the Christian faith than that of any other musical instrument.[99]

The organ is one of the most unique instruments a congregation will purchase. The mechanical complexity, even in a modestly sized organ, is enormous. It can play a range of music and provide tonal diversity unsurpassed by any other single instrument. With a range of several octaves beyond the five octaves of a typical keyboard instrument, the organ provides a delicate balance of high and low tones that defies duplication by any solo performer on another instrument.[100]

A congregation will want to exercise care when purchasing an organ or when maintaining or expanding the instrument. The location of the pipes, the placement of the instrument, and the reverberant qualities of the building should all be considered. Failing to consult a recognized organ authority may result in the purchase of a deficient instrument or the addition of pipes that are incompatible with the original instrument.[101]

Although the debate between electronic or pipe organs will undoubtedly continue, the pipe organ has proved its exceptional ability to lead congregational worship, assist in the liturgy, and serve as a solo instrument. Arguments against the purchase of a pipe organ often include the financial cost.[102] However, most electronic organs need to be updated or even replaced after about 25 years. A 25-year-old pipe organ, however, is merely beginning to develop its sound. If a pipe organ needs to be replaced, most congregations discover that the pipes are reusable and that they only need to expand the organ with newer or additional options.

OTHER INSTRUMENTS

The Scriptures are filled with numerous references to musical instruments, beginning with Genesis 4 and the record of Jubal, "the father of all who play the harp and flute" (4:21). Most biblical accounts of instrumental use are connected with worship (1 Samuel 10:1–12). From the trumpet and cymbal to the harp and lyre, God's gathered guests have used instruments in praise of His greatness and blessings (Numbers 10:8, 10; 1 Chronicles 15:16). Jewish and early Christian worship freely used instrumental music. Only during the early Middle Ages were there some concerns because pagans had used instruments for their public pageantry and sensuous celebrations.[103] However, by the time of the Reformation, instruments were again universally used in worship settings. Luther once encouraged musicians to "let their singing and playing to the praise of the Father of all grace sound forth with joy from their organs and whatever other beloved musical instruments there are."[104] The renowned Lutheran composer Michael Praetorius (1571–1621) used several voices and numerous instruments in a variety of settings.[105] Other notable Lutheran musicians, such as members of the Bach family, not only used the organ and harpsichord but also had small orchestras or instrumental ensembles accompany their cantatas. Only with the rise of extremely conservative post-Reformation Calvinists was instrumental music denigrated for several centuries among some Protestant groups. Unfortunately, such views also crept into those Lutheran circles that exhibited strong Pietistic influence.

Introducing musical instruments into the worship setting should be done carefully and caringly. Church festivals, particularly the festival season of Easter, are optimal for church musicians to present special music with instrumental accompaniment. While instrumental music requires considerably more work for the music director, the time, effort, and expense are worth it as God's gathered guests express their praise and thanksgiving.

Stringed instruments—guitar, piano, violin, and so on—are especially good for small-group worship because they work well in chamber settings. With electronic amplification, many of these instruments can be adapted to larger settings as well. Sounds from synthesizers and computer-generated sound equipment can be used to augment worship music, always to the glory of God. Drums and tympani also can enrich the music of a worship service. Handbells have become increasingly popular in North American congregations as instrumental choirs, as well as for accompaniment to chanting, hymn melodies, and in ensemble with other instruments.

A primary consideration of any instrumental music is that it "fit" the liturgy and not merely serve as concert music.[106] Because instrumental music is nearly divorced from the Word, its use requires more care. "Pure music" may be appropriate on special occasions when the festive activities of a procession are self-evident or when contemplation on a text can be prolonged and dramatically enhanced.[107] The following questions may be asked when considering instrumental music: Does the musical piece relate to the mood of the service? Will it support and unify rather than interrupt or call attention to itself? Instrumental pieces based on congregational hymns may remind worshipers of the Word. The mood should provide a sense of spiritual calm and not introduce secular elements into the service. Instrumental music presented to entertain or to exhibit a performer's special technical achievements is inappropriate. Suitable music always serves the Gospel and the whole worship service. Instrumental music should be performed well. If used in ensemble or with the congregation, the instruments should blend and balance. No one instrument should overwhelm the ensemble. When using electronic instruments, attention must be paid so decibel levels do not distract from the worship setting. Percussion instruments should not overwhelm the other instruments either.

Besides ensemble work, instrumental solos are appropriate in a variety of places in the worship structure. A prelude or interlude to a hymn offers an opportunity for the congregation to focus on the text while the instrument enhances the melodic line. A solo instrument may assist in the melody line of a new hymn tune. A violin, flute, clarinet, or trumpet soloist normally plays in the range of women's and children's voices and can assist on a hymn stanza sung by female voices. A bassoon, cello, French horn, or trombone plays in the range of men's voices and may be used while male voices sing a hymn stanza. If a small choir is missing a part or has a weak section, an instrument with the right tonal quality could "fill in." This was a typical practice during the Renaissance and Baroque periods.[108] Lutheran composers such as Heinrich Schütz (1585–1672) and Michael Praetorius gave instructions for the performance of their compositions that offered combinations of voices and instruments for variety, to support the singers, and to accent the grandeur of God's glory.[109] A solo instrument may also play a descant as the congregation sings the melody. This may heighten a doxological stanza or a specific hymn text. Music directors may want to routinely seek out members of the congregation who play instruments professionally or young people whose talents may be nurtured. Providing an opportunity to use one's talents to the Lord's glory is appreciated by these musicans.

Time is perhaps the greatest gift musicians give in worship. Not only does it require time to play during the church service, but weeks and possibly months are required to prepare for special services. In addition, a choir director needs time to select music, develop a repertoire, gather members of a choir, and rehearse adequately. Yet that time needed for worship preparation is always well spent.

Music in God's service is one of the highest forms of worship. From the Psalter to contemporary songs, believers have voiced praise to their Creator, Redeemer, and Sanctifier. Music holds an intimate place in the life of Christian worshipers. It engages the human spirit in a unique way. The place of music in Lutheran worship has a long and valued tradition. Coupled with the strength of God's promises, a hymn provides not only a teaching moment, but also an opportunity to praise, pray, and give thanks with all who call on the name of the Lord. Instruments elevate the experience of corporate worship as creation joins in a doxology with God's gathered guests.

Some Questions to Consider

1. Cite five biblical examples of incorporating music in worship.
2. What was Luther's understanding of the place of music in worship?

3. Illustrate from your experience five of the adjectives used to describe music in Lutheran worship.

4. What is the unique function of a minister of music or cantor?

5. How can chant be used in a congregation to enhance worship?

6. What parts of the liturgy were traditionally sung by worshipers? What kinds of music can be sung by the congregation in a worship service?

7. Why should hymn selection be done carefully and caringly? How can new songs be introduced to a worshiping group?

8. Describe the significance and purpose of the Hymn of the Day.

9. What is the role of the choir in the context of a local congregation? Explain how the choir in your home congregation meets some or all of the needs of a worshiping community.

10. Why is the organ often an "instrument of choice" for congregations? How can other instruments also enhance congregational worship?

Notes

1. Cited in Gehrke, *Worshiping God with Joy*, 15.

2. Paul H. Lang, *Music in Western Civilization*, 41, stated, "Music could be considered by the Church only if it served the purposes of the Church, and therefore the subject and aim of Christian cult music was and remained the *gloria Dei* and the *aedificatio hominum*."

3. Quasten, *Music and Worship*, 62–65, notes in elaborate detail the temple rites of Old Testament worship, as well as some of the negative comments by early Christian writers related to pagan instrumentation.

4. Pfatteicher and Messerli, *Manual on the Liturgy*, 213, 372 n. 8.

5. Westermeyer, *Te Deum*, 49, who cites *The Common Service Book of the Lutheran Church* (Philadelphia: Board of Publication of the United Lutheran Church in America, 1918), 215.

6. Evanson, "Service of the Word," 410.

7. Westermeyer, *Te Deum*, 49–50.

8. Dix and Chadwick, *Treatise on the Apostolic Tradition*, 50.

9. Quasten, *Music and Worship*, 1. See also Faulkner, *Wiser Than Despair*, 50–72.

10. See D. H. Tripp, "Gnosticism," 81–83, and Gelineau, "Music and Singing in the Liturgy," in *The Study of Liturgy*, rev. ed., ed. Cheslyn Jones et al. (New York: Oxford University Press, 1992), 498–99.

11. Where possible, the titles provided will be those found in *Lutheran Worship*.

12. Eskew and McElrath, *Sing with Understanding*, 75.

13. Halter, *Practice of Sacred Music*, 8.

14. Quasten, *Music and Worship*, 66–72.

15. Ignatius, "Letter to the Ephesians," 4.2, in *Apostolic Fathers*, 106.

16. Clement of Rome, "First Letter to the Corinthians," 34.7, in *Apostolic Fathers*, 23.

17. John Chrysostom, "Homily 5," as cited from Patrologia graeca 63:486–7 in Gelineau, "Music and Singing in the Liturgy," 495.

18. Dix, *Shape of the Liturgy*, 365–66, noted almost humorously that after the Gregorian reforms choirs refused to learn any new music. He also noted that few of the musical pieces that they did know well and liked were fit for the liturgy, at least if one considers the appropriateness according to the Sundays of the church year.

19. Reed, *Lutheran Liturgy* (rev. ed.), 63.

20. Dix, *Shape of the Liturgy*, 598–99, explained further that the Low Mass was extremely popular among laypeople because it eliminated most of the choral music and could be conducted within a short period of time.

21. Westermeyer, *Te Deum*, 141–49, summarizes recent views on why Luther loved and used music as a critical and Christological dimension to his theology.

22. Luther, *Sämmtliche Schriften*, 22:1541, translated in Halter, *Practice of Sacred Music*, 11.

23. Luther, *Sämmtliche Schriften*, 24a:582, translated in Halter, *Practice of Sacred Music*, 9.

24. Luther, *Sämmtliche Schriften*, 14:429–430, translated in Halter, *Practice of Sacred Music*, 10. Cf. Ulrich Leupold's translation of "Preface to Georg Rhau's *Symphoniae incundae*," LW 53:323.

25. See Pelikan, *Bach among the Theologians*, for an interesting perspective on Bach and his music.

26. Reed, *Lutheran Liturgy* (rev. ed.), 84–86, reports that the music for the new Lutheran liturgies was provided by such musical luminaries as Spangenberg, Lossius, Eler, Keuchenthal, and Ludecus in *cantionales*.

27. Howell, "From Trent to Vatican II," 289.

28. Reed, *Lutheran Liturgy* (rev. ed.), 146.

29. Westermeyer, *Te Deum*, provides a wealth of information in an easily accessible format for the casual reader, the interested student, or the church musician. In addition, Palisca, *Norton Anthology of Western Music*; Strunk, *Source Readings in Music History*; Sadie, *New Grove Dictionary of Music and Musicians*; Faulkner, *Wiser Than Despair*; and Marilyn Stulken, *Hymnal Companion to* Lutheran Book of Worship (Philadelphia: Fortress, 1981) provide much information.

30. Considered in this review were *The Lutheran Hymnal* (1942), *Service Book and Hymnal* (1958), *Worship Supplement* (1969), *Lutheran Book of Worship* (1978), *Lutheran Worship* (1982), *Christian Worship* (1993), *With One Voice* (1997), *Hymnal Supplement 98* (1998), and *This Far by Faith* (1999). Westermeyer, "Musical Leadership," 117, states: "At virtually every point the congregation is assumed to have a role as important as those in liturgical and musical leadership, and it seems to be expressed most often through musical participation."

31. Halter, *Practice of Sacred Music*, 90.

32. Kretzmann, "Pastor and Church Musician," 219.

33. Leaver, *Theological Character of Music in Worship*, 11. The use of solo instrumental music requires that the tune be associated with a text worshipers can recall.

34. Pope Paul VI, "Homily, September 24, 1972," in *Documents on the Liturgy, 1963–1979*, ed. and trans. Thomas C. O'Brien (Collegeville, Minn.: Liturgical Press, 1982), as quoted in Hansen, *Ministry of the Cantor*, 2.

35. Schalk, "Music and the Liturgy," 250.

36. These characteristics are developed from Pfatteicher and Messerli, *Manual on the Liturgy*, 78–79; they also are noted in Schalk, "Music and the Liturgy," 245–46.

37. The companion volumes Halter and Schalk, *Handbook of Church Music,* and Carl Schalk, ed., *Key Words in Church Music* (St. Louis: Concordia, 1978), offer church musicians and pastors beneficial and profitable guides to Christian and Lutheran worship resources. See also Precht, *Lutheran Worship: History and Practice*.

38. Nuechterlein, "Music of the Congregation," 123–24, provides helpful suggestions for introducing and playing hymns.

39. Pfatteicher and Messerli, *Manual on the Liturgy*, 103.

40. Westermeyer, *Church Musician*, offers many insights into the ecclesiastical position of cantor—its banes and blessings for the local parish, as well as its history, particularly in Lutheranism.

41. Westermeyer, "Musical Leadership," 130–33, points out that church musicians are often caught in the crossfire between various "camps" in worship tastes and practices, yet they must maintain a sense of personal integrity with an almost prophetic voice.

42. Halter, *Practice of Sacred Music*, 85.

43. Gehrke, *Worshiping God with Joy*, 16.

44. Pfatteicher and Messerli, *Manual on the Liturgy*, 82.

45. Gelineau, "Music and Singing in the Liturgy," 495.

46. Pfatteicher and Messerli, *Manual on the Liturgy*, 86.

47. The echo-response form of singing remains common in Christian communities in Africa.

48. Senn, "Dialogue between Liturgy and Music," 25.

49. Cobb, "Liturgy of the Word in the Early Church," 227.

50. Gelineau, "Music and Singing in the Liturgy," 505.

51. Gelineau, "Music and Singing in the Liturgy," 500.

52. Westermeyer, *Te Deum*, 102–3, 111–14.

53. "German Mass," LW 53:72–90.

54. Held, "Psalms and Their Use," and Bunjes, "Musical Carriage for the Psalms," 471–87, provide excellent background and explanation for the singing of the psalms in Lutheran congregations.

55. Bunjes, "Music of *Lutheran Worship*," 536–48, explains the details of liturgical chant as presented in *Lutheran Worship*. The chant patterns in *Lutheran Worship* are explained briefly on pp. 366–68.

56. Gorman, *Chicago Folk Service*.

57. Lutheran books of worship continue to include these hymns: "Kyrie, God Father" (*Lutheran Worship*, 209); "All Glory Be to God on High" (*Lutheran Worship*, 215); "We All Believe in One True God, Maker" (*Lutheran Worship*, 213); "Isaiah, Mighty Seer, in Spirit Soared" (*Lutheran Worship*, 214); and "O Christ, the Lamb of God" (*Lutheran Worship*, 7).

58. Messerli, "Music of the Choir," 140, provides more than a half-dozen settings of Propers for the church year that are useful for mixed choirs and congregational chanting.

59. Bunjes, "Music of *Lutheran Worship*," 543–44, distinguishes chant from song by noting that liturgical song uses a "*beat* as the unit of rhythmic measurement" (*Bunjes's emphasis*).

60. The "responsorial" form is the practice of having the people respond with a short stanza or musical phrase after a number of stanzas are sung by the choir or cantor.

61. *Antiphon* comes from the Greek word *antiphoneo*, which means "to sound in answer, to reply, or to respond." The word refers to a brief chanted scriptural sentence or phrase that frames the singing of a psalm and indicates the psalm tone to be used.

62. See Messerli, "Music of the Choir," 157–62.

63. Nuechterlein, "Music of the Congregation," 115, notes that Isaac Watts (1674–1748) wrote Christian hymns as well as extremely well-loved poetic versifications of psalms—"The Lord My Shepherd Is" (Psalm 23); "Jesus Shall Reign" (Psalm 72), "Our God, Our Help in Ages Past" (Psalm 90); "Joy to the World" (Psalm 98); and "Oh, Bless the Lord, My Soul" (Psalm 103).

64. Routley, *Words, Music, and the Church*, 191.

65. *Lutheran Worship*, 36.

66. *Lutheran Worship*, 137.

67. *Lutheran Worship*, 157 or 158.

68. Messerli, "Music of the Choir," 148.

69. Schalk, *Hymn of the Day*, 7.

70. Fremder, "Selection of Hymns," 516–19, lists more than 40 criteria for selecting hymns. These criteria are listed under three categories—Word and theology, textual considerations, and musical considerations—that substantiate many of the ideas in this section.

71. Brunner, *Worship in the Name of Jesus*, 269.

72. Precht and Severs, *Lutheran Worship Concordance*, provides the hymn number and the stanza in which particular words appear, as does E. V. Haserodt, *The Lutheran Hymnal Concordance* (St. Louis: Concordia, 1956).

73. Precht, *Lutheran Worship: Hymnal Companion*, is one of several such helps available for hymnals. More specifically, Leaver, *Come to the Feast*, provides beneficial insights into the powerfully rugged hymns and nuanced translations of the poet-theologian Martin H. Franzmann.

74. See Maschke, "Transcultural Nature of Liturgical Worship," 241–63.

75. Marcus P. B. Felde, "Nairobi Statement on Worship and Culture," in *Christian Worship*, ed. S. Anita Stauffer (Geneva: Department for Theology and Studies, Lutheran World Federation, 1996).

76. See sections of *This Far by Faith*, particularly its introductory notes on pp. 8–17.

77. See *Lutheran Worship*, pp. 994–99.

78. Eskew and McElrath, *Sing with Understanding*, provides excellent background information on the development of hymnody. Other books to consider are Stulken, *Hymnal Companion*; Seton, *Our Heritage of Hymns*; and Brooks, *Hymns as Homilies*.

79. White and White, *Church Architecture*, 109.

80. Schalk, "Music and the Liturgy," 248.

81. Schalk, *Hymn of the Day*, gives a thorough explanation of the background, purpose, and contemporary use of this key hymn in Lutheran worship.

82. Nuechterlein, "Music of the Congregation," 112–13. See also Messerli, "Music of the Choir," 162–64. These authors provide historical information on the chorale and other congregational music.

83. See Vajda, "Hymn Writing and Translating," 488–99, for an inspiring and encouraging essay on the importance of new songs.

84. Westermeyer, *Church Musician*, 131–32, explains that *Barform* was a special form of German poetry.

85. Hillert, "Music in the Church Today," 249.

86. Unfortunately, in recent years congregations have found that leaders who sing through microphones often turn the congregation into silent worshipers. Day, *Why Catholics Can't Sing*, 51–53, points this out several times in his somewhat impudent look at music in worship.

87. Messerli, "Music of the Choir," 142–43, notes that a Sequence Hymn historically followed the Alleluia and is of Gregorian origin. Used mostly on festival occasions, a few are included in modern hymnals. The Easter hymn "Victimae paschali" forms the basis for the German hymn "Christ lag in Todesbanden" ("Christ Jesus Lay in Death's Strong Bands") and is one of the most famous sequence hymns, which can be sung by the choir and congregation in a variety of settings.

88. Halter and Schalk, eds., *Handbook of Church Music*, 20.

89. Messerli, "Music of the Choir," 150, correctly warns that "choral performance of such settings in the liturgy could help a congregation in worship, but the pitfalls of vocal display, exaggerated effects, and

distraction of the worshiper are real. If used, such choral settings must not prolong the liturgy unduly at the moment the congregation awaits the consecration and reception of the Sacrament."

90. Messerli, "Music of the Choir," 133.

91. Messerli, "Music of the Choir," 131.

92. Halter and Schalk, *Handbook of Church Music*, 21.

93. Routley, *Words, Music, and the Church*, 193.

94. Hammond, *Liturgy and Architecture*, 44.

95. Gehrke, *Worshiping God with Joy*, 31.

96. Messerli, "Music of the Choir," 136–37, lists possible groups with suggested vocal ranges, as well as special-purpose choirs.

97. Halter, *Practice of Sacred Music*, 22–23.

98. Faulkner, Appendix I in *Wiser Than Despair*, 215–19.

99. Westermeyer, *Church Musician*, 129.

100. Gotsch, "Music of Instruments," 172–207, provides helpful information on organ use in worship settings.

101. John Ogasapian, *Church Organs* (Grand Rapids: Baker, 1983).

102. White and White, *Church Architecture*, 115, provides arguments from aesthetic and philosophical perspectives but finally settles for "the economic arguments": "First of all, such a purchase is a long-term investment . . . . Even the best electronic devices will not last more than ten to fifteen years . . . . By the time the electronic organ has been replaced two or three times, a small pipe organ could have been paid for. In addition, a pipe organ holds its value, whereas only a tiny fraction of the original investment in an electronic device can generally be recovered . . . . Each pipe organ is unique . . . [and] since it is tailored to the place and people who will use it, the congregation will derive the maximum benefit from it—the best sound for its dollar, so to speak."

103. Quasten, *Music and Worship*, 92.

104. Quoted in Schalk, "Music and Liturgy," 258.

105. Pfatteicher and Messerli, *Manual on the Liturgy*, 106.

106. Day, *Why Catholics Can't Sing*, 86, suggests that the best music in worship "just seemed to *take place*; it did not sound like something presented to the congregation" (*Day's emphasis*).

107. Gelineau, "Music and Singing in the Liturgy," 506.

108. Gehrke, *Worshiping God with Joy*, 17.

109. Klammer, "Orchestral Instruments," 211–12.

PART 4

FESTIVAL AND OCCASIONAL WORSHIP SERVICES

CHAPTER 13

SEASONAL WORSHIP SERVICES

Besides regular worship opportunities on Sundays, God's gathered guests come to church for special worship services throughout the church year. These seasonal services mark significant events in the liturgical year or special occasions in the life of the Christian community or the individual Christian. This chapter will explore the seasonal services offered throughout the church year. The next chapter will examine how and why we gather for other special and sacramental services.

Although Sunday is set aside for corporate Christian worship, Lutherans have followed the Christian tradition of also gathering for worship during the week to celebrate specific times in the church year. A tradition that dates back centuries before the Reformation encourages Christians to prepare their hearts for the major Christian celebrations of Christmas and Easter. Midweek services for Advent and Lent are still held in most Lutheran congregations, as they are in other Christian communities. These services help Christians express their uniqueness and distinction from the world, as well as provide opportunities to be strengthened in their spiritual pilgrimage as God's gathered guests.

MIDWEEK ADVENT SERVICES

In our contemporary society the preparation for Christmas begins long before the Advent season. Stores and shopping malls are decorated with Christmas motifs several months before December 25. Traditionally, Christians also have set aside time to prepare for Christmas. As noted in chapter 3, the Advent season is marked by themes of preparation and expectation. For generations Lutherans have gathered for Wednesday (or more recently, Thursday) evening services that highlight aspects of preparation, expectation, and hope. The four weeks of Advent usually include at least three midweek services. (There are four Sundays in Advent, but

Christmas may fall before the fourth Wednesday, thus reducing the number of mid-week services.)

Because Advent is the beginning of the new church year, some congregations choose to emphasize parish renewal. Other pastors have established a tradition of introducing new worship practices during the Advent season. For example, singing a new canticle or trying a new method of Communion distribution may be more easily introduced during these weeks as people expect different worship activities.[1]

Through the years, congregations have developed numerous patterns for mid-week Advent services. Some may offer a series of children's programs; others may develop a thematic approach based on prophecies and fulfillment or symbols of Christ's life. Whatever the pattern, the focus is always on preparation for Christ's threefold coming—as the incarnate Son of God, as our personal Savior, and as the final Judge. An acclamation that could be spoken by the congregation prior to Holy Communion affirms this eschatological theme: "Christ has come! Christ is come! Christ will come again!"[2]

Many congregations use Vespers or Evening Prayer because it emphasizes the numerous biblical images of Advent. The Magnificat, the traditional canticle for Vespers, is especially appropriate for the Advent season. A young female voice could introduce the congregation to one of the versions of Mary's Song found in *Lutheran Worship*.[3] Worship leaders may take advantage of the Advent season to make more thorough comments on and explanations of the Magnificat. Martin Luther considered the Magnificat to be an extremely stimulating source of inspiration for preaching on the Christian faith and faithful service.[4]

Although Christmas carols are occasionally used in congregations during this season, the Advent hymns of the church place more emphasis on the biblical concept of preparation. Singing the psalms in either a hymnic setting or as chant with little accompaniment can add to a sense of hope-filled anticipation as the congregation joins in words sung by believers for millennia. The singing of Christmas music will have a greater impact on a congregation if the richness of the Advent themes is emphasized during the three or four midweek services. Paul Bosch asserts: "Advent hymns are the great undiscovered treasury in most of our hymnals. To ignore such hymns in our worship in favor of four weeks of Christmas carols is liturgical overload and spiritual impoverishment. . . . Advent hymns are the best-kept secret in the liturgical year."[5]

The reintroduction of blue as the liturgical color for Advent communicates a sense of hope. The more traditional royal purple proclaims the coming King. If purple is used, the symbols on the paraments should be distinct from those used during Lent. Advent and Lent may be linked by the use of the Lamb as a symbol for both seasons, but the crucial distinction between the seasonal emphases should be explained to the gathered guests.

The grand tradition of singing the Great O Antiphons dates to the sixth or seventh century of the Christian church. The seven antiphons invite Jesus to come to us. They use Old Testament names that reflect the messianic prophecies of Christ. Jesus is addressed as O Wisdom, O Lord, O Root of Jesse, O Key of David, O Daystar, O King of Nations, and O Emmanuel.[6] These antiphons are combined in the Advent hymn "Oh, Come, Oh, Come, Emmanuel." Originally sung from December 17 through December 23, the hymn's seven stanzas may be used individually for Sunday and weekday services to provide a unifying theme for the Advent season.

Candlelight services may be considered for Advent services, though they are best suited for the Christmas and Epiphany seasons. Children's messages during these seasonal services are a worthy practice for proclaiming that the Christ of Bethlehem is the Savior of the world.[7] Because children are exemplary models of enthusiastic expression of anticipation and hope, their excitement can be directed to Christ's second coming and shared with the entire congregation. The use of an Advent wreath or progressively decorating a Christmas tree during each of the weekly evening services can involve children in the worship life of the congregation and place the focus on Christ.

The Advent wreath, or any arrangement of four candles, provides an important teaching moment in the life of God's gathered guests. While some have labeled the candles used in the Advent wreath, there is no tradition for such allegorical appellations. Similarly, the color of the candles is sometimes a concern. When purple and pink candles are used, the traditional Introits provide a clue to the appropriate color to light. The Third Sunday of Advent is called *Gaudete*, which means "rejoice." The words of the Introit,

which begins with that word, provide a glimmer of gladness in an otherwise more solemn season. As a result, a pink or rose candle is lit to emphasize this theme of joy. Most congregations now use four candles of the same color (all blue, all white, or perhaps all red). A larger center white candle may be lit on Christmas; however, if a congregation uses a paschal candle, it should be reserved for the season of Easter, for Baptisms, and for funerals.

If possible, the Advent wreath should be made from real greens as another symbol of the more austere, yet hopeful, time of year. Flowers are normally omitted until Christmas Day. The wreath itself is a circle, another symbol of eternal life and our Christian hope. It may be hung or it may be freestanding. The lighting of the candles on the wreath does not require ceremony, yet the significance of the Christian's Advent hope may be indicated by means of a note in the service folder or with a comment made by the worship leader as the candles are lit.[8]

Whatever resources are used or practices followed during Advent, the key is to gather the guests before God in anticipation of receiving His Christmas Gift and in anticipation of the return of that Gift at the end of time.

EPIPHANY

A nearly forgotten festival in the liturgical year is the Festival of the Epiphany of Our Lord. While frequently celebrated by Lutheran congregations on the Sunday following January 6, the date itself marks a significant holiday for many non-Western Christian communities, particularly the various national Orthodox churches. This festival and season is the oldest festival of the church.

An evening service for Epiphany holds great potential for introducing several memorable liturgical practices from the grander Christian tradition. One of the primary themes of Epiphany, a name that comes from the Greek word for "manifestation," is the theme of light. The Scripture readings usually assigned to this festival recall God's promise that a people who were sitting in darkness would see a great light (Isaiah 9:2; 60:1–9). Epiphany celebrates Jesus as the light of the world (John 1:5; 8:12; 9:5). Another item connected with Epiphany is frankincense, a gift brought by the Magi to the Christ Child (Matthew 2:11). It is a uniquely sensuous substance used during worship activities in many Christian communities.

A noteworthy service form for Epiphany is Evening Prayer.[9] The service begins with the *Lucernarium* or Service of Light. The congregation arrives and is seated in relative darkness, and the worship leader or cantor, holding the Christ candle, chants the opening verses as he and any other worship participants slowly process. Worshipers seated at the center aisle may light their candles from the Christ candle and pass the flame down the row.[10] By the time the leaders are assembled in the chancel, the church is bright with light. The hymn "Joyous Light of Glory"[11] is sung by the congregation or

choir as the chancel candles are lighted. Thus the Epiphany theme of light becomes a central experience in this special service.

Prior to the Psalmody, a children's message may be given in which the significance of the gifts of the Magi—gold, frankincense, and myrrh—is explained. Most pertinent to this service is an explanation of the importance and significance of incense. The vessels for incensing the altar may be brought out for the children to see. (See illustration on previous page.) After the children depart and as the congregation sings the antiphon portion of the Psalmody—"Let my prayer rise before you as incense; the lifting up of my hands as the evening sacrifice"—the altar may be incensed.[12] The incensing of the altar concludes as the minister offers a prayer that recalls the meaning of incense. If other psalms are sung or spoken, either by the congregation or choir, the incense may be brought from the altar into the midst of the congregation.

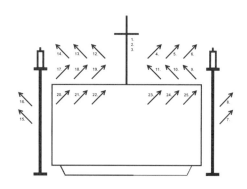

The Gospel Canticle is the Magnificat. Again the Epiphany theme can be underscored by a commentary on the text prior to singing the canticle. On a festive occasion such as Epiphany, this canticle may be sung by a solo voice, preferably by a girl. The Litany that follows helps the congregation appreciate the breadth of God's plan of salvation, particularly the Epiphany emphasis of the Word for the world. Such an emphasis recalls why Epiphany is often called the Gentiles' Christmas.

This adaptation of Evening Prayer may be introduced over several years to help the congregation recognize the significance of the Christian community in a world that so quickly forgets the meaning of Christmas and Epiphany.[13]

ASH WEDNESDAY

Lutherans join liturgical Christians around the world to set aside the six weeks prior to Easter as a time for the preparations of Lent. Ash Wednesday marks the beginning of this season. For many Lutherans, the name of this day has been lost through negligence of an expressive practice. While the use of ashes is not a necessity for Ash Wednesday, it can provide several teaching moments. Ashes may be obtained by burning the palm

branches from the previous year's celebration of Palm Sunday. A children's message can explain the significance of ashes during biblical times. The ashes are not "blessed," but a prayer spoken prior to distribution of the ashes can recall the sign of the ashes as a symbol both of our repentance and of our mortality. Such symbolism accentuates our need for Jesus and for the forgiveness and life He freely provides.

The actual imposition of ashes may be accomplished in several ways. Worshipers may come forward to the altar to receive the ashes in a manner similar to the distribution of Holy Communion. The ashes are placed on a person's forehead with the words "Dust you are and to dust you shall return" (Genesis 3:19). As an option, the ashes may be placed on the back of a person's hand instead of on the forehead.

Although the "wearing of the ashes" has a long tradition, members should not feel uncomfortable if they choose to wash off the ashes. Rather, the significance and blessings of one's Baptism should be affirmed by the minister as it is underscored by such washing; the sense of cleansing and relief should be tied to Christ's glorious cross and resurrection. The pastor's explanation, whether in the service folder or orally in the service, is crucial for the proper introduction and reception of this practice.

Many congregations offer Holy Communion on Ash Wednesday, but this may be one service when the Sacrament is not offered as a way to emphasize the solemnity of our repentance and the anticipation of the Sacrament on the first Sunday in Lent. If Holy Communion is offered, be careful that the service does not become too lengthy or the Communion liturgy too abbreviated. Pastoral sensitivities will help direct local practices.

An expanded Confessional Service (see chapter 14) would be fitting for Ash Wednesday. To that end, Psalm 51 is normally used in the Ash Wednesday service not as a response to the Old Testament Reading, but as an Entrance Psalm. A series of "scrutinies"[14] or a recital of Luther's explanations of the Ten Commandments could provide the means for self-examination. After an exhortation to confession and an explanation of absolution, the words of comfort and forgiveness spoken by the pastor will be most effective in the hearts and lives of God's people. Some congregations may consider wiping off the ash marks at the altar as a visual aid to the reality of Christ's words spoken by the pastor.

MIDWEEK LENTEN SERVICES

For centuries Lutherans have gathered as God's guests for midweek services during the Lenten season. These services focus the members of the congregation on the life,

suffering, and death of their Savior. These services also build the congregation's anticipation of the Easter festival.

Lenten services frequently vary in format. Lutherans have emphasized the Lenten season with vigor and variety, whether through a sermon series on Christ's passion; chancel dramas that recall the personal struggle of various biblical characters involved in Christ's suffering and death; film presentations; choral vespers; or the use of guest preachers from area Lutheran congregations. The opportunity to recall the Lord's great gift of Himself in the Lord's Supper is a custom many Lutheran congregations continue to enjoy throughout the Lenten season.

Catechetical sermons are traditional for the Lenten season. In the early church, candidates for Baptism were instructed on the mysteries of the faith during this season. Thus throughout the 40 days of Lent, they learned the Apostles' Creed and the Lord's Prayer, as well as the significance of the sacraments. Lent is a time of disciplined learning and preparation, and catechetical instruction for the whole congregation falls nicely into this emphasis. Faith is deepened as the story of our Lord's life is connected to the six chief parts in Luther's Small Catechism.[15] Luther prepared various series of catechetical sermons from traditional texts.[16] In many ways, this was a return to the pre-medieval and early Christian emphasis on the joy of our Lord's life, rather than a lugubrious contemplation of suffering and death. Although the Sundays of the season are "in Lent," they are still considered "little Easters." Thus they may have a somewhat lighter tone. However, the solemnities of Lent are maintained during midweek services, which are somber and meditative. Such characteristics may be easily perceived by the worshipers as they gather in the darkness of the late winter months.

Some congregations have introduced midweek suppers for those who attend the midweek evening services. Perhaps one of these meals might emphasize fasting and almsgiving. Either a sparse amount of food may be offered or a menu that features fare from a country in which the congregation supports mission work. A freewill offering could be collected for missions. The tradition of fasting dates to Old Testament practices and was continued by early Christians for centuries.[17] If fasting is done in a visible and organized way, a "hunger veil" may be introduced. First mentioned in the ninth century, this large cloth veil (*das Hungertuch* in German) reminded the congregation's members of the Lenten theme of fasting and self-sacrifice.[18] A banner may be constructed with the theme for the Lenten season or a hunger veil may be purchased as a means to promote and encourage purposeful fasting and almsgiving. The hunger veil also may be placed on the altar as a frontal.

Vespers or Compline provide meaningful Lenten worship services for the gathered guests, particularly if the celebration of the Lord's Supper is not offered at the midweek service. Either of these distinct services will benefit congregations that are seeking a deeper understanding of the church's worship tradition.

Vespers offers a specific ascription of praise and a responsory for the Lenten season. The Office Hymn should emphasize the Lenten theme chosen for the service. The sermon, which follows, should clearly speak of God's will for the Christian's life and how it is fulfilled most generously and freely in Christ. The canticle may be omitted or one of the following Lenten hymns may be used: "The Royal Banners Forward Go" (*Vexilla regis*) or "O Christ, the Lamb of God" (*Agnus Dei*).[19] The Lord's Prayer follows the Kyrie and may be sung on a single recitation note by the whole congregation after the pastor intones the first line; this approach encourages the congregation to think about each petition as it is chanted. The prayers that follow the Lord's Prayer may include a collect for Lent and normally conclude with the Collect for Peace.[20] The absence of a closing hymn after the Benediction enables the congregation to depart quietly and reverently.

Perhaps the most appropriate service for the Lenten season is Prayer at the Close of the Day or Compline.[21] The Office of Compline promotes a strikingly penitential tone among worshipers. An order of Confession and Absolution or a Declaration of Grace at each service can be augmented by a modification of the full Service of Corporate Confession and Absolution[22] for variety in Lenten worship styles. The brief reading indicated in rubric 5 of Compline can be supplemented with a reading from a portion of the Passion Narrative from one of the Gospels or from a harmony of the Gospels. It is followed by the sermon. The responsory from Psalm 31:5 and Luke 23:46 strongly echoes familiar Lenten themes and is an appropriate response to the Word as read and proclaimed. The prayers presented in rubric 8 may be supplemented with Lenten prayers, and they conclude with the Lord's Prayer, perhaps chanted on one tone. Although the Gospel Canticle may be omitted, its emphasis on watching with Christ is reminiscent of the disciples in the Garden of Gethsemane, thus it is most appropriate for the Lenten season. The service concludes with the blessing and no hymn is sung. A quiet organ postlude would communicate a sense of solemnity and devotional meditation as the congregation departs.

Kneeling for prayer during Lent is an old tradition. Kneeling was an ancient mark of humility and submission.[23] Although it is never a preferred human position—kneeling is uncomfortable—Lent is a time to involve our bodies and not merely our heads in worship. Be careful that those who are unable to kneel are not made to feel badly if they do not participate. When introducing kneeling for prayer during the Lenten season, worship leaders should be sensitive to the length of the prayers and perhaps initially have the congregation kneel only for the Lord's Prayer.

The Litany[24] is an invaluable addition to a congregation's Lenten worship practice. This classic Christian prayer, which Luther adapted for his congregation, may be used throughout the Lenten season to provide a deeper sense of continuity and to serve as a source of instruction in the Christian faith.[25]

The hymns selected for Lenten services should reflect the more solemn tone of the season. A great variety of Lutheran hymns and chorales provide substantive material both for meditation and for proclamation.[26]

SUNDAY OF THE PASSION (PALM SUNDAY)

The Sunday of the Passion begins Holy Week, sometimes referred to as the "Great Week," which is the culmination of the Lenten experience. The double emphasis of this Sunday is reflected in the Epistle for the day, Paul's great Christological hymn from Philippians 2:5–11. The reading, as should the whole service, has the double theme of holy joy and somber humility, a reminder of the reality of the coming week. Beginning with loud *hosannas* and a jubilant procession, the congregation is drawn into the joyous festivities until the sobering cry "Crucify Him!" is heard in the Gospel. Worship leaders will want to plan for such a contrast.

The use of a full procession is appropriate for this Sunday because it is practical, festive, and makes a public statement or confession. Early Christians understood such processions as a churchly enactment of the coronation processions held when new kings or emperors were crowned. A palm procession is also reminiscent of the Jerusalem crowds who welcomed Jesus as their messianic hope (Luke 19:37–40). There also may be a conscious or subtle allusion to another crowd of palmbearers: the martyrs of Revelation who have entered the heavenly gates through much tribulation (Revelation 7:9). The original practice of a Palm Sunday procession dates to fourth-century Jerusalem when Christian pilgrims gathered to reenact Christ's triumphant entry.[27]

After the pastor greets the congregation with "Blessed is he who comes in the name of the Lord," the congregation responds, "Hosanna to the Son of David."[28] After a traditional salutation, a brief prayer may be said, followed by the Gospel Reading of Jesus' triumphant entry into Jerusalem. Some liturgies provide a prefatory dialogue that includes a blessing of the branches, though this is not necessary.[29]

After this dialogue, the pastor says, "Let us go forth in peace." The people respond, "in the name of the Lord." The choir may sing the festival hymn "All Glory, Laud, and Honor" with the congregation joining in the refrain.[30] At the conclusion of the procession, the pastor again greets the people, "Blessed is he who comes in the name of the Lord." The people respond, "Amen." The service continues with the Collect of the Day. The Confession and Absolution may be placed immediately prior to the Preface for Holy Communion.

The singing of *hosanna* should not be confused with the omission of the *alleluia* during Lent. The word *hosanna* is a transliteration of the Hebrew phrase that expresses the plea "Lord, save us" (Psalm 118:25), which became a cry of joyous hope. In some congregations when the *alleluia* is omitted in a Lenten hymn, *hosanna* (pronounced *ho-zee-a-na* to coincide with the syllables of *alleluia*) or the words "Hail! Hosanna!" are sung in its place.

The color for Passion Sunday is scarlet, a royal red that is darker than the red used for Pentecost and other festivals. The color reminds worshipers of the blood of the Lamb of God. Because the Sunday of the Passion is celebrative, greens may be used to adorn the church—particularly palm branches.[31] Flowers may be absent from the chancel because it is Lent. The green palm branches were understood as symbols of victory, life, and hope in the earliest Greek and Latin practices of the Christian communities.[32]

A tradition that dates to the early church is evident in two alternate names for this Sunday: *Dominica competentium* (Sunday of the Catechumens) or *Missa in Traditio Symboli* (Mass for Passing Down the Creed). Both names refer to the practice of teaching the Apostles' Creed to catechumens on the Sunday before their Baptism, which would have occurred on Easter Eve.[33] Luther Reed suggests that this connection may explain the practice of celebrating confirmation on this date in some Lutheran churches, but he suggests that such a practice may be counterproductive to the expected emphasis on the passion of our Lord.[34]

Passion Sunday is the more descriptive name for this Sunday and comes from the traditional reading of the passion account that occurred on this day. The three-year cycle of readings enables a congregation to hear the entire passion account without duplication over three years. One fairly common catholic tradition was to have various voices read or chant Matthew 26–27 on Palm Sunday, Mark 14–15 on Tuesday, Luke 22–23 on Wednesday, and John 18–19 on Good Friday.[35] The Reading of the Passion was retained in most Lutheran congregations after the Reformation. Many sixteenth-century Lutheran congregations adopted a conflation of the passion history prepared by Johannes Bugenhagen. This tradition culminated in the dramatic musical arrangement of *St. Matthew's Passion* by Johann Sebastian Bach.[36]

Recently, Lutheran congregations have used the Gospel account of Jesus' entry into Jerusalem as a Gospel Reading for Passion Sunday. However, this is better used for the processional service and the passion account retained for the actual Gospel Reading. The passion account may be read by a single speaker, or it may be read by several readers or even groups, each voice taking a particular part in the text. The Gospel acclamations are omitted on this Sunday because acclamations were given during the entrance procession. The sermon may be a brief commentary on the significance of the events described in the lesson. Holy Communion is usually offered at this service so God's gathered guests may be refreshed for the watching and praying to come.

Some congregations hold daily services during Holy Week, and several Lutheran hymnbooks provide the Propers for each day. Brief noontime services or short Vespers services each day would speak volumes to the community, particularly in urban settings, and would offer opportunities to bring others into the church. A brief confession, the singing of a Lenten hymn verse, the chanting of a psalm between the Scripture readings, a short sermon followed by another Lenten hymn, a prayer, the Lord's Prayer, and Benediction could easily be done in 30 minutes. Such a service could provide busy individuals with a meaningful time for meditation on the most significant event in world history.[37]

MAUNDY THURSDAY (HOLY THURSDAY)

Although many worship books include readings for each day of Holy Week, most Lutheran congregations celebrate only the *Triduum*, which is Latin for "three days." The *Triduum* includes services on Maundy Thursday and Good Friday, as well as the Easter Vigil of Holy Saturday.[38] The word *Maundy* comes from the Latin *mandatum*, which means "commandment." It alludes to Jesus' new commandment in John 13:34 to love one another, which He gave after He had washed His disciples' feet. More important for sacramental churches, this is the day on which Jesus instituted the Lord's Supper.

The Sacrament of the Altar should be the key feature in a Lutheran service on Maundy Thursday. The sermon should certainly point to the significance not only of the event but also the continuing blessings imparted as we receive our Lord's body and blood in, with, and under the bread and wine. To that end, the service should not suggest that the Supper is merely a memorial meal. While this theme is a major emphasis in other Protestant denominations, Lutherans have recognized that

the Sacrament is much more. Our Lord actually comes to us and gives us His forgiveness. The fact that this is Christ's last will and testament, rather than a covenant
between two equals, may also be expressed in the service.[39]

A narrative Communion service may be considered for
Maundy Thursday because it directs the congregation's attention not only to the meaning of worship but, more important, to the significance of the Sacrament.[40] Some Lutheran
congregations have introduced their members to the similarities between the Jewish Seder and Jesus' Last Supper.[41] While
many connections can be made,[42] a Maundy Thursday service
may not be the best time to introduce them.[43] Such instruc-
tion is best reserved for a Sunday evening during Lent or another day of Holy Week.

The washing of the disciples' feet by Jesus is also recalled on this day. Therefore, another theme for Maundy Thursday worship in addition to the Lord's Supper
may be humble service, especially that expressed through parish ministries. Ser-
vice-oriented ministries might be highlighted by public recognition of the hours
donated in the congregation and community. In many denominations, the pastor
symbolically washes someone's feet.[44] Yet the pastoral ministry should also be
emphasized as one to and for everyone. Perhaps a synodical or district official could
be invited to preach a sermon that underscores the pastoral office in the congregation.[45]

A third theme, that of Lenten preparation, concludes this unique night. The
stripping of the altar ends the Maundy Thursday service, as well as the Lenten
preparations of the congregation. (Good Friday is not a preparation day; instead, it
is the recollection and celebration of Christ's selfless death on the cross.) As the
choir quietly sings Psalm 22 and the congregation silently watches, the presiding
minister and assistants remove all the paraments and furnishings from the altar
area and chancel.[46] This should be carefully planned to avoid unnecessary shuffling
by participants or inordinate moving of furnishings that may disrupt the meditation of the congregation and distract from the significance of the actions. The stripping of the altar is symbolic of Jesus' humiliation at the hands of those who
crucified Him.

Some Lutheran worship resources for Maundy Thursday suggest the omission
of the Benediction at this service because the service continues on Good Friday and
in the Easter Vigil.[47] If this practice is followed, it should be stated clearly so the congregation understands the "three days" of the Triduum are part of one service and
their meditations at home should reflect this intent and purpose.

GOOD FRIDAY

The service or services of Good Friday should be as austere and unembellished as possible, yet without a funereal gloom. The focus is on the Word or, more particularly, the fulfillment of God's promises in Christ Jesus' death, which is the full payment for the world's sin. Thus there is naturally a sense of restrained joy at the ultimate goodness of the day's events. A hymn attributed to Bernard of Clairvaux (1091–1153), "O Sacred Head, Now Wounded,"[48] may  serve as a guiding theme throughout the day. The reading of the Passion from the Gospel of John dates to fourth-century Jerusalem and is usually followed in Lutheran churches[49] with the hymn "Lamb of God, Pure and Sinless" by Nikolaus Decius (1490–1541).[50]

Lutheran Worship: Agenda provides several services for Good Friday. Each has its own particular emphasis and provides ample opportunity for adaptation to local customs and circumstances.

GOOD FRIDAY AT NOONDAY[51]

This brief order of service for Good Friday could be adapted for local congregational use throughout the Lenten season. The service begins with two Lenten responsory readings and collects. The hymn "Jesus, I Will Ponder Now"[52] is suggested. After the Scripture readings and another hymn, a sermon is indicated, followed by another hymn. Two more responsive verses and a collect are followed by the Agnus Dei, which is spoken responsorially. A special closing blessing concludes the service: "Christ crucified draw you to himself, to find in him a sure ground of faith, a firm support for hope, and the assurance of sins forgiven; and the blessing of almighty God, the Father, the (✠) Son, and the Holy Spirit, be with you now and forever."[53]

GOOD FRIDAY I[54]

Good Friday I, which includes the Bidding Prayer, emphasizes praying with Jesus. The Old Testament Reading and hymn follow an introductory collect. After the Gospel Reading, a sermon is suggested. After the sermon, the Bidding Prayer is said. This form of prayer, which Lutherans have retained, was an established Christian tradition dating to early post-apostolic times.[55] An assisting minister announces or "bids" the topic for the prayer, and the presiding minister prays the petitions. The conclusion to the Bidding Prayer leads directly to the Lord's Prayer and comes from the time of the Lutheran Reformation.[56] The congregation may be encouraged to kneel for the prayers and intervening silence and may stand or be seated for the bidding.

An option for this Good Friday service is an adaptation of the adoration of the cross. Originating in fourth-century Jerusalem, this service was popular in the Middle Ages but was eliminated in Lutheran congregations at the time of the Reformation.[57] If not already in the sanctuary at the start of the service or carried in at the beginning of the service, a rough-hewn wooden cross[58] is carried into the chancel immediately after the Bidding Prayer. It is leaned against the altar or Communion rail as the congregation responds to the sentences spoken by the presiding minister. The presiding minister may chant or say, "Behold, the life-giving cross on which was hung the salvation of the whole world." The congregation then responds, "Oh, come, let us worship him."[59] A series of Reproaches is spoken by the pastor as the people answer with a stanza from "Lamb of God, Pure and Sinless," which is followed by a time for silent reflection. The Reproaches were originally in Latin with a Greek refrain, suggesting that they originated early in the history of Christian worship.[60] The hymn "O Dearest Jesus, What Law Have You Broken,"[61] as well as a concluding responsive sentence, end the service.[62]

Be careful when using the adoration of the cross that the physical cross is not being worshiped. Such a perspective is often miscommunicated by the song "The Old Rugged Cross." It is not the cross but the one enthroned on the cross who is being worshiped. Two ancient hymns by the sixth-century hymn writer Venantius Honorius Fortunatus are ideal alternatives for use in this portion of the service: "Sing, My Tongue"[63] and "The Royal Banners Forward Go."[64]

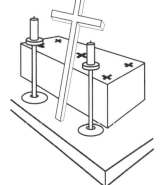

GOOD FRIDAY II

The Good Friday II service includes Communion and again the Reproaches are suggested for use after the Epistle Reading.[65] The Gospel for the Day—John 18–19—is read in sections and interspersed with seven hymn stanzas. Stanza 1 is from "Jesus, I Will Ponder Now,"[66] and six stanzas are from "O Sacred Head, Now Wounded."[67] Several readers may be used for this service. The Bidding Prayer follows the sermon and comes before the Lord's Supper.[68] Although some churches do not celebrate Communion, Lutherans at the time of the Reformation restored the reception of the Sacrament on Good Friday.[69] More recently, Roman Catholic and Anglican communities have reintroduced Communion services on Good Friday.[70]

TRE ORE SERVICE

Another Good Friday service that has become popular is the Tre Ore service. The title refers to the "three hours"—from noon to 3 P.M.—on Good Friday when there was darkness. This three-hour devotion originated in Jerusalem when the bishop presided over a service of readings, interspersed with prayers, that concluded with the reading of the passion according to St. John. Curiously, in following centuries this service of pilgrimage was not adopted by Christians outside of Jerusalem. Only in the seventeenth century did some Peruvian Jesuits introduce a devotional service on the seven words of Christ from the cross.[71] Recently, many Protestants, including Lutherans, have adopted this Roman Catholic devotional service as a time to meditate on the last words of Christ or on other themes related to the passion. Besides the seven last words, significant questions raised during the passion of our Lord, selected individuals at the cross, or other Lenten devotional thematic patterns have been developed. In addition to a commentary or homily on one of Christ's last words from the cross or another biblical text, responsive readings, prayers, and a hymn, such as "Jesus, in Your Dying Woes,"[72] complete the seven sections of the service.[73] Meditative interludes allow worshipers to come and go between the sections of the three devotional hours.

TENEBRAE SERVICE

An increasing number of Lutheran congregations conduct a service known as *Tenebrae*, which is Latin for "darkness." In the Middle Ages, Tenebrae services were held on the evenings in Holy Week preceding the Triduum as a preparation for Maundy Thursday, Good Friday, and the Easter Vigil.[74] This seems to indicate a transposition of the daily services of Holy Week to evening services so laypeople could more actively participate in the devotional services of the Triduum.[75]

The Tenebrae service for Good Friday consists of seven to ten Scripture readings, each followed by a period of meditation and, perhaps, a hymn stanza. A stand with the same number of candles as readings is placed in the chancel. After each reading, a candle is extinguished. After the final reading the church is in complete darkness. Traditionally, seven psalms were read, but adaptations have been made so selected readings from the Passion Narrative may be used in place of or in addition to the psalms.[76] The service often concludes with Jesus' last words from the cross, "It is finished." As these words are spoken, a large Bible may be slammed shut (the *strepitus*), which is symbolic of the tomb being closed. The worshipers then leave the sanctuary in silence. They may follow the eternal light, which is carried out of the sanctuary and not returned to its place until the Easter Vigil.

VIGIL OF EASTER[77]

Although a relatively new service among Lutherans, the Easter Vigil has a long and revered tradition. Perhaps dating to early Jewish-Christian practices of an evening service in preparation for Passover, the Vigil recalls the many accounts of God's deliverance of His people.[78] In *Apostolic Tradition*, Hippolytus describes the already ancient ceremony that prepared the catechumens for their Baptism on Saturday night.[79] Following the Jewish custom of reckoning the beginning of the day at sundown, the Easter Vigil began on Easter Eve with a time of prayer and meditation. The Baptism of the catechumens and their first Communion followed. As time passed, the ceremonies became more elaborate, and often the service had to begin on Saturday morning to complete the various activities prescribed for the day.[80] Over the centuries, particularly after the Reformation, the service became less prominent and was nearly eliminated. Only since about 1950 has the Easter Vigil been reinstituted among Roman Catholics.[81] It has reappeared in the worship experiences of Anglicans and Lutherans more recently.

The Easter Vigil is rich in Gospel motifs (Romans 6:3–5) and opportunities to celebrate the fullness of Christian faith, "a veritable catechism of faith's meaning and a breath-taking reenactment of faith's dramatic journey, anticipated, affirmed, and fulfilled."[82] Philip Pfatteicher explains the transhistorical nature of this service: "The Passover and the Resurrection and the church's celebration of Easter all merge and become contemporary events."[83] The Vigil consists of four parts or individual services; each is distinct yet develops a theme closely connected to the resurrection Gospel: "freedom out of slavery, life out of death, light out of darkness, and speech out of silence."[84] Many Lutherans are unfamiliar with this service, yet the Vigil offers great possibilities for the gathering of God's guests.

THE SERVICE OF LIGHT

This first service of the Easter Vigil contains three elements: the recognition of new fire, a presentation of the paschal canticle, and the first expression of Easter joy.

Adapted from earlier forms of the *Lucernarium* of Vespers, or Evening Prayer, the first element of the Service of Light features a large fire that is built outside the church. This action may recall the Jewish tradition of gathering the household on the Sabbath Eve to announce the beginning of the day as the *Shabbat* candles are lit. If community ordinances permit, a congregation may burn the trunk of the previous year's Christmas tree, which could also be used for the Good Friday cross. If the

eternal light was carried out during a Tenebrae service, the flame is now reintroduced and used to light the larger fire. The new fire is recognized by the pastor with
a short commentary and prayer. (In medieval times the fire was ignited by flint,
which was associated with Christ, the stone that had been rejected.[85])

An assisting minister then brings forward the paschal candle. The candle
should feature a cross and the Greek capital letters *alpha* (A) and *omega* (Ω), as well
as the numerals of the year. As the pastor traces the cross, letters, and year, he says:[86]

Tracing the vertical arm of the cross: Christ Jesus, the same yesterday, today, and
forever,

Tracing the horizontal arm of the cross: the beginning and the ending,

Tracing the alpha: the Alpha

Tracing the omega: and Omega.

Tracing the first numeral: His are time

Tracing the second numeral: and eternity;

Tracing the third numeral: his are the glory and dominion,

Tracing the last numeral: now and forever.

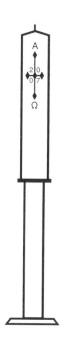

An ancient practice directs the pastor to place five pieces of
incense, which are held in place with red wax nails, into the cross
to represent Christ's five wounds:[87]

Placing a wax nail in upper vertical part of cross: By his
wounds

Placing a wax nail at the crossbeam: we have healing

Placing a wax nail in lower vertical part of cross: both now

Placing a wax nail in left arm of cross: and forever.

Placing a wax nail in right arm of cross: Amen.

The pastor lights the paschal candle from the newly kindled
fire and prays the appointed collect. Then the worshipers light
their candles from the paschal candle. In ancient times as the candles were lighted the congregation sang the hymn *Phos hilaron*
("Joyous Light of Glory").[88] This song from Evening Prayer may be used, or one of
the following hymns may be sung as the congregation enters the church: "Christ,
Whose Glory Fills the Skies," "O Gladsome Light, O Grace," "O Splendor of the
Father's Light," or "O Trinity, O Blessed Light."[89] Instead of a hymn, the assisting
minister who is carrying the paschal candle may chant "The light of Christ" three
times—at the beginning of the procession, halfway to the altar, and again at the
altar—to which the people respond, "Thanks be to God."[90] The paschal candle is
then placed in its stand. The paschal candle will remain lit for every service during
the 50 days of Easter. Placed at the liturgical north side, the candle should be lighted

before any other candle is lit, perhaps 15 minutes or more prior to the start of a service held during the season of Easter.

After everyone has assembled in the church, the assisting minister stands by the baptismal font and chants the Easter Proclamation, the *Exsultet* (Latin for "rejoice"). This early Christian hymn is a masterpiece of liturgical poetry and is filled with biblical imagery, allusions, and typologies. It encourages: "Rejoice now, all you heavenly choirs of angels; rejoice now, all creation. . . . Rejoice too, all the earth. . . . Rejoice, O Church of Christ."[91] The pastor continues with a chant that recalls the significance of this time and concludes with the petition "Let Christ, the true light and morning star, shine in our hearts."[92] After the worshipers extinguish their candles, the lights in the nave are turned low for the next service.

THE SERVICE OF READINGS

Between four (from Genesis; Exodus; Isaiah 4; and Deuteronomy 31:22–30) to twelve lessons are read to recall the history of God's people.[93] The overall theme of this service is the renewal of life through the resurrection. The eight lessons provided in the Lutheran rite[94] are: the creation (Genesis 1:1–2:2 or 1:1–3:24), the flood (Genesis 7:1–5, 11–18; 8:6–18; 9:8–13), Abraham's sacrifice of Isaac (Genesis 22:1–18), Israel's deliverance at the Red Sea (Exodus 14:10–15:1), salvation offered freely to all (Isaiah 55:1–11), a new heart and a new spirit (Ezekiel 36:24–28), faith strained but victorious (Job 19:20–27), and the gathering of God's people (Zephaniah 3:12–20). In addition to these readings, other orders suggest extra passages that can be added, if time and circumstances permit: Isaiah 4:2–6; 5:1–2a, 7a; Exodus 12:1–14 or 1–24; Jonah 3:1–10; Deuteronomy 31:19–30; and Daniel 3:1–29.[95] After a period of silent meditation, a prayer accompanies each reading.

In the early church these readings were the major component of the Easter Vigil and may have lasted throughout the night. If worshipers knelt for prayer during the Lenten season, a congregation may stand for the prayers during this service. Otherwise, the congregation may remain seated throughout the Service of Readings. A hymn stanza may also be sung in place of some readings or between readings. If hymn stanzas are included before or after each reading, they should closely reflect the theme of the reading.

Although the Service of Readings appears to be long, it is not meant to be too solemn or too slowly paced, which might result in a distracted or disinterested congregation. Egeria, the fourth-century nun who visited Jerusalem and provided the first report of this service, wrote, "For the sake of the people, everything is done rapidly, lest they be delayed too long."[96]

The canticle of the three young men, "All You Works of the Lord" (Benedicite, Omnia Opera),[97] may be sung after the completion of all the readings. Attributed to Shadrach, Meshach, and Abednego, this canticle picks up the theme of creation's rejoicing.[98] It may be sung by a soloist, choir, or by the congregation. During the singing of the canticle, the presiding and assisting ministers proceed to the baptismal font. Baptismal candidates may also be presented at this time in anticipation of the next service of the Easter Vigil.

SERVICE OF HOLY BAPTISM

If possible, the pastor should plan for at least one Baptism at the Easter Vigil.[99] After the candidates for Baptism and the sponsors have gathered at the font, the pastor addresses the congregation about the significance of Baptism (Romans 6:3–11). After the address, the congregation sings "All Who Believe and Are Baptized."[100] If the baptismal candidate, sponsors, and family have not gathered prior to the address, they may do so during this hymn. The Baptism follows according to the church's usual practice and order.[101]

If there are no baptisms, this service of the Easter Vigil can be done as a baptismal remembrance service. In that case the pastor invites the congregation to renounce the devil and all his works and ways and confess their faith with the three articles of the Apostles' Creed. The renewal of baptismal vows was an early Christian custom that occurred regularly until the sixth century. At the Vigil of Easter those who had been baptized celebrated this event with great thanksgiving and special prayers. This anniversary emphasis was an ancient prototype of a "confirmation reunion."[102] Such a reunion is a worthy practice to reinstate.

After the baptismal blessing, the Easter Vigil moves its attention to the altar for the final and main service, the Service of Holy Communion.

SERVICE OF HOLY COMMUNION

The altar is the concluding and chief focus for the Vigil and the rest of the Easter celebration. The altar may be vested prior to the service, but it is not uncommon for the altar guild or chancel care committee to bring out the white or gold paraments during the singing of the Hymn of Praise, a reversal of the Maundy Thursday stripping of the altar.

The Service of Holy Communion begins with a joyous and responsive greeting as the pastor proclaims, "Alleluia. Christ is risen." Then the worshipers respond, "The Lord is risen indeed. Alleluia."[103] The altar candles are lighted from the paschal candle during this greeting.

As the church blazes with light and color, the Hymn of Praise, traditionally "Glory to God in the Highest," is sung. The collect, readings, and Easter Gospel are then read, and the Communion service concludes in normal fashion. If other Easter services are conducted, the worship leaders may depart with a recessional hymn.

For the Easter Vigil, the pastor may wear Easter vestments throughout the services. However, for visual distinction among the various services, he may begin with the purple vesture for the Service of Light. He can change to the white or gold stole at the Service of Readings, which would be symbolic of the church's proclamatory authority. For the Service of Baptism, white robes or white aprons may be given to the baptized. Finally, a full Easter chasuble may be worn for Communion.

Various festival decorations may be evident throughout the church building. Excess is nearly impossible in celebrating the Festival of Our Lord's Resurrection! Easter lilies and banners may be displayed in the chancel, though lights should not be focused on them until the Service of Light concludes. Similarly, the music for the Vigil will move from solemn chants to the joyous sounds of the Hymn of Praise and the celebrative hymns used during the distribution of Holy Communion.

When planning this service, considerations for local customs and available personnel are important. Some congregations have used the Vigil as an Easter Eve service, similar to a Christmas Eve service. Others have emphasized the watchful nature of the Vigil and have begun the service near midnight. Another possibility is to schedule the service an hour before sunrise so the congregation begins the service in darkness but leaves in the joyous light of Easter morning. The distinctive changes in atmosphere and mood of the service cannot be missed regardless of the time set for the start of the Vigil. If attendance is a concern, consider involving neighboring congregations in a joint celebration of the Vigil.

Whatever energies and efforts are exerted for the planning of this service, worship leaders and worshipers will find it to be a memorable service. The means of grace are never more prominent in any single service than in the Easter Vigil, which makes this a particularly edifying service for Lutherans, who cherish God's Word and Sacraments. Also the message of the forgiveness of sins and God's initial, continual, and final work through Christ cannot be missed by God's gathered guests.

The suggestions for services in this chapter have centered around enhancing the special occasions in the church's life as God's gathered guests recall His gifts. While there are many other possibilities, congregation members and worship leaders will want to consider these specific suggestions to enhance the proclamation of God's wonderful works in worship and praise.

SOME QUESTIONS TO CONSIDER

1. How can your local congregation expand its celebration of Advent? What ideas suggested in this chapter would be viable this next Advent season? Describe what your congregation's worship life might be like after a three-year educational program on Advent practices.

2. What are three features of Epiphany that make the service of Evening Prayer appropriate for this festival?

3. How could Ash Wednesday become a catechetically significant service for Lutheran worshipers? Give three specific lessons that could be taught.

4. List five ways your congregation has varied its midweek Lenten services over the past several years in comparison to its Sunday routine.

5. Why is the double theme of the Sunday of the Passion a somewhat difficult emphasis to carry out? How might you assist your pastor in planning this service?

6. What is the Triduum? Why is it beneficial? How is the sense of unity maintained?

7. List five features of a Maundy Thursday service that Lutheran worship leaders may wish to emphasize.

8. Briefly describe what you consider to be the most important emphasis of a Good Friday service. Is this emphasis evident in the Good Friday services described in this chapter?

9. If you had to organize an Easter Vigil, what steps would you take to ensure the service effectively communicates the Easter Gospel? How far in advance would you begin work? Whom would you involve in the preparations? Briefly describe who would be responsible for each detail.

NOTES

1. Bosch, *Church Year Guide*, 88.

2. If used, this acclamation would be spoken by the congregation in response to the Words of Institution in the Service of the Sacrament.

3. The Magnificat in Vespers (*Lutheran Worship*, pp. 228–30), the Gospel Canticle in Evening Prayer (*Lutheran Worship*, pp. 255–57), and "My Soul Now Magnifies the Lord" (*Lutheran Worship*, 211) can be introduced over several years, then used for the midweek services.

4. LW 21:295–358. See also LW 53:176–79.

5. Bosch, *Church Year Guide*, 97.

6. Horn, *Christian Year*, 56–57, provides the Latin words: *O Sapientiae, O Adonai, O Radix Jesse, O Clavis David, O Oriens, O Rex Gentium, O Emmanuel.* See *Lutheran Worship*, 31.

7. Beginning in 1533, the first two weeks of Advent were set aside in the Wittenberg parish for preaching on the catechism. See Luther's reference in the Large Catechism to teaching children through sermons at appropriate times during the church year (LC, "The Creed," 32). However, Luther did not want to relegate such creedal information to the children's sermon only; instead, he believed it should be included in every sermon/service.

8. See Kemper, *Variety for Worship*, 15–20. While Kemper names the candles, the themes are more important.

9. *Lutheran Worship*, pp. 250–62.

10. If a congregation used candles for a Christmas Eve service, they could be used again.

11. *Lutheran Worship*, pp. 251–52.

12. See *Lutheran Worship*, pp. 253–54. The practice of incensing the altar is simple. Normally, the thurifer (the assisting minister who carries the censer, also known as the thurible or incense burner) processes into the church with the censer and keeps some incense burning on the coal during the first part of the service. When it is time to incense the altar, the thurifer may incense the altar, or, more traditionally, the thurifer hands the censer to the presiding minister. The presiding minister approaches the altar and swings the censer three times each at the center of the altar, at the right front "horn" (if a freestanding altar, at the right rear), and at the left front "horn" of the altar (if a freestanding altar, at the left rear). If desired, the presiding minister or thurifer may turn and approach the congregation and incense the front, right, and left sides of the congregation from the center aisle. He then returns to the chancel, and the censer is placed on its stand.

13. For more information on the Epiphany season, see *Gathered Guests* chapter 3.

14. The Scrutinies were a series of questions developed in the early church as a public form for examining catechumens. Such questions helped catechumens understand the significance of the Christian faith and their anticipated Baptism.

15. One schedule for a series of catechetical sermons using the Gospel of Mark might be 14:27–31 (Confession and Holy Absolution); 14:32–42 (Lord's Prayer); 14:43–52 (Holy Baptism); 14:53–64 (Ten Commandments: First Table); 14:65–72 (Ten Commandments: Second Table); 15:1–20 (Apostles' Creed); 14:12–26 (Holy Communion); 15:21–41 (Table of Duties); and 16:1–8 (Easter Sunday).

16. See Luther's 1528 series on the Ten Commandments, the Creed, and the Lord's Prayer in LW 51.

17. Dix, *Shape of the Liturgy* (2d ed.), 353–54, speaks of prebaptismal fasts that Justin mentioned as traditions in the church in A.D. 155.

18. Horn, *Christian Year*, 103–4.

19. *Lutheran Worship*, 2 and 7. After a few practices, either of these can be sung easily by a congregation.

20. See *Lutheran Worship*, p. 234.

21. *Lutheran Worship*, pp. 263–69.

22. *Lutheran Worship*, pp. 308–9.

23. Bosch, *Church Year Guide*, 63, suggests that the practice grew out of the posture of defeat and submission to one's conqueror and came straight from the battlefield.

24. *Lutheran Worship*, pp. 279–87.

25. "German Litany and Latin Litany Corrected," LW 53:153–70. See also *Gathered Guests* chapter 17 for a richer explanation of the Litany form.

26. See Graf, *Joybells of Life*.

27. Wilkinson, *Egeria's Travels*, 30.1–31.4.

28. See *Lutheran Worship: Agenda*, 35–37, for the Palm Sunday Procession with Palms.

29. Although Inter-Lutheran Commission on Worship, *Church Year*, provides a prayer of blessing, Lutheran custom is to avoid blessing objects.

30. Kemper, *Variety for Worship*, 40–44, notes that a better way for worship leaders to introduce a Palm Sunday procession is by making it a recession. The palms may be distributed to the congregation during the service and their significance explained. Then the palms are carried out as the worshipers depart into the world to witness to their faith and hope in Christ, who is our crucified yet victorious Lord.

31. Bosch, *Church Year Guide*, 67, notes that some churches use budding or leafing olive, willow, or birch branches because they are locally available.

32. Pfatteicher, *Commentary*, 233.

33. Horn, *Christian Year*, 116.

34. Reed, *Lutheran Liturgy* (rev. ed.), 498.

35. Pfatteicher, *Commentary*, 232.

36. Horn, *Christian Year*, 114.

37. Worship planners might wish to consult Wilkinson, *Egeria's Travels*; Gingras, *Egeria*; or Peters, *Jerusalem,* for other service possibilities during Holy Week.

38. Early in the fifth century, Augustine spoke of "the most holy triduum of the crucified, buried, and risen Lord" (Letter 55:24 in *Corpus scriptorum ecclesiasticorum latinuum* 34/2.195).

39. See Luther's emphasis on the nature of a "testament" in "Treatise on the New Testament," LW 35:75–111; and SD VII. More than a covenant, Luther emphasized that the testament of Christ required His death so the promises would be put into effect (Ap. XXIV, 60).

40. A variety of such services are available. Two narrative services were prepared by the LCMS Commission on Worship when *Lutheran Worship* was introduced in the early 1980s.

41. Kemper, *Variety for Worship*, 46–56, provides a narrative service that draws together the whole church year and connects it to the Passover.

42. Rosen and Rosen, *Christ in the Passover*, provide many of these connections, though they downplay the sacramental significance of Jesus' real presence in the bread and wine.

43. Senn, "Lord's Supper, Not Passover Seder," 362–68, argues against such a practice.

44. Protestant groups in the nineteenth and twentieth centuries have invested this practice with quasi-sacramental value as one of Christ's three ordinances; however, Lutherans use foot washing only as a symbolic act, "an enacted sermon" (Pfatteicher, *Commentary*, 242). It shows the meaning of Christ's call to loving service.

45. Bosch, *Church Year Guide*, 34.

46. *Lutheran Worship: Agenda* provides the following directives: "Immediately after the Benediction in the Divine Service, the Communion vessels are reverently removed from the altar, the altar is stripped, and the chancel is cleared in preparation for the solemn services of Good Friday. While this is done, one of the following psalms [Psalm 22 or Psalm 51] is sung antiphonally by the choir and congregation or by two groups within the congregation. The Gloria Patri is omitted" (39). Once the psalm is concluded, the worshipers leave the church silently.

47. Pfatteicher, *Commentary*, 243; *Lutheran Book of Worship: Ministers Desk Edition* (Minneapolis: Augsburg; Philadelphia: Board of Publication, LCA, 1978), 138; Pfatteicher and Messerli, *Manual on the Liturgy*, 319–20.

48. *Lutheran Worship,* 113.

49. Pfatteicher, *Commentary*, 247.

50. *Lutheran Worship*, 208.

51. *Lutheran Worship: Agenda*, pp. 45–47.

52. *Lutheran Worship*, 109.

53. *Lutheran Worship: Agenda*, 47.

54. *Lutheran Worship Agenda*, 48–56.

55. Pfatteicher, *Commentary*, 248. For more information on the Bidding Prayer, see *Gathered Guests* chapter 17.

56. Pfatteicher, *Commentary*, 250.

57. Horn, *Christian Year*, 125.

58. The trunk of the previous year's Christmas tree may form a suitable cross.

59. *Lutheran Worship: Agenda*, 52. The concluding sentence of the service may be more theologically appropriate. The pastor says, "We adore you, O Christ, and we bless you." The congregation responds, "By your holy cross you have redeemed the world" (*Lutheran Worship: Agenda*, 56).

60. Pfatteicher, *Commentary*, 253–54, explains that the Reproaches were eliminated in *Lutheran Book of Worship* because they were considered antisemitic, as was the hymn "O Dearest Jesus, What Law Have You Broken." The hymn also reflects pietistic individualism, rather than the more communal orientation of the Reproaches, thus it is not as suitable for use as a response. However, this hymn is suggested to conclude this portion of the service.

61. *Lutheran Worship*, 119.

62. Brauer, "Church Year," 168.

63. *Lutheran Worship*, 117.

64. *Lutheran Worship*, 103 or 104.

65. *Lutheran Worship: Agenda*, 58–71.

66. *Lutheran Worship*, 109.

67. *Lutheran Worship*, 113.

68. Brauer, "Church Year," 169.

69. Compare Brauer's comment that "generally Holy Communion is not celebrated on this day, though rubrics and pericopes are given should they be required" ("Church Year," 168) and Horn, who suggests that Communion on Good Friday is a Calvinist emphasis (*Christian Year*, 125–26), with Senn's remark that Lutherans at the time of the Reformation celebrated Communion on Good Friday (*Christian Liturgy*, 343).

70. Pfatteicher, *Commentary*, 256.

71. Whitaker, "Three Hours Devotion," 507–8.

72. *Lutheran Worship*, 112.

73. Kemper, *Variety for Worship*, 67–78.

74. Horn, *Christian Year*, 124.

75. Crichton, "Tenebrae," 503–4.

76. Kemper, *Variety for Worship*, 58–66.

77. *Lutheran Worship: Agenda*, 73–90. An offprint is available for congregational participation.

78. Pfatteicher, *Commentary*, 258, notes Exodus 12:41–42; Luke 12:35–38.

79. Dix and Chadwick, *Treatise on the Apostolic Tradition*, 32, 50.

80. Horn, *Christian Year*, 128.

81. Jungmann, *Early Liturgy*, 263, gives the official date as 1956 for the renewal of the Vigil among Roman Catholics.

82. Bosch, *Church Year Guide*, 38.

83. Pfatteicher, *Commentary*, 258.

84. Brauer, "Church Year," 169.

85. Pfatteicher, *Commentary*, 261.

86. Adapted from Pfatteicher, *Commentary*, 262–63.

87. Pfatteicher, *Commentary*, 262, 270.

88. Horn, *Christian Year*, 129, suggests that there may also be some connection with the pagan practice of *Osterfeuer* observed by the ancient Germanic tribes in Europe.

89. *Lutheran Worship*, 480, 486, 481, and 487 respectively.

90. *Lutheran Worship: Agenda*, 74–75.

91. *Lutheran Worship: Agenda*, 75–76. An alternative to the Easter Proclamation is the hymn "Rejoice, Angelic Choirs, Rejoice" (*Lutheran Book of Worship*, 146).

92. *Lutheran Worship: Agenda*, 80.

93. Pfatteicher, *Commentary*, 273–74, notes that *Lutheran Book of Worship* has twelve readings, which follows the 1570 Roman Catholic missal. In contrast, the 1969 *Roman Missal* has seven readings; *Lutheran Worship: Agenda* has eight; and the Episcopal *Book of Common Prayer* has nine. Pfatteicher recommends that the creation account in Genesis and the exodus account should be read (*Lutheran Book of Worship* lists Exodus 13:17–15:1 and suggests that Moses' and Miriam's Songs from Exodus 15 be sung). The specific use of other Scripture texts is noted for comparison. Isaiah 4:2–6; 5:1–2a, 7a is used in the *Lutheran Book of Worship* and Episcopal service (Isaiah 54:1–14 in the Roman Rite). Baruch 3:9–37 [or 3:9–15, 32–4:4] is found in *Lutheran Book of Worship* and *Roman Missal*, along with Ezekiel 37:1–14. These are also used in the Episcopal service. *Lutheran Worship: Agenda* and the Episcopal service include a passage from Zephaniah. Pastoral discretion will determine local practice.

94. *Lutheran Worship: Agenda*, 81–83.

95. Pfatteicher and Messerli, *Manual on the Liturgy*, 147–52, also suggest that canticles may be sung for some of the readings, perhaps as a change for the congregation, as well as a way to introduce Old Testament songs.

96. Gingras, *Egeria*, 114.

97. *Lutheran Worship*, 9.

98. *Lutheran Book of Worship* concludes the Service of Readings with Daniel 3:1–29, making the canticle a natural conclusion to the readings. However, Pfatteicher, *Commentary*, 281, makes no comment on the canticle's inclusion.

99. After this service becomes a traditional element in a congregation's worship life, people anticipate such an event and will ask to participate in this baptismal service.

100. *Lutheran Worship*, 225.

101. See *Lutheran Worship*, pp. 199–204, and *Gathered Guests* chapter 14.

102. Horn, *Christian Year*, 129.

103. *Lutheran Worship: Agenda*, 86.

CHAPTER 14

OCCASIONAL WORSHIP SERVICES

Gathering together for special occasions is a mark of human society, as well as a trait of the Christian community. Of the significant events in a Christian's life, most important and significant is the Holy Spirit's work in the Sacrament of Holy Baptism.[1] There also are other occasions when God's gathered guests come together to mark special occasions. Most of these are nonsacramental, yet they are related to the rhythms of congregational life: weddings, funerals, and other similar significant events for God's people. Lutherans call these "occasional" services. Although some occur occasionally, others occur with regularity. Two types of services are discussed in this chapter—sacramental and nonsacramental—yet both types are special occasions in the life of a Christian.

Sacramental services mark those occasions in a Christian's life when the Sacraments of Baptism, Holy Absolution, and the Lord's Supper are received as God's gracious gifts. We will consider the corporate significance of Baptism, as well as the significance of private Absolution and private Communion, which occur usually in the home or in a church's smaller chapel.

The nonsacramental services identify singular occasions in the life of a Christian that are highly valued but lack a sacramental quality. Most obviously, these services—confirmation, marriage, and funerals—do not grant the forgiveness of sins. Finally, a few worship services recognize significant events in the life of a congregation and will be mentioned at the end of this chapter. These include ordination, commissioning, and the installation of professional church workers.[2]

THE SACRAMENT OF HOLY BAPTISM

Lutherans recognize Holy Baptism as God's act by which He establishes a saving relationship with individual sinners. Through Baptism our sins are washed away (1 Corinthians 6:11) and we are liberated from sin, death, and the devil

(1 Corinthians 10:1–2; 12:13). Jesus revealed the vital importance of Baptism when He spoke to Nicodemus: "No one can enter the kingdom of God unless he is born of water and the Spirit" (John 3:5). Prior to His ascension, Jesus gave His oft-quoted commission: "As you go, make disciples of all nations by baptizing them in the name of the Father and of the Son and of the Holy Spirit and by teaching them to observe everything that I have commanded you" (Matthew 28:19–20, author's translation).

Besides the command and institution by Jesus, early Christians recognized the great benefits of Baptism. Peter told the Pentecost crowds, "Repent and be baptized, every one of you, in the name of Jesus Christ for the forgiveness of your sins. And you will receive the gift of the Holy Spirit. The promise is for you and your children and for all who are far off—for all whom the Lord our God will call" (Acts 2:38–39). Later Peter wrote, "Baptism . . . now saves you . . . not the removal of dirt from the body but the pledge of a good conscience toward God. It saves you by the resurrection of Jesus Christ" (1 Peter 3:21). Similarly, Paul extolled the blessings of Baptism: "All of us who were baptized into Christ Jesus were baptized into His death[.] We were therefore buried with Him through baptism into death in order that, just as Christ was raised from the dead through the glory of the Father, we too may live a new life" (Romans 6:3b–4). Paul reminded Titus that God "saved us, not because of righteous things we had done, but because of His mercy. He saved us through the washing of rebirth and renewal by the Holy Spirit, whom He poured out on us generously through Jesus Christ our Savior" (Titus 3:5–6). Baptism is clearly God's action of imparting Christ's benefits to His chosen people and He attaches great promises and blessings to this washing by water and the Word.

Early Christians observed the Sacrament of Holy Baptism regularly. Baptismal practices are addressed in the Book of Acts and the writings of Justin Martyr in the first century, as well as in the second-century writing "The Didache." In the third century, Tertullian (ca. A.D. 155–225) wrote the first treatise on the subject, *De Baptismo*. Also Hippolytus's *Apostolic Tradition* provides a rather detailed description of the baptismal service. Interestingly, Hippolytus clearly stated that infants were to be baptized first, then the men and women.[3] A generation ago Kurt Aland and Joachim Jeremias addressed the specific issue of infant baptism and its normal practice by early Christians.[4]

Besides baptizing infants, the early church baptized adult converts after a period of instruction. This catechesis typically occurred during the Lenten season and culminated in a baptismal service during the Easter Vigil. The final week of instruction began with a detailed explanation of the Apostles' Creed and ended with an exposition and recitation of the Lord's Prayer. In Jerusalem after Constantine's conversion, the catechumenate (the programmed instruction that led to Baptism) lasted for three years and was marked liturgically at various stages.[5] The Vigil of Easter was the customary service at which new Christians were baptized. More will be said of this pre-baptismal teaching process under the section on confirmation later in this chapter.

The essential elements of the order of service for Baptism have changed little over the centuries. Even when nearly all baptisms were of infants, the teaching element of the service remained. Luther reflects this educational focus in his 1523 *Little Book of Baptism*, which was a close adaptation of the common baptismal rite of his day.[6] Three years later, he prepared an abridged baptismal book from which most present-day Lutheran baptismal services are drawn.[7] Although Luther followed several practices that the church added to emphasize important aspects of Baptism, the significance of Baptism is always directed to what God does through the Word-empowered water.

LUTHER'S BAPTISMAL SERVICE

Luther's order begins with the ancient exsufflation (from the Latin word that means "to blow upon") of the catechumen, in which the pastor blows on the child three times and says, "Depart, you unclean spirit, and make room for the Holy Spirit."[8] This act is the first of three exorcisms in Luther's baptismal service. Then the pastor marks a cross on the child as he says, "Receive the sign of the holy cross upon the forehead and the breast."[9] Most Lutheran rites have commendably added the words "to mark you as one redeemed by Christ the crucified."[10] By making the sign of the cross on themselves, worshipers recall their Baptism as the Invocation is spoken.

Luther then recommended that two prayers be said, including his famous "Flood Prayer," which connects several Old Testament images with Baptism in a manner similar to 1 Peter 3. The prayer is a powerful statement of God's sole action in Baptism. Because it is not readily available in English, it is included here.

> Almighty, eternal God, who according to your strict judgment condemned the unbelieving world through the flood and according to your great mercy preserved believing Noah and the seven members of his family, and who drowned Pharaoh with his army in the Red Sea and led your people Israel through the same sea on dry ground, thereby prefiguring this bath of your Holy Baptism, and who through the baptism of your dear child, our LORD Jesus Christ, hallowed and set apart the Jordan and all water to be a blessed flood and a rich

washing away of sins: we ask for the sake of this very same boundless mercy of yours that you would look graciously upon N. and bless him with true faith in the Holy Spirit so that through this same saving flood all that has been born in him from Adam and whatever he has added thereto may be drowned in him and sink, and that he, separated from the number of the unbelieving, may be preserved dry and secure in the holy ark of the Christian church and may at all times fervent in spirit and joyful in hope serve your name, so that with all believers in your promise he may become worthy to attain eternal life through Jesus Christ our LORD. Amen.[11]

After these prayers, the pastor speaks a second exorcism: "I adjure you, you unclean spirit, in the name of the Father (✠) and of the Son (✠) and of the Holy Spirit (✠), that you come out of and depart from this servant of Jesus Christ, N. Amen."[12] The account of Jesus and the children from the Gospel of Mark is then read. Placing his hands on the child's head,[13] the pastor invites the congregation and the sponsors to pray the Lord's Prayer.

Because the practice of Christian communities in medieval times prescribed that the exorcisms occur at the door of the church, the baptismal party moved to the baptismal font after the Lord's Prayer. Luther's order then prescribed that three questions that confirmed the exorcism be asked of the child through its sponsors: "Do you renounce the devil? And all his works? And all his ways?"[14] The sponsors would answer yes to each question. The pastor then asked three more questions that conformed to the three articles of the Apostles' Creed, to which the sponsors again would answer yes. Finally, the pastor would ask the child if he or she wanted to be baptized.

In his order, Luther stated that the pastor should "take the child and immerse it in the baptismal font[15] and say: 'And I baptize you in the name of the Father and of the Son and of the Holy Spirit.' "[16] For modern Lutherans, immersion is not as common as it was in Luther's day. Yet Luther's explanation of Baptism in the Small Catechism says clearly that the picture (that is, the sign or significance) is that of drowning and rising.[17] The early church required "flowing water"[18] for Baptism, so an alternative to full immersion may be to pour water over the candidate's head. Perhaps the most common practice in churches today is to apply water to the head by sprinkling. The first and middle names alone are used for the Baptism because the "family name" of the newly baptized has become the universal name "Christian."[19]

After the application of the water, the pastor places a christening robe on the child, prays a blessing, and speaks a word of peace. The christening robe or white baptismal gown depicts the righteousness given by Christ (Galatians 3:27) and worn by the saints in heaven (Revelation 7:9). Some families have a long white heirloom baptismal dress that is used on this occasion, though it makes immersion less convenient. A white cloth with an embroidered cross, similar to a communion purificator, may be used as a towel to wipe the water from the head of the baptized and given as a reminder of the baptism. A white poncholike garment may also be placed over infants and adults as a visual image of what has occurred in God's sight.[20] In an alternate custom, a stolelike garment is placed around the neck of the newly baptized as a symbol of the "easy yoke" (Matthew 11:30).

The prayer of the congregation that follows in the modern rite is the beginning of a regular remembrance and encouragement of the young in faith so they will grow in the grace and power of the Holy Spirit. This activity of the church as it remembers and encourages the newly baptized exemplifies the continuing growth and spiritual concern of the community of faith that is gathered around Word and Sacraments. Such a prayer ministry is vital for the continuing spiritual development of God's people.

LUTHERAN BAPTISMAL PRACTICES

Baptismal services in most Lutheran congregations follow a pattern similar to Luther's order. The few differences would be evident in the omission of most of the exorcisms and the Flood Prayer. In addition, new elements have been added over time. By the 1540s, an explanation of the biblical basis of and need for Baptism was included in most German Lutheran services. An admonition to sponsors was added in the sixteenth century, which has been retained in various forms to this day.[21] The most recent addition provides a congregational greeting to welcome the newly baptized, which emphasizes the corporate nature of Baptism and the community into which the newly baptized individual has entered.[22]

Recent Lutheran baptismal services include the ritual of giving a lighted candle. Luther's *Little Book of Baptism* (1523) concluded with the candle being placed in the child's hand, recalling the necessary watchful anticipation for Christ's return (Matthew 25:1–13). The pastor would then say: "Receive this burning light and preserve your baptism blamelessly, so that when the Lord comes to the wedding you may go to meet him and enter the heavenly mansion with the saints to receive eternal life."[23] If a congregation has a paschal candle, it should be placed near the font after Ascension Day, and it should be lighted for all baptisms. The baptismal candle would be lit from the paschal candle.

Baptism is not a mere act of initiation or part of a process of becoming a Christian. The name of Jesus is placed on the baptized, and through the water and the Word, the Holy Spirit creates faith and confirms the faith of older children and adults who already believe because the Spirit has worked faith in their hearts through hearing God's Word. Where there is faith, there is life and salvation, as Luther stated.[24] There is nothing more that can be given whereby we must be saved (Acts 4:12). Therefore, it is imperative that the church's baptismal teaching and practices reflect this unitive event. As Norman Nagel states, "When Baptism is not the entire gift, then man may have his parts to do; and when man does the doing, there is never enough."[25]

Baptisms normally occur in a congregational setting. Two locations of the baptismal service have become common in the Sunday liturgy; both are frequently related to the site of the font. One places the Baptism at the beginning of the service at the entrance to the sanctuary. If an opening hymn is normally used, it should be a baptismal hymn on a Sunday with a Baptism. The questions relating to the exorcism are a miniature confession of sins, tying Holy Baptism to Holy Absolution.[26] The Divine Service continues after the Baptism with the Hymn of Praise. The Rite of Baptism may also occur after the sermon at the time of the Apostles' Creed. Such placement connects the baptismal creed with the activity of Baptism.[27] The baptismal font is often located at the front of the church in the latter situation.

Infants are not the only baptismal candidates who may have sponsors. In the early church, adults who wished to be baptized were given sponsors who nurtured and mentored the new Christian.[28] The primary sponsors of a child are the parents. Yet with the busyness of raising a family, parents need the support of other Christians, particularly to help the family develop a strong devotional life centered around God's Word. Sponsors for adults may help to integrate and assimilate the new member into the larger community of faith. Sponsors, therefore, should be mature Christians who are able to meet the demands of such responsibilities.[29]

Although private Baptisms are infrequent, there are occasions when necessity requires that a child be baptized with only parents and witnesses and/or sponsors present. Similarly, emergency Baptisms are infrequent but still necessary. When a private Baptism or an emergency Baptism occurs, the congregation benefits from being informed. When a layperson performs an emergency Baptism, a special service may be conducted to ratify and recognize the legitimacy of the lay Baptism.[30]

Baptismal anniversaries may be celebrated in a congregation or in a parochial day school to help young children recall the significance of their baptisms.[31] Such a recollection may involve a reference to the paschal candle and a prayer, mentioning the Christian names of those celebrating a baptismal anniversary. Any additional customs related to this sacrament are aids to enlarging and enhancing the significance of Baptism, yet the essential act of Baptism is the application of water in the name of the Trinity.

CONFIRMATION

As mentioned earlier, instruction in the Christian faith and life was intimately connected to Baptism among the early Christians. Growing out of the early church's practice of making disciples by baptizing and teaching, confirmation was not a special rite or worship service but a process of instruction connected directly to Baptism. The long and intensive period of study and preparation for Baptism experienced by early Christians was known as the catechumenate. However, with the gradual decline in the number of adult converts, infant baptism became commonplace. Thus a pattern developed in which the biblical model of instruction after Baptism but prior to the reception of Holy Communion was established, following the pattern of Christ's own words.[32]

Although not understood as a sacrament, the Lutheran reformers retained the medieval practice of confirmation. In his own way, Luther emphasized confirmation as preparation for the Lord's Supper.[33] Yet the purpose of confirmation has been given various interpretations and has been subject to much misunderstanding not only among Lutherans but also among most Christians. As the Anglican scholar Geoffrey Wainwright admitted, "Confirmation has remained a rite in search of a meaning."[34] Even among Lutherans confirmation is frequently considered to be either a completion or a renewal of one's Baptism; it is also depicted as a fuller reception of the benefits of Baptism.[35] To believe that confirmation supplements Baptism depreciates the full benefits God gives in and through Baptism. Donald Deffner wisely entitled a section of his chapter on confirmation in *Lutheran Worship: History and Practice* as "The Key to Understanding *Confirmation*: Baptism."[36] If any word can be used to describe confirmation, it may be appreciation—appreciation for what God has done in Baptism, appreciation of how Baptism has continuing effects in the Christian's life, and appreciation of where the Spirit produces growth and maturity, namely in the Word and Sacrament.

A study prepared by three major Lutheran church bodies a generation ago summarizes the misunderstandings related to confirmation—misundersandings that are still prevalent. From biblical and historical evidence, the study shows that confirmation

• is not a sacrament.

- does not in any sense complete Baptism.
- is not a ratification of the vows or promises made by sponsors at Baptism.
- does not add any special form of God's presence or gifts that the baptized person does not already enjoy.
- does not confer special privileges.
- is not a prerequisite to Holy Communion.
- is not essential to the Christian life.[37]

Several decades ago, the following definition was prepared: "Confirmation is a pastoral and educational ministry of the church which helps the baptized child through the Word and Sacrament identify more deeply with the Christian community and participate more fully in its mission."[38]

Confirmation actually occurs during the whole time of the catechumenate, catechesis, or, as they are often called, "confirmation classes." Confirmation provides a means to instruct the baptized about the significance of the sacraments. This was Luther's view, though he never prepared a confirmation rite.[39]

THE RITE

The Rite of Confirmation should avoid the impression that it is a graduation.[40] Rather, it is a public and personal acknowledgment of what occurred at a person's Baptism, which begins a lifetime of learning.[41] The Rite of Confirmation, then, is the public recognition of the continuing growth in the faith of the baptized as the congregation continues its prayers for faithfulness in the Christian life. Arthur Repp explains in his magisterial study that confirmation has three essential elements: "the instruction in the Word, the confession of faith, and the intercession of the congregation, accompanied by the laying on of hands."[42] Two of these three elements occur during the Rite of Confirmation: the confession of faith and the intercession of the congregation on behalf of the catechumens.[43] Instruction in the Christian faith is never completed, but a major milestone has been reached when one is confirmed.

The Rite of Confirmation includes an affirmation of the faith, vows of faithfulness, invocation of the Spirit, and corporate prayer. The rite may be conducted at any time in the church year, though most Lutheran congregations hold the service in the spring.[44] To have it coincide with a church festival, such as Palm Sunday or Pentecost, may give undue significance to the rite and overshadow the festival.

A public examination of some kind is held at which the confirmands testify to their faith and to their commitment to the ongoing life of the congregation. Some congregations provide a special time for the catechumens to be examined before the congregation or representatives of the congregation. Others offer opportunities for confirmands to give a personal testimony in a worship context. While this public examination is usually based on Luther's Small Catechism, the life of the catechumen is also observed. Whatever the local practice, it should undergird the biblical foundation of the faith.[45]

In the Divine Service, the Rite of Confirmation[46] normally occurs after the sermon. Following a hymn of invocation of the Holy Spirit, the confirmands, usually dressed in white albs or robes, gather at the altar. The pastor recalls Jesus' commission to make disciples by baptizing and teaching. He reminds the confirmands of their Baptism and Christian instruction. The purpose of confirmation is to confess before the church the faith into which they were baptized and to pledge their faithfulness to Christ. Because Baptism is complete, confirmation is only a public recognition and expression of appreciation for that fact. The confirmands are asked to affirm their baptismal faith, similar to the questions asked at the time of their baptisms: renouncing the unholy three and confessing the Holy Trinity.[47]

The vows of faithfulness begin with a question regarding the intent of the confirmands to continue faithfully in the church. The confirmands confess that the prophetic and apostolic Scriptures are inspired, and they acknowledge that the doctrines learned from Luther's Small Catechism conform to Scripture. Then the pastor asks whether the confirmands desire to be members of the Evangelical Lutheran Church.[48] This promise is a commitment to participate actively in the Lutheran Church. Finally, the confirmands promise to conform their lives to God's Word, use the means of grace faithfully, and remain true to God in faith, word, and action.

The invocation of the Spirit is then made. This is not the first time the Spirit is invoked in a Christian's life, but it is done at confirmation as a reminder of the Spirit's presence in the lives of those who have been baptized. As the pastor speaks a word of Scripture, he places his hands on the heads of the confirmands individually.[49] Care is taken that the medieval view that forgiveness comes at Baptism and the Spirit at confirmation is not conveyed by this imposition of hands.[50] Following the imposition of hands, the pastor invites the catechumens "upon this your profession and promise" to more active participation in the life of the congregation.[51]

The third element of the rite is public intercession for the newly confirmed. Prayer is a vital part of the congregation's worship life, which is exemplified in the prayer for the confirmands.[52] A moment of silence for worshipers to offer their own prayers for the confirmands would be appropriate, if explained to the congregation. After the prayer, the pastor dismisses the confirmands and the service continues with the prayers or the offering.

First Communion, though long associated with confirmation, does not need to be tied to the Rite of Confirmation. Some congregations offer Communion as part of confirmation instruction; others wait until the period of instruction has been completed. The LCMS has encouraged congregations to continue to prepare young children through confirmation instruction for reception of Holy Communion by helping them "examine oneself."[53]

In place of a specific Rite of Confirmation, some Lutheran churches use a more general service for occasions when adults are brought into the congregation.[54] Regardless of the specific practice, the key factor in confirmation is a recollection and celebration of God's work through Word and Sacraments, His precious and powerful means of grace, which He bestows on His gathered guests.

MARRIAGE

 Probably the most recognized occasional service is a wedding service, yet not every wedding service is a Christian wedding. In this section, we want to look at the particular features of a Christian wedding that provide an opportunity for God to serve His people and for them to respond to His blessings with joy and thanksgiving.

God established the lifelong union of one man and one woman in the Garden of Eden. Although sin has tarnished the estate of marriage, it still embodies a profound relationship. Paul said that the union of a man and a woman is an image of Christ, the heavenly Bridegroom, and His bride, the church (Ephesians 5). Christian couples recognize the importance of this imagery and desire that their wedding service reflect this context. As baptized believers, couples will want to express that relationship in public as more than a religious celebration with traditional trappings. A church wedding allows the couple to celebrate publicly the loving relationship that Christians have with one another and with Christ. A church wedding service reflects God's presence and purpose for marriage. Paul wrote, "Whatever you do, whether in word or deed, do it all in the name of the Lord Jesus, giving thanks to God the Father through Him" (Colossians 3:17).

A well-planned Christian wedding[55] has no spectators, only participants—the gathered guests. Imagine a wedding reception at which only the wedding party ate and drank, danced and celebrated. Imagine if all the invited guests had to sit solemnly on hard chairs, observing the festivities. A community where such practices were followed would find that few people would attend the receptions, unless required to be there. The same holds true for many wedding services: They offer few opportunities for the guests to participate. A well-planned wedding service, how-ever, provides a wide variety of ways in which the gathered guests can participate in the worship service as God's gathered guests.

Brides and grooms have the opportunity to witness to their Christian faith in their wedding service as they celebrate one of the happiest moments of their lives. Christian weddings are not only an opportunity for the bride and groom to recall the significance of being united in Christ's name and before His altar, but for all married couples to do so. The Scripture readings, prayers, and blessings indicate the responsibilities and the joys of married life, even for those who have yet to marry.

A couple should contact the church early in their planning process, not only to be sure the church is available but also to meet with the pastor for counseling[56] and with the music director to coordinate the service. As a minister of the Lord and an official of the congregation, the pastor represents the community of faith over which he is a shepherd. He will communicate the guidelines for the service that have been established by the congregation. These guidelines will help prevent mis-understandings and avoid situations that compromise the Christian faith and life.

Marriage is a Christian witness and a social contract. The pastor of the church acts as an agent of the state, and a marriage is a civil ceremony.[57] Luther endorsed this viewpoint by encouraging the practice of marrying outside the church doors and entering the sanctuary for prayer and a blessing.[58] A Lutheran service could begin with the Rite of Marriage (explained on the next pages) at a location outside the sanctuary—at the entrance to the church, a garden, or even at a park. After the rite, a service of celebration could follow in church, using Vespers or another Ser-vice of the Word.[59]

A Christian wedding is a public worship service, even when only a few guests are invited. As such, the service should conform to the practices of the local congre-gation. Although the bride and groom are important participants in the service, the choice of having a service in a church shows that Christ is central in their lives. He is the beginning and the fulfillment of all relationships; His forgiveness will aid, help, and restore situations and persons broken by sin; His cross and resurrection will provide hope for the future. Anything that distracts from Christ or from a clear witness that confesses and exalts Christ may be deemed inappropriate.[60] The ser-vices described in this section are designed to keep Christ at the center of the wed-ding by placing the Word of God and prayer in their rightful places. Paul tells us that all things are "consecrated by the word of God and prayer" (1 Timothy 4:5). A Christian wedding will have these essential features.

The shortest form of the Lutheran rite lasts only ten minutes. The Rite of Marriage includes an address from Scripture to the bride and groom, the ceremony of mutual consent, the marriage vows, a ceremony with the rings, a prayer and pronouncement, and the pastoral blessing. These basic elements of the rite may be situated at various locations in the wedding service, which allows the couple to praise and thank God and ask for His blessings.

Several orders of service follow, with options placed in parentheses. The services are similar, yet they offer a general liturgical structure to which a couple may add their own personal witness to their faith in Christ. None of the services requires the inclusion of the Apostles' Creed, but the creed can serve as a significant witness to the couple's common faith. If used, the Apostles' Creed may be placed immediately before or after the pastor's message.

ORDER 1: *LUTHERAN WORSHIP: AGENDA*[61]

  (Preservice Music)
  (Processional)
  Invocation
  (Prayer)
  Address
  (Psalm[s], sung and/or read)
  Scripture Readings
  (Hymn/Solo)
  Address/Sermon
  Hymn or Solo
  The Rite of Marriage
  (Parental Blessing)
  (Candlelighting Ceremony)
  Prayers
  Lord's Prayer
  (Hymn/Solo)
  Benediction
  (Recessional/Recessional Hymn)

ORDER 2: FROM LUTHER[62]

  (Preservice Music)
  The Rite of Marriage
  Entrance (Hymn/Solo)
  Invocation
  Scriptural Address

  (Hymn/Solo)
  Prayer(s) of the Church
  (Lord's Prayer)
  Benediction
  Recessional (Hymn)

ORDER 3: DAILY PRAYER[63]

  Processional (Hymn of Invocation)
  Verses and Responses
  Psalmody
  Scripture Readings
  Office Hymn
  Address/Sermon
  The Rite of Marriage
  The Canticle
  Prayers
  Benedicamus
  Benediction
  Recessional (Hymn)

ORDER 4: CONTEMPORARY[64]

  Preservice Music
  Entrance (Hymn)
  Apostolic Greeting
  Prayer of Invocation
  Scripture Reading(s)
  (Address/Sermon/Homily)

The Rite of Marriage
   Exhortation on Marriage
   Exchange of Promises
   Exchange of Rings
   Declaration
   Blessing by the Pastor
   (Blessing by Family and Friends)
   Prayer of Blessing
   Prayer for Life Together
   (Other Intercessions)
   Prayer for Families
   Lord's Prayer
  Benediction
  Recessional (Hymn)

BEFORE THE SERVICE

Many couples find that a printed order of service helps their guests follow the service and gives a clearer Christian witness of their intents and plans. It enables the congregation to participate in various portions of the service, such as reading a psalm, confessing the creed, singing hymn stanzas, or joining in the prayers. The service should be planned with the pastor, organist or music director, and other participants in advance so all the details may be included in the printed service. Some couples mark the places in the service bulletin when the congregation stands, sits, or kneels so guests will feel comfortable with the actions of the service. If the couple desires, special bulletin designs are available from Christian bookstores or publishing houses.

Most church sanctuaries provide a dignified, beautiful setting for a sacred service, thus minimal decoration may be required. Normally, the color of the season of the church year will be the parament color on the wedding day, so couples should ask the pastor for information on the church season in which their wedding will be held. Floral decorations may be chosen and placed in the church. Altar guilds or chancel care committees often have guidelines for wedding floral arrangements.

Members of the wedding party should arrive early so they are ready for the service at the designated time. Dressing rooms or parlors may be available for the bride and her bridesmaids. The groom and his groomsmen also may gather at a specified location and time. Ushers should be present at least thirty minutes before the start of the wedding. Normally, the specific wedding day arrangements and times are designated by the pastor or wedding hostess at the rehearsal.[65]

Preservice music is a quiet witness to the gathering guests of the importance of the anticipated worship service. Organ or piano music may be interspersed with vocal or instrumental solos or ensemble pieces. During this time, the ushers seat guests and distribute service folders. The mother of the bride is the last person to be seated, after the groom's parents, and her presence indicates to the minister that the bridal party is ready to process. A white runner is sometimes brought down the central aisle from the front of the church. The practice had a noble purpose in past centuries when the family was concerned that the bride's dress would become soiled. Most modern churches with their carpeted aisles do not require aisle runners, which means the extra expense can be eliminated.

Christian couples may consider entering the sanctuary following a processional cross. Torchbearers carrying processional candles and a banner bearer with a specially designed wedding emblem may follow the cross. The congregation should be invited to stand and face the cross as it is brought in and as the bridal party follows it down the aisle. The last person to enter the church is the bride.

In recent years several arrangements for escorting the bride have become popular. Usually the bride comes down the aisle with her father. However, some brides wish to include both parents to witness the love she has for both of them. A practice becoming more common is for the bridal party to walk down the aisle in this manner: the parents of the groom walk together, followed immediately by the parents of the bride; the attendants walk in as couples (the maid of honor and best man last); the presiding minister processes; and finally the bride and groom enter together.

If the bridesmaids walk down the aisle in single file, the groomsmen enter from a door near the chancel and meet them at the foot of the chancel. The groomsmen then escort the bridesmaids into the chancel, with the bridesmaids on the left and the groomsmen on the right at their assigned places. Flower girls or ring bearers, if they participate in the processional, may sit with their parents or other relatives in a front pew. After escorting the bride to the foot of the chancel and giving her to the groom, the father of the bride takes his seat with his wife on the "bride's side" (the left side of the church when facing the altar).

Many young couples are unsure what to do with the traditional question "Who gives this woman to be married to this man?" In some service orders, this is identified as "The Permission."[66] Obviously, they want to acknowledge everything their parents have done for them, yet the woman is not a piece of chattel being handed from one owner to another. Nor has the groom paid a dowry for his bride, at least not in most North American communities. Yet there is a sense that to omit this traditional element would be to remove something significant from the ceremony. While there is no theological significance to the giving of the bride, it is a deeply emotional moment in the life of a bride's family. Because the purpose of the practice is unclear, some services eliminate the question or make it optional. One solution takes into consideration the significance of the ritual and expands the participants to include both families in what is called "Reaffirming Family Ties."[67] Thus at the time when the bride would normally be given in marriage, the pastor asks both sets of parents to stand (perhaps behind their child) and addresses them as follows:

> Mr. and Mrs. _____ and Mr. and Mrs. _____: Today marks a significant day in the lives of your families, as well as in the lives of your children. You have raised N. and N. to this point in their lives in Christian homes. They want to acknowledge the Christlike love and care they have received from you as God's representatives in this world. You have fulfilled your God-given responsibilities and are coming to a new stage in your relationship. Your new role is to encourage and support your son and daughter in their new family. It seems right to ask you all, mothers and fathers, to make a promise, just as N. and N. will do in a few moments.
>
> I therefore ask you: Do you support N. and N. in their choice of each other? Will you encourage them in their love and care for each other? Will you pray for them regularly as you have in the past? And will you help them build a Christian home where Christ is evident in all that they say and do? If so, please say, "We promise with God's love." (*Parents answer.*)
>
> Mr. and Mrs. _____ and Mr. and Mrs. _____, thank you for your influence and Spirit-filled guidance these past years and for bringing N. and N. to this special day. God has blessed you. (*The parents may be seated and the service continues with the Invocation.*)

Lutheran Worship: Agenda does not include the question to the parents, but it provides a shorter form of this recognition of parents before the Scripture readings, which could be placed at the beginning of the service. The pastor asks the parents: "Will you, as parents, support, encourage, and strengthen _____ in their marriage, remembering at all times that God wants them to live in obedience to his holy ordinance until death parts them?" The parents' response is "We will."[68]

The Service

The Invocation begins the service.[69] The pastor speaks the name of the Trinity, recalling the blessing first received by the bride and groom at their Baptism. The Invocation assures the gathered guests of God's presence. A hymn of invocation and a prayer may also be included.

The service continues with Scripture readings that describe the origin, purpose, and blessings of marriage. The readings included in *Lutheran Worship: Agenda* establish the biblical tradition and foundation of God's loving plan for the human family. God created His human creatures male and female and gave them the gifts of sexuality and community. Christ reestablished marriage's blessed purpose, which was corrupted in the fall, so there can be true joy in what God has joined together. Other readings may be selected by the bride and groom as a personal witness to their faith in Christ. A psalm may be sung or read responsorially between pastor and people or antiphonally between the bride's side and the groom's side of the church. Following are some suggestions for Scripture readings.

Old Testament
Genesis 1:26–31
Genesis 2:18–24
Proverbs 31:10–31
Song of Songs 2:10–13
Song of Songs 8:7
Isaiah 63:7–9

Psalm
Psalm 23
Psalm 33
Psalm 67
Psalm 98
Psalm 100
Psalm 117
Psalm 119:97–105
Psalm 127
Psalm 128
Psalm 136
Psalm 150

Epistle
Acts 16:25–34
Romans 12:1–2
1 Corinthians 12:31–13:13
Galatians 5:22–6:2
Ephesians 5:21–33
Philippians 3:7–11
Colossians 3:12–19
2 Timothy 3:15–17
1 Peter 2
1 Peter 3:1–6
1 Peter 3:16
1 Peter 4:7–10
1 John 1–2; 4
Jude 21

Gospel
Matthew 19:4–5 (or 3–9)
Matthew 22:35–40
Mark 10:6–9, 13–16
Luke 6:38
Luke 6:47–49
John 2:1–11
John 15:9–12 (12–16)

After the readings, a hymn may be sung, which is another occasion for the gathered guests to participate in the service. A hymn that stresses the biblical foundation of marriage or God's promises of joy in Christ would be especially appropriate. If a solo is sung at this point in the service, it is a good idea to print the words in the worship folder so the congregation can silently pray the text of the song.

The pastor gives a sermon or homily, which will express the commands and promises God places before the bride and groom and all married couples. The sermon text may be selected by the couple from the list above, or it may be a text the pastor used in his premarital discussions with the couple. A homily (from the Greek word that means "conversation") is usually a shorter version of a sermon (no longer than ten minutes) and is recommended for a wedding.

THE RITE OF MARRIAGE

This is the part of the service in which the marriage occurs. The pastor may indicate this by leading the wedding party closer to the altar for the exchange of vows. He will probably place the best man and maid of honor one step behind and to the side of the groom and bride respectively. The bride will hand her bouquet to her maid of honor to free her hands for the vows. This movement in the chancel may be accompanied by music, or it may be done in silence. The Rite of Marriage is composed of seven elements: an address from Scripture to the bride and groom, the ceremony of mutual consent, the marriage vows, a ceremony with the rings, a prayer and pronouncement, a blessing, and final prayers, including the Lord's Prayer.

If not done earlier in the service, the pastor may now read the scriptural directives on God's will for husbands and wives. Luther's arrangement of the directives, also called the address, followed an outline of God's commandment for marriage, the troubles resulting from sin, and the consolation Christ brings.[70] Then the pastor asks the couple to pledge their mutual consent (also called the Declaration of Solemn Intent) in words similar to the following: "N., will you have this woman (man) to be your wife (husband), to live with her (him) in holy marriage according to the Word of God? Will you love her (him), comfort her (him), honor her (him), (obey him),[71] and, forsaking all others, keep with her (him) this bond of marriage holy and unbroken until death parts you? If so, declare before God and these witnesses, I will."

The actual marriage vows are the heart of the ceremony. The bride and groom face each other and join hands. While personally written vows may be considered, most couples find that wording similar to the traditional vows speaks the essence of their pledge.[72] The vows state: "I, N., in the presence of God and these witnesses, take you, N., to be my marriage partner, and pledge to you my faithfulness in every duty and not to part from you until death parts us." The more traditional vow includes after *partner* (actually, the word is *spouse*) "to have and to hold from this day forward, for better, for worse, for richer, for poorer, in sickness and in health, to love and to cherish."[73]

As a sign of the vows that have been made, wedding bands have become a traditional sign of faithfulness. While not a necessity, most couples have at least one ring.[74] The best man places the rings on the pastor's service book. The pastor tells the couple to exchange these rings "as a pledge and token of wedded love and faithfulness."[75]

The pastor places his hand and perhaps his stole over the joined hands of the couple, who then kneel. He pronounces to the gathered guests: "N. and N. have given themselves to each other by their solemn pledges to become one in holy marriage. They have declared this before God and these witnesses. I therefore pronounce them husband and wife, in the name of the Father and of the ✠ Son and of the Holy Spirit. What God has joined together, let no one put asunder. Amen." Thus the pastor testifies as a witness to the couple's vows to each other, concluding with the words of Jesus from Matthew 19:6.

The pastor speaks a short blessing over the couple who continue to kneel: "The almighty and gracious God abundantly grant you his favor and sanctify and bless you with the blessing given our first parents in paradise that you may please him in both body and soul and live together in holy love until your life's end."[76] The parents of the couple may also come forward at this time and speak a blessing.[77]

The couple may kneel for the rest of the prayers, or they may participate in a ceremonial sign of their unity.[78] In the last several decades, couples have included at this point in the rite the lighting of a candle, usually called a unity candle, while a hymn or a solo is sung. The Christological significance of a candle may be emphasized by a brief comment by the pastor or by a written note in the service folder such as the following:

> The two candles represent two distinct lives that are now brought together before Christ as one. Jesus said of Himself, "I am the light of the world" (John 8:12). With His presence in our marriage, we know our love and lives will continue to grow and be blessed. Without Him, our marriage would be a flickering ember. Jesus also said, "You are the light of the world. . . . Let your light shine before men, that they may see your good deeds and praise your Father in heaven" (Matthew 5:14, 16). We pray that this symbolic act may reflect our desire to radiate His light throughout our lives as we live with and for Him. We ask for your prayers that we may fulfill the vows we make today before Christ, our Savior and Friend.

After the unity candle is lit, the couple returns to their places at the altar and may remain standing or kneel for the prayers and Lord's Prayer. The congregation stands and joins the couple in prayer or kneels, if possible, if the couple continues to kneel. Prayers may be spoken by the pastor or by the congregation, if printed in the service folder. The following prayer, for example, may be used. It could be divided into various petitions, spoken alternatively between the pastor and the people. The whole congregation then joins together for the termination.

> Almighty God, You made a man and a woman and joined them in marriage, and You tell us that this is like the union of Your Son Jesus Christ with His bride, the Church. We ask You, don't let Your holy work be set aside by anything we do. Bless these two, and guide them by Your Holy Spirit that in every way they may do what pleases You and may live together to Your glory. Let the Word of Christ live richly in them, and make their hearts and their home Your home. Let them be united by a love that is in Christ so that they may never feel any decrease or doubt in their love. Bless them in each other, and give them the forgiveness and patience to bear with one another's faults. Give them success, and crown everything they do with Your mercy. Let even their troubles and pains bring them Your blessing and real growth in Christian living. Teach them to come to You with every difficulty and to thank You for every good thing. And when as Your faithful children they have finished their pilgrimage here on earth, give them a home with You in heaven. For the sake of Jesus, Your Son, our Savior and Lord. Amen.[79]

The Lord's Prayer follows the other prayers as the prayer that consolidates all that is necessary for the Christian life. Because the Lord's Prayer is the prayer of the whole congregation, it is best not to have the prayer sung by a soloist. If all the members of the congregation are not familiar with this prayer, the words may be printed in the service folder.

After the prayers, the pastor speaks the Benediction over the whole congregation. After the Benediction, the couple stands (if they were kneeling) and turns to face the congregation. The maid of honor gives the bride her flowers, and the couple leaves the chancel to the recessional music or hymn.[80] The wedding party should follow the bride and groom out of the sanctuary. The parents of the bride and groom may be encouraged to join this group as they recess before the ushers dismiss the worshipers.

MUSIC FOR A CHRISTIAN WEDDING

The wedding couple will benefit from consulting with the minister of music who can provide ample musical resources appropriate for the wedding service.[81] Suggestions made by the church musician will often reflect the abilities of the choir(s), the congregation, and the musicians. Instrumental music, in addition to organ or piano pieces, can provide a joyful sound and may be included at various points in the service, particularly as part of the processional or recessional.

Wedding music, as many church musicians know, can be controversial. In a Lutheran service the music will convey the dignity of God's house and the centrality of Christ in the marriage. Some traditional music that has become overused, such as the "Wedding March,"[82] may be replaced by other beautiful works, such as "Jesu, Joy of Man's Desiring," "Solemn Processional," "Sheep May Safely Graze," "Psalm 19 [The Heavens Declare]," and "Trumpet Voluntary," among others.[83]

Hymns are the most common method to include the gathered guests in a wedding service. Hymns also are another way the bride and groom can communicate their Christian faith with their gathered guests. Hymns may be sung at various places in the service as noted in the outlines. Most hymnbooks provide a selection of hymns under the topic of Christian Marriage. In addition, the categories of Worship and Praise, Christian Family, and Community in Christ may be consulted.[84] A hymn appropriate to the church year is always fitting for a wedding service.

Increasing numbers of couples are asking a choir to participate in their service. Either as a special offering or singing alternate stanzas with the congregation, a choir adds a memorable and edifying depth to the service. A choral setting of a hymn or a psalm provides a resource sometimes forgotten by busy couples. Similarly, a soloist may contribute to the service with a special setting of a psalm, such as "The Lord's My Shepherd" (Brother James' Air).[85] It should be mentioned that few popular songs have texts suitable to the Christ-centered dimension of a Christian wedding.

Gathering God's guests for a wedding involves one of the greatest witness opportunities a Christian couple can experience. God ordained marriage, and Christ blesses weddings with His presence in the Spirit's powerful Word. The time and effort involved in planning a truly Christian service will be well spent and is a means for the couple to grow together spiritually.

FUNERAL

Except for Easter Sunday, no worship service offers a greater opportunity to bear meaningful witness to Christian hope than a funeral service. Five themes should be evident in a Christian funeral service: the cause and pain of death (sin and its consequences), the reality of Jesus' physical resurrection, the forgiveness of sins with its concomitant blessings, the assurance of the resurrection of the body, and the comfort of life everlasting.

From earliest Christian times until the last century, death was viewed as a part of life. The first Christians did not celebrate the birthdays of the martyrs, but their death days were frequently recalled. Only since the Enlightenment created an alternate worldview has Western culture become a death-denying society. The church, as God's gathered guests, has the privilege to speak not only of the comfort God offers for the bereaved but also of the joys experienced by those who trust in Christ as Lord. In many ways a funeral offers a special opportunity for the Gospel to be evident in a congregation. In his Schmalkald Articles, Luther spoke of various forms of the Gospel. One phrase he used was the "mutual conversation and consolation of the brothers and sisters."[86] Thus the gathered guests console the grieved with the hope of heaven, as Paul suggested in 1 Thessalonians 4:13, "We do not want you . . . to grieve like the rest of men, who have no hope."

Naturally, funerals of Christians are typically conducted in the church in which the deceased had gathered as a guest during his or her life to receive the blessings of God through Word and Sacraments and to respond in prayer and praise. The Christian community will want to participate as much as possible in the celebration of eternal life, a unique theme in contemporary society. Music and the church setting, where the deceased received the assurance of God's forgiving grace in Christ, offers the most conducive environment for the Christian message of hope and life in Christ.

Many Lutherans are unaware of how they can shape the funeral service through the selection of Scripture readings and hymns. Some Christians may express to their pastor how they would like to witness their Christian faith after they have died. This guidance may include meeting with him or providing written instructions to a congregation's elders. Hymn selections and Scripture readings may also be noted in a personal Bible or stated in a letter given to the pastor prior to an individual's death.

The casket is closed before the processional entrance into the church so the congregation may focus on the Word of comfort in the Gospel. Luther performed several funerals in Wittenberg in the Corpus Christi Kapelle beside the Town Church of St. Mary's; such side chapels are ideal locations for small funeral gatherings of Christians.

THE SERVICE[87]

The pastor begins the funeral service with the apostolic greeting—"Grace and peace to you from God our Father and the Lord Jesus Christ" (2 Corinthians 1:2)—which may be delivered either from the entrance of the church or at the foot of the altar. This assurance of God's love amid the immediate personal uncertainties of death is a special word of hope and comfort for the bereaved.[88] The congregation may respond with "Amen."

A funeral pall[89] may then be placed on the casket. The funeral pall is removed before the casket is carried out of the church. A funeral pall is usually a white parament that is large enough to cover the casket. The pall is a reminder of the white robe of Christ's righteousness and the white baptismal garment. Frequently Christian symbols are embroidered on the pall, providing further visual witness to

the link between Baptism, death, and eternal life. As the pall is placed on the casket, an assisting minister may read Romans 6:3–5.

A procession is then formed of the following persons, though the crucifer and torchbearers are optional: crucifer, torchbearers, pallbearers with coffin, the bereaved, assisting ministers, and presiding minister. The use of a processional cross indicates that Christ not only leads the church in life but also leads the Christian through death to eternal life. During the procession, the pastor or assisting minister may sing or speak Scripture verses.[90] A psalm[91] may also be read or sung responsorially by the pastor and congregation as the casket is brought to the front of the church. The casket is usually placed at right angles to the altar.[92] The paschal candle is placed at the head of the casket as a reminder of the deceased's baptismal faith in the resurrected Lord. Torches may be used instead and would be placed at the head and foot of the casket.

The Collect of the Day or a special prayer is then said by the pastor, followed by readings from Scripture. As in other services, one reading each may be from the Old Testament, an Epistle, and a Gospel. The following are suggested readings, though many others are possible.

From the Old Testament
Job 14:1–15a
Job 19:21–27
Isaiah 25:6–9
Isaiah 61:1–3
Lamentations 3:22–33

From the Psalms
Psalm 16
Psalm 23
Psalm 27
Psalm 34
Psalm 39
Psalm 42
Psalm 46
Psalm 71
Psalm 73
Psalm 84
Psalm 91
Psalm 116
Psalm 121
Psalm 126
Psalm 139
Psalm 146

From the Epistles

Romans 5:1–5

Romans 8:31–39

1 Corinthians 15:1–26

1 Corinthians 15:35–57

1 Corinthians 15:51–57

2 Corinthians 4:14–18

2 Corinthians 5:1–8

Philippians 3:20–21

Colossians 1:9–18

1 Thessalonians 4:13–18

1 Timothy 4:6–8

2 Timothy 1:9–10

Hebrews 4:15–16

1 Peter 1:3–9

1 John 1:5–2:2

1 John 3:1–2

Revelation 1:8, 17, 18

Revelation 7:9–17

Revelation 21:2–7

From the Gospels

Matthew 11:25–30

Matthew 18:1–4

Matthew 25:1–13

Mark 5:22–24, 35–43

Mark 10:13–16

Mark 16:1–10

Luke 7:11–16

Luke 12:35–40

John 5:24–27

John 6:35–40

John 10:11–16

John 11:21–28

John 14:1–6

The congregation may sing the appointed Gospel Verse if the service is printed in a folder. As an option, a choir (or soloist) may sing a special funeral verse adapted from Colossians 1:18 or, during Lent, from 2 Timothy 2:11b–12a.[93] A hymn may be sung after the readings and prior to the sermon.

The sermon is the most important element in this Service of the Word. While some comments related to the life of the deceased are appropriate, the sermon is not a eulogy. It is particularly important to hear the sermonic themes of Law and Gospel at the time of a funeral, with emphasis on the strong and comforting Gospel accent of Christ's victory over death. The Law is clearly evident in death itself, so the comfort, hope, and joy of forgiveness, salvation, and eternal life are pertinent for the hearts and minds of the bereaved. A relevant text from Scripture—whether chosen by the deceased, a confirmation verse, or another appropriate passage—may serve as a basis for the funeral sermon.

Following the sermon is another hymn and the creed.[94] While no particular hymn is designated, several categories in a hymnbook offer possibilities, including Comfort, Communion of Saints, Hope, Holy Spirit, Resurrection, and especially Easter. The Apostles' Creed, the believer's baptismal creed, is usually spoken by the gathered guests as they articulate their own faith in "the resurrection of the body and the life everlasting."

Prayers are then said, asking for God's comfort and assurance for the bereaved and for the gathered congregation.[95] The following collect, which is followed by the Lord's Prayer, may conclude the intercessions:

> God of all grace, you sent your Son, our Savior Jesus Christ, to bring life and immortality to light. We give you thanks that by his death he destroyed the power of death and by his resurrection opened the kingdom of heaven to all believers. Strengthen us in the confidence that because he lives we shall live also and that neither death nor life nor things present nor things to come will be able to separate us from your love which is in Christ Jesus our Lord, who lives and reigns with you and the Holy Spirit, one God, now and forever. Amen.[96]

From the time of the Reformation, Lutheran services often included the Benedictus or Luther's Nunc Dimittis. A hymn may also be sung, followed by the Benediction. The recessional follows the same order as the processional. The paschal candle remains in the chancel, and the funeral pall is removed at the church door. The cross and torches may be used for the procession to the cemetery.

COMMITTAL SERVICE

A Committal Service usually follows immediately after the funeral, though local practice may vary. This service occurs at the cemetery or place of interment. When the bereaved have gathered at the site, a procession with the casket may lead the mourners to the graveside. In Luther's day, a procession was led by the cross and torches as the people sang the hymn "From Depths of Woe I Cry to You,"[97] which is based on Psalm 130. As the pastor leads the coffin and mourners to the graveside, he may read selected verses from Job 19:25–26; Psalm 23; Psalm 118; John 11:25–26a; or Romans 14:7–8.

After everyone has gathered at the gravesite, the pastor may offer a prayer and read a Scripture selection, such as John 12:23–26 or 1 Corinthians 15:51–57. The actual committal follows as the pastor says:

> We now commit N.'s body to its resting place; earth to earth, ashes to ashes, dust to dust, in the sure and certain hope of the resurrection to eternal life through our Lord Jesus Christ. He will change our lowly bodies so that they will be like his glorious body, by the power that enables him to subdue all things to himself.
>
> May the Father, who created this body, may the ✠ Son, who by his blood redeemed this body, may the Holy Spirit, who by Holy Baptism sanctified this body to be his temple, keep these remains to the day of the resurrection of all flesh.[98]

During these words the casket may be lowered and dirt or ashes sprinkled over it.

The Lord's Prayer or Psalm 23 may be said at this time by those participating at the committal, if these selections were not used earlier. Another prayer follows the Lord's Prayer, after which a blessing of the people from Hebrews 13:20–21 concludes the committal. A dismissal may follow with these words:

P: Christ is risen.
C: He is risen, indeed.

P: Let us go forth in peace
C: in the name of the Lord.[99]

Easter and baptismal themes flow throughout the funeral service and committal. Baptismal grace and the resurrection hope and victory provide the greatest comfort to bereaved Christians.

The offices of Vespers or Compline may also be used for a funeral service.[100] The canticle for Vespers, the Nunc Dimittis, is especially meaningful and fitting for the funeral of a Christian. Compline's emphasis on being prepared for sleep and death also sends a dual message of comfort and hope to the bereaved. The response in Compline—"Into your hands I commend my spirit"—becomes a miniature confession of faith as the congregation speaks the words of Jesus from the cross (Luke 23:46) and the words of the first Christian martyr, Stephen (Acts 7:59).

Brief mention should be made of some special concerns. The burial of a child or young person should include a message directed specifically to the children in attendance. After a cremation or a prior interment, a memorial service may follow the order described above with slight adaptations. If a funeral must be conducted in a mortuary, the service is usually modified. For example, at the funeral home the order of service may be: Invocation, Prayer, Scripture Lesson, Sermon, Prayer, and Benediction. For all Christian services, the casket remains closed throughout the service.

A funeral reception after the committal is frequently held, often at the church. This practice dates to the first Christians, who continued some of the familiar Roman customs, including a memorial meal. In Roman times, this meal was held at the cemetery within twenty-four hours of the death; the grave cover was referred to as a table (*mensa*). Relatives of the deceased would come again on the third day after the death and on the ninth and thirtieth days. These meetings and meals provided the bereaved with a natural occasion to be comforted.[101] Contemporary Christians consider such a meal an opportunity to celebrate the joy of Christ's victory, even in the face of death, because they are His gathered guests.

ORDINATION AND COMMISSIONING

When a person is endorsed by the church for full-time service in God's kingdom, the gathered guests in a congregation hold an ordination or commissioning service. These services are onetime rites performed by the church for an individual who has graduated from a training school of the church and who has been endorsed by that school's faculty. In addition, the individual must have been issued a call that has been accepted, which enables the person to be recognized in the church as a minister. The ordination or commissioning is authorized by the president of the District in which the new church worker is to serve.[102] All these rites usually occur in the Divine Service immediately before the prayers. Although the Rite of Ordination usually occurs in the Divine Service, sometimes an order of Vespers or Evening Prayer is used. In such situations, the rite occurs after the canticle.

Ordination is the word used for this rite in the case of a pastoral candidate. *Commissioning* is the word used for the endorsement of all auxiliary offices. These words reflect the distinction inherent in the pastor's office of the public ministry. The Rite of Ordination is an ancient rite, dating to the early church's recognition of the servants of Christ through the laying on of hands (2 Timothy 1:6).[103] A commissioning to the teaching ministry recognizes that the office has been established "to strengthen and support the office of the public ministry and its work."[104] A lay worker, such as a lay minister, deaconess, parish worker, or director of evangelism, also is recognized with a special service that is known as a consecration.

At an ordination, a processional with other clergy is encouraged. Scripture readings that describe the institution of the office of the public ministry, the responsibilities of the office, and the strength and promise connected with the office of the public ministry are read. Then the candidate is asked to pledge himself to proclaim the Scriptures faithfully and to teach the confessions of the church correctly. After the Lord's Prayer, the participating ministers lay their hands on the head of the individual who is being ordained. The newly ordained pastor may receive a stole (and chasuble), after which the congregation commits itself to supporting the ministry of Word and Sacrament in its midst. The prayers are then said, and the rite concludes.

A commissioning service also is usually held in the context of the Divine Service and is led by the pastor of the congregation. Following a short introductory statement by the pastor, a reading from one or more of the following Scripture passages occurs: Matthew 20:25–28; Romans 12:4–8; Colossians 3:16–17; or 1 Peter

4:8–11. The pastor then asks the candidate for a pledge to teach faithfully according to the Scriptures and the Lutheran Confessions. The congregation is asked to support the teacher, and the candidate, after kneeling, is commissioned. The regular congregational prayers follow this rite.

The Rite of Consecration is designed to fit the circumstances of the various kinds of full-time Christian service. Similar to the commissioning, the candidate is introduced, Scriptures are read, and the candidate pledges faithfulness to Scripture and the Lutheran Confessions. As in the other rites, the congregation promises to support the worker.

INSTALLATION

A service of installation recognizes a new opportunity for Christian ministry within the church. When a professional servant of the church accepts a new position of ministry, a request for installation is made to the president of the District in which the position is located. Church workers may be installed several times throughout their lifetime of Christian service as they move to new locations or are given different responsibilities.

The Rite of Installation occurs within the Divine Service, again immediately before the prayers. The Scripture verses that describe the public ministry and the promises by the candidate made at his or her ordination or commissioning are repeated before the new congregation. At an installation of a pastor, a laying on of hands does not occur because such an action is characteristic of ordination. The installation of a teacher or other church worker is nearly identical to the commissioning or consecration rites.

PRIVATE SERVICES

Although Lutherans usually gather together for corporate worship, special occasions occur when this is not possible. Three services may be experienced by members of Lutheran congregations in a noncorporate setting. These are sacramental services, which convey the assurance of God's forgiving grace in Christ most clearly.

INDIVIDUAL CONFESSION AND ABSOLUTION

One of the most personal opportunities for Lutheran guests to hear God's word of forgiveness is in the service of Individual Confession and Absolution.[105] The pastor exercises the Office of the Keys, which is based on Matthew 16:19; 18:18; and John 20:22–23. "The very voice of the gospel" is proclaimed to provide "a certain and firm consolation for the conscience."[106]

Forgiveness of sins has been pronounced publicly in the church for centuries. Beginning around the eighth century, individual confession of sins to a priest became common, and absolution was also spoken privately.[107] Coupled with the stipulation that only specifically enumerated sins could be forgiven, the medieval concept of "satisfactions" resulted in abusive practices. "Satisfactions" were explained as actions that showed the authenticity of one's confession, yet they were perceived differently. Because many of these actions, such as reciting assigned prayers or performing prescribed good deeds, were associated with the assurance of forgiveness, the impression was that one earned God's forgiveness through these satisfactions.[108]

Luther prepared a "Short Order of Confession," which he attached to his Small Catechism.[109] Luther wrote, "Before God one is to acknowledge the guilt for all sins, even those of which we are not aware, as we do in the Lord's Prayer. However, before the confessor we are to confess only those sins of which we have knowledge and which trouble us."[110] Yet it was not the confession of sins that was significant for Luther, but the words of "absolution, that is, forgiveness, from the confessor as from God himself."[111]

The practice of private confession continued in Lutheranism for generations. However, in 1856 a controversy developed in the LCMS. A congregation insisted on substituting a general confession for private confession. Synodical leaders Ottomar Fuerbringer and Frederick Lochner prepared a reply in which they warned that depriving Christian individuals of the blessings of private confession and absolution would harm not only the congregation but also the Synod and posterity.[112] Regrettably, this prophecy has been fulfilled in many twenty-first century Lutheran congregations.

Lutheran Book of Worship, *Lutheran Worship*, and *Christian Worship* provide an order of service for individual confession and absolution. These services all follow the basic form suggested by Luther.[113] The privacy of such confession is protected from disclosure by laws that assure confidentiality to the pastoral office.

The service begins with the penitent kneeling before the pastor. The pastor may be seated in his office or kneeling at or near the altar or at the communion rail. The trinitarian invocation reminds the penitent of his or her Baptism and the freedom that relationship has established with God. Together the pastor and penitent say a portion of Psalms 102 and 51. The penitent continues with a brief summary of the Ten Commandments, then clearly confesses the known and troubling sins.[114] The pastor should be careful not to probe for specific sins; rather, he should let the penitent freely express those sins that clearly are obstacles to God's gracious comfort. Luther suggested that the mention of one or two sins of which one is self-consciously aware is sufficient.[115]

The pastor should offer scriptural warnings regarding the continuing practice of such sins, as well as the strong and certain comfort of forgiveness for each penitent sinner who turns to the Lord. Luther's Table of Duties quotes numerous verses from Ephesians 5–6, which the pastor may use along with appropriate Gospel verses. Then pastor and penitent together say Psalm 51:10–12, and the penitent prays a general prayer of confession.

Standing beside the penitent, usually wearing his stole as a symbol of his pastoral office, the pastor asks: "Do you believe that my words of forgiveness are God's forgiveness?" The penitent responds, "I do." Placing his hands on the head of the penitent, the pastor then speaks the words of absolution: "Receive the forgiveness Christ won for you by his Passion, death, and resurrection. By the command of our Lord Jesus Christ, I, a called and ordained servant of the Word, forgive you your sins in the name of the Father and of the ✠ Son and of the Holy Spirit."[116] The penitent responds, "Amen," and the pastor joins the penitent in speaking a portion of Psalm 30. A time of silence may be observed as the absolution is savored by the penitent.

The pastor concludes the private confession and absolution with a word of encouragement as he dismisses the forgiven penitent, saying, "Go in the strength, the peace, and the joy of the Lord, and come soon to receive Christ's body and blood and, being joined to him, live toward the work and the beauty he would fulfill in you for himself and for others. Go, you are free."[117]

Before the introduction of communion cards, pastors often received members for "communion announcements," which meant increased opportunity for exercising confession and absolution. Luther commended this practice in his Formula of the Mass and Communion for the Church in Wittenberg.[118] Today, many congregation members still follow this practice as they visit the pastor for counseling or conversation in his office. Members should never feel uneasy when requesting an opportunity to confess sins to a pastor or when requesting the use of this confessional service. Congregations may wish to establish set times for such services during the Lenten season because of its particular emphasis on penitence. If such regular times are scheduled and the community of faith is aware of the practice, the pastor should wear vestments for the service.

HOLY BAPTISM

While most baptisms occur before the family of God as part of a Sunday service, sometimes a family requests a private Baptism at the church. The order of service may be identical to that conducted in a regular service, and an elder may be present to represent the congregation.

Because of an emergency, a Baptism may be performed at the home or even in a hospital room. In such situations, witnesses to the Baptism should be present as water is poured or sprinkled on the individual with the words "N., I baptize you in the name of the Father and of the ✝ Son and the Holy Spirit." If time permits, Scripture passages related to Baptism may be read and a prayer offered for the faith of the newly baptized. The Apostles' Creed and the Lord's Prayer may also be said by those witnessing the Baptism. A private Baptism should be duly recognized by the Christian community at a later date.

HOLY COMMUNION

Individuals who are unable to attend a public service of Holy Communion require special services, often in their homes. These private Communion services usually are shortened forms of the Divine Service. Normally, the Order of Holy Communion—from the Preface to the Benediction—is used.

The recipient should be encouraged to participate fully in the responses. Hymns may be sung if several individuals are communing together, which may occur in a nursing home or a family setting. The pastor may also offer a brief devotional message that emphasizes the benefits of the Sacrament or share the Scripture readings from the weekly lectionary. The use of the Nicene Creed emphasizes the communion of saints and the forgiveness of sins despite the physical separation of the individual from the larger community of God's gathered guests.

Private Communion services help isolated individuals feel connected with the larger body of Christ. It may be especially meaningful if the consecrated elements are brought from the church's altar, perhaps even on a Sunday afternoon. The congregation should be informed of such private services conducted by the pastor.

The occasional services presented in this chapter provide many opportunities for God's gathered guests to receive God's forgiveness and the assurance of His love. Faith is strengthened and hope is assured through Word and Sacraments. Even when the Sacraments are administered apart from the larger body of the gathered guests, individual Christians sense through these services that they are part of the body of Christ. Where God's Word and Sacraments are administered properly, there Christians are gathered together in faith and hope and love.

SOME QUESTIONS TO CONSIDER

1. Define "occasional services." Why are they so named? List three such services in your explanation.

2. How does Luther's Flood Prayer pick up many of the central themes of the Lutheran understanding of Baptism?

3. Define confirmation and explain why it is not a sacrament. Why is it an important rite in the Lutheran Church? What four features constitute the Rite of Confirmation?

4. Describe the Rite of Marriage. Why can it be placed in several parts of a wedding liturgy? How can a wedding service be a witness of the couple's faith?

5. Compare and contrast a wedding service you attended with the comments in this chapter. Suggest three ways the Christian witness of the service could have been enhanced.

6. Design your funeral service. Give particular attention to the choice of readings and hymns, explaining your selections.

7. Briefly explain the distinctions among an ordination, a commissioning, and a consecration. Why may a church worker be installed several times but only ordained or consecrated once?

8. How might Individual Confession and Absolution be introduced and practiced in your congregation? What reasons would you give for introducing such a practice in the twenty-first century?

9. What other private services are offered by Lutheran congregations? Why? How do these private services relate to the concept of "gathered guests"?

NOTES

1. SC, "The Creed," 6 (K-W, 355).

2. *Lutheran Worship: Agenda* presents all the occasional services, as well as special services for congregations, schools, districts, and the Synod. Only those services most often experienced by laypeople are presented in this chapter of *Gathered Guests*.

3. Dix and Chadwick, *Treatise on the Apostolic Tradition*, 33.

4. See Cullmann, *Baptism in the New Testament*; Jeremias, *Infant Baptism in the First Four Centuries*; Aland, *Did the Early Church Baptize Infants?*; Jeremias, *Origins of Infant Baptism*; and Schlink, *Doctrine of Baptism*.

5. Jungmann, *Early Liturgy*, 77.

6. Nagel, "Holy Baptism," 272–78, draws out the theological emphases of Luther's service, as well as provides a chart that compares Luther's rite with that found in *Lutheran Worship*.

7. "Order of Baptism," LW 53:95–103, provides the 1523 version. The shorter revision from 1526 is found in LW 53:106–9. The 1526 revised version omits the directions for the exsufflation, the placing

of salt on the lips, two exorcisms with the *Ephphatha*, the anointing with oil, the christening robe, and the candle. A translation by Timothy Wengert of the 1526 "Baptismal Booklet" is included in *The Book of Concord* (K-W, 371–75).

8. SC, "Baptismal Booklet," 12 (K-W, 373).

9. SC, "Baptismal Booklet," 12 (K-W, 373).

10. *Lutheran Worship*, *Christian Worship*, and *This Far by Faith* use this formula, which is revised from *The Lutheran Hymnal: Agenda* of the Synodical Conference.

11. SC, "Baptismal Booklet," 14 (K-W, 373–74). Cf. LW 53:97.

12. SC, "Baptismal Booklet," 15 (K-W, 374).

13. In Luther's 1523 order, oil was used to anoint the candidate as a recollection of the Holy Spirit and also as a symbol of Christ as the Anointed One.

14. SC, "Baptismal Booklet," 20–22 (K-W, 374–75). Pfatteicher and Messerli, *Manual on the Liturgy*, 179, say that "it is a good idea to divide the renunciation (of Satan and all that that figure represents) into three questions to parallel the three articles of the creed: Do you renounce all the forces of evil? *I do.* Do you renounce the devil? *I do.* Do you renounce all his empty promises? *I do.*" Pfatteicher, *Commentary*, 48, provides three questions from the Episcopal *Book of Common Prayer* (p. 302): "Do you renounce Satan and all the spiritual forces of wickedness that rebel against God? Do you renounce the evil powers of this world which corrupt and destroy the creatures of God? Do you renounce all sinful desires that draw you from the love of God?" It is noteworthy that these three questions correspond to the three spiritual opponents mentioned regularly by Luther—the devil, the world, and our own sinful flesh.

15. See *Gathered Guests* chapter 11 regarding the size of baptismal fonts. Increasingly, Lutheran congregations are placing larger fonts at the entry to the sanctuary.

16. SC, "Baptismal Booklet," 27–28 (K-W, 375).This formula underscores the pastoral office. Another form—"N.N. is baptized . . ."—comes from the Eastern Orthodox tradition and emphasizes God's sole activity as the water is poured on the head of the baptized. See Pfatteicher and Messerli, *Manual on the Liturgy*, 186.

17. "Holy and Blessed Sacrament of Baptism," LW 35:29–32, shows that Luther preferred immersion. Pfatteicher and Messerli, *Manual on the Liturgy*, 182, provide three methods of baptizing by immersion, only one of which requires full submersion.

18. Richardson, "The Didache," in *Early Christian Fathers*, 174. Congregations may wish to consider a larger baptismal font when renovations are planned to facilitate a greater amount of water for such drowning or flood imagery.

19. In some cultures, particularly with adult converts, a biblical name is taken to signify the new identity received in God's eyes.

20. See Pfatteicher and Messerli, *Manual on the Liturgy*, 183, for three illustrations.

21. Nagel, "Holy Baptism," 278–79, 281.

22. See *Lutheran Book of Worship*, pp. 124–25; *Lutheran Worship*, pp. 203–4; and *This Far by Faith*, p. 68.

23. LW 53:101.

24. See SC, "Sacrament of the Altar," 5–6 (K-W, 362).

25. Nagel, "Holy Baptism," 269.

26. *Christian Worship*, pp. 12–14, combines the Rite of Baptism with corporate confession, noting that "Martin Luther said that confessing sins and receiving forgiveness is nothing else than a reliving of baptism" (12).

27. Pfatteicher and Messerli, *Manual on the Liturgy*, 173–74, suggest that the Hymn of the Day sung after the sermon should be a baptismal hymn that is used as a processional hymn so the baptismal group can make its way to the font.

28. Reed, *Lutheran Liturgy* (rev. ed.), 39.

29. If non-Lutherans are desired by the parents for family reasons, they may witness the Baptism but not serve as sponsors. Also it is best that Lutherans who are members of a Lutheran church body with whom the LCMS is not in fellowship serve as witnesses, not as sponsors.

30. See *Lutheran Worship: Agenda*, 105–9, for a service of ratification.

31. Pfatteicher and Messerli, *Manual on the Liturgy*, 170, advocate limiting Baptisms to a few times a year. While limiting Baptisms is questionable, baptismal festivals may be done several times a year and the days Pfatteicher and Messerli suggest may be considered: Easter Eve or the Second Sunday of Easter, Pentecost, the Third Sunday in Advent, the Baptism of Our Lord, and All Saints' Day. In addition, each Baptism can be a recollection of every Christian's Baptism.

32. Jesus' words from Matthew 28:19–20, reveal the pattern of "making disciples" by first baptizing, then teaching.

33. Repp, *Confirmation in the Lutheran Church*, 19–20.

34. Wainwright, *Doxology*, 74. Repp, *Confirmation*, 21, identifies six types of confirmation—catechetical, hierarchical, sacramental, traditional, pietistic, and rationalistic—which he explains on pp. 22–93.

35. Pieper, *Christian Dogmatics*, 3:276, cites C. F. W. Walther, *Pastorale* (p. 266), who warned against such a view. Repp, *Confirmation*, 143, provides evidence that Karl Barth also held such a view, which influences many modern Protestant churches.

36. Deffner, "Confirmation," 394.

37. Klos, *Confirmation and First Communion*, 142.

38. "Report of the Joint Commission on the Theology and Practice of Confirmation" (repr. in *1971 Convention Workbook of The Lutheran Church—Missouri Synod*; St. Louis: Concordia, 1971), 512. Cf. Commission on Worship, the LCMS, *Lutheran Worship: Altar Book* (St. Louis: Concordia, 1982), 33, which provides an abbreviated version of this definition. The report is based on the results of the study by Klos referenced in n. 37.

39. Senn, *Christian Liturgy*, 292–93, notes that Luther rejected the sacramental understanding of confirmation but emphasized catechesis, particularly catechetical sermons.

40. Instead of *graduation*, a better word may be *commencement*, which means "beginning" in academic settings. Pfatteicher, *Commentary*, 71, notes that graduation was the emphasis that grew out of the Rationalist eighteenth century and its rigorous educational program of indoctrination. See also Senn, "Rite of Confirmation and Culture Christianity," in *Christian Liturgy*, 559–62. Repp, *Confirmation,* 195–96, suggests stages of instruction: "With confirmation instruction completed, the child enters the *third* stage of his catechumenate, which continues till he is 18. . . . The *fourth* stage of the catechumenate remains open-ended and continues throughout life" (*Repp's emphasis*).

41. Burreson, "Confirmation," 203–11.

42. Repp, *Confirmation*, 179; cf. Repp, *Confirmation,* 58.

43. Pfatteicher, *Commentary*, 71, indicates that this was the understanding of Philipp Melanchthon in *Loci communes* (1543), which was included, with Luther's approval, in the Wittenberg Church Order of 1545.

44. Pfatteicher and Messerli, *Manual on the Liturgy*, 342, suggest a fall confirmation rite so the newly confirmed may enter congregational life during its active time of year, rather than before the summer doldrums.

45. Repp, *Confirmation*, 211–13, gives similar warnings and explains that probing examinations and personal testimonies are "a product of Pietism."

46. *Lutheran Worship: Agenda*, 110–13.

47. Repp, *Confirmation*, 215, suggests that such a renunciation applies to Baptism, and if a child is ready for confirmation, it should be a continual part of the Christian life.

48. Deffner, "Confirmation," 397, makes an unnecessary distinction between *be* and *become*.

49. Pfatteicher, *Commentary*, 75, states that the laying on of hands was a common practice in the German orders and is based on Philippians 3:10; Titus 2:13; 1 Peter 2:20; 2 Peter 3:18.

50. Senn, *Christian Liturgy*, 193–95, shows the source of this distinction in the early medieval church.

51. *Lutheran Worship: Agenda*, 112.

52. Repp, *Confirmation*, 219–21, provides four possible prayers.

53. Deffner, "Confirmation," 391, cites a study presented to the 1971 LCMS Synodical Convention (see "Report of the Joint Commission on the Theology and Practice of Confirmation," in the 1971 LCMS *Convention Workbook*, 505–15). See also Klos, *Confirmation and First Communion*, 183–213. Repp, *Confirmation*, 226, found the connection beneficial. *Lutheran Worship: Agenda*, 110, simply says that, as a result of Jesus' bidding, "we now celebrate with thankful hearts, rejoicing to confess the faith into which you were baptized and which you yourselves will now confess before the Church." *The Lutheran Hymnal: Agenda*, 21–22, on the other hand, tied "The Examination" portion of the Rite of Confirmation directly to the reception of Holy Communion.

54. See "Affirmation of Baptism," in *Lutheran Worship: Agenda*, 115–16.

55. Various resources are available to couples, such as Krause, *Planning a Christian Wedding*; and Rau, *Celebrating Your Wedding*.

56. Premarital counseling by a qualified pastor is recommended not only as a forum to discuss wedding arrangements but also so the couple can discuss important issues related to their lives together and their continuing relationship with Christ and His gathered guests after the wedding day.

57. In most states, the pastor's signature, along with that of two witnesses, is sufficient for the recognition of a valid marriage.

58. "Order of Marriage," LW 53:110–15, specifically 113.

59. Sometimes Lutheran wedding services include Holy Communion, but this is neither advisable nor necessary. Issues of close(d) Communion are often involved. Similarly, a bride and groom or even the whole wedding party should not receive Communion unless the congregation participates. Moreover, a sacrament included with a ceremony often confuses the two, suggesting both are sacramental or diminishing the significance of the sacrament.

60. For example, flash pictures during the service, casual or sloppy dress, and lack of decorum by the guests or wedding party are inappropriate at a Christian service.

61. *Lutheran Worship: Agenda*, 120–28.

62. "Order of Marriage," LW 53:110–15. Luther's rite at the entrance of the church included a questioning of the couple concerning their desire to marry, an exchange of rings, the pastoral statement of Matthew 19:6, and the pronouncement of marriage.

63. Adapted from the Vespers service, *Lutheran Worship*, pp. 224–48, as suggested in *Lutheran Worship: Agenda*, 120.

64. Inter-Lutheran Commission on Worship, *Marriage Service*, 29–33.

65. A rehearsal ensures the members of the wedding party understand their responsibilities in the service. It also helps them feel comfortable in the worship area, particularly in the chancel. Usually, the entire service is rehearsed so everyone has a sense of what will occur during the wedding, which is usually the next day.

66. For example, "Service of Marriage" (Medina, Ohio: Church World Press, n.d.), calls this the "Presentation" and the parents or family answer the question "Do you present N. to be married to N.?" (8).

67. Adapted from Lincoln, "Reaffirm Your Family Ties," 32–33. Sensitivity and revision will be necessary when planning this portion of the service, especially if both parents cannot be present or if one parent has died.

68. *Lutheran Worship: Agenda*, 127, designates this exchange for the marriage of young persons, but it is appropriate at other times as well.

69. From this point on, flash photography should stop. Unobtrusive video cameras or flashless photography may occur if it doesn't disrupt the service.

70. "Order of Marriage," LW 53:114–15, includes selections from Scripture read before the altar: Genesis 2:18, 21–24 and Ephesians 5:25–29, 22–24 on God's command; Genesis 3:16–19 on the cross; and Genesis 1:27–28, 31 and Proverbs 18:22 for comfort. The address ends with a prayer. Pfatteicher, *Commentary*, 464, indicates that the present address from Genesis, Ephesians, and Matthew rearranges the order according to the *Common Service Book*.

71. Some couples voice concern over this phrase, yet if understood in the context of a Christian relationship as described by Paul in Ephesians 5:21–33, such a commitment can be made without fear. (See 1 John 4:18.)

72. In "Sermon on the Estate of Marriage," Luther mentioned a simple formula common in his day—"I am yours; you are mine"—as the essence of the consent freely given one to the other (LW 44:11).

73. *Lutheran Worship: Agenda*, 122. An alternate vow, suggested on p. 127, reads: "I take you, N., to be my wife (husband), and I pledge before God and the witnesses here present to be your faithful husband (wife), to share with you in plenty and in want, in joy and sorrow, in sickness and in health, to forgive and strengthen you, and to join with you that together we may serve God and others as long as we both shall live."

74. Pfatteicher and Messerli, *Manual on the Liturgy*, 352–53, indicate that the ancient tradition of giving the woman a ring was a sign of her household authority because the ring was used to seal contracts and to demonstrate she was in charge of all domestic affairs.

75. *Lutheran Worship: Agenda*, 122.

76. *Lutheran Worship: Agenda*, 123.

77. *Lutheran Worship: Agenda*, 127, offers the following wording for the parents' blessing: "May the Lord make you strong in faith and love, defend you on every side, and guide you in truth and peace." Pfatteicher and Messerli, *Manual on the Liturgy*, 353, suggest the words from Psalm 61:7, "May you dwell in God's presence forever." The Gradual Verse, Psalm 128:1–2, may also be used.

78. Various ceremonies that have become popular within the past generation emphasize the couple's new relationship. Caution should be taken so these activities do not distract the gathered guests from the focus on Jesus Christ. Practices such as crowning the couple, placing a wreath of flowers on their heads, presenting an item of clothing to each other, placing a rose in a clay vessel, hanging a garland of flowers around the couple's shoulders, breaking a wine glass, drinking from a chalice, or releasing balloons are best reserved for the reception, where their significance to the couple may be explained. Most of these practices are sentimental but have little theological content.

79. Beck, "Marriage Ceremony in Modern English," 7.

80. The practice of introducing the couple or announcing a kiss is inappropriate for a Christian ceremony that wishes to focus on Christ. These may be postponed until the reception.

81. Concordia Publishing House, Augsburg Fortress, and Northwestern Publishing House provide a wealth of resources for church musicians to suggest.

82. Kretzmann, *Order of the Marriage Ceremony*, 6, notes: "Usage made Wagner's 'Bridal Chorus' from the opera *Lohengrin* and Mendelssohn's 'Wedding March' from the opera *A Midsummer Night's Dream* the processional and recessional pieces at many weddings in our country. Owing to their operatic background and secular association, they have fallen into disuse in an ever increasing number of churches. The trivial character of these pieces makes them unfit for church usage. Fortunately the modern bride is less and less inclined to want these threadbare and overworked wedding marches, and desires something more stately, dignified, joyful, and more musically satisfying."

83. Most church musicians would be pleased to demonstrate alternate processional and recessional music for the couple well in advance so adequate planning can occur.

84. The following hymns from *Christian Worship*, *Lutheran Worship*, and the *Lutheran Book of Worship* are suggested: "Alleluia! Let Praises Ring"; "Beautiful Savior"; "Blest Be the Tie That Binds"; "Christ Be My Leader"; "From All that Dwell Below the Sky"; "Heavenly Father, Hear Our Prayer"; "Holy God, We Praise Thy Name"; "In You Is Gladness"; "Jesus, Lead Thou On"; "Let All Things Now Living"; "Let Us Ever Walk with Jesus"; "Lift High the Cross"; "Lord When You Came as Welcome Guest"; "Love Divine, All Love Excelling"; "Now Thank We All Our God"; "O Perfect Love"; "Praise and Thanksgiving"; "O God of Love" (Paul Bouman); "Praise to the Lord, the Almighty"; "The King of Love My Shepherd Is"; "The Lord's My Shepherd"; "The Voice That Breathed O'er Eden"; "With the Lord Begin Thy Task"; and "What God Ordains Is Always Good." In addition, "Brothers and Sisters in Christ" and "Go, My Children, with My Blessing" are available in *Lift Up Your Hearts* (St. Louis: Concordia, 1988).

85. Solo music specifically written for Christian weddings is available from Christian publishers such as Concordia, Augsburg Fortress, and Northwestern. Regarding requests for popular songs, Schalk, *Planning a Christian Wedding Service*, 11, wisely suggests that the selection of most popular music "may find a more comfortable place at the reception, the dinner, or in connection with other activities apart from the wedding itself."

86. SA III, 4 (K-W, 319).

87. The service described here is adapted from *Lutheran Worship: Agenda*, 169–96. References to early Reformation practices are from Senn, *Christian Liturgy*, 353.

88. Other verses could be used, such as Psalm 103:13; 124:8; 2 Corinthians 1:3–4; 1 Timothy 1:17.

89. Increasing numbers of Lutheran congregations are receiving donations to purchase a funeral pall. Pfatteicher and Messserli, *Manual on the Liturgy*, 357, recommend a pall for its "democratizing value, for it prevents both the display of a costly coffin and embarrassment at a simple one."

90. Suggested verses are Job 19:25; John 11:25; Romans 14:7–8; 1 Peter 1:3; 1 John 3:3; Revelation 14:13.

91. For example, Psalm 46, 90, 103, or 130.

92. Pfatteicher and Messerli, *Manual on the Liturgy*, 358, note "an old tradition, still observed in several places, for the coffin to be positioned with the head toward the altar if the deceased was a pastor and with the feet toward the altar if the deceased was a layperson. The position reflects the accustomed role of the deceased in the church—facing the people as presiding minister or facing the altar as part of the congregation."

93. See *Lutheran Worship: Agenda*, 187–88.

94. The creed and hymn may precede the sermon.

95. See *Lutheran Worship: Agenda*, 191, for a litany that could be printed in a service folder.

96. *Lutheran Worship: Agenda*, 192.

97. *Lutheran Worship*, 230.

98. *Lutheran Worship: Agenda*, 194 (*author's adaptation*).

99. *Lutheran Worship: Agenda*, 195.

100. Senn, *Christian Liturgy*, 235, reports that the offices of Vespers, Nocturns, and Lauds developed in part from a ninth-century daily Office of the Dead.

101. Senn, *Christian Liturgy*, 166, references A. C. Rush, *Death and Burial in Christian Antiquity* (Washington: Catholic University of America Press, 1941).

102. Constien, "Synod's Various Induction Rites," 7.

103. Pieper, *Christian Dogmatics*, 3:454, says, "Ordination to the ministry by the laying on of hands and prayers is not a divine ordinance, but a church custom or ceremony, for, although it is mentioned in Holy Writ, it is not commanded (1 Tim. 4:14; 5:22; 2 Tim. 1:6: Acts 6:6; 8:17)."

104. "Commissioning and Installation of One Called to the Teaching Ministry," in *Lutheran Worship: Agenda*, 255.

105. *Lutheran Worship: Agenda*, 141–43, and *Lutheran Worship*, pp. 310–11.

106. Ap. XI, 2 (K-W, 186).

107. Pfatteicher, *Commentary*, 89.

108. See Melanchthon's discussion of Confession and Satisfaction in *The Book of Concord*, particularly Ap. XII, 98–178 (K-W, 185–218).

109. SC, "Sacrament of Holy Baptism," 16 (K-W, 360–62), notes that this 1531 version replaced a shorter version from Luther's 1529 catechism. In a letter to the council and congregation in Frankfurt, Luther defended the addition. See Jon D. Vieker, trans., "An Open Letter to Those in Frankfurt on the Main, 1533," *Concordia Journal* 16 (1990): 333–51.

110. SC, "Sacrament of Holy Baptism," 16 (K-W, 360).

111. SC, "Sacrament of Holy Baptism," 16 (K-W, 360).

112. Precht, "Confession and Absolution," 339. The whole chapter, 322–86, places the issue in its historical and theological contexts.

113. *Lutheran Book of Worship*, pp. 196–97; *Lutheran Worship*, pp. 310–11; and *Christian Worship*, pp. 154–55. The order in *Gathered Guests* follows *Lutheran Worship*.

114. *Lutheran Worship*, p. 310.

115. SC, "Sacrament of Holy Baptism," 23 (K-W, 361).

116. *Lutheran Worship: Agenda*, 142.

117. *Lutheran Worship: Agenda*, 143.

118. "Order of Mass and Communion," LW 53:33–34.

CHAPTER 15

SERVICES OF THE WORD

Gathering to hear the proclamation of God's Word is a basic activity of the Christian community and a vital means for spiritual growth. The earliest Christians met regularly, according to the Book of Acts (2:42). Throughout the history of the church, great preachers have been recognized as blessings from God. Preaching played a significant role in the Lutheran Reformation and in Martin Luther's professional ministry. He acknowledged the power of the living Word when it was proclaimed in a lively fashion for God's gathered guests. Contemporary Lutherans continue to gather as God's guests to hear His Word and to respond with prayers and praises. James White has described the preacher's task as one who "speaks *for* God, *from* the scriptures, *by* the authority of the church, *to* the people."[1] Therefore, Services of the Word have always received prominence among God's gathered guests.

The earliest accounts of Christian worship report that sermons were as important as the Sacrament of the Altar. Early services of readings and prayer were often called *synaxis*, a Greek word that means "assembly." Synaxis grew from the synogogue worship of early Christians and involved three parts: reading from Scripture, singing of psalms, and corporate prayer for the greater community.[2]

Gregory Dix presented what he called "the original unchanging outline of the Christian synaxis everywhere":

1. Opening greeting by the officiant and reply of the church.
2. Lesson.
3. Psalmody.
4. Lesson (or Lessons, separated by Psalmody).
5. Sermon.
6. Dismissal of those who did not belong to the church.
7. Prayers.
8. Dismissal of the church.[3]

The similarity to the first part of a Communion service is obvious. The supposed development from the Jewish synagogue service is more difficult to document, but research continues in this area. The connection to the later monastic devotional hours is becoming increasingly apparent.

Interestingly, one North American Lutheran leader, Henry Melchior Muhlenberg, adapted synaxis (the first part of the German Mass that centered on the Word) as his preaching service.[4] Thus there developed a precedent, though not a theological rationale, for using the first part of the Communion liturgy as a Lutheran preaching service. However, there is another influence to consider.

PRONE

We have already acknowledged that preaching has always held a significant place in Christian worship. Among the notable theologians of the early church, Ambrose, Augustine, Jerome, and Chrysostom were recognized for their effective preaching. Charlemagne (ca. A.D. 742–814), in seeking a way to reform the church, mandated that catechetical sermons be offered regularly at services of Holy Communion. However, during the Middle Ages the homily (a term derived from the Greek word that means "conversation") was regularly omitted in Rome and areas under its influence.

As a result of the neglect of preaching in the regular Latin Mass, a distinctive Service of the Word had developed by the tenth century. It was conducted in the language of the people and was included in the middle of the Mass. This service was primarily a preaching service and was conducted by the priest from the pulpit. The name of the service was Prone, from the French *prône* (which means "lecture" or "sermon"). It is derived either from the Latin *praeconium*, which means "proclamation," or from *praedicatio*, which means "sermon."[5] The form of the service consisted of the bidding of prayers, an exposition of the Lord's Prayer or of a portion of the creed, notices of upcoming feasts and fasts, and the reading of the banns of marriage and ordination.[6]

Eugene Brand reports on the order of Prone (*Pronaus*) as it was conducted around the time of Luther. A composite description of such a service would include
1. Ringing the bells.
2. Singing the Ave Maria.
3. Reading the Gospel.
4. Invocation of the Holy Spirit.
5. Sermon on the Gospel reading.
6. Reading of parish notices.
7. Prayer of the Church.

8. The Our Father.
9. The Apostles' Creed.
10. Recitation of the Decalogue.
11. Confession of sins.
12. Closing Votum.[7]

Because of the bidding prayers and commentary on the catechism, the reformers used Prone to reintroduce the Prayer of the Church into the liturgy.[8]

Several Lutheran communities developed preaching services from the medieval order of Prone. A service from 1553 in Württemberg, for example, was led entirely from the pulpit. Similar services were conducted in Strasbourg and Geneva. Each began with a Latin introit by a select group of schoolboys, then the congregation sang a hymn. The Votum, a prayer, and the Lord's Prayer (prayed silently) were followed by the reading of the sermon text and the sermon. After the sermon, parish notices were read, and the Ten Commandments, the Apostles' Creed, and the Lord's Prayer were recited. A general prayer concluded with the praying of the Lord's Prayer (again), a hymn, and a Benediction.[9] There are obvious similarities between this service and the medieval order of Prone because the Lutheran reformers carefully modified and adapted Catholic practices without rejecting what was beneficial.

Swedish Lutherans incorporated Prone not only in their Communion liturgy but also whenever a sermon was desired, including Matins and Vespers.[10] Although not the intent of Prone, one cannot miss the emphasis on Holy Absolution in the Swedish service when compared with some of the German orders. The Swedish service began with an optional exhortation to communicants. The Lord's Prayer and a penitential psalm or hymn were then said or sung. A prayer was followed by a sermon. An invitation to confession led into a general confession and absolution. Intercessions concluded the service. Curiously, the reading of Scripture is not a specifically identifiable part of this Swedish service.

The Office of Prone, while offering a non-Communion alternative, did not provide the structure Lutherans desired to hear the Word. Frank C. Senn has summarized the viewpoint held by Luther and Lutherans: "The preaching of the word is sacramental, because it conveys Christ himself."[11] Therefore, Lutherans in the past decades have created several specific services for hearing and preaching God's Word so our heavenly Father can feed His gathered guests with the bread of life.

SERVICE OF THE WORD

Despite the presence of Prone, Lutherans most frequently use the first half of the Service of Holy Communion when they wish to have only a Service of the Word.

This practice is distinctly different from one among Anglicans, who adopted the morning office as a preaching service by introducing long sermons into Matins. Although Lutherans have included sermons in the Order of Matins or Morning Prayer,[12] the practice of Matins as a non-Communion service is not as prevalent in Lutheranism as it is in Anglican churches.

Although the intent of this book is to explore current worship practices among Lutherans, several basic orders for a Service of the Word have become "official" in some Lutheran circles. Maxwell Johnson reports on a "*Lutheran-Roman Catholic Service of the Word* compiled from Lutheran and Roman Catholic liturgical books under the leadership of both Lutheran bishops and the National Conference of Catholic Bishops."[13] This service is similar to many Sunday experiences in Lutheran congregations:

> Gathering/Gathering Song
> Greeting
> Promise of the Word (i.e., a short introductory dialogue)
> Penitential Rite (optional)
> Prayer
> Reading(s)
> Psalm Response (or silence)
> Acclamation to the Gospel
> Gospel
> Homily
> Silence
> Creed (optional)
> Prayers (both spoken and sung forms supplied)
> Sign of Peace
> Lord's Prayer
> Offering (optional)
> Praise (a lengthy thanksgiving prayer similar in structure to the Eucharistic
>   Prayer)
> Blessing
> Dismissal[14]

Adapting this order could provide congregations with a Service of the Word. However, the advisability of a specific Service of the Word continues to be questioned.[15] Interestingly, committees that oversee each of the three major Lutheran worship books have prepared at least one Service of the Word during the past several decades.

During the last half of the twentieth century, the LCMS prepared a worship resource with several Services of the Word. The 1969 *Worship Supplement* contains three services with the title "A Service of Prayer and Preaching."[16] The thematic structure for each service follows the acronym ACTS—Adoration, Confession, Thanksgiving, and Supplication. Although places for congregational hymns and song are included, the liturgies are all spoken.

A few years after *Worship Supplement*, the Inter-Lutheran Commission on Worship provided a set of Services of the Word.[17] Six different services were prepared for study, one each for Advent, Christmas, Lent, and Easter, and two services for the season of Pentecost or for general use. The services began with a hymn of the season, which could be used for processions, particularly with a bookbearer because the emphasis was on the reading of Scripture. An opening dialogue set the theme for the service. A recital of the Apostles' Creed, called a covenant act, provided a baptismal connection for the gathered guests. Each service featured two canticles, and a total of nine were provided to enhance the congregation's appreciation for scriptural texts in song. An announcement of the significance of the day was followed by the prayer of the day and the lessons. Two lessons were suggested, though three could be read. A psalm, hymn, or choir anthem was suggested between the readings. A variety of responses, sung by choir or congregation, reflected the theme of the season. The sermon immediately followed the response to the reading to strengthen the tie with the texts. The Hymn of the Day reinforced the message of the lessons and the sermon. The notes introducing the services suggested that "it is appropriate for it [the Hymn of the Day] to receive more elaborate musical treatment by: use of instruments other than the organ, alternation between choir and congregation, alternate harmonizations, descants. Chorale concertos or similar extended compositions based on hymns would be desirable occasionally."[18] Following the hymn, the offering was gathered and the prayers of the people were prayed. The Greek phrases *Kyrie eleison* and *Christe eleison* were suggested, along with an explanation of the significance and historic tenacity of these phrases in Lutheran worship. The service concluded with the Benediction over the gathered guests after a second canticle was sung. A closing hymn was suggested as a way to reflect the mood of the service and as a recessional hymn for the pastor and book-bearer.

Both the Services of Prayer and Preaching in *Worship Supplement* and the Inter-Lutheran Commission on Worship's Services of the Word were experimental. Yet the service patterns, perhaps because of their simple structure (as well as the unusually uncertain times), encouraged diversity of experimental worship forms.[19]

Since the development of these services, several Lutheran bodies have produced hymnbooks with a distinct Service of the Word.

In 1978, *Lutheran Book of Worship* provided the first distinctive Service of the Word.[20] The structure is as follows:

Hymn
Dialogue Readings
Apostles' Creed
Old Testament Canticle
Prayer of the Day
Old Testament Lesson
Hymn/Psalm/Anthem
Second Lesson and Response
Silence for Meditation
Sermon
Hymn
Offering
Prayers (in various forms)
Lord's Prayer
New Testament Canticle
Benediction
Closing Hymn (optional)

Lutheran Book of Worship includes the canticles among the hymns. Philip Pfatteicher suggests this service bears much similarity to early Christian worship practices, which were adapted from synogogue services.[21]

Lutheran Worship, though omitting a Service of the Word in the pew edition, provides a Brief Service of the Word in its *Conference and Convention Edition*.[22] The service includes the following:

Hymn
Invocation
Psalm (said or sung)
Old Testament Reading
New Testament Reading
Address
Collect of the Day
Prayers
Lord's Prayer
Apostolic Benediction

This service is infrequently used, even during District conventions, because it is not located in a widely available worship resource.

Christian Worship has provided WELS congregations with a service that emphasizes the proclamation of the Word of God and encourages believers to respond with prayer, praise, and thanksgiving.[23] The structure is

Hymn

Apostolic Greeting

Confession and Declaration of Grace (a baptismal service is an optional
   substitution)

Canticle "Oh, Taste and See"

Prayer of the Day

Scripture readings (including a psalm and a verse of the day sung by the choir
   or congregation)

Gospel (with an acclamation of praise)

Hymn of the Day

Sermon

Apostles' Creed

Offering

Prayer of the Church (said responsively)

Lord's Prayer

Hymn

Final Prayer

Blessing

This Far by Faith offers two simple non-Communion services that are organized around three terms: gathering, Word, and sending.[24] The central feature of these services is the public reading of God's Word and the lively speaking of God's acts in the Old and New Testaments. Both of these Services of the Word have no prescribed rubrics, but they offer a number of options that may be followed according to local custom. For example, under the section labeled "Gathering," the congregation may gather, sing songs, give testimonies, and share community concerns. Beginning with a call for worship—which could be vocal (spoken or sung), musical (vocal or instrumental, solo or ensemble), or in dance—God's name is invoked or an apostolic greeting is offered. A confession of sins may be used, along with a greeting of peace. A Scripture song, hymn, or anthem is followed by a prayer of the day or a "gathering prayer." The portion of the service identified as "Word" includes Scripture readings (including a Gospel reading), a sermon, prayers, and an offering. The "Sending" section is brief, but it includes a Benediction that may be preceded by a "Charge to the People." After a song, there is a "Dismissal." The second service is called a "Service of Prayer and Preaching" and is modeled after revival services commonly experienced in African American communities. A Lutheran emphasis on the means of grace is encouraged.

Although not integral to the Lutheran liturgical tradition, nor even that of the ancient church, a Service of the Word clearly emphasizes the Lutheran understanding of the authority and integrity of the Word of God. Listening to the proclamation of God's Word is central to Lutheran worship.[25] A comparison of the various Services of the Word underscores the general emphasis on reading the Word from both Testaments, hearing the Word proclaimed under the double emphasis of Law and Gospel, and responding with psalms, hymns, spiritual songs, and prayers. Although none of these services has become standard among all Lutheran congregations, as has the use of the first half of the Communion service, the fact that all recent hymnbooks contain a Service of the Word demonstrates that the reading of Scripture and preaching based on that Word remain prominent practices in Lutheran worship among God's gathered guests.

SOME QUESTIONS TO CONSIDER

1. What is the earliest evidence of a Service of the Word? What was its origin? What was its basic outline?

2. How did Lutherans adapt the medieval service of Prone?

3. What does Frank C. Senn mean when he speaks of the preaching of the Word in a Lutheran context as "sacramental"?

4. Where do you think a sermon would "fit" in a service structured around the acronym ACTS? (If you can find a copy of *Worship Supplement*, compare the three Services of Prayer and Preaching.)

5. Why do you think recent Lutheran worship books have included at least one Service of the Word?

NOTES

1. James White, *Introduction to Christian Worship* (rev. ed.), 157.

2. Grisbrooke, "Synaxis," 501.

3. Dix, *Shape of the Liturgy* (2d ed.), 38.

4. Brand, "Liturgical Life of the Church," 45. The term is referred to in the Lutheran Confessions regarding Holy Communion (Ap. XXIV, 79).

5. Precht, "Confession and Absolution," 365.

6. Pfatteicher, *Commentary,* 145, dubiously suggests that *prône* was a French word for a grille that identified the part of the chancel where the notices were read.

7. Adapted from Brand, "Liturgical Life of the Church," 38–39.

8. Reed, *Lutheran Liturgy* (rev. ed.), 54.

9. Brand, "Liturgical Life of the Church," 42.

10. Senn, *Christian Liturgy*, 416–17.

11. Senn, *Christian Liturgy*, 306. Senn then quotes Luther's 1526 comments in "The Sacrament of the Body and Blood of Christ against the Fanatics," LW 36:340.

12. Commission on Worship, the LCMS, *Lutheran Worship: Altar Book*, 12, acknowledges that "custom has it that they [the services of daily prayer] may also be used as 'preaching services.' "

13. Johnson, "Planning and Leading Liturgical Prayer," 192, referencing an Augsburg Publishing House (1986) document (*Johnson's emphasis*).

14. Johnson, "Planning and Leading Liturgical Prayer," 192.

15. Helge, "Services of the Word," 14–15; and Alexander, "Luther's Reform of the Daily Office," 357.

16. *Worship Supplement*, pp. 100–102, 103–5, and 106–9.

17. Inter-Lutheran Commission on Worship, *Services of the Word*. Although produced only three years later, the Contemporary Worship series, perhaps because of the sung canticles and responses, did not acquire as great a popularity as the ACTS structure found in the *Worship Supplement* services.

18. Inter-Lutheran Commission on Worship, *Services of the Word*, 8.

19. For more information on variety in worship forms, see *Gathered Guests* chapters 20 and 22.

20. The service in *Lutheran Book of Worship* (pp. 126–30) comes after the Baptismal Service and precedes Morning Prayer and Evening Prayer.

21. Pfatteicher, *Commentary*, 450.

22. Commission on Worship, the LCMS, *Lutheran Worship: Conference and Convention Edition* (St. Louis: Concordia, 1986), 68–70.

23. *Christian Worship*, pp. 38–44. The organization of the hymnal places this service after the Service of Word and Sacrament and before the Morning and Evening Praise services.

24. *This Far by Faith*, pp. 69–71.

25. *All God's People Sing!*, pp. 8–27, offers almost a dozen Services of the Word for Christian day schools and other gatherings of young people.

CHAPTER 16

MORNING, EVENING, AND DAILY SERVICES

Most Lutherans are familiar with the morning or evening service in some form of Matins or Vespers. Martin Luther commended their regular use by congregations and by Christian families and university students, who might use these services as daily devotions. The titles of these two services are from the Latin words that mean "of the morning" and "of the evening." Matins and Vespers recall the practice of believers coming to God in a daily routine of prayer at specific times throughout the day. Although not experienced universally in all Lutheran congregations, there has been a recent increase in use of these non-Communion services on a weekly or daily basis.

This chapter studies the history of the devotional services of God's gathered guests, paying particular attention to the series of daily services, known as offices, that developed in the first centuries of Christianity. Three of these services are available in *Lutheran Worship* and will be explained in detail: Matins (and its newer counterpart, Morning Prayer), Vespers (and its newer counterpart, Evening Prayer), and Prayer at the Close of the Day (also known by its more ancient name, Compline).

DEVOTIONAL DEVELOPMENTS THAT LED TO THE CANONICAL HOURS

Growing out of the devotional life of early Christians who lived in isolated locales, special services that reflected the devotional concerns of the greater Christian community gradually developed. After reciting the Our Father, *The Didache* says, "You should pray this way three times a day."[1] These set times of devotional contemplation, prayer, and praise enabled the observant to reflect on the continuing presence of Christ and to follow the Pauline directive to "pray continually" (1 Thessalonians 5:17; cf. Psalm 34:1). A central concern among many early Christians was that they would be found ready at the imminent coming of the Lord.[2]

These times grew out of the Jewish practice of specific hours of prayer.[3] Daniel 6:10 speaks of three distinct times for prayer that he observed. Psalm 55:17 also refers to prayer at three times during the day. In addition, Psalm 119:164 mentions praising God for His righteousness seven times each day and seems to be the source for later Christian monastic practices. The New Testament indicates that such ordered prayer times probably were observed by the first Christians, particularly by the apostles and disciples. For example, Acts 2:1 and 2:15 suggest the disciples prayed around 9 A.M.; Acts 10:9 indicates noon prayers; Acts 3:1 refers to prayer at 3 P.M.; and Acts 16:25, read in light of Psalm 119:62, reflects prayer at midnight. These passages would seem to indicate a regular routine of prayer among the apostles and early Christians.[4]

These times of prayer originally were done privately at home. Hippolytus's *Apostolic Tradition* (written around A.D. 200) provides several references to these periods of devotion.[5] Similarly, Jerome (A.D. 331–420), in a letter to his co-worker the virgin Eustochia, remarked that "as everyone knows, prayers ought to be said at the third, sixth and ninth hours, at dawn and at evening."[6] Such regular hours of prayer were considered a matter of routine practice among many early Christians.

By the third century, the various devotional times were considered commemorations of Christ's work.[7] John Cassian, a fourth-century theologian and monk, is credited with the following poem that illustrates the connection of the monastic hours to significant events in Christ's passion.

> At Matins bound, at Prime reviled,
> Condemned to death at Terce.
> Nailed to the Cross at Sext; at None
> His blessed side they pierce.
>
> They take him down at Vesper-tide,
> In grave at Compline lay.
> Whence thenceforth bids His Church observe
> Her sevenfold hours alway.[8]

Thus the church found a way to relate the daily life of a Christian to Christ's life. Early Christians considered their devotional times a means to recall their Savior's gracious presence, power, and purpose and to emulate His practice.

As Christianity became more established and individual believers could assemble freely, these devotional times became public services.[9] These regular periods of directed meditation came to be called the daily office, which comes from the Latin *officium*, which means "service." Each hour or service was part of the worship life of the whole community, whether monastic or lay. The Lord's Supper was not included in these orders of service because they were preparation for the daily Mass that also was celebrated in monastic communities or in cathedrals. Thus Lutherans follow a long tradition when they use one of these services as a Service of the Word when the Lord's Supper is not celebrated.

Several additional services were devised to prepare the worshiping community for the major liturgical festivals. These occasional and extended evening services were called vigils, though they later became three separate public services: Vespers, Matins, and Lauds.[10] The worship times seem to have been chosen to coincide with the Roman division of the day into four "hours" of daytime and four "watches" of the night.[11]

Two parallel developments are evident in the codification of the daily office. One involves the congregational setting, in which the services were called the "cathedral offices." The other involves the communal setting, which led to the development of the "monastic offices." Two types of books developed for the purpose of leading devotional services. The Breviary (for priests)[12] and the Book of Hours (for laypeople) contained everything necessary and appropriate to observe or lead the Divine Office, as these services became known. For laborers in the fields, church bells tolled the hours so the workers could pause in their field to pray.

While developing his influential monastic rule, St. Benedict of Nursia (A.D. 480–543) determined that his monks should practice a daily routine of *ora et labora* ("pray and work"). His rule, particularly chapters 8 through 20, describes this daily worship routine as it was practiced at the monastery at Monte Casino in central Italy. Benedict set forth a seven-part office, along with the Night Office (Office of Readings or Matins) that was divided into three nocturns.[13] The monks were to pray at cockcrow (3 A.M.), dawn (6 A.M., Lauds), *terce* (9 A.M.), *sext* (noon), *none* (3 P.M.), lamplighting (6 P.M., Vespers), *compline* (9 P.M.), and *matins* (midnight).[14] (See diagram on next page.) The influence of Benedict's rule throughout Western Christianity was extensive, especially after the monastic revival in the ninth century.[15]

Not long after the monastic adoption of canonical hours (a *canon* is a regulation or standard) under the Rule of St. Benedict, medieval cathedral schools adapted these services as "choir offices" or services sung in the chancel only by the "choir" or robed clergy. Although these hours were observed most closely and

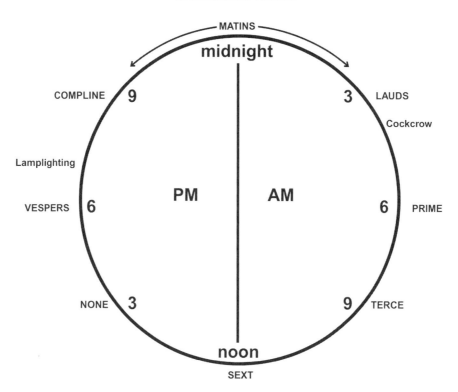

Monastic Devotional Times

MATINS

midnight

COMPLINE   9   3   LAUDS

Cockcrow

Lamplighting

PM   AM

VESPERS   6   6   PRIME

NONE   3   9   TERCE

noon

SEXT

Schedules varied depending on the seasons of the year or the monastic tradition, particularly with the placement of Matins.

scrupulously by monks of the Benedictine Order, they were followed by many others in the church as well.

> In the later Middle Ages the divine office became so elaborate that reform of it was almost continuous from the time of Gregory VII to the Council of Trent. The Gregorian Reform and the twelfth-century Renaissance did not immediately produce changes in the *Ordo Romanus* of the office, which Gregory VII confirmed against those who wished to reduce the psalmody of mattins to three psalms. . . . The *modernum officium*, used by the pope and the curia in the papal chapel, came into use during the twelfth century. This modified the calendar, abbreviated the lectionary and adopted the monastic hymnal. . . . By the fifteenth century the structure of the earlier canonical hours, based on regular recital of the psalms and scripture lections, had become so overlaid by later

accretions that council after council vied with one another "in deploring the coldness with which the clergy perform their duty of reciting the canonical office, even in choir."[16]

Even with such abuses, the services of Matins and Vespers were faithfully attended by the laity of many communities as part of their devotional piety and spiritual nurture.[17]

By the sixteenth century, the *modernum officium* was unwieldy and at times sub-Christian in its emphases on frequent recitations of "the office of the Blessed Virgin Mary and of that of the dead."[18] It was in the context of these tedious services that many of the sixteenth-century reformers were raised. Archbishop-elector Hermann von Wied of Cologne, after his conversion to Lutheranism, urged several Reformation leaders, including Philipp Melanchthon and Martin Bucer, to prepare revised orders for worship. These orders were published in *Simplex ac pia deliberatio* (*A Simple and Pious Consultation*) in 1547 and 1548. They used several German Lutheran church orders, including Andreas Osiander's Brandenburg-Nuremberg order of 1533, which contained both Matins and Vespers.[19]

Matins and Vespers were especially popular with the laity, and Lutheran reformers (including Luther and Johannes Bugenhagen) continued to use them daily and for evenings prior to church festivals (Vesper vigils). Frequently, these services were conducted by laymen in the absence of the local pastor.[20] Luther had strongly urged his congregation in Wittenberg to retain Matins and Vespers as part of the congregation's worship life because these services were filled with scriptural imagery and readings.[21] In 1523, Luther wrote:

> We should assemble daily at four or five in the morning and have [God's Word] read . . . in the same manner as the lesson is still read at Matins . . . . In like manner, come together at five or six in the evening. At this time one should really read again the Old Testament, book by book, namely the Prophets, even as Moses and the historical books are taken up in the morning. But since the New Testament is also a book, I read the Old Testament in the morning and the New Testament in the evening, or vice versa, and have reading, interpreting, praising, singing, and praying just as in the morning, also for an hour.[22]

This reading of Scripture with songs was to be done every day, though the whole congregation could not attend these services on a daily basis.

With the Anglican Church, the Lutheran Church restored modified versions of Matins and Vespers to congregational use.[23] Three hundred years later, it was the Common Service of 1888 that incorporated these services for congregational use among English-speaking North American Lutherans. The present practice in many Lutheran churches, unfortunately, has grown out of the Anglican emphasis on these services as the chief congregational services on the Lord's Day instead of the Lutheran emphasis on the Lord's Supper.[24]

The persistent popularity of Matins and Vespers lies in their rich heritage and in their adaptability to diverse congregational circumstances. The simple outline of the services provides opportunities for various liturgical and musical elaborations. Even when a sermon is replaced by a brief homily, the services provide edifying devotional thoughts based on Scripture. "The core of the Office is the praise of God in psalms and hymns, the proclamation of the Word of God in scriptural readings, and (especially in the evening) intercessory prayer."[25]

Under the heading "Toward a Wider Use of Daily Prayer," Philip Pfatteicher and Carlos Messerli state the purpose for a renewed interest in Matins and Vespers:

> When Christian people order their devotional life according to the ancient pattern developed through centuries of trial, experiment, and testing, they are, in effect, taking an advanced course in biblical and systematic theology taught by the masters of the Christian tradition. They are having their spirits stretched by some of the greatest minds of Christendom as they take their place in the earthly choir which joins the celestial praise of the citizens of heaven. These two purposes—praise and edification—are blended in that "work of God" which builds up the body of Christ.[26]

Christians who participate in these offices join a long tradition of praise and Christian growth. This may explain why increasing numbers of young Lutherans are gravitating to congregations that offer these services, particularly in the evening.

THE DAILY OFFICE

As participants in this extensive liturgical history, it is important for God's gathered guests to know not only the history of these offices but also what was included—structure and content. John Cassian's poem, noted earlier, shows the connection between the hours and Christ's life.

Four major elements of corporate worship developed within the office: psalmody, hymnody, readings, and prayers. The wealth of variety from these four sources is astounding, especially when one considers what has grown from it. The psalms (often all 150 psalms were read each week) and their antiphons (introductory Scripture verses), the creation of new hymns and songs, the readings from biblical and nonbiblical yet devotional writings,[27] and the versicles[28] and collects are evidence that the Daily Office was a wellspring for spiritual development and corporate worship.

While Matins and Compline were somewhat longer services, the basic format for an office was (bracketed portions were not used for the four midday services):[29]

Opening Versicle
Hymn or Psalm(s) with Antiphon or Canticle[30]
Sentence from Scripture: Lesson[31] (*lection*) or Chapter
Response
[Hymn]
Versicle
[Canticle]
Collect or Prayer(s)
Blessing

From this outline, one can see that the four major elements of these services were interspersed with greetings and antiphons or responses.

In each office or service, a central theme was identified, along with key or distinguishing elements of that particular order. Each service also offered a special relationship between the time of day and Jesus' life (as taken from John Cassian's writings). Philip Pfatteicher and Carlos Messerli explain that "the hours of the Office each culminate in the praying of the Lord's Prayer, and that custom suggests that the Office is part of the larger prayer of Christ the High Priest which he addresses continually to the Father."[32]

MATINS

The title of this service comes from the Latin word *matutinus,* which means "of the morning." Although usually conducted during the night, the service anticipates the morning. Traditionally prayed at midnight, this service recalls the biblical mandate to "watch and pray." Around the year A.D. 200, Hippolytus (ca. A.D. 160–235) wrote:

> About midnight, get out of your bed and wash and pray. Wash with clean water. If you have a wife, pray the psalms, alternating verses with her. If you have a wife but she is not yet a believer, go apart by yourself and pray alone, and then come back to your place with her. Even if you are bound by the bond of marital obligation, do not omit the prayer; for you are not sullied .
>
> It is very important that we pray at least once every hour; for the ancients have handed this practice down to us and taught us that this is how we are to keep watch. For at that hour all creation is at rest, praising God. Stars, trees, and waters are as if standing still. The whole host of angels keep their service together with the souls of the just. They praise almighty God in that hour; and that is why the faithful on earth must pray at this same time.

Our Lord in His parable put it this way: About midnight, He said, there came a call: Look! here comes the bridegroom! Go out to meet him! And He said more. Keep watch, then, He told them, for you do not know either the day or the hour in which the Son of Man is coming.[33]

An eschatological theme of the early church is picked up in Matins as it helps God's gathered guests focus on Christ's second coming. The church is to be like the wise young virgins who were waiting for the bridegroom with lamps burning and heads lifted (Matthew 25:1–13).

The origin of Matins is the topic of lively scholarly debate and discussion. Among the suggested hypotheses are (1) Matins was a combination of a night and a dawn office; (2) a night service was juxtaposed with the later service of Lauds; and, most likely, (3) the primitive orders of Matins or Lauds were amplified and augmented by the addition of a pre-Matins order or the Order of Prime.[34] Whatever the specific origin, the office of Matins has ancient and well-established roots in early Christian piety and practice.

The theme of Matins is preparation and watchfulness, and, if it is part of a vigil, it usually picks up the specific theme for the feast for which it serves as preparation. Key elements in Matins are the Invitatory, a powerful beginning of the Daily Office from Psalm 95, and the Venite. Similarly, the canticle Te Deum Laudamus serves as a deliberately strong element in this service, appearing prior to the prayers. These elements place the focus of the service on praising God for the new life that emerges from the darkness.

LAUDS

This service is named after the psalms that were sung in ancient times at the beginning of the day. These psalms—Psalm 148–150—were known as the *Laudate* Psalms (from the Latin word that means "praise"). The specific form of this service dates to the late fourth century in the East.[35] In its earliest stage, the Laudate Psalms concluded Matins. When the monasteries lengthened the services, combined them, then separated them again, these psalms were attached to Lauds.[36] The title of this service, *Laudes matutinales* ("morning praises"), was anglicized as *Lauds*.

The service is sometimes called the office of the "jubilant hour" because its 3 A.M. observation anticipated the sunrise.[37] A joyful theme is apparent because "Christians saw signified the resurrection of Christ, who is the rising Sun (Mal. 4:2), the true light (John 1:9), the dawn from on high (Luke 1:78, from the *Benedictus*)."[38] It may be possible for Christian worshipers to experience such a joyous hour even today, especially in the summer at an outdoor retreat setting.

The central theme of praise found in Lauds is not just any kind of praise. It is solidly and deliberately based on our Lord's victory. Jesus' resurrection is remembered at this service, as well as the resulting praise for the Christian hope of the resurrection of the body. Actually, a threefold resurrection may be considered. First, nature awakens from its sleep in a kind of natural resurrection. Second, the Savior's resurrection from the dead is clearly recalled and our own physical resurrection is anticipated. And, finally, Christians celebrate their spiritual awakening to faith in Christ by His Spirit.

The Laudate Psalms, with alleluia antiphons, are a central element to Lauds. In addition, the Benedictus, Zechariah's song as he greeted his new son, is sung. Traditionally, festival (and Sunday) services of Lauds include Psalm 93, 100, and 63, along with the Benedicite and Laudate canticles.[39] The service of Morning Prayer[40] in *Lutheran Worship* is an adaptation of Lauds with modifications from Matins.[41]

PRIME

The word *prime* comes from the Latin word *primus*, which means "the first." Prime refers to the initial hours of work that began with prayer (6 A.M.). Monks in monastic communities normally rose during the night to pray Matins and Lauds, then returned to their cells for meditation and reading. When they prepared for work, they observed a short service to consecrate the day, thus the office of Prime was developed as a second morning prayer.[42]

The origin of Prime may date to the second half of the fourth century in Bethlehem. By the beginning of the fifth century, it was used in Provence, France (Gaul) as part of the Rule of St. Benedict. Certainly, it was widespread and had become accepted practice in monasteries throughout Europe by the early sixth century.[43]

The focus of Prime is markedly different from the praises of Lauds. The attention of the worshiper is much more subjective as the sinful human worker stands before the Almighty King to whom the day is to be dedicated. Traditionally, Prime was a longer service. After the first part was completed, the monks entered the chapter or gathering room to do the "office of the chapter." This fourfold service began with a reading of a martyrology (a reading from the life of a martyr) so the accounts of the early martyrs could motivate the day's activities. Then the abbot distributed work assignments along with his prayers. Following a concisely formulated blessing—"May the almighty Lord order our days and our deeds in His peace"—a portion of Scripture or a selection from the monastic rule was read. Finally, the service ended with a blessing by the abbot, who was the house-father, as a sign that the monks were God's children and received His paternal blessing before beginning their work.[44]

The theme for Prime is preparation for the day's work. Because there is no obvious correlation to an event in Christ's life other than when the soldiers mocked and tortured Him, the theme of preparation for work is even more strikingly underscored. During the Middle Ages, the day laborers would pledge their allegiance to the lord before entering his fields. In the same way, the monks would give their "oath of allegiance" to the King of kings with "the Little Chapter" (1 Timothy 1:17). Even the concluding Benediction points to the work ahead: "The Lord bless us and keep us from all evil and bring us to everlasting life. Amen."

A longer form of Prime began with a hymn that enlisted all human efforts and abilities for the Lord's service. A lengthy set of prayers was followed by the psalmody and the Little Chapter. The responsory[45]—"Lord, have mercy"—recalls the blind man of Jericho, begging for help as Jesus passed (Mark 10:46–48; Luke 18:35–39). The final prayer "contains all the elements of a good morning prayer: thanks, petition, good intention, preparation for the coming day, and particularly the touching plea to be spared the guilt of sin throughout the day."[46]

Lutherans were reintroduced to Prime through *Worship Supplement*,[47] which provides a modified service for small groups. The service begins with the Versicle, Response, Gloria Patri, and Alleluia. A hymn is sung, followed by a psalm (Psalm 119:1–8 is suggested, along with additional psalms for each day of the week) with antiphons. Until 1955, when Prime was suppressed in the Roman Catholic Church, the Athanasian Creed was used in the Office of Prime on most Sundays as a canticle between the psalms. This can be practiced in Lutheran churches, if the worshipers desire to use Prime as a Service of the Word.[48]

The Little Chapter—"Now to the King eternal, immortal, invisible, the only God, be honor and glory forever and ever. Amen" (1 Timothy 1:17)—serves as a continuing oath of allegiance to God, dedicating the day's work to His glory. The Responsory is an adaptation of the Kyrie and Psalm 3:7, which in turn is followed by the Kyrie either in English ("Lord, have mercy") or its Greek transliteration ("*Kyrie, eleison*"). The Apostles' Creed is preceded by the Lord's Prayer. Selected portions of Scripture follow in a responsive format, leading to the final collects. The service ends with this response and blessing:

> The Lord almighty order this day and all our doings in his peace. Amen.

> V. Our help is in the name of the Lord.
> R. Who made heaven and earth.

> V. Let us bless the Lord.

R. Thanks be to God.

The Lord bless ✠ us and keep us from all evil and bring us to everlasting life. Amen.[49]

The service concludes quickly, and worshipers may leave for their daily tasks. Prime is appropriate for a retreat setting, as well as in a community setting, such as a university or a nursing home.

TERCE

The "third" hour, 9 A.M., was recognized as a necessary pause in the day's labors. Taken from the Latin word *tertius*, the Office of Terce became a time of meditation amid daily activities and a break for restful prayer. The office is short because the day is for work.[50] (This may be considered a "terse" service, though that word is not related to the title of the service.)

The theme of this service centers around the Holy Spirit and can be stated as an invitation: "Come, Holy Spirit." The correlation to Christ's life is the descent of the Holy Spirit both at the Savior's baptism and again at Pentecost.[51] This emphasis on the Holy Spirit explains why the key element of this office is the canticle Veni Creator Spiritus ("Come, Creator Spirit"[52]), which invokes the Spirit to renew His consecration of the day. The psalms (normally three were sung or said) or office hymns center on the Spirit's activities. As quickly as it begins, the service concludes so the worshipers can continue their work.

SEXT

The Latin word that means "sixth" gives the title to this service, and according to ancient reckoning, the sixth hour occurs at noon. As Pius Parsch elucidated, "The day's conflict is at its climax, the heat of passion is at its strongest, the powers of hell seem to have greater influence over man, our lower nature seems to have gained mastery."[53] Thus the theme for this service is from the Lord's Prayer: "Lead us not into temptation."

The connection to Christ's life is Good Friday. During the service, worshipers recall the Lord's suffering on the cross when the temptations of hell were meted out on Him from the sixth to the ninth hour. The shortness of the service emphasizes the temptation and crucifixion of Jesus.

A modified service, entitled Noonday Office, was reintroduced to Lutherans, again through *Worship Supplement*.[54] The service begins with the Versicle, Response, Gloria Patri and alleluia, and a psalm (Psalm 119:113–20 is suggested) with antiphon. In monastic and cathedral services at the "little hours," three psalms were said. The Little Chapter in the service of Sext is Galatians 6:2: "Carry each other's burdens, and in this way you will fulfill the law of Christ." The service continued with another Versicle and Response:

> R. Thanks be to God.
> V. The Lord is my Shepherd; I shall not want.
> R. He makes me lie down in green pastures.[55]

This is followed by the Kyrie, the Our Father, and a collect that recalls the burden of our sins that Christ bore "at this hour."[56] The service concludes with the Benedicamus.

NONE

"The ninth" (from the Latin word *none*) hour marks the last break before the end of the day's labors. A more personal note echoes through this office as worshipers look at their own futures. The theme of perseverance in the face of exhaustion from the day's toil and in the face of the end of time is evident. The last things (eschatology), and particularly one's own death, are emphasized in this office. The key element, as in the earlier two offices, is the brevity of the service and its emphasis on faithfulness to the end.

VESPERS

The title of the second-last service of the Daily Office is simply "evening" (the Latin word *vespera*). This is the church's evening prayer. It is similar to Lauds in tone and purpose, yet it looks ahead in gratitude, but not to the final rest (as does Compline). Thanksgiving for the day's accomplishments is the theme of this service, as well as preparation for the Great Thanksgiving (Eucharist). Because this is an evening service, the Lord's Supper (also an evening meal) is anticipated, as well as the hope of participating in Christ's heavenly banquet. Three key elements stand out in this service: the Service of Light, the use of incense during the psalmody and prayers, and the singing of Mary's song, the Magnificat. Because greater numbers of Lutherans use this service, more details appear later in this chapter.

COMPLINE

This final service, appropriately titled from the Latin word that means "complete," marks the conclusion of the monastic day. The service is more subjective and individualistic. It was not part of the original "hours" (three nocturns or nightwatches of Matins, including Vespers and

Lauds, and three of the day: Terce, Sext, and None) because Vespers was said in the late afternoon. Benedict of Nursia probably developed Compline as a devotional for the sleeping quarters (involving lessons, chapter of faults, and the abbot's blessing) and as a kind of second night prayer.[57] In his rule, Benedict stated: "Let Compline be limited to saying three psalms, which are to be said without antiphons. After that, let there be a hymn of that hour, a lesson, a versicle, the Kyrie, and conclude with a blessing."[58] A double theme of contrition and protection through the night is clear throughout the service. Jesus' prayer in Gethsemane is the Christocentric focus of this service.

The imagery of darkness is amplified in Compline to depict the feared darkness of night, as well as the darkness of sin and, ultimately, the darkness of death. This is evident in one of the short prayers associated with this ancient office: "Father, Redeemer, into Your hands, I commend my soul for this night-time of the day, of my life, of my soul."[59] This service also asks that God protect worshipers as the apple (pupil) of His eye and shelter them in the shadow of His wings.[60]

The confession of sins and the Gospel canticle of Simeon, the Nunc Dimittis, and its antiphon are not only memorable additions to the service but also serve as theological keys to understanding the significance of this office. Both portions of the service pick up the central theme in a straightforward biblical manner. The Gospel canticle picks up the themes of death and night, salvation and eternity, including the antiphon that brackets it. Following the canticle, the traditional order of Compline continued with a specific four-point prayer.[61] This series of prayers asked God to be present in the troubled areas of life and within the home and to be the light in the darkness. The prayers also thanked God for the day.[62] Because it is a night office, ordained leaders are not necessary to pray Compline.

The Services in *Lutheran Worship* in Detail

Lutheran Worship contains five of the services of daily prayer: Matins, Vespers, a simplified synthesis of Matins, Lauds, and Prime for Morning Prayer (Matins); and a modified compilation of Vespers and Compline itself for Evening Prayer.[63]

Matins in *Lutheran Worship* [64]

The service of Matins has been available to English-speaking Lutheran worshipers for almost a century. The English service was first included in *The Evangelical Lutheran Hymn-Book* and was used in many congregations as a Service of the Word.[65]

Although the rubrics suggest the possibility of an opening hymn, many worshipers find an opening hymn or a majestic organ prelude disturbing to the impact of the first verse: "O Lord, open my lips,"[66] which is the Versicle from Psalm 51:15. In the monasteries, after a night of silence, the first words from the lips of the gathered guests were this prayer for God's presence. Although complete silence is unnecessary, a quiet organ prelude or a single solo instrument playing a portion of the liturgy sets the tone for the beginning of this morning service.

The ancient versicle from Psalm 51 draws on the Jewish practice of reciting this psalm before the "Eighteen Benedictions."[67] Its usage in Matins dates to at least the sixth century and acknowledges the gracious fact that even worship is a work of God in us. The next versicle is from Psalm 70:1: "Make haste, O God, to deliver me; make haste to help me, O Lord."[68] According to John Pless, this "represents the survival of a fragment of the ancient monastic custom of monks chanting the whole of Psalm 70 as they walked from their sleeping quarters to the chapel."[69]

These versicles conclude with the Gloria Patri, a trinitarian affirmation that dates prior to the fourth century. The Gloria Patri is known as the "lesser Gloria"[70] and developed from a more ancient doxology. This older doxology said: "Glory to the Father through the Son in the Holy Spirit." In the fourth century, this was changed to the more familiar wording in opposition to Arius's subordinationist views of the Second Person of the Trinity.[71] The second line of the Gloria Patri was expanded from a simple "forever" to "now and forever." Finally, "as it was in the beginning" was added as a protest against those who denied the preexistence of the Son.[72]

After one of three seasonal ascriptions of praise, the service moves into the Invitatory and Venite (Psalm 95:1–7a): "Oh, come, let us sing to the Lord."[73] The Invitatory is an antiphon to the Venite. The Common Invitatory is always appropriate, though "proper" invitatories that consist of a statement and response can be found in *Lutheran Worship*.[74] The response "Oh, come, let us worship him" remains the same in all seasonal invitatories.[75] The most ancient morning psalm—Psalm 67—or an appropriate canticle may be substituted occasionally for the Venite. On weekdays a hymn that emphasizes the resurrection, a general morning hymn, or the Office Hymn may follow the response or the Venite. The Office Hymn is the principal hymn of Matins and normally reflects the thematic emphasis of praise, concluding with a trinitarian doxology.

The next part of the service is the Psalmody, which begins with a sung antiphon (by congregation or cantor). The psalm may be sung in a variety of arrangements, followed by the Gloria Patri (which adds a trinitarian ending to the psalm) and the choral repetition of the antiphon. Seasonal antiphons are also available.[76] One or more psalms were used in the cathedral or monastic offices, which reflected the usage of psalms as hymns of the church. The psalms also may be read, chanted, or sung in hymnic settings. Each psalm may be followed by a moment of silence so the congregation can meditate on God's Word. In some congregations, a prayer is said after each psalm.[77]

The lessons follow the Psalmody; each is followed by the following versicle and response:

V: O Lord, have mercy on us.
R: Thanks be to God.[78]

Matins was traditionally a reading service that incorporated longer passages of Scripture, typically at least the Old Testament and Gospel readings for the day.[79] Time to reflect and meditate on the readings is suggested. Appropriate responses in various forms may be given, whether as sung responses, as verbal comments in a short homily, as instrumental or choral works, or even as liturgical dance.[80] "Lutheran reformers retained a number of the 'pure' responsories for use after the last Scripture reading in Matins."[81] The Common Responsory is taken from Psalm 119:89; Psalm 26:8; and Luke 11:28. The Lenten Responsory comes from 1 John 2:1; Romans 8:32; and Psalm 32:1. The Easter Responsory and its alleliua is from Psalm 96:2; Psalm 29:1–2; and 1 Corinthians 15:20.

The sermon may be placed after the responsory, but a more traditional location and form encourages the worship leader to make short comments after each reading. Some commentary on Scripture that clearly proclaims the dual messages of Law and Gospel should be prepared. Luther wrote: "If this [preaching] is not done, the congregation is not benefited by the lesson, as has been the case in cloisters and in convents, where they only bawled against the walls."[82]

The Gospel canticle follows the sermon and the offering as the response of God's gathered guests to the Word and recalls their responsibility to proclaim the greatness of God. The Te Deum Laudamus is suggested as the canticle, unless it is the Easter season, at which time the Te Deum Laudamus is used in the Paschal Blessing of Morning Prayer (which is a modification of Matins). The Te Deum Laudamus is one of the ancient hymns of the church, dating to the fourth century.[83] Admiringly, Luther said in 1538 that the Te Deum Laudamus is "a fine symbol or creed composed in the form of a chant, not only for the purpose of confessing the true faith, but also for praising and thanking God."[84] As an alternative to chanting this canticle, it can be sung in a hymnic setting.[85]

The Benedictus (Zechariah's song from Luke 1:68–79) may also be used in place of the Te Deum Laudamus. The Benedictus is the traditional canticle for Lauds, and it exhibits the Jewish form of blessing (*berakah*) that begins with prophetic praises to God that have been offered since creation. Two forms of the Benedictus are provided in *Lutheran Worship*. The first[86] is appropriate for daily services because it draws attention to the new life Christians enjoy, as well as the hope believers hold for the "dawn of salvation and the dawn of the last day of fulfillment."[87] The second form of the Benedictus in *Lutheran Worship* is longer and focuses on the work of Christ's forerunner, John the Baptist.[88] This second form is most appropriate for Matins services during the seasons of Advent and Christmas.

The last major portion of Matins is the prayers of intercession. The prayers include all of the following: the Kyrie, the Our Father, a Salutation and Response, and the Collect of the Day (followed by the Collect for Grace). In less formal situations, the congregation may be invited to offer individual prayers. The Collect for Grace has been traditional in Lutheran congregations since the middle of the nineteenth century, but the prayer itself dates to the fifth century and probably was based on still earlier prayers. The Litany[89] may be substituted, especially during penitential seasons. Responsive Prayer 1 also may be used on occasion.[90] Matins concludes with the Benedicamus and the Benediction. When a pastor is not present, the Benedicamus is an appropriate conclusion to the service.[91]

The service of Matins has much to offer God's gathered guests as they hear His Word and respond with prayer and praise. The biblical content of Matins cannot be matched in providing a worthy Service of the Word for God's people.

MORNING PRAYER IN *LUTHERAN WORSHIP*[92]

An alternate version of Matins is the Service of Morning Prayer, which is a combination of Matins and Lauds. It involves several changes in the order of elements in the service (though not in content) and includes the Paschal Blessing for festival services and the Easter season. Portions of this order of service are marked with a small circle so families or small groups may use the service in a devotional setting.[93]

The service begins with the versicles and responses common for all daily offices and concludes with a double alleluia. "The invitatory antiphon for general use was composed for the *Lutheran Book of Worship* and reflects the sunrise and the renewal of life at the beginning of the daylight and recalls the Johannine equation of light and life."[94]

As in Matins, the Psalmody, Hymn of the Day, and readings are followed by the Gospel canticle, which is the Magnificat. *Lutheran Book of Worship*, from which this service is drawn, provides several canticles that may be used between the two psalms during a daily service, including the Song of the Three Young Men, a traditional canticle for Sunday Matins.[95] The Collect of the Day, as well as other prayers, are offered, concluding with the Our Father. The Benedicamus leads to the Benediction, unless the service includes a full sermon, which would typically occur on a Sunday. In this case, the service continues with the offering, another hymn, the sermon, one of three suggested prayers, and the Benediction.[96]

The Paschal Blessing,[97] which may be used to conclude Morning Prayer, echoes the Easter message and practice of the early Christians. Egeria described the reading of the Gospel at the tomb of Christ early each Sunday morning.[98] This blessing draws together the themes of Baptism, resurrection, dawn, light, and life in a commemorative recollection of the ancient cathedral office of the Easter Vigil.[99] Introduced with Galatians 3:37, the congregation responds with a sung alleluia. The leader chants the Gospel account, which is followed by the Te Deum Laudamus. The concluding prayer is an adaptation of a prayer for Easter day and serves as a psalm prayer.[100]

Morning Prayer offers the community of faith several options, thus providing variety for morning services without Holy Communion. The Easter emphasis makes it ideal for the Great Fifty Days of Easter.

VESPERS IN *LUTHERAN WORSHIP*[101]

Many Lutheran congregations use Vespers during the Lenten season. As mentioned in the discussion of Matins, Vespers can begin with the versicles and responses and the Gloria Patri rather than with an opening hymn. This approach encourages a meditative and repentant tone because Vespers can be distinguished from Matins in its quality of "contemplation, thanksgiving, and prayer . . . . It looks backward in thankfulness for the mercies of the day and invokes divine protection against all foes, and the gift of that peace which the world cannot give."[102]

The ascription of praise (the version without the alleluia is suggested for Advent and Lent) provides a note of hope and anticipated joy amid the solemnities of Lent. The ascription is a mini-reference to the Hallel Psalms (Psalm 113–118). The psalms immediately follow the ascription of praise because, unlike Matins, there is no Invitatory and Venite. Psalm 23, 110, 111, and 114 are suggested for Sundays and festivals. Psalm 6, 38, 46, 51, 105, 116, 117, 118, 126, 130, 135, 136, 138, 139, 141, 142, 143, and 146 are suggested for daily use.[103]

The reading of one or more lessons is a central feature of Vespers. Although only the Old Testament and Gospel lessons may be read, normally all three lessons are included on Sunday. A traditional daily lectionary is included in *Lutheran Worship*[104] that provides one or two readings for Vespers. Readings from the Apocrypha may also be used in this service. If used, readings from apocryphal books should be prefaced with an explanation that Luther placed these devotional materials between the two Testaments and considered them instructive for reading but not an authority for establishing doctrine.[105] Silence for contemplative meditation may follow each lesson. A brief commentary after each of the readings should be given, if no sermon is delivered.

Four responsories are provided in *Lutheran Worship*: the traditional, the Common, the Lenten, and one for Easter and its season. The traditional responsory "is a significant and impressive conclusion to the reading of Scripture . . . . It voices our constant need for mercy and our thankfulness that in God's Word, as nowhere else, we are assured of it."[106] The Common Responsory is adapted from Psalm 86:11, and the congregational response comes from Psalm 119:105. The Lenten Responsory is drawn from Psalm 144:11; Psalm 25:5; and Psalm 141:8. The Lenten congregational response comes from Psalm 143:9 and Psalm 140:1b. The Easter Responsory is adapted from Romans 6:9a and Romans 4:25 and is followed by the congregational response from Romans 6:9b and 10b and a double alleluia. Curiously, *Lutheran Worship* does not provide an Advent Responsory.[107]

The Office Hymn may be selected based on an evening theme or the season of the church year, though it may also serve as the sermon hymn in Vespers. If comments were not made at the time of the readings, the sermon should follow this hymn as an exposition of any of the texts. The offering may be gathered after the sermon.

The Versicle from Psalm 141:2 introduces the canticle, which is reminiscent of the time when the entire Psalm 141 was used.[108] The canticle for Vespers is the Magnificat (Luke 1:46–55). Luther considered this song one of the most magnificent statements of faith in all the Scriptures. He based several sermons and a major theological treatise on it.[109] The Magnificat is the song of the faithful church as she waits "quietly for the fulfillment of the word of promise. Her song of revolutionary import should be learned and pondered by all the people of God as one of the essential items of devotion."[110] Several arrangements of the Magnificat are available in *Lutheran Worship* for use as congregational hymns or as solos.[111] The singing of the Gospel canticle helps the gathered guests recall the threefold readings in the Divine Service. The Psalm reflects the Old Testament reading, and the Office Hymn (or a New Testament canticle from an epistle or from Revelation) suggests the Epistle Reading in the Divine Service.[112] The alternate canticle, the Nunc Dimittis, is more appropriate in Compline.[113]

The Kyrie, the Our Father, the Salutation, and the collects follow the canticle. The three collects provided in *Lutheran Worship* suggest various times when Vespers may be used: "At Vespers," "In Late Afternoon," or "In the Evening." The Collect for Peace traditionally completes the prayers, appearing immediately before the Benedicamus and Benediction, which close the service.

Vespers offers God's gathered guests a frequent opportunity to consider His grace, mercy, and peace. The service may be conducted in a quiet or in a festive mood, though Vespers is more conducive to Lenten meditation.

EVENING PRAYER IN *LUTHERAN WORSHIP*[114]

The introduction of Evening Prayer in *Lutheran Worship* is an ideal addition to our liturgical heritage. Although this service is often called an adaptation of Vespers, Evening Prayer is significantly different and particularly appropriate for the Christmas and Epiphany seasons.

The Service of Light ("*Lucernarium*") is the heart of this devotional service (as it is in the modern Eastern Orthodox Church). This service was used in cathedral schools and parishes in the West for centuries. Western churches also used the Service of Light on Saturdays as a preparatory service for Sunday worship, as well as on the eve of great church festivals.[115] The solemn significance of candlelighting is still evident in the activities of acolytes on Sundays and especially during Advent as the candles on the Advent wreath are lit. Although this portion of Evening Prayer is optional, it adds to a congregation's worship life during the preparatory season of Advent, the festivities of a Christmas Eve candlelight service, or during the joyous Easter season.

The Service of Light begins with a dialogue of versicles and responses that recall Jesus as the light of the world (John 8:12; John 1:5), as well as the request by the disciples from Emmaus that Jesus would remain with them (Luke 24:29). The rubrics for Evening Prayer indicate that a large lighted candle may be carried in procession to the chancel during this dialogue. If a congregation can turn the lights low prior to the service, then increase the intensity of the light during the procession, it will emphasize these words. The chancel is not lighted until the processional candle is brought into the chancel and the minister concludes the final dialogue:

L: Let your light scatter the darkness
C: and illumine your Church.[116]

The hymn "Joyous Light of Glory" ("*Phos Hilaron*" in Greek) is one of the oldest hymns still in use. Around A.D. 350, Basil the Great spoke of this ancient anonymously written hymn as a cherished tradition of the Christian church.[117] "The hymn is addressed to Christ, the brightness of the Father's glory (Hebrews 1:3). He is the glad, joy-giving, joyful, happy, blessed Light from Light as the Fourth Gospel and the Nicene Creed declare."[118] *Lutheran Worship* includes a hymnic setting and paraphrase of this song, which may be used in place of the chant.[119] After the hymn, the service continues with the Salutation and Invitatory: "Let us give thanks to the Lord our God." The congregation responds, "It is right to give him thanks and praise."[120] The prayer of thanksgiving that follows is "cast in the form of a Jewish *Berekah* which thanks God for his goodness."[121] This proclamational prayer of praise recalls God's enlightening presence in the following words:

> Blessed are you, O Lord our God, king of the universe, who led your people Israel by a pillar of cloud by day and a pillar of fire by night. Enlighten our darkness by the light of your Christ; may his Word be a lamp to our feet and a light to our path; for you are merciful, and you love your whole creation and we, your creatures, glorify you, Father, Son, and Holy Spirit.[122]

The pillars of cloud and fire recall God's protective guidance of the children of Israel in the wilderness (Exodus 13:21–22), which was based on His unilateral covenant of grace with Abraham (Genesis 15:17–18). Christ, the Word made flesh (John 1:14), became the true light of the world.

Selected verses from Psalm 141, the traditional evening psalm, are sung as the congregation asks for divine forgiveness and protection. After the antiphon for Psalm 141 is repeated, a prayer—"Let the incense of our repentant prayer ascend before you, O Lord"[123]—is spoken. The antiphon for Psalm 141 and the prayer can introduce the congregation to incense, especially on festival occasions such as Epiphany.[124] Incense symbolizes the prayers of the faithful ascending from earth to heaven, a visible and sensuous connection between the realms. A more ancient Christian understanding is that clouds of incense represent cleansing and purification (Numbers 16:46–47) and the covering over of sin with the sweetness of Christ's self-sacrifice. After incensing the altar and singing Psalm 141, the congregation may sit for the rest of the psalms, which may include periods of silence between each psalm. Reiterating the theme of thanksgiving, the Hallel Psalms (Psalm 112–117) and the Gradual Psalms (Psalm 119–131) may be sung or read.[125]

An Office Hymn appropriate for the season and the time of day is sung between the psalms and the lesson. This hymn is selected to add to the service in thought and tone.[126] A dialogue response to the readings (from Hebrews 1:1–2a) leads into the Gospel canticle. As in Vespers, the Magnificat is the canticle for Evening Prayer. The setting in Evening Prayer uses a translation by the International Consultation on English Texts, though the hymn "My Soul Now Magnifies the Lord"[127] may also be used.

Intercessory prayer was an integral part of the Daily Office of the early church. For Evening Prayer, the traditional Eastern Litany (or Deacon's Prayer) may be used, though it is not original to the service. This litany is a conflation of the Deacon's Prayer from the liturgy of John Chrysostom. The Western Litany[128] may be used instead. It is especially appropriate for Advent and Lent because it exudes a more penitential tone. Beginning in the fifth century, this prayer has been used throughout Western Christianity. It has been a part of Lutheran Vespers services since the middle of the nineteenth century. At the point of the fifth bidding, the Christian names of various church leaders may be mentioned as subjects for the congregation's prayerful consideration. In place of prayers for the dead, the litany recalls "the faithful who have gone before us and are with You" so the congregation may praise God with an alleluia.[129] A commendation of the worshipers concludes the litany, which is followed by the Collect for Peace. The Our Father concludes the prayers and is introduced with a conflation of Luke 23:41 and Luke 11:1: "Lord, remember us in your kingdom and teach us to pray."[130] After the Our Father, the service concludes with the Benedicamus and the Blessing.

In some situations it is appropriate and even necessary to include a sermon (for example, in a midweek evening service during Advent or Lent). Therefore, after the Benedicamus, an offering, hymn, sermon, prayer, and blessing may be included.[131] In this way, the integrity of the office is maintained, though the sermon becomes an obvious and beneficial "add-on."

The use of Evening Prayer during the season of Advent connects the gathered guests to the larger Christian worship tradition. The service uses images from Advent, Christmas, Epiphany, and Easter. As a result, it is appropriate for any time of the year when special evening services are offered.

PRAYER AT THE CLOSE OF THE DAY (COMPLINE)
IN *LUTHERAN WORSHIP*[132]

This fairly new service was introduced to North American Lutherans in 1969 through *Worship Supplement*. Compline is a devotional service at the end of the day rather than a preaching service. The ending of the day also brings to mind the ending of life. The familiar phrase "If I should die before I wake" has several echoes in this service. Compline could be conducted at the end of a congregational meeting or in a retreat setting.

The service in *Lutheran Worship* begins with a brief bedtime prayer: "The Lord almighty grant us a quiet night and peace at the last. Amen."[133] This prayer continues with the responsive chanting of Psalm 92:1–2, which emphasizes the conclusion of the day in God's gracious presence. After these sentences, an evening hymn of praise is sung. This hymn should be selected to establish the biblical motif for the service.[134]

The confession of sins and a declaration of grace are central features of Compline. A period of silence for self-examination may be employed after the invitation to confess. Two forms of confession are provided, though neither includes absolution. The first is a general confession by the congregation with the leader announcing a general declaration of God's forgiveness. The second form emphasizes the priesthood of all believers in a reciprocal form of confession between leader and congregation. In this confession, worshipers recognize the supertemporal nature of worship and confession "before the whole company of heaven."[135] This form is historically associated with Compline.[136] The Service of Corporate Confession and Absolution may be used on occasion.[137]

Because of Compline's emphasis on preparation for sleep, there are no lengthy Scripture readings in the service. Instead, a brief reading and a psalm are included. The traditional Compline psalms are Psalm 4, 91, and 134. *Lutheran Worship* suggests two more selections: Psalm 34 and 136. Silence and time for private prayer after each psalm may be encouraged. The brief Scripture reading that follows the psalms is sometimes called "the Little Chapter," of which only one is used on any particular night as a concise statement of the service's theme (traditionally "the Little Chapter" is taken from Jeremiah or 1 Peter, though *Lutheran Worship* suggests others). The Responsory comes from Psalm 31:5 with New Testament echoes from the lips of Jesus (Luke 23:46) and the first martyr, Stephen (Acts 7:59): "Into Your hands I commend my spirit."[138]

The Office Hymn, appropriate to the season and the time of day, is sung with little fanfare. John Pless suggests the following hymns from *Lutheran Worship*, which may be used according to the church year:

- For Advent: "O Lord of Light, Who Made the Stars" (17) and "O Savior, Rend the Heavens Wide" (32)

- For Christmas: "We Praise, O Christ, Your Holy Name" (35); "O Savior of Our Fallen Race" (45); and "On Christmas Night All Christians Sing" (65)

- For Epiphany: "From God the Father, Virgin Born" (74) and "O God of God, O Light of Light" (83)

- For Lent: "Jesus, Refuge of the Weary" (90) and "Grant, Lord Jesus, That My Healing" (95)

- For Easter: "Abide with Us, Our Savior" (287) and "Lord Jesus Christ, Will You Not Stay" (344)

- For Pentecost: "Come, Gracious Spirit, Heavenly Dove" (161)[139]

Other hymns of praise for God's gracious presence throughout the day may be used.

As an introduction to the prayers, a dialogue from Psalm 17 (vv. 1, 8, 15) is sung. One or more collects may then be chanted or said, each emphasizing preparation for sleep yet also looking forward to eternal life. These prayers conclude with the Our Father.

The traditional Gospel canticle for Compline, the Nunc Dimittis (Simeon's Song from Luke 2:29–32), picks up the themes of preparation, forgiveness, praise, and anticipation of heaven, weaving them into a perfect unity. The canticle may be used in one of several forms, including several hymnic settings.[140] The antiphon is an ancient prayer that unites the night and death imagery again: "Guide us waking, O Lord, and guard us sleeping that awake we may watch with Christ and asleep we may rest in peace."[141] The service concludes with a trinitarian blessing and a quiet dispersal of the congregation.

Throughout this chapter, the services have emphasized reading Scripture and prayer. This devotional emphasis is the key to the strong spiritual life of God's gathered guests. God feeds us with His Word and we respond in worship.

SOME QUESTIONS TO CONSIDER

1. What is the biblical basis for setting aside particular devotional times?

2. Why did Luther retain the services of Matins and Vespers? How were they used in early Lutheran worship?

3. Outline the basic format for an office, highlighting the four major elements.

4. Explain the significance of the titles of four of the daily offices. How, if at all, are they related to the life of Christ?

5. Distinguish Matins and Morning Prayer as presented in *Lutheran Worship*. Why were both services included in the same worship resource?

6. Distinguish Evening Prayer and Vespers as presented in *Lutheran Worship*. Which service would be more appropriate for midweek Lenten services? Which service would be more appropriate for midweek Advent services? Why?

7. How might Compline be a beneficial conclusion to a congregational meeting?

NOTES

1. Richardson, "The Didache," 8.3, in *Early Christian Fathers*, 174.

2. Taft, *Liturgy of the Hours*, 14–16, cites several of Origen's comments that reflect this eschatological anticipation.

3. Bradshaw, *Daily Prayer*, 6–7, reports that the Qumran community (where the Dead Sea Scrolls were found) had at least six specific times of prayer that corresponded to the Jewish method of dividing the day.

4. Dugmore, "Canonical Hours," 140, records that John Cardinal Newman reiterated this apostolic heritage (*Tracts for the Times* [6 vols.; London: Rivington, 1837], Tract 75, p. 3).

5. Taft, *Liturgy of the Hours*, 22–27, interprets the *Apostolic Tradition* as calling for prayers in the night (at midnight and at cockcrow), upon rising, three times throughout the day (the third, sixth, and ninth hours), and in the evening before bed. This totals seven prayers each day. See Dix and Chadwick, *Treatise on the Apostolic Tradition*, 62–65.

6. Dugmore, "Canonical Hours," citing Jerome, *Epistola*, 22.37.

7. Pfatteicher and Messerli, *Manual on the Liturgy*, 264 n. 4, cite Cyprian, *De oratione*, 34, and Clement of Alexandria, *Stromata*, vii.40. See also Dugmore, *Influence of the Synagogue*.

8. John Cassian, "On the Canonical System of the Daily Prayer and Psalms," Book 3 in *The Twelve Books on the Institutes of the Coenobia*, trans. E. C. S. Gibson, *Nicene and Post-Nicene Fathers of the Christian Church*, 2d ser., vol. 1 (New York: Christian Literature Society, 1894). The source of this English translation is unknown.

9. Bradshaw, *Daily Prayer*, 72, quotes Eusebius of Caesarea (ca. A.D. 260–340): "Throughout the whole world in the churches of God in the morning at sunrise and in the evening hymns and praises and truly divine pleasures [hymns] are established to God" (*Comm. in Ps.* 64.10).

10. Pius Parsch, introduction to *The Hours of the Divine Office in English and Latin* (Collegeville, Minn.: Liturgical Press, 1963–64), 3. Taft, *Liturgy of the Hours*, 165, points out that several forms of vigils for monastic and cathedral settings existed.

11. Dugmore, "Canonical Hours," 140, cites Pierre Salmon, "La prière des heures," in *L'Église en Priére*, 3d ed., ed. A. G. Martimort (Paris: Desclée, 1965), 814.

12. Parsch, introduction to *The Divine Office*, 2, notes that the two principal objectives of the breviary, "worldwide pastoral prayer and personal interior growth in prayer[,] unite and intermingle."

13. Berry, "The Divine Office," 213–14. See also Benedict, *Rule of St. Benedicct,* trans. and intro. by Anthony C. Meisel and M. L. Del Mastro (Garden City: Image Book, Doubleday, 1975), chapters 8–20, pp. 61–69.

14. Harper, *Forms and Orders*, 74, indicates that the exact times varied according to the season and geographic latitude. For example, during the winter, Vespers would be celebrated in late afternoon in a typical northern European monastery.

15. Taft, *Liturgy of the Hours*, 57–140, gives several chapters on the background of Benedict's rule.

16. Dugmore, "Canonical Hourse," 143, citing Pierre Batiffol, *History of the Roman Breviary*, trans. Atwell M. Y. Baylay (London: Longmans, Green, 1912), 173.

17. Harper, *Forms and Orders*, 74, notes that "medieval practice favoured periods of private scriptural reading and study, but this obviously excluded the illiterate."

18. Dugmore, "Canonical Hours," 144.

19. Dugmore, "Canonical Hours," 144. See also Frank C. Senn, *Christian Liturgy* (Minneapolis: Fortress, 1997), 331.

20. Reed, *Lutheran Liturgy* (rev. ed.), 390.

21. "Concerning the Order of Public Worship," LW 53:11–13.

22. "Concerning the Order of Public Worship," LW 53:12, 13.

23. Taft, *Liturgy of the Hours*, 319–20, argues that Luther was "more confident than knowledgeable in matters liturgical," thus he changed the whole focus of these services to become Services of the Word. Jungmann, *Early Liturgy*, 284, states: "The canonical Hours, therefore, began regularly with a reading from the Sacred Scriptures. A more profound theological reason, too, can be given for this order. If we assemble for the purpose of honoring God, for praying, for presenting our petitions, it is fitting that we first listen to what God wishes to tell us. In the Christian order of salvation, it is of primary importance to realize always that God is speaking to us, that God's grace is calling us. Then, and only then, can we turn to God with our own response."

24. It is interesting to note the connection that Lutherans have with Anglicans. Thomas Cranmer visited Luther in 1532, having married the niece of Andreas Osiander's wife. The following year, after becoming the Archbishop of Canterbury, he prepared the first edition of the *Book of Common Prayer*.

25. Pfatteicher and Messerli, *Manual on the Liturgy*, 268.

26. Pfatteicher and Messerli, *Manual on the Liturgy*, 269.

27. Palazzo, *History of Liturgical Books*, 121, states: "The readings at the Office (also called lessons, from *lectiones*) are of three kinds: biblical, patristic, and hagiographic . . . . The reading of the Church Fathers (homilies, sermons) and the hagiographic writings (legends about the saints, passions of the martyrs) also appeared very early in the history of the Office, in Africa and the East, and greatly developed during the Middle Ages." About the readings from the church fathers, Palazzo concludes that "these texts were intended as commentaries on sacred Scripture" (152).

28. Versicles (from the diminutive form of the Latin word *versus*), or "little verses," designate a short scriptural sentence that may be used as an introduction, conclusion, or transition in the liturgy. Versicles are often used in conjunction with Scripture readings.

29. Harper, *Forms and Orders*, 76–86.

30. Some canticles—biblical poems set to music—used in the offices come from material other than the psalms; for example, the Song of the Three Children comes from the Apocrypha.

31. Any reading done during an office is designated as a "lesson" (from the Latin word *lectio*). It may come from Scripture, a sermon by a church father, or a legendary passion of a martyr.

32. Pfatteicher and Messerli, *Manual on the Liturgy*, 267.

33. Parsch, introduction to *The Divine Office*, 5, cites *Apostolic Tradition* 32.19–27. See Dix and Chadwick, *Treatise on the Apostolic Tradition*, 65–67.

34. Dugmore, "Canonical Hours," 141–42. Taft, *Liturgy of the Hours*, 79, interpreting Cassian's monastic rule, proposes that Prime was added to the office hours to make the monks in Bethlehem wake up instead of sleep until Lauds.

35. Chadwick, "Origins of Prime," 180, cites pseudo-Athanasius, *de virginitate*, 12; Basil, *Reg. Fus. Tract.*, 37; *Peregrinatio Etheriae*, 24; and Chrysostom, *Hom.* 14 in Tim. 5, PG 62:575.

36. Bradshaw, *Daily Prayer*, 109–10. See Taft, *Liturgy of the Hours*, 191–201, for a slight variation.

37. Parsch, introduction to *The Divine Office*, 6.

38. Pfatteicher, *Commentary*, 373, citing Clement of Alexandria, *Stromata*, 7.7, 43.6–7; and Cyprian, *On the Lord's Prayer*, 35, who wrote: "We should pray in the morning to celebrate the resurrection of the Lord with morning prayer." See also Taft, *Liturgy of the Hours*, 14–15 n. 2.

39. Parsch, introduction to *The Divine Office*, 7.

40. *Lutheran Worship*, pp. 236–49.

41. Pfatteicher and Messerli, *Manual on the Liturgy*, 290–95, calls Morning Prayer a "modified Matins."

42. Parsch, introduction to *The Divine Office*, 4. Cassian, *De coenob. instit.*, 3.4, reports that Jerome introduced this service around A.D. 382 in his Bethlehem monastery to end the monks' laxity. See Dugmore, "Canonical Hours," 141.

43. Chadwick, "Origins of Prime," 182.

44. Parsch, introduction to *The Divine Office*, 8.

45. A responsory (from the Latin *responsorium*) is a Scripture verse or two that is sung by the choir or congregation after a reading.

46. Parsch, introduction to *The Divine Office*, 7.

47. *Worship Supplement*, pp. 112–15.

48. Pfatteicher, *Commentary*, 378.

49. *Worship Supplement*, 115.

50. Parsch, introduction to *The Divine Office*, 8.

51. Pfatteicher and Messerli, *Manual on the Liturgy*, 264.

52. *Lutheran Worship*, 157 or 158.

53. Parsch, introduction to *The Divine Office*, 9.

54. *Worship Supplement*, pp. 116–17.

55. *Worship Supplement*, p. 116.

56. *Worship Supplement*, p. 117.

57. Parsch, introduction to *The Divine Office*, 4.

58. Benedict, *Rule of St. Benedict*, chapter 17. In chapter 18, Benedict indicates that Psalm 4, 91, and 134 should be used every day at Compline. See also Anthony C. Meisel and M. L. del Mastro, trans., *The Rule of St. Benedict* (Garden City: Image, 1975), 67–68.

59. Parsch, introduction to *The Divine Office*, 11.

60. *Lutheran Worship*, p. 266. Taken from Psalm 17:8.

61. That is a third option in *Lutheran Worship*, p. 267.

62. Parsch, introduction to *The Divine Office*, 11.

63. Pfatteicher and Messerli, *Manual on the Liturgy*, 264.

64. *Lutheran Worship*, pp. 208–23.

65. *Evangelical Lutheran Hymn-Book*, pp. 22–26, entitled the service "The Order of Early Service or Matins." When *The Lutheran Hymnal* was published in 1942, a similar practice continued.

66. *Lutheran Worship*, p. 208.

67. Pfatteicher, *Commentary*, 374.

68. *Lutheran Worship*, p. 208.

69. Pless, "Daily Prayer," 444.

70. The "greater Gloria" is the angel's hymn, the Gloria in Excelsis.

71. Reed, *Lutheran Liturgy* (rev. ed.), 412. Pfatteicher, *Commentary*, 358, notes that "the Council of Vai-

son (529) directed the use of the Gloria Patri . . . once, after all the psalms had been sung . . . . In Gaul, each psalm was concluded with the Gloria Patri, and this became a distinguishing feature of the use of psalmody in the West."

72. The English Language Liturgical Consultation, *Praying Together* (Nashville: Abingdon, 1988), 40.

73. *Lutheran Worship*, pp. 209–11.

74. *Lutheran Worship*, pp. 288–90.

75. *Lutheran Worship*, p. 209.

76. These antiphons and chant tones can be found in *Lutheran Worship: Altar Book*, 122–25, and *Lutheran Worship*, pp. 288–290.

77. See *Lutheran Book of Worship: Minister's Desk Edition* (Minneapolis: Augsburg; Philadelphia: Board of Publication, LCA, 1978) for a complete set of psalm prayers.

78. *Lutheran Worship*, p. 211.

79. Pless, "Daily Prayer," 446, notes that *Lutheran Worship: Altar Book*, 133, provides "Readings for Daily Prayer" in a continual reading format. This list is adapted from the Church of Sweden.

80. Pfatteicher and Messerli, *Manual on the Liturgy*, 292, warns: "Whatever form it takes, the response should draw attention to the reading and not to itself."

81. Pless, "Daily Prayer," 447. *Lutheran Worship*, pp. 211–14, offers a variety of responsories.

82. "Concerning the Order of Public Worship," LW 53:12.

83. Westermeyer, *Te Deum*, 49. See also Clarke, *Liturgy and Worship*, 273.

84. LW 34:202. He also provided a Germanic paraphrase of the Te Deum Laudamus (LW 53:171–75).

85. "Holy God, We Praise Your Name" (*Lutheran Worship*, 171).

86. *Lutheran Worship*, pp. 217–18.

87. Pfatteicher, *Commentary*, 378.

88. *Lutheran Worship*, pp. 239–42.

89. *Lutheran Worship*, pp. 279–87.

90. *Lutheran Worship*, pp. 270–72.

91. See Reed, *Lutheran Liturgy* (rev. ed.), 426, and Pless, "Daily Office," 450. *Lutheran Worship* provides two forms of the Benediction for this purpose. A wise custom of the church suggests that a nonordained leader include himself in the blessing (e.g., "bless us and keep us") to uphold the Lutheran teaching on the pastoral office of the ministry. However, such a practice is not commanded by God in Scripture.

92. *Lutheran Worship*, pp. 236–49.

93. *Lutheran Worship*, p. 236.

94. Pfatteicher, *Commentary*, 375.

95. The canticle Benedicite Omnia Opera (*Lutheran Worship*, 9).

96. See Pfatteicher, *Commentary*, 375–76.

97. *Lutheran Worship*, pp. 244–49.

98. Wilkinson, *Egeria's Travels*, 27.2.

99. Pfatteicher, *Commentary*, 379.

100. Pfatteicher, *Commentary*, 381.

101. *Lutheran Worship*, pp. 224–35. Evening Prayer is a modified version of Vespers (see *Lutheran Worship*, pp. 250–62). Pfatteicher and Messerli, *Manual on the Liturgy*, 272–86, provides helpful suggestions.

102. Reed, *Lutheran Liturgy* (rev. ed.), 431.

103. *Lutheran Worship*, p. 292; *Lutheran Worship: Altar Book*, 126.

104. *Lutheran Worship*, p. 295ff.

105. "Prefaces to the Apocrypha," LW 35:335–54. LW 35:337 n. 1 cites Luther: "These books are not held equal to the Scriptures, but are useful and good to read" (WADB 2:547). See also LW 35:339 regarding the Book of Judith, which Luther calls "a fine, good, holy, useful book, well worth reading by us Christians."

106. Reed, *Lutheran Liturgy* (rev. ed.), 435.

107. The following Scripture selections, used in *Lutheran Book of Worship*, provide material for an Advent Responsory: Revelation 22:17; 2 Timothy 4:8; and Romans 8:22. The refrain of "Come, Lord Jesus" (from Revelation 22:20: *maranatha*) may also be used.

108. See Taft, *Liturgy of the Hours*, 45; and Bradshaw, *Daily Prayer*, 112. They cite the *Apostolic Constitutions* and Ambrose, respectively.

109. In 1521, Luther wrote his treatise on the Magnificat (LW 21:295–358; WA 7:538–604). In 1533, a Wittenberg hymnal included the translation and chant tones for this canticle (LW 53:176–79; WA 7:546).

110. Pfatteicher and Messerli, *Manual on the Liturgy*, 284.

111. *Lutheran Worship*, pp. 228–30, 255–57; *Lutheran Worship*, 211; and *Hymnal Supplement 98*, p. 19.

112. Pfatteicher and Messerli, *Manual on the Liturgy*, 284.

113. *Lutheran Worship: Altar Book*, 13.

114. *Lutheran Worship*, pp. 250–62. This Order of Evening Prayer is a slightly revised version of the service included in *Lutheran Book of Worship*.

115. Pfatteicher, *Commentary*, 352–53.

116. *Lutheran Worship*, p. 251.

117. Pfatteicher, *Commentary*, 353, cites Basil the Great, *Treatise on the Holy Spirit,* 29; Taft, *Liturgy of the Hours*, 38, 286; and A. Tripolitis, "*Phos hilaron*," *Vigiliae Christianae* 24 (1970): 189–96.

118. Pfatteicher, *Commentary*, 354.

119. "O Gladsome Light, O Grace" (*Lutheran Worship*, 486).

120. *Lutheran Worship*, p. 252.

121. Pfatteicher and Messerli, *Manual on the Liturgy*, 279. *Lutheran Worship: Altar Book*, 125, provides two alternate forms of the thanksgiving.

122. *Lutheran Worship*, pp. 252–53.

123. *Lutheran Worship*, p. 255.

124. One focus of Epiphany is the visit of the Magi to the Christ Child, during which they gave the family gifts of gold, frankincense, and myrrh. See Pfatteicher and Messerli, *Manual on the Liturgy*, 279–81, for more information on the use of incense in worship.

125. *Lutheran Worship*, p. 292, lists psalms appropriate for daily prayer.

126. Appendix 3 in Precht, *Lutheran Worship: History and Practice*, 569–70, suggests several hymns for Evening Prayer for each season of the church year.

127. *Lutheran Worship*, 211.

128. See *Lutheran Worship*, pp. 279–87.

129. *Lutheran Worship*, pp. 259–60.

130. *Lutheran Worship*, p. 260.

131. Pfatteicher, *Commentary*, 367, identifies this segment of Evening Prayer as "The Preaching Office."

132. *Lutheran Worship*, pp. 263–69.

133. *Lutheran Worship*, p. 263.

134. Pless, "Daily Prayer," 460, lists the following hymns included in *Lutheran Worship* as appropriate for Compline: "All Praise to Thee, My God, This Night" (484); "Now Rest Beneath Night's Shadow" (485); "O Gladsome Light, O Grace" (486); "O Trinity, O Blessed Light" (487); "Before the Ending of the Day" (489); and "God, Who Made the Earth and Heaven" (492).

135. *Lutheran Worship*, p. 264.

136. Pless, "Daily Prayer," 460.

137. *Lutheran Worship*, pp. 308–9.

138. *Lutheran Worship*, p. 265.

139. Pless, "Daily Prayer," 461.

140. See, for example, *Lutheran Worship*, 173, 193, 268, or Luther's hymn, "In Peace and Joy I Now Depart" (*Lutheran Worship*, 185).

141. *Lutheran Worship*, p. 269.

PART 5

PRAYER AND READING IN WORSHIP

CHAPTER 17

LITURGICAL PRAYER

Lutherans have always been people of prayer. Lutheran prayers often are drawn from prayer books, whether for use in a formal setting or in private devotions. Martin Luther was quick to prepare devotional guides for his friends and students to help them pray better.[1] His sermonic expositions of the Lord's Prayer and his catechisms demonstrate the importance he placed on this dimension of the Christian life in his pastoral endeavors. On one occasion, Luther said, "Indeed, the fervent prayer of a true Christian is a marvelous thing. Without it, the world wouldn't be the same. At home I lack courage and cheer, though I'd like to change that; but in the church, amidst the congregation, prayer comes directly from the heart and is triumphant."[2]

In the worship life of God's gathered guests, numerous prayers are offered in a corporate context. Prior to worship, many Christians say a silent prayer to prepare for the service. After the invocation, many Lutheran services include a prayer of confession. The Kyrie (a prayer for God's mercy) introduces the Service of the Word. The collect (a theme-setting prayer for worship) precedes the reading of Scripture. After the sermon and the creed, the Prayer of the Church is offered, which incorporates many of the concerns of God's people. The Lord's Prayer is said immediately before the consecration of the elements in the Service of the Sacrament. Prayers may also be said privately during the distribution of the Lord's Supper, either at the altar or after returning to the pew. Prior to the Benediction, a Post-Communion Collect concludes the Service of the Sacrament. And many Christians offer a silent prayer after the Benediction.

This chapter focuses on the theology and practice of prayer, with particular emphasis on how the Christian community prays during its corporate worship as God's gathered guests. Several kinds of prayers will be investigated, in particular, intercessory prayer, the collect, and the Litany. After a brief review of biblical per-

363

spectives on prayer, liturgical praying will be distinguished from other devotional methods of praying.

BIBLICAL PERSPECTIVES ON PRAYER

The Bible is filled with an incredible variety of prayers, as well as many exhortations to pray. The people of the Old Testament came to God in prayer individually and corporately on numerous significant occasions. The Psalms are recognized throughout the world as the prayer book of the Old Testament. Leslie Stradling's *Praying the Psalms* provides guidance for contemporary Christians concerning the use of the Psalter as a prayer book.[3] Linette Martin's fascinating book *Practical Praying* complements Stradling's work by listing all the prayers in the Bible (more than 200), excluding the Psalms.[4]

In the Sermon on the Mount, Jesus encouraged His disciples to pray (Matthew 6:1–18; 7:7–11). He taught His disciples to pray (Luke 11:1–13) and gave them a model prayer, the Our Father (Matthew 6:9–13; Luke 11:2–4). Jesus prayed on a regular basis during His earthly ministry and, in particular, He prayed for His disciples (Mark 1:35; John 17:6–19, 20–21). After Jesus' ascension, the apostles also prayed regularly and encouraged their fellow believers to join in prayer (Acts 1:14; 2:42). Paul frequently told the congregations he founded that he was praying for them. For example, he wrote to the Philippians: "I thank my God every time I remember you. In all my prayers for all of you, I always pray with joy" (1:3–4). The Book of Revelation includes many prayers and concludes with a prayer for Christ's return (19:1–10; 22:20). Even a position or stance for praying is indicated in Scripture (see, for example, 1 Kings 8:22, 54; 1 Timothy 2:8).

Prayer, particularly corporate prayer, is primarily a response offered in the context of God's Word. Prayer is an act of worship. God comes to us in His Word, and we respond in prayer and praise. Eugene Peterson explains that "prayer is a human word and is never the first word, never the primary word, never the initiating and shaping word simply because we are never first, never primary . . . . God has the first word. Prayer is answering speech."[5] Therefore, he repeats in his little book, "Be slow to pray."[6]

Among the first Christians, prayer was a significant act of worship and an expression of faith because they were often persecuted. In the writings of the Apostolic Fathers (Christian writers who lived immediately after the apostles), seven distinct terms refer to prayerful acts of piety and devotion: invocation, confession, prayer, request, intercession, thanksgiving, and petition.[7] Similarly, in the late third century, Origen of Alexandria followed Paul's comments in 1 Timothy 2:1 and described four kinds of prayer: request, prayer, intercession, and thanksgiving.

A theologically meaningful expression in the early church was the way God was addressed in prayer. Most prayers were addressed to the Father, as Jesus had taught and according to Jewish precedent. However, as the importance of honoring the Trinity came to the fore between the second and fourth centuries, the address in prayer changed slightly. Christians began to pray *to* the Father, *through* the Son, and *in* the Spirit.[8] This practice underscores the biblical teachings concerning Jesus' mediatorial role before the Father and the Spirit's incorporating responsibilities[9] for the Christian community. Such an expression of trinitarian devotion may easily be included in Christian prayer today.

The organized prayer of the early church, whether offered individually or corporately, became set times of prayer around the fourth century. These set times of prayer became the Daily Office.[10] Paul Bradshaw, who has studied early Christian worship and prayers, reminds us that corporate prayer was central to the daily devotional practice: "A major characteristic of the set times of daily devotion in the first few centuries was prayer . . . and especially intercession for the needs of the Church and the world."[11] Therefore, this chapter focuses on the content and form of corporate prayer. Before looking at the details of corporate prayer, two categories of prayer need to be distinguished: liturgical prayer and personal or devotional prayer.

LITURGICAL PRAYER AND PERSONAL PRAYER

There is a vast, albeit frequently unrecognized, difference between personal prayer and liturgical prayer. One author put it this way:

> In private prayer I pray, mostly for my self and my own affairs. It is the isolated person who stands in the center of the action, and the prayer is more or less individualized. But in liturgical prayer . . . it is not primarily I who am praying, but the Church, the Bride of Christ. The object of her prayer is broader, too: all the needs of God's kingdom here on earth. In liturgical prayer, I feel more like a member of a great community, like a little leaf on the great living tree of the Church.[12]

Liturgical prayer is communal, and, in many ways, it is global. It encompasses more than any one individual could fathom, yet it joins the single believer to the grandest community of faith.

Luther Reed points out that "eighteenth-century Pietism failed to distinguish between the personal, subjective prayer of the individual Christian and the objective common prayer of the assembled worshipers, or church prayer proper."[13] Such a failure led to a neglect of the content of corporate prayer and focused only on personal, emotional, and often trivial concerns, which ultimately led to a general denigration of prayer.

The Oxford Book of Prayer includes a section on the Prayer of the Church. In introducing these prayers, George Appleton describes the Prayer of the Church as prayers in which "one speaks with the voice of all, and all speak with the voice of each one."[14] The Prayer of the Church will be discussed below. For now, the emphasis is on recognizing the corporate nature of liturgical prayer and the distinction between liturgical prayer and personal devotional prayer.

The practice of praying in a public setting is different from merely addressing private concerns to God in the quiet of one's prayer closet. "At the heart of this problem is the tendency for group prayer to become a public praying of private prayers."[15] Liturgical praying gathers the thoughts, concerns, and joys of God's people who have gathered around Word and Sacrament and unites their voices before God's throne of grace. Liturgical prayer is a corporate expression of concern that flows from the whole body of Christ and is prayed by all members of the body.

THE PRAYER OF THE CHURCH

There certainly is no limit on the locations in which one can pray privately. But corporate prayer is not the same as personal prayer. The real concern is when and how to pray corporately. In the worship life of a congregation, there is a specific time in the worship service to bring the community's concerns before God and to become aware of the greater needs of God's people. In chapter 7, the Prayer of the Church was identified as a response of God's people to the proclamation of the Word and as a bridge to the Sacrament of the Altar.

The Prayer of the Church is sometimes called the Prayer of the Faithful, emphasizing that in the early church those who were not yet full members of the congregation were dismissed and only the faithful were permitted to pray corporately because prayer was understood as an exercise of faith. Many German Lutheran congregations referred to the Prayer of the Church as the General Prayer (*Allgemeine Kirchengebet*), but this prayer is anything but "general."[16] The Intercessions is another name for these prayers because the congregation intercedes on behalf of others who are in need of God's blessing and care. Luther Reed comments that the Prayer of the Church "is one of the outstanding elements in the liturgy and probably the one above all others that illustrates the congregation's active exercise of its functions as a priesthood of believers."[17]

The content of the Prayer of the Church is determined by what the church has found to be God's will, rather than by what the minister or even individual worshipers consider important. The Prayer of the Church is not merely a series of personal requests or concerns, though petitions for particular needs are included. This prayer is not a review of the sermon or a repetition of the central theme of the service, though such a thematic thread may be used to structure the prayer. Neither is the Prayer of the Church an extended period of "jabbering to God," though it is direct communication with our heavenly Father. "Nor do we find in it developed forms of adoration, confession, or even thanksgiving which are prominent features of the usual 'long prayer' of non-liturgical churches. The Lutheran Liturgy has provided for these necessary features in the earlier parts of the Service."[18]

The structure of the Prayer of the Church is in line with Christ's method of praying. In His model prayer, Jesus brought the essential needs of God's people before their heavenly Father. The Prayer of the Church brings the concerns of the whole people of God before the assembled people of God so, united in heart and voice, they may make their requests known to Him who hears all prayer through Jesus Christ. Traditionally, the Prayer of the Church has covered the following 12 areas and more or less in this order.[19] As worship leaders become more comfortable and skilled in writing their own prayers, the following twelve areas will form a general outline of the prayer.

1. Thanksgiving for what God has done.
2. For the church, God's people gathered around Word and Sacraments.
3. For the leaders of the church, both in the local congregation and in the greater church.
4. For the mission of the church.
5. For younger churches in their struggles and joys.
6. For the nation and all the peoples of the world.
7. For peace.
8. For schools.
9. For homes.
10. For all sorts and conditions of people.
11. For our economic and cultural life.
12. In anticipation of joining those in the Church Triumphant.[20]

The minister will choose whether all these items are included each time the congregation gathers to pray. However, this outline serves as a good review as the prayers are prepared. Luther Reed notes that "while the early church included the names of martyrs . . . the Reformation in Germany . . . produced general prayers which mentioned rulers by name."[21] Whatever the specific content, this corporate prayer is one of the marks of a Christian congregation as it gathers in worship around the Word (Acts 2:42).

Philip Pfatteicher reminds us that "persons involved in the local situation are best able to balance properly the universal scope proper to Christian concern with the specific petitions of a given congregation. The preparation of the prayers is no less important than the preparation of the sermon."[22] In early Christian communities, it was the deacon (or lay minister) who prepared these petitions because the deacon was aware of the community's needs. Today, a pastor will sensitively include community concerns and express the church's concerns in a manner that resonates with God's will in that locale.

Various forms of the Prayer of the Church are available to the minister. In addition to two printed prayers,[23] Divine Service II allows an assisting minister to prepare his own prayers using an intercessory form.[24] Other alternatives include the use of the Litany, the Suffrages, the Bidding Prayer, or even a selection of collects.

THE INTERCESSORY FORM

Another name for the Prayer of the Church that is particularly common in Eastern Orthodox churches is the Great Intercession. Intercessions, by definition, are prayers for other people. The Scriptures encourage prayer for others (Matthew 5:44; Colossians 4:3; James 5:16), just as Jesus did (John 17:20; Romans 8:34; Hebrews 7:25[25]). An important activity of the Holy Spirit is to be our intercessor (Romans 8:26–27). St. Paul wrote to Timothy, "I urge, then, first of all, that requests, prayers, intercession and thanksgiving be made for everyone" (1 Timothy 2:1).

Early Christians often prayed for others. The first recorded intercessory prayer used in worship by first-century Christians is quoted by Bishop Clement of Rome in his letter to the Corinthian congregation (ca. A.D. 95). He prayed: "Rescue those of our number in distress; raise up the fallen; assist the needy; heal the sick; turn back those of your people who stray; feed the hungry; release our captives; revive the weak; encourage those who lose heart."[26] When Christians gather to pray for others, particularly in a corporate setting, they join a long tradition of community intercessory prayer.

The simplest form of intercession is to indicate the person being prayed for and the desired result:

L: For [state the individual or group], that [indicate the consequence or blessing desired from God]; let us pray to the Lord.
C: Lord, have mercy.

This form of intercessory prayer entered the Western church in the fifth century when Pope Gelasius I introduced the Deacon's Prayer from the Eastern Orthodox Church into the Roman Mass.[27]

It is best to offer intercessions slowly so the congregation can offer a petition after the specific need is announced. A brief silent prayer may be offered by the minister after he says, "Let us pray to the Lord." Another method states the request, then provides a period of silence. The minister then breaks the silence by saying, "Lord," to which the congregation responds "have mercy."

Worship Supplement offered several models for intercessory prayer.[28] The following intercessions, gathered from *Worship Supplement*, were grouped under the general theme "Throughout the Year I." Each concluded with the response "Lord, hear our prayer" or "We ask you to hear us, good Lord." These intercessions may guide the minister as he prepares petitions in this simple intercessory form.

For all Christians, that beyond our divisions we seek the unity to which we are called, let us pray: [response]

For all public servants, that they zealously promote justice and the common good,

For industrial workers, that their productivity prove a blessing for all classes of society,

For favorable weather, that we may give thanks for a good harvest, let us pray: [response]

For the young men and women of our parish, that Christian idealism inspire them in the choice of a profession,

For this holy assembly, that the life-giving bread we break and the cup we bless nurture us to the full stature of Christ, let us pray: [response][29]

Other similar intercessions were prepared according to the seasons of the liturgical year. These intercessions follow the pattern of praying for various states and situations of the Christian community as indicated within the Prayer of the Church.

The appendices of Walter Huffman's *The Prayer of the Faithful* provide fifteen different forms of the Prayer of the Church.[30] Many of these forms enable the congregation to respond in a simple affirmation of the prayer as articulated by the worship leader. Other prayer models provide more extensive responses that would require inclusion in a worship folder. Huffman's examples offer excellent patterns of liturgical prayer on which ministers may further elaborate for use in corporate prayer.

A special form of the Prayer of the Church is the Bidding Prayer (sometimes called the Deacon's Litany). Traditionally prayed on Good Friday after the reading from John's Gospel, its retention in Lutheran circles from services a millennium earlier indicates the sense of continuity Lutherans share with all Christians. In the Bidding Prayer, the assisting minister takes on the traditional role of the deacon. The Bidding Prayer in *Lutheran Worship*[31] includes biddings (intentions or invitations) to pray for the following categories: the whole church, ministers of the Word and the people of God, catechumens, political authorities, evils of the world, those outside the church, enemies, and the fruits of the earth. "The Bidding Prayer is of particular interest since it is probably the prototype of all so-called 'general prayers.' In the days when Christian worship was in Greek (until about the fourth century, when it was first Latinized in North Africa), this prayer was part of the normal Sunday service."[32] The form prescribes that the deacon announces the intent of the prayer or "bids" the presiding minister to pray on a specific topic. The presiding minister then reads the appointed collect. A review of this prayer in *Lutheran Worship* accentuates the broader content and context of liturgical prayer by God's gathered guests.

THE COLLECT AND ITS FORM

According to most liturgical scholars, the collect is one of the earliest forms of liturgical prayer.[33] The origin of the title of this universally practiced form of prayer is unknown, but, more significant, it has stood the test of time. As Luther Reed notes: "The vitality and stability of this prayer form, in spite of controversies, revolutions, and reformations, constitute one of the remarkable facts in the history of Christian worship."[34] Most liturgical scholars agree that the word *collect* is functional not circumstantial. This means the prayer functions as an expression or summary of the corporate desire of the people rather than indicates the occasion of their gathering together or the reception of an offering.[35]

Originally, the collect seems to have been a prayer offered by the pastor after the deacon invited the whole congregation to pray for a particular concern, as noted in the discussion of the Bidding Prayer. The concern would be announced, the people would kneel, then a period of silent prayer would follow, after which the worshipers would rise and the pastor would speak a collect that summarized the specific concern.[36]

By definition, a collect is a short liturgical prayer of the church that ordinarily expresses a corporate need that is appropriate for a particular day in the church year. The oldest and, according to many scholars, the best collects of Christianity are also the shortest.[37] Again, citing Luther Reed, "Their humility of spirit is more than balanced by certainty of faith, and their brevity of form by breadth of thought."[38] The main thought of the collect normally centers on the thought of the day because the collect is one of the Propers for the day. The needs expressed in the collect are those of the church, not merely the personal desires of the minister or of the local congregation.

Its structure makes the collect significant. There are five clearly definable parts to a standard collect. A brief look at a series of collects in a hymnbook will reveal the following: an address, rationale, petition, result, and conclusion.

The Address

This initial phrase of a collect refers to the person of the Trinity to whom the prayer is addressed. A generic salutation such as "O God" is a simple address, but an address can refer to a specific person of the Trinity, normally the Father. Thus the prayer might begin, "O God, our heavenly Father." Occasionally, a collect will address the Son or the Spirit, though prayers are traditionally prayed *to* the Father, *through* the Son, and *in* the Spirit.

The Rationale

The collect then moves into the reason God is being addressed in prayer. This particular clause (usually a relative clause) underscores some quality, attribute, or work of God and His relationship with His people that draws them into His presence for prayer. The phrase "who sent your only-begotten Son" would be an appropriate rationale for addressing the Father. In the same way, "who is worthy of our praise and thanksgiving" would be a fitting rationale for expressing thanks and praise. Sometimes this section of the collect will be in a causal form: "because you have prepared for those who love you such good things as surpass our understanding."[39] The rationale clearly leads to the petition.

The Petition

This is the actual prayer. The petition or request mentions the gift desired, the blessing requested, or the praise offered. Usually there is only one request made in each collect. Among the older collects, "grant, we pray" may be all that is asked. The petition may also involve a variety of physical or spiritual needs of the church, which are placed in the context of the readings of the day or the season of the year.

The Result

This section of the collect refers to the expected consequence of this communal request. What is the desired outcome of the petition? This result may be introduced with "that we." The result may be spiritual or physical or a combination of various outcomes that would occur through God's activities in this world. Following the petition to grant something, a collect may have an extended clause that shows how the petition will benefit God's people. For example, "Grant that we, who celebrate with joy the day of our Lord's resurrection, may be raised from the death of sin by your life-giving Spirit."[40] The Collect for the Twenty-second Sunday after Pentecost states as a desired result of the request for grace "that we may continually be given to good works."[41]

The Conclusion

Sometimes called the termination or the doxology, this final element of the collect states "through Jesus Christ our Lord." In this statement, the biblical theology of the gathered guests shines through in the worship practice because such a conclusion reveals the community's dependence on Christ's promises (Matthew 21:22; John 14:13–14; John 16:23–24). Normally, the ending of the collect is expanded to conclude with a trinitarian affirmation to the prayer. The conclusions of collects vary distinctively according to their address.[42]

The conclusions to the collects also differ based on the location in the service. For example, when the Collect of the Day is spoken, the full conclusion as appointed is normally used. If other collects are spoken, as at Matins or Vespers, the full conclusion is used with the Collect of the Day and the final collect. To indicate that there are a series of collects, a shorter conclusion—"through Jesus Christ, Your Son, our Lord"—is said. These conclusions can be observed in prepared collects but may also be used in collects written by the minister.

Sources of Collects

The Lutheran reformers adapted and translated many of the finest ancient collects of the Roman Catholic Church. Luther translated many of these.[43] Luther often combined two or three collects into one longer German collect, following the more elaborate style of praying common in medieval France.[44] The use of these collects in contemporary congregations demonstrates a commitment to a continuity with the ancient church's biblical faith.

The collect form can be adapted easily by any minister and may be used in private prayer, as well as in corporate prayer. The simple and standardized conclusion enables the congregation to voice its "Amen" to the minister's expression of the corporate desires of God's people. No wonder that Wilhelm Löhe, one of the influential guides to North American Lutheranism, said that collects were "the breath of a soul, sprinkled with the blood of Jesus, brought to the eternal Father in the Name of his Son."[45]

OTHER FORMS OF CORPORATE PRAYER

There are several other forms of prayer used in the context of worship, including the Litany and the Suffrages. The Litany has become a classic in Lutheranism, though in recent years it is used less frequently. The Suffrages are also a beneficial form of prayer and are sometimes used as a devotional service.

THE LITANY

From the Greek word *litaneia*, which means "supplication or entreaty," the Litany is one of the most penitential prayers in Lutheran worship resources. It displays a somber meditative mood, yet it is based on a strong assurance of God's love in Christ. Philip Pfatteicher suggests that the "repeated, insistent, responsive prayer [of the litany, recalls] Jesus' parable of the importunate friend (Luke 11:5–10)."[46] By the fifth century, Roman Catholics had imported this form of prayer from Antioch and Constantinople and had incorporated it into their liturgy. Pope Gelasius (d. A.D. 496) placed it after the Introit and before the Collect of the Day,[47] similar to the placement of the Kyrie in Divine Service II in *Lutheran Worship*.

This ancient form of prayer has a long history in Lutheranism. Luther said that "next to the holy Lord's Prayer the very best that has come to earth" is the Litany.[48] In 1529, he modified the contents of this prayer, removing the doctrinally offensive phrases yet retaining the general structure and magnificent content.[49] Among the additional twenty-five petitions introduced by Luther were appeals for deliverance from error and a prayer for other Christians. Thomas Cranmer, Archbishop of Canterbury, used Luther's Litany for his English Litany of 1544, which was adapted in later editions of the *Book of Common Prayer*.[50]

The Litany manifests a multiplicity of prayer forms. It is composed of almost a half-dozen distinct kinds of prayers and contains more than sixty petitions with almost two dozen responses by the congregation. The Litany begins with a threefold Kyrie and an invocation of the Trinity, but the focus is on Christ, who hears our prayers and whose life, death, and resurrection grants us the power to approach God's gracious throne (Hebrews 4:16).

The Litany includes the Deprecations, which comes from the Latin word *deprecari*, which means "to prevent something from happening by prayer." These are specific prayers asking God to ward off evil from among His gathered guests. The Deprecations begin with "from." Included are requests that God would deliver His church from the satanic evils of sin, error, evil, crafts and assaults of the devil, and sudden and evil death (that is, one for which a person is unprepared). These prayers also include a request for deliverance from the physical harms of pestilence, famine, war, bloodshed, sedition, and rebellion; from natural disasters of lightning, tempests, and calamity by fire and water; and, finally, from everlasting death. Many of the Deprecations were added by Luther to express the Christian experience of the theology of the cross.

The Obsecrations, from the Latin word *obsecrare*, which means "to implore on religious grounds (*ob sacrum*)," establish the basis for Christian prayer on religious or theological foundations. In this portion of the Litany, the congregation asks that all its prayers be answered for Christ's sake, founded on some event in His righteous life. The Obsecrations begin with "by" and recall the mysteries of the faith and the historical facts of Jesus' incarnation, nativity, baptism, fasting and temptation, agony and sweat on the cross, death and burial, resurrection and ascension, and the sending of the Holy Spirit. Only through Christ can Christians approach the Father (John 16:23).

The Supplications, from the Latin word *supplicatio*, which means "to pray publicly as a consequence of some public event," are prayers for a variety of situations in this life, as well as for a good death. This portion of the Litany is brief and made in general terms. The Supplications begin with "in all" and God's gathered guests ask specifically for His help in tribulation, prosperity, death, and judgment, indicating that there is no condition for which prayers are not appropriate.

Finally, the Intercessions are prayers for others and are Luther's chief contribution to the Litany. Here are petitions for the church, for the weak, for the nations of the world, for humanity, and for reconciliation. They begin with "for" and conclude with "hear our prayer."

Normally, the Litany concludes with the canticle Agnus Dei—"Lamb of God"—which reminds the gathered guests that Christ is the only source for mercy and peace. The Kyrie is repeated as a bookend to the Litany. The Lord's Prayer is presented in a chanted format in *Lutheran Worship* in keeping with the chanted form of the Litany. Several collects may be added for specific needs not included in the Litany. Luther's Latin Litany, for example, has five collects with versicles, but his German Litany has only four collects with six versicles.[51] Wilhelm Löhe said of this glorious creation: "Beginning with adoration, confessing Christ in its heart, it ends in the lovely Agnus . . . how evangelical, how entirely agreeable to our church and to its temper."[52]

The Litany may be used as a specialized devotional office or as a short order of service. Adding psalms and a Scripture reading would result in the following outline:

Psalm(s)

Scripture Reading

Litany
Collect of the Day
Blessing[53]

The Litany may be used in conjunction with other services as well. In Advent and Lent, for example, the Litany may replace the Introit, Kyrie, and Hymn of Praise. The Litany may also be used with one of the other offices or with one of the Responsive Prayer services (also known as the Suffrages).

THE SUFFRAGES

The Suffrages are special prayer services that may be used alone or added to the Divine Service or the Daily Office. The title comes from a Latin word for a special form of intercession. Luther Reed explains: "The suffrages are a series of versicles and responses, chiefly from the Psalms, arranged to constitute a complete prayer much in the spirit and form of a litany, but more objective and poetic in character than the Litany itself."[54] A combination of prayers following the psalms in the daily prayer life of the church seems to date at least to the late eighth century. Lutherans continued to use these prayers in the Latin services of Matins and Vespers, though no German versions are extant. Wilhelm Löhe included the General Suffrages, as well as the Morning and Evening Suffrages, in his 1844 *Agende.*[55]

Lutheran Worship provides two forms of the Suffrages, which are designated Responsive Prayer 1 and Responsive Prayer 2.[56] Both services begin with a petition to God for mercy and the Lord's Prayer, which is followed by the Apostles' Creed. Then responsive selections from the psalter are said. Responsive Prayer 1 concludes with several specific collects, beginning with the Collect of the Day. Responsive Prayer 2 provides prayers for noon, afternoon, evening, and before travel. This last collect evokes the possibility of using Responsive Prayer 2 as an *Itinerarium* or Liturgy for Travelers. The Benedicamus and blessing conclude both devotional services.

The inclusion of Luther's Morning or Evening Prayer concludes the traditional selection of collects at the end of these services. Luther Reed notes:

> In all his Collects and prayers, Luther kept within the great Christian tradition. There was no striving for originality. On the other hand, there is every evidence of church consciousness, respect for historical continuity, and liturgical restraint. With these principles in view, Luther treated the ancient forms freely, infusing into them a warmth peculiarly his own, yet ever retaining the hard core of these expressions for centuries of Christian experience.[57]

THE MANNER OF PRAYING CORPORATELY

Praying in a congregational setting is not merely praying in a group. Corporate prayer also includes the needs of the whole people of God. Therefore, planning for these prayers is important and worthy of time and effort. Following a longstanding Christian tradition, an assisting minister may introduce the Prayer of the Church.[58] This reflects the Lutheran understanding of the priesthood of all believers. The presiding minister's conclusion of the prayer also underscores the Lutheran distinction between the priesthood of all believers and the pastoral office.

Should prayers be written out or prayed "from the heart" (*ex corde*)? Although the question is valid, "careful preparation of the prayers and Spirit-led presentation are not mutually exclusive forces."[59] An editorial in a liturgical resource several years ago was titled in part "Be Careful of Words." It stated: "To write texts [for prayers] or choose them does not necessarily mean that you have to know the intricacies of poetry and grammar, but your language must be dear to you, cherished, treated with respect, known as a treasure and a constant surprise."[60] To pray *ex corde* does not preclude preparation, thought, and even guiding notations.

Luther Reed comments about the benefits of prayers that have been passed down to the modern church:

> These prayer forms, like the Service itself, represent the discriminating thought and devotional experience of the church throughout the centuries. The survival and unbroken use, for over a thousand years, of many of these forms, is in itself a testimony to their spiritual worth and vitality. In content and form they have satisfied millions of worshipers in the past. They serve admirably as vehicles of our corporate devotion today.[61]

Thus Lutheran prayer books often present "the best" the church has to offer God in prayer.

A brief look at some of Luther's prayers (and the explanations in his Small Catechism) demonstrates that a familiarity with Scripture is one of the best resources for composing prayers. When the grammar of faith is expressed through the words of Scripture, there is a heightened sense of communication and devotion. Scriptural language is often metaphoric, thus it transcends locality. Consider the biblical imagery of this prayer from Responsive Prayer 2 that may be offered before beginning a trip:

> Lord God our Father, you kept Abraham and Sarah in safety throughout the days of their pilgrimage, you led the children of Israel through the midst of the sea, and by a star you led the Wise Men to the infant Jesus. Protect and guide us now in this time as we set out to travel, make our ways safe and our homecom-

ings joyful, and bring us at last to our heavenly home, where you dwell in glory with your Son and the Holy Spirit, God forever.[62]

Such scriptural imagery communicates beyond the experiences of a local congregation and beyond a particular culture or generation. The transcendent quality of prayer is only intensified by well-chosen and vividly descriptive eloquence.

Similarly, the manner in which one introduces the specific petitions in a prayer is as important as how the prayers are composed. The announcement of the prayers—sometimes called the intentions—should be understandable and loud enough to be heard by all. Christian names are included in the prayer.[63] If the pronunciation of a name is uncertain, help may be sought from others in the congregation or from the person submitting the request. Brief background information to the request may be included in the petition.

A comfortable format for corporate prayer would be to state the circumstances in a brief invitation, such as "Let us pray for." A time of silence may follow the intentions so the congregation can offer its prayer in accordance with God's will. Then a collect that gathers the congregation's concern may be voiced by the assisting minister or the assisting minister may say, "Lord, in your mercy." The congregation responds, "Hear our prayer."

If prayers are printed in the worship folder, alternate responses are possible, such as: "Show us your saving power"; "Bless your people with peace"; "Reveal your grace"; "Let your face shine on us"; "Strengthen us with your Spirit"; or "Give your people joy and peace."[64] Such prepared responses can more readily reflect the content of the petition, as well as the season of the church year.

No matter the format or whether the prayers are written out completely or offered *ex corde*, they should be spoken clearly. A microphone may be beneficial in a large building, especially if the minister faces the altar while praying. But volume alone is not sufficient. Articulation is important so there is no hesitation or uncertainty regarding the congregation's part in corporate prayer. Finally, the minister will want to provide adequate time for the congregation to pray silently.

Prayer is an act of worship that encompasses many categories of liturgical prayer. These prayers are part of the worship life of the body of Christ. Prayer is a response to the Word of God read and proclaimed in the worship setting. The promises attached to prayer move us to pray without ceasing. Yet we stand in a special relationship to God and to one another in public worship. What we do in worship reflects our belief and affects our belief. Therefore, our acts of corporate prayer are done with all reverence and preparation as we "storm the throne of God" as His gathered guests.

SOME QUESTIONS TO CONSIDER

1. What is the biblical basis for prayer and particularly for corporate prayer by the Christian community?

2. Briefly distinguish liturgical prayer from personal or devotional prayer.

3. Review the content of the conclusion to the Prayer of the Church in Divine Service I in *Lutheran Worship* (p. 144) or another General Prayer. Indicate which of the twelve topics are included and which are not.

4. Review the Bidding Prayer in *Lutheran Worship* (pp. 276–78). Describe how this prayer provides a broader content and context for liturgical prayer by God's gathered guests.

5. Write out two Collects of the Day from two different seasons of the church year. Indicate the five parts of a collect. If necessary, identify any part that is missing.

6. List the four unique forms of prayer included in the Litany. Describe them briefly.

7. Why is it beneficial to prepare prayers in advance for use in corporate worship? How may these prayers be introduced and said?

NOTES

1. See, for example, "Exposition of the Lord's Prayer," LW 42:15–81 (WA 2:80–130); "Personal Prayer Book," LW 43:3–45 (WA 10/2:375–28); and "Simple Way to Pray," LW 43:187–211 (WA 38:358–75).

2. WATr 3:448.

3. Stradling, *Praying the Psalms*.

4. Martin, *Practical Praying*, 160–74.

5. Peterson, *Working the Angles*, 33.

6. Peterson, *Working the Angles*, 31.

7. See Maschke, "Prayer in the Apostolic Fathers," 103–18.

8. Council of Hippo in A.D. 393, cited in Pfatteicher, *Commentary*, 127.

9. Luther's explanation of the Third Article of the Apostles' Creed says the "Holy Spirit . . . gathers . . . the whole Christian church." See 1 Corinthians 12:13; Ephesians 2:22.

10. See *Gathered Guests* chapter 16.

11. Bradshaw, *Daily Prayer*, 151.

12. Pius Parsch, introduction to *The Hours of the Divine Office in English and Latin* (Collegeville, Minn.: Liturgical Press, 1963–64), 1.

13. Reed, *Lutheran Liturgy* (rev. ed.), 319.

14. Appleton, *Oxford Book of Prayer*, 177.

15. Huffman, *Prayer of the Faithful*, 35.

16. Theodore P. Bornhoeft prepared a set of General Prayers for the three-year lectionary called *Prayers Responsively* (St. Louis: Concordia, 1984). In this collection, Bornhoeft's prayers address concerns that grow from the biblical texts, as well as from contemporary society.

17. Reed, *Lutheran Liturgy* (rev. ed.), 315.

18. Reed, *Lutheran Liturgy* (rev. ed.), 316.

19. Huffman, *Prayer of the Faithful*, 26, notes that the ancient Roman Rite had only nine biddings: for the church, the pope, all ministers, the Roman emperor, the catechumens, those in any trouble, heretics and schismatics, the Jews, and the heathen.

20. Henry Horn, *Liturgy and Life*, 63.

21. Reed, *Lutheran Liturgy* (rev. ed.), 319.

22. Pfatteicher and Messerli, *Manual on the Liturgy*, 226.

23. *Lutheran Worship*, pp. 132–33, 144.

24. *Lutheran Worship*, pp. 167–68, 175–76, 187, 195–96.

25. See also Isaiah 53:12, which prophecies Jesus' role as intercessor.

26. Clement, "Clement's First Letter," 59.4, in *Early Christian Fathers,* ed. Cyril C. Richardson, LCC 1 (New York: Macmillan, 1970), 71.

27. Pfatteicher, *Commentary*, 116.

28. *Worship Supplement*, pp. 33–42.

29. *Worship Supplement*, pp. 38–39.

30. Huffman, *Prayer of the Faithful*, 46–72, presents forms from the *Book of Common Prayer*, the Taize community, and several other liturgical resources.

31. *Lutheran Worship*, pp. 276–78.

32. Edward Horn, *Christian Year*, 125.

33. Although formally included in the Roman Mass by Pope Leo I in the middle of the fifth century, a variety of collects were employed much earlier as free compositions and improvisations.

34. Reed, *Lutheran Liturgy* (rev. ed.), 279.

35. Cobb, "Liturgy of the Word," 224 25.

36. Senn, *Christian Liturgy*, 140.

37. Reed, *Lutheran Liturgy* (rev. ed.), 577, points out that an ancient collect for Compline consists of only eleven Latin words (p. 608): *Illumina, quaesumus, Domine, tenebras nostras, et totius noctis insidias repelle propitius. Per* ["Illumine, we ask, Lord, our darkness, and throughout the night repel all treacheries by Your grace. Through . . . (Jesus Christ, our Lord)"].

38. Reed, *Lutheran Liturgy* (rev. ed.), 279.

39. From the Collect of the Day for the Sixth Sunday after Pentecost (*Lutheran Worship*, p. 67).

40. From the Collect for the Resurrection of Our Lord (*Lutheran Worship*, p. 47).

41. *Lutheran Worship*, p. 86.

42. A collect's ending depends on the person of the Trinity addressed or whether Jesus is mentioned. When a collect is addressed to the Father, which is normal, the conclusion is "through Jesus Christ, your Son, our Lord, who lives and reigns with you and the Holy Spirit, one God, now and forever." When a collect is addressed to the Son, as in the Collect for Maundy Thursday, the prayer concludes "for you live and reign with the Father and the Holy Spirit, one God, now and forever" (*Lutheran Worship*, p. 44). See also the conclusions to the collects for the Seventh Sunday of Easter and the

Eighteenth Sunday after Pentecost, which are addressed to Jesus. If the Son is mentioned in a petition addressed to the Father, the collect often ends with the indefinite pronoun "who lives and reigns with you and the Holy Spirit, one God, now and forever." If a petition is addressed to the Trinity, the prayer ends "who lives and reigns, ever one God, now and forever." *Lutheran Worship* uses a particularly distinct conclusion for the prayers in which the Spirit is specifically mentioned, as in the collects for Pentecost. The conclusion states: "through Jesus Christ, your Son, our Lord, who lives and reigns with you in communion with the same Holy Spirit, one God, now and forever" (pp. 58–60).

43. LW 53:127–46.

44. Reed, *Lutheran Liturgy* (rev. ed.), 283. Reed provides the original version, source, and an English translation of almost 150 collects (580–622).

45. Cited by Reed, *Lutheran Liturgy* (rev. ed.), 280.

46. Pfatteicher, *Commentary*, 429.

47. Pfatteicher, *Commentary*, 430.

48. Cited in Reed, *Lutheran Liturgy* (rev. ed.), 623, from Christian Gerber, *Historie der Kirchenceremonien in Sachsen* (Dresden: Sauressig, 1732), 268.

49. Luther prepared two versions of the Litany, one in German and one in Latin (WA 30/3:29–42; cf. LW 53:153–70). Reed, *Lutheran Liturgy* (rev. ed.), 736–50, provides an interesting and helpful comparison of the Roman Catholic, Anglican, and Luther's German and Latin Litanies.

50. Reed, *Lutheran Liturgy* (rev. ed.), 628–30.

51. LW 53:169–70.

52. Wilhelm Löhe, *Agende für Christliche Gemeinden des lutherischen Bekenntnisses*, 3d ed. (Nördlingen: Beck, 1884), 159, cited in Reed, *Lutheran Liturgy* (rev. ed.), 623.

53. Pless, "Daily Prayer," 467.

54. Reed, *Lutheran Liturgy* (rev. ed.), 639.

55. Pfatteicher, *Commentary*, 424.

56. See *Lutheran Worship*, pp. 270–72, 273–75.

57. Reed, *Lutheran Liturgy* (rev. ed.), 641.

58. Divine Service II, rubric 18, (*Lutheran Worship*, pp. 167, 187). See also Evanson, "Divine Service," 419.

59. Huffman, *Prayer of the Faithful*, 34.

60. Huck, "When You Pray," 3, 5.

61. Reed, *Lutheran Liturgy* (rev. ed.), 579.

62. *Lutheran Worship*, p. 275.

63. This common Christian practice accentuates the baptismal relationship that all Christians have with one another and eliminates the mutable and transitory human titles, even of ecclesiastical and political dignitaries. However, full names may be used as well.

64. Adapted from Huffman, *Prayer of the Faithful*, 40.

CHAPTER 18

LITURGICAL MINISTRIES

SERVING GOD'S GATHERED GUESTS

When Lutherans gather to form a congregation, they choose a pastor (or shepherd). This pastoral office has its roots and foundation in Christ's commands and promises (Matthew 28:16ff.; John 20:21–23; 21:15–17). Although Lutherans have refrained from establishing a rigid hierarchy of clergy, rankings of worship offices have developed throughout the two millennia of Christianity. Some congregation members were pastors, recognized as possessing a call to serve that came from God through the community.[1]

In this chapter, we will look at the origin of the offices of bishop, presbyter, and deacon. During the time of Acts, the apostles provided leadership for the fledgling church (Acts 2; 3:32–35). But there came a time when they needed assistance (Acts 6:2–4). The seven men who were chosen (Acts 6:5) are assumed by most to be the predecessors of the deacons (though the seven are not actually called "deacons" in Acts 6). Deacons were appointed to help pastors and congregations in their endeavors by taking on particular functions.[2]

The titles of "elder" (*presbyter* is derived from the Greek word that means "elder") and "overseer" (or "bishop"; we derive *episcopal* from the Greek word) were used in the early Christian congregations and communities for the same office (that of the pastor) and the same office holder (the pastor).[3] However, these titles came to designate distinct offices and responsibilities in the third century.

MAJOR ORDERS

BISHOP

After the death of the apostles, no attempt was made to replace or duplicate the office of apostle. By the second century, a recognized hierarchy of clergy already existed, and bishops served as overseers of larger congregations. Ignatius of Antioch (A.D. 50–114) was one of the first to use the word *episcopos* in this manner.[4] Sometimes referred to as the "father of the family," the bishops carried on paternal and pastoral oversight of the congregations in their region of responsibility.[5] As the church grew, the bishops were unable to supervise all the congregations under their ecclesiastical and spiritual care, especially as people settled in distant and remote locations. Thus assistants to the bishops became necessary.

PRESBYTER

Presbyters were elected from the congregations and served as assistants to the overseers or bishops, providing support primarily as rulers rather than as priests. Initially, the presbyter and bishop assumed nearly identical responsibilities: They absolved the penitent, preached the Word, and presided at Communion. Presbyters would be most closely identified with today's associate pastors in Lutheran congregations.[6] The presbyter carried out the bishop's responsibilities in his place and as his representative. In the worship setting, either the bishop or the presbyter led particular prayers, spoke the Words of Institution, and gave the final blessing over the congregation. When a bishop was present in the congregation, the presbyter assumed some of the functions of a deacon.[7] The bishops were chosen from the presbyters because these men had served as delegated representatives in the absence of the bishop. An experienced presbyter had received on-the-job training for the office of bishop. By the fourth century, presbyters were given responsibilities over their own congregations as permanent ministers. Also at that time a name change occurred and presbyters were most frequently referred to as priests.[8]

DEACON

Established early in the life of the church (1 Timothy 3:8–13 and Philippians 1:1), deacons continued to serve and became a third kind of professional minister. John Pless notes that "the office of deacon represented the link between the altar and the world."[9] This link becomes more evident when the functions performed by the deacon in the liturgy of the worshiping community are examined. Deacons led specific prayers, particularly the Prayer of the Church or the Deacon's Prayer. In praying this prayer, the deacon revealed his role as a minister of charity, expressing the church's concerns for people in need. In the structure of this prayer, the deacon asked the congregation to pray for a specific need with a short invitation, "Let us pray to the Lord." A deacon also might serve as a kind of coordinator for the whole service. As the liturgy became increasingly elaborate in some major cities and churches, the deacon arranged for all the participants and directed the service. The deacon would often read the Gospel lesson, which would form the basis for the bishop's comments in his homily. The deacon was usually responsible for preparing the Lord's Supper by bringing the Communion elements in appropriate vessels from the place of the offertory to the altar. The deacon occasionally assisted the bishop or presbyter by distributing the cup at Communion, and he sometimes dismissed the congregation at the end of the service after the bishop's Benediction.[10]

By the Middle Ages, men aspiring to these three orders were received into the ministry or were ordained through solemn rites and liturgical actions. For example, the ordination of the bishop involved the presentation of a Bible, a chalice, and the bishop's stole (and later a ring). At the ordination of a priest or presbyter, the candidate for priesthood received a chalice and paten. When a deacon was ordained or commissioned, he received a specially designed stole and book (usually of the Gospels).[11]

For centuries, these three orders of ministry were identified as the major orders of the Catholic Church. The bishops, presbyters, and deacons were considered professional ministers, though the deacons were lay assistants, rather than members of the clergy.

MINOR ORDERS

Because there were no seminaries in the early church, future leaders received on-the-job training as they participated in various activities of the church. Many of these spiritual leaders—healers, speakers in tongues, interpreters of tongues, evangelists—never became organized into specific offices. Other positions, however, attained the status of an "ordered ministry," that is, they were organized, officially recognized, and those who entered the order were ordained in some manner. In addition to the major orders of bishop, presbyter, and deacon, Hippolytus (A.D. 160–235) mentions several other offices in *Apostolic Tradition*: confessor, widow, lector, virgin, and subdeacon. Recognized for their special tasks, individuals holding these offices were appointed to their positions without these positions becoming a permanent part of the church's worship life.[12] Many of these orders had some liturgical functions, but the ministerial positions that were fixed as liturgical offices in the Middle Ages are subdeacon, acolyte, cantor, lector, exorcist, and porter.

SUBDEACON

Subdeacons evidently assisted deacons, as the title suggests. Beginning at least in the third century, these individuals worked under the direct supervision of the deacons, as mentioned by Cyprian.[13] Although not ordained into their ministerial role, these lay leaders had substantial responsibility for working on a regular part-time basis in the local congregations, perhaps comparable to volunteers in contemporary society. In the area of worship, subdeacons assisted in preparing the altar for Holy Communion and helped distribute the cup. Records from the early church indicate that subdeacons may have read the Epistle lesson, if so assigned. This last task was officially assigned to subdeacons around the seventh century.

ACOLYTE

Acolytes assisted the clergy in various capacities but most obviously in tending the lamps used in the worship environment. Jesus' parable of the wise and foolish virgins (Matthew 25) underscores the importance of this office in an era when oil lamps were the only source of light after the sun set. The office of acolyte dates to the second century and is frequently depicted by a young man holding a torch. The traditional position and present function of acolyte will be discussed later in this chapter.

EXORCIST

This class of lay leaders is closely associated with the worship life of early Christian congregations. The initial function of the exorcist was to anoint adult baptismal candidates with oil as a sign that the demons had been expelled, a necessary activity because of the prominence of pagan worship. More important, exorcists served as teachers or catechists, assisting the bishop in catechetical instruction prior to Baptism. When depicted in early Christian art, the exorcist carried a book with veiled hands. The book was probably that used for instructing the catechumens.

LECTOR

Responsible for the reading of Holy Scripture, lectors in the early church were more than merely readers.[14] They guarded and kept the precious Scripture scrolls and books. Because they were the caretakers of the books and were literate, the lectors read the first and (depending on custom) second lessons during the service. Then they gave the scroll or lectionary to the deacon, presbyter, or bishop to read the Gospel. The lector is depicted with an open book, known as a lectionary.

CANTOR

Cantors were specialists. In many ways, they were partners with lectors in proclaiming the Word, yet they served a unique function of uniting the congregation in song.[15] The office of cantor first appears in the fourth century after Constantine allowed Christianity to "go public." Around the fifth century, a series of laws was established that provided detailed guidance for cantors and other singers. As in many of the minor orders, the cantor's role diminished dramatically around the turn of the first millennium as choral music took precedence over that of solo music.[16] The role was revived among Lutherans after the Reformation in Germany. Only after Vatican II in the mid-1960s was the order reintroduced in the Roman Catholic Church.

Cantors have traditionally served as song leaders, psalmists, and teachers. This latter task grew from the need for full-time employment.[17] More important from a liturgical perspective, the cantor sang the Psalm of the Day. Cantors not only provided avenues for the congregation to join in singing from its biblical songbook, but they also led the gathered guests in their responses of musical praise and liturgical participation.[18]

PORTER

The final office included among the minor orders was that of porter. Porters were the doorkeepers to the churches or worship sites. Their practical function was necessary during times of persecution because they kept guard as early Christians met in private homes or in the catacombs. They also ensured that only those who had been baptized and instructed were able to participate in the Holy Supper. For example, at the conclusion of the Service of the Word, the porter closed the doors before the congregation continued with the Service of

the Sacrament. Among modern Eastern Orthodox Christians, at this break in the liturgy, the deacon assumes the role of porter and calls out, "The doors, the doors, the doors." This is the sign that the rest of the service is only for the faithful (those who are confirmed). Porters also looked after the needs of the congregation during the service. The actual order of doorkeeper (or *ostiarius*) had its official origin around the fourth century. The office was depicted by a person carrying a ring with two keys.[19]

CHANGES IN THE LITURGICAL MINISTRIES

Throughout the second millennium of Christianity, the liturgical offices changed as the church's needs changed. Yet the church maintained the distinct pastoral office. As the ancient world crumbled, learning ceased except within the walls of the monasteries and, later, in the cathedral schools. As a result, some offices became mere formalities, stepping stones to the ordained priesthood.

The laity became spectators as they watched the priests perform their mysterious services before a distant altar, sometimes even from behind screens and panels of religious art. One man, the priest, acted on behalf of the whole people of God. Often he communicated in a language foreign to his local community. Increasingly, the priest held the power of the Word because he alone could read (albeit poorly, according to many records). The priest claimed to possess the magical power to transform the common elements of bread and wine into the mystical body and blood of Christ. He provided the only access people had to God's forgiveness and the hope of eternal life. Thus the office of the priest became extremely powerful.

Luther believed that each Christian should be able to pray directly to God and to hear Him speak through the Bible in his or her own language.[20] Luther advocated that every believer is a priest (1 Peter 2:5), which is a distinct office (this is Luther's theology of vocation or the "offices" that all Christians hold). Lutheran theology balances the distinct office of the pastor with this priestly office. The wisdom of biblical theology is that the Office of the Keys, for example, is given to the church for use in the daily life of believers and through congregations to the pastoral office for use in the Divine Service. This practice continues into modern times.

Following Vatican II (in the mid-1960s), the Roman Catholic Church introduced varied leadership responsibilities in worship. In 1979, the Episcopal Church extended the role of the deacon beyond that of Communion assistant and usher, allowing the reading of Scripture, preparing of prayers, and leading of the confession of sins.[21]

Today, the Lutheran pastor fulfills the role of bishop and presbyter.[22] He is the presiding minister or officiant of the worship service with responsibility for over-seeing the whole service and fulfilling his pastoral role of proclaiming the Word and administering the Sacraments. The role of assisting minister may be assigned to members of the board of elders or to appropriate certified ministers of the congregation, such as male teachers or lay ministers.[23] Assisting ministers were introduced to Lutheran circles in *Lutheran Book of Worship* and *Lutheran Worship*. The "Notes on the Liturgy" in *Lutheran Worship* explains the role of these ministers: "The liturgy is the celebration of all who gather. Together with the pastor who presides, the entire congregation is involved. It is appropriate, therefore, that where it is considered necessary or desirable or both, lay persons fulfill certain functions within the service."[24] The specific functions of lay assistants in Lutheran worship services varies with congregational needs and desires.

Worship Assistants

With the gradual recognition of a biblical understanding of worship and the involvement of laypeople in the Lutheran liturgy, several activities fall under the general category of worship assistant. These include the assisting minister, acolyte, member of the chancel care committee or altar guild, and usher.

Assisting Minister

The actual duties of an assisting minister have grown out of several traditional liturgical roles but most obviously from those associated with the deacon. Thus the responsibilities of assisting ministers in a Lutheran worship service have been designated as

> Kyrie
> Hymn of Praise, introductory sentence
> Old Testament Reading
> Epistle
> Prayers (concluded by the presiding minister)
> Distribution of the cup
> Post-Communion Prayer
> Benedicamus (if included)[25]

Because there are several places in the liturgy where the assisting minister may sing or chant, musical ability is a desired quality of the man who holds the position.[26] The office of cantor is the title sometimes given to a congregation's director of music, especially if the individual has been trained in theology as well as in music.[27]

While the duties of an assisting minister are usually limited to the above elements in worship, the specific nature of the listed responsibilities are clearly diaconal and under the pastor's supervision. Other areas in which assisting ministers may render service include chanting the psalm and preparing the chancel for Communion. Assisting at Communion is a visible sign of the diaconal office.

Assisting Ministers and Communion Practice

As the offering is gathered, the assisting minister and the presiding minister prepare the altar for the distribution of the Sacrament of the Altar. If only a veiled chalice is on the altar, the assisting minister brings the Communion vessels from the credence table to the altar during the Offertory. Or the assisting minister may bring the Communion elements forward with the offering, placing the bread and wine in the appropriate vessels.

After the Words of Institution, the ministers commune during the Agnus Dei. The presiding minister normally communes first at the altar (it is not necessary to go to the Communion rail). Then the assisting minister communes at the altar. After they have communed, the presiding minister gives the chalice or individual cups and, if necessary, a second paten for the bread, to the assisting minister(s). An acolyte or another assisting minister may supply bread, wine, and clean purificators as the ministers return to the altar.[28]

During distribution, the minister may raise the bread momentarily in front of the communicant before placing it in the communicant's hand or on the tongue.[29] This is only one method of distribution. The assisting minister fills the chalice from the flagon with enough wine to complete at least one table. Shallow chalices spill easily, so care is needed when distributing the wine. The minister may hold the chalice at the middle of the stem and place the rim near the communicant's lips. Communicants may grasp the base of the chalice to regulate the amount of wine they receive.[30]

The assisting minister follows the presiding minister's decision regarding communing an individual. If a wafer or a piece of bread is dropped during distribution, the assisting minister should pick it up and place it on the corporal for proper disposal after the service. If wine is spilled, it should be blotted immediately with a purificator.

ACOLYTE

The duties of an acolyte vary considerably, depending on the circumstances and location of the congregation, as well as the time of the service and the season of the church year. Often acolytes are young people from the congregation who assume the responsibility of lighting and extinguishing the candles before and after worship services.

On a few occasions, such as during an evening service or an Easter Vigil, the candles are lighted during the service following a precise pattern. The presiding minister will inform the acolyte of such details. For most regular services, the candles on the altar are lit several minutes before the service following local customs.[31] Generally, if there are two candles on the altar, the acolyte lights the one on his right as he faces the altar first. After a slight bow at the center of the altar toward the cross, the candle on the left is lit. If six or more candles are on the altar, the same procedure is followed, beginning with the candle on the right that is closest to the center or to the cross, then continuing outward until all the candles are lit. After returning to the center and bowing slightly toward the cross, the candle on the left that is closest to the center is lit before moving outward to light the remaining candles. If two acolytes are serving, each lights the candles on his side, beginning in the center. At the end of the service, the candles are extinguished in the reverse order in which they were lit. Any other candles in the chancel are extinguished after those on the altar.

When carrying a candle in procession, called a torch, the acolyte should be careful not to tilt the torch because the wax may drip on the acolyte or on a worshiper, which could burn. Particular care is needed when walking up or down steps. The acolyte should hold the torch so the flame is above his head so worshipers may see it at all times. When standing still, the acolyte may rest the pole of the torch on the floor. An acolyte does not bow when holding a torch so wax will not drip on him or on the floor.

An acolyte may also serve as a crucifer (one who carries the cross), thurifer (one who carries the censer), bannerbearer, or bookbearer. If a large procession is planned, a thurifer leads the procession, followed by the crucifer with acolytes on either side. (It is best to use two acolytes in a procession.) The choir or other assisting ministers follow the crucifer and torchbearers. If deacons will be used in the service, they process before the presiding minister, who always comes last. The thurifer, swinging the censer gently, processes at a steady pace several pews ahead of the crucifer, who holds the cross steady and straight. If a banner is part of a procession, the acolyte places it in its stand (usually in the chancel) and straightens it. The bookbearer places the Bible on the altar or missal stand until the Gospel procession.[32] Acolytes also may assist in setting and removing communionware for the Sacrament of the Altar. In all situations, the acolytes follow the presiding minister's directions.

The acolyte role provides training for young men considering the pastoral ministry because it is an opportunity for ongoing education about the meaning of worship and the symbols, vessels, paraments, architecture, and furnishings related to worship. Worship leaders will want to encourage young people to become acolytes and nurture their understanding of the blessings of ministry and service to God's gathered guests.

Chancel Care Member (Altar Guild/Sacristan)

Members of a congregation who take care of the church building's physical maintenance follow an ancient tradition. The Holy Week narratives record that Jesus sent two of His disciples to prepare the room for the Passover meal (Mark 14:14). Whether a sacristan, a member of the chancel care committee, a trustee, or a janitor, the preparations of the building are significant and important for the worship life of a Christian congregation. This is sometimes referred to as a "ministry of liturgical environment."[33]

No one person can fulfill all the responsibilities for maintaining the worship space of a Christian congregation. Therefore, most churches have a chancel care committee, which may be called an altar guild or sacristan corps. The members of this committee—male, female, or both—are concerned with the liturgical environment, thus they will be attentive to cleanliness and aesthetics. Members may be gifted with artistic abilities in addition to a willingness to serve the gathered guests. Usually chancel care is done behind the scenes—perhaps the only exception is when the altar is stripped on Maundy Thursday. Because of their specific tasks, members of the chancel care committee work closely with the pastor.

Caring for the Worship Space

Members of the chancel care committee may take on specific tasks or arrange a schedule of duties related to care of the worship space. The proper arrangement of the space and its cleanliness are the committee's top priorities, regardless of other assigned tasks. In addition, committee members provide an aesthetically pleasing space, both in the sacristy and in the sanctuary.[34] Finally, the chancel care committee cares for the acoustical integrity, adequate and adaptable lighting, and efficient climate control in the worship area.[35]

The chancel care committee requires an adequate, well-stocked workspace. Most committees have six people, including an advisory member from the board of elders and one from the board that supervises the church building's maintenance. Each member brings a unique perspective or skill to the committee—whether in the area of art design, cleaning expertise, or organizational management. Regular meetings with the pastoral staff provide general information on the worship schedule to facilitate efficient planning.

The sacristy is the typical workspace for the chancel care committee. The ideal arrangement in a church is two sacristies, one of which is reserved for the worship participants and their vestments (sometimes called a vestry). This room also may serve as an auxiliary office for church staff. In addition to adequate closet space for hanging all the vestments, the room may have a bookshelf for hymnals, altar books, prayer books, and other worship aids, as well as chairs. A second sacristy, sometimes called a working sacristy,[36] provides storage space and workspace for the chancel care committee. Storage space is important for the multiple sets of paraments, which may be hung in specially built closets with adjustable racks or stored in shallow drawers designed so the paraments do not need to be folded. The vessels for Communion and Baptism may be stored in the sacristy, as well as extra candles and Communion elements (which are best stored in environmentally controlled cabinets). The sacristy also may house books and instructions for the committee, as well as registries, an inventory of property, and service books not needed in the vestry. A church calendar and bulletin board in the sacristy may help organize the committee's work, and a large mirror either in the vestry or sacristy is helpful for worship participants. Adequate storage for seasonal items—the Advent wreath, Christmas crèche, wedding kneeler, banner stands, etc.—may also be provided in the sacristy.

Because it is a workspace, the sacristy will have several features. First, a countertop or large table is beneficial for sorting and folding linens, laying out paraments, and preparing other items for worship. Second, the committee will want to maintain an emergency repair kit with thread and pins; a floral repair kit with scissors, wire, and a knife; a first-aid kit; matches; a fire extinguisher; and other supplies. Third, the sacristy may have space for laundering and ironing paraments, linens, and vestments and storage space for cleaning equipment and supplies—including soaps and polishes, vacuum cleaner and mops. At a minimum, the sacristy should have a sink for washing the vessels. It is also a wise practice to have a piscina for disposal of the sacramental elements, though it is not necessary.[37]

The sacristy is typically located either to the side of or directly behind the chancel. If only one sacristy is available, the committee should complete its responsibilities prior to the service so the ministers may vest in private.

Caring for Vestments and Paraments

Most chancel care committees care for several sets of altar, pulpit, and pastoral vestments. These items match the color of the liturgical year and are changed by committee members according to the church year calendar, as discussed in chapters

3 and 10. The unadorned altar is first covered with a cerecloth—literally, a waxed cloth—that is the exact size of the altar top. Then the frontal, antependium, super-frontal, or altar cloth in the color appropriate to the season of the church year is placed on the altar. Finally, the fair linen is placed over the top and sides of the altar.[38]

Vestments and paraments may be cleaned professionally. However, modern cleaning materials allow careful clean-ing of some vestments by the committee. It is best to clean paraments annually; vestments are best cleaned monthly. Soil marks from wine or wax should be cleaned immedi-ately. The committee should also inspect stoles, chasubles, cassocks, and surplices annually for frayed edges, weakened closures, and loose embroidery or fringe.

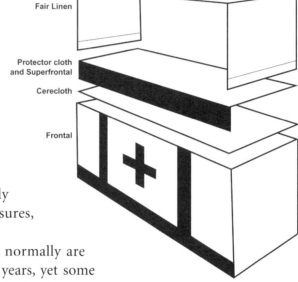

Fair Linen

Protector cloth and Superfrontal

Cerecloth

Frontal

Vestments and paraments normally are replaced every twenty to thirty years, yet some embroidered vestments from the Middle Ages remain in use. New paraments may be made or purchased. Texture, shape, color, and design should blend with the décor and architecture of the building. Local artists may produce a more appropriate vestment or parament than a ready-made item.[39]

Caring for the Furnishings

Wood furnishings in the chancel and nave are treated as one would treat household furniture. Dusting and carpet cleaning is a weekly task of the chancel care committee. Stained-glass windows may be washed and checked for repairs annually. An annual cleaning is an opportunity for the committee to involve the entire congregation and to recruit new committee members.

Rubbing briskly with a soft cloth will remove wax from candleholders or other surfaces. Tapers should be checked to ensure the wick is not jammed and is of suffi-cient length to light easily. The candlelighters may be cleaned each week to avoid getting soot on furnishings or vestments. If an eternal light is used in the chancel, a committee member should make sure the flame has not gone out, particularly before a midweek service.

Many objects in a church are made of brass, which is lacquered and does not need to be polished; rather, it can be wiped with a soft, absorbent cloth. If lacquer begins to peel or wear off, the item can be sent to a refinisher. Offering plates are the most frequently damaged item, thus an annual inspection is best. Gold and silver vessels for the Sacraments may be cleaned with soap and water. If the items are used regularly, they will need to be polished only once or twice a year.[40]

Preparation for Communion

The silver or gold communionware may be polished the day before the worship service, if necessary, then rinsed and dried the day of the service. Sufficient wafers[41] and wine are placed in their containers and set in the chancel according to local custom. If individual cups are used, these are filled and covered before the service. The altar table is set with the corporal, several purificators in a burse, the chalice or individual cups, a host box or ciborium with wafers, and a flagon of wine. (See diagram below.) Although the pastor may have a particular arrangement for the vessels, the chalice may be set on the altar and the rest of the Communion elements brought forward during the Offertory. However, if the altar is set completely, it may look like this: The chalice is veiled with the purificator, the paten is placed over the purificator, and the pall covers the paten. The veil in the liturgical color of the season is placed over all these items, and the burse is placed on top of the veil.

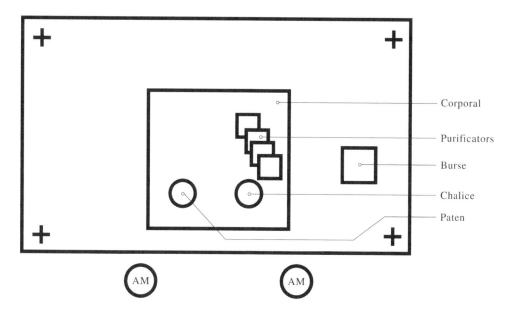

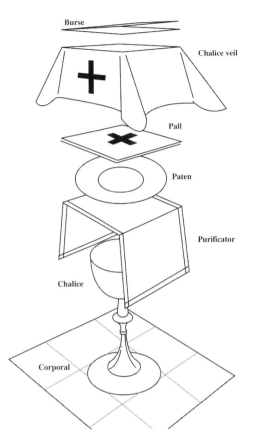

Burse

Chalice veil

Pall

Paten

Purificator

Chalice

Corporal

(See diagram at left.) The Communion vessels may be left on the altar after distribution has been completed.

The Communion vessels may be cleaned after the service by pouring water into the chalice, cups, flagon, or cruet and rinsing each three times. The water with residue wine may be poured into the piscina or on the ground. After removing the wafers or bread in the paten, ciborium, or host box, any crumbs may be rinsed out and the water poured into the piscina. After the vessels have been rinsed, they can be washed in hot soapy water and dried. Gold and silver vessels are typically stored in cloth or in a tarnish-retardant material.

Preparation for Baptism

Only two items are necessary for a Baptism—water and a cloth for drying the head of the newly baptized. If the congregation has a large baptismal font with running water, regular maintenance of the font ensures clean water. If a smaller font is used, the committee should make sure it is clean. Before the baptismal service, place warm water in a ewer (if the congregation uses one) and set a purificator or baptismal cloth near the font. If the congregation has a paschal candle, it is placed near the font to recall the Easter emphasis of Holy Baptism.

After the service, the water may be removed from the font using either a drain or a sponge. The water may be poured down the piscina or on the ground. The font, ewer, and basin may be dried and polished. The ewer may be stored with the Communion vessels.

Preparation for Other Services

A wedding is a significant event in the life of a Christian. The chancel care committee may have a significant impact on the plans made for this service of praise. Along with the pastor and elders, the committee may provide guidelines for couples to aid in their planning. These guidelines may indicate the type of floral and other decorations that are permissible, including types and placement of candlabra.

While some couples may wish to change the color of the paraments, the color reflects the liturgical season and may not be changed. One member of the chancel care committee may be designated as a wedding host or hostess to supervise the rehearsal and to assist the pastor on the wedding day.

Funerals provide another opportunity for the chancel care committee to serve God's gathered guests. If the congregation has one, the paschal candle is placed where the head of the casket will be and is lighted prior to the service. If a processional cross and torches are used, they are prepared before the service. The funeral pall, usually white to represent Easter joy and victory, is placed on the last pew, ready to be draped over the casket prior to the procession into the church or prior to the start of the service. After the service, the committee may follow the family's wishes regarding distribution of some of the flowers to shut-ins or hospitalized church members.

Seasonal services require special arrangements by the chancel care committee, including advanced planning for Advent candles and palms for Palm Sunday. Some chancel care committees make chrismons (a word developed from *Christ*'s *mono-grams*) for Christmas. Candlelight services may require the purchase of candleholders, as well as securing permission from community fire authorities. A crèche may be placed near the altar during the Christmas season. If the Maundy Thursday service will include the stripping of the altar, the chancel care committee may schedule a practice. Other special services, such as Thanksgiving, offer the committee an opportunity to decorate the chancel. If a saint day falls on a Sunday, it is observed with a change in paraments, according to pastoral preference.

General Principles for Chancel Care

Whenever possible, everything used in the worship setting of the church should be real so God's creation can be seen, heard, touched, smelled, and tasted. Flowers are usually placed on special pedestals in the chancel. Seldom, if ever, should flowers be placed directly on the altar. Normally, the only potted flowers in church are seasonal poinsettias and Easter lilies. Special greens for Christmas, Palm Sunday, or weddings are removed after the services.

Ideally, chancel candles are floorstanding. When placed on the altar, they require careful maintance. Two candles are used for the Sacrament of the Altar to symbolize Christ's two natures. A sevenfold candelabra recalls the seven-light oil lamp of the Old Testament.[42] When selecting candles, the committee should evaluate oil "candles" with caution.[43] The paschal candle is distinguished from other candles by its size. Some churches use a Christ candle as a baptismal candle and place it near the font after the Easter season. An eternal light can be found in most Lutheran churches. Traditionally, this light was a protective light in Roman Catholic churches at a time when people entered the church at all hours to worship at the altar where the reserved host was kept. The Lutheran significance of an eternal light recalls God's abiding presence as the light of the world.

A clean chancel communicates much about what is important to a congregation. The attractiveness of the paraments and the pastor's vestments also give evidence of the community's desire to do all things to God's glory. A chancel care committee has done its tasks well when the doors of the church are opened for worship and the atmosphere is peaceful and devotional.

Organization of the Chancel Care Committee

A chancel care committee requires organization. No member should feel compelled to serve for a lifetime. Changes in the committee give members an opportunity to learn, grow, and serve. In addition to several meetings each year, the committee may undertake a continuing program of education in the principles and practices of caring for the house of worship. Various resources for altar guilds or chancel care committees include information on how to conduct meetings, as well as an order of service for the induction of committee members.[44]

USHER AND GREETER

While providing a practical service, ushers and greeters follow in the long tradition of the early monastic porter. Recognition of that traditional role in the church provides a greater sense of duty and delight in serving the Lord and His gathered guests. After proper training, ushers will serve with a humble sense of joy coupled with congeniality and hospitality.

The usher does not merely stick bulletins in the hands of worshipers. Prior to the service, they check the sound system, lighting, and ventilation, and they monitor air conditioning or heating throughout the service. Ushers also are sensitive to the need of all worshipers for a reverent and orderly service. If a parent is having difficulty with a child, an usher may offer assistance. When a person leaves the nave, an usher may ask if assistance is needed, even if only to give directions to the restrooms. Ushers provide latecomers with a bulletin and information about where the congregation is in the liturgy. Often the ushers' major responsibility is the gathering of the offering, coupled with a count of the worshipers. Ushers also may have other responsibilities, depending on local customs.

The distribution of Holy Communion is a solemn yet joyous experience. Ushers direct communicants to the altar according to local custom, and they may offer an explanation of the congregation's Communion practice when guests announce to the pastor their intention to commune. Typically, four ushers assist worshipers as they approach the altar. One indicates when members are to approach the altar, another directs communicants to the altar, a third assists communicants as they return from the altar, and a fourth watches from the back of the church to supply assistance or to take care of other situations that may arise. At the end of the service, ushers escort worshipers from the church and assist in cleaning the sanctuary.

An usher or greeter is in the best position to provide help or direction to visitors. Some congregations have assistants who sit with visitors to guide them throughout the service, showing where the liturgy is printed in the hymnal or aiding in finding hymns. After the service, these assistants may introduce guests to congregation members to encourage a return visit.

The variety of liturgical ministries provides a tremendous opportunity for service in the Lord's house to, by, and for His gathered guests. Each role and responsibility has a longstanding tradition. Knowing that Christ's love is being conveyed in all acts of service to His gathered guests makes all these tasks a joy and an occasion to celebrate God's gracious presence.

SOME QUESTIONS TO CONSIDER

1. How were the major orders of church leadership distinguished in the early church's worship activities?

2. Of the "minor orders," which have a contemporary equivalent? Briefly explain these contemporary roles as they relate to the traditional orders.

3. How have liturgical ministries changed throughout the history of the church? What recent changes have affected Lutheran worship practices?

4. What areas of responsibility fall under the assisting minister's function?

5. Describe the various tasks an acolyte may perform during a midweek service. How might these tasks differ from those in a typical Sunday service?

6. Why do most congregations have a chancel care committee or altar guild?

7. How do a working sacristy, a storage sacristy, and a vesting sacristy differ? What advantage would a congregation gain by providing each of these rooms? What disadvantage might occur from such an arrangement?

8. What are the five concerns of a chancel care committee? Name some tasks that could be assigned to other members of the congregation.

9. Why are ushers and greeters important roles in contemporary North American congregations?

NOTES

1. The pastoral office has its foundation in Jesus' words in John 20:22–23 (the congregation calls a pastor to carry out the Office of the Keys publicly in Christ's name and on behalf of the congregation) and Paul's remarks in 1 Timothy 3:1–7. Paul mentions other leaders in Romans 12:3–8; 1 Corinthians 12:28; and Ephesians 4:11.

2. See 1 Timothy 3:8–10.

3. See Titus 1:5–9, for example.

4. In "Letter to the Philadelphians," 4.1, and "Letter to the Smyrnaeans," 8.1, Ignatius refers to bishops, presbyters, and deacons. See Cyril C. Richardson, ed. and trans., *Early Christian Fathers*, LCC 1 (Philadelphia: Westminster, 1953), 108, 115.

5. Dix, *Shape of the Liturgy* (2d ed.), 29–30.

6. In the Presbyterian tradition, *presbyter* or *elder* denotes the system of church government. Elected leaders serve as "teaching elders" (ministers), who have theological oversight, and "ruling elders" (laypeople), who oversee the practical administration of the congregation.

7. Volz, *Pastoral Life and Practice*, 33–36.

8. Dix, *Shape of the Liturgy* (2d ed.), 33–34.

9. Pless, "Leaders of Worship," 236.

10. Dix, *Shape of the Liturgy* (2d ed.), 34–35.

11. Jungmann, *Public Worship*, 83–87.

12. Dix and Chadwick, *Treatise on the Apostolic Tradition*, 20–21, 22. On widows, see Volz, *Pastoral Life and Practice*, 185–92.

13. Norris, *Church Vestments*, 4.

14. See *Gathered Guests* chapter 19 for more information on this ministerial position.

15. Westermeyer, *Church Musician*, provides background for the cantor's role.

16. Hansen, *Ministry of the Cantor*, 30–31.

17. Johann Sebastian Bach was the cantor in several German Lutheran congregations. Part of his responsibilities included teaching the young children who served in his choirs.

18. *Gathered Guests* chapter 12 explains the responsorial form, which is an extended solo or choral piece sung by the choir or cantor with a congregational response after a number of stanzas.

19. Norris, *Church Vestments*, 31.

20. "Babylonian Captivity of the Church," LW 36:47–56.

21. Plater, *Deacons in the Liturgy*, 11 12.

22. AC XXVIII, 53, seems to equate *bishop* and *presbyter* as referring to one office or position.

23. Commission on Theology and Church Relations, the LCMS, *Theology and Practice of the Lord's Supper*, 30, says that "while some might argue that assisting the presiding minister in the distribution of the elements is not necessarily a distinctive function of the pastoral office, the Synod's Commission on Theology and Church Relations strongly recommends that, to avoid confusion regarding the office of the public ministry and to avoid giving offense to the church, such assistance be limited to men."

24. *Lutheran Worship: Altar Book*, 25.

25. Adapted from "Duties of the Assisting Minister(s) in *Lutheran Worship*," Appendix I in *Lutheran Worship: History and Practice*, ed. Fred L. Precht (St. Louis: Concordia, 1993), 566.

26. Luther felt that musical training was so important that "before a youth is ordained into the ministry, he should practice music in school" (Plass, *What Luther Says*, 980).

27. Westermeyer, *Church Musician*, 13–17.

28. The presiding minister should distribute the bread to facilitate the practice of close(d) Communion.

29. Communicants may be instructed about the proper reception of the elements prior to communing (in confirmation classes or in new member classes). For example, the right hand may be placed on top of the left, palm up, and at chest level to receive the bread. If placed on the tongue, communicants may be instructed to tilt their heads and slightly extend their tongues to receive the bread.

30. Male communicants with mustaches and female communicants with hats may require extra assistance with the cup.

31. The general directions that follow are adapted from Michno, *Manual for Acolytes*.

32. See *Gathered Guests* chapter 7 for more information on the Gospel procession.

33. Simons and Fitzpatrick, *Ministry of Liturgical Environment*, offers the Roman Catholic perspective on the setting of the liturgy. Several ideas in this section are taken from this book.

34. Weidmann, *Manual for Altar Guilds*, 9, shows a fully vested altar with almost two dozen items placed on or alongside the altar; however, in recent years, many churches have opted to place only the necessary objects on the altar—two candles, a book (or missal) stand, and the Communion vessels.

35. These responsibilities may be subsumed under a function of the board or committee that oversees the general maintenance of the church grounds.

36. Lee Maxwell, *Altar Guild Manual*, 31.

37. Gent and Sturges, *Altar Guild Book*, 77–78.

38. Several kinds of linens are used around the chancel. The fair linen is important because it is seen, thus it is best to have at least two so a fresh fair linen can be placed on the altar each Sunday. The corporal, pall, purificators, and veil used during Communion are also normally made from linen. Each of these cloths may be embroidered with a cross. See Bockelman, *Practical Guide for Altar Guilds*, 26–33, 49–50.

39. Paul H. D. Lang, *What an Altar Guild Should Know*, 74–77, provides guidelines for planning, buying, cutting, designing, sewing, and embroidering paraments.

40. Gent and Sturges, *Altar Guild Book*, 38, suggests rubbing silver vessels with polishing gloves impregnated with jeweler's rouge to maintain the shine between polishings and to remove fingerprints.

41. Stauffer, *Altar Guild*, 32, provides a recipe for pita bread. Other recipes for wafers are available through altar guild organizations.

42. The use of two sevenfold candelabra is an innovation that exhibits symmetry of setting but lacks biblical or theological significance. A single sevenfold candelabra conforms to the Old Testament practice of a sevenfold oil lamp in the temple. In the Middle Ages, the number of altar candles ranged from one to twenty (Gent and Sturges, *Altar Guild Book*, 20). Explanations for two, three, four, or more altar candles can be found (see Bockelman, *Practical Guide for Altar Guilds*, 36).

43. While this practice can be attractive, some oil "candles" are partially translucent and the church's lighting can cause shadows in the middle of the candle. Real oil lamps might be more in keeping with the biblical objects used in worship described in Exodus 25:31–40; 37:17–24; Revelation 1:20; 4:5.

44. Paul H. D. Lang, *What an Altar Guild Should Know*, 16–32, provides ideas for devotions and meeting topics, as well as discusses the devotional life of committee members. Other sources in the notes of this section in *Gathered Guests* provide additional helps for an altar guild's organization and planning.

CHAPTER 19

THE MINISTRY OF READING

Listening is a routine activity in Lutheran worship. Each Sunday God's gathered guests hear God's Word as it is read, in addition to reading and studying it on weekdays. Lutherans typically have several Bibles at home, even in a variety of versions. But such immediate access to Holy Scripture is unique in the history of Christianity. In previous centuries, reading was a precious gift and privilege.

The reading of Scripture was an important occurrence at early Christian gatherings. At the time of the Reformation, Martin Luther grasped how important it was for the German people to read the Bible in their own language. He worked tirelessly to produce a readable translation of the Scriptures. To ensure that the Bible was heard and understood by everyone in the worship setting, Luther developed chant tones for the biblical texts in his early liturgies.[1]

In many modern Lutheran congregations, the readings are printed in a service folder for the worshipers to follow as the pastor reads. Some congregations read portions of Scripture together during the service.[2] In Lutheran churches, the pastor reads the Scripture lessons. This emphasizes the distinct office of the pastor. Sometimes laypeople will read the first two readings, but the Gospel reading is read by the pastor as a witness to the biblical teaching that God gave a distinct pastoral office to the church.

BACKGROUND AND HISTORY
OF THE PUBLIC READING OF SCRIPTURE

Reading a selection of God's Word was a regular practice in synagogue worship, as is evident in Jesus' life. First-century Jews gathered during the week for readings from the Law and the recitation of the *Shema* (Deuteronomy 6:4). On the Sabbath, an additional reading from a portion of one of the Prophets, selected either by the reader or by the synagogue ruler, was included. Luke reports that Jesus "stood up to read. The scroll of the prophet Isaiah was handed to Him. Unrolling it, He found the place where it is written . . . . Then He rolled up the scroll, gave it back to the attendant and sat down. The eyes of everyone in the synagogue were fastened on Him" (4:16ff.).

Such practices in the reading of Scripture developed during the Jewish exile in Babylon. Without land and temple, the Jewish faith became re-rooted in the Law and promises of God. Synagogues (the word is Greek for "place of meeting") developed at that time and became primary places for God's people to study and learn. After the people of Israel returned from captivity and resettled in Palestine in the sixth century before Christ's birth, they retained this practice of assembling, hearing God's Word read, and listening to comments on the passage made by the worship leaders (Nehemiah 7:73–8:8).

In the early church, reading and meditating on Scripture was important. Paul began most of his mission work in synagogues. Although not every person read, Paul encouraged Timothy to "devote yourself to the public reading of Scripture, to preaching and to teaching" (1 Timothy 4:13), indicating a close connection between Scripture reading and public proclamation and teaching. Therefore, a particular office developed in the church that was known as the lector or reader.[3] By the time of Justin Martyr (A.D. 145), the role of lector seems to have been well established in the worship life of the second-century Christian community. Justin Martyr wrote:

> And on the day called Sunday there is a meeting in one place of those who live in cities or the country, and the memoirs of the apostles or the writings of the prophets are read as long as time permits. When the reader [lector] has finished, the president [pastor] in a discourse urges and invites [us] to the imitation of these noble things. Then we all stand up together and offer prayers.[4]

The lector was already an office distinct from that of the pastor. Longer readings were suggested, either from the Old or the New Testaments. In a treatise written near the end of the second century, Tertullian criticized the heretical practice of allowing various individuals to serve as lectors, deacons, or pastors.[5] This information suggests that by A.D. 198 the offices of lector and deacon were clearly established among early orthodox Christian congregations.

In these early days of Christianity, books or scrolls were not available to every family or even to every congregation. Books or parchments were extremely expensive. Particularly during times of severe persecution, lectors probably kept the sacred books in their homes between worship occasions. Several accounts indicate that lectors were persecuted under Diocletian (around A.D. 303–304) because the authorities found a Christian scriptural scroll in their homes.[6]

As the office of lector developed, these individuals probably arranged the readings thematically throughout the year, with particular emphasis on the festival days. Later, lectors were responsible for preparing the readings of Scripture. Instead of carrying an expensive Bible to church, the lectors may have written out the readings and brought only those sheets necessary for a particular Sunday's service.

Besides being the caretakers of the scriptural texts, readers were recognized for their skill and responsibilities. The reader was a specialized evangelist, as the following qualifications for a lector from the late third century indicate.

> Let a reader be appointed, having first been subject to trial; not a buffoon, not a drunkard, not a jester, well-mannered, easy tempered, kindly, the first who makes his way to the assemblies of the Lord, easily audible, with power of narration, knowing that he fills the place of an evangelist. For he who fills the ears of those who do not understand shall be counted as a workman enrolled in the books of God.[7]

In the early church, readers were given special recognition along with their responsibilities.

After the fall of Rome in the early fifth century, lay involvement in the church diminished, particularly in the West. If trained at all, readers usually came from among the lower orders of clergy or were deacons or subdeacons preparing for clergy roles.[8] The responsibilities of the lector were to read the lessons appointed by the bishop. Usually these Scripture passages were read in a language that over the centuries became increasingly unknown to the majority of the worshipers.[9] Eventually, Scripture reading became the sole responsibility of the clergy.[10]

Lay readers were not used again in any official capacity among Christian congregations until after Vatican II (in the mid-1960s). However, Vatican II was heavily influenced by higher criticism and liberalizing social reform movements throughout the world. As a result, the church heirarchy encouraged the use of lay readers or lectors as one way to deal with many of these influences. Other Christian churches soon followed the example of the Roman Catholic Church. Unfortunately, the unique importance of the office of lector was not recognized; consequently, the oral reading of God's Word was degraded through lack of preparation. Yet Peter Brunner has correctly noted: "When reading Scripture, the reader's voice must become the vessel for the voice of the prophets and apostles and, through them, the voice of Christ Himself. In its form of expression, the voice of the reader must be a sign of the voice of prophets and apostles which it represents."[11] This Lutheran emphasis echoes Luther's emphasis on the church as the place to hear God's Word.

THE PERICOPES

Although Scripture readings were a regular part of Jewish and early Christian worship services, specifically selected and assigned readings were not prescribed in Old Testament nor New Testament times. Instead, a continuous reading of Scripture occurred on each Sabbath or during each Christian meeting.[12] Justin Martyr indicates that a precise listing of annual liturgical readings was not fixed, but "the memoirs of the apostles or the writings of the prophets were read as long as time permits."[13] Similarly, the *Apostolic Constitutions* mention the reading of lessons from the Law, the historical books, Job, the Wisdom books, the Prophets, Acts, the Epistles, and the Gospels.[14] Another historian reports events from a century later: "Augustine frequently in his sermons speaks of the lessons which have been read, sometimes only the Epistle and the Gospel, but at other times the Prophets also."[15]

An obvious need for an organized series of lessons grew from the church's emphasis on the Bible and the desire to recall the events of Christ's life. Luther Reed explains: "The three great festivals were the first to have definite lessons. Specific assignments were next made for the 'octaves' of these feasts, and then for associated seasons, and thus the scheme developed."[16] Instead of following the *lectio continua* pattern of readings, selections were "cut out" (the Greek word for a cutout portion is *pericope*) of the whole book.

Lectors probably wanted to preserve the precious and expensive biblical books by carrying in public only those readings required for a specific service. These selections were gathered into booklets of readings that were called *lectionaries*.[17] Three forms of lectionaries developed, somewhat side by side, for several centuries. The first took the form of marginal notes in a book or scroll of a particular biblical text. The notes indicated the beginning and ending of a particular reading. In the second method, the first and last words of the readings were indicated by referring to the first word of the reading. (In Latin, this initial word was called the "head" or *caput*; therefore, these books were called *capitularies*.) The final method took the form of an actual lectionary, which included the entire biblical passage and a set pattern of readings according to the developing church year.[18]

Numerous series of readings were developed during the centuries. Jerome is sometimes credited with developing the first complete list of readings for a year.[19] In the West, a series of twofold readings developed in Rome and became standard throughout most of Europe, though the Gallican (French) use of three readings—Old Testament, Epistle, and Gospel—remained common practice until the seventh century.[20] The Roman system consisted of a series of Epistle and Gospel readings for each Sunday in the liturgical year, each centering on the works and words of Christ and His apostles.[21]

At the time of the Reformation, Luther encouraged the continued use of the traditional lectionary with its assigned Gospel and Epistle readings.[22] Luther Reed explains why Luther retained these readings.

> Liturgically this was expressed in general recognition of the controlling power of the lessons in establishing the theme and tone of each day's Service; in the development of a sermon as interpreting and enforcing this central usage; and in a rich outpouring of congregational hymns (and melodies) based upon the thought of the lessons as appointed for particular Sundays and festivals in the church year.[23]

Such an ordering of the biblical texts kept the Gospel message before the gathered guests as they heard God's great plans and promises fulfilled in Christ.

After the Reformation, the Lutheran Church retained the one-year Roman lectionary, though adaptations were made in various locales.[24] Reed makes clear that

> the mature judgment of the church has retained them [the historic pericopes] because their use is a guarantee of sound and complete teaching of fundamental Christian truth. Together they constitute a solid block of fundamental material about which the services of a particular day or season are constructed. They are a most important part of the common liturgical inheritance of the universal church, with a continuous history of nearly fifteen hundred years.[25]

Thus Lutherans have maintained this historic tradition for the sake of the Gospel. With the renewed emphasis on corporate and participatory worship in the Roman Catholic Church after Vatican II, this one-year series was changed. Roman Catholic scholars and leaders from other liturgical churches, including Lutherans, developed an expanded three-year series of readings.[26]

The three-year series accomplished several things. The extended series provided an increase in the scope and the comprehensiveness of the Scripture reading that enabled worshipers to hear more of the Bible. Larger units of Scripture, sometimes entire books, could be studied over consecutive Sundays. In addition, the variety of texts for preaching increased, thus enriching the worship life of the congregation. Finally, the reintroduction of Old Testament lessons provided a sense of historical continuity with Old Testament believers, as well as a greater first-century Christian consciousness. After all, the Scriptures of the first disciples is the modern-day Old Testament.

The structure of the present three-year series is as follows: the first year (series A) features the Gospel of Matthew, the second year (series B) draws readings from Mark, and the third year (series C) uses Luke as its major source for Gospel readings. John's Gospel is used in all three years, particularly during the Easter season. For all three years, the first lesson comes from the Old Testament, except during the Easter season when it is taken from the Book of Acts. The Old Testament reading connects with or develops the theme from the Gospel reading by way of prophecies or types. The second lesson is from an epistle. Usually these Epistle readings are selected so an entire letter is read over consecutive Sundays in the continuous reading (*lectio continua*) pattern of the Jewish synagogue and early Christian worship.[27] On many occasions, the three readings "fit" together thematically in an unintentional yet serendipitous manner that enhances all the readings.

Although the three-year and one-year lectionaries continue to be altered and amended, most Protestant and Roman Catholic churches that use a lectionary follow a three-year structure of readings. The Episcopal and Lutheran Churches have followed this pattern closely. The Presbyterian and other Reformed Churches use a similar design. Occasionally, because of denominational differences or preferences, the readings may be out of synchronization by one to three weeks. For example, even among Lutherans a difference occurs during the final weeks of the church year. *Lutheran Worship* counts backward from the Third-Last Sunday in the Church Year to focus on the end times and Christ's second coming. *Lutheran Book of Worship* moves straight through the Sundays after Pentecost, and only in those years in which the season is longer does it include the common lessons on the last three Sundays of the church year.

With the general acceptance of the three-year lectionary, the purpose and process envisioned by the designers seems to have been met. Each Christian denomination may still employ particular themes, yet the ecumenical consensus for the general pattern promotes a sense of Christian unity on the Word of God in a world often out of touch with God's presence in any way.

One distinction in the Lutheran liturgical calendar is that lesser festivals, such as saint days, may take precedence over Sundays for which the assigned color is green. This occurrence is rare in the Roman Catholic Church and is not found in the Episcopal or Reformed Churches. The rationale for this practice among Lutherans is found in the Lutheran Confessions.[28] Because the Confessions encourage honoring saints and because public worship other than on a Sunday is rare, saint days may be observed when they fall on a Sunday or on the Sunday within the octave of that festival.

THE LECTOR IN MEDITATION

"The Bible is primarily intended to function in the liturgy as a text to be read aloud.

The purpose is that those who hear it are personally addressed in the concreteness of their existence," notes Dutch theologian E. H. van Olst. He continues: "Reading the Bible in the worship service—passing on the story—should lead people to faith, to the awareness that our own existence constitutes a part of the story. . . . This is how the Bible must function in the liturgy."[29]

The following steps are one way a lector may prepare for the task of reading Scripture in a public setting, whether in a church service or in a devotional context.[30]

1. PRAY FOR GUIDANCE

The Holy Spirit caused the Scriptures to be written (Ezekiel 3:27; John 20:31; 2 Timothy 3:16; Revelation 1:10–11). It is the Spirit of the Lord who also guides interpretation of the Scriptures (John 14:26; 16:13). Lectors will want to remind themselves that, like the preacher, theirs is a ministry of proclaiming God's Word to His gathered guests. Thus they may ask the Holy Spirit to use them as effective agents of His precious means of grace.

Modern society is an information-laden culture, and we forget that it is not important to be merely informed. Rather, the lector's prayer is to use the time of preparation to be "in-formed" by the Holy Spirit. That is, he prays that the Spirit who formed the Scriptures is recognized as the one who gives understanding to lector and hearers alike. The lector also may pray that the Spirit who formed his faith would also be known in his reading. Finally, lectors may recall that the Holy Spirit continues to form and reform believers as part of His sanctifying work—transforming God's people into the likeness of Christ.

2. READ THE PASSAGE

Although it would seem to go without saying, the lector should read the passage several times. Some readers (and pastors) think they can stand up and read a lesson without practice, and some can do so on a regular basis. However, lack of preparation can result in unfortunate, though sometimes humorous, misstatements. Therefore, the lector will want to read each passage aloud several times prior to reading it before the congregation. He should try to use the same Bible or printed text that will be used during the service.

As the lector reads the passage, he will determine the mood or tone of the lesson. Reading a passage slowly and reflectively helps determine whether Law or

Gospel is a primary emphasis. The biblical writer's intent may become more clear as the lector reads and notes a sense of confrontation, a call to action, or an offer of comfort. Perhaps the mood changes within the lesson. Some passages begin calmly, then develop a sense of agitation. At other times, a sense of excitement or apprehension must be communicated verbally by the reader to the hearers. For a novice lector, it may help to record the reading and play it back to discern whether the feelings expressed in the text are communicated adequately in the oral presentation.

3. RESEARCH THE BACKGROUND

A Scripture lesson is always a smaller portion of a larger work—selected verses from an Epistle, a Gospel, or another book of the Bible. The lesson is also part of the greater composite work, the Holy Bible. Thus the lesson is always taken out of its larger context and even out of its immediate context. Therefore, lectors will want to know these contexts so they may interpret the message of the lesson more accurately. For new lectors or those not acquainted with a particular book of Scripture, background reading in a commentary, Bible dictionary, or Bible handbook may prove helpful.[31]

A lector will want to draw together pertinent information about the reading by asking the following questions:

What is the literary form of the reading?

The Holy Bible is actually a library of books. Many different styles of writing are represented among the sixty-six books. Some are historical, others poetic; some are narratives, others hymns. If the reading is a letter or the law, how does this origin affect the tone of voice of the reader? If it is a biography or a prophecy, what information may be needed to explain the passage more fully so worshipers may better understand its context? If it is an apocalyptic passage or a parable, what understanding of biblical imagery will aid in the reading? If the lesson is poetry, how does the parallel structure affect the oral presentation, and what pitfalls may need to be avoided? These questions are not exhaustive; instead, they are a beginning for the reader's preparation. The style or genre of literature will affect emphasis and communication style.

What is the historical context of the passage?

World events at the time a Scripture passage was written may affect the meaning of some biblical passages. Knowing who was in political power and where the passage was written or to whom it was written will help listeners better grasp the sense of the passage. Knowing the events in the history of salvation that came before and after the passage may provide direction to the reading. Knowing the author and his audience will offer context to contemporary hearers. The lector can establish a sense of reality through this kind of research and preparation.

What is the immediate context?

The immediate context refers to the verses or chapters before and after the pericope. Knowing how the lesson fits into the context of the book provides a valuable perspective on its interpretation. For example, in the eighth chapter of Paul's letter to the Romans, Paul begins with "therefore." Without knowing the context of the previous chapters, "therefore" makes little sense. A lector who has a sense of the immediate context is better able to communicate the Gospel joy of Paul's "therefore" in this passage.

What is the larger context of the passage?

Unless one is familiar with all the books by the same author or with the theological emphasis of a particular writer, it is beneficial to see how the lesson fits into the larger context of the testament or the Bible. This does not mean the lector must read the whole Bible before a Sunday reading. However, he may wish to read an entire gospel to see where and how a pericope "fits" into the larger book. Some of Paul's letters might be read to provide context for a reading from Acts. Similarly, reading about a prophet's life in Kings or Chronicles will place many Old Testament passages into their biblical settings.

Why is this passage being read on this day in the church year?

The liturgical context of a passage provides significant but often neglected insights into a pericope. The relevance of a reading to the theme of the day should be clear. For example, the Gospel reading may function as the chief theme-setting reading. Or the Old Testament lesson may provide background for the Gospel reading. This is where a general understanding of the church year helps the lector prepare. For example, during the season of Epiphany, many of the Gospel readings focus on Jesus' miracles. Each Sunday offers a greater manifestation (the meaning of *epiphany*) of Jesus as God's only-begotten Son. Such an insight helps the lector highlight the miracle and the manifestation of Jesus on a particular Sunday.

While this step may seem complicated, it results in confidence in the biblical texts. A lector may find this step also provides personal devotional material. Believing in the certainty of God's mighty workings in the biblical past helps the lector communicate that reality in the present.

4. REFLECT ON THE THOUGHT DIVISIONS

Most biblical passages involve more than one idea. Although some short readings may only have one major thought, even a one-verse reading may have two distinct thoughts (for example, Habakkuk 2:4). Therefore, discerning thought divisions involves two steps.

After reading and studying the text, the lector marks the thoughts contained in the reading in some way. This may be done with brackets around the sentences or sections of the reading that convey specific ideas. Grammatical shifts may occur in the passage, or various speakers may be present, which should be noted. A sense of urgency in the first part of a passage may change to a sense of comfort and strength by the end. An explanatory comment may be imbedded in the text, which will be evident to the reader through punctuation but will need to be communicated by the lector verbally. Brackets provide a visual identification of these changes.

Second, the lector may record his thoughts about the reading in the margin. What spiritual insights arise? What emotions are evoked? These margin notes can direct the manner in which the passage is read. For example, a lector may record these reflections on Isaiah 2:1–2 as margin notes:

Isaiah 2:1–2	Lector's Reflections
This is what Isaiah son of Amoz saw concerning Judah and Jerusalem: In the last days the mountain of the LORD's temple will be established as chief among the mountains; it will be raised above the hills, and all nations will stream to it.	*Note that this is more than a word from God. I need to communicate the imagery too. The "last days" must refer to the end of the world or the time of Christ's appearing. From my research, I recall that this "mountain" refers to Jerusalem and the centrality of worship. Wow, I hadn't thought about how worship draws people into God's presence.*

Such insights reflect the lector's sense of awe and wonder, and they will influence his reading as voice inflection and nonverbal cues add nuance to his communication with God's gathered guests.

5. PARAPHRASE THE AUTHOR'S WORDS

One way to understand the biblical writer's words is to paraphrase the passage. Reading a passage of Scripture is often more difficult than preaching because the reader must convey someone else's ideas in that person's own words, while a preacher uses his own words. To convey the message of the verse accurately, the lector must apprehend the thoughts of the author and the context of the passage. By rewriting a passage in one's own words, the lector can ensure that the same message is being communicated. Paraphrasing may actually be more difficult with a familiar passage than with a less well-known text.

To prepare a paraphrase, the lector may wish to recreate the scene evoked by the lesson or to reflect on a personal experience related to the text. The lector may explore the contexts of the text discovered in the background research. The lector may imagine that he is the author, writing these words for the first time. Thus he may rewrite the lesson in the first person. A paraphrase of the Old Testament reading for Easter Evening (Daniel 12:1–3) might be similar to the following:

Daniel 12:1–3	Lector's Paraphrase
But at that time your people—everyone whose name is found written in the book—will be delivered. Multitudes who sleep in the dust of the earth will awake: some to everlasting life, others to shame and everlasting contempt. Those who are wise will shine like the brightness of the heavens, and those who lead many to righteousness, like the stars for ever and ever.	*Sometime in the future, at God's set time when Jesus appears, all believers will be saved. All the millions of people who have died will arise to life again: some will go to heaven, others will suffer in eternal hell. All those who know Jesus as Savior will be joyously happy in heaven, and those who teach about Jesus will shine like stars eternally.*

This paraphrase is not intended to replace the pericope; instead, it is another method by which the lector can gain a deeper appreciation for God's Word. The reading from Scripture is always the living, Spirit-powered Word from God. This step helps the lector recognize the dynamic dimensions of Scripture as the Word that continues to have an impact on both the reader and the hearer.

THE LECTOR IN PREPARATION

Around the eighth century, Charlemagne's teacher Alcuin (ca. A.D. 735–804) advised his students regarding the reading of Scripture: "Let any reader who reads the exalted words of God from the sacred body of the book make clear distinctions between meanings, titles, periods, and commas so that he may enunciate the accents with his mouth. May his pleasant voice carry far, so that everyone may hear and praise God through the reader's mouth."[32] Lectors will want

to be prepared for their responsibilities before the Lord so His Word is heard by everyone. Thus the following practical steps aid in the preparation process.

6. CHECK PRONUNCIATIONS

Some biblical names and places have unusual pronunciations or even several acceptable pronunciations. For example, one pericope from Isaiah 8 includes the name Maher-Shalal-Hash-Baz—twice! By preparing beforehand, the lector probably will not stumble across the name during the service. A lector can consult a Bible dictionary or pronunciation guide for most terms or names in Holy Scripture.[33] A pastor or teacher also may provide help.

Although people often pronounce words differently in different parts of the country, it is best to follow standard American pronunciation. Words that are repeatedly mispronounced may draw attention away from God's Word and place it on the mistake.

7. MARK APPROPRIATE PAUSES

In general, Christian worship, particularly as experienced in Lutheran congregations, suffers from too much environmental noise. Silence is almost unknown in worship settings. But in the public reading of Scripture, silence can prove beneficial. Such silence is accomplished through appropriate pauses, which are dependent on understanding the biblical writer's ideas.

Trained lectors make at least two distinct kinds of pauses. One marks major breaks in the reading; the other is a minor pause that highlights or clarifies the reading. Some lectors use slash marks (//) or prime marks (") to denote these pauses; others use asterisks (**). It is best to mark the pauses in the copy of the text that will be used for the reading, even if it is in an expensive pulpit Bible or lectionary.

Major pauses (//,", or **)

Major breaks or pauses normally correspond to the punctuation in the text. However, the lector will want to remember that the punctuation in the Bible is usually an editorial decision because the original Hebrew and Greek had no punctuation. A lector may disagree with an editor's punctuation. For example, the New International Version presents John 1:3–4 as: "Through Him all things were made; without Him nothing was made that has been made. In Him was life, and that life was the light of men." The Greek text may be translated and punctuated as: "Through Him all things were made; without Him nothing was made. That which has been made in Him was life, and that life was the light of men." The second choice emphasizes that Christ brings life to all creation.[34]

Major pauses in a text convey finality, as at the end of a sentence. On the other hand, a major pause may occur when a thought changes or a significant concept shifts the focus within a sentence. For example, the structure of Hebrew poetry repeats an idea in a succeeding line, thus a major pause may be marked after the duplicate idea is stated in the second half of a verse. This would apply in a reading from the Psalms, as well as in texts from some of the prophets. In some of Paul's letters, several major pauses may need to be marked in his long, complex sentences. Experience and the practice of reading the texts aloud will help the lector detect major pauses.

Minor pauses (/, ', or *)

Feeling, emphasis, or "color" is added through short pauses within a sentence. These pauses can make the difference between a stilted, wooden reading and one that is alive and speaks to the hearers. Minor pauses are brief and not consciously noticed. A minor pause, usually at the point of a comma, adds highlight to the sentence.

Minor pauses are more difficult to mark because they are related to pace and subtle shifts in focus. It is important to mark them, however, particularly when there is no punctuation. An essential concept can be emphasized merely by placing a minor pause after an important word. John 3:16 is familiar to most worshipers, yet well-placed pauses, especially in the first phrases, can restore a sense of awe and wonder at God's love in Christ:

For God * so loved * the world * * that He gave * His one and only * Son * * *

While this may look stilted as printed, when read fluently, the impact can be significant.

Marking pauses according to the text

There is no correct way to pause in a particular reading. Even experienced lectors mark the same text in different ways. Some lectors feel that long or frequent pauses make the lesson sound affected or choppy and the pauses exaggerated. However, what may seem exaggerated in a private reading or even in a small group may be appropriate in a larger more formal setting, especially when the human voice is amplified. For example, the following marking of Galatians 4:4–7 came from trained lectors in a published guide for reading Scripture in a worship setting.

> When the *designated* time had come, * God sent forth his *Son* * born of a *woman,* * born under the *law,* * to *deliver* from the law * those who were *subjected* to it, * so that we might receive our *status* * as adopted sons. * * The *proof* that you are sons * is the fact that God has sent forth into our *hearts* * the *spirit* of his Son * which *cries* out * * *"Abba!"* * *("Father!"). * * * You are no longer a

slave * but a *son!* * * And the fact that you *are* a son makes you an heir, * by *God's* design. * * * [35]

Although these markings are suggested by professional lectors, their approach can be followed by anyone preparing to read a Scripture verse.

Another example demonstrates the importance of pausing appropriately. Evaluate the sense of Jesus' words to the convict on the cross if pauses are placed after different words. Without marked pauses, the text reads: "I tell you the truth, today you will be with Me in paradise" (Luke 23:43). (Remember, because there is no punctuation in the original text, the punctuation in English translations has been determined by the translators and editors.) Normally, the passage is read as follows:

I tell you the truth * * * *today* * you will be with Me in *paradise.*

Some denominations, however, place the major pause after *today*:

I tell you the truth today * * * you *will be* with Me * in paradise.

This second reading suggests that Jesus was speaking only on Good Friday. It removes the promise and hope that Jesus' words pronounced from the cross offer to all believers. This illustrates that punctuation and pauses are significant communication devises for proclaiming God's Word to His gathered guests.

8. INDICATE THE EMPHASES

In everyday conversation, we naturally emphasize certain words. When we read, this natural emphasis tends to be lost. Thus the lector consciously supplies the emphasis, usually by raising the voice in volume and tone. It is important to emphasize the words that best convey the intention of the Scripture writer. For some familiar passages, this may mean emphasizing different words than those usually emphasized. It is easiest to mark emphasis by underlining a particular word or phrase.

Usually, the lector follows his natural inclination to emphasize certain words. The following suggestions, however, may help lectors know which words are best emphasized. First, when a new idea is introduced, the noun conveying the idea may be emphasized to indicate this new concept to the hearers. Second, if the main point of the sentence conveys movement or activity, the verb may be emphasized. Third, when contrasting ideas are evident in a passage, adjectives, adverbs, and even pronouns may be emphasized to clarify the contrast. Fourth, when a word is repeated (sometimes called an echo), the second appearance is not stressed. Despite these general rules, the lector places the passage in its scriptural and liturgical contexts to best determine emphasis.

9. Determine the Dramatic Elements

Perhaps the most difficult technique for a lector to use well involves changing the mood, pitch, and speed of one's voice. In one sense, reading aloud should communicate a sense of drama. Without dramatization or dramatic expression, pauses become mechanical and emphases stiff. The lector helps worshipers picture the scene in their minds. Through a change in voice, the lector communicates feelings and better illustrates the event.

To develop the dramatic elements, the lector may consider the place of the narrator, the persons in the text, and the expression of quotations. The biblical writer is usually the narrator, particularly in the Gospels and in Old Testament narrative passages. Thus the lector assumes the place of the narrator. A narrative text usually involves a number of characters. It may be helpful to think of the lectern or the reading stand as a stage, with each character having an assigned place.

Consider the Gospel account following Peter's confession (Matthew 16:21–23). The narrator, Matthew, is the lector and faces forward. Jesus could be to the left of the lector with Peter to the right of the lector. The lector as narrator faces forward for verse 21. Turning slightly to his left (to "face" Jesus), the lector reads Peter's spoken words (verse 22). Turning to face forward, the lector reads verse 23 of Matthew's narrative. The lector concludes verse 23 by turning slightly to his right as he reads Jesus' rebuke of Peter. The same method can be followed for indirect quotations. Thus by slight body shifts and subtle tonal changes much can be communicated nonverbally.

Parenthetical comments also can be indicated by shifts in tone or posture. For example, in his writing, Mark often explains terms unfamiliar to his Roman audience. Similarly, Paul makes parenthetical comments in some of his letters.[36] These parenthetical comments are most easily conveyed if the lector looks up at the congregation for these explanatory words.

Dramatic emphasis does not mean the lector takes on a multivoice presence designed to entertain the congregation. In fact, being obviously dramatic calls attention to the reader and not to God's Word. Instead, dramatic elements should enhance the reading so the meaning of the biblical text is communicated clearly. If done well, listeners will not notice this element, except in the sense that the reading is more meaningful, spirited, and animated. Scripture was written for public reading. In fact, Paul's letters were not merely personal letters but were composed for public reading.[37] There is a sense of drama communicated in the text itself that the lector can recapture as he communicates God's life-giving Word.

10. Prepare a Short Introduction

Lutherans have always believed that Scripture should be interpreted in its context. One practice, which is used in many Christian congregations, is to introduce each lesson briefly,[38] providing the liturgical rationale or the context of the reading. An introduction enables worshipers to understand the central theme of the lesson. The content of the introduction may vary from reading to reading; however, it may contain one or two of the following:

- acknowledgment and explanation of unfamiliar terms or concepts;
- background on the author and his purpose;
- comments on the main theme of the reading;
- description of the situation in which the text was first read; or
- explanation of the lesson's relationship to the theme of the day or season.

Most objections to introductions arise because of misuse. If introductions are a rambling paraphrase, they make the reading of the lesson redundant and the lector becomes a preacher. Introductions also can be too long, providing more information than is necessary to understand the text. A one-sentence statement avoids these pitfalls.

The lector prepares the introduction last, after he has a clear understanding of the biblical writer's thoughts. For the first-time lector, it may be helpful to see what others have done.[39] Sometimes the pastor will prepare the introduction to establish the theme of the service and sermon. It is best to write out the introduction but not to read it. A substantial pause is best between the introduction and the Scripture reading.

11. Practice

Although most lectors have been reading since childhood, they may not have done so in a public setting, particularly as part of corporate worship. The old adage "Practice makes perfect!" can be applied to reading Scripture too. This step involves more than reading. It involves preparing oneself spiritually for the great opportunity to give voice to God's Word before His gathered guests. Certainly, God deserves the very best that can be offered.

Practice includes reading to an audience, which may be difficult to do but will prove beneficial. The audience may evaluate the message the lector conveys, alerting him to distracting mannerisms or commenting on the tonal quality and inflections. Practice also involves knowing the setting in which the reading will occur, including double-checking the amplification system. Such practice ensures the lector is well prepared.

The Lector in Proclamation

After these preparatory steps, the lector is ready for the final step:

12. Read the Lessons Confidently

There are three critical phases in reading from Scripture—before, during, and after. Each has distinct elements for the lector to consider.[40]

Before the reading

Use a Bible that is easily read and visible to the congregation, especially if the readings are done without benefit of a reading table. A lectionary may be useful because the readings are often in a larger font and arranged for ease of reading. It is best when the Bible is already on the lectern or reading table.[41] If the reading is printed on the back of a bulletin, it may be best for the lector not to carry the page to the lectern because the nonverbal message of a sheet of paper may be that the Scripture reading is not important. However, if a single sheet of text is preferred, the lector could carry the page in an attractive folder or place it inside a larger Bible.

The lector should ensure the reading is from a translation agreed to by the pastor. In most cases all lessons are read from the same translation at every public service for the sake of continuity and consistency. If the pastor uses a different translation for the sermon, this variation can be explained by him during the sermon.

Nearly everyone who reads or speaks before a group is nervous at some point, but excessive nervousness can be an obstacle when reading Scripture publicly. Most physical and emotional characteristics of nervousness will cease with continued experience, but some suggestions to relieve nervousness include

- prepare adequately;
- practice relaxation exercises, such as deep breathing, before entering the chancel;
- warm up your voice in the sacristy by speaking nonsense syllables;
- concentrate on the reading—people want to hear God's Word;
- realize you are the agent or instrument of the Holy Spirit; and
- ask the Holy Spirit for His peace.

The lector walks at a medium pace to the place of reading, usually the lectern. If coming from the congregation, he begins walking before the lesson—during the Hymn of Praise, Psalm, or Gradual. The lectern should be at a comfortable height—about chest-high so the lector can look down at the text and up at the congregation without bobbing his head. It is not necessary to pick up the Bible when reading, though this is an alternative to a low lectern.

The lector waits for silence and the attention of the congregation before announcing the readings, especially prior to the first reading. "Deliberation at such places as this, that is to say, between major portions of the Service, adds dignity and permits thoughtful participation by the people."[42] When almost all noise has subsided, the reading may proceed.

During the reading

The lector announces the lesson using the proper liturgical format, for example, "The Old Testament Reading for _____ is from the _____ chapter of _____."[43] It is unnecessary to announce the specific starting and ending verses, unless the worshipers are using their own Bibles.[44] If the order of service does not designate how to introduce the lesson, the lector may announce the reading in a simple fashion by saying, "A reading from _____."

The lector reads distinctly and loudly so everyone can hear. If a microphone is available, the lector should not speak too softly; instead, he should concentrate on projecting his voice out over the congregation to the back corners of the room. Enunciation is crucial when one's voice is amplified.

While reading the lesson, the lector may follow along with his finger so he will not lose his place while looking up. In Jewish synagogues, an ornamental pointer is still used for this purpose so the cantor's finger will not soil the parchment. When making eye contact, it is best for the lector not to look at the same place in the congregation each time or to follow a set pattern, which can become distracting.

After the reading

When the lector has finished speaking, his body continues to communicate. He may lower the book, if it was held, or look up at the congregation after a brief pause. In many Lutheran congregations, the simple conclusion "This is the Word of the Lord" indicates the completion of the reading. The congregation may respond, "Thanks be to God." The lector returns to his seat.

A lector who reads regularly may seek a critique to highlight areas for improvement. Such an evaluation is helpful because the same readings will be used every three years. Changes or comments can be filed for the next time the reading is used.

Some Questions to Consider

1. Why is lector preparation more important in contemporary society than it was in the first three centuries of Christianity?

2. What is the biblical precedent for the role of lector? How did the role develop in the early church?

3. Define the following: lector, lectionary, pericope, and three-year series.

4. Study the Old Testament reading for the next Sunday using steps 1, 2, and 4 under the section "Lector in Meditation."

5. Research the background of the Gospel reading for the next Sunday. Write a paragraph on the historical context and one on the liturgical context of the passage.

6. Write out the Epistle reading for the previous Sunday. Follow the steps under the section "Lector in Preparation" (except step 11) as though you were going to read it.

7. List several suggestions for avoiding or curtailing nervousness prior to and while reading Scripture in the worship setting.

NOTES

1. See LW 53:73–89, 84–89. In Luther's "German Mass," he explains and illustrates the method for singing the Scripture lessons.

2. Recent discussions concerning the pastor's responsibility related to the public reading of Scripture are important and have significant implication for the understanding of the pastoral office and the priestly office (1 Peter 2:5). However, this chapter addresses a broader context for the reading of Scripture—in a day school setting, group Bible class, or committee devotion.

3. Hippolytus, *Apostolic Tradition*, xii, B. Botte, ed., *Sources chrétiennes* 11 (1968): 67, mentions individuals who were given the responsibility of reading by the pastors or bishops. See also Dix and Chadwick, *Treatise on the Apostolic Tradition*, 21.

4. Justin Martyr, "First Apology," 67, in *Early Christian Fathers*, 287.

5. Tertullian, *De Praescriptione Hereticorum*, 41. See "On Prescription against Heretics," in *Ante-Nicene Fathers*, vol. 3: Latin Christianity, trans. Peter Holmes (Christian Literature Publishing, 1885. Reprint, Peabody: Hendrickson, 1995).

6. See Eusebius, *Ecclesiastical History*, Book 8, chapter 2 (319–20); "Book of Martyrs," chapter 2 (350–51), chapter 8 (361–64), chapter 11 (369); and Book 9, chapter 6 (384–85). See Migne, Patrologia Latinae VIII:731.a. In addition, Dix, *Shape of the Liturgy*, 24–25, records details from the municipal archives of a courtroom in Africa.

7. *Apostolic Church Order* 19.3.

8. Quasten, *Music and Worship*, 91, reports that lector training began around age eight.

9. Lamb, "Place of the Bible," 574–75, notes that on more than a few occasions the readers were interpreters or even translators from the Greek into Latin or Aramaic.

10. Quasten, *Music and Worship*, 107, citing Riedel, *Die Kirchenrechtsquellen des Patriarchats Alexandrien* (Leipzig: n.p., 1900), 273, "If the deacons read well they shall read the psalms, and if the priests read well they shall read the Gospel. If they do not read well the oldest lectors shall read the psalms and the deacons the Gospel."

11. Brunner, *Worship in the Name of Jesus*, 271.

12. Langer, "From Study of Scripture to a Reenactment of Sinai," 49, cites two recent Hebew studies.

These studies suggest "that, based on the evidence of the early rabbinic texts and of Philo, the idea of a cyclical and systematic reading of all of Torah did not emerge until the period following the destruction of the Temple, and its mechanics were still being clarified in the early second century."

13. Justin Martyr, "First Apology," 67, in *Early Christian Fathers*, 287.

14. *Apostolic Constitutions* (VIII, 5, 5 and II, 57, 5, respectively) in *Ante-Nicene Fathers VII: Apostolic Teaching and Constitutions*.

15. Lamb, "Place of the Bible," 571.

16. Reed, *Lutheran Liturgy* (rev. ed.), 289.

17. Pfatteicher, *Commentary*, 132, mentions a lectionary by Venarius, who was bishop of Marseilles in the fifth century. Pfatteicher also indicates that "the first complete lectionaries date from the seventh century."

18. Folsom, "Liturgical Books of the Roman Rite," 254.

19. Reed, *Lutheran Liturgy* (rev. ed.), 290.

20. Palazzo, *History of Liturgical Books*, 84, notes that "no document before the sixth century attesting to the existence of a system of readings has reached us. But there is no doubt that such a system existed."

21. Pfatteicher, *Commentary*, 132, reports that "on weekdays one Old Testament lesson and the Gospel" were read, but in Eastern churches, the practice of two New Testament readings was established by the seventh century.

22. "Order of Mass and Communion," LW 53:23–24, suggests that later adaptations of the lectionary should include a more evangelical emphasis on faith, rather than readings that emphasized works or morality.

23. Reed, *Lutheran Liturgy* (rev. ed.), 290.

24. Pfatteicher, *Commentary*, 133, notes alternative series were used as preaching texts in Bavaria, Eisenach, and Hannover.

25. Reed, *Lutheran Liturgy* (rev. ed.), 291.

26. Pfatteicher, *Commentary*, 133, reports that a three-year cycle of lessons was standard for the Augustana Lutheran Church and was preserved in the 1967 text edition of the *Service Book and Hymnal* (pp. 651–55) and the *Altar Book* (pp. 378–85). "*The Lutheran Hymnal* (1941) also provided an alternative series of Epistles and Gospels and an optional series of Old Testament readings." A Lutheran version of the three-year lectionary was produced by the Inter-Lutheran Commission on Worship in *The Church Year, Calendar and Lectionary*.

27. *Lectio continua* occurred because scrolls could only be read one column after another. The ability to "flip" to a specific section of the text was impossible until books were developed. See P. R. Ackroyd and C. F. Evans, eds., *From the Beginnings to Jerome, Cambridge History of the Bible* vol. 1 (Cambridge: Cambridge University Press, 1970), 57–60.

28. AC XXI, 1 states: "Concerning the cult of the saints our people teach that the saints are to be remembered so that we may strengthen our faith when we see how they experienced grace and how they were helped by faith. Moreover, it is taught that each person, according to his or her calling, should take the saints' good works as an example" (K-W, 58).

29. Olst, *Bible and Liturgy*, 19, 102.

30. The following steps are summarized in *Gathered Guests* Appendix B. A wide variety of resources are available for lector training. O'Brien, *Manual for Lectors*, is a classic. Liturgy Training Publications (LTP) offers an annual workbook for lectors and readers that incorporates the same suggestions offered in this chapter. In addition, LTP produces *A Well-Trained Tongue* by Ray Lonergan, as well as a three-audiocassette program entitled *Lector Training Program*. Some of the material in this section comes from the booklet by Baumer and Wroblewski, *Celebrating Liturgy*. In addition,

an audiocassette series and an accompanying book has been prepared by Rueter, *So You're Reading the Lessons.*

31. The *Concordia Self-Study Bible* (St. Louis: Concordia, 1986) provides useful historical and theological introductions to each book of the Bible. It also furnishes some notes on most individual sections of Scripture.

32. Palazzo, *History of Liturgical Books*, 89, citing Alcuin in *Carm.* 69, lines 185–88, PGH, *Po.,* vol. 1: *Aevi Karolini*, 292.

33. Two helpful guides are Severance, *Pronouncing Bible Names*, and Walker, *Harper's Bible Pronunciation Guide.*

34. *The Holy Bible: Contemporary English Version* (New York: American Bible Society, 1995) follows this punctuation: "And with this Word, God created all things. Nothing was made without the Word. Everything that was created received its life from Him, and His life gave light to everyone."

35. Marcheschi and Marcheschi, *Workbook for Lectors and Gospel Readers*, 24. This text is from the New American Bible translation.

36. See passages such as Romans 7:1; 1 Corinthians 1:16; 7:10, 12, 14; Mark 15:34.

37. See, for example, Paul's comments in Colossians 4:16 or his astonishment in Galatians 1:6; 3:1.

38. Some individuals suggest that the Scriptures speak for themselves and need no introduction. While it is true that Scripture is perspicuitous, distortions can be unwittingly communicated when texts are removed from their contexts.

39. Brokering, *Introducing the Lessons*, may serve as a model. See also Harms, *Presenting the Lessons.*

40. DuCharme and DuCharme, *Lector Becomes Proclaimer*, emphasize this phase of lectoring.

41. If lay members serve as lectors, they may wear street clothes and sit in the congregation (near the place of reading). They may carry the reading with them or use their own Bible. For festive occasions, the lector may be vested in an alb and carry the Bible or lectionary in procession. If there is a Gospel procession, the lector may carry the Bible and hold it for the presiding minister as he reads.

42. Reed, *Lutheran Liturgy* (rev. ed.), 293.

43. *Lutheran Worship*, pp. 164, 183.

44. Verse numbering was not completed until after the Reformation and did not become common until a dozen years after Luther's death. Usually chapters and verses are indicated in the worship folder, if the listener wants to study the readings later.

PART 6

VARIETY IN WORSHIP

CHAPTER 20

PLANNING FOR PRAISE

IDEAS FOR A WORSHIP COMMITTEE

A party or a big event usually necessitates planning, which involves several people. Civic holiday celebrations, such as Fourth of July parades or Memorial Day events, sometimes require several months of planning. Careful planning is also essential for those times when God's gathered guests offer Him their prayers and praises, as well as receive His gifts through Word and Sacrament.

As congregation members and leaders become more aware of the centrality of worship in parish life, they seek to provide assistance to the pastor in the area of worship planning. Pastors may desire the involvement of laypeople in the development of a more complete program of worship, yet they may not always have the time to enlist help. Therefore, many churches establish a committee or group to aid in worship planning. This chapter focuses on the rationale for such a committee, its makeup, and its tasks and goals.

PLANNING

Why should members of a congregation or a pastor make plans for worship? Isn't "doing what we've always done" adequate? First, planning is necessary because God deserves the best His gathered guests can offer. We plan because we want to express our gratitude to God (Psalm 96:7–9). Planning also ensures a service that unites God's gathered guests with His miraculous means of grace.

Second, planning affords greater benefits to the minister. Rather than falling into a routine, a committee generates ideas about what is meaningful, what is possible, and how these ideas might be applied in the local setting. Exchanging and discussing new ideas produces cross-fertilization for a richer worship experience for God's gathered guests.

Third, planning helps avoid last-minute surprises. A lack of preparation may lead to miscommunication among worship leaders and uncertainty for worshipers. Effective planning provides protocols for communicating incidental changes or instituting contingency plans if something happens. Clearly articulated plans, particularly for occasional services, eases the nervousness of most participants. For example, a well-planned wedding service can be truly worshipful for everyone involved in contrast to one that gives little evidence of planning and in which the participants are anxious throughout.

Fourth, planning enables one to grasp the bigger picture. Through conscientious planning, an annual theme for a congregation's worship services can be implemented along with particular seasonal emphases. Weekly routine in aspects of worship can provide an opportunity to demonstrate how the overall experience of worship is significant yet varied. A systematic introduction of elements of worship can be scheduled over a period of weeks or even months when there is an overall worship plan.

Fifth, planning enables variety. People like some change in worship practices. The seasons of the church year are one opportunity to plan for and highlight such changes in worship. Liturgical worship automatically provides worshipers with exposure to various worship themes and doctrinal concepts. Similarly, introducing new hymns or liturgies initiates variety.

Finally, planning can ensure changes are meaningful. Worship leaders may forget to explain the significance of some changes. Planning will help clarify why changes are being considered, what impact changes will have, and how the gathered guests may benefit from such changes. If the changes are planned, the evaluation of those changes may be more systematic. Attention to the developmental and progressive steps required for any change will provide understanding, acceptance, and appreciation of the changes in the worship practices of God's gathered guests.

THE WORSHIP COMMITTEE

Who plans worship? Most laypeople do not consider this question. In most congregations, the pastor does most of the planning. He may communicate special concerns or needs to the chancel care committee, to the board of elders, or to the music director, but the decisions and planning are chiefly on his shoulders. The pastor prepares his sermon, selects the hymns, communicates with the organist, and has the bulletin printed. If all the responsibility for variety in worship is on the busy pastor, worship may become routine. This is why a worship committee may be necessary.

In larger congregations, a pastor may meet regularly with the director of music to make long-range plans, particularly for seasonal and festival services. These meetings are opportunities to discuss the use of choirs and instruments, as well as the introduction of new hymns or liturgical elements. However, in some relationships like this, regular planning and the consideration of several perspectives is absent.

A third option is to develop a worship committee, a group of lay leaders that works with the professional staff of the congregation to offer insights and perspectives to enhance the worship life of the gathered guests.

PURPOSES OF A WORSHIP COMMITTEE

The following areas offer opportunities for a worship committee to serve in a congregation, but not all may apply in a particular location.

Enhance worship experiences

A worship committee can provide opportunities to enrich the worship life of a congregation as it looks to improve positive worship practices, expand occasions for worship, and promote greater understanding of worship practices.

Educate congregation on worship

People want to understand what they are doing in worship and why they are doing it. Occasionally, worship practices are misunderstood or not fully appreciated. A worship committee can use numerous avenues to teach the congregation about worship, train them in new practices, or introduce different parts of the liturgy or a new hymnbook.

Provide variety through resources

No one person can keep up with the ever-increasing number of worship resources available to the church. A worship committee can assign members to watch for new resources and bring them to the attention of the committee, the music director, or the pastor.

Use the congregation's worship resources

Many individuals in a congregation have untapped abilities, whether designing bulletin covers, providing a solo, or assembling worship folders. The worship committee may keep track of individuals and their talents and invite them to participate in special worship services. The committee may encourage young people to develop specialized skills for church service. Thus the worship committee provides a means to discover and use unique gifts.

Serve as liaison for worship concerns

Almost every organization or group in a congregation is involved in worship experiences—whether it is a devotion at a meeting or active participation in a special service. Coordinating the activities of the various entities requires time and information. A worship committee can offer its services to other groups and encourage congregational organizations to become more active in the worship life of the parish. If concerns arise, members of a committee can deal with them thoughtfully and constructively with the pastoral staff.

Evaluate worship programs

Acolytes, lay readers, choirs, and musicians—as well as banner preparation, bulletin collating, drama practice, fine arts performances, and prayer ministry coordination—require supervision. A worship committee can evaluate worship-related activities in light of their effectiveness and applicability to the congregation's mission. Such evaluations may be conducted annually and reported to the board of elders or congregational assembly.

Assist elders and the chancel care committee

Policies and guidelines for occasional services are important for a congregation. While the elders and the chancel care committee have specific responsibility for the worship life of a congregation, a worship committee can help groups create a unified position on worship policies and practices. Continuing evaluation of these policies by a third-party committee, such as a worship committee, maintains a professional attitude and outlook for the whole congregation. The worship committee can also serve as a communications liaison with the congregation.

Regulate instrumental offerings

Congregations are using a greater variety of musical instruments as part of the worship service. A worship committee can review the use of musical instruments in a congregation's total worship program. Particularly, the committee can regulate requests and supervise instrument maintenance and repairs. Although this is often the responsibility of a music director, a worship committee may be in the best position to handle the supervision of instrumental music in a church service. This purpose is tied closely with the final purpose of a worship committee.

Serve as worship leaders' advocates

Both pastors and music directors need a support group. A worship committee can serve as a sounding board for the pastor and the director of music as they consider changes or improvements to the worship life of a congregation. A worship committee can be the eyes, ears, and supportive voices for the worship leaders in a congregation. Whether large or small, an understanding committee can evaluate suggestions and encourage worship leaders as they seek to serve the Lord and His gathered guests in worship.

CONSTITUTING A WORSHIP COMMITTEE

The primary responsibility for and participation in a worship committee will reside with the music director and the pastor. Even when only the pastor and music director plan the worship activities of a congregation, other laypeople may be involved occasionally. Often, a member of the board of elders sits on a worship committee because that board customarily has constitutional responsibility for the spiritual life, and particularly the worship life, of a congregation. This representative serves as liaison to the elders by communicating plans and ideas for the board's approval, as well as communicating concerns or suggestions from the board of elders to the worship committee.

A member of the chancel care committee or altar guild may serve on a worship committee because the worship committee's plans impact the activity of the chancel care committee. The enthusiastic support and willing service of the chancel care committee is invaluable for worship planning. Thus a minimal worship committee will include the pastor, director of music, an elder, and a member of the chancel care committee.

A larger committee may be advisable as the work expands and more ideas are implemented. If a congregation has a day school, a teacher may be enlisted to address the needs of children in worship and to facilitate the involvement of children's choirs or other potential means for the young people of the congregation to be part of the church service. Many teachers also have some training in the area of worship and may offer suggestions of a more general nature.

A parent of a young child may be a valuable addition to a worship committee.[1] Young parents are often frustrated by worship services that require a printed order of service because they are unable to follow ever-changing services. Seating for young families can be regularly evaluated and changes made as necessary. "Cry rooms" and baby-sitting services during worship times can be considered from a parent's perspective. Other items of local concern may be addressed with a parent who feels comfortable in such a role.

The young people of a congregation often have profound insights into the church's worship life. Creativity and enthusiasm abound as young people are enlisted to provide ideas to expand worship life. Training in the heritage of Lutheran worship often deepens commitment to the Lutheran legacy of liturgical worship. A young musician or youth leader who participates on the worship committee can communicate the church's dedication to involving the whole faith community in worship.

There are always a few people who dislike change. Asking a "silent leader" of the congregation to serve on the worship committee helps build bridges to various groups in the congregation. A "silent leader" is an individual who may not have an official leadership role but whose words and actions are followed by a majority of congregation members. This individual's service on the worship committee communicates a respect for tradition and offers a unique perspective to changes suggested by other committee members. A leader of this stature and demeanor serves both as a check on the committee and as an effective link to the congregation.

The makeup of the worship committee, though not representing the exact composition of the congregation, represents the needs of the whole congregation. Because the committee works closely with the pastoral staff and musicians, the committee may be appointed by the pastor with the approval of the congregation. Whether a change in the congregation's constitution is necessary depends on the congregation's bylaws.[2] No matter the official relationship to the voting members of a congregation, the worship committee should receive the support and encouragement of the entire congregation.

The Worship Committee's First Year

The first few months of a worship committee's existence are spent learning more about worship. However, this effort to learn and grow never stops completely; rather, it is a regular item of business for the committee. A schedule of topics ensures that as new members join the committee, material is covered or reviewed for the benefit of everyone. The following topics may be developed into specific presentations or as items for evaluation when reviewing worship practices:

- The biblical precedents of worship practices
- Church architecture and symbolism
- Customs associated with the sacraments
- Parts of the liturgy
- Meaning of the sacraments
- Nuances of occasional services
- Luther and worship
- Church or ecclesiastical art
- Musical forms and styles
- The design and construction of vestments

Depending on local tastes, personal interests, congregational needs, and collective abilities, other concerns and issues may be generated by the committee.

A major project for any new worship committee is to determine the worship needs of the congregation. A survey may be prepared to help ascertain the perception of worship practices in the congregation. Questions related to the understanding of the liturgy and particularly of the distinctive practices associated with Lutheran worship would be appropriate and beneficial. The survey should be non-threatening to worship leaders because it is an opportunity to gain feedback from the gathered guests.

When planning worship events, the committee observes the church year. Some congregations fail to see in this liturgical structure the opportunities for celebrating specific emphases. For example, in the second year of the three-year series of readings, the Sixteenth Sunday after Pentecost includes the Gospel account of Jesus healing a deaf mute (Mark 7:31–37). On that Sunday, congregations could display resources about deaf ministry. A special element in the worship services that day could provide information on this vital and specialized ministry of God's people.

Adequate planning begins six months to a year before major events so general themes and texts may be communicated to everyone involved in the congregation's worship life.[3] Some pastors meet with the music director and worship committee for an annual planning session. Others work on a seasonal basis. Once a general plan has been set, weekly details may be carried out more easily, efficiently, and effectively.

OTHER FUNCTIONS OF A WORSHIP COMMITTEE

In addition to the basic activities already mentioned, an important function of a worship committee may be to articulate a theme for each Sunday. A theme enables all participants in a worship service to understand the focus and to prepare their own parts. Although most congregations use the three-year lectionary series, worship themes may vary considerably as different texts receive emphasis. The pastor may set this theme, but the committee may communicate the theme to the congregation and work on the details of its implementation in the service.

Coupled with the task of establishing the theme is determining if members' artistic talents may be used to express further the appointed theme. Artistic expressions may include a banner, a hymn written on the theme, or an artistic rendering of the theme for a bulletin cover. Thus the committee may incorporate the fine arts into the worship service. These artistic expressions enable the whole congregation to glorify God as they use unique talents and gifts.

music

A worship committee can provide invaluable assistance to the director of music by coordinating the musical elements of a service. Particularly for festival services, sufficient time is required to prepare choral and instrumental music. The worship committee may help the music director establish schedules for all musical groups to ensure sufficient preparation and practice. The worship committee may assist the music director in other ways, depending on local situations.

Variety in the structure of Lutheran liturgical worship is often a key concern of the worship committee. Besides the variety of readings available in the lectionary, seasonal and thematic hymns may be used. There also are various settings of services that congregations may learn over the course of several months or years. For example, Matins and Morning Prayer may be used instead of an abridgment of the Divine Service. The committee may also consider omitting some parts of the ordinary or exchanging a regular part of the order of service with a hymnic setting.

Congregations are using an increasingly far-reaching variety of worship materials. Some churches print out the whole service in their worship folders so the folder looks like a Sunday newspaper insert. Others print an outline of the service that directs the worshiper to the hymnal. The worship committee may ensure the gathered guests do not experience "an octopus service"—one that requires more than two hands. Juggling a service folder, hymnal, songbook, and another book with the order of service is nearly impossible and will frustrate most worshipers. As the committee plans services, it may want to select all worship elements—order of service, hymns, etc.—from the same resource.

The preparation of special services for congregational celebrations may be expected of a worship committee. Whether a confirmation service or a series of midweek Advent or Lenten services, the worship committee may provide the leadership and the personnel to plan, organize, and implement these services. Anniversary celebrations are another joyous opportunity to commission special hymns and litanies and adapt the Divine Service. Evening services are useful as "experimental" services in preparation for these more significant celebrations. As Hugo Gehrke has wisely recommended:

> Experimentation in worship can be worthwhile, if carefully prepared and carefully executed. To do so we need to test our ideas against what the church has tried, retained, or discarded, and ask why in each instance. By knowing what has been done and by asking why, we learn better how to serve our own times. It helps us clarify our intentions by cross-checking them with a vast file of experimentation over 20 centuries and six continents.[4]

Congregations are often open to such experimental services, if they also can return

Only the Big - time!

to the older forms. Often a congregation will try an experimental service for six months, then keep the new service as one option for regular worship practices.

It is best not to adopt whole settings and services from other sources or congregations. Instead, a worship committee adapts the order of service to suit the local congregation and its abilities. In recent years, some congregations have produced model services that other congregations adopt *en masse*, leading to confusion and frustration on the part of the worshipers. This is why Lutheran hymnals provide services and settings that promote the same confession of faith but with various approaches for "personalization" to the local setting.

Several years ago, Hugo Gehrke advised: "It is essential that the planners prepare the services, but it is even more important that the planners prepare the congregation."[5] Such preparation usually takes the form of nurturing education and thorough communication, which may be accomplished through bulletin inserts, parish newsletters, and parish Web sites. Letting the congregation know about plans for and opportunities in worship activities gives each member a sense of ownership and partnership. Committee members who are sensitive listeners bring back positive and negative comments from the congregation to the committee. When done well, a worship committee creates an openness and excitement about worship. Discussions for improving the worship life of the congregation involve two-way communication.[6]

All committee members may share the responsibilities for worship services or activities, or each member may be assigned an area of special interest. If more help is needed on a project, task forces or ad hoc subcommittees may be created. The chair of the worship committee ensures that all members are involved without burdening any particular member. Although the worship committee is often comprised of volunteers, opportunities to attend worship workshops may be provided for committee members, as well as for the congregation's professional staff. Such training enhances the congregation's worship life.

The worship committee also may be responsible for securing available resources and worship aids for the congregation, including the maintenance and replacement of hymnals and other worship books and materials. This assignment necessitates keeping up to date on available resources. For example, some publishers offer a subscription service for new music or worship resources. Professional journals provide book reviews and critiques of worship materials and information on workshops.[7]

A worship committee may discover its tasks dovetail with those of other committees or organizations of the congregation. For example, though the altar guild is usually responsible for preparing the sanctuary for worship, the worship committee may also check the sound system, prepare contingency plans with ushers, analyze lighting, and monitor the temperature of the building. Thus the worship committee may establish a cooperative annual project, such as working with the chancel care committee to make a banner, design new paraments, prepare chrismons, or even make Communion bread. The worship committee also may work with the board of elders to purchase a processional cross and torches, prepare a new liturgical setting, or prepare guidelines for wedding services.

Because worship is a central activity of God's gathered guests, cooperation and communication are vital to a vibrant worship life. The worship committee has the privilege to participate in this important area of a Lutheran church's life.

Some Questions to Consider

1. Which of the six reasons for worship planning is most convincing? Why? Which is least convincing? Why? What other reasons may be given for preparing a long-range plan for the worship life of a congregation?

2. What is the minimum size and composition of a worship committee? If you were given the task of developing a worship committee in your congregation, whom would you invite to participate and why?

3. Which of the nine purposes for a worship committee do you consider to be the most important? Why?

4. Why are the first few months of a worship committee's existence so important? What may be accomplished during this time? What should never be discontinued?

5. What optional activities may a worship committee undertake?

6. How can the concept of "experimental" worship services be an advantage? What problems could develop?

7. Use the Worship Worksheet (Appendix B) to design a Reformation Day service.

Notes

1. Becker, Morgenthaler, and Bertels, "Children in Worship," *Lutheran Education* 133.4, 203–4. A congregation member could be asked to provide free baby-sitting while the parent attends meetings.

2. See *Gathered Guests* chapter 18 on the chancel care committee. Booklets mentioned in the notes have suggestions for constitutional changes that congregations may make to establish a worship committee.

3. Pfatteicher and Messerli, *Manual on the Liturgy*, 162–65, provide a checklist for the major festivals from Ash Wednesday through Pentecost as a model for further planning.

4. Gehrke, *Worshiping God with Joy*, 13.

5. Gehrke, *Worshiping God with Joy*, 13.

6. The worship committee may use the worksheet in Appendix C to communicate more formally with all entities involved in worship.

7. *Worship*; *Bride of Christ: The Journal of Lutheran Liturgical Renewal*; *Liturgy, the Journal of the Liturgical Conference*; and *The Hymn: A Journal of Congregational Song* are professional journals for worship leaders. Contact information is as follows: *Worship* (contact at The Liturgical Press, Collegeville, MN 56321 or http://www.sja.osb.org/worship); *Bride of Christ* (contact at Lutheran Liturgical Renewal, Inc., c/o St. Augustine's House, P.O. Box 125, Oxford, MI 48371 or email STAugHouse@aol.com); *Liturgy* (contact at The Liturgical Conference, 8750 Georgia Ave., Suite 123, Silver Spring, MD 20910-3621 or http://www.litconf.com; or email litconf@aol.com); and *The Hymn* (contact at The Hymn Society of Boston University School of Theology, 745 Commonwealth Ave., Boston, MA 02215-1401 or email hymnsoc@bu.edu).

Devotions

CHAPTER 21

WORSHIPING IN SMALL GROUPS

One of the most common worship experiences for Christians is small-group devotions, whether in a family setting or at a congregational meeting. Some of these devotional times are more formal, some are less formal, but all involve God's people as they gather to hear His Word of Law and Gospel and to respond with prayer, praise, and thanksgiving.

Even devotions can be prepared within a Lutheran liturgical structure and context. The purpose of this devotional form is the clear exposition of God's Word. When God's Word is used appropriately in this setting, it shines forth in all its purity, emphasizing the biblical message without distracting the worshiper. The participant in a devotional setting will hear a clear proclamation of Law and God's love and forgiveness in Christ. To prepare a meaningful worship setting for a small group, consider the purpose or goal of the devotional time, the size and the makeup of the group, and the available resources. Each factor will affect the type of devotion prepared, as well as the structure of the activity.

WHAT'S THE PURPOSE?

When preparing for a devotional time, it is best to clearly understand the purpose of the devotion. Some devotional times are for personal spiritual growth; others build up the body of believers and set the tone for further growth. Family devotions around the table serve as an anchor in the home and as a base for Christian living. Other settings have other purposes. The setting may determine the format of the devotion, as well as the content of the devotional message.

Will the devotion open or close a meeting? Will it occur at some other point in a gathering? An opening devotion may focus the event and may include a specific request for God's presence and blessing on the activities. An opening devotion often addresses the theme established for the event by the chair of the meeting or by the planning committee. A closing devotion, on the other hand, may help the group see God's hand in all their activities in addition to reiterating the theme. If conflict has occurred, a closing devotion can include confession and forgiveness.

The purpose or task of the group also may play a role in the preparation of a devotion. If the devotion will be part of a meeting of an established congregational committee, a bond already exists as members address the task assigned to the committee. These tasks may naturally lead to devotional themes. Special needs groups also provide rich opportunities to address God's Word to particular concerns within a devotional framework. In these devotional settings, God's Word of grace and forgiving love in Christ can be clearly presented in an appropriate context.

A well-prepared devotion encourages participation through the use of songs or hymns or by including spoken prayers or litanies. In this way, the group shares in its bond as God's guests gathered together in His kingdom of grace.

GROUP SIZE

Perhaps the most significant factor in devotion preparation, and the one that immediately affects worship, is group size. There are at least four sizes, each with different features.

FAMILY

A family setting features an obviously informal structure as members gather in the home. Typically, all or most of the family members participate in the devotion. Even the youngest children may fold their hands for the prayer. This may be the setting in which a child learns the Lord's Prayer or the Apostles' Creed. Older children may participate by reading prayers or Scripture passages. Usually, a parent or other adult is the leader, but various members of the family read, sing, or pray. If songs are included in a family devotion, they are familiar to the members. In this setting and group size, formal responses may be minimal but natural, such as voicing an "amen" after a prayer, Invocation, or Benediction. A conversational style predominates in a family devotion setting. Liturgy, as discussed earlier in this book, is probably minimal in a family group, though a general structure to the devotion may be evident.[1]

Although "family" may refer to a family setting, the concept may apply to any small-group devotion. Bible study groups, as well as other gatherings of fewer than 10 people, could be considered a "family" group. This size offers great flexibility in format, yet it challenges the devotion leader to prepare adequately. Spontaneity is fine, but lack of preparation can speak volumes about the group's spiritual depth.

CAMPFIRE

Most people have had some experience as part of a group gathered around a campfire. As with the family group, a devotional time around a campfire is informal. Most participants will join in the devotion, whether by singing, responding to the message, or praying. The "campfire" is distinguished from a "family" setting by a clearer differentiation between leaders and participants. A campfire setting often has a devotional leader, as well as a song leader. There also may be an instrument (usually a guitar) to aid in the singing. Seating in a campfire setting is typically directed toward a single focal point.

Although leadership may be shared by the song leader, readers, and speakers, each individual is responsible only for his or her portion of the devotion. There also are some elements in a campfire devotional that are more formal. Songsheets or written responses enable worshipers to participate more fully. This requires some planning, preparation, and coordination among the leaders.

A typical "campfire" group involves between 10 and 50 people. The larger the group, the more formal certain aspects of the devotion may become, which requires increased coordination among the worship leaders. Worship resources, such as hymnals or songbooks, may be necessary, and some training may be required before everyone in the group can participate fully. In a congregational environment, a "campfire" approach may be evident in a devotion at a voters' assembly or a congregational leadership retreat.

MISSION

As groups increase in size, the structure of the devotion contributes to the level of participation. For example, worship in a mission congregation follows a clear structure, yet a comfortable informality may be evident as the gathered guests assemble in a somewhat casual context. Such a "mission" style may involve between 50 and 150 people. In this group, leadership is evident as participants sit in a predetermined arrangement, either facing the same direction or positioned in a semicircle. A pastor or devotional leader directs the devotional time, and specialized tasks, such as music leadership or reading from Scripture, are unmistakable. Despite these more formal arrangements, there is still a looseness to the overall structure and a flexibility for spontaneous adaptations.

Because participation is strongly desired in a mission devotional setting, there is a structure, including the praying of the Lord's Prayer and the confession of a creed. Songbooks may be used, though there may be some songs that have become a common element and the members know them by heart. A printed folder may be used so everyone can participate in responsive readings or songs, though some worshipers will participate more fully than others. In this setting, personal preference may lead some people to be passive observers.

The "mission" setting may apply not only to a congregation but also to any larger group. Chapel services in day schools or devotions at professional conferences often reflect the characteristics of a mission setting.

ASSEMBLY

The final size to consider when discussing devotions is a large assembly of more than 150 people. In a setting of this size, a formal distinction between leader and participants is evident, whether through specific clothing or the position of the leader in relation to the participants. The leader may call the assembly together for the devotional time, which takes place in an environment with formal seating that most often faces the leader. The devotion, usually as a printed order, follows a specific setting that is established and directed by the leader. Group participation may be limited to specifically selected songs or hymns and speaking responsive readings.

The characteristics of these groups may vary, but the basic categories will help a devotional leader plan for the various settings. One rule of thumb: As the size of the group increases, the formality of the devotion will increase to encourage more participation by group members. This growth toward more formal worship mimics the process in early Christian history: Churches grew from family groups in the intimacy of the home to large formal assemblies in grand cathedrals.

In addition to the size of the group, a devotion leader should evaluate the affiliation or commonality of the group. Most significant in this evaluation is the age of the group's members. A grade-school devotion will be far different from a devotion prepared for a senior citizens' group. Familiarity with a variety of resources helps a devotional leader prepare appropriately. For example, favorite hymns may be meaningful to older Christians, while teaching a new song with hand gestures may be appropriate for an early childhood setting.

LITURGICAL EXPECTATIONS

When planning a devotion, many people are afraid to use even the simplest liturgy. Thus a devotion often becomes nothing more than a Bible reading, a few comments, and, occasionally, a song. If participation in the devotion is important, then it is expedient to increase the liturgical structure as the number of people in the group increases. In larger groups, liturgical settings frequently enhance devotional occasions. Morning Prayer and Evening Prayer are particularly useful for devotional settings, and *Lutheran Worship* offers a simplified form of these services for family or small-group settings.[2] Devotional leaders may explain that Christians throughout the world use these services and that participation in these historic services unites participants with many other believers in a unique expression of Christian unity. Compline (Prayer at the Close of the Day) may prove beneficial as a closing for a meeting in which conflict has occurred. As noted in chapter 16, Compline emphasizes reconciliation and God's continued presence as His gathered guests depart.[3]

Other liturgical elements may be used in various devotional settings. An Invocation and Benediction as regular parts of a devotion reflect the trinitarian faith. Similarly, a creed and the Lord's Prayer may be regular parts of a group devotion. Prayers may be in a litany or collect form, depending on the desired level of involvement by the gathered guests. Scripture readings may be selected to fit the theme of the event or to follow the liturgical structure of the church year. Music also may enhance the devotional time as worshipers unite their voices in songs, hymns, and spiritual songs.

All this should be understood as the setting for the jewel of God's Word and the message of His grace in Christ. The devotional time should not distract from God's Word; rather, it should provide a setting in which the gathered guests hear their Host speak. In that light, remember that liturgical worship directs participants to see God's gracious hand in their activities and experience the power of God's Word. A liturgical devotional setting opens worshipers to the continuing activity of the Holy Spirit as He works through the means of grace.

SMALL-GROUP AND FAMILY DEVOTIONS

In developing devotions for small groups, liturgical elements provide teaching moments about the broader Christian community.[4] Thus the devotional leader may go beyond the use of hymns and seek to include other liturgical elements. A confession of sins from the Divine Service or from Compline may be used regularly in a family setting during Lent to reinforce the theme of repentance and forgiveness. The Service of Light from Evening Prayer may be an appropriate Advent devotion setting for a family, especially when an Advent wreath is used. With repeated use, a family will become comfortable praying litanies with appropriate responses, which will enable each family member to offer his or her own petitions.

It is important to follow the laws regarding copyright. The general rule is that the copyright holder has exclusive rights to the original material for the author's or creator's lifetime plus seventy years.[5] Permission must be obtained from the copyright holder for any reproduction during this time. Thus devotion or worship planners should be aware of the legal implications of duplicating any material for a worship service or devotional setting. This is particularly important as it applies to music. Photocopies for accompanists or reproduction of texts as song sheets, transparencies, or slides is prohibited unless permission is secured prior to use.

Some worship materials are in the public domain, which means either the legal time limit has elapsed and the copyright was not renewed or the material was never copyrighted. Usually, though not always, the absence of a copyright notice indicates the material is in the public domain.

Occasionally churches or worship leaders try to apply the fair use doctrine to the use of copyrighted materials in a worship setting. This legal exception, which the courts have developed to permit limited use of copyrighted materials for scholarly critiques or academic purposes, does not apply to the worship setting.[6] Therefore, it is best to seek permission or at least legal advice prior to any performance of or reprinting of copyrighted music or texts.[7] Within the past decades, the Church Copyright Licensing International (CCLI)[8] has provided a service that covers many congregational settings. It provides affordable and legal permission to duplicate certain worship resources for local congregations.[9]

SOME QUESTIONS TO CONSIDER

1. How does group size affect the structure of a devotional liturgy? Why is some structure necessary for most group devotional times?

2. Compare and contrast a "family" devotion with an "assembly" devotion. Give an example of each from your own experience.

3. Explain what is meant by a "campfire" devotion. How does this differ from a "mission" devotion?

4. Chart the relationship between group size, involvement of leaders and participants, availability of a printed order, and seating options.

5. Why would some liturgical elements be beneficial in a small-group setting? List two possible liturgical orders that could be used in a small-group setting. How might they be used with a group of 15 youth leaders?

6. Of what copyright restrictions should worship leaders be aware? What is CCLI?

7. Design a small-group devotion using the guidelines in Appendix C.

NOTES

1. For example, the devotional booklet *Portals of Prayer* offers a setting for family use that follows a liturgical format:

   Leader: In the name of the Father and of the ✠ Son and of the Holy Spirit.

   All: Amen.

   Silent Prayer

   Leader: The Lord be with you.

   All: And also with you.

   A *Psalm* may be read by the leader or by the family in response.

   The Scripture Reading

   The Meditation

   The Prayer

   The Lord's Prayer

   Leader: Let us bless the Lord.

   All: Thanks be to God.

   Leader: The almighty and merciful God, the Father, the ✠ Son, and the Holy Spirit, bless us and keep us.

   All: Amen.

   In his Small Catechism, Luther gave suggestions on how the head of the family should lead devotions. See Luther's Morning Blessing and Evening Blessing in K-W, 363–64.

2. See *Lutheran Worship*, pp. 236ff., 250ff. The rubrics for the simplified version are identified by a small circle.

3. See *Lutheran Worship*, p. 263ff.

4. Appendix D offers "Guidelines for Constructing a Family or Small-Group Devotion." The seven points guide preparation of a devotion for various settings. Notice that the incorporation of liturgical elements is encouraged, even in family or small-group devotions.

5. The complete United States Copyright Law is available from the Copyright Office, Library of Congress, Washington, D.C. 20559.

6. Performance of material purchased legally is allowed.

7. The Church Music Publishers Association, P. O. Box 158992, Nashville, TN 37215, provides a 24-hour hotline for churches. In addition, the American Society of Composers, Authors and Publishers provides complete information on licensing performances or other copyright information. They may be contacted at ASCAP Building, One Lincoln Plaza, New York, NY 10023.

8. For further information, contact Christian Copyright Licensing International, 17201 NE Sacramento Street, Portland, OR 97230.

9. Damage recovery by a copyright holder can result in fines of as much as $50,000 per infringement.

CHAPTER 22

VARIETY IN WORSHIP

When Lutherans gather for worship, various orders of service are used. Much variety is possible both within these orders and within the larger tradition of Lutheran worship practice. Three questions need to be asked when we speak of variety in worship: Why? How? and What?

WHY SEEK VARIETY?

Why should variety in worship be considered? Why consider changing the practice of worship, particularly in a Lutheran liturgical context? There are at least seven reasons why people consider variety in worship.

First, God comes to us in myriad ways. Martin Luther described several ways the Gospel itself is present and presented to God's gathered guests: God's Good News comes to us through sermons and the sacraments of Holy Baptism, Holy Absolution, and Holy Communion. In addition, God's gracious promises are communicated and proclaimed through scripturally based hymns, personal and corporate Bible readings, and "the mutual conversation and consolation of brothers and sisters."[1] Ultimately, God's self-revelation is clearest in the message of Christ, who came to this world to suffer, die, and rise again. This variety of expression of God's love causes His creatures to pause and consider His incomprehensible ways (Romans 11:33–36; 1 Corinthians 2:16).

Second, people want to respond to such a gloriously loving God in as many ways as possible. Looking at biblical references to worship, one finds many different customs by which believers responded to God. Some people were quiet, contemplatively pondering God's blessings (1 Kings 19:12; Psalm 46:10). Others liked to interact with people so they could experience God's blessings tangibly (2 Samuel 6:14; Hebrews 10:25). Worship provides opportunities for people to respond to God's grace in diverse yet understandable ways. God invites us to explore these responses to His grace so we may interact fully with the vehicles God uses to come to His people.

Third, the full scope of the Gospel becomes evident in new settings of Word and Sacrament. Luther wrote two orders of Holy Communion and several others for special occasions in his ministry.[2] In each service Luther ensured that the Wittenberg congregation heard God's forgiving grace in Christ and was able to respond appropriately with prayers and praise. North American Lutheran experience also demonstrates that there are numerous ways to communicate the Gospel in musical settings.[3] For example, *Lutheran Worship* provides various liturgical settings and orders of service for congregational and private use. In all this diversity of expression, however, the Gospel is central in the liturgies as they focus the thoughts of the gathered guests on God's revealed Word and the Sacrament of the Altar.

Fourth, changing times require changing approaches. Society has become increasingly multicultural. Cultural variety often results in a more pluralistic outlook. Thus the church is compelled to provide diversity within its broader sense of continuity. The worship environment is the place in which a Christian can see and hear God's gracious constancy, as well as His love for all people of the world. European hymn texts and Caribbean musical settings may be blended. Irish and African texts and tunes have entered Lutheran hymnals, which have a predominantly European lineage. Despite these changes, the overall structure of the liturgy, the Christian Mass-form, remains constant because the confessional orthodoxy of Lutheran doctrine is manifested most clearly in such a setting.

Fifth, "spoiled" sinners need their "tastes" awakened. Regrettably, sinful humanity craves change. "Boredom!" is often the cry from the pew and from the sacristy. Sometimes changes are made "for change's sake," in which case the results can be disastrous.[4] Changes in style may and often do affect the substance of worship. While this may be good, unexpected side effects may result when worship activities imported from other Christian traditions become a routine part of a Lutheran worship service. Some worship planners suggest that changes should be made because people feel uncomfortable with certain traditional Lutheran practices—such as the confession of sins—and desire alternatives, such as praise songs. However, most parents know that a steady diet of sweets, though desired, will have negative long-term effects on young children. Even variety can become boring. College students may appreciate change, yet when given a diet of constant change, they will ask for more continuity.[5]

Sixth, carefully planned and executed changes in the worship life of a congregation can make "the same" more meaningful and make the old become "new."

Most congregations experience this kind of liturgical variety throughout the year as they observe changes in the church calendar. For example, the tradition of eliminating the *alleluia* during Lent adds significance to the Easter proclamation of joyful praises to God for His victory in Christ. The "old" *alleluia* becomes a joyful "new song" during the Easter season. Similarly, many Lutheran congregations have discovered that the introduction of *Lutheran Worship* has made the occasional use of hymns or services from *The Lutheran Hymnal* a refreshing change of pace.

Finally, variety enables the gathered guests to experience other Christian expressions of God's grace and forgiving love. There is a wealth of material from the rich and diverse resources of the church's traditions. Robin Leaver discerningly states: "Multiculturalism, rightly understood, has chronological as well as geographical dimensions, and our worship is enriched when we sing such hymns of faith that originate in earlier times and under different conditions than our own."[6] Lutherans have been boldly eclectic in their use of various Christian traditions. For example, a survey of hymns in any Lutheran hymnal produces a diverse list of material from an enormous variety of historical sources and national origins. From early Christian hymns to contemporary compositions, Christian artists have produced serviceable resources for Christian worshipers.[7] Minimal research of the history of Christianity will provide a wealth of material used by, for, and with Christian communities, including simple prayers and songs and extravagant seasonal or festival services.[8]

How Is Variety Introduced?

There seem to be at least seven ways in which variety in worship can be introduced and used beneficially. Some of these suggestions come from experience, others from conversations with veteran worship planners.

Most variations in a Lutheran worship service come within the structure of the traditional and ecumenical liturgy. Familiar and unfamiliar elements can be drawn together and experienced in new combinations. This is the logic behind the Propers in the regular Sunday worship service. This variety within continuity is also evident in the choices offered at various places in the liturgy. Hymns may replace some parts of the liturgy, such as the Hymn of Praise. Some congregations follow a pattern described as a "blended service" in which more contemporary-sounding songs are incorporated into the basic liturgical structure. By providing some variety within the conventional liturgy, worshipers may experience new songs and hymns, as well as a variety of scriptural forms of the Gospel, within the continuity of the grandest Christian tradition.

Variety in worship may be provided by engaging the congregation in an experiment.[9] "Experimental services" are usually new orders of worship or even new hymnal materials that the congregation is asked to study for a period of time. The congregation eventually will be given the opportunity to accept or reject the service. This gives worshipers a true sense of Gospel freedom to study the new form without feeling that it is being imposed on them.

When introducing new elements in a service or a new liturgy, some worship leaders forget to repeat the new element so the novelty becomes comfortable. Repetition establishes the new item in the memory of the worshipers. Several methods may be used to accomplish this repetition: The new element may be used as part of the choir's repertoire; the organist may use the melody as a recessional; or a children's choir may sing a stanza for a service. It is best for a new hymn to appear in a service at least quarterly for one year so the congregation accepts it as an accustomed element of worship life.[10]

When new orders of service are introduced, options within the schedule of congregational services may be offered so no one feels "forced" to worship in a new way. For example, a congregation with two Sunday services that wants to introduce Morning Prayer as an alternate order for Sunday mornings may offer it at one service and the traditional liturgy at the other. If done with care, those participating in the new order of service will naturally communicate their positive experiences with those attending the traditional service.[11]

Another practical aspect to consider when introducing variety in a congregation's worship practice is the use of the festival or seasonal services of Lent and Advent. Most people expect something different in these services. Particularly during the midweek services, most worshipers are open to the use of Vespers, Evening Prayer, or Compline. Other orders of service or unique worship elements may be used also, such as alternate hymn settings.

Finally, despite changes to the liturgy, it is imperative that the Gospel remains central. Any innovations in worship should be understood as another means to communicate God's love in Christ. For example the Gospel content may be explained prior to singing a new hymn. In the same way, the Gospel focus of a new liturgy may be demonstrated as the service is learned. The incorporation of other cultural or historical elements may be more readily accepted if they reflect particular ways of telling the Good News. Legislated or coerced changes typically result only in discord, and the Gospel message may be lost. But when variety is considered as an opportunity to speak the Gospel in a new way, God's gathered guests will see tremendous results.

What Kind of Variety?

Resources abound for providing variety in worship. The real need is for an appropriate critique of the materials to discern the soundness of the theology and their usefulness within a confessional liturgical tradition. Too frequently, worship materials prepared and distributed by corporations or prominent congregations contradict the theology of confessional Lutheranism. Conversely, some materials simply cannot be sung or are unusable in a typical congregational context. Seven areas should be considered when evalutating resources that provide variety in worship.

First, the primary resource for any variety in Lutheran worship is the church's approved worship books. *Lutheran Worship* provides a wealth of material for a variety of worship experiences within the Lutheran liturgical tradition. From hymn selections to liturgical settings, congregational worship planners have much from which to choose to offer variety to worshipers.

Within the structure of the liturgy, one can incorporate variety by selecting from the options provided in the texts of the Divine Service, such as the use of alternate Hymns of Praise, Offertories, or Post-Communion Canticles. In addition, the omission or substitution of some parts of the service may emphasize key parts of the service or the liturgical year.[12] For example, Divine Service I is a modification of the Order of Holy Communion from *The Lutheran Hymnal*. Therefore, the use of the older service may provide variety. In addition, there are distinct differences between Divine Service I and Divine Service II. Divine Service II was prepared specifically so two settings of the service could be offered for a variety of musical experiences in the congregation's worship life. Similarly, Divine Service III illustrates the possibilities of a hymnic setting proposed by Luther in his German Mass. This service involves numerous hymns in a setting that is adaptable to cultural and national situations.

The offices in *Lutheran Worship* also provide variety. Not only are the orders of Matins and Vespers included as nonsacramental services, but the modifications of these offices (Morning Prayer and Evening Prayer) may contribute to a congregation's liturgical repertoire. The service of Compline, a service that Luther cherished, has been reintroduced into hymnbooks and may be used in various worship settings. Modifications may be made to these services, but such changes should not be made only in the interests of time. When portions of the liturgy are deleted to "condense" the service, this may prevent the congregation from joining in the ancient songs of the church and experiencing the full richness of worshiping with the body of Christ.

The second source for worship materials is synodically published materials because they also will be theologically sound. For example, *Proclaim*[13] continues to be one of the best references for worship materials both in its content and form. This resource offers ideas on musical settings and incorporating variety within the liturgy throughout the whole year. *Hymnal Supplement 98* is another resource that can lend liturgical and hymnic variety. The advantage of such resources is that the LCMS has approved the doctrinal content. Although these supplements are not intended to serve as the main diet of the gathered guests, they can provide variety in worship.

A third source for variety of worship materials is in supplemental worship resources prepared by various organizations and available in printed form or on the Internet. *Creative Worship* is one such resource that provides ideas and formats for the worship service.[14] Orders of service, as well as hymn and psalm settings, are increasingly available through Web sites or on a subscription basis specifically designed to introduce variety in a congregational setting.

However, adopting another person's creative ideas into a different setting may not always prove successful. For example, a worship planner will want to understand clearly the theme of a service imported from another congregation before using it for a particular Sunday. Where adaptation is needed (which is typical), it should be done carefully by the worship planner to ensure that the sermon matches the theme of the pericopes, liturgical settings, and hymns. Adoption of a thematic service does not normally save time, but it may provide a unique worship service. In addition to the time required, some services or worship ideas borrowed from other congregations may have questionable theological content, depending on the source. Biblical integrity and Lutheran theological orthodoxy should be clearly exemplified in the worship service. The worship planner who "borrows" from resources will also want to remain vigilant of copyright laws, especially those related to Internet publications.[15]

Specialized worship resources provide a fourth source for materials that may be adapted to new contexts. For example, Terry Dittmer wrote helpful guidelines on creating "contemporary" worship experiences within the structure of the liturgy that were designed specifically for youth groups.[16] A worship planner or worship committee could adapt his basic structure to a variety of settings. Similarly, Fred Kemper offered resources from his pastoral experiences for festival worship liturgies.[17] His services may spark further creative ideas or may be adapted to a variety of congregational settings. However, keep in mind that "homemade" liturgies are subject to the idiosyncrasies of their creators despite following an established structure and reflecting a strong sense of the church's liturgical heritage.

Children's hymnbooks provide variety that may be used by a congregation. For example, *Joyful Sounds* and *All God's People Sing!* are designed specifically for children's worship, yet they can be adapted to a broader worship setting.[18] *Joyful Sounds* furnishes thematic orders of service for the Advent/Christmas, Epiphany, Lent, Easter, and Pentecost seasons, as well as a general order of service for schools.

A fifth source for variety is musical settings and instrumentation. One example of this source is a service prepared by Jaroslav Vajda. He wrote new texts for the five parts of the traditional service (Kyrie, Gloria, Creed, Sanctus, and Agnus Dei) using familiar hymn melodies.[19] As new hymnals are planned, worship commissions of the major Lutheran church bodies solicit new compositions for the Divine Service. Such new settings could be used in a variety of situations.

Sixth, one can find resources for variety by exploring earlier forms of Christian worship. Luther did not create one standard worship form, though he did encourage local Christian communities and regions to use a standardized form. After the Reformation, many Lutheran towns or districts established particular orders of service that operated within the basic framework of the catholic tradition. Thus there were orders of service specific to the communities of Brandenburg, Brunswick, Erfurt, Hesse, Münzer, Nürnberg, Schwabia, and, of course, Wittenberg. Since that time, many other orders were developed, yet all were modeled on Luther's principles for Christian worship. A review of some of these services could produce interesting elements for contemporary use.[20]

Finally, material from other denominations may have elements that can be adapted for a Lutheran service.[21] Professional journals and specialty magazines that discuss worship provide innumerable options for worship.[22] Many church bodies also prepare auxiliary resources for congregations that could be adapted for use by Lutheran worshipers. These worship elements may need to be "Lutheranized" to emphasize Word and Sacrament strongly and appropriately and to express clearly the Gospel. Thus the liturgical settings and the hymns should be evaluated carefully for doctrinal content, as well as singability.[23]

There are undoubtedly many other resources for variety in worship. Worship planners and worshipers can consider these suggestions and develop a list of sources for their own use. Whenever resources are not officially produced by the LCMS, it is important to evaluate them either with ministerial peers or in a pastoral group setting. This was a common approach among early Christians. For example, a Church Council held in Hippo (Africa) in A.D. 393 stated, "If any one should copy prayers from elsewhere, he should not use them unless he has first conferred with the more instructed brethren about them."[24] This is the kind of careful evaluation and critique that places the focus on the Gospel. What is done in worship affects the doctrines and lives of all who participate.[25]

CONCERNS AND CRITIQUES

When considering variety in worship, caution is always necessary. Composer and professor Richard Hillert stated his uneasiness with variety a generation ago: "When a congregation is always confronted with new hymnody, new worship materials, unfamiliar liturgical forms, and when it is constantly assaulted with strange new musical idioms, the virtue of newness wears thin and is reduced to the level of meaningless novelty."[26] In other words, if a congregation seeks variety merely for the sake of novelty, it will not produce a growing Christian community. God's gathered guests need a biblical foundation and a Gospel focus for their worship life, including any variations. Robert Webber wrote a broader critique a decade ago:

> Evangelicals face a crisis in worship and theology. Evangelicals, who have a high regard for a theology that is biblical, need to be particularly concerned about their worship. If worship shapes believing, as has been suggested, then evangelicals of all people, should be committed to a worship that is biblical . . . . Unfortunately, many evangelicals are drawn to a market-driven worship that views worship in a mere functional, presentational manner. Eventually, such a worship will produce shallow believers. Hence, the urgency to perfect a biblically informed worship.[27]

Webber's warning is to be heeded more today than ever because more variety is possible in our global and Internet environment. Worship planners need to understand that worship affects doctrine and doctrine should be evident in worship. Therefore, some guidelines for evaluating resources, particularly new songs and hymns, are needed. What follows is merely one attempt to provide some help for worship planners and all those who care for the worship life of God's gathered guests.

EVALUATING RESOURCES

Three components are considered when evaluating worship resources—the text, the tune, and the teaching.

THE TEXT

The text is probably the easiest to evaluate, yet it is often least analyzed. The words of any worship resource should be biblical in origin or content. Even more than biblical paraphrases, the timeless Good News of God's love and forgiveness, His grace and mercy, should be prominent in everything that is said or sung in worship. Songs and readings present, interpret, and express reactions to the workings and Word of God. For example, Lutheran hymns are noteworthy for their Christ-centeredness and objectivity. A sense of justice and concern for the world may also be evident in the text of a liturgy, prayer, or hymn.

It is best to avoid ambiguous hymns or litanies. References to God's actions in the world should be concrete and clear. The following phrase in a litany was unclear to many worshipers: "For being tempted as we are, we give you thanks." The problem was not theological because it is a phrase from Hebrews 4:15. Instead, the referent was unclear. The author intended it to refer to Jesus, but in the context of the litany, it seemed to refer to the people who were praying. Furthermore, because God is the object of our worship and praise, texts should be evaluated on how well they focus on God's actions rather than on human responses or human activities. Repeatedly telling one another to "praise the Lord" without expressing the reason for such praise (for example, God's mercy) is not only pointless, it is unbiblical.

Hymn, litany, prayer, or response texts are best when they are dignified and direct. Obsolete terms or contemporary jargon do not adequately or faithfully communicate the eternal truths of God's Word. Cumbersome phrases or long responses are often difficult for a congregation to speak in unison. Simple biblical responses that have a history in the practice of Christian worship are usually best. When social issues are addressed in a litany, they should center on biblical truths not political agendas. God's people need to hear His words of warning and comfort for society on a regular basis. However, to force a diverse congregation to speak in unison a political position may be detrimental to the unity of faith.

THE TUNE

Tunes are more than mere vehicles for a text. The ancient hymn writers knew that musical styles arouse a multiplicity of emotions and communicate subliminally. Good tunes are melodic and singable, which means they can be sung by a congregation and not only by a soloist or an ensemble of trained song leaders. However, new tunes can be taught and will bring fresh insights to traditional texts or enhance less familiar texts. New tunes may also have a more relevant sound that still connects people to God's unchanging power, presence, and purpose as expressed in the words of the text. Similarly, the mood of a tune should fit the text and communicate the content of the text without distracting the focus of the worshipers from the words that are being sung.

When considering melodies, every song need not be "happy." This is especially evident if one looks at the diversity of emotions illustrated in the Psalter, the earliest songbook of God's gathered guests. Songs of confession or those sung during the season of Lent may have a distinctly different harmonic quality than the festive hymns of Christmas and especially those of the Easter season. Funeral hymns portray a requisite solemnity, yet there is joy in the resurrection to come. Most hymnbooks provide melodic diversity that can be tapped by worship planners for the various services of the church year.

Tunes should be both singable and spiritually uplifting. They should have a quality that offers new perspectives to the singer. Finally, good tunes are repeatable without becoming predictable or petty. Just as fast food is enjoyable on occasion but is not appropriate for proper daily nutrition, a steady diet of some tunes can leave worshipers spiritually anemic. Some of the more popular hymns introduced with *Lutheran Worship* were overused and became banal and hackneyed. Similar overuse of "camp songs" or other genres of music occurs in many situations in an effort to incorporate variety in the worship setting.

THE TEACHING

What is taught is probably the most important element to evaluate in worship resources. What is said and sung not only communicates faith but also teaches faith to those who listen and learn. Worship shapes, unifies, and elevates God's people. One author on worship said, "Shallow music forms shallow people."[28] It is best to avoid shallow or vacuous songs or "catchy" liturgical settings that are empty of the deep truths of the Gospel or are even theologically erroneous. The use of the name *Jesus* or descriptions of God's attributes in a song may be correct, but the text may not teach anything. By contrast, the traditional liturgical service is filled with biblical imagery and doctrinal relevance. God's Word and the Sacraments are central to Lutherans as God's gathered guests, and the liturgy focuses on these means of grace.

Postmodern society is overly (and overtly) subjective so the objective truths of God's grace in Christ sometimes seem foreign. However, such precious and precise truths ultimately strengthen the Christian's faith in God's benevolent promises. In Lutheran hymnody, the veracity of God's forgiving love should take precedence over His sovereignty, majesty, and awesome qualities. Calvinism's emphasis on divine sovereignty, neo-Pentecostalism's stress on human emotions, and American Evangelicalism's reductionistic simplicity detract from a strong Lutheran emphasis on God's grace and mercy in Christ.[29] True praise songs grow from a recognition of humanity's sinful condition and God's amazing love and mercy in Christ.

Lutherans have called music "the living voice of the Gospel."[30] As such, new worship resources, particularly new songs, will be studied, evaluated, and critiqued on how well that Gospel voice is heard. Lutheran worshipers continue to rejoice in the Good News of God's gracious action for, with, and through us. The resources used communicate that joy. Each generation is part of a numinous "winnowing" process as God's Spirit moves the gathered guests to sing songs, hymns, and spiritual songs to our gracious Father in the name of Jesus, our Savior.

WORSHIP WARS OR WORSHIP CHOICES

The phrase "worship wars"[31] has been assigned to the discussions, decisions, and debates over acceptable forms of worship in the congregation. While much heat has been generated, not as much light has been shed on the issue by the many contributions to the conversation. By examining the "wars," one realizes this is a peculiar result of the present North American scene. However, the debate extends to Europe, Asia, and South America as well. There are more worship "choices" than ever before in the history of the Christian church, but the issue of what to use in a Lutheran worship setting is more than an issue of form—it is an issue of faith. Fifty years ago, Carl Halter addressed this concern and pointed out several ineffective ways to bridge the gap between church and society. He noted the following about individuals who seek nontraditional forms of worship:

> Modern American society does not reject the form so much as it rejects God. It fails to see the relevance of individual forms because it does not recognize the worth of God. The elimination of traditional forms in and by itself will never solve the problem, because it removes only the surface aspect of a far deeper disease. In the attempt to combat secularism this solution succumbs to it.[32]

Whether it is a matter of war or choice, social pressures and the church's witness are not always compatible.

Many worship planners believe Lutherans should have greater choice in worship practices. In one sense, this perspective has been addressed in this chapter. Luther's approach at the time of the Reformation is also worthy of consideration for twenty-first century churches. Aware of the great value of the historical church and what it had produced, Luther retained in worship anything that was beautiful, true, and valuable. He valued the church's sense of continuity with the New Testament, yet he made changes that helped the Wittenberg worshipers focus on God's graciousness in Christ. He changed the language of worship so the people could understand what was being said; he encouraged full participation by all the worshipers,

Balance

particularly through songs and hymns. Most important, he wanted sinners to meet their Savior in worship. In all of his changes, however, Luther maintained balance.

The spirit of peace directs us to look at the discussion in terms other than those of war, especially because the issue is most often expressed as "contemporary versus traditional" worship. But that "conflict" may not be what is assumed. According to Carl Halter, "If we become completely contemporary, we cut off our roots; if we become completely traditional, we clip the new flowers."[33] Balance is necessary in modern worship practices. The issue becomes one of theology, not merely worship styles and practices. The present situation in Lutheran churches is not so much a matter of the era in which a song or liturgy originated as it is how the material is communicated. In many ways, the issue is not "contemporary versus traditional" but how formal or informal the setting. How much form is necessary? What is too informal? Chaos is ungodly, but rigidity can be detrimental to the Spirit's activities.

Contemporary society is increasingly informal. Personal attire at work emphasizes comfort over image, and the same informality affects worship.[34] In one sense, this reflects the impetus of the generation raised in the 1960s and 1970s, yet those coming of age in the third millennium are different from their parents. A shift is occurring among younger generations as formality becomes more evident and strongly preferred for certain occasions. Weddings and funerals, for example, are always formal, and those attending typically exhibit a dignity of attire and a solemnity in worship practice. This return to greater formality in worship is occurring even among the young.

Lutheranism has always emphasized variety in worship, but Lutherans do not encourage variety for variety's sake. Instead, Lutheran worship leaders tend to strive for a sense of balance in worship—particularly a balanced proclamation of Law and Gospel for those who are both saints and sinners. The challenge is to create a balance between the past and the future for the sake of the present, a balance of old and new that will provide continuity with the past and hope for the future. In all settings, worship is conducted to receive God's gifts through the means of grace and to give Him glory. Worship also allows the gathered guests to respond to God in prayer, praise, and adoration.

Some Questions to Consider

1. Of the seven reasons why people seek variety in worship, which did you find to be most true? Which did you find least engaging? Suggest one other reason why variety may be desirable.

2. Do you think blended services are a good approach to introducing variety to a congregation? How would you define a "blended service"? What problems could arise with such a service?

3. What methods of introducing new material into worship would you try in your congregation? Which do you think would work well? Which might not be feasible at the present time?

4. Of the many resources for variety in worship, what are the most logical and theologically sound?

5. Analyze the text, tune, and teachings of a Christian contemporary song using the critical tools in this chapter. Make sure you identify the composer, provide any background related to the composer's religious affiliation, and write out the lyrics.

6. Why are "worship wars" more a matter of choice? How does this reflect society?

7. Describe a good balance of variety in worship. Describe the service and setting, as well as the music.

Notes

1. SA III, 4 (K-W, 319), indicates five forms of the Gospel. In other writings, Luther noted that the sung Word of God in hymns was the living voice of the Gospel and that the read Word in Scripture was the vessel for Christ ("To All the Councilmen of the Cities," LW 45:339–78).

2. See LW 53 for most of these services.

3. A comparison of the four major hymnals used in contemporary North American Lutheranism reveals that despite a general similarity, there is variety within the basic structure. Word and Sacrament are central, yet within the general Mass-form, options are possible.

4. Brand, *Rite Thing*, 29, chides those seeking variety for its own sake. He says, "The yen for variety betrays the spectator attitude. Variety does make for better entertainment . . . but it seldom results in deeper involvement."

5. See Maschke, "Lutheran Liturgical Worship." I documented this phenomenon as communicated by Lutheran campus pastors from around the United States.

6. Leaver, "Luther's Catechism Hymns: 3. Creed," 86.

7. A survey of Lutheran liturgies from the century following the Reformation produces a similar variety of services and emphases. See Fendt, *Der lutherische Gottesdienst*, as well as the two volumes edited by Richter, *Die evangelischen Kirchenordnungen*. The multivolume work *Die evangelischen Kirchenordnungen des XVI. Jahrhunderts* (vols. 1–5; Leipzig: O. R. Reisland, 1902–1913; vols. 6–15; Tubingen: J. C. B. Mohr, 1955–1977) is literally exhaustive.

8. Thompson, *Liturgies of the Western Church*, offers a glimpse of liturgies from a variety of mainline Christian traditions and eras. All are in English. A substantial amount of material from a diversity of Christian perspectives, particularly in the evangelical tradition, can be plumbed from the multivolume work edited by Webber, *Complete Library of Christian Worship*.

9. Some ideas for using this approach were given in *Gathered Guests* chapter 20.

10. *Lutheran Worship* has provided such an approach with the festive hymn by Ralph Vaughan Williams, "Hail Thee, Festival Day" (Easter text, *Lutheran Worship*, 125; Ascension text, *Lutheran Worship*, 148; and Pentecost text, *Lutheran Worship*, 159).

11. The pastoral staff will want to ensure that scheduling does not become coercive. Sometimes a contemporary worship service is scheduled to replace a well-attended traditional service, which may result in less-than-honest positive attendance reports.

12. See "Variety within the Divine Service," in *Hymnal Supplement 98 Handbook*, ed. Paul Grime and Joseph Herl (St. Louis: Commission on Worship, the LCMS, 1998), 11–14.

13. Bobb and Boehringer, *Proclaim*, provides seasonal background information, as well as information on the readings and on hymn and choral selections.

14. *Creative Worship for the Lutheran Parish* has ready-to-edit services with suggested alternatives for the main portions of the liturgy, as well as hymn suggestions.

15. See the brief discussion of copyright law in *Gathered Guests* chapter 21.

16. Dittmer, *Creating Contemporary Worship*.

17. Kemper, *Variety for Worship*, which was originally published in 1977 under the title *Change of Key*.

18. *Joyful Sounds* and *All God's People Sing!* are produced under the auspices of the LCMS. While *The Other Song Book*, compiled by Dave Anderson, has some popular material, it also has songs that are contrary to the teachings of the LCMS.

19. Vajda, "Vajda Hymn Service."

20. More than a dozen Lutheran services are presented in outline form in Halter and Schalk, *Handbook of Church Music*.

21. A resource that provides a wealth of ideas from Christian communities of the past is Thompson, *Liturgies of the Western Church*. He provides English translations of material from Justin Martyr, Hippolytus, the Roman Catholic rite, Luther's two services, two services by Zwingli and Calvin, and several English Protestant services. Other resources include Webber, *Complete Library of Christian Worship*. This multivolume work provides a wide variety of evangelical and Catholic worship resources, as well as information on the history, practice, and future of worship. Each of these resources provides ideas for worship from differing theological perspectives, so caution is needed.

22. *Liturgy, Modern Liturgy, Worship*, and *Worship Leader* are just a few of these journals or specialty magazines.

23. The LCMS doctrinal review process is designed to assure the busy worship planner that the doctrinal content of materials provided through the Synod is scriptural and confessional.

24. Cited in Wainwright, *Doxology*, 255, without documentation.

25. See *Gathered Guests* chapter 1 on the relationship between worship and doctrine.

26. Hillert, "Music in the Church Today," 252.

27. Webber, *Worship, Old and New*, 261.

28. Dawn, *Reaching Out without Dumbing Down*, 175.

29. A helpful example of how a theological critique can be done is illustrated in Fremder, "Selection of Hymns," 522–23. He documents the kind of critical integrity that was employed in a review of the popular hymn "Amazing Grace." The LCMS Commission on Worship dropped the stanza that said, " 'Twas grace that taught my heart to fear; And grace my fears relieved; How precious did that grace

appear, The hour I first believed!" Looking at the stanza from a Lutheran perspective, one can see a confusing double use of *grace*. It is used to describe both the Law, which convicts sinners, and the Gospel, which comforts sinners. In addition, the stanza suggests that human effort causes grace to appear rather than the Lutheran understanding that God's gracious work alone creates faith. This careful yet constructive critique can be used by worship planners as they evaluate other resources for worship, particularly songs and prayers.

30. Dr. Kenneth Kosche, professor of music at Concordia University Wisconsin, regularly reminds his choirs that they are singing the *viva vox evangelii* ("living voice of the Gospel").

31. The summer 1994 issue of *Dialog* (vol. 33, no. 3) used this phrase as the title of the first article by editor Ted Peters, as well as the theme for the entire issue. In Peters's article, he described some of the current issues in the area of worship in the Lutheran Church.

32. Halter, *Practice of Sacred Music*, 91.

33. Halter, *Practice of Sacred Music*, 93.

34. Wright, *Community of Joy*, 67–81.

CHAPTER 23

GATHERING OTHER GUESTS

As gathered guests who have come from a variety of nations, cultures, and backgrounds, Lutherans continue to face challenging issues related to worship, though these issues are not necessarily limited to Lutherans. Congregations in a variety of Christian denominations face common concerns about worship life as they encounter society's changes. Four practical issues are of particular concern for Lutherans: (1) how to meet the needs of children in worship; (2) how to recognize the multicultural dimensions of congregations; (3) how to remain sacramental; and (4) how to maintain doctrinal integrity for ecclesiastical identity. One dimension of worship mentioned earlier in this book indicates that Lutheran worship has an evangelism emphasis because it is an opportunity to give witness to what Lutherans believe. Worship allows others to "see and hear" what Lutherans do and say about God and His love.

CHILDREN IN WORSHIP

About two decades ago, Eldon Weisheit captured the erroneous perception held by some of the place of children in worship. He wrote: "When the flock gathers in the name of the Good Shepherd for worship, often the kids (a term consistent with the sheep analogy) are to be on the scene but not in the herd."[1] Recent studies—including one done by three major Lutheran bodies—have shown an increased need to consider children in worship.[2] Of particular interest is the documentation that worship is profoundly formative for children's spiritual development.[3]

Children's messages, though not a universal practice, are a significant part of the Sunday worship of many congregations.[4] This component bears evidence of the significance of children as members of the gathered community. While the content and appropriateness of children's messages remains a topic of discussion, it is commendable that these messages are a valid means to communicate the truths of God's forgiving love in Christ.[5]

Placement of families with children is another factor that can be beneficial for children's participation and understanding of worship. The "Children in Worship" study found that only a few congregations reserved seating in the front of church for families with children.[6] Often families with young children are seated in the rear of church so parents can exit easily. However, a child's inability to see from the rear of the church may cause increased restlessness. Seats near or in the front pews provide young children with visual access to the ritual activities and the liturgical images that may prove most interesting to them. Congregations may want to consider such a change of location for children through a worship training program for parents.

Modeling faith content is another dimension of worship to consider when evaluating children's participation in worship. Ritual is a significant element in teaching, particularly for children, yet it is a dimension of worship, especially in Protestant churches and most Lutheran congregations, that has become less recognized and used. The "Children in Worship" study states:

> The absence of the majestic elements of worship such as a processional, Gospel procession, and recessional may contribute to the lack of celebration that reportedly marks some worship experiences. Often these rituals communicate to the children present the glory and majesty of the occasion of worshiping God. Corporate gestures, such as making the sign of the cross and the exchanging of peace before reception of the sacrament also model for children the relationship that exists in the community.[7]

The use of ritual and ceremonial elements in worship provides opportunities for teaching and modeling the faith of God's gathered guests. To ignore such important practices is to deprive children of their heritage, as well as the context of their faith.

Visual images of the Christian faith are another concern that most congregations can easily remedy. Seasonal banners, liturgical symbols, stained-glass windows, religious statues, and biblical murals provide nonverbal objects that communicate the Christian faith. Placing these objects so they are visible to children can attract their interest and teach the faith. For example, as paraments are changed, the pastor can use the Sunday children's message to explain the new season of the church year, which teaches the faith and intentionally includes children in the service. The "Children in Worship" study states:

> Church environments which are planned with children in mind will "speak" to the pre-literate child in powerful ways through the visual images of color and symbol. They will also "speak" to the child through auditory messages beyond words, such as through bells, language cadences, loud/soft sounds, etc. Planned environments will also include olfactory messages through things like candles,

flowers, and wood. Child-friendly environments will also include a variety of textures which are accessible to children. These may include the smooth and shiny wood of the pew, the soft or nubby fabric of cushions, the softness of a "church book," provided for the very young child . . . . Appointments in the environment may quickly indicate whether young children are even expected to be or to stay in the worship setting.[8]

The setting of worship is significant for children. In the "Children in Worship" study, the chasuble was "considered most dramatic of the options. This element was considered most likely to catch the eye of even the very young child in worship."[9] Remarkably, more than 10 percent of the congregations visited in the "Children in Worship" study did not have a cross visible in the chancel.[10]

Teaching children how to worship is a final factor when evaluating a congregation's worship practices. Whether through active participation or specific classes on the meaning of the liturgical service, children can learn much about worship and the basic teachings of the Christian faith.[11] Recently, the LCMS Commission on Worship produced bulletin inserts for children entitled "Kids in the Divine Service."[12] Shirley Morgenthaler underscores this emphasis on teaching children the liturgy in her conclusion to the "Children in Worship" study. She states:

> In all of learning, concept development is dependent on meanings and ideas which are shared and refined in that sharing. Through their experiences, children develop conceptualizations, or individual and idiosyncratic ideas of experiences, rituals, and symbols. Only as those experiences, rituals, and symbols are shared through discussion and definition do children's conceptualizations develop into the concepts and shared meanings of the community of faith.[13]

MULTICULTURAL SENSITIVITIES

With the increased awareness of society's multicultural dimensions and increased sensitivity to unique cultural expressions, God's gathered guests will want to pay attention to positive expressions of cultural diversity. How this is done is a critical issue facing twenty-first century Christians.

Cultural diversity is part of the fabric of the Christian church, yet in the United States there is a strong emphasis on enhancing unique cultures as the church continues to serve God's gathered guests. In one sense, the Christian church, particularly at worship, is transcultural—it spans all cultures by creating its own Christian cultural expressions. By recognizing the common sinfulness of all humanity, Lutheran worshipers gather with a common need for an uncommon solution. They come as sinners in need of God's certain promise and unconditional assurance of full and free forgiveness for Christ's sake. Through Word and Sacraments, a new culture is created—that of "the saved"—which unifies worshipers (Revelation 5:9; 7:9; 14:6).

Lutheran worshipers represent diverse cultural backgrounds. Some of the diversity is represented in the church's hymnody. Lutheran hymnbooks represent a broad and eclectic base of historic, ethnic, and cultural sources.[14] Similarly, Lutherans meeting in Africa describe worship as transcultural, contextual, countercultural, and cross-cultural.[15] Through the selection and use of various hymns, this multicultural aspect of worship can be experienced beneficially.[16]

But cultural norms should not take precedence over theological correctness. Sometimes hymn texts and worship practices may not be biblical or in agreement with Lutheran confessional teachings. An American Indian student once placed an eagle feather on an altar in a prayer chapel at a Lutheran university. She thought her action would create turmoil, but the worshiping community didn't understand the significance of her action, assuming it was a symbolic offering from her native culture. Missionaries are especially sensitive to the cultural contexts of worship life as they seek to bridge the gap between cultures and the Gospel message.

Mission adaptability is the practice of using some cultural elements that are compatible with the biblical and confessional theology of Christian worship. Adaptability is always a careful process and does not always work. A missionary who worked in Taiwan reported: "One of my church's Chinese leaders . . . felt that using Chinese melodies with Christian words has not generally caught on in Taiwan because people have difficulty forgetting the usage of the melodies in their non-Christian settings."[17] Instead, he reported that new melodies written to communicate Christianity in a Chinese context were being created by gifted Chinese Christians.

Although cultural diversity can be celebrated, it should not be divisive. Rather than separation, the ultimate hope for God's gathered guests is that each time they gather to hear God's grace in Christ within a liturgical context there is an enrichment recognized from many cultures. Frank C. Senn wrote: "In the array of ethnic customs and experiences which make up American society we have the possibility of experiencing the catholicity or wholeness of the church, especially in congregations which intentionally reach out to embrace all sorts of people in their fellowship."[18] Such a perspective is necessary as congregations consider gathering other guests into God's presence.

SACRAMENTAL SERVICES

Whether the Sacrament of the Altar should be offered regularly, particularly in a setting in which many visitors are present, is becoming increasingly questioned. A strong argument can be made for weekly Communion in a Lutheran congregation. Jesus encouraged His disciples to celebrate this meal often and to do it in "remembrance of Me" (1 Corinthians 11:23–25). Perhaps such remembrances occurred whenever the disciples ate together. As the church grew, the apostles continued frequent services, including the Lord's Supper (Acts 2:46; 20:7). Early Christians carried on a similar practice of weekly mealtime services that became Communion services. However, as the frequency of the Communion services increased, participation by laypeople diminished. At the Fourth Lateran Council in 1215, the church ruled that Christians must commune at least annually, with the suggestion that it be done during the season of Easter. The joyful weekly practice had become merely an annual obligation.

Although Luther's reformation centered on the teaching of God's gracious declaration that sinful human beings were forgiven for Christ's sake, he also reformed some of the church's worship practices. He restored preaching to balance the offering of Word and Sacrament to God's gathered guests, retaining the celebration of the Sacrament of the Altar as a weekly, and in some locales, as a daily practice.[19] This was not a reformation as much as a restoration of Holy Communion to God's gathered guests.

With the rise of Rationalism in the eighteenth century, many "enlightened" Christians turned away from the Lord's Supper, considering it a ritual, something that could be eliminated without undue harm to the intellectual approach to Christianity. In contrast and at the same time, Pietism emphasized an emotional and inward religious experience that did not require outward and formal worship practices. Lutherans were influenced by both movements. In Lutheran parishes in Europe and North America, Communion was reduced to a quarterly or a monthly celebration. Particularly in North America, Lutherans wanted to show their New World perspective, so they copied the practices of other Protestant churches, many of which described the Lord's Supper as a memorial meal. However, recent decades have brought an increased appreciation for Holy Communion and a subsequent increase in the opportunities for Lutherans to receive the Sacrament. Weekly celebrations of the Lord's Supper have become almost standard in Lutheran congregations.

With the novel emphasis of Sunday worship as a major evangelism tool of the church, a legitimate concern has been raised regarding the frequency of Holy Communion. Of particular importance among WELS and LCMS congregations is the practice of close(d) Communion. This practice emphasizes the Lord's Supper as a confession of faith as well as a means of grace. Those of the same confession of faith commune together as a statement of that common belief. But some ask what visitors might think if they cannot attend Communion. Although a valid concern, the elimination of the Lord's Supper for the sake of visitors misses the purpose of the Sacrament. Normally, guests at one's home do not set the meal schedule or determine the menu. Holy Communion is for the faith-full. It is a statement of what is important for Lutheran believers. Lutheran congregations need to consider how to celebrate the Lord's Supper in ways that clearly express hospitality to the stranger while maintaining the biblical and Lutheran practice of close(d) Communion.

DENOMINATIONAL IDENTITY

Lutheran worship services are object lessons of who Lutherans are and what they believe. To do otherwise is to fail to live the substance of the Lutheran Confessions. As the United States becomes more of a "stew pot" than a "melting pot," denominational distinctions are less significant to new church members and less recognized by nonmembers. Lutherans, however, have traditionally offered a particular emphasis on the Gospel that the world needs. "The Lutheran church, as a confessing movement in the church catholic, . . . has a particular view of the gospel, communicated through Word and sacrament and expressed in the liturgy, and it must hold on to these things in order to be faithful to and maintain its identity."[20] As God's guests who gather around His altar and hear His Word, the strength of this Lutheran witness is necessary because of what Lutherans are—liturgical and evangelical, traditional and contemporary.

LITURGICAL AND EVANGELICAL

The liturgy is part of the historic heritage that Lutherans have cherished for the past half-millennium. Its unique form that brings Word and Sacrament to God's gathered guests has served generations of Lutherans. The Gospel emphasis on the Word and the Sacraments gives Lutheranism its particularly evangelical emphasis (after all, the Lutheran Church was the first to be called "evangelical"). This unique tension between liturgical and evangelical has been maintained throughout the history of Lutheranism. And Lutherans continue to bring this tension between continuity and freshness to present ecumenical discussions.

TRADITIONAL AND CONTEMPORARY

The Lutheran tradition is not a moribund love for the past or even a clinging to the old. Rather, the tradition is a passing down of the Good News of God's love and forgiveness in Christ for present and future generations. Lutherans want to share this Good News with their children and their neighbors. In the same way, Lutherans are contemporary Christians, living in the world with all the contemporary concerns of life—surviving crises, making the world a better place, enjoying family, serving the community, and reaching out to others. Lutherans understand that the unchanging Gospel is relevant to an ever-changing society, and they want the Good News heard by family members, friends, co-workers, and neighbors.

Lutheran liturgy teaches the doctrines of Word and Sacraments. God's Law clearly condemns sin and sinners; His Gospel graciously forgives the repentant sinner because of Christ's meritorious death and resurrection. In the liturgy, believers experience firsthand the blessings of absolution, the washing of Baptism, and the assurance of forgiveness and life in Communion. This experience moves worshipers to speak the Good News throughout the week at work, play, and through service to others. Worship is relevant for contemporary living.

As God's gathered guests, Lutheran worshipers manifest the truths of the faith and express to the world a joyous commitment to Christ our Savior, who is present every time we meet in His name. This response of faith is a gift from God Himself and provides the continuing incentive for worship and service until He calls us to Himself. With the ancient church, God's gathered guests exclaim, "Come, O Lord!" (*Marana tha*! [1 Corinthians 16:22]).

SOME QUESTIONS TO CONSIDER

1. Describe what a young child might see and experience during a worship service if seated or standing in the last pew of your church. What would a 3-foot tall child face when the congregation stands for prayer or the creed? What chancel items are visible from the back of church? What does the pastor look like when in the chancel or pulpit? What visually engaging objects might a child see? Be as concrete as possible.

2. How could visual aids not only help children learn more about worship and about God but also aid older members in their worship practices?

3. How is worship transcultural? Provide illustrations from your experience.

4. What problems are connected with cultural adaptation? How could cultural adaptation enhance worship? How could it distort or dilute worship activities?

5. Provide one reason for weekly celebration of the Lord's Supper. Does your congregation follow a weekly practice? Ask your pastor why or why not.

6. How is Lutheran identity maintained and enhanced through a liturgical practice of worship? What problems could arise from such an emphasis?

7. How are Lutherans liturgical and evangelical, traditional and contemporary?

NOTES

1. Weisheit, "Place of Children in the Worship Life," 1.

2. Becker, Morgenthaler, and Bertels, "Children in Worship," *Lutheran Education* 133.1–5, 19–26, 78–85, 157–64, 203–12, 252–60, and their subsequent book, describe the work done with 100 Lutheran congregations.

3. John H. Westerhoff, "The School of the Church," in *Schooling Christians*, ed. Stanley Hauerwas and John H. Westerhoff (Grand Rapids: Eerdmans, 1992), provides the theoretical basis for the "Children in Worship" study.

4. Becker, Morgenthaler, and Bertels, "Children in Worship," *Lutheran Education* 133:1, 24, indicates that "the children's message is a common form of including children in worship (40%)."

5. Becker, Morgenthaler, and Bertels, "Children in Worship," *Lutheran Education* 133:4, 206. However, the authors note that "anecdotal comments from the research associates indicate that many well intentioned children's messages are just not developmentally appropriate for children. Since this is the major vehicle for involvement of children, attention should be given to aiding those delivering the children's message in making them as appropriate as possible" (212). A discussion of the content of children's messages and the method of delivery are beyond this book but are worthy of continuing consideration.

6. Becker, Morgenthaler, and Bertels, "Children in Worship," *Lutheran Education* 133:2, 81. From personal experience with three sons, sitting near the front proved beneficial for training them in worship practices and appropriate behavior.

7. Becker, Morgenthaler, and Bertels, "Children in Worship," *Lutheran Education* 133:3, 163.

8. Becker, Morgenthaler, and Bertels, "Children in Worship," *Lutheran Education* 133:2, 79–80.

9. Becker, Morgenthaler, and Bertels, "Children in Worship," *Lutheran Education* 133:2, 82.

10. Becker, Morgenthaler, and Bertels, "Children in Worship," *Lutheran Education* 133:2, 83.

11. Earlier generations understood the necessity of teaching children how to worship and included resources in hymnals for teaching about worship. The editors of the *Service Book and Hymnal* also offered a child's book: Herzel, *Christians at Worship*.

12. Commission on Worship, the LCMS (St. Louis: LCMS, 2000).

13. Becker, Morgenthaler, and Bertels, "Children in Worship," *Lutheran Education* 133:5, 253.

14. Pfatteicher and Messerli, *Manual on the Liturgy*, 86. See also Maschke, "Transcultural Nature of Liturgical Worship," 241–63.

15. Lutheran World Federation, "Nairobi Statement on Worship and Culture," in *Christian Worship*, ed. S. Anita Stauffer (Geneva: Department for Theology and Studies, LWF, 1996).

16. See sections of *This Far by Faith*, particularly its introductory notes, 8–17.

17. Found, "Contemporary Worship," 41.

18. Senn, *Christian Worship and Its Cultural Setting*, 51.

19. SC, "Preface"; LC "Sacrament of the Altar"; AC XXIV; Ap. XXIV.

20. David A. Gustafson, *Lutherans in Crisis* (Minneapolis: Fortress, 1993), 179.

CHAPTER 24

AFTER THE BENEDICTION

When guests leave our home, my family and I usually give them a parting wish. It may be "See you again," "Come again," or "Good-bye." These parting wishes often linger in our memory as we anticipate a return visit.

God's gathered guests also receive a blessing, the Benediction, before they depart from His house. William Willimon makes an important distinction between the Benediction and a parting wish: "It is not a petition or a prayer, nor a pious wish for God's presence: it is a statement of faith, a statement of fact. God is with you."[1] Many cultures express this sentiment in departure greetings, such as the English word *good-bye*, which is short for "God be with ye." The French say "Adieu," the Italians "Addio," and the Spanish "Adiós," each recalling the Benediction that has been spoken over many centuries and over thousands of Christian believers.

After looking at the Benediction as part of the liturgy, we now will look at it as something ongoing. "Throughout the Hebrew Bible and at numerous crucial points in the New Testament," continues William Willimon, "blessing is not something that is on the periphery, but rather it is a sign that symbolizes the all-encompassing significance of religion. Blessing is always an act that transfers power, an effective sign of God's sustaining presence and present power."[2] The Benediction sends us forth as God's redeemed people and reminds us that God first placed His mark on us at our Baptism. We leave and live as God's new creations, remembering the power of His baptismal blessing. The Benediction is not a wish but a reminder of who we are and whose we are. But worship does not end after the Benediction.

LITURGY AND LIFE

In the Lutheran Confessions, worship is frequently defined as faith[3]—a living, busy, active, mighty thing.[4] For Martin Luther and for Lutherans, worship goes beyond Sunday or those routine activities that occur in church.[5] Worship certainly occurs after the Benediction. Our lives exemplify what we believe. When God's gathered guests are full of faith, they are worship-full as well. Spirit-created faith gives God's guests the ability to respond to His Word in praise and activity.

There is a dynamic quality to Christian worship that is demonstrated by our gathering and scattering. Melva Wilson Costen describes it succinctly: "Empowered gatherings evoke the need to go forth into the world to love and serve . . . . Life in the world always calls one back to mutual companionship in gatherings, confession of sin, pardon, and renewal."[6] This vigorous dynamic is always operative as God's guests gather around the means of grace, then scatter for service in the world.

Liturgical services are designed to propel the spoken and proclaimed words beyond the ears of the believers and into their hearts to produce a lively response. In that sense, worship is peculiarly faith-filling. Through the working of His Spirit, God strengthens faith to overflowing. The faith-fullness of God's gathered guests cannot stop at the end of the service; instead, it continues throughout the week as the life-instilling Gospel takes root and produces fruit after the Benediction.

The greatest worship in daily life is to repent and to be forgiven. The Gospel creates the fruit of faith, which is summarized in "love." Christ says, "Love the Lord your God with all your heart and with all your soul and with all your mind. . . . Love your neighbor as yourself" (Matthew 22:37, 39). When Christians take the commandments of God into daily life and live them, they see their sin. Only Christ could keep perfectly all God's commands. Thus Christians repent of their sin and through faith in Christ have forgiveness. Christians rise from the death of sin daily to live out their vocation, whatever it may be. Through the means of grace, Christians have the hope and strength they need to continue in this world.

Many do not understand the influence worship has on the daily lives of the gathered guests. They turn Jesus into only an example by which Christians ought to live. But the gathered guests do not worship so they can live better lives. Instead, they gather to be confronted with their sin and to receive forgiveness. Because our Lord expects us to be holy or perfect in our daily lives, doing our best does not count in Christ's kingdom. This is where the weekly gathering for worship affects life during the rest of the week. Forgiveness is necessary every moment. Christians confidently live out the Ten Commandments because they know failure to live by God's commands will not condemn them to everlasting punishment. As baptized children of God, they will live, even in the face of the Law that shows them their sin, because theirs is a life of daily repentance and forgiveness.

In the light of God's Word and the sacramental life, Christians are free to live each day as the parent, child, custodian, churchworker, doctor, or construction worker God has called them to be. God blesses the Christian's work through the power of His Word and Baptism. Thus in a Christian's daily life, Christ is not merely the example, He is the Redeemer. This reality provides Christians with the strength and ability to love the Lord and their neighbors. And we love our Lord each day as we show love to our neighbors. In this way, weekly worship influences the daily activities of the family and community.

LIVING WHAT HAS BEEN HEARD

Jesus reminded His disciples that they were not only to hear the Word of God, they were to "keep it" (Luke 11:28). Protestant worship services in general are often overly word-oriented. We speak prayers, we hear Scripture read, we recite creeds, we listen to sermons, we sing verses of hymns. Word-oriented worship is essential. If worship is only word-oriented (lowercase "w") and there is no Gospel-motivated activity, no liturgy throughout the week, then people will fail to connect liturgy with life after the Benediction.

Lutheran worship is centered around God's gifts to His people and their joyful response. God feeds His gathered guests through the means of grace: Word and Sacraments. God's people are invigorated by the Holy Spirit to live their specific calling with commitment and care as well as to live their universal calling as God's representatives in the world. Having been fed, God's gathered guests scatter to feed others the bread of life, the Word made flesh.

CALLING OTHERS TO GATHER IN HIS NAME

Christ comes to us in worship so we can carry Him to others. Through believers, the transforming power of the Gospel—the forgiveness of sins and the presence of the Spirit—becomes a transforming reality in the world. This transforming reality is evident in faith-produced actions. James White asked and answered his own rhetorical question several years ago in *New Forms of Worship*:

> We are forced, at least, to question the importance of worship for the Christian life. Does worship merit the expenditure of as much time and talent as preparation for it now seems to demand? Our answer is "yes" because of conviction that worship is at the very center of the church's mission. Evangelism, social action, nurture, education, all grow out of worship like the petals from the center of a flower.[7]

During the week, God's gathered guests respond to a variety of situations by drawing strength and insights from what they heard on Sunday and what they experienced in a liturgy of Word and Sacrament. As the Holy Spirit works through His means of grace, faith-strengthening worship brings responses after the Benediction. After hearing from God, particularly the Good News of His love in Christ, worshipers want to tell that Good News. It may be a specific message from the pastor that bears repeating, or it may be a thought from a reading that addresses a specific situation, or it may be the frequently spoken words in the liturgy or the creed that echo in conversation. The opportunities to witness are many after the Benediction.

Telling is extremely important because faith comes by hearing (Romans 10:17). However, part of living the liturgy is evident as others are invited to God's house. Many people enter a worship situation because a friend or acquaintance brought them. Telling is important, but bringing guests to church is one of the best ways to manifest the power of the Gospel after the Benediction.

Christians are never isolated. No matter how alone one may feel or even be during the week, we are assured that others also believe in the same Lord Jesus Christ. Although we may unknowingly pass fellow believers in a store, on the street, at work, or during recreational activities, we will join together again to receive and respond, to hear and to sing, to pray and to praise as God's gathered guests.

Looking Forward to Gathering

Worship is transcultural, but it is also supertemporal. Worship bridges time and enables all believers living in the "now" to glimpse eternity. Whether it is in the Preface of the Holy Communion liturgy when we join "with angels and archangels and all the company of heaven" or in the private moments of Compline as we confess our sins "before the whole company of heaven," worship goes beyond the present and joins with that of the great throng of angels and heavenly hosts.

Lutheran worship links those present as God's gathered guests to the eternal truths of God's people of all time and all places. The messages of the prophets and apostles still speak to today's situations. The Old and New Testaments still bring hope, comfort, and joy. We hear the Father's forgiving voice in the words of Holy Absolution. The Holy Spirit still comes in the sacramental waters of Holy Baptism to create faith. Jesus continues to be present in, with, and under the elements of Holy Communion to grant us forgiveness, life, and salvation.

Yet this weekly celebration is only a foretaste of the feast to come. Worship reminds us of the heavenly glory that will someday be ours. The writer to the Hebrews says: "Spur one another on toward love and good deeds. Let us not give up meeting together, as some are in the habit of doing, but let us encourage one another—and all the more as you see the Day approaching" (10:24–25). More significant, the Revelation of John shows us the continuing worship of God's people (Revelation 19:1–10). The heavenly banquet is being prepared by Jesus, and He will return to bring us to celebrate with Him eternally (Revelation 22:12).

After the last Benediction is spoken here on earth, there will still be the everlasting worship in the new creation of the Lamb who sits on the throne with psalms, hymns, and songs of joyous victory by all God's gathered guests.

Some Questions to Consider

1. How does the Benediction differ from a parting wish to a guest leaving your home? Why is this significant for understanding what occurs "after the Benediction"?

2. How does Christian worship affect the daily Christian life?

3. How is worship formative and transformative?

4. How is there a liturgy after the liturgy? What does it mean to live what has been heard?

5. What elements of a worship service that you have recently attended could you speak about to a friend who does not attend church regularly?

Notes

1. Willimon, "Peace of God Go with You," 68.
2. Willimon, "Peace of God Go with You," 68.
3. See Ap. IV, 49 (K-W, 128), and Ap. XXIV, 27 (K-W, 263).
4. "Preface to St. Paul's Epistle to the Romans," cited in SD IV, 10 (K-W, 576).
5. Ap. IV, 49 (K-W, 144).
6. Costen, *African American Christian Worship*, 127–28.
7. James White, *New Forms of Worship*, 51.

APPENDIX A

PREPARATORY STEPS FOR LECTORS

1. PRAY

Ask the Holy Spirit who brought these Scriptures into being to grant you wisdom as you prepare.

2. PREPARE

Read the text several times silently and aloud to analyze and "hear" it.

3. PROBE

Background information about the author or the event (or Old Testament prophecy for a New Testament fulfillment or vice versa) may make the passage more meaningful. What might the author or subjects be feeling?

4. PONDER

This is especially important for readings of more than five verses. Clearly delineate dialogue and discussion. Distinguish sections with brackets in one margin. In the other margin, write your thoughts about the text.

5. PARAPHRASE

After becoming familiar with the text, paraphrase the verses to ensure you understand the meaning of the text.

6. PRONOUNCE

Determine the proper way to say a name or word in the text. Also be aware of and avoid, if possible, "regionalisms" in pronunciation.

7. PAUSE

Silence is as meaningful as words. Two kinds of pauses can be marked in the text: highlight (/, ', or *), which indicates short pauses that create a mood, feeling, or emphasis; and clarification (//, ", or **), which follows punctuation or indicates longer pauses. Each phrase projects one image or thought and is spoken in one breath. Always keep words together that belong together.

8. PHRASE

Underline words that need to be emphasized, but ask, "Do the words I choose to emphasize communicate the passage's feeling and meaning?" Emphasize nouns when they introduce a new idea. Stress verbs when movement within the text is a priority. Emphasize adjectives, adverbs, and pronouns when the text presents contrasting ideas. Do not emphasize a word that is repeated (echo-phrasing).

9. PRODUCE

Help the congregation picture the scene by reading expressively. A change of pitch, speed, or tone communicates feelings and illustrates events. Consider narrator, persona, and quotations when reading. The lector is the narrator, especially for the Gospels. Each character of a text (persona) may have a place on the "stage" of the presentation. When reading quotations, the voice may change from narrator to speaker in some way. Indirect quotations may be introduced by the narrator before shifting in persona to let the speaker speak the actual words. Parenthetical comments can be read in the same manner.

10. PREPARE

Although not universally practiced, an introduction of one to three sentences may be prepared for each reading. Such an introduction may include background on the author or situation, the main theme, the liturgical context, or the biblical context.

11. PRACTICE

Practice in front of others, especially those who can provide constructive criticism.

12. PRESENT

On the day of the reading, be confident that you have prepared adequately. Before reading, ensure the reading material is at a comfortable height. Breathe comfortably. Concentrate on the message, not on the worshipers. When completed, say, "This is the Word of the Lord," pick up the materials, and be seated.

APPENDIX B

WORKSHEET FOR PLANNING A SERVICE OF HOLY COMMUNION

The following worksheet may be duplicated and used for each Sunday or festival in the church year.

Date of Service:_____ Time:_____

Place:_____

Sunday/Festival: _____

Themes, motifs, tone: _____

_____

Special actions or visuals: _____

_____

_____

Musical setting:_____ page: _____

Ministers:

    Presiding: _____

    Assisting I (deacon):_____

    Assisting II (subdeacon): _____

    Lector: _____

    Acolyte(s): _____

    Host(s):_____

    Usher(s): _____

    Others: _____

General announcements:

    ___ before the Confession   ___ before the Offertory

    ___ after the Confession   ___ before the Benediction

    ___ before the Lessons   ___ after the Benediction

(It is best to print announcements in the worship folder. Changes may be noted or emergency information announced before or after the service.)

Organ Prelude:

    ___ before the Confession

    ___ after the Confession

    Title:_____

    ___ omit (give reason): _____

Opening Hymn: _____

(A hymn here may disrupt the preparatory nature of the confessional service; therefore, it is not used in these planning sheets.)

Preparatory Service

Confession and Forgiveness:

    ___ from Divine Service II, p. _____ OR

    ___ from Divine Service I, p. ____OR

    ___ an expanded form prepared by _____

AND

    ___ Absolution OR

    ___ Declaration of Grace

Entrance Rite

Entrance:

    ___ Hymn #_____ OR

    ___ Introit, p. _____ OR

    ___ Psalm #_____ p._____ *(Preferably use the Psalm later as the Gradual)*

Procession:

    ___ participants include: _____

    _____

    ___ omit (give reason): _____

Kyrie:

    ___ sung OR

    ___ spoken

    ___ special version: _____

    sung by_____

    ___ omit (give reason): _____

Hymn of Praise:

    ___ Glory to God in the Highest (*Gloria in excelsis*) OR

    ___ This Is the Feast OR

___ other:_____

sung by: _____

___ omit (give reason): _____

Collect of the Day: p._____

Service of the Word

First Lesson: _____

    lector: _____

Gradual/Psalm: _____ page: _____

    ___ sung OR

    ___ spoken OR

    ___ replaced by: _____

Second Lesson: _____

    lector: _____

The Verse:

    ___ Alleluia OR

    ___ Lenten OR

    ___ proper, _____ page: _____

    musical setting: _____

    sung by: _____

Gospel: _____

    ___ procession

    participants include:

    Bookbearer: _____

    Torchbearers: _____

    _____

    Reader: _____

    ___ omit (give reason): _____

Hymn of the Day: _____ #:_____

    ___ sung now

    ___ sung after the Sermon

    ___ special manner of singing: _____

Sermon theme/title: _____

    text: _____

    preacher: _____

Creed:

    ___ Apostles' OR

    ___ Nicene OR

    ___ hymnic version:_____

    ___ Athanasian

    ___ omit (give reason): _____

The Prayers: _____

    written by: _____

    led by: _____

    form/response:

    ___ "Lord, in your mercy"

    ___ "Let us pray to the Lord"

    ___ other:_____

Special events (optional):

    ___ installation

    ___ confirmation

    ___ reception of members

    ___ other:_____

(Normally, a Baptism occurs at the beginning of a service.)

During the gathering of the Offering:

    ___ choir

    ___ solo

    ___ other:_____

        Title: _____

    ___ omit (give reason):_____

Offertory:

    ___ "Let the vineyards be fruitful"

    ___ "What shall I render to the Lord"

    ___ "Create in me"

    ___ other:_____

        sung by:_____

Offertory procession includes:

    ___ ushers

    ___ gift bearers: _____

    ___ others: _____

___ omit (give reason): _____

(An Offertory prayer or hymn may be said or sung here, after the offerings are received.)

___ speaker: _____

___ form: _____

___ hymn:_____ stanzas: _____

Service of the Sacrament

Communion Preface begins on page:_____

Proper Preface:

Season: _____

Altarbook or hymnal page _____

___ sung

___ spoken

Sanctus:

___ sung

___ spoken

___ special version:_____

sung by:_____

Eucharistic Prayer:

___ "Blessed are you"

___ other:_____

___ omit (give reason): _____

Words of Institution:

___ sung

___ spoken

Lord's Prayer:

___ traditional

___ contemporary

___ spoken

___ sung: p._____

The Peace:

___ greeting only

___ shared with members of the congregation

___ omit (give reason):

(Note: The exchange of peace may be placed before the Offertory.)

Communion Distribution:

    assisting ministers: _____

Distribution hymns/music:

Agnus Dei:

    ___ sung

    ___ spoken

    ___ special version: _____

    sung by: _____

Anthem/special music (optional):

    Title:_____

    performed by: _____

Additional hymns during distribution:

_____

_____

Post-Communion Canticle:

    ___ "Thank the Lord"

    ___ Nunc Dimittis

    ___ other:_____

Post-Communion prayer:

    ___ "We give [you] thanks"

    ___ "O God, from whom"

    ___ other:_____

Benediction:

    ___ "The Lord bless you"

    ___ other:_____

Dismissal (optional): _____

    by: _____

Closing Hymn (*if there needs to be a recessional*): _____

Additional notes (*for sacristans, ushers, asst. ministers, musicians, etc.*):

APPENDIX C

GUIDELINES FOR CONSTRUCTING A FAMILY OR SMALL-GROUP DEVOTION

1. Consider the group for which the devotional service is intended (age, size, sex, etc.). Who will lead the devotion? How much participation by group members is desired?

2. Reflect on the particular time of the church year in which this devotion will occur. What liturgical elements are specifically related to this season?

3. Analyze the physical setting in which the devotion will be delivered. How will this setting contribute to the structure of the devotion? What accommodation to the setting may need to be made?

4. Determine the theme(s) of the devotion. How was this theme determined? How will it be expressed?

5. What worship resources will be needed (Bible, hymnal, songbook, etc.)? Will copies be needed for each group member? Could a devotion be developed in which group members could participate without printed orders or other books? (Adhere to copyright law.) If a portion of the devotional service comes from a published resource, such as a hymnal or prayer book, and group members would have copies, list the resource and the appropriate page number on the service outline.

6. Ensure that God's Word and its exposition are the central features of the devotion. Determine what portion of Scripture will be included as a lesson. In a setting with young children, a paraphrase or a retelling of the Bible story specifically written for children (such as an Arch Book from Concordia Publishing House) might be used. In a group of older adults, the King James Version of the Bible might be appropriate. Be sensitive to the abilities and knowledge base of the group that will be participating in the devotion.

7. Structure the entire devotional time. Drawing on the Lutheran liturgical tradition, what elements (other than a hymn) can be incorporated in the devotion? How will these elements enhance participation? Identify an appropriate beginning and ending to the devotion, such as an Invocation and Benediction.

Glossary

Aaronic Benediction: *see* **Benediction**

Absolution, Holy: the full and free forgiveness announced to a sorrowful sinner by the pastor in God's or Christ's place; follows a private or corporate confession of sins; considered a third sacrament among many Lutherans.

acolyte: Greek for "a follower"; a designated ministerial assistant; usually lights and extinguishes candles but may assist in other liturgical acts.

adiaphoron: Greek for "something indifferent"; things neither commanded nor forbidden in God's Word that remain provisionally neutral until the context causes that neutrality to cease; many acts of worship are adiaphora (plural), meaning that Christians are free to do them or not, depending on the context. One example is the choice to kneel or to stand for prayer.

adoration: a special form of prayer in which God is praised for specific attributes or acts He performs; more generally, may refer to a worshipful attitude of praise and awe.

Adoration of the Cross: a Good Friday exercise in which the congregation contemplates Christ's self-sacrifice on the cross; may be observed on Holy Cross Day (September 14).

Advent: Latin for "coming"; refers to the four-Sunday season that begins the church year and prepares worshipers for Christmas; begins the first Sunday after the feast day of St. Andrew (November 30); a contemplative mood dominates.

agenda: Latin for "things to be done"; denotes an auxiliary worship book that contains directions for the rites and special services not included in an altar book; coordinates with a denomination's official hymnal.

Agnus Dei: Latin for "Lamb of God"; designation given to Jesus by John the Baptist (John 1:29); more specifically, refers to the canticle in the Communion liturgy that begins with those words; the first Communion distribution hymn during which the officiants may commune.

alb: Latin for "white"; refers to an ankle-length robe with sleeves and a cincture worn by anyone helping in a worship service; symbolic of Christ's righteousness given at Baptism; reminiscent of the white-robed martyrs of Revelation.

alleluia: *see* **hallelujah**

alpha and omega: A and Ω, the first and last capital letters of the Greek alphabet; a symbol of eternity or of Christ.

altar: ornate or simple stone or wooden table on which the Lord's Supper is prepared and distributed; the sacramental focus from which God gives His gifts; the sacrificial focus for the congregation's prayer and praise; may be freestanding.

altar book: official book for a denomination's hymnal; provides the orders of service, the Propers for each day, and extra materials for conducting a service; includes additional prayers and directions; sometimes called a missal (from the Latin for "mass").

altar guild: *see* **chancel care committee**

ambo: may be from the Latin for "both"; refers to a raised desk or table in the chancel used for Scripture reading and preaching; may replace the lectern and pulpit.

amen: Hebrew for "certainly, truly"; expresses worshipers' concurrence with what is spoken or sung by worship leaders; particularly used at the end of prayers.

anamnesis: Greek for "remembering" what God has done for the world's salvation; the first part of the Eucharistic Prayer.

antependium: Latin for "hanging before"; refers to the ornamental cloth hanging suspended in front of an altar, pulpit, or lectern.

anthem: anglicization of "antiphon"; refers to attendant choir music; developed to a high level in English worship services; often challenging musically; in Lutheran services, it is usually an element of the liturgy (Hymn of Praise or Offertory).

antiphon: Greek for "responsive"; refers to a Scripture verse sung before and after a psalm or canticle; sometimes used as congregational responses during a longer psalm sung by the choir; may provide a central theme of the psalm.

antiphonal: a responsive singing of the psalm by two choirs or two sides of the congregation; may refer to any response back and forth between two groups.

Apocrypha: books of the Bible not included in Protestant versions of Scripture; Roman Catholics call these deuterocanonical (pertaining to a second canon as defined by the Council of Trent); Luther retained them in his German Bible as worthy of reading but not to establish doctrine; used for some hymn texts; may be used for one reading in Vespers.

Apostolic Blessing: *see* **Benediction**

apse: semicircular structure with a half-dome roof in a basilica-style church; often forms the chancel; early basilicas located the bishop's chair in the apse for acoustical purposes.

Ascension: festival during the Easter season; celebrates Christ's return to heaven; occurs 40 days after Easter.

Ash Wednesday: first day of the Lenten season; may be marked by the imposition of ashes on worshipers.

assisting minister: any person who assists in worship; may be ordained or a layperson, in some cases specifically a man; often reads the Old Testament and Epistle readings, as well as distributes the wine at Communion.

attendant: refers to music not directly part of the Divine Service, such as an anthem; refers to members of a wedding party.

auditory: Latin for "hearing"; refers to a church designed by Sir Christopher Wren with balconies or galleries so crowds could easily hear.

Ave Maria: Latin for "Hail Mary"; the angel Gabriel's greeting to Mary at the time of the Annunciation; said or sung in Roman Catholic worship; retained for several decades by a few Lutheran congregations after the Reformation.

bands: "preaching tabs" of white linen; also know by the German word *Beffchen*; worn as a collar in the front of a black preaching gown; Lutheran preachers presumably wore them to symbolize the proclamation of Law and Gospel.

Baptism, Holy: sacrament by which the Holy Spirit creates faith through the Word connected to water; water is poured or sprinkled on the baptismal candidate (infant or adult) or the candidate is immersed; usually conducted before the congregation, though private and emergency Baptisms may occur.

baptistery: an often elaborately decorated room containing a baptismal font; may also refer to a large pool of water used for baptisms; structured with six or eight sides, symbolizing creation or resurrection.

basilica: Greek for "king's hall"; describes the earliest accepted form of church building; features an apse, transepts, and large nave for the assembly.

bema: Greek for "platform or step"; a platform extending from the chancel into the nave either with or without a pulpit; a raised chancel area for choir and altar.

Benedicamus: Latin for "bless we [the Lord]"; the concluding responses in Matins and Vespers.

Benediction: Latin for "[The Lord] bless [you]"; refers to two forms of the blessing or proclamation of God's presence on His people; the Aaronic blessing (Numbers 6:24–26) is usually used at Holy Communion; the Apostolic blessing (2 Corinthians 13:14) is used at other times.

Benedicite Omnia Opera: Latin for "All you works [of the Lord] bless [the Lord]"; an ancient canticle from Daniel 3 in the Apocrypha; also called the Song of the Three Children or the Song of Creation; appropriate for Matins or retreat settings; sometimes concludes the Easter Vigil.

Benedictus: Latin for "Blessed be"; from Zechariah's song in Luke 1; the Gospel Canticle for Matins; particularly appropriate for Advent and Christmas; also may refer to the second part of the Sanctus in the Divine Service ("Blessed is [He who comes]"); the song of the Jerusalem crowd on Palm Sunday (Matthew 21:9).

Bidding Prayer: see **Deacon's Prayer**

bishop: the ecclesiastical overseer of a congregation or congregations; interchangeable with presbyters in the early church; developed as the highest order of clergy; sometimes describes District or denomination presidents.

blessing: an authoritative declaration of God's favor; a verbal formula to set aside objects for religious purposes; *see also* **Benediction**.

blue: *see* **liturgical colors**

burial of the dead: *see* **funeral**

burse: a cloth envelop to store and carry Communion cloths, such as the corporal, purificators, and veil; placed on top of a veiled chalice, which covers the Communion pall.

Canon of the Mass: Greek for "rule or fixed part"; refers to a long prayer used in the Roman Mass, which included the Words of Institution; Luther removed this prayer because it emphasized sacrifice and prayer to saints; Luther replaced it with the Verba.

canonical hours: set hours of prayer in the monasteries, but also followed by laypeople; includes Matins, Lauds, Prime, Terce, Sext, None, Vespers, and Compline; morning and evening hours sometimes called "cockcrow" and "lamplighting"; also called Divine Office or Daily Office.

canticles: Latin for "little song"; designates Scripture texts (but not psalms) sung in a liturgical setting, usually at Matins (Zechariah's Song, the Benedictus) or at Vespers (the Magnificat, the Nunc Dimittis); sometimes called Gospel canticles.

cantor: Latin for "singer"; refers to a song leader who usually offers unaccompanied music in a liturgy; may refer to a choral leader or minister of music; Lutherans retained this office after the Reformation.

cassock: a black garment worn under a cotta or surplice; similar in style to an alb.

catechesis: Greek for "oral instruction"; refers to organized scriptural and confessional instruction prior to Baptism or confirmation, as well as continuing Christian nurture of the faith through the Word; in the early church, this instruction took between three months and three years.

catechumen: Greek for "one under instruction"; denotes young adults or adults undergoing instruction in the Christian faith before Baptism or confirmation.

cathedra: Greek for "chair"; refers to the bishop's chair or "throne"; normally placed in the basilica's apse.

cathedral: bishop's church in which his throne or chair was located; usually the largest church in an area or diocese (though size is not the only criterion).

catholic: Greek for "throughout or according to the whole"; implies the universal nature of the church and its unaltered biblical faith; Luther translated this word as *Christian* because the church is not a denomination but the entire body of those who acknowledge Jesus as Lord and Savior.

celebrant: the presiding minister responsible for conducting the liturgy and distributing the Sacrament of the Altar; the minister who performs a marriage.

censer: a metal container in which incense is burned; also called a thurible; often has a chain attached.

cerecloth: from the Latin for "wax"; heavy linen cloth treated with wax to resist moisture; placed over the top of the altar (mensa); fair linen is placed on top of this cloth.

ceremony: the actions, gestures, and movements that accompany the rite of a service; all actions involved in a worship service, including music, words, and objects.

chalice: from the Latin for "cup"; traditionally a gold or silver cup lined with gold; used to distribute wine at Holy Communion; may be made of ceramic, glass, or even wood.

chalice veil: cloth in the liturgical color of the season placed over the chalice and paten; burse is placed over this cloth.

chancel: liturgical space around the altar from the rail to the liturgical "east" wall; usually includes the pulpit and the lectern; sometimes called the choir in cathedrals.

chancel care committee: laypeople responsible for maintaining the cleanliness and décor of the chancel, including preparation for the sacraments; also called an altar guild.

chant: Latin for "sing"; unaccompanied liturgical singing, usually in unison (though harmony may be used); text always takes precedence over music; styles of chant include Ambrosian, Gregorian (also called plainchant or plainsong), and that of Joseph Gelineau.

chasuble: from the Latin for "little house"; the outer liturgical garment that may be worn by the presiding minister when celebrating Holy Communion; poncholike garment in the liturgical color of the season; symbols may be included on the back and front.

chi rho: the Greek capital letters X and P; represents Christ's title as the Anointed One.

choir: vocalists who supplement and augment the music of the liturgy; may sing parts of the liturgy with the congregation or for the congregation; architecturally, refers to the chancel.

chorale: strongly didactic yet melodically popular Lutheran hymns of the Reformation period; originally sung in unison and unaccompanied, though later composers, such as Bach, developed harmonic choral and instrumental accompaniments.

chrism: fragrant oil used to anoint, usually at Baptism; a symbol of the Holy Spirit.

chrismon: shortened form of "Christ's monogram"; symbols of Christ often used as Christmas tree ornaments.

Christological: having to do with the person and work of Jesus Christ, particularly the divine and human natures in the one person of Christ, but also His conception, birth, anointing, obedience, redeeming death, resurrection, ascension, and session at God's right hand on behalf of His church.

Christmas: the Nativity of Our Lord (December 25).

church: the body of Christ; the congregation of all the saints called forth by the Holy Spirit from the lost race of humanity that confesses Jesus Christ as Lord and Savior; the people who gather around Word and Sacraments to receive blessings and express gratitude with prayers and praises; the building in which God's guests gather; a worship service.

church year: the liturgical arrangement of the great teaching moments in Christ's life, particularly His birth, death, and resurrection; begins with the Sundays of Advent and continues through Pentecost as the Lord's half; ends with the Sunday of the Fulfillment after more than two dozen Sundays after Pentecost in the church half of the year.

ciborium: a chalicelike container with a cover; holds the bread or wafers for Holy Communion; may also be used for distribution during Communion.

cincture: a fabric or ropelike belt worn around the waist to gird someone wearing an alb or cassock.

close(d) Communion: the pastoral practice of giving Holy Communion only to those who are known to share the same faith; practiced by early Christians and reclaimed by Lutherans at the time of the Reformation; still followed by churches that recognize the real presence in Holy Communion—conservative Lutherans, many Roman Catholics, and most Eastern Orthodox communities.

collect: a prayer form that consists of an address, reason, request, result, and conclusion; a Proper in the liturgy that reflects the pericopes.

color: *see* **liturgical colors**

committal service: concluding portion of a funeral service; usually held at the place of interment or burial; includes a reminder of Baptism and the resurrection of the body.

Common Service: a service envisioned by Henry Melchior Muehlenberg and prepared in 1888 by U.S. Lutherans for English-speaking worshipers; followed the historic liturgy of the Lutheran Church; retained by many Lutheran congregations.

Communion, Holy: the celebration of Christ's true body and blood in, with, and under the bread and wine; Christians eat and drink this sacrament for the forgiveness of sins; also called the Eucharist, the Lord's Supper, and the Meal.

Communion pall: a 7- or 9-inch square sheet of plastic, metal, or glass covered with white linen or stiff cloth; covers the paten and chalice when vested.

Communion rail: a railing separating the altar from the nave; usually communicants kneel or stand at the rail to receive Holy Communion; also called altar rail or chancel rail.

Compline: Latin for "complete"; the last hour of Daily Prayer; emphasizes confession and preparation for sleep and death; also called Prayer at the Close of the Day.

confessor: a pastor or individual Christian to whom one confesses sins and receives the assurance of God's forgiveness; a pastor will speak a word of absolution.

confirmand: a young adult who is in the process of being confirmed; usually refers to those in the last weeks of instruction; *see also* **catechumen**.

confirmation: a pastoral and educational work of the church that edifies the faith of the baptized child through a more intensive teaching of the Word and of the basic tenets of the faith as compiled in a catechism, such as Luther's Small Catechism; it also prepares one to examine oneself prior to the reception of the Sacrament; it helps one identify more deeply with the Christian community and participate more fully in its mission.

contemporary: things related to the present culture and social setting; used to describe a less-formal worship style that follows a pattern adopted from 19th-century revivalism.

cope: festive liturgical capelike vestment in the liturgical color of the season; includes a hood or stylized hood; may be worn by the presiding or assisting minister; worn over an alb or surplice for non-Communion services; may be worn by a lay leader in Matins or Vespers.

corporal: a square linen cloth placed over the fair linen; sacramental vessels are placed on this after the Offertory; often has a cross embroidered on the front.

corpus: Latin for "body"; refers to a depiction of Christ's body; a cross with a corpus is called a crucifix.

Corpus Christi: Latin for "body of Christ"; a Roman Catholic celebration on the Thursday following Trinity Sunday that recalls Holy Communion; Lutherans do not observe this festival because it encourages inappropriate devotion to the elements.

cotta: Latin for "coat"; a waist-length surplice; sometimes has split sleeves; often worn by acolytes or musicians.

creed: Latin for "I believe"; refers to any of three confessions of faith used in worship; the Apostles' Creed is said at baptisms, funerals, and non-Communion services; the Nicene Creed is said at Communion services; the Athanasian Creed (or Quicunque Vult) may be said on Trinity Sunday.

credence: a table or shelf covered with a linen cloth placed behind or beside the altar; may hold the sacramental elements until the Offertory; may be where the offerings are placed.

cross: the instrument on which Jesus was crucified; a Christian symbol of salvation and victory; may be carried in procession, suspended over the altar, or worn on a chain around the neck; the act of making the sign of the cross by touching the forehead, chest, and right and left shoulders during the Invocation or at other times in the Divine Service.

crucifer: one who carries the processional cross during festival services.

crucifix: a cross with a corpus; emphasizes the central message of Lutheran preaching: "Christ crucified."

cruet: from medieval French for "little jug"; a small glass pitcher for Communion wine or baptismal water.

Curia: legislative body comprised of Roman Catholic ecclesiastical authorities; the body through which the pope governs the Roman Catholic Church.

Daily Prayer: also called Divine Office; *see* **canonical hours**.

dalmatic: vestment in the liturgical color of the season; worn by deacons; sleeved garment worn over the alb and deacon's stole.

deacon: Greek for "servant, messenger, or attendant"; "lay minister" or attendant who assists in the worship services of the church; often reads lessons and distributes Communion wine; other activities may be assigned by the presiding minister; lowest rank of ordained clergy in the early church.

Deacon's Prayer: ancient prayer in which the lay assistant invites or bids the congregation to pray for specific needs; also called the Bidding Prayer.

declaration of grace: minister's statement after a general confession by which God's forgiveness is assured to those who have repented; *compare* **Absolution**.

Deprecations: from the Latin "to prevent something from happening by prayer"; specific prayers asking God to ward off evil from His church.

diaconal: that which is related to deacons; *see* **deacon**.

diptych: from the Greek "folded or doubled"; refers to liturgical pictures painted or carved on two hinged boards or tablets, such as an altarpiece.

Divine Service: the chief Order of Holy Communion; includes the Service of the Word and the Service of the Sacrament; a translation of the German *Gottesdienst*.

domus dei: Latin for "house of God"; church building that emphasizes the mystery and awe of entering God's presence.

domus ecclesiae: Latin for "house of the church"; adapted from the Greek designation for house churches in early Christianity; the building housed the people who are the church, the body of Christ.

doorkeeper: *see* **porter**

dossal curtain: large ornamental cloth drapery suspended on the wall behind the altar; originated when some worshipers, particularly monks or nuns, were cloistered and had to be separated from the lay congregation in the nave; sometimes referred to as dorsal curtain.

doxology: from the Greek "words of praise"; any short ascription of praise to the Trinity, whether a final hymn stanza or other liturgical conclusion to a prayer or psalm.

east, liturgical: direction the congregation looks when facing the altar; used whether or not the altar is geographically on the east end of the building; *see* **orienting**.

Easter: The Festival of the Resurrection of Our Lord; celebrated on a date roughly defined as the first Sunday after the first full moon that falls on or after the vernal equinox; the word *Easter* is derived from the Teutonic goddess of spring, Eostre.

Easter season: *see* **Great Fifty Days**

Easter Vigil: four-part preparatory service for the Easter celebration; includes a Service of Light, Readings, Baptism, and Holy Communion.

ecumenical: from the Greek for "inhabited world"; the scope of Christian outreach; a worldwide church event; recently applied to a movement that seeks Christian unity without doctrinal unity.

elevation: lifting the bread and the cup during the Words of Institution; Luther retained this practice to highlight Christ's real presence.

Entrance Hymn: opening hymn of the Divine Service; sung after the conclusion of the preparatory confessional service; unifies the gathered guests and, if replacing the Introit, establishes the service's theme; often used as a processional hymn for choir and clergy.

epiclesis: Greek for "invoking" the Holy Spirit; some churches pray that the Holy Spirit would enter the Communion elements; Lutherans ask the Spirit to prepare the hearts of the communicants to receive the Sacrament with faith; the second part of the Eucharistic Prayer.

Epiphany: Greek for "manifestation"; the festival of Christ's manifestation of His divinity; early Christians celebrated January 6 as Christ's birthday; contemporary Christians celebrate January 6 as the arrival of the Magi (Matthew 2); also called "the Gentiles' Christmas"; the Epiphany season varies in length but concludes with the Sunday of the Transfiguration.

episcopos: Latin, from the Greek for "overseer"; translated most often as bishop.

Epistle: usually the second reading in a liturgical service; a reading from a letter of an apostle; *see also* **south, liturgical.**

eschatological: Greek for "words about the end times"; any topic connected to the end of the world, for example, death, Christ's return, judgment.

eternal light: candle in a glass container or electric light kept burning throughout the week; implies God's presence; the Roman Catholic practice recalled the presence of the Communion host on the tabernacle of the altar; sometimes called the sanctuary light.

Eucharist: Greek for "thanksgiving"; another name for Holy Communion; emphasizes the fact that Jesus gave thanks and broke the bread on numerous occasions in His ministry.

evangelical: Greek for "gospel"; the Lutheran emphasis on Christ's saving work on the cross and His victorious resurrection to assure believers forgiveness, life, and salvation.

Evangelical: Greek for "gospel"; used by many Protestants who rely on the Bible but have a weak sacramental theology; in the early 20th century, they were called Fundamentalists.

Evening Prayer: an adaptation of Vespers; includes the Service of Light (*Lucernarium*).

ewer: brass, silver, or gold pitcher that holds the baptismal water.

ex corde: Latin for "from the heart"; devotional prayer not prepared in advance, though the thoughts may be considered beforehand.

exorcism: the liturgical and ecclesiastical expulsion of the devil from a nonbeliever; ancient forms of Baptism and catechetical instruction included elaborate oaths by which spirits were driven out; Luther retained the practice; a remnant of this ritual is retained in the present baptismal formula of renunciation.

exsufflation: Latin for "blow upon"; a ritual breathing on a baptismal candidate by the officiant at the time of the exorcism; retained by Luther but no longer present in modern Lutheran orders.

Exsultet: Latin for "rejoice"; the Easter proclamation from the Easter Vigil; begins with "Rejoice now, all heavenly choirs."

fair linen: long fine linen cloth placed over the cerecloth and frontal on the altar; drapes over the side nearly to the floor; usually features five embroidered crosses; symbolizes Christ's burial cloth.

flagon: covered gold or silver pitcher that holds Communion wine.

Flood Prayer: Luther's baptismal prayer; connects the saving of Noah and his family with the waters of Baptism; follows the imagery in 1 Peter.

footwashing: an act of humility following Christ's example (John 13); presiding minister may wash the feet of several members on Maundy Thursday; while some denominations consider this act almost sacramental, Lutherans do not regularly observe it because the emphasis of Maundy Thursday is on the Lord's Supper.

font: large basin or pool, often made of stone, that holds the water for Baptism; smaller wooden fonts may include a metal basin for the water; located either near the chancel or at the church's entrance; serves either as a reminder of the sacramental community into which the baptized is brought or to underscore the act by which God brings believers into His family of faith.

"Formula of the Mass and Communion": Luther's first liturgy; removed elements from the Roman Mass that distracted from the Gospel; prepared in 1523 for the Wittenberg congregation.

fresco: painting technique in which a nearly finished plaster surface was painted with pigment to penetrate the plaster coat; used in many medieval churches.

frontal: altar hanging or parament in the liturgical color of the season; covers the entire front of the altar; usually includes seasonal symbols.

frontlet: altar hanging or parament in the liturgical color of the season; covers only a portion of the front of the altar.

funeral pall: large draping material placed over a coffin when it enters the sanctuary; usually white to symbolize Christ's righteousness received at Baptism; may be in the liturgical color of the season; usually includes a large cross or other resurrection symbol.

Gallican rite: form of liturgy common in early medieval Gaul (France); allowed diversity, variation, and elaboration; provided a wide repertoire of readings and prayers for feasts and local celebrations; also called the Frankish rite; *see also* **rite.**

General Prayer: *see* **Prayer of the Church**

Geneva gown: long, full, black robe worn as an academic garment by Luther and many of the reformers; adopted as the vestment by Calvinists; adapted during Pietist and Rationalist periods by Lutherans; sometimes called a preaching gown.

"German Mass": Luther's second liturgy; removed elements in the Roman Mass that distracted from the Gospel; included greater congregational involvement through the singing of hymns; prepared in 1526 for the Wittenberg congregation.

-gesima: Greek ending for decades; refers to the three Sundays before Lent (Septuagesima [seventieth], Sexigesima [sixtieth], and Quinquagesima [fiftieth]); generally, these are no longer observed in North American Lutheranism because of redundancy, though they are still present in European Lutheran one-year lectionaries.

Gloria in Excelsis: Latin for "Glory [to God] in the highest"; the angels' song (Luke 2); the traditional Hymn of Praise in the Divine Service; also called the "greater Gloria."

Gloria Patri: Latin for "Glory to the Father"; the doxological phrase ending the psalms and most canticles; emphasizes the trinitarian faith; also known as the "lesser Gloria."

gold: *see* liturgical colors

Good Friday: the most solemn day of the Christian year; includes a note of joy as Christians realize that Christ's death brings life; the name may be a mutation of "God's Friday."

Gospel: the good news of God's gracious love in Christ for the redemption of the world; one of the first four books of the New Testament from which a selection is read by the presiding minister; an ornate lectionary used for Gospel processions.

Gospel canticle: *see* canticles

Gospel procession: a procession into the nave prior to the Gospel Reading by the presiding minister; includes torchbearers and possibly a crucifer and thurifer: occurs during the Alleluia verse; signifies Christ's incarnation.

Gospel side: *see* orienting

Gothic: originally a pejorative term related to the barbaric Goths, Germanic tribes that moved through Europe in the fourth through sixth centuries; describes the architecture of the high Middle Ages (twelfth to fifteenth centuries); characterized by pointed arches and towering buttressed walls.

Gottesdienst: German for "God's service" or "service of God"; connotes both the Divine Service by which God serves His people through Word and Sacrament and the setting in which worshipers serve God with prayers and praises.

Gradual: Latin for "step"; a liturgical chant from a psalm; usually sung after the Old Testament Reading or between the Epistle and Gospel; the Psalm of the Day may be substituted for this as one of the Propers for the Day.

Great Fifty Days: fifty-day celebration of Easter that begins on Easter Sunday and continues through the eve of Pentecost; the Sundays are identified as "of Easter."

Greek: the language of worship for the first four centuries of Christianity; many traditions and terms originate in this classical language.

green: *see* liturgical colors

hallelujah: Hebrew for "Praise the Lord"; expression of praise and thanksgiving to God; the Greek spelling is transliterated as "alleluia"; a central theme of the Hallel Psalms.

Hauptgottesdienst: German for "chief divine service"; the main worship event on a Sunday morning (if more than one service is offered); the Order of Holy Communion.

Holy Friday: *see* **Good Friday**

Holy Saturday: the day after Good Friday, often the Easter Vigil begins this evening; sometimes called "shut-in Saturday."

Holy Thursday: *see* **Maundy Thursday**

Holy Trinity: the doctrinal confession that God is three persons in one essence; the celebration of this doctrine occurs on the Sunday after Pentecost; doxologies affirm this confession.

Holy Week: the highly solemn week that begins with Palm Sunday and goes through the Vigil of Easter; marks the final events in Christ's earthly life; includes His teachings, the institution of the Lord's Supper, and His death on Calvary; anticipates Easter.

homily: Greek for "conversation"; usually a shorter sermon in which the essence of the day and the texts are expounded; includes a Gospel emphasis on Christ.

hosanna: Hebrew for "save [us] now"; a messianic acclamation of praise and joy shouted by the people in Jerusalem; repeated in the Sanctus of the Communion liturgy; may be sung as part of hymn texts.

host: Latin for "sacrifice or victim"; individual Communion wafers; sometimes embossed with a cross or other symbol; Christ Himself, who serves His gathered guests.

Hungertuch: German for "hunger veil"; large altar frontal used during the Lenten season to emphasize the self-discipline of fasting; may serve as a mission emphasis by depicting Christian symbols from other cultures.

hymn: Greek for "song"; distinct from psalms and more recent compositions because these Christian songs of prayer and praise have remained popular among worshipers for centuries.

Hymn of Praise: song following the Introit or Kyrie in the Divine Service; affirms God's actions for the world; the Gloria in Excelsis is traditionally sung; "This Is the Feast" or "Worthy Is Christ" (Dignus est Agnus) are two recent compositions; other appropriate hymns may be used.

Hymn of the Day: a hymn specifically selected to coincide with the pericopal Scripture readings; is more than a sermon hymn or a paraphrase of the Gospel; many are Lutheran chorales; could be considered a Proper in the Lutheran liturgy.

hymnody: Greek for "singing hymns"; refers to hymns collectively or to the collection of hymns available for congregational singing.

icon: Greek for "image"; early Christian two-dimensional stylized art form; depicts biblical scenes or figures; Eastern Orthodox Christians call them "windows into heaven."

iconostasis: Greek for "icon screen"; refers to the screen or wall on which icons are displayed in an Eastern Orthodox church; the screen originally was a railing but later became a wall separating the nave and chancel; depicts the Old Testament Holy of holies; icons are assigned to precise locations on this wall.

incense: sweet smelling resin burned during worship; associated with Old Testament sacrifices of praise and thanksgiving; New Testament images of heaven portray clouds of incense; symbolizes both God's presence and the church's prayers and praises; adds another sensual dimension to worship.

installation: service officially recognizing the introduction of a person into a place of service to the church; also signifies a new opportunity for Christian ministry as a professional servant of the church accepts a new position; may occur several times throughout a professional churchworker's lifetime.

intercession: prayers for others; in Luther's Litany, he offered petitions for the church, for the weak, for the nations of the world, for humanity, and for reconciliation; any prayer beginning with "for" can be concluded with "Lord, have mercy."

Introit: Latin for "he enters"; the music sung as the presiding minister enters the chancel; usually a psalm verse, which is preceded by an Antiphon and followed by the Gloria Patri.

Invitatory: seasonal verse that serves in place of an Antiphon for the Venite as an invitation to praise God.

Invocation: Latin for "call upon"; the words that begin worship and confess that God is present by speaking His name; in many cases, the pastor and people make the sign of the cross as a reminder of their Baptism.

Itinerarium: *see* **Liturgy for Travelers**

Kanzelaltar: German for "chancel-altar or pulpit altar"; refers to the practice of European Lutherans and some other Protestant groups of positioning the pulpit directly above the altar so both Word and Sacrament are equally emphasized; some 19th-century U.S. Lutheran churches also followed this style.

Kyrie: Greek for "Lord"; short for "Kyrie eleison" (Lord, have mercy); the short hymn following the Entrance Hymn or Introit; in an expanded form, part of the Deacon's Prayer.

Latin: language of the Western Christian church for almost two millennia; source of many worship terms and concepts; sometimes used to refer to Roman Catholic rites.

Lauds: from the Latin for "praise"; emphasizes the resurrection hope of Christians; sung prior to sunrise; named for the Laudate Psalms, which were frequently sung during this office.

Laudate Psalms: Psalm 148–150; originally concluded Matins but were transferred to the morning office of Lauds.

lay reader: *see* **lector**

lectern: from Latin for "reading"; a piece of liturgical furniture that serves as a stand for the lectionary; place from which the Scripture readings are read; particularly popular among Anglicans; may be replaced with an ambo.

lectio continua: Latin for "continuous reading"; reminiscent of Hebrew reading patterns in which a book is read from beginning to end because it is on a scroll; Christians adapted this practice (evident in readings for the Sundays after Pentecost).

lection: from the Latin for "reading"; any of several liturgical readings, though usually not the Gospel; assigned for a particular Sunday.

lectionary: book containing the Scripture readings for each Sunday or festival; may also identify the appointed readings developed during the church's history; a recent ecumenical three-year series is available for adaptation or adoption by church bodies.

lector: Latin for "reader"; assisting minister who usually reads the first two Scripture readings—the Old Testament and the Epistle.

Lent: liturgical season of preparation for Easter; solemn time during which the Alleluia is not sung; most Lutheran congregations hold midweek services to aid this devotional time.

Lenten veil: a white, off-white, black, or purple cloth placed over all statuary in a church during the Lenten season; *compare* **Hungertuch.**

Lenten verse: Scripture verse that replaces the Alleluia verse during the Lenten season.

linens: white cloths used on the altar and for Holy Communion; originally made of fine linen, cotton is now more generally used; linens include the cerecloth, credence table cloth, fair linen, purificators, chalice pall, corporal, and baptismal napkins.

litany: specialized prayer in which the congregation responds to petitions and intercessions.

Litany, The: Greek for "supplication or entreaty"; one of the most penitential liturgical prayers; displays a somber meditative mood; based on a strong assurance of God's love in Christ; Luther slightly modified the prayer's contents.

Little Chapter: brief reading from Scripture in the Daily Office; found especially in the shorter offices and in Compline.

liturgical art: creative artistic expressions specifically for use in worship life; any medium may be acceptable, though the scriptural message must take precedence over the medium.

liturgical colors: seven colors used for paraments and vestments; each color is associated with a season of the church year; green is used for Sundays after Pentecost and Epiphany; red is used for Pentecost Sunday, Lutheran ordinations, and martyred saint days (scarlet may be used for Holy Week); blue is used during Advent (though Roman Catholics use it for Mary too); purple is used for Lent and possibly Advent (violet is sometimes used for Advent); white is used for the Easter and Christmas seasons; gold may be used for Easter and Christmas Day; black may be used for Ash Wednesday (and Good Friday, if the altar is not stripped).

liturgical prayer: prayer that emphasizes the Christian church's activities; may be in various forms, such as collects or intercessions.

liturgy: Greek for "work of the people"; the worship activity of the Divine Service; for Lutherans, the activity also includes God's work through the means of grace and the people's responses of hymns and prayers.

Liturgy of the Word: *see* **Service of the Word**

Liturgy of the Sacrament: *see* **Service of the Sacrament**

Liturgy for Travelers: special service in anticipation of a journey; may follow Responsive Prayer II; sometimes called Itinerarium.

Lord's Day: Sunday; emphasizes that God created this day as His first act and that Jesus rose on this day.

Lord's Prayer: *see* **Our Father**

Lord's Supper: *see* **Communion, Holy**

Lucernarium: *see* **Service of Light**

Lutheran Confessions: official doctrinal statements adopted by territorial princes and their Lutheran churches in the sixteenth century that still serve as the interpretive norm for the Scripture-based faith and life of Lutheran Christians; the Augsburg Confession in 1530 was the first "confession"; other documents were added until *The Book of Concord* was published in 1580.

Magnificat: Latin for "[it does] magnify"; title of Mary's Song (Luke 1); traditionally sung as the Gospel canticle for Vespers.

marriage: occasional service in which a Christian bride and groom give witness to their biblical faith and ask God's blessings on their life together; *see* **occasional service.**

Mass: from the Latin for "dismissal"; historically designates the service of Holy Communion after which the people were dismissed; used among some Lutherans following the Reformation; vestiges of the term are evident in names such as *Christmas.*

Mass of the Catechumens: *see* **Service of the Word**

Mass of the Faithful: *see* **Service of the Sacrament**

Matins: from the Latin for "of the morning"; first canonical hour; sung around midnight; Lutherans adapted this as a Sunday morning service without Holy Communion; *see also* **Morning Prayer.**

matzo: Hebrew for "unleavened"; unleavened Passover bread; sometimes used in Lutheran congregations for Communion bread.

Maundy Thursday: comes from Latin for "command," recalling Jesus' command to "love one another"; Thursday in Holy Week; first day of the Triduum; central feature is the institution of the Lord's Supper; the altar may be stripped in anticipation of Good Friday.

means of grace: *see* **Word and Sacraments**

mensa: Latin for "table"; refers to the top of the altar on which the Communion elements and the altar book are placed.

mikvah: Hebrew for "bath"; ceremonial washings required by Jewish law; early Christians may have used these ceremonial pools in synagogues for baptismal services.

minister of music: *see* **cantor**

missal: *see* **altar book**

missal stand: short wooden or metal stand on which the altar book (or missal) may be placed; some Anglicans and Roman Catholics use an elaborately decorated cushion.

Morning Prayer: Lutheran adaptation of Matins; includes portions of Lauds and Prime; used as a Service of the Word.

mosaic: small glass or ceramic pieces placed on a floor, wall, or ceiling as decoration; used in Christian churches to portray biblical and liturgical scenes.

napkin: linen cloth used to wipe the water from the head or body of a newly baptized Christian.

narrative service: a form of Divine Service in which the parts of the liturgy are explained with brief comments by the pastor or other assisting minister; may be used as one service or over several Sundays.

narthex: Greek for a reedy plant carried by officials who would gather outside public basilicas; the gathering space of a church outside the nave; the baptismal font may be located here.

Nativity of Our Lord, The: *see* **Christmas**

nave: Latin for "ship"; architecturally, the main portion of a church; place in which the assembly offers prayers and songs; early Christians portrayed the church as an ark into which the saved were brought by Baptism.

nocturns: from the Latin for "of the night"; collectively, the evening offices conducted in anticipation of festivals; sometimes called vigils.

None: Latin for "nine"; the canonical hour of afternoon prayer (corresponds to 3 P.M.).

Noonday Office: *see* Sext

north, liturgical: *see* orienting

Nunc Dimittis: Latin for "now [you] dismiss"; Simeon's song (Luke 1); traditionally sung as an alternate Gospel canticle for Vespers; Lutherans use it as the post-Communion canticle.

O Antiphons: Seven Advent antiphons; presented in the hymn, "Oh, Come, Oh, Come, Emmanuel"; each antiphon calls on Jesus to fulfill His Messianic role: O Wisdom (*Sapientiae*), O Lord (*Adonai*), O Root of Jesse (*Radix Jesse*), O Key of David (*Clavis David*), O Daystar (*Oriens*), O King of Nations (*Rex Gentium*), and O Emmanuel.

Obsecrations: from the Latin for "imploring on religious grounds"; special prayers in the Litany to be answered because of who Christ is or what He has done.

occasional service: a service that marks special occasions in the lives of Christians, such as a marriage or funeral; a service that marks special occasions in the life of a congregation, such as an anniversary or installation; some are sacramental, such as Baptism and private Communion.

octave: Latin for "eighth"; the fullness of a festive week; usually used in regards to a church festival as a week-long celebration or a celebration of a festival within the week of the festival date.

Offertory: verses sung by choir or congregation after an offering is gathered and while the Communion elements are prepared; Lutherans use "Create in Me," "What Shall I Render to the Lord," and "Thank the Lord and Sing His Praise."

offerings: the gifts of gratitude that God's gathered guests present to the Lord during the Divine Service; usually music or another activity accompanies this gathering.

office: from the Latin for "service"; refers to the services of the canonical hours; sometimes called the Divine Office; each may be titled "The Office of . . ."

officiant: *see* presiding minister

orans: Latin for "praying"; the position of standing for prayer with outstretched hands raised approximately to shoulder level.

ordinary: sung or spoken parts of the liturgy that do not change each Sunday or season; includes the Kyrie, the Gloria in Excelsis, the Creed, the Sanctus, and the Agnus Dei.

ordination: public rite of the confirmation of a man's calling into the public ministry of Word and Sacraments by a congregation; occurs only once in a pastor's life of ministry.

orienting: traditionally, churches were built on an east-west axis with the altar at the east (orient) and the narthex at the west; when facing the altar, the right side (the Epistle side) was south and the left (the Gospel side) was north; these directions are used in church architecture and in the placement of church furnishings even if the building does not face east.

orphrey: decorative band along a seam or hem of a liturgical vestment; sometimes used to distinguish a deacon's dalmatic from a subdeacon's tunic.

orthodox: Greek for "straight praise" or "straight [right] doctrine"; teachings that are biblical and confessional; if capitalized, refers to Eastern Christians who broke with the Roman Catholic Church in the eleventh century.

Our Father: Jesus' model prayer that He taught to His disciples (Matthew 6:9–13; Luke 11:2–4); called the Lord's Prayer in English-speaking countries.

pall: *see* **communion pall** or **funeral pall**

Palm Sunday: commemorative Sunday recalling Jesus' triumphant entry into Jerusalem; begins Holy Week; also called Sunday of the Passion.

paraments: cloth in the liturgical color of the season; used on various chancel furnishings; made of fine textiles; often decorated with symbols pertaining to the church season; *see also* **antependium, burse, frontal, pall,** and **superfrontal.**

paschal: Greek for "Passover"; refers particularly to the celebration of Jesus' passion, death, and resurrection; sometimes refers to the time of the Easter vigil (Saturday night through Easter morning); often refers to anything related to Easter.

paschal candle: large candle used during Easter to symbolize Christ's presence among His people; also used for funerals and baptisms.

pastor: Latin for "shepherd"; title for a congregation's public minister who is called as spiritual supervisor over the "flock" that gathers around Word and Sacrament in a particular place.

Passion Sunday: Sunday of Holy Week; on this day, the Passion of Our Lord according to one of the evangelists may be read; *see also* **Palm Sunday.**

paten: from the Latin and Greek for "plate"; sacramental vessel of gold or silver, lined with gold, on which consecrated bread is placed for distribution; usually fits on top of the chalice when the chalice is vested.

Peace, Exchange of or **Sharing of**: greeting between pastor and congregation after the Words of Institution; follows biblical precedence among early Christians of greeting one another with a holy kiss; opportunity for the congregation to be reconciled to each other and to express love for one another.

pectoral cross: large cross made from a precious metal worn on a chain over the chest; a symbol of the episcopal or bishop's office in many denominations; frequently worn by Lutheran pastors when vested with alb and stole.

Pentecost: Greek for "fiftieth"; celebrates the gift of the Holy Spirit fifty days after Easter and the founding of the church; coincides with a Jewish harvest festival.

pericope: Greek for "section or selection"; the portion of Scripture appointed to be read on a particular Sunday or festival; included in a lectionary.

petition: prayer that is a basic request to the Triune God.

Pietism: religious movement in the late 17th century that had a strong effect on Lutherans and other Christians; stressed emotional spirituality over doctrine as a supposed corrective to perceived doctrinal coldness; resulted in a neglect of the sacraments and, in its extreme form, a rejection of scriptural authority.

piscina: Latin for "pool"; a basin built in a sacristy that connects with the earth; used to dispose of unused consecrated wine and baptismal water; also called a sacrarium.

porter: one of the lower orders of ministers; in the early church, these assisting ministers guarded the doors during times of persecution; modern greeters may serve in a similar capacity.

prayer, liturgical: *see* **liturgical prayer**

prayer, devotional or **personal:** prayer that emphasizes personal needs and concerns; though in various forms, most often *ex corde* and informal.

Prayer of the Church: the major corporate expression of prayer in the Divine Service; expresses the will of God for His gathered guests throughout the world; an historic general format that addresses a wide range of topics; also called Prayer of the Faithful, the General Prayer, or The Intercessions.

Prayer of the Faithful: *see* **Prayer of the Church**

preservice: activities, usually musical, that occur prior to a worship service.

Preface: beginning of the Service of the Sacrament; opens with a dialogue between pastor and people; concludes with the Proper Preface, which is a seasonal sentence that connects the Lord's Supper with Jesus' life.

presbyter: Greek for "elder"; an early Christian leader who worked with a bishop; became those who worked under the supervision of a bishop as a priest in a local congregation; congregational leaders in the Presbyterian denomination who serve as teaching or ruling elders.

presiding minister: chief minister or officiant in a service; ordained pastor who carries out the sacramental responsibilities of the pastoral office or public ministry.

prie dieu: French for "pray God"; individual kneelers placed in the chancel for ministers; may be used for private confession or personal prayer in other locations.

priest: from Greek "elder"; refers to Old Testament worship leaders from the house of Levi who offered sacrifices; in the early church, referred to presbyters serving under a bishop; Roman Catholic parish pastors were designated "priests" because they were said to be sacrificing Christ in the Sacrament of the Altar; Lutheran pastors do not use this title.

Prime: Latin for "first"; first daytime service of the canonical hours; emphasizes allegiance to God for the day's work.

procession: any ceremonial movement of a group of people in or out of church: includes Entrance and Gospel processions and recessions; order of participants varies by occasion but crucifer (if used) is first and the most honored person (usually the presiding minister, though in weddings it is the bride) comes last.

processional cross: crucifix mounted on a long staff; carried during Entrance processions and recessions; normally not used during Gospel processions.

Prone: from the French for "lecture or sermon"; Service of the Word conducted from the pulpit; developed in the tenth century; consists of prayers, an exposition of the Word or creed, and announcements; used by some Lutherans for a century after the Reformation.

propers: parts of the Divine Service that vary according to the Sunday or festival; includes the Introit, Collect of the Day; Psalm of the Day; Gradual; Readings; and (in Lutheran churches) the Hymn of the Day.

Psalm of the Day: appointed psalm to be read or sung in the Divine Service; may be used instead of the Introit or, preferably, as the response to the First Reading; psalms were the hymns of God's people in the Old Testament.

pulpit: from the Latin for "stage"; the elevated and enclosed platform from which preachers proclaim God's Word; may be used in certain services as the place from which prayers are led; usually a parament in the liturgical color of the season hangs from the front.

purificator: linen sacramental napkin used to wipe the rim of the chalice after each use; placed over the cup and under the plate when the chalice may be vested; several may be used during the distribution of the Sacrament.

purple: *see* **liturgical colors**

pyx: Greek for "box"; small covered container of gold or silver; holds wafers prior to Communion distribution; also called a Host Box; an alternate container is the ciborium.

Quicunque Vult: *see* **Creed, Athanasian**

reading table: *see* **ambo**

Real Presence: Lutheran understanding of Christ's sacramental union with the physical elements in the Sacrament of the Altar; stated most simply, Christ's body and blood are in, with, and under the physical elements of bread and wine.

red: *see* **liturgical colors**

Reproaches: powerfully emotional hymn of the early church in which God reproaches His people (Micah 6:3–4) with a rhetorically disappointed voice by mentioning the benefits they received at His expense; may be used during a Good Friday service.

reredos: decorative wood, stone, or brick screen or altar backdrop; often embellished with carvings or mosaics; *see also* **dossal curtain**.

Response: *see* **Versicles**

Responsive Prayer: prayer used alone or as part of a longer devotional service; series of Versicles and Responses, chiefly from the Psalms; though in the form of a litany, it is more objective and poetic.

responsorial: an extended solo or choral piece with congregational response after a number of stanzas; sung by choir or cantor; a group response in answer to a single voice.

Resurrection of Our Lord, The Festival of the: *see* **Easter**

retable: steplike shelf positioned against the wall behind an altar; candles, flowers, and a crucifix are placed on this instead of on the altar; also known as a gradine.

rite: prescribed liturgical form containing the words (liturgy) and the action (ceremony), such as a Rite of Baptism or a Rite of Confirmation; *see also* **Gallican rite** and **Western Rite**.

rochet: close-fitting linen vestment similar to a surplice; originally worn by bishops but later adapted by musicians.

romanesque: architectural style popular from the tenth to twelfth centuries; followed a Roman style of round archways and vaults yet was elaborately carved and ornamented.

rood screen: large elaborately carved divider between chancel and nave above which was located the rood (Anglo-Saxon word for "cross") or crucifix; some screens were large enough to carry a loft or gallery.

rubrics: Latin for "red"; instructions for minister and congregation on how to conduct a service; often printed in red.

Sabbath: Hebrew for "rest"; the seventh day of creation that God assigned as a day of rest; Christians adapted this command to Sunday in remembrance of Jesus' victorious resurrection.

sacrament: from the Latin for "mystery;"; an action of God through the attachment of His Word of promise and forgiveness to a physical element; the Lutheran church recognizes Absolution, Baptism, and Communion as sacraments, though the first is not universally admitted.

sacramental: those portions of the Divine Service directed to the congregation from God by His representative, the minister; includes the Scripture readings; something that pertains to a sacrament, such as candles (sacramental lights) or chasuble (sacramental vestment).

sacrarium: *see* **piscina**

sacrifice: any offering made to God in thanksgiving or for reconciliation; Christ's sacrifice is the once-for-all sacrifice, an atoning sacrifice; other sacrifices of praise and thanksgiving are responses to what God has done.

sacrificial: those portions of the Divine Service directed to God by the congregation, such as prayers; anything that pertains to offerings made to God in grateful thanksgiving.

sacristy: room for preparing for a worship service, usually next to the chancel; room for preparing the altar and Communion vessels and for storing vestments (a working sacristy); *see also* **vestry**.

saints: all members of the body of Christ who have by the power of the Holy Spirit been cleansed in the waters of Baptism and been declared holy by the Father; often describes those Christians who have died after giving an exemplary witness to their faith.

salutation: from the Latin for "greeting of health or safety"; exchanged greeting in the Divine Service in which the pastor wishes the Lord's presence with His people and the people respond.

sanctuary: area around the altar in the chancel; improperly used to refer to the entire worship space.

Sanctus: Latin for "holy"; liturgical song sung by the six-winged seraphim before God's throne (Isaiah 6); sung by worshipers in the Preface of Holy Communion immediately before the Communion prayer.

scarlet: *see* **liturgical colors**

scrutinies: Latin for "examine"; public questions developed in the early church for examining catechumens; may be used as a Lenten discipline.

seder: order of service for a Jewish Passover meal.

sermon: Latin for "a discourse or speech"; refers to the pastor's message of Law and Gospel based on the Scripture readings for a particular Sunday or festival.

server: may refer to assisting ministers who help with distributing the Lord's Supper; specifically used for an acolyte, torchbearer, thurifer, or crucifer.

Service of Light: first part of Evening Prayer; also known as *Lucernarium*; during this portion of the service, a processional candle is brought into the church to affirm God's protective presence; first service of the Easter Vigil in which a new fire is brought into church and the paschal candle is lighted as the Easter proclamation is chanted or said.

Service of the Sacrament: second half of the Divine Service; begins with the Preface, includes the consecration and distribution of the Sacrament, and concludes with the post-Communion canticle and collect.

Service of the Word: first half of the Divine Service; begins with the Introit, includes the Hymn of Praise and readings, and concludes with the Sermon and Creed.

Sext: Latin for "sixth"; a short devotional time in the canonical hours for prayer held at noon (the sixth hour); also known as the Noonday Office.

south, liturgical: *see* **orienting**

sponsor: baptized Christian who mentors a baptismal candidate through the catechumenate; sponsors in a Lutheran Church confess the baptismal faith of the infant and promise to raise the child according to the Lutheran Confessions.

stanza: from Latin "stand"; group of poetic verses that form a unit in a hymn; erroneously called a *verse*; many Christians stand for the final doxological stanza of a hymn.

stole: pastor's identifying vestment; long band of material in the liturgical color of the season that runs over the neck and down the front; may include seasonal symbols; worn over the alb and under the chasuble at Communion; deacons may wear a special stole over one shoulder.

strepitus: Latin for "crashing sound"; loud noise made at the end of a Tenebrae service to represent the closing of Christ's tomb on Good Friday.

stripping of the altar: liturgical exercise in which all furnishings and paraments are removed from the altar and chancel on Maundy Thursday in anticipation of Good Friday.

subdeacon: nonordained minister; assists the deacon in reading and distributing Communion elements.

suffrages: *see* **Responsive Prayer**

Sunday of the Passion: *see* **Palm Sunday** and **Passion Sunday**

superfrontal: narrow parament that covers only the top front part of an altar; usually embroidered with scriptural words; *see also* **frontal**.

Supplications: Latin for "asking publicly"; brief general prayers in the Litany for various situations in the Christian life; also a request for a good death; general prayers and requests to God for personal needs.

sursum corda: Latin for "[Lift] up [your] hearts"; brief statement in the Preface of Holy Communion that reflects a responsive anticipation of God's personal gift.

surplice: from Latin for "over the fur"; full white vestment that extends below the knees or to the floor; worn over the cassock by clergy or assisting ministers for Matins or Vespers.

synagogue: Greek for "place of meeting"; traditional Jewish place for assembly to study, pray, and discuss spiritual, biblical, and community concerns; early Christians met here for worship.

synaxis: Greek for "assembly"; modern use refers to the most ancient and typical order of service preceding the Lord's Supper; a service of readings and prayers.

Table of the Word: *see* ambo

Table of the Sacrament: *see* altar

Te Deum Laudamus: Latin for "You, God, we praise"; ancient creedlike canticle used during Matins; only nonscriptural canticle; *Gloria patri* is not added to this canticle; Luther's favorite morning hymn.

Terce: Latin for "third"; midmorning break for prayer and devotion in the canonical hours (the third hour of daylight, around 9 A.M.).

Tenebrae: Latin for "darkness"; Good Friday service of readings and meditations that move from light to darkness as candles are extinguished until the service ends with the strepitus.

thanksgiving: form of prayer that expresses gratitude to God for physical benefits and spiritual blessings received.

Thanksgiving, Great: Communion prayer; includes several sentences of thanksgiving to God, a narrative of the institution, a remembrance and an invocation of the Holy Spirit, and a summary of the Christian faith; originally part of the Canon of the Mass that Luther removed from his liturgies.

theophany: Greek for "God manifested"; God's appearance in the flesh, Jesus Christ; associated most often with the Epiphany season, though occasionally used for Christ's post-resurrection appearances.

thurible: *see* censer

thurifer: assisting minister or server who carries the censer, keeps the coals burning, and places incense onto the coals.

torch: candle on a stave or pole used in processions; may flank the altar for Holy Communion or be placed next to the reading table for an office.

torchbearer: assisting minister or server who carries a torch; usually two torchbearers serve for processions, including the Gospel procession.

traditional: things related to the entire church; describes a more formal worship style that follows an historic yet relevant pattern.

traditions: that which is passed down from parents or previous generations; a hierarchy exists in the area of worship that includes biblical, catholic, confessional, denominational, parochial, and personal tradition.

transept: in a cross-shaped church, the arm of the cross; location in which the choir or congregation may sit.

Transfiguration of Our Lord, The: festival of the Lutheran Church celebrated on the last Sunday in the Epiphany season; a few other denominations have adopted the practice.

transubstantiation: Roman Catholic doctrine of the Lord's Supper that states the natures or essences of the bread and wine are replaced by the natures of the body and blood of Christ through the priest's consecration of the elements.

Tre Ore Service: Latin for "three hours"; Good Friday devotion held from noon until 3 P.M.; recalls Christ's suffering on the cross; usually the seven last words from the cross serve as the devotional theme.

Triduum: Latin for "three days"; these are the three days of Holy Week—Maundy Thursday, Good Friday, and Easter Saturday; the services comprise the whole action of devotional meditation on the suffering and death of Christ.

veil: large white cloth made from a variety of materials, usually of fine linen, that covers the Communion elements prior to the Offertory and after the distribution; *see also* **Lenten veil, chalice veil,** and **Hungertuch.**

Venite: Latin for "O, come"; the invitation from Psalm 95 that introduces selected verses to the psalm as sung by the congregation at the beginning of Matins.

Verba: Latin for "words"; the Words of Institution spoken by Christ when He instituted the Sacrament of the Altar; the words repeated by the presiding minister at the consecration of the Communion elements.

versicles: from the Latin for "little verses"; refers to short psalm verses spoken by the worship leader to which the congregation responds; often designated with a V and R.

Vespers: from the Latin for "evening"; second last of the canonical hours; sung at sunset; consists of psalms, readings, hymns, a canticle, a sermon, and prayers.

vestments: ecclesiastical garments worn by the presiding minister and assisting ministers to identify their liturgical function.

vestry: sacristy designed for worship participants to vest in a devotional atmosphere; *see also* **sacristy.**

Vigil of Easter: *see* **Easter Vigil**

violet: *see* **liturgical colors**

Votum: Latin for "vow or wish"; mini-Benediction (Philippians 4:7) often spoken at the conclusion of the sermon.

watches: nighttime hours for prayer (Vespers, Matins, and Lauds); sometimes called nocturns or nightwatches.

west, liturgical: *see* **orienting**

Western rite: form of liturgy common in late-medieval Europe; promoted by the papal curia; popularized by the mendicant orders; also called the Roman rite; *see also* **Gallican rite** and **rite.**

Whitsunday: Literally, "White Sunday"; another name for Pentecost; so-named for the white robes worn by the catechumens who were confirmed on that date.

Word and Sacrament: Lutheran emphasis on the tangible vehicles through which God's Spirit is actively working to produce and nurture faith in Christ; the preached Word from Scripture as Law and Gospel and the sacraments of Absolution, Baptism, and Communion.

worship: the setting in which God calls together His people to bestow on them the gifts of life and salvation by means of Word and Sacrament; the dynamic experience of Christians who receive God's promised gifts then respond faith-fully to Him in Christ; an opportunity to grow and develop as a community and for the community to go out into the world; *see* **Divine Service.**

Yom Kippur: Hebrew for "Day of Atonement"; the most solemn day of the Jewish year on which Jews confess and make amends for all their wrongs.

BIBLIOGRAPHY

Abbott, Walter M., ed. "Constitution on the Sacred Liturgy." In *The Documents of Vatican II*, translated by Joseph Gallagher. New York: Herder & Herder, 1966.

Aland, Kurt. *Did the Early Church Baptize Infants?* Translated by G. R. Beasley-Murray. Philadelphia: Westminster, 1963.

Alexander, J. Neil. "Luther's Reform of the Daily Office." *Worship* 57 (July 1983): 348–60.

All God's People Sing! St. Louis: Concordia, 1992.

Allen, Ronald, and Gordon Borror. *Worship: Rediscovering the Missing Jewel*. Portland: Multnomah, 1982.

Allmen, Jean Jacques von. *Worship: Its Theology and Practice*. New York: Oxford University Press, 1965.

Anderson, Dave, comp. *The Other Song Book*. Phoenix, Ariz.: The Fellowship Publications, 1987.

Appleton, George, ed. *The Oxford Book of Prayer*. New York: Oxford University Press, 1988.

Appleton, LeRoy H., and Stephen Bridges. *Symbolism in Liturgical Art*. New York: Scribner, 1959.

Augustine. *The Confessions of Saint Augustine*. Translated by John K. Ryan. Garden City: Image Books, 1960.

Barnett, James M. *The Diaconate—A Full and Equal Order*. New York: Seabury, 1981.

Barr, Browne. "Prayers of Confession: Let's Get Unspecific." *The Christian Century* 104 (7 October 1987): 844.

Barry, A. L. "Lutheran Worship: 2000 and Beyond—Seven Theses on Lutheran Worship." Paper presented at the Real Life Worship Conference, Denver, Colorado, February 1998.

———. *The Unchanging Feast: The Nature and Basis of Lutheran Worship*. St. Louis: Office of the President, the LCMS, 1995.

Baumer, Fred A., and Stephen Wroblewski. *Celebrating Liturgy*. Chicago: Liturgy Training Publications, 1986.

Beck, William F. "A Marriage Ceremony in Modern English." *Christian News* (3 May 1982): 7.

Becker, Peter M., Shirley K. Morgenthaler, and Gary L. Bertels. "Children in Worship." Parts 1–5. *Lutheran Education* 133:1 (September/October 1997): 19–26; 133:2 (November/December 1997): 78–85; 133:3 (January/February 1998): 157–64; 133:4 (March/April 1998): 203–12; 133:5 (May/June 1998): 252–60.

Benedict. *The Rule of St. Benedict*. Translated by Anthony C. Meisel and M. L. del Mastro. Garden City: Image Books, 1975.

Berry, Mary. "The Divine Office." In *The New Westminster Dictionary of Liturgy and Worship*, edited by J. G. Davies. Philadelphia: Westminster, 1986.

Bobb, Barry L., and Hans Boehringer, eds. *Proclaim: A Guide for Planning Liturgy and Music*. St. Louis: Concordia, 1985 and subsequent years.

Bockelman, Eleanor. *A Practical Guide for Altar Guilds*. Minneapolis: Augsburg, 1962.

Bosch, Paul F. *Church Year Guide*. Minneapolis: Augsburg, 1987.

———. *A Worship Workbench*. Chicago: Lutheran Council in the USA, Department of Campus Ministry, 1971.

Bouwsma, William J. *John Calvin: A Sixteenth Century Portrait*. New York: Oxford University Press, 1988.

Boyd, Kevin R. "Vestments." *Modern Liturgy* 9:7 (October 1982): 34.

Bradshaw, Paul F. *Daily Prayer in the Early Church: A Study of the Origin and Early Development of the Divine Office*. New York: Oxford University Press, 1982.

———. "The Use of the Bible in Liturgy: Some Historical Perspectives." *Studia Liturgica* 22 (1992): 35–52.

Brand, Eugene L. "The Liturgical Life of the Church." In *A Handbook of Church Music*, edited by Carl Halter and Carl Schalk. St. Louis: Concordia, 1978.

———. *The Rite Thing*. Minneapolis: Augsburg, 1970.

Brauer, James L. "The Church Year." In *Lutheran Worship: History and Practice*, edited by Fred L. Precht. St. Louis: Concordia, 1993.

———. *Meaningful Worship: A Guide to the Lutheran Service*. St. Louis: Concordia, 1994.

Brecht, Martin. *Martin Luther: Shaping and Defining the Reformation, 1521–1532*. Translated by James L. Schaaf. Minneapolis: Fortress, 1990.

Brokering, Herbert F. *Introducing the Lessons: Brief Introductory Statements for Lectors*. Minneapolis: Augsburg, 1983.

Brooks, Peter Newman. *Hymns as Homilies*. Leominster, England: Gracewing, 1997.

Bruggink, Donald J., and Carl H. Droppers. *Christ and Architecture: Building Presbyterian/Reformed Churches*. Grand Rapids: Eerdmans, 1965.

Brunner, Peter. *Worship in the Name of Jesus*. Translated by M. H. Bertram. St. Louis: Concordia, 1968.

Bunjes, Paul G. "The Music of *Lutheran Worship*." In *Lutheran Worship: History and Practice*, edited by Fred L. Precht. St. Louis: Concordia, 1993.

———. "The Musical Carriage for the Psalms." In *Lutheran Worship: History and Practice*, edited by Fred L. Precht. St. Louis: Concordia, 1993.

Burreson, Kent J. "Confirmation: Living and Rejoicing in the Sacramental Life." In *Through the Church the Song Goes On: Preparing a Lutheran Hymnal for the 21st Century*, edited by Paul J. Grime, D. Richard Stuckwisch, and Jon D. Vieker. St. Louis: Commission on Worship, the LCMS, 1999.

Buszin, Walter E. *The Doctrine of the Universal Priesthood and Its Influence upon the Liturgies and Music of the Lutheran Church*. St. Louis: Concordia, n.d.

———. "The Genius of Lutheran Corporate Worship." *Concordia Theological Monthly* (April 1950): 269–75.

Buxton, R. F. "Advent." In *The New Westminster Dictionary of Liturgy and Worship*, edited by J. G. Davies. Philadelphia: Westminster, 1986.

Cabrol, Fernand. *The Prayer of the Early Christians*. Translated by Ernest Graf. New York: Benziger Brothers, 1930.

———. *The Year's Liturgy: The Sundays, Feriæ and Feasts of the Liturgical Year*. 2 vols. London: Burns, Oates & Washbourne, 1938–1940.

Calvin, John. *Institutes of the Christian Religion*. Edited by John T. McNeill. Translated by Ford Lewis Battles. Philadelphia: Westminster, 1960.

Cassian, John. *The Twelve Books on the Institutes of the Coenobia*. Book III, "On the Canonical System of the Daily Prayer and Psalms." Translated by E. C. S. Gibson. The Nicene and Post-Nicene Fathers, 2d ser., vol. 1. New York: Christian Literature Society, 1894.

Chadwick, O. "The Origins of Prime." *The Journal of Theological Studies* XLIX (1948): 180.

Chamberlain, John V. "Eucharist Nonessential." *Christian Century* 106:30 (18 October 1989): 941–42.

Chemnitz, Martin. "Second Topic: Concerning Traditions." In *Examination of the Council of Trent*. Vol. 1, translated by Fred Kramer. St. Louis: Concordia, 1971.

Chesterton, Gilbert K. "The Ethics of Elfdom." In *Orthodoxy*. New York: Dodd, Mead, 1908. Reprint, New York: Doubleday Image, 1990.

Christian, Robert, and Walter Schoedel. *Worship Is: Celebrating as Lutherans*. St. Louis: Concordia, 1990.

Chupungco, Anscar J. "History of the Liturgy until the Fourth Century." In *Introduction to the Liturgy*. Vol. 1 of *Handbook for Liturgical Studies*, edited by Anscar J. Chupungco. Collegeville, Minn.: Liturgical Press, 1997.

———. "History of the Roman Liturgy until the Fifteenth Century." In *Introduction to the Liturgy*. Vol. 1 of *Handbook for Liturgical Studies*, edited by Anscar J. Chupungco. Collegeville, Minn.: Liturgical Press, 1997.

Church, Michael G. L. "The Law of Begging: Prosper at the End of the Day." *Worship* 73:5 (September 1999): 443–53.

Clarke, W. K. L., ed. *Liturgy and Worship: A Companion to the Prayer Books of the Anglican Communion*. London: SPCK, 1932.

Clement of Rome. "To the Corinthians." In vol. 2, part 1 of *The Apostolic Fathers*, edited and translated by J. B. Lightfoot. New York: Macmillan, 1890. Reprint, Peabody, Mass.: Hendrickson, 1989.

———. "First Letter to the Corinthians." In *The Apostolic Fathers*, edited by J. B. Lightfoot and J. R. Harmer. London: Macmillan, 1891. Reprint, Grand Rapids: Baker, 1984.

Clowney, Paul, and Tessa Clowney. *Exploring Churches*. Grand Rapids: Eerdmans, 1982.

Cobb, Peter G. "The History of the Christian Year." In *The New Westminster Dictionary of Liturgy and Worship*, edited by J. G. Davies. Philadelphia: Westminster, 1986.

———. "The Liturgy of the Word in the Early Church." In *The Study of Liturgy*. Rev. ed. Edited by Cheslyn Jones, Geoffrey Wainwright, Edward Yarnold, and Paul Bradshaw. New York: Oxford University Press, 1992.

Commission on Church Architecture, the LCMS. *Architecture and the Church*. St. Louis: Concordia, 1965.

Commission on Theology and Church Relations, the LCMS. *The Nature and Implications of the Concept of Fellowship*. St. Louis: Commission on Theology and Church Relations, the LCMS, 1981.

———. *Women in the Church: Scriptural Principles and Ecclesial Practice*. St. Louis: Commission on Theology and Church Relations, the LCMS, 1985.

———. *Theology and Practice of the Lord's Supper*. St. Louis: Concordia, 1983.

———. *Admission to the Lord's Supper: Basics of Biblical and Confessional Teaching*. St. Louis: Concordia, 1999.

Commission on Worship, the LCMS. *Guide to Introducing* Lutheran Worship. St. Louis: Concordia, 1981.

———. *Hymnal Supplement 98*. St. Louis: Concordia, 1998.

———. *Through the Church the Song Goes On: Preparing a Lutheran Hymnal for the 21st Century*. Edited by Paul J. Grime, D. Richard Stuckwisch, and Jon D. Vieker. St. Louis: The LCMS, 1999.

———. *Narrative for Adults.* St. Louis: Concordia, 1981.

———. "What Is Liturgy?" *Lutheran Worship Notes* 24 (Spring 1992).

———. *Lutheran Worship.* St. Louis: Concordia, 1982.

———. *Lutheran Worship: Agenda.* St. Louis: Concordia, 1984.

———. *Lutheran Worship: Altar Book.* St. Louis: Concordia, 1982.

———. *Worship Supplement.* St. Louis: Concordia, 1969.

Constien, Victor A. "Here's a Handy Guide to Explain Synod's Various Induction Rites." *Reporter* 12:1 (6 January 1986): 7.

Consultation on Common Texts. *Common Lectionary: The Lectionary Proposed by the Consultation on Common Texts.* New York: Church Hymnal Corporation, 1983.

Cope, Gilbert. "Vestments." In *The New Westminster Dictionary of Liturgy and Worship*, edited by J. G. Davies. Philadelphia: Westminster, 1986.

Costen, Melva Wilson. *African American Christian Worship.* Nashville: Abingdon, 1993.

Creative Worship for the Lutheran Parish. St. Louis: Concordia, current years.

Crichton, J. D. "Tenebrae." In *The New Westminster Dictionary of Liturgy and Worship*, edited by J. G. Davies. Philadelphia: Westminster, 1986.

Cullmann, Oscar. *Baptism in the New Testament.* Translated by J. K. S. Reid. London: SCM, 1950.

———. "The Tradition." In *The Early Church: Studies in Early Christian History and Theology*, edited by A. J. B. Higgins. Philadelphia: Westminster, 1956.

Davies, J. G. "Architectural Setting." In *The New Westminster Dictionary of Liturgy and Worship*, edited by J. G. Davies. Philadelphia: Westminster, 1986.

Dawn, Marva J. *Reaching Out without Dumbing Down: A Theology of Worship for the Turn-of-the-Century Culture.* Grand Rapids: Eerdmans, 1995.

Day, Thomas. *Why Catholics Can't Sing: The Culture of Catholicism and the Triumph of Bad Taste.* New York: Crossroad, 1990.

Deffner, Donald L. "Confirmation." In *Lutheran Worship: History and Practice*, edited by Fred L. Precht. St. Louis: Concordia, 1993.

The Department of Systematic Theology, Concordia Seminary, St. Louis. "Is 'Non-Alcoholic Wine' Really Wine?" *Concordia Journal* 17:1 (January 1991): 4–6.

Die evangelischen Kirchenordnungen des XVI. Jahrhunderts. 15 vols. Vols. 1–5, Leipzig: O. R. Reisland, 1902–13, vols. 6–15, Tubingen: J. C. B. Mohr, 1955–77.

Di Sante, Carmine. *Jewish Prayer: The Origins of the Christian Liturgy.* Translated by Matthew J. O'Connell. New York: Paulist Press, 1985.

Dittmer, Terry. *Creating Contemporary Worship: A Workbook for Understanding and Writing Youth-led Worship Services.* St. Louis: Concordia, 1985.

Dix, Gregory. *The Shape of the Liturgy.* Westminster: Dacre Press, 1945.

———. *The Shape of the Liturgy.* 2d ed. Westminster: Dacre Press, 1954.

———, and Henry Chadwick, eds. *The Treatise on the Apostolic Tradition of St. Hippolytus of Rome, Bishop and Martyr.* London: Alban Press, 1991.

Dolby, Anastasia. *Church Vestments: Their Origin, Use, and Ornament Practically Illustrated.* London: Chapman & Hall, 1868.

DuCharme, Jerry, and Gail DuCharme. *Lector Becomes Proclaimer.* San Jose: Resource Publications, 1989.

Dugmore, C. W. "Canonical Hours." In *The New Westminster Dictionary of Liturgy and Worship*, edited by J. G. Davies. Philadelphia: Westminster, 1986.

———.*The Influence of the Synagogue upon the Divine Office.* London: Oxford University Press, 1945.

Elert, Werner. *Eucharist and Church Fellowship in the First Four Centuries.* Translated by Norman E. Nagel. St. Louis: Concordia, 1966.

Eskew, Harry, and Hugh T. McElrath. *Sing with Understanding: An Introduction to Christian Hymnology.* Nashville: Broadman, 1980.

Eusebius. *Ecclesiastical History.* Translated by C. F. Cruse. Grand Rapids: Baker, 1955. Reprint, 1988.

———. *The History of the Church from Christ to Constantine.* Translated by G. A. Williamson. Baltimore: Penguin, 1965.

———. *The Life of Constantine the Great.* Translated by E. C. Richardson. Nicene and Post-Nicene Fathers, 2d ser, vol. 1. New York: Christian Literature, 1890.

The Evangelical Lutheran Hymn-Book. St. Louis: Concordia, 1927.

Evanson, Charles J. "The Service of the Word." In *Lutheran Worship: History and Practice*, edited by Fred L. Precht. St. Louis: Concordia, 1993.

Fagerberg, David W. *What Is Liturgical Theology? A Study in Methodology.* Collegeville, Minn.: Liturgical Press, 1992.

Faulkner, Quentin. *Wiser Than Despair: The Evolution of Ideas in the Relationship of Music and the Christian Church.* Westport, Conn.: Greenwood, 1996.

Federer, Karl. *Liturgie und Glaube: Eine theologie-geschichtliche Untersuchung.* Paradosis 4. Freiburg, Switzerland: Paulusverlag, 1950.

Fendt, Leonhard. *Der lutherische Gottesdienst des 16. Jahrhunderts: Sein Werden und Sein Wachsen.* Munich: Reinhardt, 1923.

Ferguson, George W. *Signs and Symbols in Christian Art.* New York: Oxford University Press, 1954.

Finney, Paul Corby, ed. *Seeing beyond the Word: Visual Arts and the Calvinist Tradition.* Grand Rapids: Eerdmans, 1999.

Folsom, Cassian. "The Liturgical Books of the Roman Rite." In *Introduction to the Liturgy.* Vol. 1 of *Handbook for Liturgical Studies*, edited by Anscar J. Chupungco. Collegeville, Minn.: Liturgical Press, 1997.

Found, James. "Contemporary Worship: Learning from the Early Church." *Taiwan Mission* (Summer 1996): 41.

Fremder, Alfred E. "The Selection of Hymns." In *Lutheran Worship: History and Practice*, edited by Fred L. Precht. St. Louis: Concordia, 1993.

Gehrke, Hugo J. *Worshiping God with Joy: A Planning Guide for the Worship Committee.* God's People at Work in the Parish. St. Louis: Concordia, 1979.

Gelineau, Joseph. "Music and Singing in the Liturgy." In *The Study of Liturgy.* Rev. ed. Edited by Cheslyn Jones et al. New York: Oxford University Press, 1992.

Gent, Barbara, and Betty Sturges. *The Altar Guild Book.* Wilton, Conn.: Morehouse-Barlow, 1982.

Gerson, Paula Lieber, ed. *Abbot Suger and Saint-Denis: A Symposium.* New York: Metropolitan Museum of Art, 1986.

Gingras, George E., trans. *Egeria: Diary of a Pilgrimage.* Ancient Christian Writers 38. New York: Newman, 1970.

Gleason, David Paul. "Liturgy: An Evangelism Advantage." In *Encountering God: The Legacy of* Lutheran Book of Worship *for the 21st Century*, edited by Ralph R. Van Loon. Minneapolis: Kirk House, 1998.

González, Justo L. *A History of Christian Thought*. Rev. ed. Nashville: Abingdon, 1987.

Goranson, Stephen. "7 vs. 8: The Battle over the Holy Day at Dura-Europos." *Bible Review* (August 1996): 22–33, 44.

Gorman, Art. *Chicago Folk Service*. Park Ridge, Ill.: Kjos Music, 1972.

Gotsch, Herbert. "The Music of Instruments." In *A Handbook of Church Music*, edited by Carl Halter and Carl Schalk. St. Louis: Concordia, 1978.

Graf, Arthur E. *Joybells of Life*. Giddings, Tex.: Faith Publications, 1973.

Grillmeier, Alois. *Christ in Christian Tradition*. Vol. 1. 2d rev. ed. Translated by John Bowden. Atlanta: John Knox, 1975.

Grime, Paul, and Joseph Herl, eds. "Variety within the Divine Service." In *Hymnal Supplement 98 Handbook*. St. Louis: Commission on Worship, the LCMS, 1998.

Grisbrooke, E. Jardine. "Synaxis." In *The New Westminster Dictionary of Liturgy and Worship*, edited by J. G. Davies. Philadelphia: Westminster, 1986.

Gritsch, Eric W. "Martin Luther's View of Tradition." In *The Quadrilog: Tradition and the Future of Ecumenism: Essays in Honor of George H. Tavard*, edited by Kenneth Hagen. Collegeville, Minn.: Liturgical Press, 1994.

Gustafson, David A. *Lutherans in Crisis: The Question of Identity in the American Republic*. Minneapolis: Fortress, 1993.

Hagen, Kenneth. Introduction to *The Quadrilog: Tradition and the Future of Ecumenism: Essays in Honor of George H. Tavard*, edited by Kenneth Hagen. Collegeville, Minn.: Liturgical Press, 1994.

Halter, Carl. *The Practice of Sacred Music*. St. Louis: Concordia, 1955.

———, and Carl Schalk, eds. *A Handbook of Church Music*. St. Louis: Concordia, 1978.

Hammond, Peter. *Liturgy and Architecture*. New York: Columbia University Press, 1961.

Hansen, James. *The Ministry of the Cantor*. Collegeville, Minn.: Liturgical Press, 1985.

Harms, Paul. *Presenting the Lessons: A Guide for Lectors*. Minneapolis: Augsburg, 1980.

Harper, John. *The Forms and Orders of Western Liturgy from the Tenth to the Eighteenth Century: A Historical Introduction and Guide for Students and Musicians*. Oxford: Clarendon, 1991.

Held, David. "The Psalms and Their Use." In *Lutheran Worship: History and Practice*, edited by Fred L. Precht. St. Louis: Concordia, 1993.

Helge, Brian L. "Services of the Word: Good, Bad, Unnecessary." *Lutheran Forum* 7 (August 1973): 14–15.

Herzel, Catherine. *Christians at Worship: Helps for Using the Service Book and Hymn in Sunday Worship and at Home*. Edited by Gustav K. Wiencke. Philadelphia: Lutheran Church Press, 1964.

Hickman, Hoyt L., Don E. Saliers, Laurence Hull Stookey, and James F. White. *Handbook of the Christian Year*. Nashville: Abingdon, 1986.

Hillert, Richard. "Music in the Church Today: An Appraisal." In *A Handbook of Church Music*, edited by Carl Halter and Carl Schalk. St. Louis: Concordia, 1978.

Hippolytus. *The Treatise on the Apostolic Tradition of St. Hippolytus of Rome, Bishop and Martyr*. Edited by Gregory Dix and Henry Chadwick. London: Alban Press, 1992.

Hoon, Paul W. *The Integrity of Worship: Ecumenical and Pastoral Studies in Liturgical Theology*. Nashville: Abingdon, 1971.

Hopkins, C., and P. V. C. Baur. *The Excavations at Dura-Europos.* New Haven: Yale University Press, 1934.

Horn, Edward T. *The Christian Year.* Philadelphia: Muhlenberg, 1957.

Horn, Henry E. *Liturgy and Life.* Philadelphia: Lutheran Church Press, 1966.

Howell, Clifford. "From Trent to Vatican II." In *The Study of Liturgy.* Rev. ed. Edited by Cheslyn Jones et al. New York: Oxford University Press, 1992.

Huck, Gabe. "When You Pray: 'Be Careful of Words . . .'" *Accent on Worship: The Liturgical Conference* 4.4 (1986).

Huffman, Walter C. *The Prayer of the Faithful: Understanding and Creatively Using the Prayer of the Church.* Minneapolis: Augsburg, 1986.

Hummel, Horace D. *The Word Becoming Flesh: An Introduction to the Origin, Purpose, and Meaning of the Old Testament.* St. Louis: Concordia, 1979.

Ignatius of Antioch. "Letter to the Ephesians." In *The Apostolic Fathers,* edited by J. B. Lightfoot and J. R. Harmer. London: Macmillan, 1891. Reprint, Grand Rapids: Baker, 1984.

———. "Letter to the Magnesians." Edited and translated by Cyril C. Richardson. In *Early Christian Fathers,* edited by Cyril C. Richardson. Library of Christian Classics, vol. 1. Philadelphia: Westminster, 1953.

———. "Letter to the Philadelphians." In *Early Christian Fathers,* edited and translated by Cyril C. Richardson. Library of Christian Classics, vol. 1. Philadelphia: Westminster, 1953.

———. "Letter to the Smyrnaeans." In *Early Christian Fathers,* edited and translated by Cyril C. Richardson. Library of Christian Classics, vol. 1. Philadelphia: Westminster, 1953.

Inter-Lutheran Commission on Worship. *The Church Year, Calendar and Lectionary.* Contemporary Worship 6. Minneapolis: Augsburg, 1973.

———. *The Marriage Service.* Contemporary Worship 3. Minneapolis: Augsburg, 1972.

———. *Services of the Word.* Contemporary Worship 5. Minneapolis: Augsburg, 1972.

International Consultation on English Texts. *Prayers We Have in Common: Agreed Liturgical Texts.* Rev. ed. Philadelphia: Fortress, 1972.

Irenaeus. "Selections from the Work *Against Heresies* by Irenaeus, Bishop of Lyons." Edited and translated by Edward Rochie Hardy. In *Early Christian Fathers,* edited by Cyril C. Richardson. Library of Christian Classics, vol. 1. Philadelphia: Westminster, 1953.

Jay, Eric George, trans. *Origen's Treatise on Prayer.* London: SPCK, 1954.

Jeremias, Joachim. *Infant Baptism in the First Four Centuries.* Translated by David Cairns. Philadelphia: Westminster, 1960.

———. *The Origins of Infant Baptism: A Further Study in Reply to Kurt Aland.* Translated by Dorothea M. Barton. Naperville, Ill.: A. R. Allenson, 1963.

Johnson, Maxwell E. "Planning and Leading Liturgical Prayer in an Ecumenical Context." *Pro Ecclesia* VIII:2 (Spring 1999): 192.

Joint Commission on the Theology and Practice of Confirmation, the LCMS. "Confirmation and First Communion." In *1971 Convention Workbook of The Lutheran Church—Missouri Synod.* St. Louis: The LCMS, 1971.

Joyful Sounds. St. Louis: Concordia, 1977.

Jungmann, Josef A. *The Early Liturgy: To the Time of Gregory the Great.* Translated by Francis A. Brunner. Liturgical Studies VI. South Bend: University of Notre Dame Press, 1959.

———. *Public Worship: A Survey.* Translated by Clifford Howell. Collegeville, Minn.: Liturgical Press, 1957.

Justin Martyr. "The First Apology of Justin, the Martyr." Edited and translated by Edward Rochie Hardy. In *Early Christian Fathers*, edited by Cyril C. Richardson. Library of Christian Classics, vol. 1. Philadelphia: Westminster, 1953.

Kalb, Friedrich. *Theology of Worship in 17th-Century Lutheranism.* Translated by Henry P. A. Hamann. St. Louis: Concordia, 1965.

Kalokyris, Constantine. *The Essence of Orthodox Iconography.* Translated by Peter A. Chamberas. Brookline, Mass.: Holy Cross Orthodox Press, 1985.

Kavanagh, Aidan. *Elements of Rite: A Handbook of Liturgical Style.* New York: Pueblo, 1982.

———. *On Liturgical Theology.* New York: Pueblo, 1984.

Kelly, J. N. D. *Early Christian Creeds.* 3d ed. London: Longman, 1972.

Kemper, Frederick W. *Variety for Worship: Resources for Festival Worship Liturgies.* St. Louis: Concordia, 1984. Formerly titled *Change of Key: Models for Festival Worship.* St. Louis: Concordia, 1977.

Kiefert, Patrick R. *Worship and Evangelism: A Pastoral Handbook.* Burnsville, Minn.: Prince of Peace Publishing, 1990.

Klammer, Edward W. "Orchestral Instruments." In *A Handbook of Church Music*, edited by Carl Halter and Carl Schalk. St. Louis: Concordia, 1978.

Klauser, Theodor. *A Short History of the Western Liturgy: An Account and Some Reflections.* 2d ed. Translated by John Halliburton. New York: Oxford University Press, 1979.

Klos, Frank W. *Confirmation and First Communion: A Study Book.* Minneapolis: Augsburg, 1968.

Koenker, Ernest Benjamin. *The Liturgical Renaissance in the Roman Catholic Church.* 2d ed. St. Louis: Concordia, 1966.

Kolb, Robert, and Timothy J. Wengert, eds. *The Book of Concord.* Translated by Charles Arand et al. Minneapolis: Augsburg Fortress, 2000.

Kraeling, C. H. *The Christian Building.* Excavations at Dura-Europus 8:2. New Haven: Dura-Europus Publications, 1967.

Krause, Paul M. *Planning a Christian Wedding.* St. Louis: Concordia, 1963.

Kretzmann, Adalbert Raphael. *The Order of the Marriage Ceremony for Church Weddings.* 5th rev. ed. Chicago: The Evangelical Lutheran Church of Saint Luke, 1969.

———. "The Pastor and the Church Musician." In *A Handbook of Church Music*, edited by Carl Halter and Carl Schalk. St. Louis: Concordia, 1978.

Lake, Kirsopp, trans. "The Didache." In *The Apostolic Fathers.* 2 vols. Cambridge: Harvard University Press, 1965.

Lamb, J. A. "The Place of the Bible in the Liturgy." In *From the Beginnings to Jerome*, edited by P. R. Ackroyd and C. F. Evans. Vol. 1 of *The Cambridge History of the Bible.* Cambridge: Cambridge University Press, 1970.

Lane, Margaret. "Parson's Plumage." Review of *A History of Ecclesiastical Dress*, by Janet Mayo. *The [London] Daily Telegraph* (25 January 1985): 12.

Lang, Paul H. *Music in Western Civilization.* New York: Norton, 1941.

Lang, Paul H. D. *What an Altar Guild Should Know.* St. Louis: Concordia, 1964.

Langer, Ruth. "From Study of Scripture to a Reenactment of Sinai." *Worship* 72:1 (January 1998): 43–67.

Lathrop, Gordon W. *Holy People: A Liturgical Ecclesiology.* Minneapolis: Fortress, 1999.

———. *Holy Things: A Liturgical Theology.* Minneapolis: Fortress, 1993.

Leaver, Robin A. "Luther's Catechism Hymns: 3. Creed." *Lutheran Quarterly* XII:1 (Spring 1998): 79–88.

———. *The Theological Character of Music in Worship.* Church Music Pamphlet, edited by Carl Schalk. St. Louis: Concordia, 1989.

———, ed. Introduction to *Come to the Feast: The Original and Translated Hymns of Martin H. Franzmann.* St. Louis: Morning Star Music Publishers, 1994.

Leonard, John Brook. "The Gallican Liturgy." In *Twenty Centuries of Christian Worship.* Vol. 2 of *The Complete Library of Christian Worship*, edited by Robert E. Webber. Nashville: Star Song, 1994.

Lincoln, Edwin R. "Reaffirming Family Ties." *Christianity Today* 23:8 (19 January 1979): 32–33.

Liturgical Commission of the Roman Catholic diocese of Superior, Wisc., "Diocesan Building Directives." *Liturgical Arts* XXVI (1957): 7–9, 43–44.

Lochner, Friedrich. *Der Hauptgottesdienst der Evangelisch-Lutherischen Kirche.* St. Louis: Concordia, 1895.

Lonergan, Ray. *A Well-Trained Tongue: A Workbook for Lectors.* Chicago: Liturgy Training Publications, 1982.

Ludwig, Theodore M. *The Sacred Paths: Understanding the Religions of the World.* 2d ed. Upper Saddle River: Prentice Hall, 1996.

Luecke, David S. *Evangelical Style and Lutheran Substance: Facing America's Mission Challenge.* St. Louis: Concordia, 1988.

Luther, Martin. ———. "The Babylonian Captivity of the Church, 1520." Translated by A. T. W. Steinhäuser. Revised by Frederick C. Ahrens and Abdel Ross Wentz. Vol. 36 of *Luther's Works.* Philadelphia: Muhlenberg, 1959.

———. "A Brief Instruction on What to Look for and Expect in the Gospels, 1521." Translated and edited by E. Theodore Bachman. Vol. 35 of *Luther's Works.* Philadelphia: Fortress, 1960.

———. "A Christian Exhortation to the Livonians Concerning Public Worship and Concord." Translated by Paul Zeller Strodach. Revised by Ulrich S. Leupold. Vol. 53 of *Luther's Works.* Philadelphia: Fortress, 1965.

———. "Concerning the Order of Public Worship, 1523." Translated by Paul Zeller Strodach. Revised by Ulrich S. Leupold. Vol. 53 of *Luther's Works.* Philadelphia: Fortress, 1965.

———. "An Exposition of the Lord's Prayer for Simple Laymen, 1519." Translated by Martin H. Bertram. Edited by Martin O. Dietrich. Vol. 42 of *Luther's Works.* Philadelphia: Fortress, 1969.

———. "The German Litany and the Latin Litany Corrected." Translated by Paul Zeller Strodach. Revised by Ulrich S. Leupold. Vol. 53 of *Luther's Works.* Philadelphia: Fortress, 1965.

———. "The German Mass and Order of Service, 1526." Translated by Augustus Steimle and Ulrich S. Leupold. Vol. 53 of *Luther's Works.* Philadelphia: Fortress, 1965.

———. "How One Should Teach Common Folk to Shrive Themselves." Translated by Joseph Stump. Revised by Ulrich S. Leupuld. Vol. 53 of *Luther's Works.* Philadelphia: Fortress, 1965.

———. "The Holy and Blessed Sacrament of Baptism." Translated by Charles M. Jacobs. Revised by E. Theodore Bachmann. Vol. 35 of *Luther's Works.* Philadelphia: Fortress, 1960.

———. "The Magnificat." Translated by A. T. W. Steinhäuser. Vol. 21 of *Luther's Works.* St. Louis: Concordia, 1956.

———. "Morning Blessing and Evening Blessing." In *The Book of Concord*, edited by Robert Kolb and Timothy J. Wengert. Translated by Charles Arand et al. Minneapolis: Augsb urg Fortress, 2000.

———. "Ninety-Five Theses, 1517." Translated by C. M. Jacobs. Revised by Harold J. Grimm. Vol. 31 of *Luther's Works*. Philadelphia: Muhlenberg, 1957.

———. "On the Councils and the Church." Translated by Charles M. Jacobs. Revised by Eric W. Gritsch. Vol. 41 of *Luther's Works*. Philadelphia: Fortress, 1966.

———. "An Open Letter to Those in Frankfurt on the Main, 1533." Translated by Jon D. Vieker. *Concordia Journal* 16 (1990): 333–51.

———. "Order of Baptism." Translated by Paul Zeller Strodach. Revised by Ulrich S. Leupold. Vol. 53 of *Luther's Works*. Philadelphia: Fortress, 1965.

———. "The Order of Marriage for Common Pastors, 1529." Translated by P. Z. Strodach. Revised and edied by Ulrich S. Leupold. Vol. 53 of *Luther's Works*. Philadelphia: Fortress, 1965.

———. "An Order of Mass and Communion for the Church at Wittenberg, 1523." Translated by Paul Zeller Strodach. Revised by Ulrich S. Leupold. Vol. 53 of *Luther's Works*. Philadelphia: Fortress, 1965.

———. "Personal Prayer Book, 1522." Translated by Martin H. Bertram. Vol. 43 of *Luther's Works*. Philadelphia: Fortress, 1968.

———. "Preface to Georg Rhau's *Symphoniae Iucundae*, 1538." Translated by Ulrich S. Leupold. Vol. 53 of *Luther's Works*. Philadelphia: Fortress, 1965.

———. "Prefaces to the Apocrypha." Translated by E. Theodore Bachmann. Vol. 35 of *Luther's Works*. Philadelphia: Fortress, 1960.

———. *Sämmtliche Schriften*. Vol. 10. Edited by J. G. Walch. St. Louis: Concordia, 1880.

———. "A Short Order of Confession before the Priest for the Common Man." Translated by Paul Zeller Strodach. Revised by Ulrich S. Leupold. Vol. 53 of *Luther's Works*. Philadelphia: Fortress, 1965.

———. "A Simple Way to Pray, 1535." Translated by Carl. J. Schindler. Vol. 43 of *Luther's Works*. Philadelphia: Fortress, 1968.

———. "Ten Sermons on the Catechism, November 30 to December 18, 1528." Edited and translated by John W. Doberstein. Vol. 51 of *Luther's Works*. Philadelphia: Muhlenberg, 1959.

———. "A Treatise on the New Testament, That Is the Holy Mass, 1520." Translated by Jeremioah J. Schindel. Revised by E. Theodore Bachmann. Vol. 35 of *Luther's Work*. Philadelphia: Fortress, 1960.

MacDonald, William L. *Early Christian and Byzantine Architecture*. New York: George Braziller, 1962.

Maertens, Thierry. *Assembly for Christ: From Biblical Theology to Pastoral Theology in the Twentieth Century*. London: Darton, Longman & Todd, 1970.

Magirius, Heinrich. *Dresden: Die Frauenkirche*. Regensburg: Scheel & Steiner, 1999.

Mai, Harmut. *Der Evangelische Kanzelaltar: Geschichte und Bedeutung*. Halle: M. Niemeyer, 1969.

Marcheschi, Graziano, and Nancy Marcheschi. *Workbook for Lectors and Gospel Readers*. Chicago: Liturgy Training Publications, 1991.

Martin, Linette. *Practical Praying*. Grand Rapids: Eerdmans, 1997.

Martin, Ralph P. *Worship in the Early Church*. Rev. ed. Grand Rapids: Eerdmans, 1964.

———. *The Worship of God: Some Theological, Pastoral, and Practical Reflections*. Grand Rapids: Eerdmans, 1982.

"The Martyrdom of Polycarp, Bishop of Smyrna, as Told in the Letter of the Church of Smyrna to the

Church of Philomelium." Edited and translated by Massey H. Shepherd Jr. In *Early Christian Fathers*, edited by Cyril C. Richardson. Library of Christian Classics, vol. 1. Philadelphia: Westminster, 1953.

Maschke, Timothy. "Contemporaneity: A Hermeneutical Perspective in Martin Luther." In *Ad Fontes Lutheri: Toward the Recovery of the Real Luther: Essays in Honor of Kenneth Hagen's Sixty-Fifth Birthday*, edited by Timothy Maschke, Franz Posset, and Joan Skocir. Milwaukee: Marquette University Press, 2001.

———. "Lutheran Liturgical Worship on a Christian College Campus." D.Min. thesis. Deerfield, Ill.: Trinity Evangelical Divinity School, 1984.

———. "Prayer in the Apostolic Fathers." *The Second Century: A Journal of Early Christian Studies* 9:2 (Summer 1992): 103–18.

———. "The Transcultural Nature of Liturgical Worship." In *Christ and Culture in Dialogue: Constructive Themes and Practical Applications*, edited by Angus J. L. Menuge et al. St. Louis: Concordia Academic Press, 1999.

Mauk, Marchita B. *Places for Worship: A Guide to Building and Renovating*. American Essays in Liturgy. Collegeville, Minn.: Liturgical Press, 1995.

Maxwell, Lee A. *The Altar Guild Manual*. St. Louis: Concordia, 1996.

Maxwell, William D. *A History of Christian Worship: An Outline of Its Development and Forms*. Grand Rapids: Baker, 1982. Reprint of *Outlines of Christian Worship*. London: Oxford University Press, 1936.

McClean, Charles. *The Conduct of the Services*. St. Louis: Concordia Seminary Print Shop, 1972.

Messerli, Carlos R. "The Music of the Choir." In *A Handbook of Church Music*, edited by Carl Halter and Carl Schalk. St. Louis: Concordia, 1978.

Michno, Dennis G. *A Manual for Acolytes: The Duties of the Server at Liturgical Celebrations*. Wilton, Conn.: Morehouse-Barlow, 1981.

Milburn, Robert. *Early Christian Art and Architecture*. Berkeley: University of California Press, 1988.

Muller, Richard A. *Dictionary of Latin and Greek Theological Terms: Drawn Principally from Protestant Scholastic Theology*. Grand Rapids: Baker, 1985.

Nagel, Norman E. "Holy Baptism." In *Lutheran Worship: History and Practice*, edited by Fred L. Precht. St. Louis: Concordia, 1993.

[Nagel, Norman E.] Introduction to *Lutheran Worship*. St. Louis: Concordia, 1982.

Newton, Eric, and William Neil. *2000 Years of Christian Art*. New York: Harper & Row, 1966.

Norris, Herbert. *Church Vestments: Their Origin and Development*. New York: E. P. Dutton, 1950.

Nuechterlein, Louis G. "The Music of the Congregation." In *A Handbook of Church Music*, edited by Carl Halter and Carl Schalk. St. Louis: Concordia, 1978.

O'Brien, Judith Tate. *Manual for Lectors*. Dayton: Pflaum, 1975.

Oesterly, W. O. E. *The Jewish Background of Christian Liturgy*. Oxford: Clarendon, 1925.

Olst, E. H. van. *The Bible and Liturgy*. Translated by John Vriend. Grand Rapids: Eerdmans, 1991.

Palazzo, Eric. *A History of Liturgical Books from the Beginning to the Thirteenth Century*. Translated by Madeleine Beaumont. Collegeville, Minn.: Liturgical Press, 1998.

Palisca, Claude V., ed. *The Norton Anthology of Western Music*. New York: Norton, 1988.

Parker, Sean. "Worship Wars: Traditional Worship vs. Contemporary: What's Right? And, Is Anyone

Wrong?" [*Lutheran Witness*] news release of the LCMS. Accessed 23 November 1996 at http://lcmsnews@crf.cuis.edu.

Parsch, Pius. Introduction to *The Hours of the Divine Office in English and Latin*. Collegeville, Minn.: Liturgical Press, 1963–64.

Pecklers, Keith F. "History of the Roman Liturgy from the Sixteenth until the Twentieth Centuries." In *Introduction to the Liturgy*. Vol. 1 of *Handbook for Liturgical Studies*, edited by Anscar J. Chupungco. Collegeville, Minn.: Liturgical Press, 1997.

Pelikan, Jaroslav. *Bach among the Theologians*. Philadelpha: Fortress, 1986.

Peters, F. E. *Jerusalem: The Holy City in the Eyes of Chroniclers, Visitors, Pilgrims, and Prophets from the Days of Abraham to the Beginnings of Modern Times*. Princeton: Princeton University Press, 1985.

Peters, Ted, ed. "Worship Wars." *Dialog* 33:3 (Summer 1994).

Peterson, Eugene H. *Working the Angles: The Shaping of Pastoral Integrity*. Grand Rapids: Eerdmans, 1987.

Pfatteicher, Philip H. *Commentary on the* Lutheran Book of Worship: *Lutheran Liturgy in Its Ecumenical Context*. Minneapolis: Augsburg Fortress, 1990.

———. *Festivals and Commemorations: Handbook to the Calendar in* Lutheran Book of Worship. Minneapolis: Augsburg, 1980.

———. *Liturgical Spirituality*. Valley Forge: Trinity Press International, 1997.

———. *The School of the Church: Worship and Christian Formation*. Valley Forge: Trinity Press International, 1995.

———. "Still to Be Tried." *Lutheran Forum* 27:4 (November 1993): 22–24.

———, and Carlos R. Messerli. *Manual on the Liturgy*. Minneapolis: Augsburg, 1979.

Pieper, Francis. *Christian Dogmatics*. 4 vols. St. Louis: Concordia, 1950–57.

Piepkorn, Arthur Carl. *Roman Catholic, Old Catholic, Eastern Orthodox*. Vol. 1 of *Profiles in Belief: The Religious Bodies of the United States and Canada*. New York: Harper & Row, 1977.

———. *The Survival of the Historic Vestments in the Lutheran Church after 1555*. Graduate Study 1. St. Louis: School for Graduate Studies, Concordia Seminary, 1956.

Pittelko, Roger D. *Worship and Liturgy: God Speaks We Respond*. St. Louis: Concordia, 1995.

Plass, Ewald, ed. and comp. *What Luther Says: An Anthology*. 3 vols. St. Louis: Concordia, 1959.

Plater, Ormonde. *Deacons in the Liturgy*. Harrisburg, Penn.: Morehouse, 1992.

Pless, John T. "Daily Prayer." In *Lutheran Worship: History and Practice,* edited by Fred L. Precht. St. Louis: Concordia, 1993.

———. "The Leaders of Worship." In *Lutheran Worship: History and Practice*, edited by Fred L. Precht. St. Louis: Concordia, 1993.

Pocknee, C. E., and G. D. W. Randall. "Candles, Lamps and Lights." In *The New Westminster Dictionary of Liturgy and Worship*, edited by J. G. Davies. Philadelphia: Westminster, 1986.

Pope Paul VI. "Homily, September 24, 1972." In *Documents on the Liturgy, 1963–1979: Conciliar, Papal, and Curial Texts*, edited and translated by Thomas C. O'Brien. Collegeville, Minn.: Liturgical Press, 1982.

Portals of Prayer. St. Louis: Concordia, various issues.

Precht, Fred L. "Confession and Absolution: Sin and Forgiveness." In *Lutheran Worship: History and Practice*, edited by Fred L. Precht. St. Louis: Concordia, 1993.

———. *Lutheran Worship: Hymnal Companion.* St. Louis: Concordia, 1992.

———. "Worship Resources in Missouri Synod's History." In *Lutheran Worship: History and Practice*, edited by Fred L. Precht. St. Louis: Concordia, 1993.

———, ed. *Lutheran Worship: History and Practice.* St. Louis: Concordia, 1993.

———, and Michelle Severs. *Lutheran Worship Concordance.* St. Louis: Concordia, 1994.

Prenter, Regin. "Liturgy and Theology." In *Liturgy, Theology, and Music in the Lutheran Church*, edited by Mandus A. Egge. Minneapolis: International Choral Union, 1959.

Preus, Robert D. *The Theology of Post-Reformation Lutheranism.* St. Louis: Concordia, 1970.

Quasten, Johannes. *Music and Worship in Pagan and Christian Antiquity.* Translated by Boniface Ramsey. Washington, D.C.: National Association of Pastoral Musicians, 1983.

Rathmann, Rodney L., and Anthony L. Smith. *Worship: Celebrating God's Grace.* Edited by Thomas J. Doyle. St. Louis: Concordia, 1990.

Rau, Harold M. *Celebrating Your Wedding: A Personal Planning Guide.* St. Louis: Concordia, 1992.

Reed, Luther D. *The Lutheran Liturgy: A Study of the Common Liturgy of the Lutheran Church in America.* Philadelphia: Muhlenberg, 1947.

———. *The Lutheran Liturgy: A Study of the Common Liturgy of the Lutheran Church in America.* Rev. ed. Philadelphia: Muhlenberg, 1959.

Repp, Arthur C. *Confirmation in the Lutheran Church.* St. Louis: Concordia, 1964.

Richardson, Cyril C., ed. and trans. "The Teaching of the Twelve Apostles, Commonly Called the Didache." In *Early Christian Fathers*, edited by Cyril C. Richardson. Library of Christian Classics, vol. 1. Philadelphia: Westminster, 1953.

Richter, Aemelius L., ed. *Die evangelischen Kirchenordnungen des sechszehnten Jahrhunderts.* Weimar: Landes-Industriecomptoirs, 1846.

Roll, Susan K. "Christmas Then and Now: Reflections on Its Origins and Contemporary Pastoral Problems." *Worship* 73:6 (November 1999): 505–21.

Rosen, Ceil, and Moishe Rosen. *Christ in the Passover: Why Is This Night Different?* Chicago: Moody, 1978.

Rostovtzeff, Michael. *Dura-Europos and its Art.* Oxford: Clarendon, 1938.

Routley, Erik. *Words, Music, and the Church.* Nashville: Abingdon, 1968.

Rueter, Alvin. *So You're Reading the Lessons: Helps for Sunday Morning Lectors.* Audiotape. Minneapolis: Augsburg, 1986.

Sadie, Stanley, ed. *The New Grove Dictionary of Music and Musicians.* London: Macmillan, 1980.

Sauer, Robert. "The Special Hymnal Review Committee." In *Lutheran Worship: History and Practice*, edited by Fred L. Precht. St. Louis: Concordia, 1993.

Schalk, Carl F. *God's Song in a New Land: Lutheran Hymnals in America.* St. Louis: Concordia, 1995.

———. *The Hymn of the Day and Its Use in Lutheran Worship.* Church Music Pamphlet. St. Louis: Concordia, 1983.

———. "Music and the Liturgy: The Lutheran Tradition." In *Lutheran Worship: History and Practice*, edited by Fred L. Precht. St. Louis: Concordia, 1993.

———. *Planning a Christian Wedding Service.* St. Louis: Concordia, 1981.

Schattauer, Thomas H., ed. *InSide Out: Worship in an Age of Mission.* Minneapolis: Fortress, 1999.

Schlink, Edmund. *The Doctrine of Baptism.* Translated by Herbert J. A. Bouman. St. Louis: Concordia, 1972.

Schloeder, Steven J. *Architecture in Communion: Implementing the Second Vatican Council through Liturgy and Architecture.* San Francisco: Ignatius Press, 1998.

Schneidau, Herbert N. *Sacred Discontent: The Bible and Western Tradition.* Berkeley: University of California Press, 1976.

Senn, Frank C. *Christian Liturgy: Catholic and Evangelical.* Minneapolis: Fortress, 1997.

———. *Christian Worship and Its Cultural Setting.* Philadelphia: Fortress, 1983.

———. "The Dialogue between Liturgy and Music." *The Hymn* 38:2 (April 1987): 25.

———. "The Lord's Supper, Not the Passover Seder." *Worship* 60 (July 1986): 362–68.

———. "Martin Luther's Revision of the Eucharistic Canon in the *Formula Missae* of 1523." *Concordia Theological Monthly* XLIV:2 (March 1973).

———. "The Spirit of the Liturgy: A Wonderland Revisited." *Liturgy* 5:3 (Winter 1986): 25–29.

———. *The Witness of the Worshiping Community: Liturgy and the Practice of Evangelism.* New York: Paulist, 1993.

Seton, Bernard E. *Our Heritage of Hymns: A Swift Survey.* Berrien Springs, Mich.: Andrews University Press, 1984.

Severance, W. Murray. *Pronouncing Bible Names.* Nashville: Holman Bible Publishers, 1985.

Simons, Thomas G., and James M. Fitzpatrick. *The Ministry of Liturgical Environment.* Collegeville, Minn.: Liturgical Press, 1984.

Smith, Ralph F. "Worship as Transformation." *Currents in Theology and Mission* 18:5 (October 1991): 345–50.

Spener, Philip Jacob. *Pia Desideria.* Translated with introduction by Theodore G. Tappert. Philadelphia: Fortress, 1964.

Spinks, Bryan D. *Luther's Liturgical Criteria and His Reform of the Canon of the Mass.* Grove Liturgical Study 30. Bramcote Notts, England: Grove Books, 1982.

Stauffer, S. Anita. *The Altar Guild: A Guide for the Ministry of Liturgical Preparations.* Philadelphia: Fortress, 1980.

Stradling, Leslie E. *Praying the Psalms.* Philadelphia: Fortress, 1977.

Strathmann, H. "*leitourgeo, leitourgia, leitorgos, leitourgikos.*" In vol. 4 of *Theological Dictionary of the New Testament,* edited by G. Kittel. Translated by G. W. Bromiley. Grand Rapids: Eerdmans, 1967.

Strunk, W. Oliver. *Source Readings in Music History from Classical Antiquity through the Romantic Era.* New York: Norton, 1950.

Strzygowski, Josef. *Early Church Art in Northern Europe, with Special Reference to Timber Construction and Decoration.* New York: Hacker Art Books, 1980.

Taft, Robert. *The Liturgy of the Hours in East and West: The Origins of the Divine Office and Its Meaning for Today.* 2d rev. ed. Collegeville, Minn.: Liturgical Press, 1993.

Talley, Thomas J. *The Origins of the Liturgical Year.* 2d em. ed. Collegeville, Minn.: Liturgical Press, 1991.

Tappert, Theodore G., and John W. Doberstein, trans. *Journals of Henry Melchoir Muhlenberg.* Philadelphia: Muhlenberg, 1942–58.

Tertullian. "On Baptism." The Ante-Nicene Fathers, vol. 3. Edited by Alexander Roberts and James Donaldson. New York: Scribner, 1899.

This Far by Faith: An African American Resource for Worship. Minneapolis: Augsburg Fortress, 1999.

Thompson, Bard. *Liturgies of the Western Church.* Cleveland: Meridian, 1961.

Truemper, David G. "Evangelism: Liturgy *versus* Church Growth." *Lutheran Forum* 24:1 (Lent/February 1991): 30–33.

Underhill, Evelyn. *Worship.* New York: Harper, 1936.

Vajda, Jaroslav J. "Hymn Writing and Translating." In *Lutheran Worship: History and Practice*, edited by Fred L. Precht. St. Louis: Concordia, 1993.

———. "The Vajda Hymn Service." Prepared under the auspices of the Commission on Worship, the LCMS. St. Louis: Concordia, 1990.

Vajta, Vilmos. *Luther on Worship: An Interpretation.* Translated by U. S. Leupold. Philadelphia: Muhlenberg, 1958.

Van Dijk, S. J. P. "The Bible in Liturgical Use." In *The West from the Fathers to the Reformation*, edited by G. W. H. Lampe. Vol. 2 of *The Cambridge History of the Bible.* Cambridge: Cambridge University Press, 1969.

Van Loon, Ralph R., ed. *Encountering God: The Legacy of* Lutheran Book of Worship *for the 21st Century.* Minneapolis: Kirk House, 1998.

Vincie, Catherine. "The Liturgical Assembly: Review and Reassessment." *Worship* 67:2 (March 1993): 123–43.

Volz, Carl A. *Pastoral Life and Practice in the Early Church.* Minneapolis: Augsburg, 1990.

Wainwright, Geoffrey. *Doxology: The Praise of God in Worship, Doctrine, and Life: A Systematic Theology.* New York: Oxford University Press, 1980.

Walker, William O., ed. *Harper's Bible Pronunciation Guide.* San Francisco: Harper & Row, 1989.

Walsh, C. J. "Rosary." In *The New Westminster Dictionary of Liturgy and Worship*, edited by J. G. Davies. Philadelphia: Westminster, 1979.

Walther, C. F. W. *The Proper Distinction between Law and Gospel: Thirty-nine Evening Lectures.* Translated by W. H. T. Dau. St. Louis: Concordia, 1929.

Ware, Timothy. *The Orthodox Church.* Baltimore: Penguin, 1963.

Webber, Robert E., ed. *The Complete Library of Christian Worship.* 7 vols. in 8. Nashville: Star Song, 1993–1994.

———. *Signs of Wonder: The Phenomenon of Convergence in Modern Liturgical and Charismatic Churches.* Nashville: Abbot-Martyn, 1992.

———. *Worship, Old and New: A Biblical, Historical, and Practical Introduction.* Rev. ed. Grand Rapids: Zondervan, 1994.

Weidmann, Carl F. *A Manual for Altar Guilds.* 2d ed. New York: Ernst Kaufmann, 1941.

Weisheit, Eldon. "The Place of Children in the Worship Life of a Christian Congregation." Lutheran Education Association Monograph 9:1 (Fall 1983).

Weitzmann, Kurt, Manolis Chatzidakis, and Svetozar Radojcic. *Icons.* New York: Alpine Fine Arts Collection, 1980.

Wengert, Timothy J., trans. "The Baptismal Booklet." In *The Book of Concord*, edited by Robert Kolb and Timothy J. Wengert. Minneapolis: Augsburg Fortress, 2000.

Werning, Waldo J. *L.C.M.S. Worship: The Rest of the Story.* Ft. Wayne, Ind.: Biblical Renewal Publications, 2000.

Westerhoff, John H. "Fashioning Christians in Our Day." In *Schooling Christians: "Holy Experiments" in American Education*, edited by Stanley Hauerwas and John H. Westerhoff. Grand Rapids: Eerdmans, 1992.

Westermeyer, Paul. *The Church Musician.* Rev. ed. Minneapolis: Augsburg Fortress, 1997.

———. "Musical Leadership." In *Encountering God: The Legacy of* Lutheran Book of Worship *for the 21st Century*, edited by Ralph R. Van Loon. Minneapolis: Kirk House, 1998.

———. *Te Deum: The Church and Music.* Minneapolis: Fortress, 1998.

Whaley, Vernon M. *The Dynamics of Corporate Worship.* Grand Rapids: Baker, 2001.

Whitaker, E. C. "Three Hours Devotion." In *The New Westminster Dictionary of Liturgy and Worship*, edited by J. G. Davies. Philadelphia: Westminster, 1986.

White, James F. "The Classification of Protestant Traditions of Worship." *Studia Liturgica* 17 (1987): 264–72.

———. *Documents of Christian Worship: Descriptive and Interpretive Sources.* Louisville: Westminster/John Knox, 1992.

———. *Introduction to Christian Worship.* Nashville: Abingdon, 1980.

———. *Introduction to Christian Worship.* Rev. ed. Nashville: Abingdon, 1990.

———. "Lutheran Worship." In *Twenty Centuries of Christian Worship.* Vol. 2 of *The Complete Library of Christian Worship*, edited by Robert E. Webber. Nashville: Star Song, 1994.

———. *New Forms of Worship.* Nashville: Abingdon, 1971.

———. *Protestant Worship and Church Architecture: Theological and Historical Considerations.* New York: Oxford University Press, 1964.

———, and Susan J. White. *Church Architecture: Building and Renovating for Christian Worship.* Nashville: Abingdon, 1988.

White, Susan J. *Christian Worship and Technological Change.* Nashville: Abingdon, 1994.

Wilkinson, John, trans. and ed. *Egeria's Travels.* London: SPCK, 1971.

Willimon, William H. "The Peace of God Go with You." *Liturgy* 1:4 (1981): 68.

Wright, Tim. *A Community of Joy: How to Create Contemporary Worship.* Edited by Herb Miller. Nashville: Abingdon, 1994.

Zemler-Cizewski, Wanda. "The Eucharist and the Consequences of Celiac Disease: A Question of Access to Holy Communion." *Worship* 74:3 (May 2000): 237–48.

TOPICAL INDEX

Hymn Title and Name Index

SCRIPTURE INDEX

Revelation